Irish Women Writers

Irish Women Writers

An A-to-Z Guide

EDITED BY

Alexander G. Gonzalez

GREENWOOD PRESS

Westport, Connecticut • London

Library of Congress Cataloging-in-Publication Data

Irish women writers : an A-to-Z guide / edited by Alexander G. Gonzalez.
   p.   cm.
  Includes bibliographical references and index.
  ISBN 0–313–32883–8 (alk. paper)
  1. English literature—Irish authors—Bio-bibliography—Dictionaries.   2. English
literature—Women authors—Bio-bibliography—Dictionaries.   3. Irish
literature—Women authors—Bio-bibliography—Dictionaries.   4. Women and
literature—Northern Ireland—Dictionaries.   5. English literature—Irish
authors—Dictionaries.   6. English literature—Women authors—Dictionaries.   7.
Irish literature—Women authors—Dictionaries.   8. Northern Ireland—In
literature—Dictionaries.   9. Women and literature—Ireland—Dictionaries.   10.
Ireland—In literature—Dictionaries.   I. Gonzalez, Alexander G.
  PR8733.I75   2006
  820.9'9287'09417—dc22   2005018723

British Library Cataloguing in Publication Data is available.

Library of Congress Catalog Card Number: 2005018723
ISBN 0–313–32883–8

First published in 2006

Greenwood Press, 88 Post Road West, Westport, CT 06881
An imprint of Greenwood Publishing Group, Inc.
www.greenwood.com

Printed in the United States of America

The paper used in this book complies with the
Permanent Paper Standard issued by the National
Information Standards Organization (Z39.48–1984).

10 9 8 7 6 5 4 3 2 1

For my loving wife, Michele

CONTENTS

Preface   xi

Introduction *by Mary Fitzgerald-Hoyt*   1

Linda Anderson (1949–) *by Anthea Cordner*   9

Ivy Bannister (1951–) *by Maryanne Felter*   12

Mary Beckett (1926–) *by Virginia B. Mack*   14

Sara Berkeley (1967–) *by Claire McEwen*   17

Maeve Binchy (1940–) *by Rebecca Steinberger*   20

Caroline Blackwood (1931–1996) *by Coleen Comerford*   23

Eavan Boland (1944–) *by Patricia Hagen and Thomas Zelman*   26

Angela Bourke (1952–) *by Christie Fox*   35

Elizabeth Bowen (1899–1973) *by Christine Cusick*   39

Clare Boylan (1948–) *by John J. Han*   44

Elizabeth Brennan (1907–) *by Paul Marchbanks*   48

Frances Browne (1816–1879) *by Paul Marchbanks*   51

Mary Rose Callaghan (1944–) *by Maryanne Felter*   54

Moya Cannon (1956–) *by Christine Cusick*   57

Marina Carr (1964–) *by Gerald C. Wood*   61

Juanita Casey (1925–) *by Rebecca Steinberger*   67

Mary (Catherine Gunning Maguire) Colum (1884–1957) *by Paige Reynolds*   69

Julia M. Crottie (1853–1930?) *by Paul Marchbanks*   72

Geraldine Cummins (1890–1969) *by Shelia Odak*   75

Ita Daly (1945–) *by John J. Han*   79

Suzanne Day (1890–1964) *by Tom Keegan*   82

Teresa Deevy (1894–1963) *by Christie Fox*   84

Anne Devlin (1951–) *by Sara E. Stenson*   88

Eilis Dillon (1920–1994) *by Maryanne Felter*   94

Emma Donoghue (1969–) *by Maureen E. Mulvihill*   98

Mary Dorcey (1950–) *by John J. Han*   102

Ellen Mary Patrick Downing (1828–1869) *by Katherine Parr*   106

Maria Edgeworth (1767–1849) *by Claire Denelle Cowart*   109

Ruth Dudley Edwards (1944–) *by Shelia Odak*   117

Anne Enright (1962–) *by Sara E. Stenson*   120

Mary E. Frances (Mary Blundell) (1859–1930) *by Tom Keegan*   124

Miriam Gallagher (1940–) *by John L. Murphy*   127

Sarah Grand (1854–1943) *by Tina O'Toole*   131

Lady Gregory (née [Isabella] Augusta Persse) (1852–1932)
   by Martin F. Kearney   134

Anne Le Marquand Hartigan (1937–) *by Joseph Heininger*   140

Rita Ann Higgins (1955–) *by Rita Barnes*   145

Norah Hoult (1898–1984) *by Karen O'Brien*   151

Biddy Jenkinson (1949–) *by Maureen E. Mulvihill*   154

Jennifer Johnston (1930–) *by Shawn O'Hare*   158

Marie Jones (1955–) *by Patrick Lonergan*   164

Molly Keane (1904–1996) *by Ann Owens Weekes*   168

Eva Kelly (1830–1910) *by Katherine Parr*   172

Rita Kelly (1953–) *by Joseph Heininger*   175

Mary Lavin (1912–1996) *by Maryanne Felter*   179

Emily Lawless (1845–1913) *by Matthew J. Goodman*   185

Joan Lingard (1932–) *by Joseph Heininger*   190

Deirdre Madden (1960–) *by Shawn O'Hare*   193

Joy Martin (1937–) *by Susan Bazargan*   197

Medbh McGuckian (1950–) *by Sara E. Stenson*   200

Janet McNeill (1907–) *by Tom Keegan*   208

Paula Meehan (1955–) *by Sara E. Stenson*   211

Máire Mhac an tSaoi (1922–) *by Cóilín D. Owens*   216

Alice Milligan (1866–1953) *by Rita Barnes*   219

Susan L. Mitchell (1866–1926) *by Paul Marchbanks*   224

Lady Morgan (1776?–1859) *by John J. Han*   228

Val Mulkerns (1925–) *by Virginia B. Mack*   232

Iris Murdoch (1919–1999) *by Lisa Weihman*   236

Eilean Ni Chuilleanain (1942–) *by Sara E. Stenson*   241

Nuala Ní Dhomhnaill (1952–) *by Oona Frawley*   248

Éilís ní Dhuibhne (1954–) *by Beth Wightman*   256

Áine Ní Ghlinn (1955–) *by Coleen Comerford*   262

Máiréad Ní Ghráda (1896–1971) *by Coleen Comerford*   265

Edna O'Brien (1930–) *by Sandra Manoogian Pearce*   268

Kate O'Brien (1897–1974) *by Elizabeth Gilmartin*   276

Mary O'Donnell (1954–) *by Coleen Comerford*   280

Julia O'Faolain (1932–) *by Ann Owens Weekes*   283

Nuala O'Faolain (1940–) *by Mary Fitzgerald-Hoyt*   286

Mary O'Malley (1954–) *by Mary Fitzgerald-Hoyt*   290

Christina Reid (1942–) *by Patrick Lonergan*   294

Somerville and Ross (E.O.E. Somerville [1858–1949] and
  Violet Martin [1862–1915]) *by Ann Owens Weekes*   298

Eithne Strong (1923–1999) *by Joseph Heininger*   303

Mary Tighe (née Blachford) (1772–1810) *by Maureen E. Mulvihill*   308

Katharine Tynan (1861–1931) *by Colette Epplé*   314

Lady Wilde (1821–1896) *by Katherine Parr*   319

Sheila Wingfield (1906–1992) *by Coleen Comerford*   323

Selected Bibliography   327

Index   333

About the Editor and Contributors   341

PREFACE

This book is intended to serve as a reference work for scholars studying Irish women writers, whether those scholars be entirely new to the field or experienced researchers simply moving on to study the work of authors new to them. Arranged alphabetically, the entries are written by contributors who are experts on their authors and who are fully up-to-date on the latest research available relevant to their entries. Each entry contains a brief biography, a concise, detailed discussion of the author's major works and themes, a review of the author's critical reception, and a bibliography of primary and secondary sources. Appended to the book is a selected bibliography that lists the most significant general secondary sources in the field.

The idea for this guide to Irish women writers evolved from my work editing *Modern Irish Writers* (1997). In that book's preface I listed writers who could not be included because of space limitations. Despite that book's inclusion of 22 women writers (out of 78 total), enough of those left out were women that I decided to edit a similar book dedicated entirely to women writers. Also compelling was the emergence of so many women writers over the past twenty years; I wanted to facilitate as much as possible the study of their work. And, of course, I was motivated by sheer admiration of the work of many of these writers. Unfortunately, I still have a list of writers I could not include, again purely because of space limitations.

I did not include Leland Bardwell, Eva Gore-Booth, and Maire Aine Nic Ghearailt because despite casting a wide net I simply could not find any scholar willing to write on them; I assigned the space allotted to them to other worthy writers. Also suggested to me but omitted, solely for the reason of having limited space, were Jane Barlow, Margaret Brew, Celia de Freine, George Egerton, Mary Laffan Hartley, Emily Hickey, Lady Caroline Lamb, Mary Manning, Gina Moxley, and Enda Wylie.

As always in a book of this scope and nature, I have many persons to thank. For her pioneering work on Irish women writers and her three essays written for this book I must thank Ann Weekes, whose seminal *Unveiling Treasures* (1993) is still a starting place for anyone wanting to explore the primary works of many little-known Irish women writers. Indeed, my own tome, with its emphasis on secondary sources, is intended to be, as far as is possible, a complement to Ann's.

For generously granting permission to quote from their poetry I must thank Eavan Boland and Biddy Jenkinson. For stepping in to write essays on short notice when the original contributors were either unwilling or unable to honor their commitments I must express great gratitude to Maryanne Felter, who picked up several authors in addition to her own original assignments, and also to Oona Frawley, Matthew Goodman, John

Han, Martin Kearney, Maureen Mulvihill, and Katherine Parr. For steering contributors my way I am grateful to Mary Rose Callaghan, Claire Cowart, Peter Dempsey, Paul Dolan, Mary Fitzgerald-Hoyt, Mark Hall, Cheryl Herr, Christina Hunt Mahony, Maureen Mulvihill, Shane Murphy, George O'Brien, Stephen Regan, Marilyn Richtarik, Ruth Sherry, Jim Smith, Sara Stenson, Paddy Sullivan, Kim Summers, Beverly Taylor, George Watson, and Stephen Watt.

I must thank also Mary Fitzgerald-Hoyt, not only for the quality of her original assignment and her willingness to take on another on short notice, but also for having written this book's inspiring introduction; her work for me absorbed a good deal of her sabbatical leave time—so a particular thank-you to her. For her friendship and encouragement all along I owe her a further debt of gratitude. In fact, a book such as this would not be possible without the help of many scholars, quite a few of whom I consider friends. Thank you.

INTRODUCTION

Mary Fitzgerald-Hoyt

Of one thing I am certain: to make any kind of statement, pronouncement, or commentary that will adequately address the vast subject of Irish women writers is impossible. But as a means of introducing this important, ambitious, and so necessary volume, I shall focus on a poster, a quotation, and a personal habit.

Visitors to Irish and Irish American bookstores, pubs, and shops have no doubt seen the ubiquitous Irish Writers poster, which features the usual suspects: Yeats, O'Casey, Joyce, Kavanagh, and so on. And although there is no denying that the writers depicted have shaped, even defined, Irish literary history, all of the featured literary figures are male, as if the designer believed that no Irish woman ever expressed herself in writing. Indeed, the faces of several of these notable men have assumed iconic status, commodified into coffee mugs, T-shirts, and similar kitsch aimed at the foreign tourist; their homes have been transformed into museums. The tourist can "experience" a slice of literary Ireland without taking the trouble to read a book.

A couple of years ago, I noticed in the Trinity College book shop that an attempt had been made to redress this injustice of equating Irish literature with male writers: there was a poster titled Irish Women Writers. Yet admirable as it may have been to remind or even inform the populace that there *is* such a creature as an Irish woman writer, it perhaps unconsciously underlines the fundamental problem. The cultural assumptions lurking behind the soi-disant Irish Writers poster infiltrate its female counterpart. To state "writer" and assume "male" bespeaks privilege and arrogance; to qualify "writer" with "women" suggests at once defiance and apology, for surely Eavan Boland, Nuala Ní Dhomhnaill, Somerville and Ross, Jennifer Johnston, and a host of other spectacular talents, as diverse as they are stylistically and culturally, deserve a place on any Irish Writers poster.

My promised quotation appears in Nuala O'Faolain's first volume of autobiography, *Are You Somebody* (1996). Having once been a friend and colleague of Seamus Deane, the Northern Irish critic, poet, and novelist who became the general editor of the original *The Field Day Anthology of Irish Writing* (1991), O'Faolain, a late-blooming feminist just discovering a personal sense of her own Irishness, was dismayed and wounded at the anthology's now-infamous exclusion and underrepresentation of women writers. When she questioned Deane in a television interview, she recalls that "he said words to the effect that he really hadn't noticed what he was doing" (104). O'Faolain concluded that he was "weary" and "baffled" and "didn't want an argument" (104).

The editors of volumes 4 and 5 of *The Field Day Anthology of Irish Writing* (2002) acknowledge Deane's support and assistance in making those additional volumes possible, volumes that feature writing by and about women and whose organizing principles depart from traditional rubrics of chronological periods and literary schools or movements. Yet while it is heartening to know that people are capable of attempting to rectify injustices and reconsider past attitudes, it remains unnerving that such an eminent critic could have failed to notice the terrible inequity of such an exclusion of women writers. More to the point, something is radically wrong that the literary hierarchy morphed into such an omnipotent "boys' club" to begin with. Fiction writer Anne Enright has flatly dismissed the entire *Field Day Anthology* enterprise, even expressing reluctance about being included in the new volumes. When interviewed by Caitriona Moloney about the Irish literary canon and the *Field Day* controversy, Enright retorted, "*The Field Day Anthology* got it so spectacularly wrong that anyone would know that they had no credibility; therefore it doesn't matter" (*Irish Women Writers Speak Out*, 55).

The personal habit I suppose I might call the "index reflex." It's the impulse that overcomes me when I pick up a new book theorizing about Irish national identity or the complexities of Irish culture. The index often disappoints, for too often the examples drawn are chosen exclusively from male writers. How, one wonders, can a discussion of contemporary ideas of the Irish "nation" fail to consider Eavan Boland's writing? How can interrogations of historiography and mythmaking ignore Julia O'Faolain's *No Country for Young Men* (1980)? How can discussions of politics in Northern Irish life overlook the plays of Anne Devlin and Christina Reid?

Too often critics' and anthologists' vision has been clouded by the cataracts of entitlement and unimaginativeness. That reflex action of "WWJS"—not, What would Jesus say, but, What would *Joyce* say—or Yeats, or O'Casey, or Heaney—hobbles the ongoing discussion of what it means to be Irish, of how to define Irish literature.

Of course, the resistance to women writers reaches beyond the island of Ireland. Women writers worldwide have long been caught in the coils of an old contradiction. Writers transform the familiar with creative vision, but women's familiar world has historically been devalued, the hearth and home to which they were relegated deemed intrinsically less important than the more public world of "masculine" pursuit, which has variously meant moneymaking, empire building, war waging, and the like. In another century and another nation, Elizabeth Barrett Browning's eponymous Aurora Leigh, attempting to be both woman and poet in a resisting, sometimes hostile society, excoriated the superficial education and time-wasting busywork accorded to women in the Victorian age, both designed to render women "good" wives and mothers, angels in the house. At the same time, she asserted the validity of the quotidien world that women occupied as a fit subject for epic poetry, a genre stuck in the groove of antiquity. Generations later, Virginia Woolf revealed that behind the apparent shallowness of an upper-class woman's party-giving lurked a terrifying vision of a world laid waste; in *Mrs. Dalloway* (1925) the minutiae of domestic life are rendered luminous, a brave attempt to beat back the void.

Ironically, because women were devalued, so was their work, and to write about domestic chores, childbearing and child rearing, the woman's body, was too often deemed trivial, not the stuff of literature. For countless other women, literacy itself was a locked room, education deemed only for men. And as much as we might like to think of these attitudes as historical injustices, relics of the past, to do so is to be perilously ignorant of the lives of so many contemporary women oppressed by patriarchal civil and religious power structures, domestic abuse, and economic and sexual exploitation. Irish American writer Valerie Miner has been one of many to voice a cautionary note about contemporary women's lives, noting current dangers: "There is a smugness among some men and women that we are enlightened and inclusive and we are neither" (Moloney and Thompson, 195).

When Eavan Boland, now regarded as a major poet who has transformed Irish literature and literary criticism, rendered her then-world of suburban homekeeping and child rearing into poetry, dared to write frankly about women's bodies and women's self-images, she was variously ignored and reviled. I once heard her attempts to foster other women's self-expression by conducting community writing workshops dismissed in a derisive, ad feminam attack by one of Ireland's leading literary critics—herself a woman. The inimitable imagination of Medbh McGuckian has produced a poetry that while often drawing inspiration from the traditional realms of women—home and garden—demands that its reader dismantle any traditional notions of reading and responding to literature. Yet this dazzling originality has often roused hostility, accusations of opacity, even incomprehensibility. WWJS, indeed!

And yet, there is much cause for hope. The political, economic, social, and cultural sea changes that have transformed Ireland in the last few decades have rippled into women's literature and how that literature is written, written about, and published. Irish women's literature is simply more *available* than it once was. An explosion of anthologies, critical studies, biographies, and interviews insists upon women's massive contribution to Irish literature. Not long ago, the visionary Attic Press was once one of the few publishing houses eager to promote literature by women, and among its fine offerings was Ailbhe Smyth's anthology of women's writing, *Wildish Things* (1989), which not only offered a diverse and innovative array of writers but also exploded traditional notions of Irish women and Irish literature. Attic also published Ann Owens Weekes's groundbreaking *Unveiling Treasures: The Attic Guide to the Published Works of Irish Women Literary Writers: Drama, Fiction, Poetry* (1993), an invaluable reference guide of biographical, critical, and bibliographical information.

Yet the Attic Press lacked both the clout and the war chest of larger publishing houses, and the gratification of having one's work published did not guarantee that that work gained the notice accorded to the writings of Irish male authors. Irish women writers remained—and often still are—under-reviewed; outrageous though it may be, some were treated as tainted because of their association with feminist presses; many found sympathetic audiences not at home in Ireland but on the Irish studies circuit in the United States, offering readings at academic conferences and for Irish literature programs at American colleges and universities.

Many readers' first exposure to Irish women writers had its genesis in reading works *about* them rather than *by* them, a strangely ironic twist on Eavan Boland's complaint that Irish women traditionally were written about rather than heard, transformed into mythical figures by male writers and not allowed to speak in their own voices. *Unveiling Treasures*, personal interviews, the occasional piece of literary criticism or biography, and even the academic conference paper were for many of us the introduction to Irish women writers, and for those of us living outside of Ireland, that intellectual seduction was an often frustrating event, for we discovered the difficulties of gaining access to the primary works; for those of us attempting to woo a new audience in our college and university classrooms, the fickleness of book distribution provided an often insurmountable obstacle, forcing us into the awkwardness of leaving works on library reserve or, in extremis, resorting to sheaves of photocopied poems and short stories. The occasional anthology, such as Smyth's above-mentioned *Wildish Things; Territories of the Voice*, a collection of contemporary Irish women's fiction (edited by

De Salvo, Hogan, and D'Arcy, 1989); or Daniel and Linda Casey's *Stories by Contemporary Irish Women* (1990), was an oasis. A. A. Kelly's *Pillars of the House: An Anthology of Verse by Irish Women from 1690 to the Present* (1988) opened a new window on Irish poetry. Wake Forest University Press provided beautifully produced editions of several Irish women poets—though not, alas, Eavan Boland. Novels and plays were often paradise unattainable.

Yet even in those hungry years, it is clear that Irish women writers were having an impact on the writing of Irish literary history. Academic books are time-consuming in their researching, writing, and production, and the fact that a number of fine critical works about Irish women writers emerged at the turn of the twentieth century suggests that those writers had ignited these scholars' imaginations years earlier. Ann Owens Weekes's *Irish Women Writers: An Uncharted Tradition* (1990) transformed the reading of Irish fiction by asserting women's contribution. Patricia Boyle Haberstroh's *Women Creating Women: Contemporary Irish Women Poets* (1996), a study of the Irish female poetic imagination, and *My Self, My Muse: Irish Women Poets Reflect on Life and Art* (2001), an anthology of poets' meditations on their own creative processes, have had a crucial part in redefining traditional notions of Irish poetry. Alexander G. Gonzalez, editor of the present volume, attempted in *Contemporary Irish Women Poets: Some Male Perspectives* to redress former prejudicial, wrongheaded critiques of Irish women poets. Collections of interviews, such as Rebecca E. Wilson and Gillean S. Arjat's *Sleeping with Monsters: Conversations with Scottish and Irish Women Poets* (1990) and Caitriona Moloney and Helen Thompson's *Irish Women Writers Speak Out: Voices from the Field* (2003), have both provided women writers with the opportunity to illuminate their lives and artistry and introduced readers to underconsidered or even unfamiliar writers. Previously male-writer-dominated topics have been reexamined to include women writers in *The Comic Tradition in Irish Women Writers* (edited by Theresa O'Connor, 1996), C. L. Innes's *Woman and Nation in Irish Literature and Society: 1880–1935* (1993), and *Border Crossings: Irish Women Writers and National Identities* (edited by Kathryn Kirkpatrick, 2000).

Other scholars have revised, even revolutionized our readings of familiar figures or illuminated the context in which we read the history that shaped women's lives. Ann Saddlemyer's important scholarship on Isabella Augusta Persse, Lady Gregory, and the Penguin edition of selected works of Lady Gregory, edited by Lucy McDiarmid and Maureen Waters, have foregrounded the achievement of a major figure too often treated patronizingly in studies of the male writers she encouraged and supported. Margaret MacCurtain, Margaret Ward, and a number of other fine historians have transformed the reading of Irish history by writing women's experiences into it; Angela Bourke's feminist interpretations of Irish folklore have provided a new lens through which to view the past.

The recent blossoming of works by and about Irish women is heartening; so much more needs to be said and done. In a world where critical studies of Seamus Heaney's poetry constitute their own cottage industry, as of this writing only one full-length study of Eavan Boland's work has been published. Ann Owens Weekes's work on Irish women's fiction, mentioned above, and Christine St. Peter's *Changing Ireland: Strategies in Contemporary Women's Fiction* (2000) have made vital inroads; luminaries such as Kate O'Brien, Edna O'Brien, and Jennifer Johnston deserve several critical studies all their own. Irish women dramatists merit more representation in anthologies, more space in critical studies of Irish drama.

Of course, that splendid motherlode of Irish women's writing, volumes 4 and 5 of *The Field Day Anthology of Irish Writing,* subtitled *Irish Women's Writing and Traditions* (edited by Angela Bourke, Máirin Ní Dhonneadha, Siobhán Kilfeather, Maria Luddy, Margaret MacCurtain, Gerardine Meaney, Mary O'Dowd, and Clair Wills), is already transforming Irish literary history, not only because it reveals that women's writing in Ireland is neither a recent nor a monolithic enterprise, but also because it attempts to refashion how Irish literature is read, how it is defined. Not only is it a monumental work of scholarship, but it is also a triumphant imaginative achievement, challenging its readers to rethink their assumptions about Irish literature. In the two newest volumes of *The Field Day Anthology of Irish Writing* the traditional rejection of women's experience in the domestic sphere as fit topic for literature is replaced with an embracing of that experience through sections on sexuality, childbirth, the rituals of grieving, yet a refusal to define those experiences narrowly: sexuality is not limited to heterosexuality; maternity is also examined through infanticide. Writings on diverse expressions of spirituality are included, as are women's traditionally overlooked place in the public spheres of politics, education, philanthropy, and scientific inquiry. The arbitrary business of literary periodization is abandoned in favor of thematic connections across centuries. The very definition of "literature" is stretched and challenged by the interdisciplinarity of both the editors and the texts they have selected and by the inclusion of works that elude easy categorization.

Essential and gripping debates about Irish identity and Irish historiography have burgeoned in recent years, debates with such open-ended gerunds as "inventing Ireland," "writing Ireland," and the like, suggesting process rather than product, fluidity rather than immobility. In their various ways, Declan Kiberd, John Wilson Foster, Eavan Boland, Nuala Ní Dhomhnaill, the founders of Field Day, the writers and actors involved in Charabanc, and a host of others have called for, as Declan Kiberd has argued, an abandonment of "binary thinking" and a more flexible definition of Irishness, acknowledging that to say "Irish" and mean "Nationalist," to say "Irish" and mean "Catholic," to say "Irish writer" and mean "man," simply will not do anymore. The founders of Field Day, seeing their Northern Irish home under siege literally and figuratively, called for a "Fifth Province" of the imagination as a way of extricating Northern Ireland from the religious bigotry, political violence, and cultural stagnation corroding it.

"Revision," "imagination," and "redefinition" have become the shibboleths of discussions that embrace such far-reaching issues as the future of Northern Ireland, the writing of Irish history, and the transformation of a national self-image marked by victimhood into a forward-looking, progressive identity. One would think that women would be a natural part of this process and discussion. What better way to revise the past than to amplify the voices of those who were shouted down in its official written version? What better way to redefine Irish identity than to include those who were excluded from the original definition? What better way to address the much-discussed "silences" of the past than to acknowledge, as the recent volumes of *The Field Day Anthology* attest, that perhaps silence was not the overarching issue but rather the failure of the men in charge to turn up the volume enough to hear the women speaking?

To attempt to redefine or rewrite Ireland while neglecting the contributions of women is as wrongheaded as attempting to paint a portrait with the artist keeping one eye closed and one arm tied behind his or her back. To go back to my three opening examples, what a triumph it would be if posters and anthologies no longer had to be revised to make up for the overlooking of women. What a day it would be if editors of anthologies would find it unimaginable *not* to think of including women's writing as more than a token sample. What a pleasure it would be to begin critical books at the beginning, not needing to check the index first because it would be unthinkable not to find women's names there.

Becoming aware of Irish women's literature was for many of us a transformative event, akin to one's discovery of feminism or postcolonial literature. Once those doors are opened, there is no going back. Previously loved books become problematic, even distasteful, when viewed through these new lenses. Read alongside Jean Rhys's *Wide Sargasso Sea* (1966), the former female triumphalism of *Jane Eyre* (1847) is tarnished. Yet these moments of metamorphosis may be exhilarating as well. Perhaps it was discovering the stunning short stories in *Territories of the Voice* or the bold originality of the writers anthologized in *Wildish Things*; perhaps it was hearing Nuala Ní Dhomhnaill read her exuberant poetry in the Irish language she inhabits rather than speaks; perhaps it was identifying with the lonely young poet searching for a voice while sitting at her kitchen table, a young woman whom Eavan Boland describes as herself. That first splash of cold water in the face that revealed that women in Irish literature not only were Molly Bloom or Deirdre of the Sorrows or that mythic figure that Yeats made of Maud Gonne, but were, as Boland has asserted, the *authors* rather than merely the *subjects* of Irish literature.

Ann Owens Weekes recalls in her introduction to *Unveiling Treasures* that growing up in Ireland she developed a passion for reading, but that that passion was strangely unsatisfying: "Yet enjoyment was often tinged with a sense of unease I could not articulate, an Irish Catholic enchanted by the experiences of British Protestants, an Irish girl excluded from a world of and for Irish men; I was not 'at home' in fiction" (6). Weekes's own defining moment as a reader arrived with her adolescent discovery of Mary Lavin's fiction: "I knew that something extraordinary had occurred in my world" (6). When she went on years later to write *Unveiling Treasures*, Weekes in effect both shared and enhanced that moment of discovery, for the entries contained in her work offered a glimpse into the lives and works of an array of writers, the short entries occasioned by space constraints tempting the reader to look further, to seek out the works listed in the bibliography, to discover the writing behind the teasing biographical information and critical commentary.

Alexander G. Gonzalez's present volume both fills a void and provides an occasion for rejoicing. *Unveiling Treasures* first appeared over a decade ago, and massive changes, from the controversial economic explosion known as the Celtic Tiger, to the legalization of divorce, changed policies regarding reproductive rights, the fraught but guardedly hopeful evolution of the Good Friday Agreement, and the presidencies of Mary Robinson and Mary McAleese, have been accompanied by transformative new works by familiar writers and a torrent of new talents. Readers wanting to keep current with those who long ago earned their place on the Irish Writers poster will find entries on Edgeworth, Somerville and Ross, Lady Gregory, O'Brien, Johnston, and others whose exclusion from discussions of Irish literature, written by women or men, would be unthinkable; the Republic of Ireland and Northern Ireland, English-language writers and Irish-language writers, poets, fiction writers, dramatists, critics, and memoirists are included. And there is room here, too, for the discovery of a previously unknown or unread author.

In "That the Science of Cartography Is Limited" (1994), Eavan Boland argued the limitations of printed maps, their inability to convey the flesh and vegetation, the suffering and silence, of a landscape. Her speaker laments the absence of the so-called famine roads on the map, those ill-conceived, abortive public-works projects spawned by a British Victorian belief that providing free relief to the starving Irish would corrupt their characters and imperil their immortal souls. As the poem argues, both those who died building the roads and the roads themselves, unfinished and abandoned, have no existence on the map.

Women have long had such a shadowy half-life on the Irish map and in the Irish literary anthology. For all that remains to be done, this reference work and the work of the many scholars illuminating the lives and writing of Irish women are evidence of change. The writer Kate O'Riordan commented in an interview that even though she was born in England and after spending her childhood in Ireland returned to England to live, her publishers prefer to categorize her as an "Irish woman writer"—because they can consequently sell more books (Moloney and Thompson, 208)! Of course, there's irony to be had, if we want to go there. But on the occasion of this marvelous new reference book, perhaps it is preferable to focus on the fact that those readers who do discover new names in *Irish Women Writers: An A-to-Z Guide* will not experience that old frustration of the unavailable text. Internet book services, expanding opportunities for publication, and, yes, the dubious pleasure of the "Irish woman writer" designation having achieved a certain cachet, have guaranteed that the map is not vacant, the anthology is expanding, and perhaps someday, the poster will no longer be lopsided.

BIBLIOGRAPHY

Boland, Eavan. "That the Science of Cartography Is Limited." In *In a Time of Violence*. New York: Norton, 1994, 7–8.

Bourke, Angela, Máirin Ní Dhonneadha, Siobhan Kilfeather, Maria Luddy, Margaret MacCurtain, Gerardine Meaney, Mary O'Dowd, and Clair Wills, eds. *The Field Day Anthology of Irish Writing*. Vols. 4 and 5, *Irish Women's Writing and Traditions*. Cork: Cork University Press, 2002.

Casey, Daniel J., and Linda M. Casey, eds. *Stories by Contemporary Irish Women*. Syracuse, NY: Syracuse University Press, 1990.

De Salvo, Louise, Katherine Hogan, and Kathleen D'Arcy, eds. *Territories of the Voice: Contemporary Stories by Irish Women Writers*. Boston: Beacon, 1989.

Gonzalez, Alexander G., ed. *Contemporary Irish Women Poets: Some Male Perspectives*. Westport, CT: Greenwood, 1999.

Haberstroh, Patricia Boyle, ed. *My Self, My Muse: Irish Women Poets Reflect on Life and Art*. Syracuse, NY: Syracuse University Press, 2001.

———. *Women Creating Women: Contemporary Irish Women Poets*. Syracuse, NY: Syracuse University Press, 1996.

Innes, C. L. *Woman and Nation in Irish Literature and Society: 1880–1935*. London: Harvester Wheatsheaf, 1993.

Kelly, A. A. *Pillars of the House: An Anthology of Verse by Irish Women from 1690 to the Present*. Dublin: Wolfhound, 1988.

Kiberd, Declan. *Inventing Ireland: The Literature of a Modern Nation*. London: Cape, 1995.

Kirkpatrick, Kathryn, ed. *Border Crossings: Irish Women Writers and National Identities*. Tuscaloosa: University of Alabama Press, 2000.

Moloney, Caitriona, and Helen Thompson, eds. *Irish Women Writers Speak Out: Voices from the Field*. With a foreword by Ann Owens Weekes. Syracuse, NY: Syracuse University Press, 2003.

O'Connor, Theresa, ed. *The Comic Tradition in Irish Women Writers*. Gainesville: University Press of Florida, 1996.

O'Faolain, Nuala. *Are You Somebody?: The Accidental Memoir of a Dublin Woman.* New York: Holt, 1996.

Smyth, Ailbhe, ed. *Wildish Things: An Anthology of New Irish Women's Writing.* Dublin: Attic, 1989.

St. Peter, Christine. *Changing Ireland: Strategies in Contemporary Women's Fiction.* New York: Palgrave Macmillan, 2000.

Weekes, Ann Owens. *Irish Women Writers: An Uncharted Tradition.* Lexington: University of Kentucky Press, 1990.

———. *Unveiling Treasures: The Attic Guide to the Published Works of Irish Women Literary Writers: Drama, Fiction, Poetry.* Dublin: Attic, 1993.

Wilson, Rebecca E., and Gillean Somerville-Arjat, eds. *Sleeping with Monsters: Conversations with Scottish and Irish Women Poets.* Dublin: Wolfhound, 1990.

LINDA ANDERSON
(1949–   )

Anthea Cordner

BIOGRAPHY

Linda Anderson was one of five children born to a Protestant working-class family in Belfast, County Down, Northern Ireland. Although her childhood experiences included incidents of religious bigotry, her relationship with her Canadian mother and close childhood friendship with a Catholic girl allowed her to expand her views beyond those of her contemporaries. She was educated in a girls' grammar school, graduated from Queen's University Belfast with a BA in philosophy and French, and received a postgraduate diploma in education. In 1968 she participated in the civil rights movement before emigrating to England and settling in North London in 1972.

Along with several other jobs, she taught in a comprehensive school before tutoring creative writing at several universities, including Nottingham Trent and Goldsmiths' College. This culminated in her appointment as head of creative writing at Lancaster University from 1995 to 2002. Linda Anderson began her career as a poet; however, although she then proceeded to write plays for stage and radio production while pursuing her interest in short stories, she is best known for her two novels about the Troubles. She considers herself "very much" a Northern Irish writer, situated in a specific region and era, and admires fiction that combines historical exactitude with technical innovation to convey the complexities of contemporary problems. She is currently working for the Open University as a reader in creative writing, has recently completed a creative writing PhD at Lancaster, and is working on a new novel.

MAJOR WORKS AND THEMES

Linda Anderson's first novel, *To Stay Alive* (1984), centers around the domestic and public lives of Dan and Rosaleen, a young married couple who are caught up not only in inner-city poverty but also in the Belfast Troubles. Dan, a medical student, is coerced into attending a wounded IRA gunman and escapes death only to be taken in for questioning by the British army. Rosaleen tries to jolt herself back to reality from her death-in-life state through a sexual relationship with Gerry, a British soldier isolated from his peers. She tells him, "I think about death all the time. It drives me insane" (190). The novel evokes the madness, the fear, and the suffocating atmosphere of Belfast during the IRA prisoners' hunger and dirty protests. It focuses on the struggle by the women, the soldiers, and the Catholic working and middle classes to "stay alive," both physically and mentally.

Her second novel, *Cuckoo* (1986), continues the themes of birth, death, sex, and love. It has an adventurous style that incorporates time shifts, a diary extract, and a funeral scene set out as a play. In the beginning the reader is lost in the peculiar narrative stance of Fran, the main female protagonist, as she walks out of her job, moves into a council flat, and lets her "beefy black" neighbor verbally abuse her before passively complying to sex. Her indifference continues through her relationship with Caroline and Dominic, and the birth of her daughter. At a Greenham nuclear protest she awakens to activity and ends her affair with Dominic in a confrontation about Northern Ireland. In this she is acknowledging her "cuckoo" identity: "I felt I had no right to be there. I didn't belong. And now you're telling me I have no right to be here. Well, you're wrong. I can't be dispossessed any more" (88).

Fran's Northern Ireland displacement and trauma widen to become inclusive of the threatening nuclear war and South African apartheid. Lloyd, the "Black Briton" who fathers her baby, shares her identity crisis: "See, Britain not my home! Jamaica not my home! No place my home!" (90). Through writing and protest she hopes to find a place for her child by turning her "words" into a "sword." Her diary relates her traumatic childhood, the death of her boyfriend, her destructive marriage, and the forced abortion of her first child. Literature in words, or silence, is another major theme throughout this novel, which takes the Northern Ireland identity problem and transposes it into the overarching life, death, and crisis themes.

Anderson's poetry and drama pursue similar themes with strong female protagonists "suffocating" or "sleepwalking" through traumatic experiences relating to contemporary Northern Ireland. Several of Anderson's short stories describe the effects on family life of incidents of violence and death, which frequently include an examination of traditional gender divides. The dead become powerful symbols and in turn blank signifiers on which future generations can "read" the results of violence. There is, alternatively, a sense that women can escape this inevitable historic patterning. This concept is exemplified in "The Death of Men" and "Waste," when the tribal rituals surrounding death expose scarred responses to sectarian violence.

Linda Anderson notes how her interaction with the violent Troubles often binds the private to the public persona. She depicts her obsessive linkage between domestic "privacies" and "the mutilating world" of political violence (Anderson, quoted in Weekes, 16). An example of this can be found in her only canonical poem, "Gang-Bang Ulster Style," which is based on the 1974 "Romper Room Killing" of Ann Ogilby and reenacts the story of a woman who is brutally murdered as a punishment for an extramarital affair while her husband is held as a political prisoner. Anderson's novels, stories, plays, and poems all respond to similar acts of violence while commenting effectively on the female responses to such traumas.

CRITICAL RECEPTION

Thus far, in keeping with the fate of other female prose writers in the North of Ireland, there has been little critical engagement with Anderson's work. Early reviews tended to point to her "analyses of hatred" (*Kaleidoscope*, BBC Radio Four, March 5, 1986). Her first novel received hostile reviews in Northern Ireland yet was widely appreciated in Britain and America. Reviews from the *Irish Times* and the *Belfast Telegraph* acknowledged the powerful negative imagery evocative of regional tragedies. The novel proved popular not only when short-listed for the David Higham and Sinclair prizes, but also on winning awards from the Arts Councils of Great Britain and

Northern Ireland. In 1997 Anderson received the Write Out Loud, a BBC and Arts Council award for radio work. She also received the Testimony Award from the Sunday Playhouse in 1990 and Radio Four's Book at Bedtime Award in 1992.

Cuckoo drew rave reviews for its technical merits and ability to expose harsh truths about identity, bigotry, and belonging. Its publication led to the author being chosen as one of the top ten new authors in 1988 by W. H. Smith and *Cosmopolitan.* Claire Buck notes the postmodern and deconstructive nature of Anderson's work, which she describes as "boldly experimental and subversive" (279–80). Ruth Carr's *The Field Day Anthology* includes Linda Anderson among her list of female writers who can "challenge the forces opposed to social change in ways that avoid simplistic polemics" (1133). With an impending new novel to follow several short stories, Anderson continues to have much to convey about the Troubles and proves to be an important Northern Irish woman writer.

BIBLIOGRAPHY

Works by Linda Anderson

Fiction

Cuckoo. London: Bodley Head, 1986.
The Nurse's Wife and Other Stories. London: True North, 2004.
To Stay Alive. London: Bodley Head, 1984; London: Futura, 1985. Also published as *We Can't All Be Heroes, You Know.* New York: Ticknor and Fields, 1985.

Unpublished Plays

Blinding, 1990. (For Etherton and Stern Gallery in Tucson, Arizona, to accompany paintings by Margaret Bailey Doogan, and later in Belfast Arts Festival in Queen's University.)
Charmed Lives, 1988. (Runner-up in Wandsworth All-London Competition.)
The Flight Response, 1995. (Rocket Theatre Company production for Square Albert Theatre, Manchester.)

Poetry

Anderson's poetry has been included in several anthologies in Ireland, Britain, and America. Examples include *Women on War,* Daniello Gioseffi, ed. (New York: Simon and Schuster, 1988); *Pillars of the House,* A. A. Kelly, ed. (Dublin: Wolfhound, 1987); *The Field Day Anthology of Irish Writing V,* Angela Bourke, Mairin Ni Dhonneadha, Siobhan Kilfeather, Maria Luddy, Margaret MacCurtain, Gerardine Meaney, Mary O'Dowd, and Clair Wills, eds. (Cork: Cork University Press, 2002). In addition, Anderson has been published in creative writing magazines and journals such as *Cyphers, Iron, Symbolic Interaction,* and *Mslexia.*

Studies of Linda Anderson

Buck, Claire, ed. *Bloomsbury Guide to Women's Literature.* London: Bloomsbury, 1994.
Carr, Ruth. "Contemporary Fiction" and "Biography." In *The Field Day Anthology of Irish Writing.* Vol. 5, edited by Angela Bourke et al., 1130–38, 1231. Cork: Cork University Press, 2002.
Weekes, Ann Owens. *Unveiling Treasures: The Attic Guide to the Published Works of Irish Women Literary Writers.* Dublin: Attic, 1993, 15–17.

IVY BANNISTER
(1951–   )

Maryanne Felter

BIOGRAPHY

Born in New York on July 11, 1951, Ivy Bannister emigrated to Ireland when she was nineteen years old, having no Irish background or heritage but wanting "to live in a place where even the most mundane conversations are lyrical" (Moloney and Thompson, 147). Bannister grew up in Connecticut, took her BA at Smith College, and did her PhD at Trinity College in Dublin. Although Bannister admits to being "half German, and French, Swedish, Norwegian, and a little bit of Cherokee [she] mostly feel[s] Irish" (quoted in Moloney and Thompson, 148). Today she is included in the lists of modern Irish short-story writers and playwrights.

MAJOR WORKS AND THEMES

Ivy Bannister has worked in all genres. Early on Bannister tended to write plays, and her dissertation on Bernard Shaw was, as she says herself, "a fantastic training ground—learning his plays back to front was an education; familiarity with reasonable, lucid, witty prose style was a preparation for writing everything and anything" (e-mail message to author, September 21, 2003). Most of her dramatic work has been done for radio and hence is difficult to find in print; even the dates of broadcast are unavailable, according to Bannister. But one of her earliest works, *The Wilde Circus Show* (1990), a play about Oscar Wilde's father, published by the *Journal of Irish Literature,* focuses on the triangular marital situation that included Sir William Wilde, Speranza, and Mary Travers. *The Wall* (no date), a play about family relationships, won the Mobil Ireland Playwrighting Award. Some of Bannister's stories also became plays; she herself tells of "Lift Me Up and Pour Me Out," a play based on a short story, that was done by three actresses in Germany "on a double bill with a Beckett play" and also as "a radio play by RTE with one actress as a monologue" (e-mail message to author, September 29, 2003). Hogan mentions an early play about Constance Markiewicz, *The Rebel Countess* (no date; Hogan, 118), a radio monologue about Countess Markiewicz's life and nationalist work. *Traveller's Tales* (no date) uses Beatrice Grimshaw, the Irish explorer, as a character and was performed in Derry as a full-length stage play, while an earlier, shorter version was used by the BBC for a production for schoolchildren. Bannister has won a number of awards for her plays, including the O.Z. Whitehead Award (1986), the Listowel Award (1987), and the P.J. O'Connor Award (1991).

Bannister's fiction, writes Moloney, "has been complimented for its understanding of difficult relationships" (148). And in fact almost all of her works deal with the quirks, idiosyncrasies, and sometimes horrors of relationships. Short stories explore the theme of marital infidelity, including "The Magician," the title story of her 1996 collection

The Magician and Other Stories, as well as her "remake" of the Oberon-Titania-Bottom story from *Midsummer Night's Dream* in "The King, the Queen, and the Donkey Man" in *Ride on Rapunzel* (1992), and "What Big Teeth," in *In Sunshine or in Shadow* (1998). She writes hauntingly of parent-child relationships as well in "My Mother's Daughter" and "Blood Relations" in *Prize Winning Radio Stories* (1994), "In My Father's Garage" in *Home—An Anthology of Modern Irish Writing* (1996), and "The Woman Who Had Difficulty Answering the Phone" (2001). In most of her works, Bannister's play with language is evident, and she has developed a style that is colorful and sometimes magical in its inventiveness. Improbable and inexplicable characters and plots pepper the collection *Magician*: "The Family of Jimmy McManus" with Finbar the spider-boy, "Seduced" with the artist Vincent, "The Chiropodist" with a foot-fetishing murderer, all twist questions of parental, sexual, and romantic relationship to grotesque ends. "Love," which won the Francis MacManus Award in 1999, is a beautifully touching story about a mother and her three children, one of whom is mentally disabled, and the hopes and fears she has for them, while "Help Wanted" takes on the question of surrogate motherhood. Bannister's world is a quirky one, but one that explores humanity from many different perspectives. Although she has described herself as "mid-Atlantic," being part neither of Ireland nor of America, very little in her work dissects the intersection of national identities; instead her focus appears to be on the individual character in a specific situation or relationship.

Most recently, Bannister has been writing and publishing poetry. Many of her poems have been published in some collections of Irish works as well as in the *Irish Times,* the *Sunday Tribune, Poetry Ireland Review,* and *The Shop.* Her poetry tends to be well wrought, often more formal than free verse, with a real attention to sound, wordplay, and striking imagery. Bannister's keen ear may be the result of her writing for so long for stage and radio. Bannister is currently working on a memoir, *Blunt Trauma*, as yet unpublished, a hauntingly provocative story of her sister's death in the Swissair disaster of 1998. The memoir explores family relations from a nonfiction point of view and goes far toward glossing some of Bannister's other work. *Blunt Trauma* is a powerful and memorable piece of nonfiction.

CRITICAL RECEPTION

Although Bannister continues to write and has been fairly prolific in her play and story writing, she has not been picked up by the major critical reference sources. She has a short biographical note in *The Dictionary of Irish Literature* but no mention in *Contemporary Authors* or other resources in the Gale series. Reviews of her works, as well as the works themselves, are difficult to come by in the United States. In 1997, the *Irish Independent* said of *Magician*: "This enchanting and occasionally macabre accumulation of stories mirrors [Bannister's] own personal battles between the traditional and the contemporary, the old and the new," while *Books Ireland* said the stories were "quirky and offbeat and usually pack a surprise." In all, Bannister deserves more critical attention than she is currently receiving.

BIBLIOGRAPHY

Works by Ivy Bannister

"Blood Relations." In *Prize-Winning Radio Stories*, edited by Michael Littleton, 91–96. Dublin: Mercier, 1994.

"The Dancing Chicken of Chinatown." In *Prize-Winning Radio Stories*, edited by Michael Littleton, 61–66. Dublin: Mercier, 1994.

"In My Father's Garage." In *Home—An Anthology of Modern Irish Writing*, edited by Siobhan Parkinson, 6–7. Dublin: A. & A. Farmar, 1996.

"The King, the Queen and the Donkey-Man." In *Ride on Rapunzel: Fairytales for Feminists*. Dublin: Attic, 1992, 103–7.

Magician and Other Stories. Dublin: Poolbeg, 1996.

"My Mother's Daughter." In *Prize-Winning Radio Stories*, edited by Michael Littleton, 27–32. Dublin: Mercier, 1994.

"A Place Called Tubingen." In *The State of Irish Theatre in the 'Nineties*, edited by Eberhard Bort, 6–8. Trier: Wissenschaftlicher Verlag, 1996.

"Seduced." *Virgins and Hyacinths: An Attic Press Book of Fiction*. Ed. Caroline Walsh. Dublin: Poolbeg, 1993. 123–139.

"Sloughing Off." In *A Dream Recurring and Other Stories and Poems: Maxwell House Winners 2*. Dublin: Arlen House, 1980, 68–69.

Various entries. In *Dictionary of Irish Literature*, edited by Robert Hogan. Westport, CT: Greenwood, 1996.

"What Big Teeth." In *In Shadow or in Sunshine*, edited by Kate Cuise O'Brien and Mary Maher, 1–12. New York: Delacorte, 1998.

"The Woman Who Had Difficulty Answering the Phone." In *Loose Horses: Stories from South Dublin*, 2001. http://homepage.eircom.net/~loosehorses/stories/woman.htm (accessed August 25, 2005).

Interviews with Ivy Bannister

"Ivy Bannister." Interview by Caitriona Moloney. In *Irish Women Speak Out: Voices from the Field*, edited by Catriona Moloney and Helen Thompson, 147–55. Syracuse, NY: Syracuse University Press, 2003.

Studies of Ivy Bannister

Hogan, Robert. "Ivy Bannister." In *Dictionary of Irish Literature*. Vol. 1. 2nd ed. Westport, CT: Greenwood, 1996, 117–18.

Sweeney, Eamon. "Review of Magician." *Irish Times*, January 15, 1997, 16.

Weekes, Ann Owens. *Unveiling Treasures: The Attic Guide to the Published Work of Irish Women Literary Writers: Drama, Fiction, Poetry*. Dublin: Attic, 1993, 21–22.

MARY BECKETT
(1926–   )

Virginia B. Mack

BIOGRAPHY

Mary Beckett was born, and grew up as a Catholic, in Belfast, but, as she has noted, she has a Protestant name because her grandfather was a Protestant, and when she was growing up, her family lived in a Protestant neighborhood (Perry). In this respect, as in many others, her life and work embody what I refer to as "radical ambiguity." She was educated at St. Columban's National School, St. Dominic's High School, and St. Mary's Teacher Training College and worked as a primary teacher in Holy Cross, Ardoyne, for eleven years. She and her husband, Peter Gaffey, met in the Aran Islands, were married in 1956, and shortly after that moved to Dublin. They have five children; another, the first, died at birth.

Her first short story, "The Excursion," was on BBC Northern Ireland in 1949. Like Val Mulkerns and James Plunkett, she was one of the *Bell* writers, publishing several short stories there in the early 1950s and contributing a nonfiction piece, "The Young Writer," along with John Montague, Valentin Iremonger, John Ryan, and James Plunkett. She has noted in conversation that she was encouraged to write by Peadar O'Donnell, who was then editor of the *Bell*. When she wrote "Theresa," published in the *Bell* in 1951, O'Donnell came to Belfast and told her not to stop writing (Beckett, interview with the author, January 24, 1996). She also contributed a short story, "Three Dreams Cross," to David Marcus's *Irish Writing: Women Writers Issue*, the first journal published in Ireland to be dedicated entirely to women. Beckett remembers quite a bit of encouragement and support from her parents, especially her father, who was a teacher.

Beckett has commented that in Ireland "women wrote, then faded out" (Beckett, interview). Her own life follows the pattern she described: after a successful beginning, she had a twenty-year literary silence. She attributes this to her displacement from Belfast to Dublin, the rigors of rearing five small children, and the collapse of the *Bell* and *Irish Writing*, the magazines for which she wrote (Perry, 64).

MAJOR WORKS AND THEMES

Beckett broke her literary silence with the publication of *A Belfast Woman* (1980). This collection is composed of eleven stories set in Northern Ireland near or in Belfast and characterized by themes of isolation and emotional paralysis, regret for past mistakes, hostility between husbands and wives—all often mitigated only by love for children. "The Excursion," first in the collection, takes place in the late 1940s and sets the tone of the book. Eleanor, a wife, wants to go on the Young Farmers Club excursion to Dublin; however, her husband, James, goes instead. When he returns, drunk, having spent the entire day in Dublin in a bar, Eleanor is so angry that she tries to push him into the fire. The love of children prevails in "Theresa," set in 1946. This is the tale of a young girl (Theresa) and her baby, Deirdre, the illegitimate daughter of an American soldier. Deirdre's "otherness" is compounded by the fact that she is black, but rather than becoming an outcast, she is accepted by the community and by the Belfast man that Theresa eventually marries. "A Belfast Woman," the title story, takes place after 1972. It is a first-person narration by a Catholic woman in Belfast who chronicles the Troubles as well as the story of a search for a proper home and a denunciation of the violence that displaces homeowners.

The protest against the violence in the North that is a central theme of "A Belfast Woman" is extended in *Give Them Stones* (1987). The most well received critically of all Beckett's works, the novel is narrated by Martha Murtagh, the protagonist, and set in Belfast between 1941 and the 1970s. A primary theme is the condemnation of violence and the hope for a united Ireland combined with Martha's developing independence by establishing herself as a baker.

A Literary Woman (1990), a collection of ten short stories set in Dublin in the late 1970s and 1980s, is Beckett's latest and most accomplished work. These stories move away from the explicit theme of violence in the North to an eerie, generalized sense of danger that suggests the work of Henry James, whom Beckett has mentioned as an influence (Beckett, interview). This element is particularly obvious in "Ghosts," the second story, in the inexplicable presence of "two old ladies knitting" who appear on an unplugged television in a small detached house in Dublin. It is developed further through anonymous, threatening letters that appear in five stories. Beckett's use of the device culminates in "A Literary Woman," the title story. Narrated by Winifred Teeling, a spinster from Dublin who plays the role of an evil god attempting to change people's lives by writing anonymous letters filled with false accusations, it is the story of the woman writer as outlaw. In addition to her novels and short stories, Beckett has published four children's books, which are set in Ireland.

CRITICAL RECEPTION

Beckett's short stories were initially received warmly by Peadar O'Donnell and David Marcus. However, after the *Bell* and *Irish Writing* ceased publication, Beckett's literary work did not appear publicly, and she seemed to have been forgotten until the 1970s, when Marcus published "A Belfast Woman" in the literary section of the *Irish Times* (Perry, 69). Since then, critical commentary has focused on the feminist content of her work and her stance against the violence in the North. She has given two substantial published interviews, by Donna Perry and by Megan Sullivan. Her work has frequently been anthologized in collections of short stories by Irish women. In one of the earliest collections (1984), Janet Madden-Simpson notes that she allows "currents of feminine revolt to come to the surface" (9). Ailbhe Smyth cites Beckett in her comments on Irish women writers' concern with language and voice in her introduction to *Wildish Things: An Anthology of New Irish Women's Writing* (1989, 9). Jeanette Shumaker in "Irish 'Fallen Women' in Stories by Mary Beckett, Lilian Roberts Finlay and Emma Cooke" looks at Beckett's short story "Ruth" (*A Belfast Woman*) using the literary theory of Carol Gilligan, Julia Kristeva, and Luce Irigaray. In a later article Shumaker is concerned with mother-daughter rivalries specifically ("Mother-Daughter Rivalries").

Beckett has been recognized in several articles as a voice of the women of Northern Ireland in advocating against violence on both sides. In a positive treatment of *Give Them Stones,* Gerry Smyth points out Beckett's concern with the relationship among the individual, the family, and the larger social and political systems of the state. In her article " 'Instead I Said I Am a Home Baker': Nationalist Ideology and Materialist Politics in Mary Beckett's *Give Them Stones*," Megan Sullivan is concerned with Martha Murtagh's move from her identification with nationalism to a "gender-based class politics" (227). Sullivan also includes a discussion of Martha's emerging criticism of the Republican movement in *Give Them Stones* in *Women in Northern Ireland: Cultural Studies and Material Conditions.*

BIBLIOGRAPHY

Works by Mary Beckett

A Belfast Woman. Dublin: Poolbeg, 1980; New York: William Morrow, 1989.
A Family Tree. Dublin: Poolbeg, 1992.

Give Them Stones. London: Bloomsbury, 1987; New York: William Morrow, 1988; New York: Harper and Row, 1989.

Hannah or Pink Balloons. Dublin: Merino, 1995.

A Literary Woman. London: Bloomsbury, 1990, 1991.

Orla at School. Dublin: Poolbeg, 1991.

Orla Was Six. Dublin: Poolbeg, 1989, 1992.

Studies of Mary Beckett

Madden-Simpson, Janet. "Introduction: Anglo-Irish Literature: The Received Tradition." In *Woman's Part: An Anthology of Short Fiction by and about Irishwomen 1890–1960*. Dublin: Arlen House, 1984, 1–19.

Perry, Donna Marie. "Mary Beckett." In *Backtalk: Women Writers Speak Out: Interviews*. New Brunswick, NJ: Rutgers University Press, 1993, 63–82.

Shumaker, Jeanette. "Irish 'Fallen Women' in Stories by Mary Beckett, Lilian Roberts Finlay and Emma Cooke." *Short Story* 7, no. 2 (Fall 1999): 91–98.

———. "Mother-Daughter Rivalries in Stories by Irish Women: Elizabeth Bowen, Edna O'Brien, Mary Beckett, and Helen Lucy Burke." *North Dakota Quarterly* 68, no. 1 (Winter 2001): 70–85.

Smyth, Ailbhe. "Introduction." In *Wildish Things*. Dublin: Attic, 1989, 7–16.

Smyth, Gerry. *The Novel and the Nation*. London: Pluto, 1997.

Sullivan, Megan. "'Instead I Said I Am a Home Baker': Nationalist Ideology and Materialist Politics in Mary Beckett's *Give Them Stones*." In *Border Crossings: Irish Women Writers and National Identities*, edited by Kathryn Kirkpatrick, 227–49. Tuskaloosa: University of Alabama Press, 2000.

———. "Mary Beckett: An Interview." *Irish Literary Supplement* 14, no. 2 (Fall 1995): 10–12.

———. *Women in Northern Ireland: Cultural Studies and Material Conditions*. Gainesville: University of Florida Press, 1999.

Weekes, Ann Owens. *Unveiling Treasures: The Attic Guide to the Published Works of Irish Women Literary Writers: Drama, Fiction, Poetry*. Dublin: Attic, 1993, 29–31.

SARA BERKELEY
(1967–   )

Claire McEwen

BIOGRAPHY

Sara Berkeley was born in North Dublin in 1967, where she was brought up with her three brothers by her Irish father and English mother. She was educated at Manor House, Raheny, and at Trinity College, Dublin, where she attained a BA in English literature and German in 1989. She received a scholarship from the Education Abroad Program for the academic year 1989–1990 and spent that time at the University of California at Berkeley. She moved to London in 1990 and graduated with an MSc in technical communication from Southbank Polytechnic University the following year. In

1991 she received an Irish Arts Council writing bursary, which she used to travel to America to research *Shadowing Hannah* (1999). She then returned to London to work for Exley Publications as a freelance writer and spent the next two years writing nonfiction educational books for children. From then until 1999 she worked for a San Francisco computer company as a technical writer and editor. Eventually, she moved back to London for a while with her then-boyfriend, but after the relationship ended she returned to San Francisco.

Now Sara Tolchin, she lives in San Francisco with her husband and daughter, although she continues to use her maiden name for her writing. She works as a freelance technical writer and editor under the name of Quarto Writing and has her own Web site, which contains examples of her technical and business writing and also carries several uncollected poems written between 1995 and 1999. Her creative writing career began at the age of sixteen when Dermot Bolger published a selection of her poems in Raven Arts Press's *Raven Introductions 3* (1983). Since then she has published three collections of poetry, a book of short stories, and a novel, as well as publishing widely in journals, magazines, and anthologies. She has also published a number of translations from Irish, including "Sweeney's Eyes," a translation of Cathal Ó'Searcaigh's poem "Súile Shuibhne," which was included in volume 3 of the *Field Day Anthology of Irish Writing* (1991). Having spent most of the last few years taking care of her daughter, she now has an almost-completed manuscript for a further poetry collection; a second novel is with her New York–based agent, and she is currently at work on a third.

MAJOR WORKS AND THEMES

Berkeley's first collection of poetry, *Penn* (1986), was followed by *Home Movie Nights* (1989). Her most recent collection, *Facts About Water* (1994), contains a selection of poems from her first two books as well as an entire new section. There is no specifically Irish resonance in these collections, something that Berkeley attributes to her feelings of being an "outsider" even while growing up in Ireland, and she views herself as part of a female literary tradition rather than an Irish one. Indeed, much of the thematic content of the poems is specifically feminine, centering on motherhood, water, blood, and bones, but the most striking theme that runs throughout her poetic work is the fragile relationship between life and death. This is particularly notable in the intensity of the many love poems, including "The Parting" and "He Isn't There," and in the heavy preoccupation with death and the process of remembrance and commemoration in poems such as "I Don't Want His Name in Here" and "Herjia." There is an extensive use of pronouns in Berkeley's poetry, which creates a sense of intimacy and involvement, drawing the reader into the poetry and creating a feeling of shared experiences. It is not until *Facts About Water* that the influence of Berkeley's geographical changes are most evident, with poems such as "Zoo Gardens, Berlin," "Paddington," and the coupled "Fault" and "Valley," indicative of her international experiences.

Berkeley has said, "Poetry will always be my first love, and I like to write it best of all" (Berkeley, personal correspondence). Her poetic language, however, translates exceptionally well into her prose, creating powerful and hauntingly beautiful short stories, which are concerned with the intimate relationships between the private and public selves, between silence and articulation. In all of the stories collected in *The Swimmer in the Deep Blue Dream* (1992), there is a sense of the impossibility of real communication reinforced by the inner torments or confusion suffered by the characters. The problematic nature of conveying this is demonstrated in the lack of resolution and the suppression of details in the stories. In "The Sky's Gone Out," for example, a man is captivated by a young woman on the London Underground and impulsively decides to follow her until finally she stops and howls an inarticulate sentence to the wind. At the end of the story he realizes what she has said but the reader is kept in the dark in order to convey the protagonist's confusion. Berkeley frequently repeats names, places, and circumstances in the collection, which not only holds the collection together but also creates a sense of universality.

Shadowing Hannah developed out of the title story of *The Swimmer in the Deep Blue Dream* and deals with Ireland's last taboo: incest. The novel charts the life of Hannah as she tries to escape her past and her incestuous relationship with her elder brother, Rene. Hannah, in an echo of Berkeley's own migration, moves from Dublin to London and then finally to America in search of a new and untainted life. The nature of Hannah and Rene's relationship is not made clear until the latter part of the novel and focuses instead on Hannah's attempts to fit into her new life and to cope with the secret that haunts her. Her inability to communicate with the people she meets in London is in stark contrast to the articulacy of the letters that she and Rene exchange, and this functions to dispel much of the sense of impropriety about the relationship. Indeed, Berkeley treats the subject with such compassion and tenderness that the awfulness of the situation evinces sympathy rather than revulsion in what is essentially a tragic love story. Again, there is little indication of Berkeley's Irish identity in this work and it is perhaps notable that both Hannah and Rene leave Ireland to escape their guilt. In personal correspondence Berkeley herself has said that she left Ireland "partly to move away from the stifling Church/State relationship and the parochial nature of society in the 80s," finally finding her "freedom" in America. In this novel, and for Berkeley, it seems that the age-old process of Irish emigration is, ultimately, the means of escape once again.

CRITICAL RECEPTION

Despite some excellent reviews, Sara Berkeley's work has received very little critical attention, and her prose work, in particular, appears to have been largely overlooked. However, her novel was favorably reviewed by the *Read Ireland Book Review,* which described *Shadowing Hannah* as "captivating, controversial and deeply felt," while the *New York Times* called it a "disturbing yet vibrant first novel." Her poetry has been highly acclaimed by reviewers writing for, among others, the *Times*, the *Irish Times*, the *Sunday Press*, the *Irish Literary Supplement*, and the *Irish Literary Review*. Her debut collection, *Penn* (1986), was short-listed for the Irish Book Awards and the Sunday Tribune Arts Award. Berkeley was also nominated for the *Pushcart Prize Anthology* in 2001 for a poem called "Great Basin, April 1997," which was published in the *Birmingham Poetry Review*. She has been extremely well received by other Irish poets including Eavan Boland, Joan McBreen, and Paul Durcan, who remarked that Berkeley "is the most naturally gifted poet to emerge in Ireland since Michael Hartnett in 1960." Sarah Fulford devotes a whole chapter of her recent critical study, *Gendered Spaces in Contemporary Irish Poetry* (2002), to a discussion of "Sara Berkeley's Nomadic Subjects." In this critical essay, Fulford examines the ways in which Berkeley's emigrant experience shape her sense of national identity and how this is then represented in her poetry. In addition to reviews and criticism, it is also important to note the extent to which Berkeley's work has been anthologized as a measure of how highly her work is regarded. Of particular note is the inclusion of her work in major publications such as *The Picador Book of Contemporary Irish Fiction* (1993) and *The Penguin Book of Contemporary Irish Poetry* (1991).

BIBLIOGRAPHY

Works by Sara Berkeley

Facts About Water. Dublin: New Island; Newcastle upon Tyne, UK: Bloodaxe; Saskatchewan: Thistledown, 1994.
Home-Movie Nights. Dublin: Raven Arts; Saskatchewan: Thistledown, 1989.
Penn. Dublin: Raven Arts; Saskatchewan: Thistledown, 1986.
Shadowing Hannah. Dublin: New Island, 1999.
The Swimmer in the Deep Blue Dream. Dublin: Raven Arts; Saskatchewan: Thistledown, 1992.

Interview with Sara Berkeley

Donovan, Katie. "Poetry in Motion." *Irish Times*, October 12, 1994, 12.

Studies of Sara Berkeley

Fulford, Sarah. "Sara Berkeley's Nomadic Subjects." In *Gendered Spaces in Contemporary Irish Poetry*. Bern: Peter Lang, 2002, 215–46.
Meaney, Gerardine. "History Gasps: Myth in Contemporary Irish Women's Poetry." In *Poetry in Contemporary Irish Literature*, edited by Michael Kenneally, 99–113. Gerrards Cross, UK: Smythe, 1995.
Wilson, Rebecca E., and Gillean Somerville-Arjat, eds. *Sleeping with Monsters: Conversations with Scottish and Irish Women Poets*. Dublin: Wolfhound, 1990, 158–64.

MAEVE BINCHY
(1940–   )

Rebecca Steinberger

BIOGRAPHY

Formerly a journalist, Maeve Binchy has achieved international success with her fiction's accessible characters, story lines, and themes. But the affable Binchy could not have predicted that she would become one of the most recognizable Irish women writers of the late twentieth century. Born in Dalkey, Ireland, in 1940, Binchy was the eldest of four children of Maureen Blackmore Binchy, a nurse, and William T. Binchy, a lawyer. She received her education from a local convent school and graduated in 1961 from University College Dublin with degrees in French and history. After graduation, Binchy taught for the Zion Schools in Dublin. However, following a monumental trip to Israel, where she was on a kibbutz, Binchy became engaged in the writing process.

It was her father, impressed with her descriptions of a foreign land, who was responsible for her initial publication; the *Irish Independent* printed her letters, and when Binchy returned from Israel, she gave up teaching in lieu of a writing career. In 1968, Binchy was offered an editorial position with the *Irish Times* covering women's issues. After the death of her parents, Binchy became a correspondent for the *Irish Times* in London. In 1975, she married children's author Gordon Snell and began writing her own brand of fiction.

Binchy began writing plays and short stories, but she did not obtain eminence until the publication of her first novel, *Light a Penny Candle* (1982). Twelve novels later, Binchy has realized her success through her books' translations in numerous languages, the making of *Circle of Friends* (1990) into a hit film, and the adaptations of her stories into made-for-television movies. In 1999, Binchy was awarded a Lifetime Achievement Award at the Nibbies (British Book Awards). In an interview with Lewis Burke Frumkes, she notes the growing pool of celebrated Irish writers: "I think it has a lot to do with the Irish having become a lot more confident in themselves. . . . Ireland is a country that has come out into the sunshine. I never feel that the past is always looking over my shoulder because I think that everybody is writing differently. New people are writing, young people are writing. They've found a voice for themselves: their own voice" (15). With the announcement that she will retire in order to spend more time traveling in Ireland and abroad with her husband, Binchy's statement seems to invite her devoted readers to engage in the works of new voices in the literary world—and Irish voices at that.

MAJOR WORKS AND THEMES

The number and popularity of Binchy's novels, in particular, are a testament to her ability to connect to her reading public—from Ireland and abroad. While her novels are situated in Ireland, her themes of romance, opportunity, and taking chances remain readily accessible to any reader who approaches her fiction. In addition, the strength of Ireland—through setting and characters—is not fixed in one location, but rather spreads across the island nation and thus examines both rural and urban life. And while romance blossoms for many of her characters, her love plots embody a sense of realism.

While popular culture tends to focus on the universal qualities in Binchy's novels, her works importantly engage controversial issues inherent in Irish society. Her ongoing examination of contemporary Ireland begins in her first novel, *Light a Penny Candle*, which investigates the relationship between Ireland and England through its two main characters during World War II and postwar Europe. This is followed by *The Lilac Bus* (1984), which exposes oppression and nationalism in an Ireland faced with an emergent identity as social mores shift and the culture attempts to modernize. Also, class issues become paramount in her highly acclaimed *Circle of Friends* as the urban is diametrically opposed to the rural.

Binchy exposes her readers to other lands throughout her cadre of "Irish" novels; for example, the main character in *Glass Lake* (1994) runs away to England to escape a confining marriage, and a Dubliner befriends a New Englander in *Tara Road* (1998). Therefore, by giving her readers glimpses of life in other countries by women from those countries, she highlights the "Irishness" of her protagonists. In doing so, Binchy lends a voice to the typical Irish woman who reads—and identifies with—her accessible fiction.

CRITICAL RECEPTION

In an interview with Mike Burns, Binchy asserts, "I'm not an academic writer. I'm no Booker Prize winner writer. I'm really at the popular end, which is no bad place to be. But I'm not like a writer people would read and be able to quote and would study in universities. So I don't think I just have the Irish market. I think I have mainly the women's market" (346). Binchy does not apologize for the absence of erudite material in her texts; as a result, the reception of her works has been less than critical and primarily focused on the pop-Irishness of her tales.

However, she has received serious applause from women who find value in her portrayal of confident, clever, and average female characters. As Cristina Odone bemoans Binchy's retirement, she explains that the importance of her writing—as opposed to that of other contemporary women writers—is that "she never marginalises us. . . . We do not have to measure up to impossible feats of acrobatics or aspire to unattainable levels of emotional toughness" (24). The real success for Binchy, then, is her ability to create realistic characters who do not fall prey to the sexual and social constraints that pervade our twenty-first-century culture. Ultimately, she affords the everyday reader the capacity to voice her own mantra of individualism and self-assuredness.

BIBLIOGRAPHY

Works by Maeve Binchy

Central Line. Dublin: Ward River, 1977.
Central Line: Stories of Big City Life. London: London Quartet, 1978.
Circle of Friends. New York: Dell, 1991.
The Copper Beach. New York: Bantam Doubleday Dell, 1993.
Deeply Regretted. Dublin: Turoe, 1979.
Dublin 4. Minneapolis, MN: Irish Books and Media, 1982.
Echoes. New York: Viking, 1986.
End of Term. Dublin: Peacock Theater, 1976.
Evening Class. New York: Delacorte, 1996.
Firefly Summer. New York: Delacorte, 1996.
"For the Irish, Long-Windedness Serves as a Literary Virtue." *New York Times*, November 4, 2002, E1.
Glass Lake. New York: Delacorte, 1988.
The Half Promised Land. Dublin: Peacock Theater, 1979.
Light a Penny Candle. New York: Viking, 1983.
The Lilac Bus. Minneapolis, MN: Irish Books and Media, 1984.
"Maeve's Diary." Dublin: Irish Times, 1979, 118.
"My First Book." Dublin: Irish Times, 1976, 131.
Quentins. New York: Dutton, 2002.
Scarlet Feather. New York: Dutton, 2000.
Silver Wedding. New York: Delacorte, 1999.
This Year It Will Be Different and Other Stories. New York: Delacorte, 1996.
Victoria Line. Minneapolis, MN: Irish Books and Media, 1980.

Studies of Maeve Binchy

Burns, Mike. "Maeve Binchy (Bestselling Irish Author)." *Europe* 345 (1995): 22–25.
Current Biography Index 56 (1995): 6–12.

Frumkes, Lewis Burke. "A Conversation with Maeve Binchy." *Writer* 113, no. 2 (Winter 2000): 14–15.

Kirby, Anthony. "Pupil of the Storyteller Tradition." *Christian Science Monitor*, March 11, 1999, 19.

Odone, Cristina. "Don't Allow the Clitterati to Make You Feel Inadequate." *New Statesman* 129, no. 4485 (2000): 24–26.

Walters, Kate. "Queen *Maeve*." *World of Hibernia* 6, no. 4 (March 2001): 177.

Weber, Katharine. "Maeve Binchy." *Publishers Weekly* 239, no. 47 (1992): 42, 44.

CAROLINE BLACKWOOD
(1931–1996)

Coleen Comerford

BIOGRAPHY

Caroline Blackwood is as well known for her spectacular life as for her literary career. Born Lady Caroline Hamilton-Temple-Blackwood on July 16, 1931, outside Belfast, she was a descendant of the playwright Richard Brinsley Sheridan, daughter of the Marquess of Dufferin and Ava, and heiress to the Guinness fortune. Her father, who died while Blackwood was young, was a politician and fierce drinker, and her mother a narcissist. She was raised mainly by neglectful nannies in a rickety Georgian mansion on a five-thousand-acre estate. As a young woman, Blackwood was educated in boarding schools and later worked as a reader at Hulton Press. Her first journalistic piece, an article on beatniks, was published in *Encounter*. This piece led to other assignments and Blackwood was soon writing for periodicals such as the *Observer*. As an adult, Blackwood was intelligent, beautiful, rich, and witty, but she suffered dramatically from her childhood neglect. In addition to inheriting the wit and literary flair of her ancestors, she inherited alcoholism, which afflicted both of her parents. Blackwood's heavy drinking added to her depression and moody, reckless personality.

Blackwood had three tumultuous marriages. At eighteen, she eloped with painter Lucien Freud, the grandson of Sigmund Freud. A strikingly beautiful woman, Blackwood posed for several of Freud's finest paintings. After two years, Blackwood deserted Freud and departed for Hollywood, where she hoped to become an actor. Instead, she established herself in the social circle of Christopher Isherwood, Cecil Beaton, and Kenneth Tynan, tried LSD with Carey Grant, and soon left for New York without having taken a screen test. Blackwood met her second husband, composer Israel Citkowitz, in New York. The couple raised three daughters, although one daughter, Ivana, was in reality fathered by English screenwriter Ivan Moffat. Like her own mother, Blackwood was cruel and neglectful toward her daughters and, also like her mother, hired inept and uncaring nannies to take care of them. One of her daughters eventually became a heroin addict and committed suicide. During her marriage to Citkowitz, Blackwood

and her surroundings became seamy; friends described her home as littered with cigarette butts and empty bottles of liquor and pill cases. Blackwood became known for
sordid public incidents, and years of heavy drinking began to mar her beauty. Blackwood and Citkowitz divorced in 1959. In 1972, Blackwood was married for the third
time, to poet Robert Lowell, Citkowitz remaining in the house to guard their children
from Lowell, whose manic attacks were frightening. During the years of their marriage, Blackwood and Lowell were faced with hospitalizations for his mental break-
downs and her nervous depression and alcoholism. However, Blackwood and Lowell's
chaotic and destructive relationship inspired both of their work. In Lowell's book *The
Dolphin,* Blackwood is portrayed as various seductive and devouring aquatic beings.
Lowell finally left Blackwood to return to his former wife, Elizabeth Hardwick, but he
died in a taxicab on his way to Hardwick's flat, reportedly clutching one of Freud's
paintings of Blackwood.

In the years following Lowell's death, Blackwood produced her best work, which
includes novels, novellas, stories, memoirs, essays, and a book dealing with the
women's peace movement. Blackwood died in New York at sixty-four of cervical cancer.

MAJOR WORKS AND THEMES

Blackwood's first novella, *The Stepdaughter* (1976), establishes the morbid subject
matter and despairing tone that characterizes her fiction. Blackwood addresses the
themes of obsession, anguish, dementia, isolation, and insanity, which in this story
occur as a result of marital failure. Recently abandoned by her husband, who has moved
to France with his lover, the protagonist, "K," obsesses over the presence of her husband's teenage daughter, whom he has left in the apartment without explanation. *The
Stepdaughter* follows the protagonist's psychological breakdown. The story is constructed as a series of letters that "K" writes to herself in her head, which she does to
compete with her miserable au pair, who sends and receives letters from France. The
au pair has been hired to take care of the protagonist's infant daughter, whose crying
"K" cannot tolerate. "K" congratulates herself on tormenting her au pair, and imagines
what kind of horrible things the girl writes about her in her letters. Meanwhile, "K"
fixates on her stepdaughter, who, according to "K," creeps silently around her spectacular Manhattan apartment, emerging from in front of her television set only to bake
and consume cupcakes. "K" imagines that she punishes her stepdaughter by deliberately not speaking to her, and Blackwood's first-person narrator allows the reader to
agree that the stepdaughter is indeed a hideous, monstrously overweight ogress. However, when "K" finally works up the courage to speak to her stepdaughter, the girl seems
composed and rational. Her stepdaughter's discomfiture has actually been a projection
of the protagonist's own extreme anxiety. After revealing that she is not actually the
daughter of the man "K" married, the stepdaughter disappears, and "K," devoid of the
object of her obsession, continues her descent into madness.

Blackwood's next novella, *Great Granny Webster* (1977), displays her comic wit
and talent for characterization. The protagonist, a young girl recovering from an illness, is sent to stay with Great Granny Webster to be near the curative sea air. Granny
lives in a ramshackle mansion similar to the one in which Blackwood grew up. She is
a miserable, miserly old woman who has outlived her contemporaries and resentfully
awaits her own death. Granny believes that humans are born to suffer and thus does
not attempt to generate pleasure in herself or others. She allows the house to become

damp, dark, and unwelcoming, and she allows only the most disgusting food to be served. She sits in the most uncomfortable chair in the house—a stiff, high-backed chair—and is opposed to any modern convenience. In stark contrast to Granny stands the protagonist's Aunt Lavinia, a dashing socialite, like Blackwood herself. Lavinia has striking good looks, fabulous friends, a thirst for booze, and stylish clothes. Lavinia, however, is suicidal. She finally manages to kill herself in the end, which occurs without warning. The narrator also tells the story of her grandmother, Great Granny Webster's daughter, who, like many of Blackwood's characters, went insane. Both Lavinia and Granny's daughter are described as otherworldly, beautiful, almost mythic creatures. That they both suffer and retreat from reality conveys Blackwood's belief that such beauty is only trampled by the meanness and cruelty of the world, epitomized by Granny. Blackwood distinctively treats her themes of insanity, isolation, paranoia, and cruelty with a dispassionate, almost indifferent tone.

Blackwood's characteristic themes and style were well established by the time she wrote *Corrigan* (1984). This novel, however, focuses more on the theme of exploitation than on insanity. Devina, an elderly woman who lives in the country outside London, literally waits for death to reunite her with her beloved husband. Nadine, her daughter, lives in town with her insensitive, domineering husband and has stopped visiting her mother because she feels her mother has become too dismal. Devina lives in total isolation save her housekeeper, Mrs. Murphy, whose absurdly raucous physical presence exhibits Blackwood's humorous side. Devina is reawakened after a visit from a charismatic disabled man, Corrigan, who is supposedly collecting funds to help St. Crispin's, a hospital for invalids. Corrigan begins to visit Devina regularly, and she eventually invites him to live with her. To Nadine's shock and chagrin, Devina makes radical alterations to her beautiful home to accommodate Corrigan, buys him a van so that he can more easily travel the countryside in search of donations, and buys large tracts of land and arranges for them to be farmed, so that she can send fresh vegetables to the St. Crispin's patients. The relationship between Corrigan and Devina is oddly romantic; together they drink champagne and read poetry, and since Corrigan's arrival, Devina's interest in gourmet cooking has revived. Eventually, Devina dies and it is revealed that Corrigan is not disabled, and that Devina knew all along that he was faking. The lie, Blackwood suggests, was incidental to the joy and sense of purpose that Corrigan's presence added to the last months of Devina's life. Moreover, Blackwood implies that Corrigan was in fact exploited by Devina, who recognized Corrigan's jealousy and used it to her benefit. The most harmful exploitation, however, occurs in Nadine's life, and, after her mother's death, she finally gathers the strength to leave her egocentric and uncaring husband.

In addition to fiction, Blackwood wrote many journalistic pieces and works of nonfiction, such as *In the Pink: Caroline Blackwood on Hunting* (1987) and *The Last of the Duchess* (1995), her final work. *The Last of the Duchess*, which chronicles Blackwood's failed attempts to meet the intensely private Wallis Simpson, Duchess of Windsor, paints a keen and comical portrait of the high society of the Windsors.

CRITICAL RECEPTION

Blackwood is well known as a writer, but she is recognized more for her brilliant husbands and riotous lifestyle than for her work. Many reviewers have insisted that Blackwood's importance lies not in her own art, but in the art that she inspired in others, like Lowell. The title of Nancy Schoenberger's biography, *Dangerous Muse* (2002), conveys this opinion. When her work has been addressed, especially her fiction, it has generally garnered favorable reviews. Critics have recognized the power of Blackwood's direct, elegant, and detached prose, and have expressed interest in her macabre subject matter.

BIBLIOGRAPHY

Works by Caroline Blackwood

Corrigan. London: Heinemann, 1984; New York: Viking, 1985.
Darling, You Shouldn't Have Gone to So Much Trouble. London: Cape, 1980. (With Anna Haycraft.)
The Fate of Mary Rose. New York: Summit, 1981.
For All That I Found There. London: Duckworth, 1973; New York: Braziller, 1974.
Goodnight Sweet Ladies. London: Heinemann, 1983.
Great Granny Webster. New York: Scribner, 1977.
In the Pink: Caroline Blackwood on Hunting. London: Bloomsbury, 1987.
The Last of the Duchess. New York: Pantheon, 1995.
On the Perimeter. London: Heinemann, 1984; New York: Penguin, 1985.
The Stepdaughter. London: Duckworth, 1976; New York: Scribner, 1977.

Studies of Caroline Blackwood

Herman, Carol. "Helen or Circe, Take Your Pick." *Washington Times*, July 8, 2001, 6.
Meyers, Jeffrey. "Dangerous Muse: The Life of Lady Caroline Blackwood." Review of biography. *New Criterion* 20, no. 1 (September 2001): 120.
Schoenberger, Nancy. *Dangerous Muse: The Life of Lady Caroline Blackwood.* Cambridge, MA: Da Capo, 2002.

EAVAN BOLAND
(1944–   )

Patricia Hagen and Thomas Zelman

BIOGRAPHY

Eavan Boland was born in Dublin in 1944; her mother, Frances Kelley, was a painter, and her father, Frederick Boland, a diplomat. After the creation of the Republic of Ireland, Frederick Boland became its ambassador to England in 1950 and moved his family to London. Five years later, his diplomatic posting took the family to New York; the young Eavan, therefore, lived outside Ireland from the ages of six to fourteen. This childhood exile from Ireland was a noteworthy formative influence, the subject of ruminations in *Object Lessons* and in numerous poems.

Back in Dublin, Boland attended Trinity College, graduating in 1967 with first-class honors in English literature. In 1969 she married novelist Kevin Casey; they moved to the suburbs—a significant locale in her poetry—and raised two daughters. Her public life has included frequent radio broadcasts, reviews in the *Irish Times*, teaching positions at Trinity College, Bowdoin College, and the University of Iowa, and writing workshops, particularly for women, throughout Ireland. Boland currently divides her time between Dublin and Stanford University in Palo Alto, California, where she is director of the creative writing program.

MAJOR WORKS AND THEMES

Boland's first significant volume of poetry, *New Territory* (1967), was published when she was only twenty-two, a recent graduate of Trinity College. The volume's central trope is the poet as explorer; unsurprisingly for a young writer fresh from the academy and part of a poetic circle that included such developing poets as Derek Mahon and Brendan Kennelly, Boland generally celebrates canonical (male) literary heroes, though with an occasional Irish twist. The few representations of women in the volume, for example, "The Winning of Etain," collude with the mythic underpinnings of Irish poetry Boland was later adamantly to reject in *A Kind of Scar* (1989). While thematically conventional, *New Territory* nevertheless plants the seeds of Boland's subsequent concerns: the role of the poet, the source of poetic authority, the power and limits of the imagination. Formally, the volume is a tour de force.

The War Horse (1975) centers on conflicts past and present, political and personal, and marks the beginning of what has become one of Boland's most significant quests: the creation of an ethical relation between the image and the poetic imagination. Unlike the Celtic twilight mythos of *New Territory*, the subversive allusions in *The War Horse* frequently center on the damage that has been done by unquestioned collusion with mythologies of heroism and sacrifice. In "A Soldier's Son," for example, family tradition becomes a metaphor for a larger cultural tradition of insane violence that attacks one's own future. Similarly, both "The Greek Experience" and "Naoise at Four" affirm that violence creates sterility, not continuity with a glorious past. Unlike earlier bards, who glamorized the fallen warriors, Boland asserts that poets today must recognize that mythologizing fuels the violence.

While several of the finest poems in *The War Horse* are a response to public violence ("Famine Road" and "Child of Our Time" in particular), Boland also explores the way in which violence invades the private sphere in such poems as "The Botanic Gardens," "The War Horse," "Sisters," and "Suburban Woman." In "The Botanic Gardens," the trope of marriage operates in both the private and the public realms; although the garden was planted by a foreigner, recalling the plantation of Ireland, the many diverse plants forced into proximity are sheltered and nurtured—and flourish— together. Significantly, the poem ends with a picture not of the garden but of its interpreter, struggling to decipher its meaning. Interpreting this locale—valorizing the peace in diversity embodied in the botanical garden—requires a fundamentally different sensibility than that of the politician or the traditional poet writing in the heroic tradition. The poem is not only a lovely work in its own right, but a harbinger of the "muse of the ordinary" Boland will claim for herself in *The Journey and Other Poems* (1986).

Like the poems in *New Territory*, those in *The War Horse* demonstrate Boland's mastery of form; the volume contains sonnets, quatrains, couplets, and experiments with line length, rhythm, and rhyme. Despite a section of poems "after"—after Nelly Sachs, after Mayakovsky—and translations, including one of the delightful Irish poem

"Pangur Ban," *The War Horse* demonstrates a new, significantly more subversive, relationship with the inherited poem.

Although *In Her Own Image* (1980) and *Night Feed* (1982) are almost oppositional in style and tone, Boland wrote poems for both volumes simultaneously. Both stem from the same root: a thoroughly gendered poetic stance that stakes a claim in subject matter rarely seen in the Irish poem until this time: anorexia, mastectomy, masturbation, and menstruation in the former collection, and suburban life in the latter. While the subjects of *In Her Own Image* are more obviously a matter of gender politics, more explicitly feminist than those in *Night Feed*, Boland notes that suburban life is perhaps even further outside the realm of acceptable subject matter for poetry than the more dramatic taboo subjects of *In Her Own Image*.

A central concern of both volumes is that of representation. Having asserted the way in which the conventional mythologies undergirding the Irish literary tradition comprise mutilating fantasies that collude with violence, Boland examines, in "Tirade for the Mimic Muse," the ways in which Irish poets have reduced real women to icons and hollow mouthpieces, denying them voice. "In His Own Image" explores the violence inherent in men's representations of women through the trope of abusive man as a sculptor, shaping his woman into a desirable form by beating her; "Mastectomy" considers men's needs to excise signs of women's sexuality and nurturing. In "Anorexic" Boland suggests that women have internalized cultural representations so strongly that they burn themselves to finally become free of men's demands. "Solitary," a masturbation poem, centers on the metaphor of a priestess at a shrine who violates the taboos passed on by male culture. By taking control of her own sexuality, she creates—and represents—herself, calling out in her own voice.

In *Night Feed*, the companion to *In Her Own Image*, poems about masturbation and anorexia yield to lyrics about suburban motherhood. In the "Domestic Interior" section, meditations on domestic life give rise to another of Boland's archetypal concerns, the passage of time. Indeed, the very locale deemed most unsuitable to poetry, the suburb, becomes in Boland's work an effective vehicle for expressing the time-bound nature of love, life, and death. As she affirms in "The New Pastoral," she has developed a new aesthetic as indoor nature poet and suburban nature poet, not merely describing but revealing—without romanticizing—the essence of ordinary life. As a counterbalance to the monotony of suburban routine, several poems in the collection center on transformation. Both "A Woman Transforms Herself into a Fish" and "The Woman Changes Her Skin" have the feel of legend as the speaker escapes the routines and pains of motherhood by becoming fish and snake, but it is significant to note the agency signaled in the titles: the woman is not passive subject but active shaper of the legends, controlling the terms of transformation, the terms of representation. *Night Feed* also continues Boland's examination of authority and representation through a series of poems about representation in paintings: "Degas's Laundresses," "Pose," "Fruit on a Straight-Sided Tray," and "Domestic Interior."

While the three volumes prior to *The Journey and Other Poems* implicitly critique the Irish poetic tradition, in *The Journey* this critique becomes explicit in such poems as "The Glass King," in which the Irish lyric is likened to the mad Charles VI of France, and "Mise Eire," in which Mother Ireland refuses her emblematic role. By the time *The Journey* was published, in 1986, Boland had written widely about the changes that occur when women stop being subjects and objects of poems and start becoming their authors; during this time (for a period of more than ten years) she had also become active in leading women's poetry workshops, another source of her growing articulation of the difficulties for a woman poet trying to work within a national tradition. Having explored issues of her own womanhood and contemporary womanhood in the previous two volumes, Boland expands her explorations in *The Journey* to "find and repossess" the idea of the nation, allowing the voices of women to enter and overtake the tradition.

As in the previous volumes, we find in *The Journey* meditations on authority and representation in paintings and drawings by Chardin, Canaletto, Renoir, and Boland's own mother, Frances Kelly; in these poems Boland subverts the representation by giving voice to the women who were merely subjects of the paintings. This volume also contains several autobiographical lyrics about the poet's childhood exile in England and the simplified, sanitized representations of Ireland she, like many exiles, brought with her. "The Oral Tradition" suggests an alternative to the Ireland of literary tradition; "Fever" is a compelling testimony to the kind of experience invisible in the Ireland constructed by its male writers. Linking all these poems, underlying this entire volume, and weaving through all future ones, is Boland's affirmation, in "Envoi," of a muse that will "bless the ordinary" and "sanctify the common." Thus, the speaker of the title poem in *The Journey* begins by remarking that no poems have been written about antibiotics: like the lives of women, the subject is too mundane, too unliterary. In this poem, which combines elements of Dante's *Purgatorio* (1311), Virgil's *Aeneid* (29–19 B.C.E.), and the Irish Aisling tradition, Boland finds a female mentor in Sappho, who takes her on a dream vision in which she sees other mothers, women from the past before antibiotics, their suffering untold, their voices silent.

Expressing these silences is the driving force behind *Outside History* (1990). The title of the first section of this volume, "Object Lessons" (the title as well of Boland's 1995 prose work), is a literal description of Boland's operating method as she meditates on a series of objects—a piece of silver, a fan, a book, a doll—to see what lessons they may yield about the "silent and fugitive" past. The subjects of these lessons are wide ranging, but the issue of representation is the common thread weaving them together into a meta-lesson on poetic methods, poetic ethics. In the second section of the volume, "Outside History," Boland recombines the elements of the first section to concentrate more specifically on the gaps between representation and time, myth and history, stasis and fluidity. In the title poem of this section, Boland uses stellar light, which reaches us thousands of years after it happens, as a metaphor for the "darkness" of history, which likewise reaches us only across gaps of time and space, when the actual happenings are long over. Time marches on as we try to capture it, give voice to it, rendering even our most honest attempts fictitious in some sense.

This is true even in our own lifetimes, as we see in "A False Spring," in which the poet wants to advise her younger self but recognizes that it is too late for this dialogue to occur. But although we cannot change the past, we have an obligation to reexamine our images of it and remediate our narratives and our myths to create an appropriate ethical relationship between past and present. "An Old Steel Engraving" establishes a powerful contrast between a wounded patriot who cannot die because he has been transformed into an icon in an engraving and the flowing river, which reflected the battle but moves on. The patriot's unfinished action carries into the present as historic images inspire patriotic deaths; it will continue to structure the present until we can learn to honor the past without romanticizing it—to let it become truly past.

The final section of *Outside History*, "Distances," recombines elements from the earlier sections into poems centering on memory, the personal version of both history and mythology. The central tension here is perhaps best stated as preserving (mummifying) something to withstand time as opposed to conserving something within the flux of time. "Contingencies" ends with an image of candles placed in jars, now empty, but, last summer, full with freshly made preserves. Since "conserves" and "preserves" are synonyms for these concoctions, the double meaning structures the poem's aesthetic ethics. On the one hand, the image suggests the private, domestic (female) realm as a shelter preserving women from danger by secluding them; thus, the women speak mildly and keep their hungers private, advising children to stay safe by staying in their place. On the other hand, the image suggests conservation of neighborliness and women's friendships; the "preserves" are not monuments that exist outside time, but "conserves" that provide nourishment as they are consumed.

While *In a Time of Violence* (1994) returns to themes and forms explored in Boland's earlier volumes, from *The War Horse* through *Outside History*, the volume is not so much repetitive as culminative, as if the disparate threads Boland has been weaving throughout her career have pulled together into a tapestry that reveals its pattern with power and grace. The section titles of this volume—"Writing in a Time of Violence," "Legends," and "Anna Liffey"—suggest variations on such concerns as the power of gaps and silences, the potencies and dangers of myth, the ethics of representation, and the limits of art, though now expanded to include the ethics and limits of interpretation as well. Stylistically, gaps and implications, always part of Boland's thematic concerns, become increasingly important elements of poetic structure as she examines the violent subtexts or shadows that haunt images of beauty and elegance. In "The Death of Reason," for example, the speaker reads an eighteenth-century portrait against the grain to represent its "negative space": the system of economic and political violence that enabled this refined elegance to exist. As the Peep-O-Day Boys torch the big house, they are destroying not merely the property of a hated landlord but also the images that represented and supported a hated system. "In a Bad Light" continues Boland's remediation of images as she points to the Irish seamstresses who stitched a silk, crepe, and satin garment on display in a St. Louis museum; similarly, "The Dolls [*sic*] Museum in Dublin" reflects on the way in which the visible remnants of the past tend to ornamentalize it, suppressing our recognition of the invisible—and frequently violent—conditions that created it. "Writing in a Time of Violence" considers the shadow side of language, the way in which linguistic beauty, like its visual counterpart, suppresses our recognition of the violence that often underlies it.

While not specifically feminist, poems in this volume are thoroughly gendered. Boland contrasts the male tradition, in which women are featured largely as erotic object, with her female enterprise; thus, in "Story" she notes how much our legends depend on the woman being young and beautiful, preserved outside time and therefore disconnected from a woman's real life. Boland's rejection of the Yeatsian yearning for immortality through the unchanging medium of art dominates such poems as "What Language Did," "We Are the Only Animals Who Do This," and "A Woman Painted on a Leaf." In this, her finest volume, Boland is at the height of her powers.

Object Lessons: The Life of the Woman and the Poet in Our Time (1995) is a graceful prose volume of personal and artistic reflections in which Boland explores the situation of a woman poet in Ireland. In a sense, this is her *Portrait of the Artist*, as she speaks autobiographically, considering the impact influential traditions—familial, national, gender—have had on her artistic growth. The book begins with a series of illuminations in which Boland re-envisions herself first as child, then as a young woman, trying to come to grips with her fragmented sense of self. With a simple beauty, she speaks of the consequences of living abroad as a child, of the slow and often confusing process of piecing together an identity, of returning to Ireland as a teenager and feeling like an outsider, of studying the court poets in a land that sanctified its rebels, of becoming a woman poet in a literary tradition that lacked any such niche. Her task then, as she identifies it, was to develop a poetic language that could integrate and reconcile.

The second half of *Object Lessons* focuses more specifically on Boland's growth toward a comprehensive ethos. Chapter 6, "Outside History," reprises her influential pamphlet *A Kind of Scar: The Woman Poet in a National Tradition* (1989); in later chapters she explores the dangers of subordinating aesthetic judgment to romantic, nationalist, or feminist agendas. A poem written in support of such political movements, she claims, runs the risk of becoming a coercive gesture that curtails inquiry. Rather, the Irish political poem should fuse the personal and the political in a startling and unpredictable way. *Object Lessons* itself is entertainingly unpredictable. In the course of working out a poetic ideology, Boland brings into the discussion her consideration of her father's diplomatic work, her meetings with Padraic Colum and Patrick Kavanagh, her readings of poems by other past and contemporary writers, and some useful glosses to her own poems ("Lava Cameo," "The Black Lace Fan My Mother Gave Me").

The Lost Land (1998), dedicated to Mary Robinson and divided into two sections, "Colony" and "The Lost Land," represents Boland's most sustained engagement in dialogue with the idea of a nation, its ordeal and fragmentations. Like "The Death of Reason" from *In a Time of Violence*, the first poem in this volume, "My Country in Darkness," locates the end of an ideology in the loss of the image, or art, that had represented it. In this poem, darkness falls on Gaelic Ireland not with the exile of the Wild Geese but with the death of the last bard. If we are indeed constructed by our constructs, the death of the construct must signal a parallel death to a particular form of identity. Subsequent poems in the "Colony" section explore the fragmented identities that followed Gaelic Ireland, identities drawn from both sides of the Pale: "The Colonists," "Daughters of Colony," "The Mother Tongue," and "The Scar" express a fragmented culture, a "lost land" that is lost to colonist and native alike. As we would expect, Boland identifies a dissonance between the nation memorialized in statuary and song and the country experienced by ordinary people from both sides of the Pale, who are wounded, divided, unhealed, at best denizens of "A Habitable Grief."

In the second section of the volume, the "lost land" becomes more personal than historical or political in lyrics of lost youth ("Happiness," "Dublin, 1959," "Watching Old Movies When They Were New") and melancholic elegies on a daughter's growing up and away ("The Lost Land," "The Blossom," "Daughter," "The Loss," "The Bargain," "Ceres Looks at the Morning," "Escape"). While Boland occasionally creates syntactic and imagistic surprises in these poems, the ingenuity and unpredictability that characterize earlier volumes are generally absent from *The Lost Land,* and Boland's signature dense syntax, with its unanchored references, multiple negatives, short silences, and strings of modification, generally gives way in this volume to plain, unadorned statement. There is no doubt that *The Lost Land* is a flatter and narrower collection of poems, both stylistically and thematically, than any of Boland's earlier volumes. This flatness may be a flaw born of exhaustion—many of the poems in *The Lost Land* seem repetitive, paler versions of lyrics she has already written. Or it may signal that Boland has purposely and willingly stripped away the technical brilliance in order to experience anew the anxiety and fragmentations of not only her subject matter but also her art, thus conveying her poetic processes more honestly.

In "Love," from the "Legends" section of *In a Time of Violence*, the speaker reflects on a time in her marriage when emotions were extremely concentrated, wondering whether she and her husband will ever feel so intensely again. The answer in *Against Love Poetry* (2001; published in Europe as *Code*) is a resounding but far from despairing no. Two central concerns throughout Boland's career—suburban, ordinary life and the silences and gaps of the past—are woven together in *Against Love Poetry* as Boland interrogates marriage in much the same way as she has interrogated paintings, literature, personal objects, and history in earlier volumes. Unlike the conventional love poem, which centers on an intense spot of time, the poems in this volume, both individually and collectively, focus attention on the quotidian. Thus "Marriage for the Millennium" depicts a wife talking to a husband who is absorbed in his newspaper and does not hear her. "Embers" portrays a similar scene as the speaker retells the Irish legend she is reading to her husband who is absorbed in his own book and uninterested in the story she is telling. In other hands, both poems could easily become indictments of the husband or of the institution of marriage, but in Boland's hands they are affirmations: it is not the singular, romantic moments but the daily rituals of love that ease our hearts and keep the embers warm. *Against Love Poetry* is a logical extension of Boland's oeuvre, proclaiming yet again her fidelity to the "muse of the ordinary" invoked in *The Journey*. In this newest volume she affirms that the true story of a marriage, like the true story of a nation, lies not in the singular, extraordinary, intense moments of heroism or passion but rather in the ordinary rituals, the daily stoicisms, the regular human sufferings and small triumphs that over time create patterns that are themselves witness and tribute to what is important in human experience. "Quarantine," a poem about a couple who leave the workhouse in the worst year of the famine, fuses the "ordinary" heroism of the past with the "ordinary" passion of marriage. The couple dies after falling asleep in freezing weather; when they are found, it is clear that he died while trying to warm her feet.

Against Love Poetry stands above all against the boast that poetry has the power to stop time and fend off decay; Boland firmly rejects representations that valorize an unchanging surface. Thus, "Lines for a Thirtieth Wedding Anniversary" uses the metaphor of a granite wall slowly eroding to suggest the way in which both partners have changed individually as they take into themselves the influence of the other, thus changing the marriage relationship as well; all three elements of the equation are also reformed by the passage of time. What preserves the marriage has its source not in art but in the rituals of daily life.

The remarkable ethical and thematic coherence of Boland's poetic work is a proverbial two-edged sword. On the one hand, it creates an accretive energy by which individual poems and indeed whole volumes are woven together into a complex matrix in which the whole has a resonance much greater than any of its individual parts, however excellent they are in their own right. On the other hand, it can degenerate into redundancy as the reader encounters poems that seem mere shadows of earlier, more powerful works. Both effects are present in *Against Love Poetry*, the latter perhaps more pronounced because Boland's style, as in *The Lost Land*, is pared down, her imagery and syntax more restrictive than in earlier volumes. It seems that in these later volumes Boland's long-standing ambivalence about the power and exhilaration of language has crystallized into a sparer aesthetic. Ironically, although both of her most recent volumes contain some excellent individual poems, Boland's attempts to pare down her rhetoric, tone down her imagery, and unpack her syntax have resulted in a rather vacant feeling in a number of poems in both *The Lost Land* and *Against Love Poetry*.

CRITICAL RECEPTION

Almost from the beginning, Boland's work has drawn highly polarized responses. Given the nature of Boland's poetic enterprise, and the way in which she links a subversive agenda with a dedication to the formal elements of poetry, it is inevitable that she would be criticized for being too feminine, too feminist, not feminist enough, too nationalist, not nationalist enough, too political, not political enough, and, of course, elitist. Thus her work has drawn reviews ranging from the wildly celebratory, epitomized by the *Poetry Ireland* 32 review in which Áine Ní Ghlinn calls *Outside History* "beyond praise" to the thoroughly dismissive, epitomized by William Logan's masculinist assertion that the "bard of fabric" must find a different (and, one presumes, either genderless or masculine) subject matter in order to be true to her (undefined) culture. Edna Longley takes Boland to task for her "nationalism" (alias for anti-English sentiments) and accuses Boland of re-creating the very Mother Ireland figure she critiques in *A Kind of Scar*. Considering *Outside History* from a feminist perspective, Mary O'Connor grants Boland's transformative efforts but echoes the notion that Boland has created herself into an emblematic figure who presumes to speak for all her countrywomen.

While ideology is a factor in reviews of any poet's work, Boland's seems to bring it to the foreground with particular force, at least in part because she has consciously chosen to reject two ideologies that have been sacred cows in a number of literary circles, the Romantic Heresy, as she terms it—the notion that ordinary subjects must be glamorized and romanticized in order to become fit for poetic treatment—and feminist aesthetics, whose proponents frequently view formal and technical virtuosity with deep suspicion.

This rejection has left her vulnerable to critics operating out of both masculinist and feminist ideologies. Asserting that the poem is a place of experience, not convictions, Boland distinguishes between being a feminist (which definition she firmly acknowledges) and being a feminist poet (which definition she rejects). While her reputation is less contested in the United States and England than in Ireland, Boland is generally acknowledged as the preeminent female poet in contemporary Ireland. More recently, she is coming to be recognized as one of the preeminent poets of either gender writing in English today.

The editor and the publisher gratefully acknowledge permission of Eavan Boland for quotes from her work.

BIBLIOGRAPHY

Works by Eavan Boland

Against Love Poetry. New York: Norton, 2001.
Code. Manchester, UK: Carcanet, 2001.
"Finding Anne Bradstreet." In *Green Thoughts, Green Shades: Essays by Contemporary Poets on the Early Modern Lyric*, edited by Jonathan F. S. Post, 176–90. Berkeley: University of California Press, 2002.
In a Time of Violence. Manchester, UK: Carcanet, 1994; New York: Norton, 1994.
In Her Own Image. Dublin: Arlen House, 1980.
Introducing Eavan Boland. Toronto: Ontario Review Press Poetry Series, 1981.
The Journey. Dublin: Gallery, 1982.
The Journey and Other Poems. Dublin: Arlen House, 1986; Manchester, UK: Carcanet, 1987.
A Kind of Scar: The Woman Poet in a National Tradition. LIP pamphlet. Dublin: Attic, 1989.
The Lost Land. New York: Norton, 1998.
The Making of a Poem: A Norton Anthology of Poetic Forms. New York: Norton, 2001. (Editor, with Mark Strand.)
New Territory. Dublin: Allen Figgis, 1967.

Night Feed. Dublin: Arlen House, 1982; London: Boyars, 1982; Manchester, UK: Carcanet, 1994.

Object Lessons: The Life of the Woman and the Poet in Our Time. New York: Norton; Manchester, UK: Carcanet, 1995.

An Origin Like Water: Collected Poems 1967–1987. New York: Norton, 1996.

Outside History. Manchester, UK: Carcanet, 1990.

Outside History: Selected Poems 1980–1990. New York: Norton, 1990.

Selected Poems. Manchester, UK: Carcanet, 1989.

Three Irish Poets. Manchester, UK: Carcanet, 2003. (With Mary O'Malley and Paula Meehan.)

23 Poems. Dublin: Gallagher, 1962.

The War Horse. London: Gollancz, 1975; Dublin: Arlen House, 1980.

Interviews with Eavan Boland

Boland, Eavan. Interview. By Caffeine Destiny. http://www.caffeinedestiny.com/boland.html.

———. Interview. In *Writing Irish: Selected Interviews with Writers from the* Irish Literary Supplement. With Nancy Means Wright and Dennis Hannan. Syracuse, NY: Syracuse University Press, 1999, 173–83.

"An Interview with Eavan Boland." With Jody Allen-Randolph. *Irish University Review* 23, no. 1 (Spring–Summer 1993): 117–30.

———. Interview. By Alice Quinn. New Yorker On-line. October 22, 2001. http://www.new yorker.com/ONLINE_ONLY/ARCHIVES/?011029on_onlineonly01a.

Studies of Eavan Boland

Allen-Randolph, Jody. "Private Worlds, Public Realities: Eavan Boland's Poetry 1967–1990." *Irish University Review* 23, no. 1 (Spring–Summer 1993): 5–22.

Atfield, Rose. "'The Stain of Absolute Possession': The Postcolonial in the Work of Eavan Boland." In *Contemporary Women's Poetry: Reading/Writing/Practice,* edited by Alison Mark, 189–207. New York: Palgrave-Macmillan, 2001.

Clutterbuck, Catriona. "Irish Critical Responses to Self-Representation in Eavan Boland, 1987–1995." *Colby Quarterly* 35, no. 4 (December 1999): 275–87.

Ghlinn, Áine Ní. "Beyond Praise." *Poetry Ireland Review,* no. 32 (Summer 1991): 93–94.

Haberstroh, Patricia Boyle. "Woman, Artist, and Image in Night Feed." *Irish University Review* 23, no. 1 (Spring–Summer 1993): 67–74.

———. *Women Creating Women: Contemporary Irish Women Poets.* Syracuse, NY: Syracuse University Press, 1996.

Hagen, Patricia, and Thomas Zelman. *Eavan Boland and the History of the Ordinary.* Dublin: Maunsel, 2004.

———. "'We Were Never on the Scene of the Crime': Eavan Boland's Reclamation of History." *Twentieth Century Literature* 37, no. 4 (Winter 1991): 442–53.

Hannan, Dennis J., and Nancy Means Wright. "Irish Women Poets: Breaking the Silence." *Canadian Journal of Irish Studies* 16, no. 2 (December 1990): 57–65.

Kupillas, Peter. "Bringing It All Back Home: Unity and Meaning in Eavan Boland's 'Domestic Interior' Sequence." *Contemporary Irish Women Poets: Some Male Perspectives*, edited by Alexander G. Gonzalez, 13–32. Westport, CT: Greenwood, 1999.

Logan, William. "Animal Instincts and Natural Powers." *New York Times Book Review*, April 21, 1992, 22.

Mark, Alison, ed. *Contemporary Women's Poetry: Reading/Writing/Practice.* New York: Palgrave-Macmillan, 2001.

O'Connor, Mary. "Chronicles of Impeded Growth: Eavan Boland and the Reconstruction of Identity." *Post Identity,* 45–76. http://liberalarts.udmercy.edu/pi/PI2.2/PI22_OConnor.pdf.

O'Donnell, Mary. "In Her Own Image—An Assertion That Myths Are Made by Men, by the Poet in Transition." *Irish University Review* 23, no. 1 (Spring–Summer 1993): 40–44.

Roche, Anthony. "Introduction." *Irish University Review* 23, no. 1 (Spring–Summer 1993): 1–4.

Roche, Anthony, and Jody Allen-Randolph, guest eds. "Eavan Boland." Special issue, *Irish University Review* 23, no. 1 (Spring–Summer 1993).

Smith, R. T. "Altered Light: *Outside History.*" *Irish University Review* 23, no. 1 (Spring–Summer 1993): 86–99.

Somerville-Arjat, Gillean, and Rebecca E. Wilson. *Sleeping with Monsters: Conversations with Scottish and Irish Women Poets.* Dublin: Wolfhound, 1990, 79–90.

Weekes, Ann Owen. " 'An Origin Like Water': The Poetry of Eavan Boland and Modernist Critiques of Irish Literature." In *Irishness and (Post)Modernism*, edited by John S. Rickard, 159–76. Lewisburg, PA: Bucknell University Press, 1994.

ANGELA BOURKE
(1952–   )

Christie Fox

BIOGRAPHY

Born in Dublin, Angela Bourke (née Partridge) did not grow up in an Irish-speaking household, although she now publishes in both English and Irish. Her parents used Irish to communicate things they did not want the children to understand, and it was not until Bourke began the common Irish childhood ritual of summers in the Connemara Gaeltacht that her love of the Irish language blossomed.

Often sick as a child, Bourke spent sick days in her parents' bedroom, reading whatever she could get her hands on, until she lit upon Maud Joynt's *The Golden Legends of the Gael* (1925), which ignited her interest in Irish folklore, especially the tales concerning women. Joynt, a contemporary of William Butler Yeats, published early English translations of medieval Irish manuscripts. Interestingly, the Royal Irish Academy engaged Joynt to work on an Irish dictionary project; a language scholar who knew Sanskrit and Hindi, she was a Buddhist and a vegetarian as well as a feminist. It seems no accident that Bourke found feminist leanings in the strong women portrayed by Joynt's text.

Bourke's interest in the Irish language had to be kept separate from her interest in feminism and women's studies, she felt, as her third-level study of Irish coincided with the escalation of violence in Northern Ireland and the appropriation of nationalist literature by the Republican movement. Yet she found a strong intersection between tales of brave, young, smart warrior women, such as the Ulster Queen Medb and Airmed (who stored healing herbs in precise order on her cloak), and contemporary feminist studies, which she felt ignored the Irish language, deeming it patriarchal and old-fashioned. Bourke found that there was often at least a proto-feminist subtext to many of the Irish texts, and that the stories she heard in Irish gave her comfort and a way into another Irish world, one filled with bogs and fairy forts, and quite alien from her own urban existence.

Bourke received her education at University College Dublin (UCD), where she received a bursary that allowed her to travel to the Université de Bretagne Occidentale, Brest, in France. Her doctoral dissertation, "Caoineadh na dTri Muire" (1982), focused on women's religious poetry in Irish folklore. Now a lecturer in modern Irish at UCD, Bourke has held visiting-professor positions at Harvard and the University of Minnesota, and has lectured throughout Europe, Japan, and North America. She was also the plenary speaker at "Ideology and Ireland in the Nineteenth Century" at University College Galway in 1996. English-language-only scholars are somewhat hampered in receiving a full picture of Bourke's career, as her Irish-language articles are rarely translated.

MAJOR WORKS AND THEMES

Bourke started her career writing about women's Irish-language oral poetry, transforming her doctoral dissertation into a book, *Caoineadh na dTrí Muire: Téama na Páise i bhfílocht bhéil na Gaeilge* (1983). She later expanded on women's Irish-language poetry to include two works about Nuala Ní Dhomnnaill, one in English and one in Irish. Her first publication, however, grew out of her interest in Irish folklore: the pamphlet "One Hundred Irish Proverbs and Sayings" (1978) appeared under the name Angela Partridge.

Focusing on the connection between Irish folklore texts and feminism, Bourke found that Irish women used keening as a site of resistance and a way to assert control over grief and women's status. She has published several articles on this subject, each exploring a different aspect of the keen. Bourke tells us that women used the moment of the keen—when the keener is said to be out of her mind with grief—to complain about poor treatment from husbands, fathers, and sons. Voicing this kind of dissent at any other time would have been inappropriate and socially unacceptable, but the boundaries of the keen were much more fluid. Bourke also discusses keening as a profession that included novices and, essentially, trainees. She expanded this work to include keening in Scots Gaelic for the UCD women's studies working papers series in 1998.

After winning the Frank O'Connor Award for Short Fiction in 1992 (awarded to the writer of an unpublished short story), Bourke published a longer foray into fiction writing, *By Salt Water* (1996); the collection of short stories contains a line through several stories about a young girl named Una. The reader watches Una mature, starting with "Pinkeens," when she is quite young, and brave distant cousins visit. Una learns about being a girl throughout these stories, clearly drawn from Bourke's own childhood. Una lives in Dublin and, as Bourke herself related in "Language, Stories, Healing," she cannot imagine the countryside, with its different accents, livestock in the yard, and secular schools. Una's world consists of red brick row houses, paved alleyways that serve as playgrounds, and a local slaughterhouse, all taken from Bourke's childhood.

A "medium bold girl," Una watches a favorite nun in her Catholic school leave the order, and later suffers a schoolgirl crush on an older cousin. Bourke uses all the stories to explore women's relationships; even as Una develops the crush, she meets Bernie, her cousin's intended, and watches her, learning about courtship and the mysteries of the teenage years. She also learns about the dangers of womanhood in "Majella's Quilt," which deals with miscarriage and the toll of multiple births on women. Although Una doesn't age much throughout the stories, we get a sense of her maturing quickly, as children must do as they move from childhood into adolescence. The salt water of the title refers to all types of salty water, from the sea to tears to amniotic fluid. Bourke attempts to cover specific moments of Irish women's experience, using this water as a consistent backdrop.

Her best-known and most widely received work, *The Burning of Bridget Cleary: A True Story* (1999), combines her interest in fairies, feminism, and folklore; the resulting book examines the circumstances of Bridget Cleary's death through the lens of the political and social landscape of the time. In Tipperary in 1895, Bridget Cleary was twenty-six and married to a man much older than she was. She dressed well, made her own money, and did not always fit into the social hierarchies of rural Ireland.

The historical record reports that Bridget Cleary caught cold around March 4, 1895; her family, seeing her illness worsen, reported that she had been taken by the fairies and would emerge from their stronghold, riding a white horse. The shallow grave containing a horribly burned body told another story. Bourke claims that members of her family, including her husband, father, aunt, and cousins, tortured Bridget over several days, and then finally Michael Cleary doused his wife with paraffin and set her on fire, ostensibly to drive out the fairy tormentors who controlled her. Cleary was convicted, sentenced to twenty years in prison, and served fifteen.

Bourke uses newspaper accounts, census reports, and Irish parliament debates to provide a picture of turn-of-the-century Ireland, emphasizing details such as the way the Tories of the time used Cleary's alleged actions as evidence against Home Rule; surely a people whose belief in the supernatural was so strong that they would permit this gruesome death, they argued, should not be allowed self-government. The great benefit of the book, in fact, is that it provides this kind of larger context, showing a world caught between "new" science and the more familiar "herb doctors"; between colonization and the promise of Home Rule; and between stories of fairies and stories of medicine.

The book follows the trials of Michael Cleary and Bridget's family, including actual court testimony as reported in the newspapers, both urban and rural. Bourke also indicates the difference in reporting of newspapers with different political bents. The book is somewhat of a spellbinding page-turner, although reviewers have noted that it contains more than just Bridget Cleary's story, which is also one of its strengths. Noted scholar Declan Kiberd observes that this "century-old tale becomes in [Bourke's] telling as troubling and mysterious as the news of the last half-hour." Seamus Deane calls it "brilliantly researched and narrated." In fact, the book won the Irish Times Non-Fiction Award and the American Conference for Irish Studies James S. Donnelly Prize (both quotations are from the back book jacket of *The Burning of Bridget Cleary*).

Bourke also co-edited volumes 4 and 5 of the *The Field Day Anthology of Irish Writing: Irish Women's Writing and Traditions* (2002). When the first three volumes of the *The Field Day Anthology of Irish Writing* were published in 1992, representing more than 1500 years of Irish historical, literary, political, and social writings, the editors gave woefully little attention to women's writings. The furor over this glaring omission resulted in the promise of a volume dedicated exclusively to women, but over the next ten years the volume doubled in size and now includes contributions from more than 750 writers covering the same scope of texts as the first three volumes.

Bourke's biography of Maeve Brennan, a journalist born in Ireland who became a popular writer for the *New Yorker* magazine, appeared in 2004. Intriguingly, Brennan died in 1993, poor, homeless, and generally forgotten. Her papers are held at UCD.

CRITICAL RECEPTION

At more or less the same time as *The Burning of Bridget Cleary*, Joan Hoff and Marian Yeates published *The Cooper's Wife Is Missing* (2001). Different in tone and scope, the book raised some controversy as its publication date was very close to Bourke's in the United States, and Hoff and Yeates had access to Bourke's papers before they finished their work. The two books were often reviewed together, permitting readers to compare their strengths and weaknesses, but Bourke's is generally commended for being more focused on Ireland and Irish concerns, as well as for its gripping writing style. Bourke generally received commendation for the book, although some reviewers thought it raised more questions than it answered.

Reviews of *Bridget Cleary* appeared in the *New York Times Book Review*, *Newsday*, the *Times Literary Supplement*, and Salon.com. Declan Kiberd has praised Bourke's insight into and commentary on Ireland's folk beliefs and traditions, and reviewers hailed this knowledge and acuity.

Bourke's first book, *By Salt Water,* received far less critical notice and is generally considered a slight, if interesting, group of stories. Reviews appeared in *Booklist* and *Kirkus Reviews*.

BIBLIOGRAPHY

Works by Angela Bourke

The Burning of Bridget Cleary: A True Story. London: Pimlico, 1999; New York: Penguin, 2001.
By Salt Water. Dublin: Dufour, 1996.
Caoineadh na dTrí Muire: Téama na Páise i bhfilíocht bhéil na Gaeilge. Dublin: An Clóchomhar Tra, 1983.
The Field Day Anthology of Irish Writing. Vols. 4 and 5, Women's Writing and Traditions. (Editor, with Mairin Ni Dhonneadha, Siobhan Kilfeather, Maria Luddy, Margaret MacCurtain, Gerardine Meaney, Mary O'Dowd, and Clair Wills.) New York: New York University Press, 2002.
A Hundred Irish Proverbs and Sayings. Dublin: Folens, 1978. (As Angela Partridge.)
"Introduction." In *Fish Stone Water*, by Anna Rackard. Dublin: Attic, 2002.
"Language, Stories, Healing." In *Gender and Sexuality in Modern Ireland*, edited by Anthony Bradley and Maryann Gialanella Valiulis, 299–314. Amherst, MA: University of Massachusetts Press, 1997.
"More in Anger Than in Sorrow: Irish Women's Lament Poetry." In *Feminist Messages: Coding in Women's Folk Culture*, edited by Joan Newlon Radner, 160–82. Urbana: University of Illinois Press, 1993.
"Working and Weeping: Women's Oral Poetry in Irish and Scottish Gaelic." UCD Women's Studies Forum, Working Papers No. 7. Dublin: University College Dublin, 1988.

Studies of Angela Bourke

Mulvihill, Maureen E. "Fourteen Hundred Years of Irish Women Writers." Review of *The Field Day Anthology of Irish Writing*. Vols. 4 and 5, *Irish Women's Writing and Traditions,* edited by Angela Bourke et al. *Eighteenth-Century Studies* 36, no. 4 (Summer 2003): 607–10.
Murphy, Cliona. "Review of Books: Europe: Early and Modern." Review of *The Cooper's Wife Is Missing,* by Joan Hoff and Marian Yeates, and *The Burning of Bridget Cleary,* by Angela Bourke. *American Historical Review* 6, no. 3 (June 2001): 1049–51.

Warner, Marina. "International Books of the Year—and the Millennium." *Times Literary Supplement*, December 3, 1999, 9–15.

ELIZABETH BOWEN
(1899–1973)
Christine Cusick

BIOGRAPHY

Critical attention to the work of Elizabeth Bowen has flourished over the last decade of the twentieth century and well into the first years of the twenty-first. This recent acclaim for the legacy of Bowen's fiction, short fiction, essays, reviews, and literary endeavor, as well as the release of new editions of all her novels and autobiographical writings, can be attributed in part to a renewed academic commitment to uncovering the work of Irish women writers. However, Bowen's place within a specific literary history and culture is not so easily categorized. For, in addition to her place as an Irish woman writer and as one of the last Anglo-Irish ascendancy writers, she is also recognized as a major figure of British modernist thought and innovation.

The only child of parents Henry Cole Bowen and Florence Colley Bowen, both members of the Protestant Anglo-Irish gentry, Elizabeth Bowen was born in Dublin. Although the first seven years of her life were spent mostly in Dublin, the Ireland Bowen would come to know and inscribe is not Ireland's urban center but her ancestral demesne in rural County Cork, Bowen's Court, which would become formative as a part of Bowen's imaginative sensibilities. At the same time, Bowen's family history within the Protestant ascendancy, as well as her geographic transience between Ireland and England, offered Bowen a distinctly Janus-like vision of Irish place, history, and literary endeavor.

Bowen's nomadic lifestyle began at the young age of seven when she and her mother moved to England's coast of Kent to stay with relatives while her father recovered from a mental breakdown. Bowen's time with her mother was soon cut short, however. Florence Collins Bowen died of cancer when Elizabeth was just thirteen years old. And as friends and biographers such as Victoria Glendinning point out, this loss would always remain an unarticulated source of pain for Elizabeth. After her mother's death, Bowen was placed in the care of aunts and eventually her father and stepmother, with whom she stayed at Bowen's Court.

Bowen studied art for a brief time in London before finding her voice in a literary imagination that was initially confined to short stories and that was first encouraged by novelist Rose Macaulay. After a year in Italy, Bowen returned to London in 1923. This year marked both her first publication, *Encounters*, a collection of short fiction, and her marriage to Alan Cameron, who was the director of education for Northamptonshire, where they first lived before moving to Old Headington in 1925 for his subsequent post of secretary of education for the city of Oxford. It was in Oxford that Bowen found a literary community and social circle that inspired and sustained her work.

The influence of the intellectual energy of the Oxford circles is evident in Bowen's publication record of this time. In 1929 she completed a collection of short stories, *Joining Charles,* and her first novel, *The Last September,* which would be her most distinctly "Anglo-Irish" novel. A year later, Bowen's father died in County Cork, leaving Elizabeth with the inheritance of Bowen's Court and all of the fiscal and cultural responsibilities that accompany ownership of an Irish Big House.

In the years following her time in Oxford, Bowen found a familiar literary circle in London, associating with figures such as Cyril Connolly, Rosamond Lehmann, Iris Murdoch, Sean O'Faolain, and Virginia Woolf. The destruction and impact of World War II, however, was perhaps the most significant influence on Bowen during her time in London. Bowen became engaged with political activism through her involvement as an air raid precautions warden and her work for the Ministry of Information. Bowen also traveled to Ireland to survey opinion on Ireland's status of neutrality during World War II. War and violent unrest were not in any way foreign to Bowen, who had historical ties to a volatile Irish history and witnessed the consequences of the Irish Civil War. The immediacy of London's place in World War II, however, offered Bowen a new perspective on the nature of violence and war-related suffering.

Interestingly, this war experience inspired Bowen's primary autobiographical texts, *Seven Winters* (1942) and *Bowen's Court* (1942), both of which suggest an impulse to represent her time and experience of Ireland, from her childlike perspective of Dublin in the former text, to a mature perspective of a family legacy that was inevitably marked by social and political connotations and divisions in the latter. The death of her husband as well as the burden of maintaining Bowen's Court created a great sense of financial instability that led to the sale and eventual demolition of Bowen's Court. Bowen's final home was in Hythe, Kent, where she would spend her final days of life composing, but not completing, *Pictures and Conversations,* which would be published posthumously in 1975. In 1973, Elizabeth Bowen died of cancer at the age of seventy-three. Her request to be buried in Ireland, close to Bowen's Court, as well as the response of the villages of the surrounding community, suggests that despite her frequent identification with England, she indeed felt most at home in her family's Anglo-Irish heritage.

MAJOR WORKS AND THEMES

Unlike that of her predecessors of the Anglo-Irish literary elite, such as William Butler Yeats and Lady Gregory, Bowen's writing is not directly associated with that of the Irish Revival's cultural legacy. And while Bowen's work is more typically identified with the English tradition of the comedy of manners and social satire, her "Irish texts" are important records of the cultural, psychological, and political identities of the fading Anglo-Irish ascendancy of the early twentieth century. More specifically, these texts chart the experiences of young women who come to terms with their limited opportunities within the boundaries of the traditional gender and political norms that govern their lives.

The Last September, Bowen's first published novel, constructs a world that is largely defined by the nuances and isolation of the Big House as they indicate the dualities of Anglo-Irish identity. Chronicling the fall of the Anglo-Irish gentry in Ireland during the Irish Civil War, this novel maps the tennis games and dance parties of Danielstown as they coexist with the darkness of Ireland's struggle for independence. The political turmoil is a subtle undertone of the more prominent personal story of Lois Farquar, a young woman on the cusp of adulthood as she attempts to come to terms with what it means to exist in the liminal spaces of both personal and political marginalization. Under the care of the Naylors, her uncle and aunt, Lois's orphan status is not only familial, but also national, which Bowen highlights through Lois's desire to be away from Danielstown, an escape that seems viable only through her marriage to a British soldier. Bowen carefully positions these personal deliberations about coming of age against Lois's Anglo-Irish life of leisure that attempts to persist despite the encroaching realities of war just beyond the windows. Though these attempts at escape linger throughout the novel, their futility becomes increasingly apparent as the novel progresses and makes clear that political and cultural boundaries are ultimately destructive and divisive.

A World of Love (1955) is perhaps less concerned with the place of the Anglo-Irish gentry than it is with the intricacies of a young woman's unwilling engagement with a past in which she is at first uninterested. The Big House of *The Last September* is replaced with the Irish country house, Montefort, which biographer Victoria Glendinning reminds us is based on a deserted farmhouse near Bowen's *Bowen's Court*. More impressionistic and moody than *The Last September*, *A World of Love* evocatively charts Jane's youthful anticipation of a world spurred by more than war and politics. It is Jane's rummaging through attic corners and her discovery of love letters written by Montefort's former owner that propel her into human relationship and communion. And yet, Jane's discovery remains that of anticipation; even at the novel's end, while there is more indication of promise than in *The Last September*, there remains little certainty of what her fate will be.

In addition to the thematic similarity of a young woman's search for adulthood, *A World of Love*, like *The Last September*, purposefully invokes place as participant in the novel's development and imaginative impulse. In Bowen's "Notes on Writing a Novel," from *Pictures and Conversations* (1975), she writes: "Scene, much more than character, is inside the novelist's conscious power. . . . Scene is only justified in the novel where it can be shown, or at least felt, to act upon action or character" (178). Bowen's valuing of place as a participant in plot is perhaps most significantly revealed in her Irish novels. Although she spent the majority of her days in England, her memory of the nuances of Irish place clearly informs her literary mappings of Anglo-Irish identity. In stark contrast to the structure of *The Last September*, the worn and tattered walls of Montefort that she crafts in *A World of Love* mirror the decline of its inhabitants: the often absent owner, Antonia, and the very present Lilia, who works tenaciously to maintain the already lost respectability of Montefort. In comparison to *The Last September*, her inscription of place in *A World of Love* shows that she is more astutely aware of the landscape beyond the house, however, perhaps the figurative and literal decay of its walls forcing the eye beyond the no longer effective safety of class and social boundaries espoused by the Anglo-Irish family. Both *The Last September* and *A World of Love* offer an incisive telling of the young Anglo-Irish woman's place on the peripheries of two conflicting cultures. Their experiences are mirrored by their settings, which offer a physical enactment of an identity that is constantly negotiated by the political moment.

Bowen's primary autobiographical writings, *Seven Winters* and *Bowen's Court*, are most accurately described as family histories of culture and place. *Seven Winters* is a recollection of her childhood in Dublin, a mnemonic mapping that traces the influences of an Irish dwelling on the formation of a young girl's imagination. Integrating a record of her memories of dance lessons and walks to church services at St. Stephens with a consideration of the Anglo-Irish legacy of the land and the house, *Seven Winters* makes clear that the life of Anglo-Irish community, leisure, and festivity, which she so clearly valued in her adult years, had early beginnings in Bowen's life.

Bowen's Court is perhaps the more historically informed of Bowen's autobiographical pieces, the social and political engagement of such a desmesne inevitably infusing itself into the more personal family relationships within its walls. Bowen's personal and emotional investment in the duality of an Anglo-Irish position becomes clear from the text's mapping of the familial past as defined by the edifice of this Big-House structure, as well as by the surrounding village of Kildorrery. Within the context of this piece, one can return to *The Last September* with a keen understanding of why Bowen was able to create Lois's psychological interiority with such precision.

Bowen's vision of the moment is perhaps most clearly expressed in her short fiction, which relies on an understanding of the simultaneity of human awareness and time. In much of her short fiction, Bowen is less concerned with the construction of the interaction between place and person than she is with capturing the nuances of human disillusionment with a life that remains constant only in its changes. From the return of a fantastical lover within wartime London in "The Demon Lover" to the moments of desire and escape in "A Walk in the Woods" and the revelatory critique of the Anglo-Irish in "Her Table Spread," Bowen's short fiction relies less on her skilled creation of a place and more on her attuned sensibility of the human impulse to turn away from the limits of the present and seek understanding in the past.

CRITICAL RECEPTION

As literary scholars more readily turn to questions of place and identity politics in the late twentieth and early twenty-first centuries, critical consideration of Bowen's work has experienced significant growth. Attention to Bowen's Irish novels is most often concerned with Bowen's treatment of the dual marginalization and dislocation, and eventual decline of the Anglo-Irish ascendancy in Ireland. More recent scholarship positions these questions against analyses of Bowen's use of the physical setting—that is, the Big House and the Irish landscape—as a lens through which to understand both the political, as in the case of Lois in *The Last September*, and the personal, as in the case of Jane in *A World of Love,* tenuousness of an Anglo-Irish existence. Critics such as Gearóid Cronin suggest that the presence of the Big House inescapably lingers in much of Bowen's fiction and links the isolated presence of the Big House to Bowen's treatment of history, suggesting that Bowen's descriptions of Danielstown's interior mirrors the family's altered relationship with an Anglo-Irish past that clearly has no future in Ireland.

Scholars have also found resonance between Bowen's constructions of place and sociocultural contexts of tradition. C. L. Innes, for example, places Bowen's treatment of the Big House within the cultural legacy of Yeats, exploring the ways Bowen's *The Last September* positions a young woman against a house that represents specific political structures and at the same time implies traditional gender roles in an otherwise changing Ireland. Josette Leray is also concerned with Bowen's treatment of place, particularly as it is expressed in *A World of Love*. Leray argues, however, that while the setting of this novel might very well be Ireland, its themes and symbols, including that of the Big House, are in no way particular to Ireland.

Critical reviews also reveal that scholars are increasingly concerned with Bowen's work as the subject of feminist critique. While Bowen openly rejected the women's movement within her historical moment, critics have successfully complicated her literary response to women's roles and relationships. Harriet Chessman begins to explore female anxieties of authority through an analysis of Bowen's position with regard to narrative and language. However, Phyllis Lassner's study, which examines Bowen's treatment of female subjectivity, is perhaps the first clearly feminist reading of Bowen's work. Such studies have been expanded upon by scholars such as Renée Hoogland, who carefully explores Bowen's work from a lesbian feminist perspective, making the important gesture of problematizing such a reading with Bowen's own vehement dismissal of a specifically feminist undertone in her work. Maud Ellman attributes the growth in scholarly attention to Bowen's work to the development of feminist criticism and of Irish studies, as well as the reconsideration of the cultural impact of World War II. Ellman proceeds to engage in this critical discussion by offering a psychoanalytic and deconstructive method of interpretation in *Elizabeth Bowen: The Shadow across the Page.*

BIBLIOGRAPHY

Works by Elizabeth Bowen

Bowen's Court. London: Longmans, Green, 1942.
Collected Impressions. London: Longmans, Green, 1950.
A Day in the Dark and Other Stories. London: Cape, 1969.
The Death of the Heart. London: Gollancz, 1938.
Elizabeth Bowen's Irish Stories. Dublin: Poolbeg, 1978. (With an introduction by Victoria Glendinning.)
Encounters. London: Sidgwick and Jackson, 1923.
Eva Trout, or Changing Scenes. New York: Knopf, 1968.
Friends and Relations. London: Constable, 1931.
The Heat of the Day. New York: Knopf, 1949.
The House in Paris. London: Gollancz, 1934.
Ivy Gripped the Steps and Other Stories. New York: Knopf, 1946.
The Last September. London: Constable, 1929.
The Little Girls. London: Cape, 1964.
Pictures and Conversations. New York: Knopf, 1975.
Seven Winters. Dublin: Cuala, 1942
The Shelbourne Hotel. New York: Knopf, 1951.
A Time in Rome. London: Longmans, 1960.
To the North. London: Gollancz, 1932.
A World of Love. New York: Knopf, 1955.

Studies of Elizabeth Bowen

Chessman, Harriet S. "Women and Language in the Fiction of Elizabeth Bowen." *Twentieth Century Literature* 29, no. 1 (Spring 1983): 69–85.
Coates, John. "Elizabeth Bowen's *The Last September*: The Loss of the Past and the Modern Consciousness." *Durham University Journal* 51 (1990): 205–16.

Concilo, Carmen. "Things That Do Speak in Elizabeth Bowen's *The Last September.*" In *Moments of Moment: Aspects of the Literary Epiphany,* edited by Wim Tigges, 279–92. Amsterdam: Rodopi, 1999.

Corcoran, Neil. "Discovery of a Lack: History and Ellipsis in Elizabeth Bowen's *The Last September.*" *Irish University Review* 31, no. 2 (Autumn–Winter 2001): 315–33.

Cronin, Gearóid. "The Big House and the Irish Landscape in the Work of Elizabeth Bowen." In *The Big House in Ireland: Reality and Representation,* edited by Jacqueline Genet, 143–61. Dingle, Ire.: Brandon, 1991.

Ellman, Maud. *Elizabeth Bowen: The Shadow across the Page.* Edinburgh: Edinburgh University Press, 2003.

Glendinning, Victoria. *Elizabeth Bowen: A Life.* New York: Knopf/Random House, 1978.

Gonzalez, Alexander G. "Elizabeth Bowen's 'Her Table Spread': A Joycean Irish Story." *Studies in Short Fiction* 30, no. 3 (Summer 1993): 343–48.

Hoogland, Renee C. *Elizabeth Bowen: A Reputation in Writing.* New York: New York University Press, 1994.

Hopkins, Chris. "Elizabeth Bowen." *Review of Contemporary Fiction* 21, no. 2 (Summer 2001): 114–51.

Innes, C.L. "Custom, Ceremony, and Innocence: Elizabeth Bowen's *The Last September.*" In *Woman and Nation in Irish Literature and Society, 1880–1945.* Athens: University of Georgia Press, 1993, 165–77.

Jordan, Heather Bryant. *How Will the Heart Endure: Elizabeth Bowen and the Landscape of War.* Ann Arbor: University of Michigan Press, 1992.

Kiberd, Declan. "Elizabeth Bowen—The Dandy in Revolt." In *Inventing Ireland: The Literature of the Modern Nation.* Cambridge, MA: Harvard University Press, 1995, 364–79.

Kitagawa, Yoriko. "Anticipating the Postmodern Self: Elizabeth Bowen's *The Death of the Heart.*" *English Studies* 81 (2000): 484–96.

Lassner, Phyllis. *Elizabeth Bowen.* Savage, MD: Barnes and Noble, 1990.

Leray, Josette. "Elizabeth Bowen's *A World of Love.*" In *The Big House in Ireland: Reality and Representation*, edited by Jacqueline Genet, 163–77. Dingle, Ire.: Brandon, 1991.

Sarisalmi, Tiina. "Instances of Strangeness and Disruption: Women and Language in Elizabeth Bowen's Fiction." In *Voicing Gender*, edited by Yvonne Hyrynen, 151–62. Tampere, Finland: University of Tampere Press, 1996.

Sellery, J'nan M., and William O. Harris. *Elizabeth Bowen: A Bibliography.* Austin: University of Texas Press, 1981.

CLARE BOYLAN
(1948–)

John J. Han

BIOGRAPHY

Fiction writer and journalist, Clare Boylan was born in Dublin, daughter of Patrick and Evelyn (née Selby) Boylan. Educated in suburban Dublin, Clare Boylan started her professional career as a journalist. From 1966 to 1968, she worked for the *Dublin*

Evening Press as a reporter. After that, until 1970, she worked as editor of *Young Women*, a Dublin magazine; in September 1970, she married journalist Alan Wilkes. For the next seven years Boylan worked for the *Evening Press*, this time as a feature editor, and then from 1981 to 1984 she served as the editor of *Image* magazine, in Dublin.

Boylan gained prominence as a fiction writer with the 1983 publication of her first work, *Holy Pictures*, a novel about a fourteen-year-old Irish girl's entry into adulthood. The same year saw the publication of Boylan's first short-story collection, *A Nail on the Head*. It was soon followed by *Last Resorts* (1984), a novel dealing with a middle-aged woman's disillusioned life. In the succeeding novel, *Black Baby* (1988), Boylan deals with an elderly Irish woman's chance encounter with a black woman in her mid-thirties. Her second collection of short stories, *Concerning Virgins* (1990), was followed by her fourth novel, *Home Rule* (1992). Published with the title of *11 Edward Street* in the United States, it chronicles the hardships that befall a Dublin family in the 1890s. Next appeared *Room for a Single Day* (1997), a comic novel about a deprived Irish family living on the outskirts of Dublin in the 1950s. *Beloved Stranger* (1999) is based partly on the mental illness of Boylan's own father. In 2000, Abacus Books in London published Boylan's *The Collected Stories*, which was published also by Counterpart in New York in 2002; the collection compiles Boylan's thirty-eight stories from *A Nail on the Head*, *Concerning Virgins*, and *That Bad Woman* (1995). Boylan's most recent work of fiction, *Emma Brown: A Novel from the Unfinished Manuscript* (2003), expands on the twenty-page fragment left by Charlotte Brontë and tentatively titled *Emma*.

Boylan's stories have been widely anthologized in such books as *Winters Tales* (1978), *Territories of the Voice* (1989), and *The Penguin Book of Modern Women's Short Stories* (1990). Her stories have also been published in numerous magazines in the United States, England, Australia, Sweden, and Norway. Several of her stories have been made into films. Boylan is editor of two books of nonfiction: *The Agony and the Ego: The Art and Strategy of Fiction Writing Explored* (essays, 1993) and *The Literary Companion to Cats: An Anthology of Prose and Poetry* (1994), compiling literary works on cat love and hate from the past twenty-five centuries. In 1974, Boylan received the Journalist of the Year Award (Ireland) from Benson & Hedges; her novel *Room for a Single Lady* was the winner of the Spirit of Life Award. A member of Aosdána, Boylan currently resides in Kilbride, County Wicklow, Ireland.

MAJOR WORKS AND THEMES

Boylan's mostly modern Irish characters, particularly women, struggle with economic, social, familial, or interpersonal issues. Her favorite themes include the dreariness of poverty-stricken life, male chauvinism, the mother-daughter relationship, sex and love, and the loneliness of old age. *Holy Pictures*, set in mid-1920s Dublin and dedicated to the author's husband, is a tragicomic domestic story written from the perspective of the Catholic teenager Nan Cantwell. A good student at a strict Catholic school, Nan observes the adult world around her and finds it disappointing. Her father, who runs the Cantwell Corset factory, is rude and overbearing. He remarks, "Names do not matter to women. They are only of interest to people in the world. Women do not have a name until they marry" (86). Nan's mother accepts her fate as an inferior marital partner, explaining to Nan, "When you're my age, you'll put up with a lot of things that you don't like" (6–7). The church condemns women and girls participating in men's sports—tennis, swimming, golfing, and others—because it leads them to dress skimpily; the bishops of the whole diocese decree that this excessive liking for masculine sports "exposes women to moral dangers, to habits of conduct wholly at variance with the mission of women in family and society" (17). After her husband's death, with the family in dire poverty, Nan's mother decides to open a rooming house. A wealthy tenant, Mr. Finnucane, starts courting Nan's mother, but he also tries to seduce Nan. Nan tearfully reports Mr. Finnucane's inexcusable behavior to her mother, who replies, "Every man will attempt that. It's up to the woman," visibly upset that she has lost a rich tenant.

Harriet Bell, the heroine of *Last Resorts*, is a forty-year-old English painter whose husband deserted her and their three children years ago. She vacations at a cottage on a Greek holiday island with her family and her married lover, Joe Fisher. Harriet is known among the locals for being bohemian. Hungry for affection, she sleeps around; once, she was impregnated by one of the men she fell in love with, and the child was stillborn and looked "reproachfully monstrous" (10). Her children, whom Harriet has raised all alone, are uncontrollable. Lulu walks around half-naked, inviting condemnation from old people; Tim "[lies] on the bed in his boiling and barred room masturbating all day" (10); and Kitty is pregnant and has no qualms about saying the *f* word to Harriet's face. Although her lover, Joe, sleeps with her, he refuses to divorce his wife. Harriet's lot is to be depressed, hurt, and lonely.

Boylan quotes a verse from St. Paul's letter to the Hebrews as the epigram for *Black Baby*: "Be not forgetful to entertain strangers: for thereby some have entertained angels unawares." In this hilarious novel, the author tells the story of a sixty-seven-year-old Irish spinster's chance encounter with Dinah, a cheerful, burly black woman from Africa, and of their meeting's effect on their lives. Before the friendship is formed, Alice has little zest for life. Recalling the black baby she "purchased" from a Catholic mission in Africa decades ago, Alice allows Dinah—who identifies herself as "[Alice's] daughter in Christ" (16)—into her home. Dinah is a fraud, but she still revives Alice's appetite for life and frees her from boredom and cynicism. Alice has found salvation in Dinah—an "angel" whom she entertained unawares.

Beloved Strangers focuses on a Dublin couple, Dick and Lily Butler, who have been married for fifty years. Married life has been good overall, mainly because Lily patiently endured Dick's hot temper, submitting graciously to the authority of her overbearing husband. As he ages, Dick mellows but begins to lose his mind. Diagnosed suddenly as manic-depressive, he is committed to a mental institution. Faced with a reality never experienced before, Lily falters but eventually musters strength to live alone.

CRITICAL RECEPTION

Although Boylan worked as a journalist for more than two decades, her fame rests on her novels and short stories. Once an emerging star in fiction writing, she is now considered one of the finest Irish storytellers. Boylan's fiction has been reviewed in a considerable number of prominent newspapers, magazines, and library publications. The works that receive the most critical attention are *Holy Pictures*, *A Nail on the Head*, *Last Resorts*, *Black Baby*, *11 Edward Street* (*Home Rule*), *Beloved Stranger*, and *The Collected Stories*.

Most critics praise Boylan for her sympathetic treatment of Irish women who undergo hardships and for her skillful use of figurative language, sensory details, and humor. Katy Emick comments that Clare Boylan is "a rare combination of worldly wise aplomb and refreshing sincerity" (82). Boylan's skill as displayed in *Room for a Single Lady* "shows in the way she makes the reader sentimentally nostalgic for poverty at the same time as terrified by its bleakness" (82). Gail Pool finds the storyline of *Beloved Stranger* both "engaging" and "absorbing" (30). In his review of *The Collected Stories*, Jeff Zaleski considers Boylan "an appealing and idiosyncratic chronicler of the quirks and foibles of the Irish working class" (56). Barbara Love finds melodramatic elements in *Emma Brown* but adds that "this successor to *Jane Eyre* is still entertaining and should be popular with readers who cannot get their fill of Victoriana" (159).

Some critics, however, find fault, complaining of the superficial plot, shallow characterization, and forced social messages in Boylan's fiction. Ellen Kaye Stoppel, in her commentary on *11 Edward Street*, writes that the novel "attempts to cover too much material and too many years." According to Stoppel, "The narrative is superficial, the characters little more than stick figures, and outside events so casually handled that even World War I makes little impact" (118). Regarding *Room for a Single Lady*, Nicholas Clee criticizes its plot: "Consisting of a series of genial (and sometimes strenuously farcical) episodes, the novel lacks direction and shape" (23). Meanwhile, Claudia Pugh-Thomas sees a lack of character development in *Beloved Stranger*, which, she feels, "reads like a detached case study; the three central characters emerge as examples of a type, rather than fully-formed individuals" (23).

BIBLIOGRAPHY

Works by Clare Boylan

Novels and Short Stories

Another Family Christmas: A Collection of Short Stories. Dublin: Poolbeg, 1997.
Beloved Stranger. London: Little, Brown, 1999.
Black Baby. London: Hamish Hamilton, 1988.
The Collected Stories. London: Abacus, 2000; New York: Counterpart, 2002.
Concerning Virgins. London: Hamish Hamilton, 1990.
Emma Brown: A Novel from the Unfinished Manuscript. London: Little, Brown, 2003.
Holy Pictures. New York: Summit, 1983.
Home Rule. London: Hamish Hamilton, 1992. Also published as *11 Edward Street*. New York: Doubleday, 1992.
Last Resorts. London: Hamish Hamilton, 1984.
A Nail on the Head. London: Hamish Hamilton, 1983.
Room for a Single Lady. London: Little, Brown, 1997.
That Bad Woman: Short Stories. London: Little, Brown, 1995.

Coauthored Novel

Ladies' Night at Finbar's Hotel, with Kate O'Riordan, Maeve Binchy, Emma Donoghue, Anne Haverty, Éilis Ní Dhuibhne, and Deirdre Purcell. Edited by Dermot Bolger. London: Picador, 1999.

Edited Volumes

The Agony and the Ego: The Art and Strategy of Fiction Writing Explored. New York: Penguin, 1993.
The Literary Companion to Cats: An Anthology of Prose and Poetry. London: Sinclair-Stevenson, 1994.

Studies of Clare Boylan

Clee, Nicholas. "A Child Among the Lodgers." Review of *Room for a Single Lady*. *TLS: The Times Literary Supplement* September 26, 1997, 23.

Emick, Katy. Review of *Room for a Single Lady*. *New Statesman* December 19–26, 1997, 82–83.

Love, Barbara. Review of *Emma Brown: A Novel from the Unfinished Manuscript by Charlotte Brontë*. *Library Journal* February 15, 2004, 159.

Pool, Gail. "Things Fall Apart." Review of *Beloved Stranger*. *Women's Review of Books*, July 2001, 30–31.

Pugh-Thomas, Claudia. "Acts of Betrayal." Review of *Beloved Stranger*. *TLS: The Times Literary Supplement* September 17, 1999, 23.

Stoppel, Ellen Kaye. Review of *11 Edward Street*. *Library Journal* May 15, 1992, 118.

Zaleski, Jeff. Review of *The Collected Stories*. *Publishers Weekly* October 21, 2002, 56.

ELIZABETH BRENNAN
(1907–   )

Paul Marchbanks

BIOGRAPHY

Born in Clonmel County, Tipperary, in 1907 and raised in Dublin, Elizabeth Brennan made the first of two significant moves upon marrying an Englishman, relocating to the southwest country of England, and there beginning to craft carefully a number of short novels, primarily for a younger audience. Upon the death of her husband, she returned to her homeland and, now a single mother, supported her family by working in a Dublin newspaper office. A second marriage allowed her to redirect her energies toward romantic novelettes and a number of historical projects, one of which dealt with the history of St. Patrick's Cathedral, while another explored in detail the characters of Lady Gore-Booth and Lady Londonderry.

MAJOR WORKS AND THEMES

Brennan's early writing career demonstrated remarkable productivity and a diversity of interests. Between 1945 and 1950 she published four novels, two sets of children stories, and one collection of poetry. The same year that she released *Am I My Brother's Keeper* (1946), a hospital novel set in England and Ireland that considered the immediately relevant emigration of professionals from Ireland, she provided her younger public the whimsically illustrated *The Wind Fairies* (1946), a piece popular enough to demand an immediate sequel.

Two years later, another work for children appeared. The novel *The Mystery of Hermit's Crest* (1948) is a finely wrought adventure dedicated at some length to those nephews and nieces whom Brennan claims to have translated faithfully into the rambunctious sleuths of her tale. This particular adventure appears modeled after such teen fare as the then well-known American Hardy Boys series, its plot replete with such dramatic staples as a missing child, an undying jealousy over a long-dead beauty, and a burning mansion. The characters populating the novel are equally fabulous and include an emotionally abusive guardian uncle, a constitutionally nervous politician whose power and prestige rest on a series of hidden misdeeds, a wandering ancient whose cryptic murmurings belie his apparent dotage, and the requisite artist in hiding whose breathtaking works provide the key to unlocking the central mystery—that he and the wandering ancient are one and the same. A small crew of teenagers uncovers this mystery as a way to enliven their dull vacation from college. They snoop about dressed like specters, frightening their guilty targets and anonymously providing the public with their discoveries, earmarking each clue with their mysterious moniker, "The Sign of Four." Predictably gothic locales here include an old town immediately established as "desolate" and "grim" and surrounded by mountains (one of which resembles an ancient, round tower), the requisite grange, cave, and old quarry (9–10), and an abbey-turned-manor in which "the famous Four Masters spent some time . . . while [travelling] Ireland" (64).

Such occasional Irish touches proliferate in Brennan's later work, providing the fundamental structure for some of her more quickly written romances. Young women in need of male companionship inevitably find their mate in the most "Irish" of geographies, among the cottages and green hills of western, rural Ireland. For instance, though the opportunity to become a professional dancer pulls her toward the urban east, the heroine of *A Girl Called Debbie* (1975) makes sure to balance her life ambitions by securing the well-off, widowed proprietor of Abbey Farm in the small western town of Rockinish. The earlier *Love in the Glade* (1968), released at a time when the politically correct vision of romantic Ireland had not yet been occluded by the prolonged, gritty realism of the Troubles, provides perhaps the best sampling of this romantic, sentimental mode.

When the perpetually late, apparently flighty heroine inherits the quaint cottage of a great-aunt dismissed as "foolish" and "poetic" by her family, Sally Carroll suddenly finds her comfortable plans to marry a businessman to be inconsistent with what she now recognizes as her deeper, truer self. (She will later claim, with sappily endearing tears, that she is a country girl who had the *misfortune* to be born in the city.) We discover that the twenty-one-year-old's long-lasting dream of living in the country—one quietly shared by a habitually compliant mother—has been buried repeatedly by Ireland's new pragmatic patriarchs, the responsible, teetotalist father concerned primarily with his "silly" daughter's security, and, more recently, the charmingly condescending fiancé who must have central heating. Demanding a mode of living less dominated by clocks and an array of stifling expectations, Sally disappears to her new abode across the country and finds in "Innisfree Cottage" (of course), the "timeless world of her dreams," complete with Victorian parlor and all the Aran accoutrements and antique reliquaries she could desire (43). Better yet is Eskey Vale itself, with its misty blue sky and "bee-loud" glades that inspire the occasional, impulsive quoting of poems from W. B. Yeats's mythic, 1890s mode (135). The male lover who necessarily appears with her new environs proves at least as patronizing as his Dublin counterpart, but more vitally alive and engagingly capricious, qualities that ultimately doom Peter Brandon's brash presumption in planning a wedding without having yet asked Sally to do him the honor (190).

The sequel to this tale, with its wonderfully politically incorrect title *Patrick's Woman* (1969), appears even more hastily constructed and executed than its predecessor, suggesting that the acclaimed *Girl on an Island* (1984), with which she ended her writing career, was a gem only slowly uncovered from beneath assorted stones of lesser color and carat.

CRITICAL RECEPTION

In such cursory reference texts as *A Biographical Dictionary of Irish Writers* (1985) and the *Electronic Irish Records Dataset*, Brennan is primarily regarded as a writer of light, romantic fiction, her creation of children's stories and the occasional play receiving the briefest of mentions. Her plays were obviously appreciated enough to be broadcast over irish radio, and *Girl on an Island* received an Irish Countrywoman's Association (ICA) Prize. There is, however, a definite dearth of critical material regarding her work beyond the most obviously ebullient, terse comments with which her works were advertised and published.

BIBLIOGRAPHY

Works by Elizabeth Brennan

Am I My Brother's Keeper? Dublin: Metropolitan, 1946.
The Children's Book of Irish Saints. London: Harrap, 1963.
A Girl Called Debbie. London: Robert Hale, 1975.
Girl on an Island. London: Robert Hale, 1984.
Her Lucky Mistake. London: Robert Hale, 1966.
His Glamorous Cousin. London: Hale; Toronto: Thomas Allen, 1963.
Innocent in Eden. London: Robert Hale, 1971.
Love in the Glade. London: Robert Hale, 1968.
Love's Loom. London: Robert Hale, 1973.
Mountain of Desire. London: Robert Hale, 1970.
The Mystery of Hermits Crest. Dublin: Metropolitan, 1948.
No Roses for Jo. London: Robert Hale, 1972.
Out of the Darkness. Dublin: Metropolitan, 1945.
Patrick's Woman. London: Robert Hale, 1969.
Retreat from Love. London: Robert Hale, 1967.
Sweet Love of Youth. London: Robert Hale, 1978
Whispering Walls. Dublin: Metropolitan, 1948.
The Wind Fairies. Dublin: Metropolitan, 1946.
The Wind Fairies Again. Dublin, Metropolitan, 1948.
Wind Over the Bogs. Dublin: Metropolitan, 1950.

Studies of Elizabeth Brennan

Brady, Anne M., and Brian Cleeve, eds. *A Biographical Dictionary of Irish Writers*. New York: St. Martin's, 1985, 19.

"Elizabeth Brennan." Princess Grace Irish Library (Monaco). Electronic Irish Records Dataset. http://www.pgil-eirdata.org/html/pgil_datasets/authors/b/Brennan,E/life.htm   (accessed August 2003).

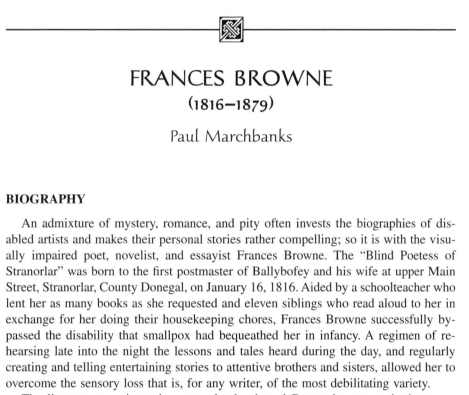

FRANCES BROWNE
(1816–1879)

Paul Marchbanks

BIOGRAPHY

An admixture of mystery, romance, and pity often invests the biographies of disabled artists and makes their personal stories rather compelling; so it is with the visually impaired poet, novelist, and essayist Frances Browne. The "Blind Poetess of Stranorlar" was born to the first postmaster of Ballybofey and his wife at upper Main Street, Stranorlar, County Donegal, on January 16, 1816. Aided by a schoolteacher who lent her as many books as she requested and eleven siblings who read aloud to her in exchange for her doing their housekeeping chores, Frances Browne successfully bypassed the disability that smallpox had bequeathed her in infancy. A regimen of rehearsing late into the night the lessons and tales heard during the day, and regularly creating and telling entertaining stories to attentive brothers and sisters, allowed her to overcome the sensory loss that is, for any writer, of the most debilitating variety.

The literary progenitor who most clearly shaped Browne's own aspirations was Homer. (Her most famous heroine would be a highly educated Russian of Greek descent whose pride in her lineage was matched only by her close knowledge of Greek culture and art.) After she had consumed Pope's translation of *The Iliad*, the budding poetess's artistic notions did an about-face, and she hastily threw a cherished manuscript into the nearest fireplace. While the dynamic tales of Sir Walter Scott continued to stir her artistic impulses, however, the enormity of Byron's *Childe Harold* effectively squelched her poetic ambitions, so overwhelming the fifteen-year-old enthusiast that she shelved verse making for a decade.

In 1840, an oral reading of collected Irish songs parted the air for her and she wrote the lyric "The Songs of Our Land," published in the *Irish Penny Journal* the following year. Numerous poems followed and established for her a reputation in such British periodicals as *Hoods* magazine, the *Athenaeum*, and Lady Blessington's *Keepsake*. She used the meager funds from these publications to help educate one of her sisters, who thereafter acted as her amanuensis. With only a small civil list pension of twenty pounds from the Royal Bounty Fund, she and her sister removed to Edinburgh in 1847. Over the next five years, Browne published numerous stories, poems, reviews, and essays, though health difficulties and a commitment to sending much of her earnings back to her family precluded financial security for herself. In 1852, however, a one-hundred-pound gift from the Marquis of Lansdowne allowed her to move to London and begin focusing her powers on fiction, both short stories for children and more serious, extended fare for her peers. Over the next thirty years she produced a few melodramatic novels, such as the popular *The Hidden Sin* (1866), as well as many children's tales. The collection of interwoven parables, "Granny's Wonderful Chair" (1856), proved to have the longest legs, returning to print twenty-five years after its initial publication and running through six editions in only eight years.

MAJOR WORKS AND THEMES

Though temporarily cowed by the feats of poetic superstars like Byron, when Browne came of age she renewed her artistic production with a vengeance, audaciously writing of climes and cultures she could never see and would never have the opportunity to visit except via the many histories read to her. Unlike her Romantic idol, whose fictional journeys reflected his own travels through Europe, only Browne's mind would prove mobile. Her imagination took the narrative lyric "The Star of Attéghéi" far into the Circassian region of Russia, while other poems ventured into medieval monasteries, Arabia, the Italy of Tasso, and the ancient road of Simplon down which Napoleon marched. Her mind's eye even sailed the Atlantic, making landfall in America as she wrote of the Protestant Union in New England and the abolition of slavery. It was the poetry of her native country, however, that would linger most deliciously in the Irish psyche, whether she called the hidden avian folk to "Sing on by fane and forest old," or evoked those songs that coursed through the nation's shared consciousness like "some far flowing river." In the dominant Irish mode of the time, her poems echoed the romantic ardor and evocative melancholia of similar poetry by such well-remembered contemporaries as James Clarence Mangan and the other poets of *The Nation*.

While Frances Browne began her professional career as a poet, publishing her first volume of poetry in 1844 and a second collection in 1848, her fiction output soon overtook the lyrical. Children's stories provided yet another means of exploring geographies and walks of life untouched by her feet. While *The Exile's Trust* (1869) explored the vicissitudes of the French Revolution in southern Normandy, *The First of the African Diamonds* (1887) stepped with the Dutch onto the banks of the Orange River. *Granny's Wonderful Chair and Its Tales of Fairy Times* (1856), a popular collection of parables still making its way into print as late as the 1920s, preached selflessness and contentment with simple material conditions in a far-off, magical land. Told by a self-propelled armchair, one shod with wheels, capped by a talking seat cushion, and accompanied by the young heroine, Snowflower, these tales of mysterious forests and shape-changing sheep gradually win the humble girl the accoutrements of court and a prince for husband.

Browne's novels targeted a decidedly older audience and replaced neatly packaged didacticism with sensational plots and complex characters. The best known of her novels, *The Hidden Sin* (1866), relates the adventures of one Lucien La Touche, whose family's misfortunes result in his removal to a wealthy uncle in America. There, Lucien quickly forgets his Irish heritage and learns to avoid interacting with the poorer Irish immigrants landing on Maryland's shores. As an adult, he re-crosses the Atlantic and plays out his adventures in London with one of literature's most unjustly forgotten femme fatales, Madame Palivez, returning to Ireland only at the novel's end, and then but temporarily. His latent Irishness does, however, provide a consistent albeit muted backdrop for the action, emerging in his comments on Irish honor (92), or on his sister's reliance on Irish superstitions (109) and legends (113), or on the old rosary from home (156).

CRITICAL RECEPTION

Browne's status as a perpetually poor, visually impaired artisan with hard-won learning and compelling storytelling skills earned her the hagiographic notice of many. The kind treatment the *Dublin Review* gave to this "blind poetess" was rather representative of the criticism she received at the hands of those who knew both her biography as well as her art. In 1904, twenty-five years after her death, she was still earning effusive praise, the editor of yet another edition of her most famous children's tales taking every opportunity to eulogize this "one of the elect" whose imaginative powers of visualization overcame her disability, allowing "no blurred lines or uncertainties." While her longer fiction received little attention then or since, her children's stories still receive professional attention.

BIBLIOGRAPHY

Works by Frances Browne

The Castleford Case. London: Hurst and Blackett, 1862.
The Dangerous Guest: A Story of 1745. London, Religious Tracts Society, 1886.
The Ericksons and The Clever Boy, or Consider One Another. Edinburgh: Paton and Ritchie, 1852.
The Exile's Trust: A Tale of the French Revolution, and Other Stories. London: Leisure Hour, 1869.
The First of the African Diamonds. London: Religious Tracts Society, 1887.
The Foundling of the Fens: A Story of a Flood. London: Religious Tracts Society, 1886.
Granny's Wonderful Chair, and Its Tales of Fairy Times. 1856. London: Griffith and Farran, 1857.
The Hidden Sin: A Novel. London: Bentley, 1866.
Lyrics and Miscellaneous Poems. Edinburgh: Sutherland and Knox, 1848.
My Nearest Neighbour, and Other Stories. London: Religious Tracts Society, 1875.
My Share of the World: An Autobiography. London: Hurst and Blackett, 1861.
The Orphans of Elfholm. Magnet Stories. 1860. London: Groombridge, 1862.
Our Uncle the Traveller's Stories. London: Kent, 1859.
Pictures and Songs of Home. London: Nelson, 1856.
The Star of Attéghéi. The Vision of Schwartz and Other Poems. London: Moxon, 1844.
The Young Foresters. London: Groombridge, 1864.

Studies of Frances Browne

Avery, Gillian. "Frances Browne." In *Dictionary of National Biography: Missing Persons*, edited by C. S. Nicholls. Oxford: Oxford University Press, 1993.
Burnett, Frances Hodgson. "The Story of the Lost Fairy Book." Introduction to *Granny's Wonderful Chair*, by Frances Browne. London: McClure, Phillips, 1904.
The Cabinet Irish Literature: Selections from the Works of the Chief Poets, Orators, and Prose Writers of Ireland. With Biographical Sketches and Literary Notices. 4 Vols. London: Blackie, 1879–80.
"Frances Browne." *The Field Day Anthology of Irish Writing*. Vols. 4 and 5, *Women's Writing and Traditions*, edited by Angela Bourke, Mairin Ni Dhonneadha, Siobhan Kilfeather,

Maria Luddy, Margaret MacCurtain, Gerardine Meaney, Mary O'Dowd, and Clair Wills, 861–64, 893, 1156–57. New York: New York University Press, 2002.

"The Life and Writings of Miss Browne, the Blind Poetess." *Dublin Review* 17 (1844): 517–60.

Manlove, Colin. "George MacDonald and the Fairy Tales of Francis Paget and Frances Browne." *North Wind: Journal of the George MacDonald Society* 18 (1999): 17–32.

Nelson, Claudia. "Art for Man's Sake: Frances Browne's Magic and Victorian Social Aesthetics." *Bookbird: A Journal of International Children's Literature* 36 (Summer 1998): 19–24.

"Our Poets: No. 29 Frances Browne." *Irish Monthly* 24 (1896): 262–68.

Radford, Dollie. Preface. In *Granny's Wonderful Chair and Its Tales of Fairy Times*, by Frances Browne. Everyman's Library. London: Dent, 1906.

MARY ROSE CALLAGHAN
(1944–   )

Maryanne Felter

BIOGRAPHY

Novelist and biographer Mary Rose Callaghan, the second of six children, was born in Dublin and educated from the age of nine mostly in convent boarding schools, leaving school in 1962. Enrolling as a medical student at University College Dublin she took her BA in English, history, and ethics/politics in 1968 and received a diploma in education in 1969. After teaching in various secondary schools both in England and in Ireland, she became assistant editor of the *Arts in Ireland* from 1973 to 1975. She has done some journalism, publishing in the *Irish Times*, the *Sunday Tribune*, *Hibernia*, the *Irish Independent*, and the *Catholic Standard*. Some of her shorter creative pieces have been published in *U* magazine, the *Irish Times*, *Image* magazine, and the *Journal of Irish Literature*. Her move to America in 1975 allowed her to focus on her writing, and she finished her first novel, *Mothers*, in 1978 (published in 1982). While continuing to write fiction, Callaghan also worked as a contributing editor for the *Journal of Irish Literature* from 1975 to 1993, was associate editor for the first and second editions of the *Dictionary of Irish Literature*, and taught writing classes at the University of Delaware. Callaghan and her husband, Robert Hogan, traversed the Atlantic yearly, spending half their time in Newark, Delaware, and half in Dublin, finally settling permanently in Bray in 1993. Since her husband's death, Callaghan has continued to live in Bray, writing, taking classes in art history, and teaching.

MAJOR WORKS AND THEMES

Callaghan is noted for her control of point of view, her characterization, her penchant for literary allusion, and her humor. The plots are often wild and quirky even though they take on serious themes. *Mothers*, a powerful first novel, chronicles, in dramatic monologues, the lives of three Irishwomen from three generations. It explores marriage, adoption, pregnancy out of wedlock, and female sisterhood and created quite a stir during abortion debates in Ireland when it was first published. *Confessions of a Prodigal Daughter* (1985) is a portrait of an artist as a young girl. Modeled loosely on Dante's *Comedia* and highly allusive, the novel, with its large cast of Dickensian characters, is comic but not as successful aesthetically as *Mothers*. Taking a break from fiction, Callaghan was commissioned to write *Kitty O'Shea: A Life of Katherine Parnell* (1989). Callaghan's purpose here is to show Katherine Parnell's life as a noble and courageous one, not simply one linked by chance to her famous husband's. The biography is readable and well researched, a fine work showing her background in history. Callaghan's next novel, *The Awkward Girl* (1990), demonstrates her control of narration and plot structure, which allows her to interweave thirty-six minor characters and apparently fragmented short "stories" around one major title character. She balances biting comedy with sympathetic characterization, manipulates aesthetic distance, and pulls her readers into her main character's subtle epiphanies. In 1990, Callaghan published a novel for young adults, *Has Anyone Seen Heather?*, a murder mystery that is fast-paced and action-filled, with a strong, suspenseful plot and likable characters. It was followed in 1997 by a sequel, *The Last Summer*, which transcends its designation as "young adult fiction." A novel that explores sibling rivalry, family relations, and artistic ambition in a comic, allusive manner, it can be read by all adults, young and old. In 1996, Callaghan published *Emigrant Dreams* (published in the United States as *I Met a Man who Wasn't There*), a novel that epitomizes all her strengths. Here, her Irish narrator (Anne O'Brien from *Confessions*, now a middle-aged writer), haunted by her dead Irish American grandfather, explores questions of reputation, political correctness, emigration, memory, and the close relationship between creativity and insanity. The novel depicts the emotional problems of an Irish writer teaching in an American college, as she attempts to untangle the dubious involvement of an Irish American ancestor who was involved in the real-life Becker murder trial of 1912. *The Visitors' Book* (2001) continues Callaghan's interest in trans-Atlantic comic possibilities as each of twelve chapters chronicles how the narrator's Bray home becomes a kind of bed-and-breakfast establishment for visiting American friends and family. While her earlier novels tended to concentrate on specifically Irish situations and characters, the later novels move out to embrace trans-Atlantic themes, making use of both her Irish and her American experiences.

CRITICAL RECEPTION

From the start, critical response to Callaghan has been mostly positive. Although Marion Glastonbury in the *New Statesman* called *Mothers* a "sentimental, conventional and predictable tale," Anne Donovan in *Library Journal* said it is "engaging, as both an Irish and a feminist novel," while *Kirkus Reviews* reported that it is "grounded in genuine affection and lifted above mere soap by charm and wit." Callaghan's second novel did not fare as well as her first. Although *Publishers Weekly* called *Confessions of a Prodigal Daughter* a "graceful touching tale," *Booklist* saw it as a "thin novel" and Anne Haverty in the *Times Literary Supplement* said that the novel "frequently takes refuge in a contrived charm, and the result is diminishing and curiously juvenile." Jay Halio in *DLB*, however, argued that *Confessions* "did not receive the widespread notice and acclaim that *Mothers* did, probably because its subjects were less controversial." *The Awkward Girl* has fared better, with the *Sunday Independent* noting that it is a "profoundly moving book," and *Eire-Ireland* calling it "quite an exceptional novel. . . . [Mary Rose Callaghan's work] may well place her in the ranks of the Irish writers of the twentieth century." Unfortunately out of print now, *Emigrant Dreams*, probably Callaghan's best novel, was received with almost unanimous good press. *Publishers Weekly* noted that Callaghan "fuses intriguing historical detail onto a psychological thriller that features more than one superbly wrought character. Eccentric and thoroughly enjoyable, this novel offers intelligent, witty entertainment." Halio (*DLB*) observed that "while the novel succeeds as entertaining fiction, it also offers perceptive comments about the writing process and how it is affected by the difficulties of married life and other relationships." Callaghan's seventh novel, *The Visitors' Book*, has also met with good reviews. The *Irish Tatler* called it "a wry and amusing look at Celtic Tiger Ireland" that is "written in the easy personal style of a journal." Edel Coffey, in the *Sunday Tribune*, noted that "Callaghan takes the romantic visions some Americans have of Ireland and dismantles them with great comic effect." In all, reviewers have liked Callaghan's work. As Coffey says, she is "a seasoned writer and has established a reputation for her comic fiction."

BIBLIOGRAPHY

Works by Mary Rose Callaghan

Full-Length Works

The Awkward Girl. Dublin: Attic, 1990.
Confessions of a Prodigal Daughter. London: Marion Boyars, 1985.
Emigrant Dreams. Dublin: Poolbeg, 1996. Published in the United States as *I Met a Man Who Wasn't There*. New York: Marion Boyars, 1996.
Has Anyone Seen Heather? Dublin: Attic, 1990.
A House for Fools. *Journal of Irish Literature* 12, no. 3 (September 1983): 3–67.
Kitty O'Shea: A Life of Katherine Parnell. London: Pandora, 1989.
The Last Summer. Dublin: Poolbeg, 1997.
Mothers. Dublin: Arlen House, 1982.
The Visitors' Book. Dingle, Ire.: Brandon, 2001.

Shorter Works

"Breakfast with Turgenev." *Journal of Irish Literature* 6, no. 2 (May 1977): 14–20.
"Crybaby." *Shenandoah* 46 (Fall 1996): 74–79.
"A Far, Far Better Thing." *Image*, May 1986, 96–102.
"Hold It! These Things Don't Happen in Real Life." *Irish Independent*, February 10, 1987, 9.
"How I Saved Thirteen Thousand Pounds." *Journal of Irish Literature* 17, no. 1 (January 1988): 14–31.
"I Hate Christmas." In *A Woman's Christmas*, edited by Terry Prone. 146–55. Dublin: Martello Press, 1994.
"Julia O'Faolain." In *DLB 14: British Novelists Since 1960*, edited by Jay Halio, 580–84. Detroit: Gale, 1983.
"My First Bra." *Irish Times*, August 27, 1979, 12.
"A Novel Way of Cooking." *Woman's Way*, October 28, 1983, 6, 8, 38–40.
"Ronnie." *Journal of Irish Literature* 5, no. 3 (September 1976): 89–121.
"The Siege of Fort Bathtub." In *Modern Irish Stories*, edited by Caroline Walsh, 70–75. Dublin: Irish Times, 1985.
"Sisters—The Pain and Joy of a Lifelong Bond." *Irish Times*, September 13, 1985, 13.

"Underwear." In *Wall Reader and Other Stories*. Dublin: Arlen House, 1979, 94–101.
"Windfalls." In *If Only*, edited by Kate Cruise O'Brien and Mary Maher, 47–60. Dublin: Poolbeg, 1997.

Studies of Mary Rose Callaghan

"Callaghan, Mary Rose." *Beacham's Guide to Literature for Young Adults* 7, edited by Kirk H. Beetz. Washington, D.C.: Beacham, 1990.
"Callaghan, Mary Rose." *Cambridge Guide to Women's Writing in English*, edited by Lorna Sage. Cambridge: Cambridge University Press, 1999.
"Callaghan, Mary Rose." *Contemporary Authors* 118. Detroit: Gale, 1986, 74.
"Callaghan, Mary Rose." *Contemporary Authors New Revision Series* 43. Detroit: Gale, 1994, 56–57.
Felter, Maryanne. "Callaghan, Mary Rose." *Dictionary of Irish Literature*. 2nd ed. Westport, CT: Greenwood, 1996, 214–15.
———. "An Interview with Mary Rose Callaghan." *Nua: Studies in Contemporary Irish Writing* 4, nos. 1–2 (2003): 159–68.
Halio, Jay. "Mary Rose Callaghan." *DLB 207: British Novelists since 1960*. 3rd series, edited by Merritt Moseley, 66–71. Detroit: Gale Group, 1999.
———. "Contemplation, Fiction, and the Writer's Sensibility." *Southern Review* 19 (Winter 1983): 203–18 (passim).
Weekes, Ann Owens. "Mary Rose Callaghan." *Unveiling Treasures: The Attic Guide to the Published Works of Irish Women Literary Writers: Drama, Fiction, Poetry*, edited by Ann Owens Weekes, 66–68. Dublin: Attic, 1993.
Wessel-Felter, Maryanne. "*Commedia*: The Fiction of Mary Rose Callaghan." *Eire-Ireland* 29, no. 2 (Summer 1994): 139–45.

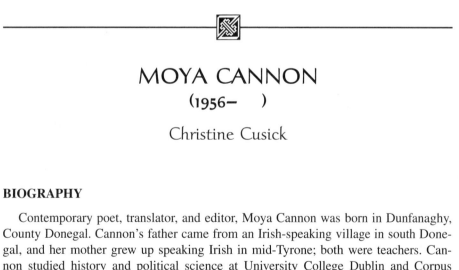

MOYA CANNON
(1956–   )

Christine Cusick

BIOGRAPHY

Contemporary poet, translator, and editor, Moya Cannon was born in Dunfanaghy, County Donegal. Cannon's father came from an Irish-speaking village in south Donegal, and her mother grew up speaking Irish in mid-Tyrone; both were teachers. Cannon studied history and political science at University College Dublin and Corpus Christi College, Cambridge. Awakening to poetry in her late teens, she immediately experienced a visceral response to poetry's engagement with the spiritual and organic. Cannon's exposure to the values of translation and rhythm espoused by canonical figures such as Ezra Pound inspired her to embrace the traditions of Irish song and verse. Attention to the dynamics of language and intonation remain present in Cannon's collaborative work with contemporary classical musicians such as Philip Martin (*Echoes under the Stones*, 1994) and translation work with traditional Irish musicians such as

Maighread and Tríona Ní Dhomhnaill (*Idir an Dá Sholas: Between the Two Lights*, 2000). Moreover, thematic threads in both her published volumes concern the inadequacy of language, as she seems to surrender to music and performance as the more careful arbiters of meaning.

In recognition of *Oar* (1990), Cannon was awarded the 1991 Brendan Behan Award for a first collection. She was writer-in-residence at Champlain College, Trent University, Ontario, in 1994–95 and in 2003 and edited *Poetry Ireland Review* in 1995. Cannon has given many poetry readings in Ireland, Britain, Germany, Austria, Canada, and the United States and has broadcast on RTE radio and television and on BBC radio. In 2001 Cannon was awarded the fifth annual poetry award of the Center for Irish Studies at the University of St. Thomas in Minnesota. This award places Cannon in the company of poets such as Louis de Paor, Peter Sirr, John F. Deane, and Eavan Boland. Cannon is currently completing a translation of traditional Irish songs from Gaelic and Old Irish into modern Irish as well as a third volume of poetry. Teaching in a school for adolescent travelers in Galway, where she holds her permanent residence, she is actively involved in various poetry workshops, including international programs sponsored by University College Galway.

MAJOR WORKS AND THEMES

While editor of *Poetry Ireland Review,* Cannon chose as themes of two of her issues "Poetry and Survival" and "The Sacred and the Secular." Joan McBreen has appropriately suggested that these choices are in fact reflective of Cannon's poetic vision. And such themes as poetic and linguistic endurance, as well as the points of contact between the spiritual and physical spheres, are indeed present in Cannon's poetry. With subtle complexity, *Oar* inscribes the rugged terrain of Ireland's coastal corridors with the ambulation and reflections of her personae. Exact and deceivingly sparse, Cannon's poetry maps Ireland's Galway coasts and Clare's Burren limestone through its emphasis on an experiential knowledge of place. Her personae traverse and continuously rediscover the natural world, thereby enacting an engagement with the physicality of the terrain. In poems such as "West," Cannon's speaker is perceptively aware of the natural nuances of terrain that suggest "that these limestone walls have no need of gates." Cannon's emphasis on the geological and topographical complexity of Ireland's western terrain and coasts simultaneously engages with questions of human perspective of nature's grand scale and history. Cannon's poetry gestures toward the metaphysical implications of a magnificent physical world that so carefully records the modest acts of human histories. Her poetry clearly espouses an affinity between humans and nature, however, juxtaposing human and natural desires in poems like "Thirst in the Burren," where she aligns the thirst of the fern and human thirst. In this poem, Cannon skillfully conflates the physicality of the Burren with the spiritual needs of an ambler, the pounding of the stone reverberating their connection. In its expression of the specificity and materiality of the landscape, Cannon's work is a refreshing contribution to the Irish literary tradition of the Revival that often neglects the physical details of the landscape as it emphasizes instead its abstract cultural ties, both mythic and national.

Cannon's second published volume, *The Parchment Boat* (1997), continues the poetic ambulation of Ireland's western seascape that began in *Oar* and offers poignant reflections on human memory of place, the findings of archaeological navigation, and the remnants of a fading native language. While poems such as "Winter Paths" suggests that through both a physical and mnemonic return to a specific landscape humans gain understanding of it, others, such as "Isolde's Tower, Essex Quay," position a contemporary excavation site against the layers of a myth. Although poems such as "Song in Windsor, Ontario," "Patched Kayak," and "Ontario Drumlin" are clear reflections in a Canadian context, the majority of the poems in this volume are closely infused with the language and nuances of Ireland's westernmost shores. More specifically, this verse explores the relationship between these shores and the fading Irish language that ties them to a human past. In poems such as "Murdering the Language," for example, Cannon compares the endurance of the Irish language to that of the shore against countless tides. Even in clear references to a colonial past, Cannon's verse refuses to oversimplify questions of language and politics. In the same way, while Cannon chooses to write in English, in poems such as "Scríob" and " 'Taom' " her verse gracefully turns to the Irish language and uses it with careful purpose, enacting what it means to live and write between two languages.

In her generous reflections upon her craft in "The Poetry of What Happens," Cannon writes, "Almost from the start the metaphors available to me related to landscape, language, and place-names, that most tangible of etymologies, the interface between language and landscape" (128). Such metaphors infuse the themes of both of Cannon's volumes and ask the reader to envision the organic and elemental realities of an Ireland that struggles to balance a layered past with the often uninterested development that accompanies contemporary technological and economic advancements. In poems such as "Foundations" Cannon reminds the reader that regardless of the pace of human construction, the forms of life are inevitably fragile, undeniably controlled by forces that are grander than the blades and shovels that turn the sand.

Both *Oar* and *The Parchment Boat* resist overtly political themes; the reader will find few direct references to battle, twentieth-century Irish nationalism, or the Troubles. In fact, Cannon's verse positions the natural world as the primary subject of its text, with political concerns existing as only pieces of a too-often-simplified physical place. Cannon's poetry does not name Ireland as nation or state, for politics are only slight allusions among the more central themes of human existence amid nonhuman nature. In addition, Cannon's poetry pays attention to detail, maps personae's traversing of the land, remembers the stories and myths that have shaped it, and honors unreachable presences of the natural world. These gestures, however, do not privilege the stories of humans over those of natural history; rather, they position them as echoes and interpreters of one another. In this way, Cannon's poetry complicates the Irish poem and releases it from the sometimes stifling legacy of the Irish Revival that wrote the landscape into simplified symbol within the cultural imagination and in so doing neglected the land's material mutability. Like the Revivalists' literature, Cannon's poetry values the natural terrain and the myths that inscribe it, but, as is clear in poems such as "Mountain," Cannon's respect takes a very different form, suggests humility in the face of the natural world, confronts its disintegration, and is open to a human connection and interaction with nature that is cultural, material, *and* spiritual. Cannon's poetry extends a liberating commitment to the materiality of Ireland's physical landscape as something that both contains stories and exists as an archeological and geological reality. In this way, her poetry recognizes the intersecting constructions of cultural scripts and material place. As such, excavation of the past requires a turn not only to the concepts and theories used to describe it, but also to the active experience of its natural gritty places. Less explicitly concerned with the woman's inscription of land than are contemporaries such as Eavan Boland, Cannon's poetry in both *Oar* and *The Parchment Boat* offers a representation of landscape as a vast terrain of history and of stories that is intricately connected to human experience more by recurrent patterns than by any overt emphasis on mythic importance.

CRITICAL RECEPTION

Attention to Moya Cannon's poetry has unfolded with energy and enthusiasm on both sides of the Atlantic and across Europe. Scholars and general readers alike recognize Cannon as a major voice in contemporary Irish poetry. In addition to her two published volumes, Cannon's poetry has been published in international journals and anthologies, including *The Field Day Anthology of Irish Writing*, Volumes 4 and 5, *Irish Women's Writing and Traditions* (2002), *The Wake Forest Book of Irish Women's Poetry* (1999), *The White Page: An Bhileog Bhán* (1999), and *Human Rights Have No Borders: Voices of Irish Poets* (1998). The diversity and scope of these collections, as well as the critical responses to her work, indicate the intellectual and imaginative quality of Cannon's poetry.

Cannon's poetic grappling with questions of language, landscape, and history are at the center of her critical reception, her provocative and reverential use of words drawing attention and receiving consideration. In a contemporary Ireland that struggles to confront both the positive and negative effects of Ireland's economic resurgence, technological revolution, and participation in the European Union, Cannon's poetic voice puts Ireland's contemporary historic moment within its proper context of a dense and layered natural and cultural continuum. And yet, Cannon's turn to Ireland's terrain and mythology is not one of wistful longing. Rather, her turn is ever concerned with the present realities that make necessary the lessons and awareness of the past. And so, Cannon's poetry purposely and convincingly brings us beyond the linearity of human progress and economy and reminds us that such systems of understanding and conception are inevitably limited. Patricia Haberstroh calls our attention to such a gesture made in "The Poetry of What Happens," in which Cannon writes about the appeal of a break between the rational and irrational that is found in the older Irish nature lyrics (13). Cannon's poetry successfully maps the possibilities of such a break through its reconsideration of a natural and mythical past within the seemingly ordinary moments of her speakers' wanderings and wonderings.

In addition to Cannon's unique perspective on the current moment of Irish culture, her work is largely anthologized in part because of its encounters with the Irish language. Haberstroh notes that "Cannon foregrounds linguistic issues, influenced as she was, and is, by growing up and continuing to live between two languages" ("Women Poets," 183). This wavering is indeed clear in Cannon's poetry. A fluent speaker of Irish, Cannon chooses to write in English, but she often incorporates Irish words into her poetry. Identifying Cannon's use of the word "mother" to refer to language in "Prodigal," Haberstroh sees such treatment of the Irish language as explorations in "female creativity" that might be read "as a woman poet defining her own struggles with language" (*Women Creating Women*, 216). Within the context of Haberstroh's critique, the Irish language is not only a subject for Cannon's poetry but also a vehicle, her verse turning to the Irish language amid an otherwise English-language verse. This gesture of a turn to the Irish is not a romantic attempt to regain an unchanged culture. Rather, it is an attempt to claim this culture for a contemporary woman poet. Haberstroh places this within what has been a traditionally male endeavor, the conflation of Irish words into English verse performed by poets such as Paul Muldoon as an artistic and political statement of linguistic preservation. And so Haberstroh recognizes in Cannon's poems such as " 'Taom' " a "giant leap" in reclaiming that "tongue for women as well, writing in English about the value of the mother language" (*Women Creating Women*, 217). Such critical explorations of Cannon's poetry are especially useful in situating her within the canon of contemporary Irish poetry. For while she does not approach questions of language with the same voice as Nuala Ní Dhomhnaill, who writes only in Irish, Cannon's concern with questions of language nevertheless illustrates the extent to which Irish continues to engage and articulate the contemporary Irish imagination.

BIBLIOGRAPHY

Works by Moya Cannon

Oar. Cliffs of Moher, Ire.: Salmon, 1990; Oldcastle, Ire.: Gallery, 2000.
The Parchment Boat. Oldcastle, Ire.: Gallery, 1997.
"The Poetry of What Happens." In *My Self. My Muse: Irish Women Poets Reflect on Life and Art,* edited by Patricia Boyle Haberstroh, 122–34. Syracuse, NY: Syracuse University Press, 2001.

Studies of Moya Cannon

Bourke, Angela, Mairin Ni Dhonneadha, Siobhan Kilfeather, Maria Luddy, Margaret MacCurtain, Gerardine Meaney, Mary O'Dowd, and Clair Wills, eds. *The Field Day Anthology of Irish Writing.* Vols. 4 and 5, *Irish Women Writers and Traditions.* Cork: Cork University Press, 2002.
Cusick, Christine L. "Memory and the Ecological Promise of Story in Irish Texts." PhD diss., Duquesne University, 2002.
Haberstroh, Patricia Boyle. "New Directions in Irish Women's Poetry." In *Women Creating Women: Contemporary Irish Women Poets.* Syracuse, NY: Syracuse University Press, 1995, 197–224.
———. "Women Poets of the West: Moya Cannon and Mary O'Malley." *Nua: New Studies in Contemporary Irish Writing* 2, nos. 1–2 (1998–1999): 181–91.
McBreen, Joan, ed. *The White Page/An Bhileog Bhán: Twentieth-Century Irish Women Poets.* Cliffs of Moher, Ire.: Salmon, 1999.
Morgan, Kenneth, and Almut Schlepper, eds. *Human Rights Have No Borders: Voices of Irish Poets.* Dublin: Marino, 1998.
O'Brien, Peggy, ed. *The Wake Forest Book of Irish Women's Poetry: 1967–2000.* Winston-Salem, NC: Wake Forest University Press, 1999.

MARINA CARR
(1964–)

Gerald C. Wood

BIOGRAPHY

Marina Carr is from the Midlands, raised in Gortnamona, near Tullamore, and Pallas Lake, County Offaly. She attended Sacred Heart School in Tullamore. While Carr was growing up, her mother was the principal in a national school, and her father, Hugh Carr, wrote novels and plays, including ones staged at the Abbey, Peacock, and Gate theaters in Dublin. Carr was the second oldest of six children. Her mother, who also wrote poetry in Irish, died when the playwright was seventeen. Carr attended University College Dublin (UCD), where she read philosophy and English and participated in the Drama Society, as both an actress and a writer. She graduated in 1987, teaching first grade for a year at St. Anselm's School in Bay Ridge, Brooklyn, before returning to Dublin. Her first play, *Ullaloo* (1991), was written at UCD, though not performed at the Peacock until more than three years later and two years after *Low in the Dark*.

She also writes short stories, including "Grow Mermaid," which won the Hennessy Prize in 1995. But Carr's plays are indisputably the basis for her international fame. *The Mai* (1994) received the Dublin Theatre Festival Best New Play Award, and *Portia Coughlan* (1996) won the Susan Smith Blackburn Award in 1997. The next year *By the Bog of Cats . . .* won the Irish Times/ESB Award for Best New Play. She was elected to Aosdána in 1996 and has served as writer in residence at the Abbey Theatre and Trinity College, as well as Heimbold Professor of Irish Studies at Villanova University during the spring of 2003. For her body of work, Carr also received the E. M. Forster Award from the American Academy of Arts and Letters. Marina Carr is married and the mother of two children, both boys. She lives in Dublin.

MAJOR WORKS AND THEMES

Marina Carr's works are usually divided into two periods. In her first four plays she wrote genderized versions of Beckett's absurdist plays. For example, in *Low in the Dark* the stage is initially separated into a men's side, where a wall is being built, and a women's bathroom. At the beginning of the play the women knit a scarf and feed many babies, or primp to attract men. As the play progresses, the roles become interchanged. The men play at being a married couple and even become pregnant themselves. Bender, one of the women, has a proliferation of babies, even claiming one (whom she has misplaced) will become the pope. Most Beckett-like are passages of meaninglessness, such as Baxter's declaration to Bone (the other man), "We're all abortions. . . . But look on the good side Bone. Life is short, soon we'll be dead." Throughout *Low in the Dark*, Curtains (a character literally covered in curtains) narrates the story of archetypal men and women who, like the men in *Waiting for Godot* (1952), were "walking low in the dark through a dead universe. There seemed no reason to go on. There seemed no reason to stop."

With *The Mai*, Carr returned to the Midlands of her childhood as inspiration for a more realistic theater. It is a memory play (influenced by Tennessee Williams's *The Glass Menagerie*, 1945) in which Millie, a thirty-year-old woman, remembers her family, especially Mai, her mother. The setting is a house built by Mai on the edge of Owl Lake, primarily for her husband Robert, who wanders and womanizes. He returns at the beginning of the play, erotically playing a bow over his wife, who substitutes for his cello. But he becomes involved again, this time with a local woman, leading Mai to suicide by drowning at the end of the first act. Central to Millie's memories is the legend of "The Pool of the Dark Witch," in which Coillte perishes in a lake of her own tears when her love, Bláth, leaves her temporarily for the dark witch. Among the family members recalled is Grandma Fraochlán, a hundred-year-old, who, like Mai, betrayed the needs of her children to fuse with her husband-lover, the nine-fingered fisherman. She fills her old age with mulberry wine and opium. During the final act, the women, including Millie's aunts, one who is married but longs for affairs and one who has slept with too many men to count, share the sadness in their lives. And Millie admits to the audience that she, too, was frustrated in love, having conceived her son, Joseph, in New York with a married man.

Portia Coughlan follows a similar tragic structure in which the death of the major character is revealed at the end of the first act of the three-act play. It begins on the thirtieth birthday of Portia, an unhappily married woman who drinks heavily and has casual affairs while obsessively imagining the ghost of her dead twin brother, Gabriel. Neglecting her three sons and supported by her one-eyed friend, Stacia (the Cyclops of Coolinarney), Portia feels connected to the Belmont River, where Gabriel died fifteen years earlier in a failed suicide pact of the twins. With hints of gypsy blood on her mother's side and rumors that her father and mother shared the same father, Portia drowns herself at the spot of her brother's death. After the funeral, Carr returns the audience to the day after the birthday party, when Portia withdraws, explaining, there's "a wolf tooth growin' in me heart and it's turnin' me from everyone and everythin' I am." In the final scenes, relatives confirm the blood ties between Portia's parents and the sexual ties between Portia and Gabriel. The play ends with Portia telling her husband that she married him hoping he would bring her into the real world.

While *Portia Coughlin* made a passing reference to Shakespeare's *Merchant of Venice* in the names of its heroine and place (Belmont), *By the Bog of Cats . . .* is loosely based on Euripides' *Medea*. It opens with Hester Swane pulling a dead black swan across the frozen bog and declaring her love for Carthage Kilbride, the lover who jilted her. The bog is haunted by a Ghost Fancier and a Catwoman, dressed in cat eyes and fur, who says she and Hester share "the gift of seein' things as they are, not as they should be." Hester's daughter, Josie, seven years old, is ridiculed by her grandmother, Mrs. Kilbride, for being a bastard and a tinker. At end of the first act, Hester confesses that she was abandoned on her Communion day by her mother, but Hester longs for the return of her mother, who is lost to the bog. The second act begins with the ghost of Hester's brother, Joseph, visiting the Catwoman as the guests ready for the marriage of Carthage and Caroline, the daughter of a wealthy landowner. At the wedding reception, Mrs. Kilbride and Hester both appear in wedding dresses, Hester refusing to move from her caravan, saying she is waiting for her mother to return. In the third act, Hester burns her home and livestock and converses with the ghost of her brother, whom she killed out of jealousy over their mother. Hester accuses Caroline's father of poisoning his son, then kills her daughter and herself, motivated by the desire to keep her daughter from being haunted by an absent mother.

On Raftery's Hill (2000) is set on a remote farm, where the Raftery son, Ded, hides in the cowshed playing his fiddle while grandmother Shalome repeatedly packs her suitcase for a trip to Kinneygar. Red, the father, enters with two dead hares around his neck, having left other dead animals to rot in the fields and streams. The younger daughter, Sorrel, is engaged to Dara Mood, a local farmer. Rumors of incest and insanity are rife in the village, and Shalome tells Red he is a bastard, the son of an English officer. Red imagines a plot by Sorrel and Dara to take over the farm and rapes her, describing his attack as the way he guts a hare. In the second act, which starts three weeks later, Sorrel asks Dinah, her older sister, about their mother, who died giving birth to Sorrel, and washes compulsively after the attack by Red. In an emotional fit, Ded declares that his father once sent him to the barn to molest Dinah. Red offers Dara land and money, but he refuses, which leads Sorrel to call off the wedding. Shalome appears in Sorrel's wedding dress, and Dinah admits to a sexual relationship with her father since she was twelve. Sorrel declares the family as "a band of gorillas swingin' from the trees" but promises to break from Dara as Red tears a piece from the wedding dress to use in cleaning his gun.

In the writing of *Ariel* (2002), Marina Carr once again returned to Euripides, this time choosing *Iphigenia at Aulis* as the point of departure. It begins with the sixteenth birthday party for Ariel, the daughter of Fermoy Fitzgerald, the owner of a cement company and a politician inspired by his belief that the age of compassion is over and God now demands "blood sacrifice." The family is haunted by the death of his mother thirty-five years before, apparently at the hands of his father. Also, his wife, Frances, mourns the death of her son, James, and Hannafin, Fermoy's political opponent, threatens to reveal the sordid details from the Fitzgerald past. The second act takes place ten years later, Fermoy having won the previous election after a scandal that drove Hannafin to suicide and the timely disappearance of Ariel, which gave Fermoy the sympathy vote. Suspecting that her husband is behind the loss of Ariel, Frances stabs her husband, who admits with his dying words that Ariel's body is in Cuura Lake. Two months later, in act three, each of the remaining children, Stephen and Elaine, sides with the parent of the opposite sex. Before the coffin of Ariel, the ghost of Fermoy appears to Elaine, who then murders her mother by stabbing her in the throat.

Marina Carr's plays tend to focus on intimacy issues between the sexes. The women tend to be "obsessed with the artistic or the romantic" while men "are preoccupied with the land or the accumulation of money" (Scaife, 12). The result is at best a confusion of gender roles and at worst a pattern of disappointment and violence. In part such ignorance and aggression can be attributed to the isolated Irish landscape, but the characters are also trapped by a sense of fate, reflected in a biological, racial, and even mythical determinism. They are haunted by ghosts and visions, which relieve them of some burdens of the present but also suggest that their conflicts transcend all places and times.

The dominant motifs in Marina Carr's plays are the burden of the past; women caught between lovers and children; neglected or abandoned children; and the search for freedom and identity. While storytelling is central to her work, it is not always liberating. In Carr's plays the stories can be both a form of communal, even mythical, sharing and the fate against which the characters struggle. Black humor energizes her best work, often capped by violent acts that simultaneously purify the action—by returning to a necessary order—and mark the final loss of freedom.

CRITICAL RECEPTION

There is general agreement that Marina Carr is one of the most distinctive voices among contemporary Irish playwrights, male or female. Like Martin McDonagh and Conor McPherson, she has declared her independence from traditional Irish theater (despite her respect for Brian Friel, Tom Murphy, Tom Mac Intyre, Sebastian Barry, and Frank McGuinness). But unlike McDonagh and McPherson, Carr pays regular homage to her dramatic predecessors, looking to Samuel Beckett, Tennessee Williams, and the Greeks for her inspiration. As Tom Mac Intyre has summarized, Carr's work is "a poetry compounded of myth and folklore, dream and fantasy, the breeze from the sea, the currach on the shore. It's the stuff of romance, story-telling and a mode of survival, and also, story-telling as a mode of escape from demanding imperatives" (75). Restless, she is a "quest writer," who continually experiments with the poetics of staging and theatrical form (77).

Since this experimentation makes her hard to classify, Marina Carr repeatedly disappoints critics with aesthetic or political agendas. For those who prefer the avant-garde, her recent dependence on classical theater is nostalgia, a step backward. Similarly, her strong and willful female characters are, in Carr's words, "natural feminists" who "feel their worth, and know their rights, and [have] a certain strength and sense of themselves" (Carr, interview by Murphy, 52). She "dislodges assumed ideas of belonging and identity for women" (Cerquoni, 199). And yet Carr's women seem trapped by the Greek sense of repetition. Unable to act nobly in society or imagine significant choices in their private worlds, the Carr females can also be "limited, damaged women, unable to transcend their circumstances" and, worse yet, "more problematic than her men . . . not conquering the world or even surviving, for that matter" (Harris, 229). As Clare Wallace observes, Marina Carr creates women who are both "strong-willed" and "haunting because of their chronic inability to imagine freedom" ("Tragic Destiny," 435). Some critics view the violence in her plays as an indication of the "rage . . . of a colonized culture" (Fouéré, 169–70). But her poetic interest in rural Ireland and her respect for the ancients limit her investigation of impediments to Irish identity and liberation; in her works, postcolonial critics believe, "class and entitlement are ignored, and gender [is] defined in reactionary terms" (Merriman, " 'Poetry Shite,' " 158).

The key to evaluating Marina Carr's plays is whether the critic can accept that her theatrical space is purgatorial, not rhetorical. Her women are passionate and bold, but they also are obsessive and narcissistic, mothers who "just cannot seem to provide any real sustenance for their offspring" (Scaife, 11). The materialism of Carthage Kilbride in *By the Bog of Cats* . . . may hint at Ireland's struggles with global capitalism, but primarily it indicates Kilbride's ignorance of the transcendent, no small matter to a playwright who has fought with a ghost, believes in angels, and communicates with animals (Carr, interview by Murphy, 48–50). And while the Midland plays resonate with images, personalities, and dramas of historical Ireland, they are haunted by myths that move across all boundaries. The impossibility of categorizing Marina Carr makes her maddening for doctrinaire critics but fascinating to those who look for a personal voice in Irish theater.

BIBLIOGRAPHY

Works by Marina Carr

Articles

"Afterword to *Portia Coughlan.*" In *The Dazzling Dark: New Irish Plays*, edited by Frank McGuinness, 310–11. London: Faber, 1996.
"Dealing with the Dead." *Irish University Review* 28, no. 1 (Spring–Summer 1998): 190–96.
"Introduction." In *Marina Carr: Plays*. Vol. 1. London: Faber and Faber, 1999, ix–x.

Published Plays

Ariel. Loughcrew, Ire.: Gallery, 2002.
By the Bog of Cats . . . Loughcrew, Ire.: Gallery, 1998; New York: Dramatists Play Service, 2002.
Low in the Dark. In *The Crack in the Emerald: New Irish Plays*, edited by David Grant, 63–140. London: Nick Herne, 1990; Reissued, 1994.
The Mai. Loughcrew, Ire.: Gallery; Syracuse, NY: Syracuse University Press, 1995; New York: Dramatists Play Service, 2003.
Marina Carr: Plays. Vol. 1. London: Faber and Faber, 1999. (Includes *Low in the Dark*, *The Mai*, *Portia Coughlan*, and *By the Bog of Cats* . . .)

On Raftery's Hill. Loughcrew, Ire.: Gallery, 2000; New York: Dramatists Play Service, 2002.
Portia Coughlan. London: Faber and Faber, 1996.
Portia Coughlan. In *The Dazzling Dark*, edited by Frank McGuinness, 235–311. London: Faber and Faber, 1996.
Portia Coughlan Rev. ed. Loughcrew, Ire.: Gallery, 1998; New York: Dramatists Play Service, 2003.

Interviews with Marina Carr

Battersby, Eileen. "Marina of the Midlands." *Irish Times*, May 4, 2000, 15.
Clarity, James F. "A Playwright's Post-Beckett Period." *New York Times*, November 3, 1994, C23.
Murphy, Mike. "Marina Carr." In *Reading the Future: Irish Writers in Conversation with Mike Murphy*, edited by Mike Murphy and Cliodhna Ní Anluain, 43–57. Dublin: Lilliput, 2000.
Sihra, Melissa. "Marina Carr in Conversation with Melissa Sihra." In *Theatre Talk: Voices of Irish Theatre Practitioners*, edited by Lilian Chambers, Ger FitzGibbon, and Eamonn Jordan, 55–63. Dublin: Carysfort, 2001.
Stephenson, Heidi, and Natasha Langridge. "Interview with Marina Carr." In *Rage and Reason: Women Playwrights on Playwriting*, edited by Heidi Stephenson and Natasha Langridge, 146–55. London: Methuen, 1997.

Studies of Marina Carr

Becket, Fiona. "A Theatrical Matrilineage? Problems of the Familial in the Drama of Teresa Deevy and Marina Carr." In *Ireland in Proximity: History, Gender, Space*, edited by Scott Brewster, Virginia Crossman, Fiona Becket, and David Alderson, 80–93. London: Routledge, 1999.
Burke, Patrick. "A Dream of Fair Women: Marina Carr's *The Mai* and Ní Dhuibhne's *Dún na mBan Trí Thine*." *Hungarian Journal of English and American Studies* 2, no. 2 (1996): 123–27.
Cerquoni, Enrica. " 'One Bog, Many Bogs': Theatrical Space, Visual Image and Meaning in Some Productions of Marina Carr's *By the Bog of Cats . . .*" In *The Theatre of Marina Carr*, edited by Cathy Leeney and Anna McMullan, 172–99. Dublin: Carysfort, 2003.
Dhuibhne, Eilis Ní. "Playing the Story: Narrative Technique in *The Mai*." In Leeney and McMullan, *Theatre of Carr*, 65–73.
Fouéré, Olwen. "Journeys in Performance: On Playing in *The Mai* and *By the Bog of Cats*." In Leeney and McMullan, *Theatre of Carr*, 160–71.
Harris, Claudia W. "Rising Out of the Miasmal Mists: Marina Carr's Ireland." In Leeney and McMullan, *Theatre of Carr*, 216–32.
Kurdi, Maria. "Alternative Articulations of Female Subjectivity and Gender Relations in Contemporary Irish Women's Plays: The Example of Marina Carr." In *Codes and Masks: Aspects of Identity in Contemporary Irish Plays in an Intercultural Context*. Frankfort: Peter Lang, 2000, 59–72.
Leeney, Cathy, and Anna McMullan, eds. *The Theatre of Marina Carr: "Before Rules Was Made."* Dublin: Carysfort, 2003.
Mac Intyre, Tom. "Where Your Treasure Is: *The Mai*." In Leeney and McMullan, *Theatre of Carr*, 75–77.
McDonald, Marianne. "Classics as Celtic Firebrand: Greek Tragedy, Irish Playwrights, and Colonialism." In *Theatre Stuff: Critical Essays on Contemporary Irish Theatre*, edited by Eamonn Jordan, 16–26. Dublin: Carysfort, 2000.
McMullan, Anna. "Gender, Authorship and Performance in Selected Plays by Contemporary Irish Women Playwrights: Mary Elizabeth Burke-Kennedy, Marie Jones, Marina Carr, Emma Donoghue." In Jordan, *Theatre Stuff*, 34–46.
———. "Marina Carr's Unhomely Women." *Irish Theatre Magazine* 1, no. 1 (Autumn 1998): 14–16.

Merriman, Victor. "Decolonisation Postponed: The Theatre of Tiger Trash." *Irish University Review* 29, no. 2 (Autumn–Winter 1999): 305–17.

———. " 'Poetry shite': A Postcolonial Reading of Portia Coughlan and Hester Swayne." In Leeney and McMullan, *Theatre of Carr*, 145–59.

Morse, Donald E. "Sleepwalkers Along a Precipice: Staging Memory in Marina Carr's *The Mai*." *Hungarian Journal of English and American Studies* 2, no. 2 (1996): 111–22.

O'Brien, Matt. "Always the Best Man, Never the Groom: The Role of the Fantasy Male in Marina Carr's Plays." In Leeney and McMullan, *Theatre of Carr*, 200–215.

O'Dwyer, Riana. "The Imagination of Women's Reality: Christina Reid and Marina Carr." In Jordan *Theatre Stuff*, 236–48.

Roche, Anthony. "Woman on the Threshold: J.M. Synge's *The Shadow of the Glen*, Teresa Deevy's *Katie Roche* and Marina Carr's *The Mai*." *Irish University Review* 25, no. 1 (Spring/Summer 1995): 143–62. Reprinted in Leeney and McMullan, *Theatre of Carr*, 17–42.

Scaife, Sarahjane. "Mutual Beginnings: Marina Carr's *Low in the Dark*." In Leeney and McMullan, *Theatre of Carr*, 1–16.

Sihra, Melissa. "A Cautionary Tale: Marina Carr's *By the Bog of Cats*." In Jordan, *Theatre Stuff*, 257–68.

———. "Reflections Across Water: New Stages of Performing Carr." In Leeney and McMullan, *Theatre of Carr*, 92–113.

Wallace, Clare. "Authentic Reproductions: Marina Carr and the Inevitable." In Leeney and McMullan, *Theatre of Carr*, 43–64.

———. "A Crossroads Between Worlds: Marina Carr and the Use of Tragedy." *Litteraria Pragensia* 10, no. 20 (2000): 76–89.

———. "Tragic Destiny and Abjection in Marina Carr's *The Mai, Portia Coughlan* and *By the Bog of Cats . . .*" *Irish University Review* 31, no. 2 (Autumn–Winter 2001): 431–49.

JUANITA CASEY
(1925–   )

Rebecca Steinberger

BIOGRAPHY

Poet, playwright, novelist, and artist, Juanita Casey was born in England. Her mother, Annie Maloney, died in childbirth, and Casey was abandoned by her father, Jobey Smith, when she was only a year old. As she has explained in an interview with Gordon Henderson, "I was born of Traveling People" (42). While Casey lived with the Traveling People in England and Ireland, she received a quality education in four different private boarding schools. Before cultivating her writing skills, Casey worked in a number of eclectic jobs on farms, racetracks, and circuses.

Casey married three times—farmer John Fisher in 1945, Sven Berlin, a poet and sculptor, in 1953, and Fergus Casey, a journalist, in 1971. She has one child from each of her marriages: William, Jasper, and Sheba. She resides in Gloragh, Sneem, County Kerry.

MAJOR WORKS AND THEMES

Casey's fascination with horses, a frequent subject in her paintings and writings, undoubtedly stems from her involvement with animals as well as her early employment experiences. As such, her first major publication, *Hath the Rain a Father?* (1966), is a collection of realistic and supernatural short stories and illustrations that revolve around animals. Arguably, the horse can be considered a common thread in Casey's motley publications, as evidenced in her first novel, *The Horse of Selene* (1973)—which she wrote in six weeks—her artwork, and her various collections of poetry. In addition to its role in Casey's novels, the horse serves as a central figure in her poetry, *Horse by the River, and Other Poems* (1968), and the BBC-produced television play *Stallion Eternity* (n.d.).

Perhaps Casey's writing can best be categorized as experimental, as evidenced in her second novel, *The Circus* (1974), which is written in stream-of-consciousness style and, as such, creates stylistic and linguistic comparisons with James Joyce. As Casey asserts, "I tried to write this book where words, really, are meaningless and meaningful at the same time" (Henderson, 47). In addition to her television plays, Casey wrote the play *30 Gnu Pence*, which was read at the Abbey Theatre in 1973.

While Casey is generally accepted as possessing a nonconforming, individualistic writing style, she clearly shines in her ability to transcend genres and forms and, at the same time, lead the way for a newfound inclusion of a more liberal definition of Irish womanhood.

CRITICAL RECEPTION

In addition to Gordon Henderson's "An Interview with Juanita Casey" (1972), Patricia Boyle Haberstroh's *Women Creating Women: Contemporary Irish Women Poets* examines Casey's poetry in a chapter titled "New Directions in Irish Women's Poetry." Haberstroh contends that "class boundaries . . . collapse" in her poems as they "detail life on the edge" (203). Through Casey's depiction and celebration of the Traveling People with whom she lived, her poems suggest a freedom and liberty afforded to the Irish female Traveler that serves as a stark contrast to the traditional role of an Irish woman.

While criticism on Juanita Casey is scarce, the archives of the Proscenium Press, housed in the Special Collections Department of the University of Delaware Library, contain the Irish writer's collected letters from 1972 to 1988 as well as poems, short stories, and illustrations.

BIBLIOGRAPHY

Works by Juanita Casey

The Circus. Dublin: Dolmen, 1974.
Eternity Smith and Other Poems. Dublin: Dolmen, 1985.
Fields of Praise. London: British Broadcasting Corporation, n.d.
Hath the Rain a Father? London: Phoenix House, 1966.
Horse by the River, and Other Poems. Chester Springs, PA: Dufour, 1968.
The Horse of Selene. Dublin: Dolmen, 1971.

Juanita Casey: A Sampling. Newark, NJ: Proscenium, 1981.
The New Forest. Manchester, UK: Gallery, 1960.
Paddy No More. Dublin: Wolfhound, 1978.
Stallion Eternity. London: British Broadcasting Corporation, n.d.
30 Gnu Pence. Dublin: Peacock Theatre, 1973.

Studies of Juanita Casey

Haberstroh, Patricia Boyle. *Women Creating Women: Contemporary Irish Women Poets*. Syracuse, NY: Syracuse University Press, 1996, 203–4.
Henderson, Gordon. "An Interview with Juanita Casey." *Journal of Irish Literature* 1, no. 3 (September 1972): 42–54.
"Juanita Casey." *Dictionary of Literary Biography*. Vol. 14, *British Novelists since 1960*. Detroit, MI: Gale, 1982.

MARY (CATHERINE GUNNING MAGUIRE) COLUM
(1884–1957)

Paige Reynolds

BIOGRAPHY

A memoirist, political activist, creative writer, literary critic, biographer, and journalist, Mary Colum was born in Collooney, County Sligo, the first of five children to middle-class parents from Catholic farming families. Colum's mother died when she was ten, and her father, a district inspector for the Royal Irish Constabulary, was frequently absent from the family. Consequently, she spent her childhood in the care of her grandmother, and at age thirteen became a boarding student at the Convent of St. Louis, excelling in literature and modern languages. Upon graduation, Colum attended the National University of Ireland, where she headed the Twilight Literary Society.

Colum contributed actively to the political and cultural foment of the Irish Literary Revival. After university, she taught modern languages at Patrick Pearse's St. Ida's, the sister school to St. Enda's. In 1911, she established the monthly intellectual journal the *Irish Review*, with Padraic Colum, David Houston, Thomas MacDonough, and James Stephens. As an editor, Colum published her own articles, as well as work by Pearse, George Russell, and Hanna Sheehy Skeffington, until the *Review* ceased publication in 1914. Along with Maud Gonne and other women nationalists, she also helped found Cumann na mBan, an auxiliary of the Irish Volunteers, and fought for women's suffrage.

She married Padraic Colum in 1912, and two years later, the penurious couple embarked for America—their fare to Pittsburgh paid by Padraic's generous aunt Josephine. They soon moved to New York City, where Mary was largely responsible for the couple's financial support. She worked as a private tutor, a translator, and an editor and fashion writer for the garment industry periodical *Women's Wear*. Meanwhile, she initiated her career as a prolific contributor to leading American journals, newspapers, and magazines.

Just as Colum placed herself in the center of Dublin cultural life, she likewise affiliated herself with influential American and continental intellectual circles. Both in New York and during a sojourn in Chicago, she interacted with members of the avant-garde, including Sherwood Anderson, Van Wyck Brooks, Amy Lowell, Harriet Monroe, Edward Arlington Robinson, and Elinor Wylie. Colum made contact with additional American writers during summers she and her husband spent writing at the McDowell Colony in New Hampshire. In 1922, the Colums returned briefly to the newly independent Irish Free State, and continued on to Paris and to Hawaii, where Padraic gathered native Polynesian folklore on behalf of the Hawaiian legislature. Upon returning to America in 1925, the Colums took up residence in Connecticut, where they became friends with Eugene O'Neill and Maxwell Perkins, the influential editor who published her comparative critical study, *From These Roots: The Ideas That Have Made Modern Literature* (1937). The Colums returned to Europe in 1930, settling in France, where she once again cultivated talented associates and developed a deeper friendship with James Joyce. Not only did Colum contribute to and help edit *Finnegans Wake*, but also she and her husband provided personal support to Joyce: they were godparents to his son and helped care for his schizophrenic daughter.

After three years in France, the Colums returned to New York so that Mary could edit the *Forum*. When it ceased publication in 1941, she accepted with her husband a joint appointment at Columbia, and together they taught comparative literature courses there until her death. Peripatetic to the end, the Colums also taught at the University of Wisconsin and the University of Miami in Florida. Mary Colum died in 1957 and is buried with her husband in St. Fintan Cemetery in Dublin.

MAJOR WORKS AND THEMES

Though not yet collected in a single volume, Colum's critical and creative work can be found throughout the important journals, magazines, and newspapers of the early twentieth century. Her early work appeared in Irish literary and political publications such as the *Irish Statesman*, *Tomorrow,* and the *United Irishman*. As a founder of and critic for the *Irish Review*, Colum published in this journal important analyses of writers as diverse as Synge and Strindberg. During this same period, she also wrote articles and short stories for the *English Review* and the *London Nation*. Once in America, she contributed over her lifetime almost 200 articles and reviews to publications such as the *American Mercury*, the *Dial*, *Freeman*, the *Nation*, the *New Republic*, *Poetry*, *Saturday Review of Literature*, *Scribners*, and the *Yale Review*. And she served as literary editor of the *Forum* and the poetry review of the *New York Times Book Review*.

Colum also published three book-length studies, each capturing the cultural landscape through a different critical lens. Colum's *Life and the Dream* (1928, 1947; rev. 1966) not only provides a compelling personal memoir, but also sketches an anecdotal portrait of life in early twentieth-century Dublin, London, Paris, and America. This autobiography, which concludes roughly around the Second World War, continues to be mined for information about more famous political and cultural luminaries, but as recent critics have demonstrated, it stands alone as a rich coming-of-age narrative. In the strictly Irish context, it reveals Colum to be a dedicated suffragist, committed nationalist, and active participant in the cultural revival.

In *From These Roots: The Ideas That Have Made Modern Literature* (1937), Colum deployed her talent for addressing rigorous intellectual questions in a voice accessible to those outside the academy. This ambitious study explains the origins of modernism through Colum's survey of Western literature from the mid-eighteenth to the early twentieth centuries. In her substantive analysis, Colum traces the development of modern literature through ideas voiced by a diverse set of writers including Madame de Staël, Poe, Tolstoy, Woolf, and Joyce, and argues for the comparative study of literature. Her study describes the groundwork for future formal and thematic experimentation laid by these authors, as well as introducing provocative influences on modern literature, ranging from the U.S. Declaration of Independence to Freud's work with the unconscious. Colum's argument culminates in the familiar modernist championing of a literature free from market forces; she concludes by insisting that readers and critics distinguish between writing as a trade and writing as an art.

Until recently, Colum was recognized largely for the perceptive chronicle of James Joyce's life that she coauthored with her husband. In *Our Friend James Joyce* (1958), Padraic describes their early life in Dublin, while Mary focuses on their Paris friendship with Joyce. Though Mary Colum received the contract for this memoir of friendship, her husband necessarily edited the book after her death. Nonetheless, she planned the shape of the narrative and wrote one-third of the text.

CRITICAL RECEPTION

During her lifetime, Colum's critical work was well received, garnering high praise from Eugene O'Neill and William Rose Benét, who likened her to Rebecca West and celebrated her as "the best woman critic in America" (220). She received prestigious teaching appointments in the States and was awarded Guggenheim Fellowships in 1930 and 1938. As the founder and editor of both the *Irish Review* and the poetry review column of the *New York Times Book Review*, Colum played a significant role in shaping early-twentieth-century intellectual culture in Ireland and America.

Despite her profound influence on her contemporaries, Colum's work continues to be underrated. For instance, while Padraic Colum acknowledged that his wife was the more accomplished teacher, he alone received an honorary degree from Columbia University in 1958. Her memoirs have been mined for information about more famous (often male) writers, and her biographical information must frequently be derived from accounts of her husband's life. In recent years, Colum and her work have begun to attract more scholarly attention, with useful studies published by Taura Napier, Patricia Rimo, and Sanford Sternlicht. In particular, these critics celebrate Colum's capacity to negotiate between seeming oppositions. Her work, they claim, seeks to demonstrate connections linking the elite and the popular, the aesthetic and the social, the continental and the American, the male and the female.

BIBLIOGRAPHY

Works by Mary Colum

Articles and Reviews

"The Allies of the Volunteers." *Irish Freedom* (September 1914). In *In Their Own Voice: Women and Irish Nationalism*, edited by Margaret Ward. 49–51. Dublin: Attic, 1995.
"An American Critic: Van Wyck Brooks." *Dial* 76 (1924): 246–48.

"John Synge." *The Irish Review* 1, no. 1 (March 1911): 38–42.
"On Thinking Critically." *Forum* (February 1934): 75–80.

Regular Columns

"Life and Literature." *Forum*. December 1933–April 1940.
"The New Books of Poetry." *New York Times Book Review*. November 1941–March 1943.

Books

From these Roots: The Ideas That Have Made Modern Literature. New York: Scribner's, 1937.
Life and the Dream: Memories of a Literary Life in Europe and America. 1928. London: Macmillan, 1947. Rev. 1966.
Our Friend James Joyce. New York: Doubleday, 1958.

Studies of Mary Colum

Benét, William Rose. "A Colum as Columnist." *Saturday Review of Literature*, October 28, 1933, 220–21.
Napier, Taura S. "Critic as Artist: Mary Colum and the Ideals of Literary Expression." *Canadian Journal of Irish Studies* 19, no. 1 (July 1993): 54–66.
———. "The Mosaic 'I': Mary Colum and Modern Irish Autobiography." *Irish University Review* 28, no. 1 (Spring–Summer 1998): 37–55.
Rimo, Patricia. "Mollie Colum and Her Circle." *Irish Literary Supplement* 4, no. 2 (Fall 1985): 27–28.
Sternlicht, Sanford. "Padraic and Mary Colum: Bridging Worlds—Dublin and New York, Poetry and Criticism, Men and Women." In *Politics and the Rhetoric of Poetry: Perspectives on Modern Anglo-Irish Poetry*, edited by Tjebbe A. Westendorp and Jane Mallinson, 199–205. Amsterdam: Rodopi, 1995.
Wilson, Edmund. "The Memoirs of Mary Colum." Review of *Life and the Dream*, by Mary Colum. *New Yorker*, March 22, 1947, 111.

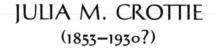

JULIA M. CROTTIE
(1853–1930?)

Paul Marchbanks

BIOGRAPHY

Julia M. Crottie was born in 1853, a period of increasing public mistrust of Irish political and constitutional systems. The horrors of the Great Famine remained open wounds in the national consciousness, and those economic hopes recently lifted by the Irish Tenant League party were disintegrating along with the tenuous alliance between champions of religious equality and those more concerned with tenant rights. Anxieties concerning the poor Catholic Irishman's position in a society ruled by the Anglo-Irish Protestant entered Crottie's bloodstream at a formative age and surfaced repeatedly in her later fiction.

Born and raised in Lismore, County Waterford, she received a private education under the Presentation Convent nuns. As an adult she lived in both Ramsay, Isle of Man, and then the United States, contributing to such American Catholic journals as the *Catholic World*, the *Month*, and the *Rosary*.

Crottie's production of novel-length fiction proved limited in quantity, if not chronological scope. In *Neighbours: Annals of a Dull Town* (1900) and *Innisdoyle Neighbours* (1920), Crottie illuminated with light satire and social acumen the frustrated hopes of the late-Victorian, rural Irish, both the firmly rooted variety insulated from the changing world and those who emigrated only to return. *The Lost Land* (1901), set in a considerably earlier period, explored the societal dynamics between wealthy, transplanted oppressor and indigenous, working poor during the failed United Irishmen movement of the late eighteenth-century, a period of rising hopes abbreviated by the Act of Union in 1801.

MAJOR WORKS AND THEMES

Crottie so enjoyed populating the fictional Innisdoyle with closely detailed townspeople that she both began and ended her novel-writing career with collections of such characters. Much like its companion work published two decades later, *Neighbours: Annals of a Dull Town* traces the interwoven stories of country folk living in sometimes suffocating proximity to one another. As of the opening chapter, their seedy and scarred town still retains something of a close, communal feel. As the narrator interjects midway through the third tale, however, this particular town's cloistered space lends itself more to conflict than to community. When the Irish American emigrant Miss Dunne returns with a carefully wrought air of mystery, wealth, and condescension, she craftily succeeds at turning the town gossips onto everyone's business but her own. The narrator confides in us with uncharacteristic directness, "Nobody who has not lived in a stagnant town like Innisdoyle can know to what blackness of malice . . . suspicion may lead." As might be predicted from the narrator's own assessment of this ambitious antiheroine, Miss Dunne's malice backfires, landing her in the workhouse inhabited by so many of her impoverished neighbors. This universally feared location, along with ubiquitous male drinking problems, lingering memories of the great hunger, and a pattern of problematic, returning émigrés, creates a sobering picture of hardship in the 1870s. The wit and humor Crottie injects into these neighbors' attempts to talk with their deceased loved ones, marry one another's children off, or complete exorbitant town projects that far exceed their means significantly lightens but never effaces her rendering of the era's social and material hardships.

Crottie' second novel, *The Lost Land: A Tale of a Cromwellian-Irish Town, Being the Autobiography of Miss Annita Lombard, 1780–87*, maps the adolescent experience of a sensitive but spirited female narrator appalled at the changes slowly degrading the idealized Ireland of her childhood. The narrative begins by vividly imaging hard-earned turf fires, a golden-haired songbird of a mother not long for this world, a caste-blind and actively supportive community, and an altruistic priest who practices what he preaches in the locals' dwindling Irish Gaelic language. The heroine's relocation from this rural neighborhood of the Knock with its misty hills and Skoogh neighbors to Curraglen, one of many towns constricted by the "soul-killing Penal Laws" (7), introduces the antithesis for every cherished element of community. In this new, strangely asocial village, the clannish, Protestant rich use the increasingly dominant English tongue to denigrate the presumably backward majority.

The narrator, Miss Lombard, rarely articulates her own opinions directly, instead relying on detailed portraitures of heroic and villainous characters who alternately convict or vindicate themselves by their words and actions. Few gray characters populate this novel. The Murdstone-like doctor who marries Annita's mother and proceeds to stamp out domestic joy proves himself an alcoholic, a vicious tyrant, a Catholic-turned-Protestant sycophant, and a murderer. Annita's elder brother Thad Lombard provides a stark contrast for his stepfather. He attempts to educate local youth via *seanchus* and Gaelic Irish, loudly vocalizes political opposition to his powerful Protestant neighbors, and ultimately loses his life while running from the oppressors he had hoped to overthrow. The narrator's two primary caregivers provide further examples of Crottie's effective employment of familiar archetypes, the obsequious Eliza's deference to all customs and rulings of the Protestant ascendancy providing a neat foil for her vocal female counterpart, "The Barrister." This second matriarch sees through superstition, popular fashion, and empty tradition, peering right into her neighbors' secret agendas and innermost motivations. During the Sodality Festival, she correctly interprets the wealthy Devines' acts of pity towards the poor for what they are, grudging displays of condescension laced with insult (78–85).

In her illuminating preface to the novel, Crottie anticipates criticism of the lugubrious tone that dominates the novel, claiming it impossible for a soul like Annita's "to discover much of gaiety or light" in this "rainy, old-world Munster town, with no life stirring but the ugly life born of stagnation and rottenness" (vi). And to make sure we do not miss the obvious parallels between Annita's depressed era and Crottie's own (Irish independence still lay twenty years in the future), our author draws the connection for us herself, articulating a call to awareness that approaches a call to action: "How do we know that these [similar conditions] are not pressing their heaviness and hopelessness on thoughtful souls in Irish towns to-day?" (vi).

CRITICAL RECEPTION

Though largely unknown to today's Irish scholar—a situation due in part to her small oeuvre, the difficulty of finding those few novels she did write, and the absence of any full-length studies of Crottie's works—this artisan's fictions were recognized in their time for their honest, incisive portrayal of those religious and socioeconomic prejudices that continued to divide urban communities in early modern Ireland. Justin McCarthy wrote three years after Crottie's initial publication of *The Lost Land* that she had reproduced the impressions of her childhood, small-town experience with "appalling faithfulness," and ranked her with William Carleton as one of a handful willing to reveal with brutal honesty and "fearless realism" her own people's failings in addition to their commonly eulogized strengths (758). Stephen Brown wrote similarly of this mimetic mode in 1919, calling Crottie's *Neighbours* a realistic portrait that faithfully collects "pictures of very unlovely aspects of life in a small stagnant town" (77), including the "petty unpleasant sides of human nature" and the "gossip of the back lane" (78). Both editors recognized Crottie's skill at presenting a balanced view of the Irish, one that fondly represented their whistful and romantic leanings while employing that "sardonic humour" (McCarthy, 758) necessary to mark and fairly evaluate their embittered lives and frequently myopic social judgments.

Some unnumbered pages in *Neighbours* contain excerpts from reviews of her work. These magazines and journals of the day registered even more enthusiastic praise of such works as Crottie's *Neighbours*, a work celebrated by the *St. James's Gazette* and classed as "exceedingly true to the life" by the *Belfast News Letter*. Critics at the *Academy* and the *Bookman* appreciated the humor and pathos Crottie interjected into such authentic representations of Irish life, realistic portrayals the latter critic attributed in part to Crottie's "rare instinct for dialogue which alone can make such stories absolutely faithful." Justin McCarthy, writing at the *All Ireland Review*, offered an optimistic if condescending assessment of Crottie's potential when he wrote, "Unless I am greatly mistaken Miss Crottie is destined to make an abiding mark on the literature of the country which is both hers and mine."

BIBLIOGRAPHY

Works by Julia M. Crottie

Innisdoyle Neighbours. Manchester, UK: Magnificat Press, 1920.
The Lost Land. London: T. Fisher Unwin, 1901.
Neighbours: Annals of a Dull Town. London: T. Fisher Unwin, 1900. (Unnumbered additional pages contain excerpts from reviews of her work.)

Studies of Julia M. Crottie

Brown, Stephen J. "Julia Crottie." In *Ireland in Fiction: A Guide to Irish Novels, Tales, Romances, and Folk-Lore*. Dublin: S. J. Maunsel, 1919, 77–78.
McCarthy, Justin, Maurice Francis Egan, Charles Welsh, Douglas Hyde, Lady Gregory, and James Jeffrey Roche, eds. "Julia Crotty." In *Irish Literature*. Vol. 2. 1904. Philadelphia: Morris, 2004, 758.
Stewart, Bruce. "Julia Crottie." *Princess Grace Irish Library* (Monaco). Electronic Irish Records Dataset. http://www.pgil-eirdata.org/html/pgil_datasets/authors/c/Crottie,JM/life.htm (accessed September 2003).
Walker, Brian, Art Ó Broin, and Seán McMahon, eds. *The Faces of Ireland*. Belfast: Appletree, 1980.
Welch, Robert, ed. "Julia Crotty." In *The Oxford Companion to Irish Literature*. Oxford: Oxford University Press, 1996, 123.

GERALDINE CUMMINS
(1890–1969)

Shelia Odak

BIOGRAPHY

Geraldine Dorothy Cummins was born in Cork, the fifth child and first daughter of Jane and Dr. Ashley Cummins, a physician and Professor of Medicine at National University, Ireland. Cummins's education consisted of instruction from a series of often uneducated governesses and what she read on her own at the Cork Public Library, where she gravitated toward books of Irish literature and drama. However, many of her ten siblings received university degrees, including her sisters.

As an athletic young woman, Cummins sought to emulate her father, who had been a rugby football international player. At eighteen, Cummins became a member of the Irish Women's International Hockey Team. She also wished to follow her father into medicine, but Cummins's mother was displeased at the idea of her eldest daughter choosing this profession, so Cummins explored other occupations. During her late teens and early twenties, Cummins was a suffragette and served as an officer in the Munster Women's Franchise League. She worked at the National Library in Dublin during World War I and had a stint as a journalist in London during the 1920s. Also to please her mother, Cummins started writing fiction during these years, often collaborating with Suzanne R. Day. The two wrote three plays together, and later, Cummins wrote a fourth drama independently.

During the final years of World War I, Cummins began pursuing an interest in psychic phenomena that shaped the rest of her life and career. She became acquainted with the psychic arts while staying as a paying guest in the Dublin home of Hester Dowden. Dowden, a medium who became famous for communications she said were received from the deceased Oscar Wilde, introduced Cummins to the Ouija board, where the two performed psychic experiments.

As Cummins began conducting her own psychic research she felt she could foresee future events and read objects, though she was most skilled at automatic writing, a process in which, in a trancelike state, she would fill up pages with script deemed to have come from the dead. Cummins described this process by saying, "I am a mere listener, and through my stillness and passivity I lend my aid to the stranger who is speaking" (*The Road to Immortality*, 21). Using her automatic writing, Cummins gave sittings to such figures as W. B. Yeats and E. Œ. Somerville, among others. Interestingly, in February 1939, just days after his death, Cummins claimed she received a message from Yeats through her automatic writing. Upon meeting E. B. Gibbes in 1923, Cummins was able to concentrate more fully on her work in psychic studies due to Gibbes's generous offer to let Cummins live with her.

In 1926, Cummins was at the center of a landmark legal case regarding the ownership of "spirit writings" when Bligh Bond, who had typed up some of Cummins's automatic writings, alleged that he was entitled to the copyright for the sittings. The ruling in the case established that the medium would hold the copyright for such writings.

While pursuing her psychic endeavors, Cummins continued her literary writing, producing two novels. However, a month before Gibbes's death in 1951, she encouraged Cummins to give up her literary efforts in order to devote herself to automatic writing. Cummins promised to do so, a promise she kept for the remainder of her life. Cummins produced only one other book of fiction, *Variety Show*, a volume of short stories, which was published in 1959 but likely written much earlier. Cummins died in 1969 and is buried on Little Island in St. Lappan's churchyard.

MAJOR WORKS AND THEMES

Cummins's writing revolves around Irish characters and themes. *Broken Faith* (1913), her first collaboration with Suzanne Day, is a family tragedy featuring a hard-working, heroic wife who finds she must surrender her worthless husband to the police. Critics denounced the play for portraying men negatively. However, Cummins recalls that Yeats felt the drama had "a strength and directness" that he associated with masculinity (*Unseen Adventures*, 88). *Fox and Geese* (1917), which was the final collaborative effort for Cummins and Day, was the pair's greatest success and gives a comedic take on peasant life featuring matchmaking schemes and lively dialogue. As with much of Cummins's work, the female characters are the strongest and initiate the action.

Cummins's novels often deal with life in Munster. In her first novel, *The Land They Loved* (1919), Cummins tells the story of a young woman who returns to Ireland after several years working in America. The two brothers who were her childhood sweethearts, one of whom she had hoped to marry, have been killed. The plot focuses on their younger brother, who now wishes to marry the young woman himself. *Fires of Beltane* (1936) features a young Irish woman who becomes pregnant by an aristocrat from the neighborhood Big House. After he deserts her and flees to America, the young woman has the child and settles into an unhappy and abusive marriage with a local farmer.

The volume of short stories, *Variety Show* (1959), contains tales ranging from glimpses of peasant life to the workings of an upper-middle-class marriage. The finest of these stories is "The Tragedy of Eight Pence," which chronicles a happily married woman trying to shield her ill husband from the knowledge that his death will leave her penniless and destined to work as a servant for a pair of despised, miserly relatives.

Cummins's work shows the influence of Somerville and Ross, and in 1952 Cummins published the first biography of Somerville, who was also her close friend. Cummins recognized the limitations of the themes in her fiction, saying that she had "only successfully composed fiction or plays about Irish characters and Irish country scenes" (*Unseen Adventures*, 76). However, she is also the author of over a dozen books that stem from her automatic writings, and these bear no resemblance to her fiction. Cummins's subjects in these works are as diverse as a messenger from early Christian history (*The Scripts of Cleophas*, 1928), an explorer who disappeared in the jungles of South America (*The Fate of Colonel Fawcett*, 1955), a classical lecturer (*The Road to Immortality*, 1933, and *Beyond Human Personality*, 1935), a woman who had been a successful psychic during her own lifetime (*Swan on a Black Sea*, 1965), and a former U.S. president (*Mind in Life and Death*, 1956).

CRITICAL RECEPTION

There has been little critical work done on Cummins's writing, especially her fiction. As Janet Madden-Simpson states in her introduction to Cummins's short story "The Tragedy of Eight Pence," included in Madden-Simpson's anthology *Woman's Part* (1984), Cummins's "work has been forgotten" (209). Charles Fryer, who wrote a study concentrating on Cummins's psychical works, feels that she is "part of the Irish literary heritage, along with Synge, Joyce, Yeats and Bernard Shaw" (4), though even his enthusiasm is tempered when discussing her fiction and her biography of E. Œ. Somerville, which reflects Cummins's boundless affection for her friend, often to the detriment of the work. Gifford Lewis, author of the biography *Somerville and Ross*, calls Cummins's book "awkwardly written," a charge with which most critics seem to agree (184). Bette London, who has written an academic study that looks at Cummins's mediumship as an act of authorial collaboration and a serious writing practice with feminist implications, states that Cummins's psychical writings "could be said to have transformed a run-of-the-mill author into an author of exceptional abilities" (153).

BIBLIOGRAPHY

Works by Geraldine Cummins

Drama

Broken Faith. Produced at Abbey Theatre, Dublin, 1913. (With Suzanne R. Day.)
Fox and Geese. Dublin: Maunsel, 1917. Produced at Abbey Theatre, Dublin, 1917; produced at Court Theatre, London, 1917. (With Suzanne R. Day.)
Till Yesterday Comes Again. Produced at Chanticleer Theatre, London, 1938.
The Way of the World. Produced at Abbey Theatre, Dublin, 1914. (With Suzanne R. Day.)

Fiction

Fires of Beltane. London: Michael Joseph, 1936.
The Land They Loved. London: Macmillan, 1919.
Variety Show. London: Barrie and Rockliff, 1959.

Nonfiction

Dr. E. Œ. Somerville, a Biography. London: Dakers, 1952.

Psychical Works

After Pentecost. London: Rider, 1944.
Beyond Human Personality. London: I. Nicholson and Watson, 1935.
The Childhood of Jesus. London: F. Muller, 1937.
The Fate of Colonel Fawcett. London: Aquarian, 1955.
The Great Days of Ephesus. London: Rider, 1933.
Healing the Mind. London: Aquarian, 1957.
I Appeal Unto Caesar. London: Psychic Press, 1950.
The Manhood of Jesus. London: Andrew Dakers, 1949.
Mind in Life and Death. London: Aquarian, 1956.
Paul in Athens. London: Rider, 1930.
Perceptive Healing. London: Rider, 1945.
The Resurrection of Christ. London: L.S.A. Publications, 1947.
The Road to Immortality. London: I. Nicholson and Watson, 1933.
The Scripts of Cleophas. London: Rider, 1928.
Swan on a Black Sea. London: Routledge and Kegan Paul, 1965.
They Survive. London: Rider, 1946.
Travellers in Eternity. London: Psychic Press, 1948.
Unseen Adventures. London: Rider, 1951. (Autobiography)
When Nero Was Dictator. London: F. Muller, 1939.

Studies of Geraldine Cummins

Fryer, Charles. *Geraldine Cummins*. Tasburgh, UK: Pelegrin Trust in association with Pilgrim Books, 1990.
Lewis, Gifford. *Somerville and Ross*. Harmondsworth, UK: Penguin, 1987.
London, Bette. *Writing Double*. Ithaca, NY: Cornell University Press, 1999.
Madden-Simpson, Janet. Introduction to "The Tragedy of Eight Pence." In *Woman's Part*. Dublin: Arlen House, 1984, 209.

ITA DALY
(1945–   )

John J. Han

BIOGRAPHY

A contemporary novelist and short-story writer residing in Dublin, Ita Daly was born in County Leitrim. After graduating from St. Louis High School in Dublin, Ita majored in English and Spanish at University College Dublin, earning a BA (1965), an MA (1966), and a higher diploma in education (1968). She belonged to the Workers' Party (later Communist Party of Ireland) until 1968, although her political inclination has remained leftist. A nonpracticing Catholic, Daly taught English literature and Spanish at St. Louis High School, her alma mater, in 1968–79. She married David Marcus, a writer and literary editor, in 1972. In 1979, when her only daughter, Sarah Patricia, was born, Daly made writing her full-time profession.

Daly started her writing career with the publication of *The Lady with the Red Shoes and Other Stories* (1980), her only collection of short stories, which includes such works as "Virginibus Puerisque," "Hey Nonny No," and "Compassion." In 1986, Daly published her first novel, *Ellen*, a bizarre romantic story narrated by a young woman who abruptly murders her girlfriend and roommate. *Ellen* was followed by another strange novel, *A Singular Attraction* (1987), in which the middle-aged female protagonist disgusts her Danish lover after sex by saying that her bleeding results from sexually transmitted disease. The year 1989 saw the publication of *Candy on the DART*, her first children's book. In the same year, Daly published her third novel, *Dangerous Fictions*, portraying the lonely life of an emotionally troubled woman. *All Fall Down* (1992), a comic novel, describes some of the irregularities and scandals found in twentieth-century Ireland. *Unholy Ghosts* (1996) focuses on a German Jewish girl who is haunted by memories from the Nazi era and converts to Catholicism and then to revolutionary socialism. *Irish Myths and Legends*, retold by Ita Daly and illustrated by Bee Willey, was published in 2001. Daly is currently working on another novel.

Daly's short stories have been published in various magazines and literary anthologies, including *The Penguin Book of Irish Short Stories*, on both sides of the Atlantic. She earned two Hennessy Literary Awards—one in 1972 for the story "Virginibus Pueresque" and the other in 1975 for "The Lady with the Red Shoes. She also won the *Irish Times* Short Story Competition in 1975 for "Compassion."

MAJOR WORKS AND THEMES

Although Ita Daly has written in several genres, she is known primarily for novels about twentieth-century Irish women who are introspective, solitary, and alienated. The title character of *Ellen* grows up in a caring family in Dublin. Having failed her Leaving Certificate, she is disqualified from entering university. She leads a dull, friendless life until she miraculously strikes up a friendship with Myra, a librarian originally from Sligo. Myra suggests—and Ellen agrees—that they live together in a flat for more freedom and privacy. Living without parental protection makes Ellen feel invigorated and rewarded. The relationship between the two young women is strained, however, when Myra breaks her promise not to have any boyfriends. Myra spends less time with Ellen as she falls in love with Adrien. Soon Ellen finds her own boyfriend in Bobbie, Myra's cousin. One day, Ellen notices Myra entertaining Bobbie in her absence. Outraged that Myra is attempting to steal Bobbie from her, Ellen suddenly murders Myra with a bread knife. Ellen eventually marries Adrien not because she loves him but because she craves companionship and new pleasures: "But, though I had no affection for Adrien, I could see that there was a bargain to be kept. He would provide me with a shelter so I must endeavour to provide him with whatever it was he needed in a wife" (139).

A Singular Attraction and *Dangerous Fictions* continue to showcase odd women who lead dull, solitary lives. The protagonist of *A Singular Attraction*, Pauline, is a thirty-eight-year-old spinster ashamed of her long-held virginity. After having sex with a Danish man, she tells him that the blood on the bedsheet is because of her venereal disease. She is spurned by him and returns to her lonely celibate lifestyle. *Dangerous Fictions* focuses on an emotionally unstable woman named Martina. Although she has been married for twenty years, she is incapable of behaving naturally. At one point she desecrates her mother-in-law's grave by defecating on it. Estranged from her family, Martina eventually lives a lonesome life in Spain.

Unholy Ghosts chronicles the turbulent life stories of a German family in the mid-twentieth century through the narration of Belle Meyers, the gardener at a Dublin mental hospital. Belle, her grandmother (Buba), and her mother (Mutti) immigrated to Ireland in the early 1940s. Buba and Mutti refuse to talk about life in Germany and mislead Belle to believe that they are Jews. Indeed, the Meyers are Germans who lived in the expropriated apartment of their neighboring Jewish family, gone after the Nazis rounded them up. After the war, the Meyers feared persecution by the American troops and thus adopted the Jewish identity. At the novel's end, the conversation between Belle and Father Jack reveals the true story, which drives Belle to insanity. Disillusioned by conventional religion and seeking companionship, Belle secretly joins the Socialist Workers Party, and indeed much of the novel focuses on Belle's involvement in the socialist movement in Ireland. She is mentored by the hard-core revolutionary Mona McCarthy, who recommends that she read *A Life of Rosa Luxemburg*, a book about the prominent German socialist leader (1870–1919). When Mona is killed by a sniper on the street in Budapest, Hungary, the Right as well as the Left in Ireland consider her death "a glorious death as both sides vied with one another to claim her as an official martyr" (199).

Irish Myths and Legends, which retells the magical stories of kings, fairies, and heroes prominent in Celtic mythology and Irish legends and tales, is divided into four sections: the mythological cycle, the Cuchulain cycle, the Fianna cycle, and the traditional tales. According to the author, she learned many of these tales during her childhood from her mother. "Balor of the Evil Eye" focuses on the savage tyrant with a single fiery eye in his forehead whose daughter gives birth to the mythical hero Lugh. "Children of Lir" concerns the tragic fate of the mythical chieftain's four children. Lir's first wife, Aobh, dies while delivering their second set of twins. Then Lir remarries Aoife, Aobh's sister. Jealous of Lir's affection for the four stepsons, she plots to kill them, but, fortunately for them, she strikes them with a magic wand, not with a sword, thus instead turning them into swans at Loch Dairbhreach (Lake Derravarragh in County Westmeath). The book also includes the story of Deirdre, the lady of great beauty who eloped rather than marry the old king, and the story of the king of leprechauns.

CRITICAL RECEPTION

Considered a popular fiction writer, Ita Daly has received little scholarly attention. A critical book about her has yet to be published, and scholarly journals generally seem to disregard work on her fiction. Relatively brief critical comments on her individual works have appeared in such popular periodicals as the *Spectator*, *New Statesman*, *London Review of Books*, *Times Literary Supplement* (London), and *Observer*.

Critical comments on Daly's works tend to be qualified. Favorable reviewers focus on her strong plot, writing style, and Irish themes. In his review of *Unholy Ghosts*, for instance, Nick Dent feels that some parts "get a bit corny" (as exemplified by the passages about casual sexual intercourse between Belle and Max). Also, Daly's "fluent, somewhat unmodulated style and cheerful matter-of-factness" do not measure up to the emotional impact provided by the novel's epigraph from Gerard Manley Hopkins's sonnet "Carrion Comfort": "O the mind, mind has mountains; cliffs of fall/Frightful, sheer, no-man-fathomed." However, Dent points out, "the world of the radical left in postwar Dublin, complete with its ironies and contradictions, is particularly well portrayed. . . . *Unholy Ghosts* has a strong plot, containing one of the dramatic twists that are Daly's trademark. It is in many ways a powerful tale" (27, 30). In another review of *Unholy Ghosts*, Carlo Gébler praises Daly's excellent ability to narrate the story, to achieve the dénouement, and to allow her characters to have their own autonomy. On the other hand, Gébler notes, Daly misrepresents historical facts when she touches on the subject of Nazi Germany, the German Democratic Republic riots, and the Hungarian revolt (24).

Christine St. Peter includes Ita Daly's *Dangerous Fictions* in the category of Irish women's exilic fiction. Each work in this category is "the narrative of the adult protagonist living in another country whose story inscribes her self-exile" (45). In addition to Daly's novel, this diverse group includes works by Edna O'Brien, Julia O'Faolain, Mary Rose Callaghan, Deirdre Madden, and Linda Anderson. Peters also praises Daly's *Unholy Ghosts* and Mary Dorcey's *Biography of Desire* (1997) as "two fine examples of letter or journal novels by Irish women" (173). In his 2001 review of *Irish Myths and Legends*, John Peters comments that those who have not read such earlier collections as Marie Heaney's *Names upon the Harp* (2000) or Neil Phillip's *Celtic Fairy Tales* (1999) will "get a good sense of the range and richness of the Irish folk tradition" from Daly's book (1866).

While Daly's fiction does have moments of brilliance, most reviewers comment on her stories' bizarre, incoherent, caricatural, and excessively political elements. In his review of *Ellen*, Adelware Maja-Pearce observes that the novel is marred by organic disunity: "Myra betrays [Ellen] in one of the most unconvincing scenes I have ever come across and Ellen kills her. Whereupon, and quite mysteriously, Ellen herself gradually inherits Myra's beauty, a comment I suppose on the symbiotic relationship between them that continues after Myra's death. Alternatively, the author might be trying to suggest that Ellen could only begin to emerge from her bondage once she had disposed of her crutch. Either way one isn't inclined to look too deeply into the matter. It all seems rather pointless and not particularly well written." (26). Although Daly's fiction may occasionally lack plausibility, unity, and coherence, her lively writing style (especially dialogue) renders her fiction an engaging read. She deals with subjects that are important in understanding contemporary Irish society, and her feminist and socialist concerns are particularly worthy of further critical study.

BIBLIOGRAPHY

Works by Ita Daly

All Fall Down. London: Bloomsbury, 1992.
Andy and Sharon, Olé. Dublin: Poolbeg, 1990.
Candy on the DART. Dublin: Poolbeg, 1989.
Dangerous Fictions. London: Bloomsbury, 1989.
Ellen. London: Cape, 1986.
Irish Myths & Legends. Oxford: Oxford University Press, 2001.
The Lady with the Red Shoes and Other Stories. Dublin: Poolbeg, 1980.
A Singular Attraction. London: Cape, 1987.
Unholy Ghosts. London: Bloomsbury, 1996.

Studies of Ita Daly

Dent, Nick. "Seeking and Finding Asylum." Review of *Unholy Ghost*. *Spectator*, March 16, 1996, 27.
Gébler, Carlo. "A Child of History." Review of *Unholy Ghosts*. *Times Literary Supplement*, March 1, 1996, 24.
Maja-Pearce, Adewale. "Identity Problems." Review of *Ellen*. *New Statesman*, March 14, 1986, 26.
Peters, John. Review of *Irish Myths and Legends*. *Booklist*, June 1 and 15, 2001, 1866.
St. Peter, Christine. *Changing Ireland: Strategies in Contemporary Fiction*. New York: Palgrave, 2000.

SUZANNE DAY
(1890–1964)

Tom Keegan

BIOGRAPHY

Suzanne Rouvier Day was born in Cork in 1890. An outspoken advocate of women's suffrage, at the age of twenty she helped create a branch of the Irish Women Franchise League in Cork. She later left this branch in favor of the more militant Munster Women's Franchise League (MWFL). The following year, 1911, she successfully ran for a position on the Cork Board of Guardians, winning again in 1914. Yet with the start of the First World War she resigned from the MWFL, opting to spend more than a year aiding refugees in northern France. Her philanthropic nature found work again years later when she participated in the London Fire Service during the Second World War. Suzanne Day died in London in 1964.

MAJOR WORKS AND THEMES

Day's epistolary novel, *The Amazing Philanthropists* (1916) provides a satirical account of her experience running for the Cork Board of Guardians. With her friend Geraldine Cummins, Day wrote three plays for the Abbey Theatre, *Fox and Geese*, *The Way of the World*, and *Broken Faith*. This first play, *Broken Faith,* is perhaps her best-known work. A marriage plot, the play invokes a number of typical comedic devices, role reversals, and so on. Set in a rural community, the play also makes use of mild dialect and touches lightly on the issues of religion and anti-English sentiment. Composed of forty-four letters, *The Amazing Philanthropists* turns a satirical tongue on not only the politics of the day, but the gender politics as well. Juxtaposing dialect with polished prose, Day highlights the ideological differences between her male peers and herself—often carving her opponents on both the personal and intellectual cutting boards. Day and Cummins's play *Fox and Geese* likewise examines the feminist bent underlying rural Irish womanhood. The play utilizes a comedic marriage plot that takes under its satirical gaze myths of class, religion both Christian and pagan, and gender politics. With some assistance from the widowed Biddy Maguire, Katie Downey and Mary Fitzgibbon overtake the objects of their desire, Malachi Phelan and Timothy James Maguire, respectively. The two female protagonists appear in shades of Oliver Goldsmith's Kate Hardcastle and J.M. Synge's Pegeen Mike, witty and lovestruck. Meanwhile, the male characters, for the most part, remain as they were in *The Amazing Philanthropists*, rhetorical blunderers tied to notions of class and tradition increasingly meaningless in the contemporary landscape.

CRITICAL RECEPTION

No serious critical appraisal of Day's work has appeared, despite the quality of her work.

BIBLIOGRAPHY

Works by Suzanne Day

The Amazing Philanthropists. London: Sidgwick and Jackson, 1916.
Broken Faith. Unpublished. Produced at Abbey Theatre, Dublin, 1913. (With Geraldine Cummins.)
Fox and Geese. Dublin: Maunsel, 1917. (With Geraldine Cummins.)
Round About Bar le Duc. London: Skeffington, 1918.
The Way of the World. Produced at Abbey Theatre, Dublin, 1914. (With Geraldine Cummins.)
Where the Mistral Blows: Impressions of Provence. London: Methuen, 1933.

Studies of Suzanne Day

Bourke, Angela, Mairin Ni Dhonneadha, Siobhan Kilfeather, Maria Luddy, Margaret MacCurtain, Gerardine Meaney, Mary O'Dowd, and Clair Wills, eds. *The Field Day Anthology of Irish Writing*. Vols. 4 and 5, *Women's Writing and Traditions*. Cork: Cork University Press, 2002.

Clarke, Desmond. *Ireland in Fiction: A Guide to Irish Novels, Tales, Romances and Folklore.* Part 2. Cork: Royal Carbery, 1985.

Cleeve, Brian, and Anne Brady. *A Dictionary of Irish Writers.* Dublin: Lilliput, 1985.

Deane, Seamus, Andrew Carpenter, and Jonathan Williams, eds. *The Field Day Anthology of Irish Writing.* Vol. 3. Derry, Ire.: Field Day, 1991.

TERESA DEEVY
(1894–1963)

Christie Fox

BIOGRAPHY

The youngest of thirteen children, Teresa Deevy was born on January 19, 1894, at her family home, Landscape, in Waterford. Her father, Edward, ran a drapery business that was successful enough to permit the purchase of a rather grand home. Her mother, Mary Feehan Deevy, left to raise the children alone when Edward died in 1897, passed on her strong religious beliefs to her children. Deevy was exposed to religious and political influences even as a child. Her maternal uncle was a parish priest who had enough involvement with the Land League to be chastised by the bishop, eventually serving time in prison. One of Teresa's brothers was a Jesuit priest, and two of her sisters became nuns, including one in the Ursuline convent where Teresa attended boarding school. This sister died during the Waterford influenza epidemic in 1917, after Teresa (known as "Tessa") left the school. The influence of the Catholic Church remained strong throughout her life, and even when she disagreed with certain church decisions, Deevy remained a daily communicant.

She excelled in school, receiving honors in English and piano, a fact both ironic and poignant for one who lost her hearing as a young adult. Teresa had enrolled in University College Dublin, planning to become a teacher, but contracted Ménière's disease, which strikes the inner ear and sometimes, although not always, causes deafness. Unfortunately, Deevy did become completely deaf and had to change her plans to teach. She transferred to University College Cork and finished her degree there, but it was a trip to London to learn lip-reading that inspired in Deevy a love of the theater. There, she attended plays as often as she could, reading the scripts in advance whenever possible and lip-reading the dialogue. It was here that she discovered Shaw and Chekhov; later, she was often referred to as the "Irish Chekhov."

When Deevy returned to Ireland, she began writing plays but also became increasingly interested in politics. She joined Cumann na mBan, an Irish women's nationalist organization, and visited prisoners in Waterford Jail, although her mother disapproved. It is likely that her political fervor cooled in light of the less-than-savory cultural politics of the time: for example, she objected to censorship on religious grounds. Turning thus to playwrighting, she joined the ranks of many young Irish playwrights initially rejected by the Abbey Theatre.

By the time of her success in the National Theatre, Deevy had moved to Dublin with her sister, Nell, who served as an indispensable help in Teresa's lip-reading: they developed a way to communicate even in poor light, and whenever Teresa had trouble lip-reading, Nell would translate for her. They shared a flat on Waterloo Road, just south of the Grand Canal. The flat saw many visitors from the arts world, including Lennox Robinson, her patron of sorts, actress Ria Mooney, who appeared in several of Deevy's plays, painter Patrick Hennessy, playwright M. J. Molloy, and painter Jack B. Yeats, brother of William Butler Yeats. After her sister's death in 1954, Deevy returned to Waterford, where she fearlessly rode her bike through the streets, mindless of drivers' angry horns. Passersby could not understand how she avoided being hit, nor why her clothes often didn't match each other or the season, an indication, according to Sean Dunne, of "her lack of interest in her personal appearance" (10).

Deevy believed that poor productions lacking strong actors led to her plays' loss in popularity. The "Irish Chekhov" died in Maypark Nursing Home in Waterford in January 1963, after having tried her hand at various different kinds of works, including a ballet.

MAJOR WORKS AND THEMES

After a series of rejections, Deevy learned that Lennox Robinson had taken an interest in her plays and in 1930, her three-act play *Reapers* was accepted and produced. Critical response favored this play, but her next full-length play really made her mark on the Irish theatrical landscape. Her script *Temporal Powers* won an Abbey Award for the best play submitted that year (she shared the award with Paul Vincent Carroll's *Things That Are Caesar's*). Produced in 1932, the play generated acclaim from critics as well as short-story writer and novelist Frank O'Connor, who wrote her a note comparing the play favorably to J. M. Synge's *The Playboy of the Western World* (1907). The play took a hard look at poverty, its main characters destitute until they find some money that proves to be their downfall. It was Deevy's first attempt to write directly about social issues.

The Abbey produced one of her strongest and most published one-act plays, *The King of Spain's Daughter*, in 1935. This short play set up a narrative pattern that Deevy followed with her best-known play, *Katie Roche* (1936), in which a confused young woman must choose between fairly limiting options presented to her by a father figure, who generally inflicts physical violence on her to ensure that the woman makes a proper choice. *The King of Spain's Daughter* focuses on Annie Kinsella, who must choose between what is essentially indentured slavery at the local factory or marriage to Jim Harris, a man she does not love. The play contains a startling indictment of marriage itself when one character, who is saddened by the sight of a wedding in the distance, observes, "What have bad or good to do with it? For twenty years you're thinking of that day, an' for thirty you're lookin' back at it. After that you don't mind—you haven't the feelin'—excepting maybe an odd day, like to-day" (126). Annie ultimately chooses marriage after learning of Jim's diligent preparation: "He put by two shillin's every week for two hundred weeks. I think he is a man that—supposin' he was jealous—might cut your throat" (142). The audience sees that Annie has not left behind the threat of violence entirely. The wedding in the distance, incidentally, was the original inspiration for the play after Deevy witnessed a wedding on "An April Day," to which the play is dedicated.

Her most popular play, *Katie Roche*, earned two revivals at the Abbey (1975 and 1994) after its original production in 1936. Katie, another heroine pulled in multiple directions, must find her self-fulfillment independently of her family and her society. Katie is a "foundling," who—we later learn—was an unclaimed child of the local gentry. The name "Roche" belongs to neither of her parents, but to the woman who took her in after her mother died and who refused to give her any specific details about her real parents. Katie finds herself engaged and then married to her employer, Stanislaus Gregg, who once proposed to her mother. Once she accepts, she finds that not much in her life has changed. Although she is no longer the Greggs' maid, her husband spends most of his time in Dublin and the marriage lacks a physical relationship. She is denied her previous flirtations with the local boys, and when Stanislaus finds her in a compromising situation, he decrees that they will immediately move to the Continent. Again, the ending proves problematic for modern audiences, as Katie moves from "self-pitying" to "brave" in a few lines, and decides abruptly: "I'm a great beauty . . . after all my talk—crying now . . . (*grows exultant*). I *will* be brave!" (113).

The two actors who played Katie in the revivals provide some insight into this turn at the end. Jeananne Crowley, who played her in the 1975 revival directed by Joe Dowling, found that Katie had few options, as women of that time were pressured to do what was "expected" of them, with little room for dissent (Katie Donovan, quoted in Murray, 3). Derbhle Crotty, who played her in 1994, stated in an interview with the *Irish Times* that despite the seeming inevitability of the play's ending, she found that Katie had more freedom than Hedda Gabler or Nora from Ibsen's *A Doll's House* (1879) (Katie Donovan, cited in Murray, 3). Katie "just keeps going," which, Crotty notes, can be more difficult and require more courage than leaving. Both productions mined the play for insights into the lives of Irishwomen in the 1930s, in de Valera's world of comely maidens at the crossroads. *Katie Roche* was included in the prestigious *Famous Plays of 1935–6*, published by Victor Gollancz.

Deevy's next play, *The Wild Goose* (1936), was her first with a male protagonist. Set in the seventeenth century after the momentous Battle of the Boyne, the play concerns Martin Shea's indecision among marriage, church, and the army. This would be Deevy's last Abbey play. In 1941 Ernest Blythe became managing director at the Abbey and, as Christopher Murray has noted, female playwrights no longer found a welcome there. Blythe and the Gate rejected Deevy's next major play, *Wife to James Whelan*, and although it was produced on the radio by both Radio Eireann and the BBC, the manuscript was not published until the 1995 special issue of *Irish University Review* dedicated to Deevy. In it, the play's central character, Nan, must decide which man to marry and whether or not be "wife to James Whelan." In the end, she marries the other man, who owns property but who dies quickly and leaves her penniless; Whelan marries another woman, which humiliates Nan. The play centers around the high price of independence for women in traditional Irish society.

Once the Abbey stopped producing her plays, Deevy spent her energies on radio plays, which she had been writing alongside traditional plays. Deevy made regular trips to London and Belfast to supervise the recordings of these plays, and it is interesting to imagine a deaf playwright overseeing the performance of radio plays, but as long as she was able to read the actors' lips, she was able to follow along.

CRITICAL RECEPTION

In 1928, Deevy submitted the one-act *Reserved Ground* to the Abbey Theatre, and although the Abbey rejected it, they included a note that stated "the author showed power and promise, that she had the gift of writing but that everything in the play should be psychologically true and that it should not have the sentimental ending of a third-rate novel" (R.M. Fox, quoted in Kearney, 81). Deevy took this as encouragement, and the note may in fact help explain Deevy's continuing trouble with endings. Deevy had a successful career as a playwright during her lifetime, and participated in Dublin artistic society. Audiences and critics alike enjoyed her plays. She has not endured, however, as a revived or particularly well-known member of the Irish theatrical canon.

Many of her plays are not revived now because contemporary audiences and practitioners are uncertain how to interpret her conclusions. Christopher Murray describes her writing as seeking something elusive: "Deevy's task as a playwright is to reconcile subjectivity with authority perceived as patriarchal. . . . In a sense what is searched for in Deevy is legitimacy itself, the space to be free. It is achieved only ironically, a feature of her work not commented on in her own day and felt to be too compromised by conventional endings in our day" (9). Although the Abbey has staged two revivals of *Katie Roche*, Deevy's critical acclaim has waned and she was not included, for example, in influential studies of modern Irish drama until the late-twentieth-century movement to include women.

Deevy paid astonishing attention to timing and pauses, leading critics to suggest that her deafness contributed to her fascination with pauses. She often required silences to regulate passion. *Katie Roche* includes fifty-nine silences and forty-three pauses. Murray refers to it as "scoring" her work, and notes that no other Irish playwright does so (8). Deevy makes a distinction between "pause" and "silence"; these silences mute the temperature of the play, ensuring that the female characters—in this case, Katie—never get too far out of the bounds of convention.

In the late twentieth century, some scholars moved to credit Deevy as the "Second Lady of the Abbey Theatre," after Lady Gregory. In 1986, the *Journal of Irish Literature* devoted an entire issue to Deevy, including a list of Deevy's complete works, compiled by Eileen Kearney, who had access to private papers of Deevy's family. Unfortunately, many original dates of production have been lost, as have several of the original manuscripts. Sean Dunne notes that some short stories by "D.V. Goode" were found among her papers and suggests that this might have been a pseudonym for Deevy (10).

Then in 1995, the *Irish University Review* published their jubilee issue, "Teresa Deevy and Irish Women Playwrights." This issue came on the heels of a successful revival of *Katie Roche* and was part of a renewed interest in her career. Scholarly publication on Deevy's work has continued to grow.

BIBLIOGRAPHY

Works by Teresa Deevy

Published Plays

Going Beyond Alma's Glory. Irish Writing 17 (December 1951): 21–32.
Katie Roche. In *Famous Plays of 1935–36*. London: Victor Gollancz, 1936, 607–701.
The King of Spain's Daughter and Other One-Act Plays. Dublin: New Frontiers, 1947. (Included: *The King of Spain's Daughter, In Search of Valour* [published previously as *A Disciple*], and *Strange Birth*.)
Temporal Powers. The Journal of Irish Literature 14, no. 2 (May 1985): 18–75.

Three Plays. London: Macmillan, 1939. (Included: *Katie Roche*, *The Wild Goose*, and *The King of Spain's Daughter*.)
Wife to James Whelan. In Special issue, *Irish University Review*, edited by Christopher Murray, 25, no. 1 (Spring–Summer 1995): 29–87.

Unpublished Radio Plays

Dignity.
Holiday House. (A version of *Going Beyond Alma's Glory*.)
Iníon Rí na Spáinne (*The King of Spain's Daughter*). Translated by Máirtín Ó Diréain.
Light Falling.
One Look—And What It Led To. (A version of *In the Cellar of My Friend*; the title comes from *Crotchet Castle* [1831] by Thomas Love Peacock.)
Polinka. (Adapted from Chekhov's story "Polinka" [1887].)
Strange Birth.
Supreme Dominion.
Within a Marble City.

Studies of Teresa Deevy

Dunne, Sean. "Rediscovering Teresa Deevy." *Cork Examiner*, March 20, 1984, 10.
Fox, Christie. "Neither Here nor There: The Liminal Position of Teresa Deevy and Her Female Characters." In *A Century of Irish Drama: Widening the Stage*, edited by Stephen Watt, Eileen Morgan, and Shakir Mustafa, 193–203. Bloomington: Indiana University Press, 2000.
Hogan, Robert, ed. "A Teresa Deevy Number." Special issue, *Journal of Irish Literature* 14, no. 2 (May 1985).
Kearney, Eileen M. "Teresa Deevy (1894–1963): Ireland's Forgotten Second Lady of the Abbey Theatre." *Theatre Annual* 40 (1985): 77–90.
Murray, Christopher. "Introduction: The Stifled Voice." *Irish University Review* 25, no. 1 (Spring–Summer 1995): 1–10.
Richards, Shaun. " 'Suffocated in the Green Flag': The Drama of Teresa Deevy and 1930s Ireland." *Literature and History* 4, no. 1 (Spring 1995): 65–80.
Robinson, Lennox. *Ireland's Abbey Theatre: A History 1899–1951*. London: Sidgwick, 1951.

ANNE DEVLIN
(1951–   )

Sara E. Stenson

BIOGRAPHY

Anne Maria Devlin, daughter of socialist politician Paddy Devlin, was raised in Andersontown, a largely Catholic town outside of Belfast. Though she now lives in Birmingham with her son, she continues to write fiction and plays about women from Northern Ireland. She taught at Bushmill's Comprehensive School in Antrim for two years before moving in 1976 with her first husband to Freiburg, Germany. In 1982 she received the Hennessy Literary Award for her short story "Passages," which was later published in the collection *The Way Paver* (1986). Devlin often traveled back to Belfast after the end of her first marriage. In 1984 she moved with her second husband, producer Chris Parr, to Birmingham and their son was born. In 1985 she earned the Beckett Award for Best First Play for Television for *A Woman Calling* (adapted from "Passages") and *The Long March* (1982).

Also in 1985, one of her most well-known plays, *Ourselves Alone*, was produced at London's Royal Court Theatre, whose associate director she went on to become. The play won critical acclaim and several prizes including the George Devine Award, the Irish Post Award, the Time Out Fringe Theater Award, and the Susan Smith Blackburn Prize for best play by a female playwright. Devlin also received two Lawrence Olivier Award nominations in 1986 for Best Newcomer and Best Play. The play was also produced in Liverpool, Dublin, and Washington, D.C. Her first collection of plays, including *Ourselves Alone*, *A Woman Calling*, and *The Long March*, was published in 1986. Along with *After Easter* (1994), *Ourselves Alone* continues to draw the majority of Devlin's scholarly attention.

Devlin's *Mainly After Dark* (translation of a play by Arlette Niamand) was produced in Edinburgh in 1986. She lectured at Birmingham from 1987 to 1989 while writing several radio and television screenplays, including *Naming the Names*, which aired on the BBC in 1987 and again in 1989. In 1988 she won another award for Best Drama at the Eighth International Celtic Film Festival. The Birmingham-based play *Heartlanders* is a collaborative effort by Devlin, Stephen Bill, and David Edgar and was produced in 1989. Devlin was writer in residence at Lund University in Sweden in 1990. Her second major work, *After Easter*, was produced in Stratford-upon-Avon and in Belfast.

More recently, Devlin has created screenplays that have been produced as motion pictures. *Titanic Town*, based on the novel by Mary Costello, George Faber, and Charlie Pattinson, was produced by the BBC and others in 1998. That same year saw the production of Devlin's work with Peter Ettedgui and Julien Temple on the film *Vigo*, which recounts the life of French filmmaker Jean Vigo (1905–1934). The version created by Devlin and others is based on Chris Ward's *Love's a Revolution* (n.d.), adapted from Paulo Emilio Salles Gomez's *Jean Vigo* (1971).

MAJOR WORKS AND MAJOR THEMES

Devlin's writing career is marked by her ability to adapt and transform work to a variety of forms, including prose, plays, and screenplays for television and radio. Though Devlin is known primarily for her major plays and screenwriting, she began writing short stories. From the outset, she has continued to maintain an interest in women's lives in relation to sectarian struggle in Northern Ireland. In *Naming the Names* (1987) Finnula McQuillen is jailed for her involvement in the death of her lover. Finn falls for a young English student studying Irish history in Belfast, causing an instantaneous clash of personal and political relations. She reflects upon her own interrogation, recounting the ghosts of her past and her battle to keep her involvement and the names of other members in a secret organization anonymous. Detached yet no longer disillusioned, Finn ponders the nature of her own accountability and that of her interrogators, recalling the violence and the intricate web of accusers and accused.

Ourselves Alone (1985) recounts the sectarian struggle in Belfast through the eyes of three young women who live among IRA volunteers. The play's title draws from the motto of the Irish Republican Party, Sinn Fein. However, Devlin draws a pun on the party's motto in her depiction of women's isolation and their communal strength. The hunger strikes of the 1980s serve as a haunting backdrop that illuminates the tenuous intersection of personal and political turmoil and loss.

Josie, Frieda, and Donna's lives are bound to political struggle as they run messages and harbor suspicious persons, yet their lives are marked by personal challenges albeit with the inability to reach their own goals or to establish fulfilling intimate relationships with lovers. Frieda, the outspoken rebel, sings in Republican clubs but longs for her own career singing her own songs. Her relationship with John McDermott of the Worker's Party is ultimately unsatisfying and she leaves for England. Josie, her sister, is highly committed to the IRA's violent campaign and in love with leader Cathal O'Donnell, who is already married. Though Devlin initially had only these two sisters in mind for the play, in an author's note she claims to have heard another voice, "that of the woman waiting." Donna emerges as a quiet though sharp observer who sees each of these women as somehow waiting as well. Donna has a child with Josie and Frieda's brother Liam. Their relationship frays as they each seek new lovers.

The play's main conflict begins when Josie and Frieda's father, Malachy, brings home Joe Conran, a potential volunteer for the Provisional IRA, whose British background is held suspect, so Josie is asked to interview him. They begin a love affair, whereupon Josie changes to disfavor the violent campaign just before Joe is exposed as an informer. Tension comes to a head as Josie reveals she is pregnant with Joe's child. The paternity debate that ensues as father, brother, and ex-lover react exposes ways in which Nationalist politics influence sexual and reproductive control of women and their potential families.

Rather than end with departures and broken families, *Heartlanders* (1989) celebrates arrivals and unites families. The play was collaboratively written by Devlin, Stephen Bill, and David Edgar to celebrate Birmingham's centenary. Set in the fall of 1989, it highlights the journeys of three individuals passing through the city. Tom looks for an old love, Margaret searches for her missing daughter, and Aan emigrates from India.

In her second major work, *After Easter* (1994), Devlin returns to explore Irish identities. The play has also been well received, earning her a nomination for the Lloyd's Playwright of the Year Award. Greta, the play's protagonist, struggles to come to terms with her past and begins to assert her own voice. Early on, Greta struggles with postnatal depression after the birth of her third child. She moved to England fifteen years ago, married her English Marxist husband, George, and had twins, now eleven years old. Her doctor releases her from the hospital to visit her sister Helen in London for Easter. They are joined by a third sister, Aoife, shortly before hearing of their father's death.

Upon their return to Northern Ireland for his funeral, the remaining family members seek safety from sectarian street violence under the table where their father is laid out. They argue, along with their mother and brother, over whom the father loved the most. When Greta finds herself alone with her father's remains, he instantly comes to life, desperately reaching out of the coffin for her throat. The moment brings Greta back to her terrible childhood, much as the visions and nightmares that plague her as a result of her mother's frequent drunken beatings.

Though other characters, such as Finn from *Naming the Names* and Josie from *Ourselves Alone* often confront their visions, Greta's emerge in a more dynamic form, invoking Catholicism and mysticism as well as violence. Greta's hallucinations relate to her Irish Catholic upbringing, especially the events surrounding Easter, including Pentecost Sunday, death, and resurrection. One particularly intriguing night vision is the dark mysterious figure that appears to her as either the devil or a banshee. This intense dream reappears when Greta considers suicide during her return to London after her father's funeral. Greta's visions do not, however, ultimately restrict her life. Similarly, although she seeks the advice of Elish, a cousin who is the prioress of a convent, she finds it unhelpful because of its narrow definition of motherhood. By the play's end Greta enables her own resolution; her voice symbolically comes to life in an ethereal moment when she recalls for her baby her encounter with a mythical stag. The stag, she claims, brought her to the origins of life because she was unafraid to feed it. Greta is self-actualized, choosing to embrace the new life of motherhood rather than concede, paralyzed and possibly dead from the burden of her past. In this moment, Greta can finally recall a vision with clarity and meaning in her own voice. The stag vision is the culmination of Devlin's efforts to capture both the mystical and the mundane, often oscillating somewhere in between.

In her recent work, Devlin continues to examine the intersection of personal and political struggle. Her screenplay for *Titanic Town* was released as a motion picture in 1998; the material is adopted from Maria Costello's novel. Her main character, the charismatic and determined Bernie McPhelimy, takes up the cause for peace amid the fear and confusion of West Belfast's violent sectarian climate of 1972. The life of Bernie, mother of four and wife of a sick husband, is irreparably altered as her friend is shot and killed by IRA gunmen in front of her son. Disgusted with the loss of innocent lives and the implications of violence on all sides of the conflict, Bernie calls for a ceasefire. Her statement is taken as an attack on the IRA, which immediately spins her family into the midst of sectarian violence and chaos. Ostracized by her community, Bernie attempts to communicate with both IRA volunteers and British police. Devlin's screenplay charts familiar territory of the public and personal in West Belfast, similar to her earlier work.

Marking a change from her earlier work, Devlin's most recent undertaking, the screenplay for *Vigo*, is a biographical account of famed French filmmaker Jean Vigo, who made only four movies before his early death. Jean Vigo, the son of a leader of the French anarchist movement, led a life plagued by illness, most notably tuberculosis. Vigo met his wife, Lydu Lozinska, during treatment in a sanitarium. He worked through his disease, creating a short series of controversial films, most notably *A Propos de Nice* (1929), whose premier resulted in riots. Similarly *Zero for Conduct* (1932) was immediately banned for its antiauthoritarianism. Vigo fell while making *L'Atalante* and the injuries that resulted required him to edit the work from his home, as he was too ill to travel. Though this most recent work changes in scope and setting, Vigo, like many of her other characters, struggles to assert his voice through his art despite prevailing political ideologies. Like many of her previous characters, Devlin asserts the differentiation of Vigo's voice in order to establish the necessity and ability of individuals to claim a space outside that defined by political rhetoric.

CRITICAL RECEPTION

Critics often cite Devlin's strength in depicting individual plights in response to external controls. The outside forces most frequently addressed by Devlin are the ideologies that promote and sustain sectarian violence in the North. Furthermore, she cautiously examines individuals' abilities to explore and realize their own subjectivity through themes of exile and return and relationships between men and women. England appears as a place to which to escape, though it is not always a safe haven. Devlin repeatedly explores the nuanced ways in which individuals must fight to find and articulate their own voices. Catriona Clutterbuck investigates community life amid imperialist politics in Devlin's *After Easter* and Brian Friel's *Dancing At Lughnasa* (1990). Clutterback asserts that Devlin's Greta begins where Friel's Michael ends his role of the prophet. Devlin deliberately applies a naiveté to Greta, invoking unrealistic visions in order to demand that she reexamine her childhood. Furthermore, Greta must speak of these dreams in order to work through memories so that she can find a greater self-realization.

Devlin's specific focus on women's lives has drawn sustained interest by scholars, many of whom, like Anne Rea, find her depiction of the domestic powerful and evocative. Rea looks at the exclusion of women from the public realm, their isolation in the home, the gendering of the IRA's campaign, and its influence over the politics of gender. Devlin's men, frequently controlling and apathetic, often are more committed to the prospect of becoming martyrs than establishing a fulfilling relationship with women. Critics address men primarily in terms of women's detachment from them and their ideals. According to Rea, Devlin's work superimposes patriarchal authority with militarism in which "the home becomes the metonym for the nation" (222). Devlin recalls the Nationalist ideal of women not only as unquestioning supporters of the men they love but also as devoted even to the point of willingly placing themselves in danger.

Devlin also often explores the role of motherhood, challenging the highly symbolic role of women as mothers and caretakers when she depicts unidealized pregnancies. Ann Rea asserts that the main conflict in *Ourselves Alone* is symbolized by Josie's unborn baby, whose father is a known informer; the birth of her child threatens "racial purity." Motherhood becomes problematic and threatens Greta's very sense of self in *After Easter*. Although her plight centers on her horrific childhood, her struggle is marred by her inability to raise her children, as illness strips her from her family.

In their struggle to articulate experiences, Devlin's women frequently contend with visions, memories, and dreams. Helen Lojek claims that these reflections often haunt characters and relate to their feelings of powerlessness. Chris Wood's work looks at women's need to tell stories and examines their relationship to visions and dreams in four of her plays. Wood asserts that Devlin's work illustrates that the potential for peace in Northern Ireland is inextricably bound to the necessity for women to tell their own stories. Memories for Devlin's women are marked by absent fathers and absent mothers; however, they must be explored, articulated, and repeated in order for women to lay claim to their past, understand the present, and envision a future. According to Devlin, the future depends on understanding and cooperation as much among men and women as it does among political communities.

BIBLIOGRAPHY

Works by Anne Devlin

Publications

After Easter. London: Faber and Faber, 1994; New York: Dramatists Play Service, 1999.
Heartlanders: A Community Play to Celebrate Birmingham's Centenary. London: Hern, 1989.
    (With Stephen Bill and David Edgar.)
Ourselves Alone, with *The Long March* and *A Woman Calling.* London: Faber and Faber, 1986.
Titanic Town: Based on the Novel by Mary Costello. London: Faber and Faber, 1998.
The Way-Paver. London: Faber and Faber, 1986.

Scripts

After Easter. BBC Radio 4, June 30, 1996.
First Bite. BBC Radio 4, 1990.
Five Notes after a Visit. BBC Radio 4, 1986.
The Long March. BBC Radio 4, November 8, 1982.
The Long March. BBC One, November 20, 1984.
Naming the Names. BBC Two, February 8, 1987.
Naming the Names. BBC Radio 4, December 8, 1987.
The Rainbow. Adapted from the novel by D. H. Lawrence. BBC One, December 4, 1988. 3
    episodes.
Titanic Town. Adapted from the novel by Mary Costello, George Faber, and Charlie Pattinson.
    BBC/British Screen/Company Pictures/Arts Council of Northern Ireland Lottery Fund/
    Hollywood Partners/Pandora Cinema, 1998.
The Uncle from a Miracle. BBC Radio 4, June 28, 1991.
The Venus de Milo Instead. BBC One, September 9, 1987.
Vigo. Based on the play *Love's a Revolution,* adapted by Chris Ward from Paulo Emilio Salles
    Gomez's *Jean Vigo.* Impact Pictures/Nitrate Film, 1998. (With Peter Ettedgui and Julien
    Temple.)
A Woman Calling. BBC Two, April 18, 1984.
Wuthering Heights. Adapted from the novel by Emily Brontë. London, Paramount, 1992. Di-
    rector: Peter Kosminsky.

Studies of Anne Devlin

Anderson, Lisa M. "Anne Devlin (19?–   )". In *Irish Playwrights, 1880–1995: A Research and
    Production Sourcebook*, edited by Bernice Schrank and William Demastes, xii, 93–96.
    Westport, CT: Greenwood, 1997.
Clutterbuck, Catriona. "Lughnasa After Easter: Treatments of Narrative Imperialism in Friel and
    Devlin." *Irish University Review* 29, no. 1 (Spring–Summer 1999): 101–18.
Connolly, Clara. "*Ourselves Alone*? Clar na mBan Conference Report." *Feminist Review* 50
    (Summer 1995): 120.
Cottreau, Deborah. "Matriarchy Ascending: The Feminist Mytho-Poetics of Anne Devlin's
    After Easter." *Hungarian Journal of English and American Studies* 5, no. 1 (1999):
    199–223.
Kurdi, Maria. "Female Self-Cure Through Revisioning and Refashioning Male/Master Narra-
    tives in Anne Devlin's *After Easter.*" *Hungarian Journal of English and American Stud-
    ies* 2, no. 2 (1996): 97–110.
Lojek, Helen. "Difference without Indifference: The Drama of Frank McGuinness and Anne De-
    vlin." *Eire-Ireland* 25, no. 2 (Summer 1990): 56–68.
MacGurk, Brendan. "Commitment and Risk in Anne Devlin's *Ourselves Alone* and *After Easter.*"
    In *The State of the Play: Irish Theater in the "Nineties,"* edited by Eberhard Bort, 51–
    61. Trier: Wissenschaftlicher Verlag, 1996.
Rea, Ann. "Reproducing the Nation: Nationalism, Reproduction, and Paternalism in Anne De-
    vlin's *Ourselves Alone.*" In *Border Crossings: Irish Women Writers and National Identi-
    ties*, edited by Kathryn Kirkpatrick, 204–26. Tuscaloosa: University of Alabama Press,
    2000.
Sullivan, Esther-Beth. "What Is 'Left to a Woman of the House' When the Irish Situation Is
    Staged?" In *Staging Resistance: Essays on Political Theater*, edited by Jeanne
    Colleran and Jenny Spencer, viii, 213–26. Ann Arbor: University of Michigan Press,
    1998.
Sullivan, Megan. " 'I'll Not Swear One Word Against You; It's Not for You I Did It': Anne De-
    vlin and Irish Cinema." *Canadian Journal of Irish Studies* 25, nos. 1–2 (July–December
    1999): 277–90.

Wood, Chris. "'My Own Story': Woman's Place, Divided Loyalty, and Patriarchal Hegemony in the Plays of Anne Devlin." *Canadian Journal of Irish Studies* 25, nos. 1–2 (July–December 1999): 291–308.

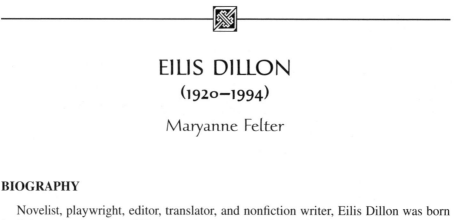

EILIS DILLON
(1920–1994)

Maryanne Felter

BIOGRAPHY

Novelist, playwright, editor, translator, and nonfiction writer, Eilis Dillon was born in Galway, the daughter of Thomas Dillon, a university professor, and Geraldine (Plunkett) Dillon, sister of 1916 hero Joseph Maria Plunkett. Educated in a convent school in Sligo, Dillon first planned to study music with the goal of being a professional cellist. But having composed her first story at the age of seven, Dillon says she "never remember[ed] a time when [she] did not want to write" (*Something About The Author*, 74:67). As a professional writer, Dillon lectured on creative writing at Trinity College Dublin (1971–72) and University College Dublin (1988) as well as in various American colleges. In the 1960s, when her first husband, Cormac O'Cuilleanain, a university professor, took ill, the couple retired to Rome, where O'Cuilleanain died in 1970. In 1974, Dillon married Vivian Mercier; they wintered in California, where Mercier was a professor, and spent their springs and summers in Ireland until Mercier's retirement in 1987. Dillon suffered Mercier's death in 1989 and her daughter's death in 1990, but she continued to write until her own death on July 19, 1994. Although most are currently out of print, Dillon wrote more than fifty books, won a number of literary awards, and was celebrated with an honorary doctorate from University College Cork in 1992.

MAJOR WORKS AND THEMES

Dillon's first novel, *An Choill bheo,* was published in 1948. Her work since then has been in both English and Irish and has spanned genres and aimed at different age groups. Dillon's adolescent books are quite fresh and exciting even though some were written almost thirty years ago. Adventure stories full of daring feats and improbable plots, the stories are action-packed, the life-and-death plots centering around romantic, fantastical situations. Dillon writes of potential shipwreck (*The Cruise of the Santa Maria,* 1967), cattle stampedes (*The Singing Cave,* 1959), and treasure hunting (*The Fort of Gold,* 1961) among other things. Dillon sets many of her books on the west coast of Ireland and its islands, evoking mystery, folklore, and local legends in domestic scenes of Irish-speaking peasants in thatched cottages. Dillon maintains suspense as her young heroes defy all odds and adult prohibitions. She makes her children heroes and problem solvers with strength of character and great fortitude. But some-times when Dillon sets her historical fiction for children outside Ireland, her books lack life and vigor. *The Shadow of Vesuvius* (1978) and *Living in Imperial Rome* (1974) are flat and schoolbookish. Even *Children of Bach* (1992), which is suspenseful, lacks the grip of her Irish books. But given her output in children's fiction (thirty-five books), the quality of these books, in general, is impressive.

Dillon's adult fiction is not always as successful. She turned to mystery writing to focus on strengthening her plots, but her mystery *Death at Crane's Court* (1963) lacks the typical suspense and horror of the genre; *Sent to His Account* (1969) and *Death in the Quadrangle* (1956) are somewhat better. *The Bitter Glass* (1959) is the first in a series of historical novels to use Irish political events as the center of romantic love stories. In this novel, an Irish-Catholic member of the gentry is set against the strug-gles between nationalists and the Black and Tans. The book was highly acclaimed in England and America, though too close to the events for Irish readers. *Blood Relations* (1977) is a rambling, episodic historical romance set against the background of the Easter Rebellion. Her earlier novel *Across the Bitter Sea* (1973) was a more success-ful blend of love story and historical novel, and became a blockbuster that also received critical praise. Here, the daughter of the tallywoman of a local, wealthy, Protestant land-lord marries the son of that landlord and is torn between her affection for her husband and her romantic passion for Morgan, a patriot during the rebellion. Other novels, *The Head of the Family* (1960), *Bold John Henebry* (1965), *Wild Geese* (1980), *Citizen Burke* (1984), and *The Interloper* (1987) also explore historical and nationalist themes.

Dillon has also written plays and nonfiction as well as some translations. She edited Vivian Mercier's incomplete *Modern Irish Literature* (1994) after his death, admirably organizing his extensive drafts and notes. *Inside Ireland* (1982) chronicles Dillon's fam-ily history as representative of Irish history in general.

CRITICAL RECEPTION

From the start, reviews of Dillon's children's fiction were excellent. Most review-ers recommend the children's books highly, using such terms as "suspenseful," "fast-paced," "lively," "remarkable," and "superb storytelling." Early on, the *Cleveland Open Shelf*, for instance, said that the *Lost Island* (1952) "holds the reader enthralled to its conclusion." the *New Statesman* noted of *San Sebastian* (1953) that it "provide[s] the kind of action and suspense younger teenagers enjoy." Of *The House on the Shore* (1955), Pamela Whitlock of the *New York Times* wrote, "There are several authors pro-ducing good, well-worked-out adventure stories today. Eilis Dillon should be noticed for being, imaginatively, a jump ahead of the rest of them." Suzanne Rahn, in the only major critical article published to date on Dillon, argues that the well-crafted children's novels appeal to both Irish and American children. Her detective stories were also praised. Maurice Richardson in the *Observer* called *Death at Crane's Court* (1953) a "cosy, chatty, Irish whodunit," and said that *Sent to His Account* (1969) had a "good surprise finish." The historical novels received mixed reviews though the later ones were on the best-seller lists. Of *The Bitter Glass* (1958) Elizabeth Cade, in the *Philadelphia Enquirer*, complains that "a kind of static feeling seems to shackle the whole narrative despite the author's talent for realistic writing." Eudora Welty, on the other hand, according to a current Web site, called *The Bitter Glass* an "excellent piece of work . . . full of reality, full of poetry." Most of the reviews of *The Head of the Fam-ily* (1960) and *Bold John Henebry* (1965) stress Dillon's understanding of human nature and her ability, as the *Sunday Times* reports, to evoke her characters "with precision and great tenderness." Roger Garfitt, in the *Listener*, praised the early chapters of *Across the Bitter Sea* (1973) as "hav[ing] an authentic documentary power," but complained that as the story of the family moves into the "second and third generations, the whole structure begins irresistibly, and incongruously, to suggest a Fenian Forsyte Saga. The Easter Rising becomes rather like a Sports Gala, with Morgan's grand-nieces running messages round every corner, and his grandson doing well in the Sniping Event. When a national legend begins to put on weight in this way, it is perhaps a sign that it is finally slipping into past history." But the *Sunday Times* called it "a quite remarkable novel . . . one of the most compelling and convincing love stories. . . . a novel of which Zola might have been proud." the *Catholic Herald* called *Citizen Burke* (1984) "a first class historical novel." And Declan Kiberd wrote in the *Irish Times* that "all other books were researched with scholarly scruple and written with a tremendous attention to exactitude of language. Of none was this more true than *Citizen Burke*; many will concur with her late husband, the critic Vivian Mercier, in judging it her finest achievement. . . . [It] is a work of imaginative reconstruction, but one in which the pressure of felt experience is registered on every page." Although some reviewers criticized her historical fiction for being sentimental, most agree that it is powerfully felt and imaginatively realized. For one as prolific as Eilis Dillon, the positive reviews outnumber the negative, and, particularly concerning her children's books, she has been and continues to be an underrated Irish author.

BIBLIOGRAPHY

Works by Eilis Dillon

Children's Books

Aunt Bedelia's Cats. London: Hamish Hamilton, 1957.
The Cats' Opera. London: Faber and Faber, 1962.
Children of Bach. New York: Macmillan, 1992.
The Coriander. London: Faber and Faber, 1963.
The Cruise of the Santa Maria. New York: Funk and Wagnalls, 1967.
Down in the World. London: Hodder and Stoughton, 1983.
A Family of Foxes. London: Faber and Faber, 1963.
The Five Hundred. London: Hamish Hamilton, 1972.
The Fort of Gold. London: Faber and Faber, 1962.
A Herd of Deer. London: Faber and Faber, 1969.
The Horse Fancier. Basingstoke: Macmillan Education, 1985.
The House on the Shore. London: Faber and Faber, 1955.
The Island of Ghosts. New York: Macmillan, 1989.
The Island of Horses. London: Faber and Faber, 1956.
The Key. London: Faber and Faber, 1967.
King Big-Ears. London: Faber and Faber, 1961.
The King's Room. London: Hamish Hamilton, 1970.
The Lion Cub. Dublin: Poolbeg, 1966.
The Little Wild House. London: Faber and Faber, 1955.
Living in Imperial Rome. London: Faber and Faber, 1974.
The Lost Island. London: Faber and Faber, 1952.
Midsummer Magic. New York: Macmillan, 1949.
Plover Hill. London: Hamish Hamilton, 1957.
Pony and a Trap. London: Hamish Hamilton, 1962.

The Road to Dunmore. London: Faber and Faber, 1966.
The San Sebastian. London: Faber and Faber, 1953.
The Seals. London: Faber and Faber, 1968.
The Sea Wall. New York: Farrar Strauss, 1965.
The Seekers. New York: Scribner, 1986.
The Shadow of Vesuvius. New York: Thomas Nelson, 1978.
The Singing Cave. London: Faber and Faber, 1959.
Under the Orange Grove. London: Faber and Faber, 1968.
The Voyage of Mael Duin. London: Faber and Faber, 1969.
The Wise Man on the Mountain. London: Hamish Hamilton, 1969.

Adult Fiction

Across the Bitter Sea. New York: Simon and Schuster, 1973.
The Bitter Glass. London: Faber and Faber, 1958.
Blood Relations. New York: Simon and Schuster, 1977.
Bold John Henebry. London: Faber and Faber, 1965.
Citizen Burke. London: Hodder and Stoughton, 1984.
Death at Crane's Court. London: Faber and Faber, 1953.
Death in the Quadrangle. London: Faber and Faber, 1956.
The Head of the Family. London: Faber and Faber, 1960.
The Interloper. London: Hodder and Stoughton, 1987.
Sent to His Account. London: Faber and Faber, 1954.
Wild Geese. New York: Simon and Schuster, 1980.

Plays

The Cat's Opera. Performed at Abbey Theatre, Dublin, 1981.
Manna. Performed on Radio Éireann, Dublin, 1962.
A Page of History. Performed at Abbey Theatre, Dublin, 1966.

Irish Works

Ceol na Coille (The Song of the Forest). Dublin: Oifig an tSolathair, 1955.
An Choill bheo (The Living Forest). Dublin: Oifig an tSolathair, 1948.
Oscar agus an Coiste se nEasog (Oscar and the Six-Weasel Coach). Dublin: Oifig an tSolathair, 1952.

Other

The Hamish Hamilton Book of Wise Animals. London: Hamish Hamilton, 1973. (Editor.)
Inside Ireland. London: Hodder and Stoughton, 1982.
The Lucky Bag: Classic Irish Children's Stories. Dublin: O'Brien, 1985. (Editor, with Pat Donlon, Patricia Egan, and Peter Fallon.)
Modern Irish Literature, by Vivian Mercier. Oxford: Clarendon, 1994. (Editor.)

Translations

The Lament of Arthur O'Leary (from the eighteenth-century Irish of Eibhlin Ni Chonaill). *Irish University Review* 1, no. 2 (Spring 1971): 198–210.

Studies of Eilis Dillon

"Dillon, Eilis." In *Contemporary Authors: Autobiography Series.* Vol. 3, edited by Adele Sarkissian. Detroit: Gale, 1986.
"Dillon, Eilis." In *Major Authors and Illustrators for Children and Young Adults*, edited by Laurie Collier. Detroit: Gale, 1993.

"Dillon, Eilis." In *Something About the Author*. Vol. 74, edited by Diane Telger. Detroit: Gale, 1993.

"Dillon, Eilis." In *Something About the Author*. Vol. 83, edited by Alan Hedblad. Detroit: Gale, 1996.

"Dillon, Eilis." In *Something about the Author*. Vol. 105, edited by Alan Hedblad. Detroit: Gale, 1999.

Felter, Maryanne. "Eilis Dillon." In *Dictionary of Irish Literature*, edited by Robert Hogan. Westport, CT: Greenwood, 1996.

Rahn, Suzanne. " 'Inishrone Is Our Island': Rediscovering the Irish Novels of Eilis Dillon." *Lion and the Unicorn* 21, no. 3 (1997): 347–68.

EMMA DONOGHUE
(1969–)

Maureen E. Mulvihill

BIOGRAPHY

Dublin-born novelist, anthologist, short-story writer, playwright, and literary historian, Emma Donoghue was born on October 24, 1969 into a large, educated Irish-Catholic family. By virtue of her upbringing and training, she was destined for a literary career. Donoghue benefited from a stimulating childhood as the youngest in a family of eight children, but she benefited in greater measure from the inspiration of two literary parents: Frances Donoghue née Rutledge, a secondary-level English teacher, and Denis Donoghue, literary critic and professor, University College Dublin (1966–79), and thereafter Henry James Professor of Letters, New York University.

Following her early training at Catholic convent schools in Dublin, Emma Donoghue was educated at University College Dublin, where in 1990 she earned a first-class honors BA in English and French. In 1997, she earned a PhD in English from Cambridge University, with a thesis on friendship between men and women in eighteenth-century English fiction. In 1993, Donoghue launched her career as a writer with the publication of *Passions Between Women: British Lesbian Culture, 1668–1801*. The publication of Donoghue's writings is presently managed by the Caroline Davidson Literary Agency, London, and, in the United States, Anderson/Grinberg Literary Management, New York City. Donoghue's chief interest in 2003 was maternity. According to the Emma Donoghue Web site, Donoghue's latest production, of November 15, 2003, in "collaboration with her lover," Christine (Chris) Roulston, a professor of French at the University of Western Ontario, is a baby son, Finn ("News" link, "Special Event" heading, 2004, http://www.emmadonoghue.com/news.htm).

In addition to her prolific writing schedule, Donoghue has taught creative writing for the Cheltenham Literary Festival, the Arvon Foundation, the University of Western Ontario, and the University of York. She also has been a judge for the *Irish Times* Literature Prizes, and she has been a presenter of a prime-time literary series on Irish television. A shareholder of the National Theatre of Ireland, Donoghue is also a member of the Society of Authors, the Writer's Union of Canada, and the Playwright's Union of Canada.

Donoghue is an interesting case of intersecting national identities. By birth and rearing, she considers herself an Irish writer, though she has been an official resident of Ontario, Canada, since 1998; on her Web site she admits that her literary muse is not Irish, but English: "I'm writing in the tradition of Jane Austen, for whose novel *Emma* I am named . . . [but] I would never have let anyone call me 'British' " (see "Frequently Asked Questions" link, "The Writer" section, 2004, http://www.emmadonoghue.com/FAQ.htm). Her "enduring obsession with the eighteenth century" began in graduate school in England (see "Frequently Asked Questions" link, "The Writer" section, 2004, http://www.emmadonoghue.com/FAQ.htm). Donoghue speaks candidly of her rich and productive mix of national allegiances in several interviews, published in *Conversations with Irish Women Writers*, by Helen Thompson and Caitriona Moloney (Syracuse University Press, 2002); *Irish Studies Review* 8, no. 1 (2000); *Sunday Independent* (Ireland) (September 14, 1997); *Sunday Times* (March 26, 1995); and the *Irish Times* (April 14, 1993). Donoghue's autobiographical articles appeared in *Women's News* (Belfast), November 1997; and an ongoing account of her credits and activities is duly recorded in painstaking detail on the Emma Donoghue Web site at http://www.emmadonoghue.com.

MAJOR WORKS AND THEMES

Though she is often judged narrowly as a popular lesbian writer, Donoghue's best work is inspired by her knowledge of the history and literature of seventeenth- and eighteenth-century Ireland and England. Surrealism, fantasy, and humor are also engaging features in her work, primarily in her short stories and reconstructed folk (or fairy) tales.

Passions between Women, Donoghue's début title, pointed the way for her PhD thesis at Cambridge University in 1997 and, more important, her eventual focus on lesbian material. This award-winning historical monograph is a serious survey of same-sex relationships between British women, 1668–1803, and one of the first interrogations of early-modern British lesbian culture. *Stir-Fry* (1994) is an autobiographically inspired coming-of-age novel set in the 1980s and early 1990s that captures the ethos of campus life in south Dublin. *Hood* (1995), which also draws on Donoghue's personal experience, is a poignant chronicle of lesbian Irish identity. Its folktale framing has been praised by commentators as an especially effective narrative technique. *Kissing the Witch* (1997) is a diverting collection of "lesbian revisionist" fairy tales (*Dictionary of Literary Biography vol.* 267, 71), all structurally interlinked and reconstructed through the eyes of a modern (lesbian) woman. In this volume, Donoghue exploits selected themes in the canon of European folk literature, particularly the nineteenth-century tales of the brothers Grimm. *We Are Michael Field* (1998), a spectacular biographical account of the twenty-five-year lesbian relationship of Edith Cooper and Katherine Bradley, two lesbian Victorian writers who published collaboratively (thirty plays, eleven volumes of poetry) under the single pseudonym of Michael Field, is one of Donoghue's best-sellers. It also is the first critical study of the couple's hefty corpus of unpublished journals and letters. *Slammerkin* (2000), arguably Donoghue's most commercially successful book, is a reliably researched historical novel on the louche society of a late-eighteenth-century London seamstress and former prostitute, one Mary

Saunders, who murdered her Welsh employer with a meat cleaver. The narrative is especially riveting in its reconstruction of Saunders's historically documented capture, arrest, and public hanging. *The Woman Who Gave Birth to Rabbits* (2002), Donoghue's first successful collection of short stories, features a memorable narrative about one Mary Toft, who in 1726 devised the amusing and rather successful hoax of being able to produce not babies but rabbits. In 2004, *Life Mask* was added to Donoghue's ambitious repertoire; this novel, according to the author's extensive Web site, "is about a love triangle in 1790s London, among the élite who moved through the overlapping worlds of art, politics, sport, and theatre." She also is one of several authors in the collaborative novel *Like a Charm: A Novel in Voices* (2004), a crime novel whose unsolved mysteries are ingeniously linked to a charm bracelet; Donoghue's contribution, "Veritas," concerns a girl in 1830s Louisiana, who probes her cousin's mysterious death.

Donoghue's work as a dramatist and writer of radio plays often draws on her publications in historical fiction and other writings. She also has edited two collections of lesbian literature, *What Sappho Would Have Said* (published in the United States as *Poems Between Women: Four Centuries of Love, Romantic Friendship, and Desire*, 1997) and *The Mammoth Book of Lesbian Short Stories* (1999).

Donoghue's work in progress, according to her Web site, includes a contemporary novel about emigration, set in Ireland and Canada; a book of short stories inspired by biblical narratives; a short-story collection on social taboos; a play on an early Canadian vigilante killing; and a study of lesbian narrative motifs in English literature.

CRITICAL RECEPTION

Within a few years on the literary market, Donoghue was judged a broadly talented writer of her generation. As finely documented on her Web site (http://www.emmadonoghue.com/bio.htm; see "What the Critics Say" link), the *Irish Times* judged her a "writer of great skill, wit and intelligence" (1996); the *Seattle Times* wrote, "Every now and again, a writer comes along with a fully loaded brain and a nature so fanciful that she simply must spin out truly original and transporting stuff . . . [an] eccentric, untethered genius" (2002); and the *Washington Post* wrote, "A loving chronicler of the physical world, especially the lost physical world of the past; and a sensitive compass in the arena of moral and emotional dilemma" (2002). Her awards include finalist, 2002 Stonewall Award, for *The Woman Who Gave Birth to Rabbits*; 2002 Ferro-Grumley Award for Lesbian Fiction, for *Slammerkin*; finalist, 2001 *Irish Times* Fiction Prize, for *Slammerkin*; finalist, 1997 James L. Tiptree Award, for *Kissing the Witch*; recipient, 1997 American Library Association's Gay, Lesbian and Bisexual Book Award, for *Hood*; and three-time finalist, Lambda Awards, for *Passions between Women, Stir-Fry*, and *Poems between Women*. To date, Donoghue's writings have been translated into Catalan, Dutch, German, Hebrew, Spanish, and Swedish.

BIBLIOGRAPHY

Works by Emma Donoghue

Books

Hood. London: Hamilton, 1995; New York: HarperCollins, 1996.

Kissing the Witch. London: Hamilton, 1997. Republished as *Kissing the Witch: Old Tales in New Skins.* New York: HarperCollins, 1997.

Ladies and Gentlemen. Dublin: New Island, 1998.

Ladies' Night at Finbar's Hotel, edited by Dermot Bolger. London: Picador, 1999. Dublin: New Island, 1999. San Diego, CA: Harcourt Brace, 2000. (A collaborative novel, of several unsigned chapters by Maeve Binchy, Dermot Bolger, Clare Boylan, Emma Donoghue, Anne Haverty, Yilis N' Dhuibhne, Kate O'Riordan, and Deirdre Purcell.)

Life Mask. London: Virago (Time Warner), 2004; New York: Harcourt, Brace, 2004.

The Mammoth Book of Lesbian Short Stories. London: Robinson, 1999; New York: Carroll and Graf, 1999. (Editor.)

Passions between Women: British Lesbian Culture, 1668–1801. London: Scarlet, 1993; New York: HarperCollins, 1995.

Slammerkin. London: Virago, 2000. New York: Harcourt Brace, 2001.

Stir-Fry. London: Hamilton, 1994. New York: HarperCollins, 1994.

"Veritas," in the collaborative novel *Like a Charm: A Novel in Voices.* London: Morrow, 2004.

We Are Michael Field. Bath, UK: Absolute, 1998.

What Sappho Would Have Said: Four Centuries of Love Poems between Women. London: Hamilton, 1997. Republished as *Poems between Women: Four Generations of Love, Romantic Friendship, and Desire.* New York: Columbia University Press, 1997. (Editor.)

The Woman Who Gave Birth to Rabbits. New York: Harcourt, Brace, 2002. London: Virago, 2002.

Produced Plays

I Know My Own Heart. Dublin: Glasshouse Productions, March 1993.

Kissing the Witch. San Francisco, CA: Magic Theatre, June 9, 2000.

Ladies and Gentlemen. Dublin: Glasshouse Productions, April 18, 1996; Minneapolis: Outward Spiral Theatre, April 14, 2000.

Radio and Film Scripts

Daddy's Girl. BBC Radio 4, 2000.

Don't Die Wondering. BBC Radio 4, 2000.

Error Messages. RTÉ, 1999.

Exes. BBC Radio 4, 2001.

Expecting. BBC Radio 4, 1996.

Figures of Speech. BBC Radio 4, 2000.

Humans and Other Animals. BBC Radio 4, 2003.

The Lost Seed. BBC Radio 4, 2000.

Mix. BBC Radio 3, 2003.

Night Vision. BBC Radio 4, 2000.

Pluck. Film script. Zanzibar Productions, 2001.

A Short Story. BBC Radio 4, 2000.

Trespasses. RTÉ, 1996.

Selected Studies of Emma Donoghue

Bensyl, Stacia L. "Emma Donoghue." *Dictionary of Literary Biography* 267, 68–74. Detroit: Gale, 2002. With author photo and other images.

Quinn, Antoinette. "New Noises from the Woodshed: The Novels of Emma Donoghue." In *Contemporary Irish Fiction: Themes, Tropes, Theories,* edited by Liam Harte and Michael Parker, 145–67. New York: St. Martin's, 2000.

Smyth, Gerry. *The Novel and the Nation: Studies in the New Irish Fiction.* London: Pluto, 1997.

Van Marle, Tonie. "Emma Donoghue." In *Gay and Lesbian Literature.* Vol. 2, edited by Tom Pendergast and Sara Pendergast, 123–24. Detroit: St. James, 1998.

Wingfield, Rachel. "Lesbian Writers in the Mainstream: Sarah Maitland, Jeanette Winterson, and Emma Donoghue." In *Beyond Sex and Romance: The Politics of Contemporary Lesbian Fiction*, edited by Elaine Hutton, 60–80. London: Women's Press, 1998.

MARY DORCEY
(1950–   )

John J. Han

BIOGRAPHY

Poet, fiction writer, and lesbian feminist, Mary Dorcey was born in County Dublin, where she was raised and educated. Dorcey attended the Open University in Great Britain as its first Irish student, and the University of Paris. In 1972 she joined the Irish Women's Liberation Movement; she has also served as a founding member of Women for Radical Change, of Irish Women United, and of the Irish Gay Rights movement. Dorcey currently lectures at the Centre for Gender and Women's Studies at Trinity College Dublin, where she also serves as Research Associate. Her research interests include "sexual orientation and romantic vision in the writing of contemporary British and American women" (Web site). Dorcey has lived in the United States, England, France, Spain, and Japan, and currently resides in County Wicklow.

In 1982, Dorcey published her first collection of poetry celebrating lesbian love, *Kindling*. In 1990, she won the Rooney Prize for Irish Literature for the critically acclaimed *A Noise from the Woodshed: Short Stories* (1989), a compilation of highly sensuous stories wherein the author continues her exploration of lesbian sexuality. Dorcey's exploration of lesbian themes continued in the next two collections of verse, *Moving into the Space Cleared by Our Mothers* (1991) and *The River That Carries Me* (1995). The September of 1997 saw the publication of her best-selling novel, *Biography of Desire*, in which the author deals with the complexity of bisexuality. Her most recent published book-length work is *Like Joy in Season, Like Sorrow* (2001), primarily focused on women's aging and approach to eventual mortality. Dorcey has completed writing her second novel, *Death and Family Affairs*, and is awaiting its publication.

Dorcey's poems, stories, and novel in progress have been anthologized in numerous books, including *Mad and Bad Fairies: A Collection of Feminist Fairytales* (1989), *Beautiful Barbarians: Lesbian Feminist Poetry* (1991), *Virgins and Hyacinths: The Attic Book of Fiction* (1993), *New Writing from Ireland* (1994), and *Wee Girls: Women Writing from an Irish Perspective* (1996). Her poems have been performed on stage, radio, and television. *In the Pink* and *Sunny Side Plucked*—the two dramatizations of Dorcey's poetry—toured Ireland, England, Europe, and Australia. Her lesbian poetry and fiction are being studied internationally, especially in university courses on gender and sexuality in contemporary Irish writing; her works have also been translated into Italian, Spanish, Dutch, and Japanese. Dorcey was awarded three Arts Council bursaries for literature, in 1990, 1995, and 1999. She has delivered many keynote speeches and has read her works at conferences and art festivals nationally and internationally.

MAJOR WORKS AND THEMES

Dorcey's poetry and fiction deal mostly with erotic lesbian sexuality, the suffering of women, the solidarity of women, and aging and death as related to women. She celebrates lesbian relationships in many of her fictional works. "A Noise from the Woodshed," for example, is a study of bisexuality focused on the romantic relationship between two women. Another story, "The Husband," is about a woman who refuses to renounce her newly found lesbian desire and is written from the perspective of the man who still loves her. In *Biography of Desire*, Dorcey uses three main characters—the American Katherine, her Irish husband, Malachy, and the Irish lesbian Nina—to examine how bisexual desire is transformed into lesbian desire. Katherine, who has two children by Malachy, falls in love with Nina, who has engaged in a seven-year relationship with Elinor. Katherine is eventually deserted by Nina, and Malachy urges her to come back to him. Katherine, however, refuses her husband's plea after she realizes that, as a lesbian, she has crossed the river of no return: "I can't fit any of what's happened to me in the last months into your words. Into the words I had for my life before this happened. But I'm not the woman I was when this life was right for me. And I can't fit back again. I've been changed forever. It's not just about love or happiness. It's about a way of being in the world, a vision, a sense of communication and sharing" (270).

"I Cannot Love You as You Want to Be Loved" is one of many poems in *The River That Carries Me* that celebrate erotic lesbian sexuality. Elements of sensuality pervade the work, as when the speaker declares that she cannot love her lover without loving her thighs, "[w]ithout wanting to run [her] hand along the length of them" (4). In "A Leather Jacket," the speaker recalls how the sleeves of a leather jacket created "a steady, soft moan" (32) when her arms tightened about her lover. "Walking on Air" deals with the power of lesbian desire. The speaker recalls how she was encouraged by her lover to gather herself and cross over to her world; after a moment's hesitation, she closed her eyes, disregarded the chasm and the "raging torrent," and "stepped into her bare arms" (30).

Some poems express the pain of separation from a partner. In "Crocus," for example, a six-line work recalling an East Asian lyric poem, the speaker reveals how the full-bloomed crocuses they planted together last fall accentuate her lover's absence. "Tell Me How You Carry It Off" is a plea for the estranged lover to teach her how she can live without the presence of the other. In "The Train," the speaker remembers the lover's hands drawing back from hers; she wonders why there are so many partings in this world.

Some of Dorcey's poems graphically portray the sufferings women undergo and their need for solidarity. "A Woman in Another War" depicts the brutalities committed against women in a war-torn country. Soldiers rape women repeatedly. A newborn baby cries while its mother is being raped; when the mother begs the rapist to allow her to feed the baby, he picks up the baby, slits its throat, and hands the severed head back to her. In "Reading the Newspaper," the poet lists all the things that she and her partner were doing in a safe country on the day when women were being raped and their children were being killed in foreign wars. In "The Breath of History," the poet appreciates the extraordinary safety of her daily existence, but history reminds her that there is no guarantee of continued safety.

Dorcey's *Like Joy in Season, Like Sorrow* includes poems about aging, dying, and death—the ultimate issues that face every human being. In "Uncharted Passage," the speaker compares her mother to the "flagship" and to the "masthead" that has guided her life (3). The mother's death reminds her offspring of the cycle of birth, aging, and death that strikes every human being. In "Sweet Melancholy," the adult female speaker remembers the elegies her mother used to sing; she values all the sacrifices that her mother made for the next generation. Finally, the daughter in "Time Has Made a Mirror" eulogizes her deceased mother, whose fond memories she is compelled not to lose.

CRITICAL RECEPTION

Dorcey is considered one of the best short-story writers in contemporary Ireland, alongside writers such as Maeve Binchy, Éilís Ní Dhuibhne, Anne Enright, and Ivy Bannister. Critics also view her as a forerunner of the lesbian and gay rights movement and of lesbian writing in modern Ireland. In the introduction to *Wildish Things: An Anthology of New Irish Women's Writing* (1989), Ailbhe Smyth comments that Mary Dorcey's writing of lesbian sexuality is "a rare voice from a deeply hidden pool" (10). In the foreword to the book *Alternative Loves* (1994), Smyth also recognizes the remarkable contributions Dorcey has made to the cause of Irish gay and lesbian literature: "[T]here is now a space which Irish lesbian and gay writers can inhabit with some dignity, if not yet absolute ease" (vi). According to Christina Hunt Mahony, lesbian fiction of the fellow Irish writer Emma Donoghue "would not in a sense have been possible without the pioneering work of Mary Dorcey, whose *A Noise from the Woodshed* is a seminal collection of this genre" (24). Ann Owens Weekes has examined Mary Dorcey as a crucial leader of lesbian politics and literature in the late twentieth century: Kate O'Brien, author of the pioneering lesbian novel *Music and Splendour* (1958), had "a worthy successor" in Dorcey; *A Noise from the Woodshed* broke the thirty-year drought in lesbian writing in Ireland (146). Jessie Lendennie also praises Dorcey as "one of Ireland's most exciting poets" (Web site).

In her review of *The River That Carries Me*, Patricia Monaghan points out that readers need to do more than locate the poet in the context of contemporary lesbian poetry. Indeed, Dorcey's poetry "is informed by the struggle to articulate lesbian sexuality, but it is her style that ravishes." Dorcey writes in English and her language has the "starkness and sensuality" of her fellow Irish authors who write in English. Specifically, Dorcey's "meandering repetitions give a liturgical flavor to her love poems (and most of these poems, even when about loss, are love poems) that is appropriate to Dorcey's pagan sense of the sacramentality of sex" (37). Paula R. Pratt has demonstrated how Dorcey's *Biography of Desire* illuminates bisexual identity, which has been considered as deviant from both homosexuality and heterosexuality: the novel reflects a kind of "hybridity" in the author's own identity—"the rather fluid movement from bisexuality to lesbian identity." According to Pratt, Dorcey's novel is significant in two ways: first, it has "[reshaped] contemporary Irish literature"; second and more important, it has "[made] a contribution to the shaping of the perceptions and understanding of bisexuality in all its richness and humanity" (Web site).

Although Dorcey is internationally known for her lesbian activism and writing, her works are rarely reviewed by scholarly journals. She has also been virtually ignored by such popular periodicals as the *Times Literary Supplement*, *New York Times*, and

Washington Post, among others. Few reference books on contemporary Irish writing cover Dorcey. As a lesbian activist and writer, her fame is firmly established, but it will take more time before her literary works are fully accepted by mainstream critics.

BIBLIOGRAPHY

Works by Mary Dorcey

Poetry

Kindling. London: Onlywomen, 1982.
Like Joy in Season, Like Sorrow. Cliffs of Moher, Ire.: Salmon, 2001.
Moving into the Space Cleared by Our Mothers. Galway, Ire.: Salmon, 1991.
The River That Carries Me. Galway, Ire.: Salmon, 1995.

Fiction

Biography of Desire. Dublin: Poolbeg, 1997.
A Noise from the Woodshed: Short Stories. London: Onlywomen, 1989.

Studies of Mary Dorcey

Lendennie, Jessie. "Salmon Poetry." Accessed March 22, 2004. http://www.thedrunkenboat.com/salmon.htm.
Mahony, Christina Hunt. Introduction. In *Contemporary Irish Literature: Transforming Tradition.* New York: St. Martin's, 1998, 1–25.
Monaghan, Patricia. "A Pride of Gay Books: Nonfiction." Review of *The River That Carries Me. Booklist,* June 1–15, 1996, 37.
Pratt, Paula R. "Bisexuality, Queer Theory and Mary Dorcey's *Biography of Desire*: An Outlaw Reading." Accessed May 31, 2001 and March 22, 2004. http://www.thecore.nus.edu/landow/post/poldiscourse/casablanca/pratt2.html.
Quinn, Antoinette. "Speaking of the Unspoken: The Poetry of Mary Dorcey." *Colby Quarterly* 28, no. 4 (December 1992): 227–38.
Smyth, Ailbhe. Foreword. In *Alternative Loves*, edited by David Marcus, v–vii. Dublin: Martello, 1994.
———, ed. Introduction. In *Wildish Things: An Anthology of New Irish Women's Writing.* Dublin: Attic, 1989, 7–16.
"Trinity College, Dublin: Centre for Gender and Women's Studies." Accessed October 9, 2003. March 22, 2004. http://www.tcd.ie/Womens_Studies/cfws_staff.html.
Weekes, Ann Owens. "A Trackless Road: Irish Nationalisms and Lesbian Writing." In *Border Crossings: Irish Women Writers and National Identities*, edited by Kathryn Kirkpatrick, 123–56. Tuscaloosa: University of Alabama Press, 2000.

ELLEN MARY PATRICK DOWNING
(1828–1869)

Katherine Parr

BIOGRAPHY

The poet known as "Mary of the Nation" was born Ellen Mary Patrick Downing to Julia Eliza Barry and John Barry Downing in the parish of St. Mary Shandon, Cork City. John Barry was the resident medical officer at the Cork Fever Hospital, where Julia also served as matron. Ellen, known affectionately as Ellie, was a sickly child, afflicted by an unnamed and debilitating neural condition that included extreme sensitivity to noise and light. She spent her childhood as an invalid, nursed by her mother and treated by her father. During her convalescence, she read the classics, including Homer and Virgil, as well as the poets Gerald Griffin, Thomas Moore, and Lord Byron. She is reputed to have put to memory extensive passages of poetry long before she could read. Downing began writing her own verses as a young girl, and at age sixteen saw her first poem published in "Answers to Correspondents," the *Nation,* May 10, 1845. She signed that poem under the pseudonym "Kate" but submitted her next using her initials, E.M.P.D. That year she saw four more poems published in that journal, including "A Farewell to Elia," which addressed the essayist Charles Lamb. In April of 1846, however, she chose the signature "Mary" for a poem about the river Lee, which runs through her native Cork, and the young poet soon became recognized as "Mary of the Nation." She continued to use that signature until 1850, when she entered the convent of the Presentation Sisters, in Cork, and took the name Sister Alphonsus Liguori.

Over the course of her affiliation with the *Nation,* 1845–1848, Ellen Downing contributed forty-one poems. In February of 1848, however, she broke with the editor and her mentor, Charles Gavan Duffy, to follow the more radical John Mitchel to the *United Irishman.* The rift between editors came about because of Duffy's conservative political stance with regard to the leadership of the Irish Confederation. The famine and the reported abuses of rents charged by English estate holders caused Mitchel to opine that the colonial government was engaged in a deliberate plan to rid Ireland of its peasant population; Mitchel went so far as to call famine policies genocide. "Mary" agonized over the rift with Duffy, yet her sympathies compelled her agreement with Mitchel, so on February 26, the *Nation* ran the last of her contributions. On the eve of St. Valentine's Day, Mitchel had welcomed "Mary" with a preface to her poem "To-Day," calling it "a simple little Valentine" (Markham, 10). "Mary" contributed six more poems to the *United Irishman* before Mitchel's newspaper was suppressed by the government and Mitchel himself was tried and deported. An essay written by Downing, "To the Women of Ireland," remains the centerpiece of her anticolonial ideology. It is a revolutionary call for armed rebellion and for the participation of women in the revolt.

In the fall of 1848, a rebellion against the government was quashed, and "Mary," one of its most vocal advocates, succumbed to her childhood illness, falling into a depressive state. After her recovery, she determined to follow a new vocation and entered the North Presentation Convent on October 14, 1849, taking the habit and her new name in 1850. Her service as a nun, however, was cut short four months later by the recurrence of her illness, and she was forced to leave the convent. She lived, instead, with her mother and her sister, a widow. Recovered once again, she joined the Third Order of St. Dominic in order to maintain her affiliation with a religious order. Unable to write in verse after the shock of the failure of the 1848 rebellion, she began writing religious tracts and children's poetry.

In 1860, Julia Barry Downing passed away and Ellen was appointed to her mother's position as matron at the Cork Fever Hospital. Under jealous criticism from her peers, she served only until the end of that year, although her work was praised by physicians and trustees of the hospital. In 1868 her religious poems were collected by Dr. Patrick Leahy, S. J., and published as *Voices from the Heart*, which brought her the Vatican's notice. News of her pious life and deteriorating health reached the rector of the Irish College, who ordered a *triduum* of prayer for her in January of 1869. On the twenty-seventh day of that month, Ellen Mary Patrick Downing passed away.

One myth surrounds the persona "Mary of the Nation" and involves an engagement to the poet and Young Ireland patriot Joseph Brennan. Both Downing and Brennan belonged to the Cork Historical Society and contributed to its magazine. The engagement supposedly ended tragically when Brennan's participation in the 1848 rebellion forced him to flee to America. The story was sensationalized by the Young Ireland historian A. M. Sullivan and repeated in turn-of-the-century anthologies that held her poetry, yet Downing's biographers contradict the legend that her supposed broken heart was caused by Brennan's emigration. Father Russell confirms this account as told to him by Ellen's sister, Mrs. William Reed, who claimed that the engagement was broken off by Ellen herself. In a letter to her sister dated before Brennan's flight, "Mary" recalled the engagement as "'swept so far into the past that I begin to doubt if it ever was a real present'" (quoted in Russell, "Ellen Downing," 507). Brennan did not flee the country until 1849.

MAJOR WORKS AND THEMES

As "Mary of the Nation," Ellen Downing addressed a variety of themes. Her poems about the rivers Lee and Blackwater describe the Cork landscape, while "The Old Castle" recalls the Castle Blackrock, on the river Lee, as emblematic of Ireland's Celtic past. But it was the famine that held her attention and inspired her poetry written between 1846 and 1848. "Mary" addressed social issues such as forced emigration and exorbitant land rents. Applying the traditional *caoine*, she mourned the famine dead with the rest of the nation. She also chastised Ireland's leaders and England's government for failed economic and social policies. Loyal to the politics of Young Ireland, she criticized Ireland's Repeal Association under the leadership of Daniel O'Connell and his son John. Most remarkable in her work for the *Nation,* however, is her feminist stance. She inverted the *aisling* form, taking as the objects of her poems youthful Irish men rather than women. Likewise, Downing portrayed her women characters as strong and equal to the fight for independence, and she addressed the women of Ireland in editorials invoking their participation in the planned rebellion of 1848. Yet even while writing such politically charged verses, she included devotional poems that reflected her deep religious faith. Her later religious tracts signed "Mary Alphonsus" were published in *Meditations and Prayers: In Honour of St. Catherine of Sienna* (1879), and her religious verses were collected as *Verses from the Heart*. She is also reported to have published a collection called *Poems for Children* (1881), although no copies seem to survive.

CRITICAL RECEPTION

When the sixteen-year-old Ellen submitted her first poems to the *Nation*, its editor praised her for her patriotism and talent. She quickly advanced to the prestigious column the "Poets Corner" with the appearance of "A Farewell to Elia." Not all of her poems received such praise, however. Her polemic verses brought criticism by another Young Ireland poet, Richard Dalton Williams, who remonstrated that "Mary" should abandon her war songs and return instead to sweeter verses (424).

Her best-remembered poems remain in turn-of-the-century anthologies of Irish literature: the sonnet "My Owen," "Talk by the Blackwater," and "Past and Present." The editor of *Irish Literature*, Justin McCarthy, called her poetry "simple and graceful" (916), while T. P. O'Connor described her poetry, and that of her sister poets Eva Kelly and Jane Elgee-Wilde, as powerful. The most lavish praise, however, came from the religious community. Dr. Patrick Leahy, the bishop of Dromore, undertook the publication of *Voices from the Heart* and included her biography in its preface. Her friend Sr. Mary Imelda Magee added a heartfelt preface to *Meditations and Prayers*. Archbishop Kirby, the rector of the Irish College in Rome, was so deeply impressed by her collection of poems that he arranged for her a papal blessing. More extensive examinations of her work were undertaken by Father Matthew Russell, editor of the *Irish Monthly*, who included four critical essays in the 1878 edition of that magazine, three more in 1884, and another in 1908. Later biographers Thomas Markham and T. F. O'Sullivan recount her significance and include samples of her poetry as exemplary.

BIBLIOGRAPHY

Works by Ellen Mary Downing

Meditations and Prayers: In Honour of St. Catherine of Sienna, and Other Saints. Dublin: M. H. Gill, 1879.
Poems for Children. Dublin: Gill, 1881.
Voices from the Heart. Dublin: M'Kernan, 1868.

Studies of Ellen Mary Downing

Markham, Thomas. *Ellen Mary Downing*. *"Mary of the Nation."* Dublin: Catholic Truth Society of Ireland, 1913.
M'Carthy, Justin, ed. "Ellen Mary Patrick Downing." In *Irish Literature*. Vol. 3. Chicago: DeBower-Elliott, 1904, 916–17.
O'Connor, T. P., ed. "Eva Mary Kelly—Ellen Downing." In *The Cabinet of Irish Literature: Selections from the Works of the Chief Poets, Orators, and Prose Writers of Ireland*. Vol. 6. London: Blackie, n.d., 145–48.
O'Sullivan, T. F. "Ellen Mary Patrick Downing." In *The Young Irelanders*. Tralee, Ire.: Kerryman, 1944, 115–21.

Russell, Matthew, S. J. "Ellen Downing—'Mary' of the Nation." *Irish Monthly* 6 (1878): 459–
    65, 506–12.
———. "The Late Ellen Downing of Cork—'Mary' of the Nation." *Irish Monthly* 6 (1878): 573–
    630, 661–67.
———. "More About 'Mary' of the Nation." *Irish Monthly* 36 (1908): 69–81.
———. "The Unpublished Relics of Ellen Downing—'Mary' of the Nation." *Irish Monthly* 12
    (1884): 315–29, 425–32, 534–40.
Williams, Richard D. "Shamrock to Mary." *Nation*, April 10, 1847, 424.

MARIA EDGEWORTH
(1767–1849)

Claire Denelle Cowart

BIOGRAPHY

Maria Edgeworth was born in Oxfordshire, England. Her Anglo-Irish father, Richard Lovell Edgeworth, eventually became the dominant influence in Edgeworth's life, but she saw little of him during her early childhood years in England. She spent her first five years with her mother, Anna Maria Elers, at her mother's family home, Black Bourton, while her father traveled extensively. Her parents' marriage was not happy, and when Edgeworth's mother died in 1773, her father remarried after only four months.

Richard Edgeworth's second marriage, to Honora Sneyd, brought significant changes to his daughter's life. Scholars Marilyn Butler and Ann Weekes have argued convincingly that these early years affected both the development of Edgeworth's character and the course of her writing career. Edgeworth's father and stepmother were devoted to each other and paid little attention to Maria, his second child and only daughter at that time. When they took her to Ireland to visit Edgeworthstown, her father's estate in County Longford, she became very difficult to control. In her biography of Edgeworth, Marilyn Butler describes an episode in which the child Maria expressed a desire for her own death, saying "I'm very unhappy" (quoted by Butler, 47). Both Richard and Honora had studied theories of childhood education and behavior, but they failed to recognize the six-year-old's difficulties in adjusting to her new circumstances. After two years they sent her to boarding school in London.

During her school years Edgeworth made a determined effort to please her father and stepmother. She corresponded faithfully with both, expressing a strong desire for approval and a wish to modify her behavior to be more acceptable to them. After his second wife's death, in 1780, Richard Edgeworth married Elizabeth Sneyd, Honora's sister, who proved kinder, and Edgeworth's situation improved noticeably. In 1782, when the family returned to Edgworthstown, she made herself indispensable to her father as his secretary and bookkeeper and also began teaching the younger children in her father's growing family. Richard Edgeworth married four times, fathering a total of twenty-two children. Maria's third stepmother, Frances Beaufort, was a year younger than Maria herself, and the two became close friends.

When Edgeworth was fourteen years old, her father began to give her writing assignments; one of her first tasks was to write "an inquiry into the causes of poverty in Ireland" (Weekes, 36). She returned to this theme in her Irish novels, but most of her early writing focused on education for children. Her first publication was *Letters for Literary Ladies* (1795), followed the year after with *The Parent's Assistant* (1796). Two years later came *Practical Education*, cowritten with her father. Edgeworth wrote educational primers throughout her career, filling these books with illustrative stories about children whose moral choices are rewarded or punished according to how deserving they are. Interspersed with these educational works were "tales," such as the very popular *Castle Rackrent* (1800), and fictional works set in England, such as *Belinda* (1801) and *Leonora* (1806); these last two are modeled on the "novel of manners" and usually criticize fashionable life.

Her early works were first published anonymously, but Edgeworth did not remain unknown for long, and when she traveled she received a great deal of attention. Although most of her adult life was spent at Edgeworthstown, she occasionally made extended visits to England, Scotland, and the Continent. An especially significant journey took place in 1802, when Richard Edgeworth took his family abroad. In Paris, Edgeworth met Abraham Edelcrantz, a Swedish diplomat who proposed to her in January of 1803. Although some evidence exists that her father hoped she would marry, Edgeworth refused the proposal, claiming reluctance to leave her home and family. At the time, Edgeworth was thirty-three and Edelcrantz was forty-six. Neither ever married, but references in Edgeworth's letters and journals make it clear that she kept track of developments in his life.

Her fame as a writer, plus her father's involvement in the Enlightenment movement of eighteenth-century Britain, put Edgeworth in contact with leading intellectual and literary figures of the time. These include Elizabeth Hamilton, Lord Byron, Etienne Dumont, Thomas Malthus, and others. In 1823 she traveled to Scotland and met Sir Walter Scott, whose own novels were strongly influenced by her fiction. Their friendship endured, and Scott visited her in Edgeworthstown in 1825.

After the death of Edgeworth's father in 1825, her brother Lovell began managing the family property but was not successful. With the backing of the rest of her family, Edgeworth took control from the mid-1820s until 1839. During these years she concentrated on running the estate. She continued to write, although not quite so prolifically as before, and avoided fiction, with the exception of one late novel, *Helen* (1834). When the Great Famine struck in 1846, Edgeworth applied herself to the relief efforts with vigor and practicality. She sent out successful appeals for assistance to England and the United States, provided grain as a substitute crop for potato farmers in her area, and supplied many of the poor with shoes. In May of 1849, after a short illness, Maria Edgeworth died at her home in Edgeworthstown.

MAJOR WORKS AND THEMES

Many of Edgeworth's books for adult audiences were labeled "tales" by the author, who thought that her father disapproved of novels and would prefer all her writing to make a moral point. The first book she composed without her father's input was *Castle*

Rackrent, An Hibernian Tale: Taken from the Facts, and from the Manners of the Irish Squires, Before the Year 1782. For feedback on this book, Edgeworth went to her aunt Ruxton and her cousin Sophy. The freedom and encouragement she experienced in their company led her to experiment with technique and content in this short novel detailing the history of the Rackrents, Anglo-Irish landlords who ruin their estate through four generations of riotous living, neglect, and poor judgment.

Castle Rackrent is narrated by Thady Quirk, a long-time retainer of the Rackrent family who presents himself as a trusted and admiring servant of the family. Gradually the reader realizes that his judgments are often faulty, and that the Rackrents have been failures as landlords. Thady's dialect and idioms, combined with the irony of his observations, make this character one of the most memorable in Edgeworth's fiction. Another unusual feature of the novel is the glossary with explanatory notes that Edgeworth appends to the story. These explanations of the vernacular English spoken by Irishmen demonstrate both Edgeworth's interest in language and her preoccupation with improving understanding between Ireland and England.

Another theme of *Castle Rackrent*, the Big House in decay, became a recurring subject for Anglo-Irish writers who followed Edgeworth. For Edgeworth herself, the relationship between landlord and tenants had been significant since her early days of assisting her father at Edgeworthstown. Her belief that a landlord owes a responsibility to the land and its tenants derives from her father's teaching and example and is explored further in her other Irish fiction.

In *Ennui* (1809), the plot revolves around two young men who are exchanged at birth, so that the supposed Earl of Glenthorn is in fact the son of the true earl's old nurse. The false earl has been living in England for most of his life and suffers from "ennui" as a result of his empty, meaningless lifestyle. A visit from his old nurse, Ellinor, prompts him to visit Ireland, where a series of encounters and conversations with Irishmen, visiting Englishmen, and his Scots agent prompt him to revise both his own character and his opinions of Ireland. After some plot twists involving the 1798 rebellion, Glenthorn learns the truth of his birth and hands the property over to his foster-brother. The plot ends happily when a wiser and better Glenthorn regains the property through marriage.

Another landlord is at the center of *The Absentee* (1812). In this "tale," Lord Colambre returns from London to Ireland; like Glenthorn, he moves from the unimportant round of fashionable life into social responsibility. In the course of traveling throughout Ireland in an attempt to learn about his own nation, Colambre encounters some properties as ruined as Castle Rackrent and others as successfully managed as Edgeworthstown. Upon discovering that his own estate has fallen into a deplorable condition through the mismanagement of a corrupt agent, he convinces his family to return home from England and become responsible landlords.

Ennui and *The Absentee* were originally published as part of Edgeworth's series, *Tales of Fashionable Life* (1809–12), which uses didactic methods similar to those in Edgeworth's illustrative stories for children. The central male characters both learn how to be praiseworthy landlords from characters who practice the theories Maria Edgeworth learned from her father. Ireland itself also becomes a subject of the novels as Glenthorn and Colambre travel throughout the country and interact with vivid characters drawn from all levels of society. Edgeworth's ability to engage readers with her depiction of the country inspired Sir Walter Scott and others to follow her example and write their own "national" novels; Scott was particularly inspired by *The Absentee*.

Ormond (1817), the last of Edgeworth's four novels of Irish life, shares the themes and basic premise of *Ennui* and *The Absentee*, but is longer and more complex. Like her previous heroes, Harry Ormond learns by observation. However, he also participates more fully in Irish life by living for long periods with his two O'Shane uncles: Ulick, a politician, who is urban and sophisticated, and Corny, whose domain is the isolated Black Islands, where he lives like a tribal chieftain from Ireland's feudal past. Harry finds traits to admire in each man but realizes that Corny has given up the benefits of civilization and that Ulick has been corrupted. A third role model is Sir Herbert Annaly, an English-educated landlord whose main concern is justice. After the deaths of Ulick and Corny, Harry marries Annaly's daughter and returns to the Black Islands, resolved to run them in the responsible, enlightened manner he has learned from Annaly. This novel shows the influence of the Romantic movement in literature, particularly in the primitive, natural appeal of the Black Islands.

The didacticism of the novels is directed to the English as well as to the Anglo-Irish, as in many ways Edgeworth defends and justifies the Irish way of life to an English audience. Her *Essay on Irish Bulls* (1802), cowritten with Richard Edgeworth, delivers a similar message: to explain the meanings behind Irish expressions that have been taken to be blunders, or "bulls," by the English. In the process, the authors use stories, often humorous, to suggest that the English attitude toward the Irish is both unjust and ignorant, in terms of politics as well as language.

CRITICAL RECEPTION

Initial reaction to Maria Edgeworth's Irish writing came in the form of positive reviews and praise from her contemporaries. Sir Walter Scott cited her Irish novels as the inspiration for his own national literature: "I felt that something might be attempted for my own country of the same kind with that which Miss Edgeworth so fortunately achieved for Ireland" (Scott's preface to *Waverley* [Franklin Center, PA: Franklin Library, 1981], p. 419). William Carleton appreciated her efforts to improve English opinions of the Irish: "When the Irishman was made to stand forth as the butt of ridicule to his neighbours, the first that undertook his vindication was Maria Edgeworth" (iv). Some evidence suggests that the Russian writer Ivan Turgenev also was influenced by Edgeworth.

Although most critics regard *Castle Rackrent* as Edgeworth's finest work, interpretations of the novel vary, particularly regarding the novel's unreliable narrator, Thady Quirk. In his introduction to the 1964 edition, George Watson describes Thady as "this absurdly loyal family retainer" (xxi). Although Thomas Flanagan acknowledges that Thady has "his own wry view of the matter," he also states that Thady "does not fully understand the story which he is telling" (77). Later critics have viewed Thady as more complex. In Alan Warner's view, "Thady is not consistent, and his behaviour is certainly ambiguous" (47). James Newcomer argues that a conniving Thady uses "guile . . . to turn his employers' weaknesses to his own advantage" (*Maria Edgeworth*, 66). Terry Eagleton hypothesizes that Thady may be fooling not only the readers of the novel but also the "Editor," Edgeworth herself: "In this sense, curiously, it is Maria Edgeworth who is being taken for a ride by one of her own creations" (167). John Cronin is among several critics with a more neutral view; he sees Thady as "neither ingenious nor malign," but "a magnificently realized slave, a terrifying vision of the results of colonial misrule" (36).

Edgeworth's use of the Irish vernacular also has sparked disagreement. According to Brian Hollingworth, "Edgeworth's treatment of the vernacular in the Irish tales remains deeply ambivalent . . . [as] we cannot find an unqualified endorsement of the vernacular voice" (220). Other critics view Edgeworth's use of language in *Castle Rackrent* as an effective means of "revealing a society" to her readers (Kiely, 5).

Much discussion has centered around Edgeworth's attitudes on political and class issues. One of the first critics to characterize her as a colonialist was Daniel Corkery: "It was natural for the Ascendancy folk of this second period to write in this colonial manner, for what are all their books but travellers' tales?" (8). Later critics have approached Edgeworth's Irish novels from a postcolonialist perspective. Seamus Deane sees *Castle Rackrent* as "a demonstration of the ruin which an irresponsible aristocracy brings upon itself and upon its descendants" (92). Mary Jean Corbett points out that the author herself experienced colonized status. Brian Hollingworth concludes "that Edgeworth by birth, breeding, social role and conviction, remains a committed member of the Irish establishment [Anglo-Irish Protestant]" (218). Others find conflict within Edgeworth's own authorial stance. Eagleton suggests that "*Castle Rackrent* can be read as embodying an ideological conflict we can discern elsewhere in Edgeworth, between the values of a vital if anarchic ruling class which is able, whatever its moral shabbiness, to secure the allegiance of its underlings, and the rational virtues of a more sober social order whose austere utility will win it few ardent adherents" (163). Robert Tracy's analysis of political and social attitudes in Edgeworth's fiction concludes that Edgeworth's instincts as a writer and her awareness of the flaws of the Anglo-Irish "impel her toward . . . an endorsement of Irish tradition and identity," but her grounding in her father's principles prevents her from finally making such an endorsement (9). Detailed discussions of Edgeworth's reaction to major political events of her time, such as the 1798 rebellion and the 1800 Act of Union, can be found in articles by many critics, including Brian Hollingworth, Michael Hurst, Mitzi Myers, and Tom Dunne. Additional analysis of Edgeworth's national and political attitudes, as embedded in the *Essay on Irish Bulls,* can be found in articles by Martin Croghan and Marilyn Butler.

A feminist reading has been applied to Edgeworth's texts by a number of recent critics. Both Ann Weekes and Terry Eagleton point out that Thady Quirk, in *Castle Rackrent*, has a feminine function in the novel; as a servant, he is subject to his masters in much the same way that women of the time period were subject to men. Weekes also argues that Edgeworth continually draws attention to the marriages in *Castle Rackrent* to show that the Rackrent men fail not only as landlords but as husbands. Bonnie Blackwell objects to earlier critics' defining Edgeworth in terms of her father's influence on her and delves at length into the relationship in *Ennui* between the main character, Glenthorn, and the Irish wet nurse, Ellinor, who turns out to be his mother. Marilyn Butler also discusses *Ennui* from a feminist standpoint, pointing out that in the novel "three powerful women, each representing a different strand of the Irish people in history, capture [Glenthorn] and transform him" (283). Additionally, a special issue of *Women's Studies: An Interdisciplinary Journal* (31, no. 3) was devoted to Edgeworth in the spring of 2002.

While most modern critics agree on the originality and artistic worth of *Castle Rackrent*, they disagree on the merit of Edgeworth's other Irish fiction. Some dismiss everything but *Castle Rackrent* as didactic and humorless. In the late 1990s and early part of the twenty-first century, however, several critics have reexamined the later texts. Marilyn Butler, Katie Trumpener, and Bonnie Blackwell have found value in *Ennui,* which many previous analysts dismissed as overly preachy. Butler asserts that *Ennui* is "a story with strong characters and scenes, and a foray into magic realism and the hidden Ireland" (280). *The Absentee* has advocates in Robert Tracy and W. J. McCormack. *Ormond* is much admired by Flanagan, Butler, and a number of other critics for its strong characters and dramatic scenes. Flanagan praises *Ormond* as Edgeworth's "finest work after *Castle Rackrent*" and the O'Shanes as her "most brilliant creations" (93). These later novels have also been examined for their Romantic elements by some critics, including Siobhan Kilfeather and Katie Trumpener.

Despite the wide range of critical writing on Edgeworth available, great potential exists for further interpretations of her work. As W. J. McCormack writes in the introduction to Edgeworth in *The Field Day Anthology*, full justice has not yet been done "to the questions raised by her exemplary fiction" (*Field Day*, vol. 1, 1013).

BIBLIOGRAPHY

Works by Maria Edgeworth

Selected Collections

Tales and Miscellaneous Pieces. 14 vols. London: R. Hunter and Baldwin, Cradock and Joy, 1825.
Tales and Novels. 18 vols. London: Baldwin and Cradock, 1832–33.
Tales and Novels. 9 vols. London: Whitaker, 1848.
The Works of Maria Edgeworth, edited by Marilyn Butler et al. 12 vols. London: Pickering and Chatto, 2003.

Selected Individual Works

Belinda. 3 vols. London: J. Johnson, 1801.
Castle Rackrent, An Hibernian Tale; Taken from Facts, and from the Manners of the Irish Squires, Before the Year 1782. London: J. Johnson, 1800.
Comic Dramas in Three Acts: Love and Law, The Two Guardians, and The Rose, The Thistle, and the Shamrock. London: Hunter, 1817.
Essay on Irish Bulls. London: J. Johnson, 1802. (With R. L. Edgeworth.)
Harrington, A Tale and *Ormond: A Tale*. 3 vols. London: Hunter and Baldwin, Cradock and Joy, 1817.
Helen: A Tale. 3 vols. London: Bentley, 1834.
Leonora. 2 vols. London: J. Johnson, 1806.
Letters for Literary Ladies, to Which Is Added an Essay on the Noble Science of Self-Justification. London: J. Johnson, 1795.
The Modern Griselda: A Tale. London: J. Johnson, 1805.
The Parent's Assistant; or Stories for Children. 3 vols. London: J. Johnson, 1796.
Patronage. 4 vols. London: J. Johnson, 1814.
Popular Tales. 3 vols. London: J. Johnson, 1804.
Practical Education. 2 vols. London: J. Johnson, 1798. (With R. L. Edgeworth.)
Tales of Fashionable Life. 6 vols. London: J. Johnson, 1809–1812.

Selected Letters

The Life and Letters of Maria Edgeworth. Edited by Augustus J. C. Hare. 2 vols. London: Arnold, 1894.
Maria Edgeworth: Letters from England 1813–1844. Edited by Christina Colvin. Oxford: Clarendon, 1971.
Maria Edgeworth in France and Switzerland: Selections from the Edgeworth Family Letters. Edited by Christina Colvin. Oxford: Clarendon, 1979.

A Memoir of Maria Edgeworth, with a Selection from Her Letters. Edited by Frances Edgeworth. 3 vols. London: Masters, 1867.

Studies of Maria Edgeworth

Altieri, J. "Style and Purpose in Maria Edgeworth's Fiction." *Nineteenth-Century Fiction* 23, no. 2 (September 1968): 265–78.

Bilger, Audrey. *Laughing Feminism: Subversive Comedy in Frances Burney, Maria Edgeworth, and Jane Austen*. Detroit: Wayne State University Press, 1999.

Blackwell, Bonnie. "War in the Nursery, 1798: The Persecuting Breast and the Melancholy Babe in Maria Edgeworth's *Ennui*." *Women's Studies: An Interdisciplinary Journal* 31, no. 3 (May/June 2002): 349–97.

Brookes, Gerry H. "The Didacticism of Edgeworth's *Castle Rackrent*." *Studies in English Literature, 1500–1900* 17, no. 4 (Autumn 1977): 593–605.

Butler, Marilyn. "Edgeworth's Ireland: History, Popular Culture, and Secret Codes." *Novel: A Forum on Fiction* 34, no. 2 (Spring 2001): 267–92.

Butler, Marilyn. *Maria Edgeworth: A Literary Biography*. Oxford: Clarendon, 1972.

Cahalan, James M. *Great Hatred, Little Room: The Irish Historical Novel*. Syracuse, NY: Syracuse University Press, 1983.

———. *The Irish Novel: A Critical History*. Boston: Twayne, 1998.

Carleton, William. General Introduction. In *Traits and Stories of the Irish Peasantry*. Vol. 1. London: Tegg, 1843, i–xxiv.

Colgan, Maurice. "After Rackrent: Ascendancy Nationalism in Maria Edgeworth's Later Irish Novels." In *Studies in Anglo-Irish Literature*, edited by Heinz Kosok. Bonn: Bouvier, 1982.

Corbett, Mary Jean. "Another Tale to Tell: Postcolonial Theory and the Case of *Castle Rackrent*." *Criticism* 36, no. 3 (Summer 1994): 383–400.

Corkery, Daniel. *Synge and Anglo-Irish Literature*. Cork: Cork University Press, 1931.

Croghan, Martin J. "Maria Edgeworth and the Tradition of Irish Semiotics." In *A Small Nation's Contribution to the World*, edited by Donald E. Morse, Csilla Bertha, and István Pálffy, 194–206. Gerrards Cross, UK: Smythe, 1993.

Cronin, John. *The Anglo-Irish Novel*. Belfast: Appletree, 1980.

Deane, Seamus. *A Short History of Irish Literature*. London: Hutchinson, 1982.

Dunne, Tom. "Edgeworthstown in Fact and Fiction, 1760–1840." In *Longford: Essays in County History*, edited by Raymond Gillespie and Gerard Moran, 95–121. Dublin: Lilliput, 1991.

Eagleton, Terry. "Form and Ideology in the Anglo-Irish Novel." In *Heathcliff and the Great Hunger*. London: Verso, 1995, 124–44.

Flanagan, Thomas. *The Irish Novelists 1800–1850*. New York: Columbia University Press, 1958.

Gonda, Caroline. *Reading Daughters' Fictions, 1709–1834*. Cambridge: Cambridge University Press, 1996.

Hack, Daniel. "Inter-Nationalism: *Castle Rackrent* and Anglo-Irish Union." *Novel: A Forum on Fiction* 29, no. 2 (Winter 1996): 145–64.

Harden, O. Elizabeth M. *Maria Edgeworth*. Boston: Twayne, 1984.

———. *Maria Edgeworth's Art of Prose Fiction*. The Hague: Mouton, 1971.

Hollingworth, Brian. *Maria Edgeworth's Irish Writing: Language, History, Politics*. New York: St. Martin's, 1997.

Hurst, Michael. *Maria Edgeworth and the Public Scene: Intellect, Fine Feeling and Landlordism in the Age of Reform*. London: Macmillan, 1969.

Inglis-Jones, Elizabeth. *The Great Maria: A Portrait of Maria Edgeworth*. London: Faber and Faber, 1959.

Kiberd, Declan. "Native Informants: Maria Edgeworth and *Castle Rackrent*." In *Irish Classics*. London: Granta, 2000, 243–64.

Kiely, Benedict. *A Raid into Dark Corners and Other Essays*. Cork: Cork University Press, 1999.

Kilfeather, Siobhan. "Origins of Female Gothic." *Bullan: An Irish Studies Journal* 1, no. 2 (Autumn 1994): 35–45.

Kirkpatrick, Kathryn. "Putting Down the Rebellion: Notes and Glosses on *Castle Rackrent, 1800.*" *Eire-Ireland* 30, no. 1 (Spring 1995): 75–90.

Kowaleski-Wallace, Elizabeth. *Their Fathers' Daughters: Hannah More, Maria Edgeworth, and Patriarchal Complicity.* New York: Oxford University Press, 1991.

Lawless, Emily. *Maria Edgeworth.* London: Macmillan, 1904.

McCormack, W. J. *Ascendancy and Tradition in Anglo-Irish Literary History from 1789 to 1939.* Oxford: Clarendon, 1985.

———. "Maria Edgeworth." In *The Field Day Anthology of Irish Writing.* Vol. 1, edited by Seamus Deane, 1011–13. Derry, Ire.: Field Day, 1991.

Murphy, Willa. "A Queen of Hearts or an Old Maid? Maria Edgeworth's Fictions of Union." In *Acts of Union: The Causes, Contexts and Consequences of the Act of Union,* edited by Daire Keogh and Kevin Whelan, 187–201. Dublin: Four Courts, 2001.

Murray, Patrick. "The Irish Novels of Maria Edgeworth." *Studies* 59, no. 235 (Autumn 1970): 267–68.

———. "Maria Edgeworth and Her Father: The Literary Partnership." *Eire-Ireland* 6, no. 3 (Fall 1971): 39–50.

Myers, Mitzi. " 'Completing the Union': Critical Ennui, the Politics of Narrative, and The Reformation of Irish Cultural Identity." *Prose Studies: History, Theory, Criticism* 18, no. 3 (December 1995): 41–77.

———. " 'Like the Pictures in a Magic Lantern': Gender, History, and Edgeworth's Rebellion Narratives." *Nineteenth Century Contexts* 19, no. 4 (1996): 373–412.

———. "War Correspondence: Maria Edgeworth and the En-Gendering of Revolution, Rebellion, and Union." *Eighteenth Century Life* 22, no. 3 (November 1998): 74–91.

Newby, P. H. *Maria Edgeworth.* Denver, CO: Swallow, 1950.

Newcomer, James. "*Castle Rackrent*: Its Structure and Its Irony." *Criticism* 8, no. 2 (Spring 1996): 170–79.

———. *Maria Edgeworth.* Lewisburg, PA: Bucknell University Press, 1973.

———. *Maria Edgeworth the Novelist: A Bicentenary Study.* Fort Worth: Texas Christian University Press, 1967.

Ni Chuilleanain, Eilean. "The Voices of Maria Edgeworth's Comedy." In *The Comic Tradition in Irish Women Writers,* edited by Theresa O'Connor, 21–39. Gainesville: University Press of Florida, 1996.

Owens, Coilin. "Irish Bulls and *Castle Rackrent.*" In *Family Chronicles: Maria Edgeworth's* Castle Rackrent, edited by Coilin Owens, 70–78. Dublin: Wolfhound, 1987.

Slade, B. C. *Maria Edgeworth, 1767–1849: A Bibliographical Tribute.* London: Constable, 1937.

Tracy, Robert. "Maria Edgeworth and Lady Morgan: Legality versus Legitimacy." *Nineteenth Century Fiction* 40, no. 1 (June 1985): 1–22.

Trumpener, Katie. *Bardic Nationalism: The Romantic Novel and the British Empire.* Princeton, NJ: Princeton University Press, 1997.

Warner, Alan. *A Guide to Anglo-Irish Literature.* Dublin: Gill and Macmillan, 1981.

Watson, George. Introduction to *Castle Rackrent,* by Maria Edgeworth. London: Oxford University Press, 1964.

Weekes, Ann Owen. *Irish Women Writers: An Uncharted Tradition.* Lexington: Kentucky University Press, 1990.

RUTH DUDLEY EDWARDS
(1944–   )
Shelia Odak

BIOGRAPHY

Born in 1944, Ruth Dudley Edwards is a member of a Dublin family of academics who specialize in history, including her father, Robert Dudley Edwards, and her brother Owen. Dudley Edwards herself was educated in history at University College Dublin and completed postgraduate work at Cambridge University, studying fifteenth-century ecclesiastical relations. Her early career is a diverse one: She served as a lecturer of history and English at further-education institutions in Cambridge, as a marketing executive for the post office, and from 1975 to 1979 as an employee of the British Department of Industry.

Dudley Edwards states that she "became a writer for the most traditional of reasons: someone offered me an advance" (Web site). Her supervisor at Cambridge suggested her to a publisher as someone who could write *An Atlas of Irish History*. Needing the money, she accepted the assignment. Her second book, a biography of Patrick Pearse, leader of the 1916 Irish rebellion, won the National University of Ireland Prize for Historical Research. Writing the book, Dudley Edwards discovered that she loved the process of researching and composing a biography. This love translated into biographies of such diverse figures as publisher Victor Gollancz, whose biography won her the James Tait Black Memorial Prize for Biography, socialist James Connolly, and British prime minister Harold Macmillan. Dudley Edwards's work as the company historian of the *Economist*, a post she held from 1982 to 2000, led to the writing of what she terms the "biggest and fattest" of her works, *The Pursuit of Reason: The Economist, 1843–1993* (Web site).

In her teens, Dudley Edwards developed a passion for detective stories, devouring works by Agatha Christie, Raymond Chandler, Ian Fleming, and other mystery writers. However, she never planned to become an author of crime fiction. Like the unanticipated beginnings of her nonfiction career, Dudley Edwards received an unexpected offer to write a detective novel. As she tried to complete the task and write a "straight," serious story, she found herself falling into writing satire and farce, traits that mark all of her crime fiction. Three of Dudley Edwards's mysteries have been shortlisted for Crime Writers' Association awards.

In addition to writing histories, biographies, and crime fiction, Dudley Edwards has been a freelance journalist and broadcaster since 1993. Her first extensive journalistic effort was as a humorous diarist for the *Independent*, though she had written book reviews since her twenties. Her entry into a more serious type of journalism started with an article she wrote, run by the *Sunday Times*, that detailed her ideas on the situation in Northern Ireland. Dudley Edwards has continued her political journalism, writing for almost every national paper in the United Kingdom and every national newspaper in the Republic of Ireland. She also serves as a commentator on BBC news programs and the BBC World Service. Her controversial views on Northern Ireland, which show more sympathy for the Northern Irish people than is expected from a person with a Dublin Catholic Nationalist background, often mark her as a pundit on this subject, though she says she is also interested in politics in the United Kingdom, the United States, and Europe (Web site).

Dudley Edwards is currently working on an account of the victims of the 1998 Omagh bombing, telling the story from their point of view and chronicling their civil case filed against the Irish Republican Army and five individuals.

MAJOR WORKS AND THEMES

While the subjects of her nonfiction books cover several areas, two of her strongest works center on Irish people and concerns. Her biography of Patrick Pearse (1977) uses recently available material to offer a view of this Irish patriot that encompasses both his faults and his virtues. Portraying him as a man driven by ambition and by flawed views on the needs of the Irish people, Dudley Edwards shows how Pearse unquestioningly moved forward with his own ideas, falling victim to that Irish trait of failing "to combine pragmatism and idealism" (339). As Dudley Edwards put it, this was a man who "wrote, acted and died for a people that did not exist" (343).

The Faithful Tribe (1999) looks at how the Protestant parades of the Orange Order in Northern Ireland have become distorted by the media, who portray only the violent side of the marches. Blending her personal experiences with the marchers, as well as historical and political commentary, Dudley Edwards works to show the Orange Order as a group of individual, ordinary people, rather than a monolith of intolerance. She chronicles what the parades mean, and how they affect the thousands of Protestants who see this ritual as a way to honor their community, religion, and traditions.

Dudley Edwards's detective fiction often chronicles the adventures of solid Scotland Yard detective James Milton, lapsed civil servant Robert Amiss, and irrepressible Ida "Jack" Troutbeck. Interestingly, Dudley Edwards also draws on the subjects of her nonfiction books for her fiction; for example, aspects of the *Economist* (1993) appear in *Publish and Be Murdered* (1998). Relying on dialogue rather than action, these satirical mysteries skewer everything from the civil service to gentlemen's clubs, from the academic world to the Anglo-Irish peace process, though her favorite target is the British establishment. She notes that members of these communities "co-operate in making fun of themselves" and are more than willing to help her research her biting takes on their institutions. When asked why her wit is not pointed more often toward her own countrymen, Dudley Edwards notes that Ireland "lacks a sense of humor about itself. Every time I make a joke in print about some aspect of Irishness, I get furious letters accusing me of being patronising, disloyal or a lickspittle to the British establishment" ("Our Exhibitionist Establishment," *Spectator*, June 6, 1998, 20–21).

CRITICAL RECEPTION

Little academic work has been done on Dudley Edwards. In a collection of essays on college mystery novels, Uwe Baumann places Dudley Edwards's *Matricide at St. Martha's* (1994) alongside novels by Charlotte MacLeod and Robert Robinson in order to examine her use of humor, noting Dudley Edwards's satirical take on the women's movement on college campuses.

Other critical notice comes from book reviews of her various works. Dudley Edwards's biographies and histories, notably her life of Victor Gollancz and history of the *Economist*, have been both praised and criticized for their comprehensiveness. Specifically, some critics wish for more editing of her research, especially that derived from primary sources. However, reviewers also note that her contributions to the views on her subjects, especially regarding her biography of Patrick Pearse, are both illuminating and sensitive. A. C. Hepburn notes that Dudley Edwards's portrayal of Pearse is "on a different level" from previous partisan works on Irish political figures (1391).

Reviews for *The Faithful Tribe* have praised it as an important book that gives an often unheard perspective on Northern Irish politics. However, several reviewers feel Dudley Edwards's sympathy for her subject is a detriment to the work. For example, Stephen Howe finds the book "engrossing and illuminating, if sometimes infuriating," because he believes that in her efforts to portray fairly members of the Orange Order, Dudley Edwards goes too far and ignores many of their faults. C.D.C. Armstrong also cites this problem but notes that the book contains a message "of urgency as well as interest" (40).

BIBLIOGRAPHY

Works by Ruth Dudley Edwards

Nonfiction

An Atlas of Irish History. London: Methuen, 1973.
The Best of Bagehot. London: Hamish Hamilton, 1993.
The Faithful Tribe: An Intimate Portrait of the Loyal Institutions. London: Harper, 1999.
Harold Macmillan: A Life in Pictures. London: Macmillan, 1983.
James Connolly. Dublin: Gill and Macmillan, 1981.
Newspapermen: Hugh Cudlipp, Cecil Harmsworth King, and the Glory Days of Fleet Street. London: Secker and Warburg, 2003.
Patrick Pearse: The Triumph of Failure. London: Gollancz, 1977.
The Pursuit of Reason: The Economist, 1843–1993. London: Hamish Hamilton, 1993.
True Brits: Inside the Foreign Office. London: BBC Books, 1994.
Victor Gollancz: A Biography. London: Gollancz, 1987.

Fiction

The Anglo-Irish Murders. London: Harper, 2000.
Carnage on the Committee. London: Harper, 2004.
Clubbed to Death. London: Gollancz, 1992.
Corridors of Death. London: Quartet, 1981.
Matricide at St. Martha's. London: Harper, 1994.
Murder in a Cathedral. London: Harper, 1996.
Publish and Be Murdered. London: Harper, 1998.
Ruth Dudley Edwards Web site. http://www.ruthdudleyedwards.co.uk/bigfatbooks.htm (accessed July 12, 2004).
The Saint Valentine's Day Murders. London: Quartet, 1984.
The School of English Murder. London: Gollancz, 1990.
Ten Lords A-Leaping. London: Harper, 1995.

Studies of Ruth Dudley Edwards

Armstrong, C.D.C. "The Many Shades of Orange." Review of *The Faithful Tribe*. *Spectator*, June 19, 1999, 39–40.

Baumann, Uwe. "The Campus—A Cozy Place Where Comedy Meets Crime." In *The Great Good Place?* edited by Peter Nover. Frankfurt: Lang, 1999.

Hepburn, A.C. Review of *Patrick Pearse*. *American Historical Review* 84, no. 5 (December 1979): 1391–92.

Howe, Stephen. "Marching Boys." Review of *The Faithful Tribe*. *New Statesman* June 6, 1999, 47–48.

"Moreover: Green, Orange, 10% Black." Review of *The Faithful Tribe*. *Economist* July 10, 1999, 78–79.

Rees, Matthew. "Bookshelf: 'Paper' with a British Accent." Review of *The Pursuit of Reason*. *Wall Street Journal*, June 6, 1995, A16.

ANNE ENRIGHT
(1962–   )

Sara E. Stenson

BIOGRAPHY

Anne Enright grew up in the Dublin suburbs and attended St. Louis High School in Rathmines. She later studied at Pearson College in Canada and at Trinity College Dublin, where she completed her degree in modern English and philosophy in 1985. Acting with Dublin's Rough Magic Theatre and the Abbey, she also wrote *Thank God, Fasting* for Dublin Youth Theatre and "Revenge" for the RTE television series *Two Lives* (produced in 1994). She earned another scholarship for her MA in creative writing at the University of East Anglia. Enright then returned to Dublin and worked as producer and director for RTE's show *Nighthawks*. She began to write her first volume of short stories, *The Portable Virgin*, in 1991, which won critical acclaim and the Rooney Prize. After the book's publication, Enright left television to write full-time. In 1993, she married actor and director Martin Murphy and began to work on her first novel, *The Wig My Father Wore* (1995), which displays a strong cinematic influence. The book has since been translated into four major languages.

Enright collaborated with Dermot Bolger, Jennifer Johnston, Colm Toibin, Hugo Hamilton, and Joseph O'Connor in the group novel *Finbar's Hotel* in 1997. Bolger arranged the anonymous chapters into a narrative concerning one night in a derelict Dublin hotel.

Enright's second novel, *What Are You Like?* (2000), which depicts the reunion of female twins separated at birth, was published on both sides of the Atlantic. Enright's stunning effort won the Encore Prize of the Society of Authors. The work was also short-listed for the Whitbread Award and received the Kerry Ingredients Listowel Writer's Week Prize. Enright and Murphy celebrated the birth of their first child, Rachel Chris Murphy, in 2000. Enright wrote two essays for the *London Review of Books* that year, one titled "Diary" (also republished as "My Milk" in *Harper's* magazine) and the other "What Is It That Henrietta Lacks?" Her most recent work, *The Pleasure of Eliza*

Lynch (2002), is based on the infamous lover of Paraguay's revolutionary, Francisco Solano Lopez. Enright and her family moved in the spring of 2001 from central Dublin to County Wicklow.

MAJOR WORKS AND THEMES

Critics complain about her intensely sarcastic sense of humor, which Enright blames on her mother. Sharp, often dark, and yet relentlessly innovative, Anne Enright's un-hinging irony and decentered writing style capture the momentum, multiplicity, and veracity of the Irish identities in the postmodern age. Writing short stories, novels, and essays for both print and broadcast outlets such as Radio 4, RTE, the *London Review of Books*, and the *New Yorker*, she centers much of her work on Irishwomen, particu-larly parent-child relationships. Enright often explores and exposes the need to main-tain family secrets within Irish contexts. She aligns everyday lived experiences of individuals with an analysis of broad themes such as exile and cosmopolitanism.

Many critics still hold that Enright's first collection of short stories is her best. *The Portable Virgin* (1991) reveals a series of character studies that are witty, fearlessly in-terrogative, and grotesque. In "(She Owns) Everything," Cathy works behind the counter in a Dublin shop and is obsessed with matching each customer with a suitable handbag. In "Juggling Oranges," Billy is a mime by profession who "embarrasses" himself by falling in love at forty-nine. In "Luck Be a Lady," Mrs. Hanratty sees her life only in terms of numbers. Enright's signature satirical take on the ordinary, coupled with her retreat to surreal flights of fancy, often recall Jonathan Swift, Flann O'Brien, and others. Her tragic humor all too often exposes the modernist preoccupation with consciousness, for which she has been compared to Joyce. The collection's title story offers an unflinchingly close perspective of Mary, who claims that what follows will not be a "usual" betrayal story. Enright's meticulously crafted monologue explores the consciousness of this middle-aged Dublin woman, re-creating and decentering notions of Dublin commercialism and Irish Catholicism to question the viability of patriarchy and love within contemporary Irish society.

Enright attributes her ability to portray aptly the "insideness" of her characters to the influences of Samuel Beckett, Maeve Brennan (writer for the *New Yorker*), and Americanists such as De Lillo. A hip cinematic influence also pervades her first novel, *The Wig My Father Wore* (1995). Enright's fragmented prose style imitates the zoom-lens effects of camera work and the angular framing work of television editing. One character, Grace, works for a troubled television quiz show called *Love Quiz*. In an-other plot, an angel named Stephen moves in and impregnates her. Meanwhile, her fa-ther falls ill from a stroke; her mother secretly cares for his wig in order to ensure that his sense of identity remains unchanged. The wig is a great example of Enright's hu-morous and fetishistic examination of material objects. The presence of human hair, flesh, yarn, and even cow udders reflects Enright's interest in contemporary visual artists Kathy Prendergast and Dorothy Cross.

In her next novel, *What Are You Like?* (2000), everyday items take on the legacy of memory and forgetting as twin sisters reunite. The novel spans the reaches of Ireland, England, and America, exploring themes of dislocation, loss, exile, multiple identities, Irish Catholicism, and motherhood. Employing a fragmented plot structure and a se-ries of alternating narrative voices that recall her earlier work, Enright reaches deep into dark spaces as the novel recalls and recovers a hidden adoption and a mother's si-lence. The twins' mother dies in childbirth and as a result the Catholic Church calls for their separation. Maria grows up in Dublin with her father, Berts, and stepmother, Evelyn, before emigrating to New York in her twenties; meanwhile, Rose is adopted by English parents and comes of age in Surrey. Eventually Maria returns to Dublin and suffers a mental breakdown. Rose searches for her family through a Catholic adoption agency in London and arrives at her biological family's doorstep by the novel's end. Anne, the twins' mother, returns from the dead to recount her life and blame the survivors who "walk over" her for stifling her voice and mystifying her life. Enright resurrects the buried voice of what she terms the "dead mother" in Irish literature (Enright, interview by Moloney, 61). Through the voices of Maria, Rose, and Evelyn and her fascination with domestic objects, Anne Enright emphasizes what she calls the female sense of being "bewildered" in the world (Enright, interview by Padel, 8). For Enright, disorientation is the key; women are perplexed rather than merely angry or victimized.

Enright's most recent novel, *The Pleasure of Eliza Lynch* (2002), recovers the voice of one woman in particular, San Lopez's infamous mistress from Cork. The novel takes place in the second half of the nineteenth century during Paraguay's nation-building wars. Francisco San Lopez, the dictator's eldest son, travels to France on a diplomatic tour, where he and Eliza have an affair in Paris, during which she becomes pregnant and returns with him to Paraguay. The novel then divides its focus between Eliza and Stewart, her drunken doctor, who witnesses the war. Enright's Eliza is proud, beautiful, charming, and intelligent, but she is ostracized by her lover's family and the society of Asuncion. Although Eliza indulges in luxury, she also endures the death of her lover and favorite son. Enright again explores the relationship between sex and power, but this time at a leisurely pace.

CRITICAL RECEPTION

Even though Enright calls the current climate of Irish writing "such a boy's world," she has received attention in various outlets and numerous literary awards. Her first collection of short stories, *The Portable Virgin*, was celebrated. Anne Weekes has noted strength and originality in Enright's fragmented writing style composed of "precisely focused shots into a character's consciousness" (120), which has also been noted in her later work. Caitriona Moloney finds Joycean qualities in the short story "The Brat" reminiscent of Farrington from Joyce's "Counterparts" (1914). Maryanne Felter appreciates Enright's use of "surrealistic" and "disjointed" images.

Despite the opinions of Felter and others who prefer Enright's short stories for content and style, Enright's first novel, *The Wig My Father Wore*, received positive reviews for its pop-culture-induced imagery and style. Her second novel, *What Are You Like?*, was met with enthusiasm. Penelope Fitzgerald hails the novel's "fluid" effect of time and space dimensions (8). Reviewers also sense a difficulty for readership to "put the pieces together," which Weekes cautions against in her evaluation of Enright's first book (121). Fast paced and decentered in form, Enright's writing style allows for a complex exploration of family relations and media culture.

Reception of Enright's *The Pleasure of Eliza Lynch* (2002) continues to develop. Critics debate the overall effect of the novel's slower pace and historically based figure. In a recent review, William Skidelsky identifies a connection between the portrayal of Eliza's lush physical traits and Enright's experiences raising her first child while writing the novel (55). Enright wrote a series of shorter pieces, based on her own pregnancy, just before the novel's release. She embraces the stylistic change in an interview with Joanne Hayden (Web site). Despite numerous book reviews and interviews, critics have yet to explore fully the ways in which Enright recalls and resists a familiar gendered story resonant within Irish contexts. Her satiric tone, dynamic technical skill, and powerful use of language evoke Joyce, O'Brien, and others. Meanwhile, her attention to the effect of visual imagery calls on the aesthetics of contemporary women artists Prendergast and Cross. Enright's work provides a mirror to Irish society that reflects and refracts new understandings of Irishness.

BIBLIOGRAPHY

Works by Anne Enright

Fiction

Finbar's Hotel. Edited by Dermot Bolger. London: Picador; Dublin: New Island, 1997; San Diego: Harcourt Brace, 1999. (With Dermot Bolger, Roddy Doyle, Hugo Hamilton, Jennifer Johnston, Joseph O'Connor, and Colm Toibin.)
The Pleasure of Eliza Lynch. London: Cape, 2002.
The Portable Virgin. London: Secker and Warburg, 1991.
What Are You Like? London: Cape; New York: Atlantic Monthly Press, 2000.
The Wig My Father Wore. London: Cape, 1995; New York: Grove, 2001.

Play

Thank God, Fasting. Dublin Youth Theatre, 1994.

Selected Short Stories

"Felix." In *Class Work: The Best of Contemporary Short Fiction*, edited by Malcom Bradbury, 141–51. London: Sceptre, 1995.
"Seascape." In *Irish Love Stories*, edited by David Marcus, 125–30. London: Sceptre, 1994.

Selected Periodical Publications

"Diary." *London Review of Books* 22, no. 9 (October 5, 2000): 34–35. Republished as "My Milk." *Harpers*, (May 14, 2001): 26.
"Holles Street Revisited." *Dublin Review* 12 (Autumn 2003). http://www.thedublinreview.com/archive/twelve.
"In the Bed Department." *New Yorker* 77 (May 2001): 92–95.
"Pale Hands I Loved, Beside the Shalimar." *Paris Review* 42 (Winter 2000–2001): 269–79.
"What's Left of Henrietta Lacks?" *London Review of Books* 22, no. 8 (April 13, 2000). http://www.lrb.co.uk/v22/no8/enrio1_htm.

Interviews with Anne Enright

Hayden, Joanne. Interview. *The Sunday Business Post* (Dublin), December 29, 2000. http://archives.tcm.ie/businesspost/2002/12/29/story812503528.asp.
Moloney, Caitriona. "Anne Enright." *Irish Women Writers Speak Out: Voices from the Field*, edited by Caitriona Moloney and Helen Thompson, 51–64. Syracuse, NY: Syracuse University Press, 2003.
O'Flanagan, Mary Kate. "Reclaiming Ireland's Eva Peron: An Interview with Anne Enright." *Sunday Business Post* (Dublin), November 11, 2003. http://archives.tcm.ie/businesspost/2002/11/03story526976528.asp.
Padel, Ruth. "Anne Enright: Twin Tracks and Double Visions." *Independent* (London), February 26, 2000, 9.

Studies of Anne Enright

Felter, Maryanne. "Anne Enright." *Dictionary of Irish Literature, Revised and Enlarged Edition.* Vol. 1, edited by Robert Hogan, 410–11. Westport, CT: Greenwood, 1996.

Fitzgerald, Penelope. "Bringers of Ill Luck and Bad Weather." Review of *What Are You Like? London Review of Books* 22, no. 5 (March 5, 2000): 8.

Moloney, Caitriona. "Anne Enright." *Dictionary of Literary Biography.* Vol. 267, *Twenty-first-Century British and Irish Novelists*, edited by Michael R. Molino, 88–93. Detroit: Gale, 2002.

Skidelsky, William. Review of *The Pleasure of Eliza Lynch. New Statesman* 131 (October 7, 2000): 55.

Weekes, Anne Owens, ed. "Anne Enright." *Unveiling Treasures: The Atlantic Guide to The Published Works of Irish Women Literary Writers: Drama, Fiction, Poetry.* Dublin: Attic, 1993, 120–21.

MARY E. FRANCES (MARY BLUNDELL)
(1859–1930)

Tom Keegan

BIOGRAPHY

Mary E. Frances was born in Killiney Park, near Dublin. As a young girl she was educated in Lamberton Park, County Laois, and Belgium. A prolific writer from a young age, Mary wrote *True Joy*, a children's novel, at the age of eight. The second of four daughters, Mary coauthored a number of novels with her sisters Agnes and Margaret. In 1873 she moved to Brussels with her family, spending her summers in Switzerland. In 1879 she married Francis Blundell, a son of English Catholic gentry in Lancashire, and on the same day had her first story published in *Irish Monthly*. The couple eventually moved to Crosby, near Liverpool, a location that became a common setting for her novels. Her husband died in 1884 and Mary remained a widow until her death in 1930.

MAJOR WORKS AND THEMES

A commingling of sentimentalism and nationalism, M. E. Frances's many works embrace a melodramatic aesthetic while evincing shades of what would later be termed the "Big House novel." Her first book, *Little Rosary of the Sacred Heart*, a collection of meditations for each day of the year, aimed at a child audience, appeared in 1886. This work was followed in 1892 by *Whither?: A Novel*, which appeared in three volumes. She went on to publish almost a work a year for the next thirty-five years. Of these, many are novels or collections of stories, often in a pastoral setting, often showcasing a young heroine, and often involving a romance plot—for instance, *The Pas-*

torals of Dorset (1901), *Fiander's Widow* (1901), *The Tender Passion* (1910), and *Napoleon of the Looms* (1925). However, this is not always the case, and her 1915 novel, *Dark Rosaleen*, broaches the particularly divisive matter of religion in rural Ireland. Set in the village of Cloon-na-hinch, the novel follows two firstborn sons, Patsy Burke and Hector McTavish, over a twenty-five year span. Frances chronicles their childhood friendship, the influential zealotry of Hector's father—a Protestant minister—Patsy's decision to become a priest, Hector's marriage to Norah Burke, and the violent result of their interfaith marriage. The novel wears its sentimentality garishly at times but maintains an interestingly objective regard for notions of Irishness. Here, perhaps more so than in any of Frances's other works, we can observe the unity of landscape, sentimentality, and nationalism that underlie much of the author's oeuvre. Notably these themes are not limited simply to an Irish setting, and works such as *The Runaway* (1923) and *Wood Sanctuary* (1930) explore the lives and loves of Welsh heroines. Perhaps disingenuously on the author's part, the latter work begins with this statement: "This very simple story is concerned with everyday happenings in the lives of everyday people. It contains no mysteries except those revealed to lovers of wild nature, no complexities save the complexities of the human heart" (1).

CRITICAL RECEPTION

In 1894, W. P. Ryan wrote of her first novel, "*Whither?*, published over her pseudonym of M. E. Frances, made a stir of no transient kind a couple of years ago" (117). Similarly, D. J. O'Donoghue refers to Frances in 1912's *Poets of Ireland: A Biographical Dictionary* as "one of the best-known women novelists of the day" (152). Yet while Frances's work seems to suggest at the very least a moderate degree of controversy and literary weight, it has received scant critical attention of late. In 1935, a now rare and relatively unacknowledged autobiography, *An Irish Novelist's Own Story*, was published posthumously. Terry Eagleton's claim in *Heathcliff and the Great Hunger, Studies in Irish Culture* (London: Verso, 1995, 227) that for nineteenth-century Ireland, "the sexual culture of the nation belonged to a complex economy of land and inheritance, property and procreation," finds ample support in Frances's works. She remains a chronicler of sexual and religious politics within the domestic sphere, occasionally venturing outside the home to address issues such as the white slave trade, as in *The Story of Mary Dunne* (1913). Yet, the most recently published edition of any of her novels was a 1971 reprint of *The Pastorals of Dorset*. It is both surprising and disappointing to see an arguably feminist novelist, who wrote astride the century and facilitated a transition out of the sentimental nineteenth century and into the nationalism and religious fervor of the twentieth, fall so easily out of print.

BIBLIOGRAPHY

Works by Mary E. Frances

Among the Untrodden Ways. London: Blackwood, 1896.
Cousin Christopher. London: T. Fisher Unwin, [1925?].
Dark Rosaleen. London: Cassell, 1915.
A Daughter of the Soil. London: Osgood and McIlwaine, 1895.
Fiander's Widow. London: Longmans, 1901.
Galatea of the Wheatfield. London: Methuen, 1909.
Gentleman Roger. London: Sands, 1911.

Golden Sally. London: Sands, 1925. (With Agnes Blundell.)
Honesty. London: Hodder and Stoughton, [1912?].
In a North Country Village. London: Osgood and McIlwaine, 1893.
An Irish Novelist's Own Story. Dublin: CTSI, 1935.
Lychgate Hall: A Romance. London: Longmans, 1904.
A Maid o'Dorset. London: Cassell, 1917.
The Manor Farm: A Novel. London: Longmans, 1902.
Mary Waters. London: Hutchinson, [1921?].
Miss Erin. London: Methuen, 1905.
Mossoo: A Comedy of a Lancashire Village. London: Hutchinson, [1927?].
Napoleon of the Looms. London: Hutchinson, [1925?].
Noblesse Oblige. London: Long, 1909.
North, South and Over the Sea. London: Newnes, 1902.
Our Alty. London: Long, 1912.
The Pastorals of Dorset. London: Longmans, Green, 1901.
Penton's Captain. London: Chapman and Hall, 1916.
Renewal. London: Allen and Unwin, 1921.
The Runaway. London: Hutchinson, [1923?].
Stepping Westward. London: Methuen, 1907.
The Story of Dan. London: Osgood and McIlwaine, 1894.
The Story of Mary Dunne. London: Murray, 1913.
The Tender Passion. London: Long, 1910.
Tyrer's Lass. London: Sands, 1926. (With Agnes Blundell.)
Whither?: A Novel. London: Griffith and Farran, 1892.
Wild Wheat: A Dorset Romance. London: Longmans, Green, 1905.
Wood Sanctuary. London: Allen and Unwin, 1930. (With Margaret Blundell.)

Studies of Mary E. Francis

Bourke, Angela, Mairin Ni Dhonneadha, Siobhan Kilfeather, Maria Luddy, Margaret MacCurtain, Gerardine Meaney, Mary O'Dowd, and Clair Wills, eds. *The Field Day Anthology of Irish Writing.* Vol. 4 and 5, *Irish Women Writers and Traditions.* Cork: Cork University Press, 2002.

Brown, Stephen. *Ireland in Fiction: A Guide to Irish Novels, Tales, Romances and Folklore.* Part 1. Dublin: Maunsel, 1919.

Deane, Seamus, Andrew Carpenter, and Jonathan Williams, eds. *The Field Day Anthology of Irish Writing.* Vol. 3. Cork: Cork University Press, 2002.

Murphy, James H. *Catholic Fiction and Social Reality in Ireland, 1873–1922.* Westport, CT: Greenwood, 1997.

O'Donoghue, D. J. *The Poets of Ireland: A Biographical Dictionary.* Dublin: Hodges, Figgis, 1912.

Ryan, W. P. *The Irish Literary Revival.* London: Privately published, 1894.

Weekes, Ann Owens. "Mary E. Frances." In *The Attic Guide to Irish Women Writers.* Dublin: Attic, 1993, 129–30.

MIRIAM GALLAGHER
(1940–   )

John L. Murphy

BIOGRAPHY

Born in Waterford, educated in Dublin, London, and Austria, Miriam Gallagher lives in Dublin, working as a speech and language therapist. *Let's Help Our Children Talk* (1977) explains her methods. Having authored twenty-five produced plays to date, she has also written, produced, and directed the 1994 short film *Gypsies*, screened in Dublin, New York, and San Francisco. In 1988 and 1989, she received Arts Council and European Script Fund awards for her screenplay, *Girls in Silk Kimonos*. In 1993, she visited Finland on a writer's exchange; her work has been translated and performed there, as well as in Estonia. Dutch, Russian, and Irish translations of her work have also appeared. She is married to the artist Gerhardt Gallagher; they have two daughters and a son.

Gallagher is a member of the Society of Irish Playwrights and Artists Without Frontiers. Her workshops at Mountjoy and Arbour Hill prisons led to her first playwriting commission; *Fancy Footwork* (1983) was probably the first production allowed by the Irish government to be staged by prisoners in a professional theater. Its success at the Dublin Theatre Festival marked her debut as a playwright, and her concern with human rights continued in her service on the committee and as vice president of Irish PEN (Poets, Playwrights, Essayists, Editors, and Novelists). She has given dramatic workshops around the world for adults and children, as her online essay "Drama in Education" illustrates.

MAJOR WORKS AND THEMES

The commentary on and citations from thirteen plays follow Gallagher's arrangement as *Fancy Footwork: Selected Plays*. In *Labels* (full-length stage play; Dublin Theatre Festival, 1985), themes of departed children, lonely mothers, and escapist daydreams emerge. These concerns, along with their expression through a damaged female protagonist, resurface in *Shyllag*. Gallagher explores organized medicine's damage to both its harried practitioners and its dehumanized patients in a Dublin facility. With sympathy, humor, and compassion for those in Hooterstown's Wellenough Clinic, her jittery dialogue reveals tensions while mostly avoiding sentiment. Still, at times the plot lapses into melodrama. Gallagher dramatizes societal dependence on pharmaceutical relief in its sanctioned doses. She alludes to the impact legal prescriptions have on the illegal drug culture within inner-city Dublin.

Gallagher wrote her first play, *Fancy Footwork* (one act; Dublin Theater Festival, 1983), for Exit, a theater group at Mountjoy Prison. Transferring comic-book caricatures to a lurid stage set, performers mimic political machinations through their own battles within the boxing ring. Concise in action and theme, this play concentrates on a contest well suited to dramatization in a confined, intensified setting. As with many of Gallagher's dramas, the true bout matches up illusion versus reality. Such a clash often ends with its survivor worsened or softened by mind-altering drugs or psychological withdrawal from trauma.

Just Desserts blends three earlier pieces, *Omlettes* (a forty-five minute play, 1985) with *Lemon Soufflé* (fifty minutes, 1985) and a brief opener, *Easter Eggs*. These were combined at an Andrews Lane Theatre production in Dublin in 1990. In her introduction, Gallagher states, "As children we say YES to life—*Easter Eggs* is fast, fun, and messy with the text in verse. As confused adolescents we say both YES and NO to Life. *Lemon Soufflé* is dreamy, romantic, mysterious. As adults the choice is already made. *Omlettes* (consciously misspelt) is potent, controlled, sinister" (156). Eggs serve as an ingredient in all three "desserts," and unite the dramatic trilogy. In the last of the plays that Gallagher describes above, adults and students wait for delayed "omlettes," while menaced by waiters acting as mimes and counseled by a visiting tramp, under a portrait of the departed manager whose whims the staff serve. Allusions to Charlie Chaplin and Samuel Beckett and scores from Sibelius and Rimski-Korsakov flip light comedic morsels into a queasy scramble of earlier twentieth-century modernism. For *Lemon Soufflé*, Elizabethan tunes sweeten reveries rather than arouse nightmares. Unlike the "omlettes," soufflés arrive but turn out unpredictably, for the secret of a successful dessert—or a meaningful life ahead—eludes most of the young couples who face a dinner of "musical chairs" within a castle of many rooms and courses. The commands of the feast's unseen Lord of the Old Abbey again connect the play to the similarly absent manager of *Omlettes*. Music, fantasy, and continental allusions are sprinkled into both texts. Gallagher's ambition to place her subjects in the larger European legacy often infuses her dramas. The final piece, *Easter Eggs,* set in the early twentieth century, merges the Pearl of Great Price gospel parable with fairy-tale magic. It hints at adult power and ensuing despair—"Black Pollution"—while reinforcing happy endings, as with the Christian holiday that the children's party celebrates, mixing pagan and folk imagery.

Continuing the fairy-tale mood, the one-act *Dreamkeeper* premiered at ContemporÉire in 1984. This two-person allegory equates a mountain climb to personal struggle—while enacting violence, theology, and mutual reliance. This play debuted as twinned with another one-act, *The Sealwoman and the Fisher*, which adapts the Scots legend of the "selkie." Inclusion of bones and bodhran for musical accompaniment, with barefoot and stylized movements of dancing performers, recalls Celtic Revival productions. Hoods, robes, and chants suggest early Abbey efforts. Echoes of *Riders to the Sea*, dirges to Mananan MacLir, and invocations to the Sea Child recall Yeats, Synge, and Lady Gregory. An Irish translation by Margaret Birmingham, *An Beanríon agus t-Iascaire*, appeared at Scoil Aengus in Dublin the following year.

The first of three musical subjects, *Carolan's Cap* commemorates Turlough O'Carolan (1670–1738), with an "interlude" to be played in "a good ale house," village square, or castle that integrates eleven compositions into its portrayal of their blind harpist's life. Reviving the convivial spirit of Carolan's tunes, this one-actor piece seeks to restore the atmosphere of the Big House that its itinerant inspiration enlivened, for Carolan served as the last of the ancient Irish bards. Commissioned for the Dublin Crisis Conference, this interlude premiered at Synod Hall, Christchurch, in early 1986. On Christmas Day of the same year, an RTÉ adaptation aired. The following year, a

Finnish translation debuted in Helsinki, backed by Finnish musicians. During 1986 and 1987, concert-hall appearances and a performance at the Keadue O'Carolan festival were given, with inclusion of a harpist supplementing the original drama's classical guitar and flute accompaniment.

Gallagher's next interlude, *Nocturne*, is about the creator of the nocturne, Dublin-born John Field (1782–1837). With his Irish origins, London apprenticeship, and Russian residence, Field elevates the musical and dramatic possibilities inherent in Carolan's circumscribed career into an elegant ambience "for performance in a concert hall, theatre, or Big House" (*Fancy Footwork*, 212). The play debuted in the John Field Room of Dublin's National Concert Hall in 1987; it returned at the Dublin Millennium John Field Celebration in 1988. A Russian translation followed. Gallagher, by costume and decor, brings 1820s Russia into Field's impressionistic recollections, countered by an actress who plays three female roles against his two. The emergence of a determined woman, Ehktarina Karaminskova, against a male antagonist's straying affections, as well as compression of multiple characters into fewer actors, anticipates Gallagher's *Shyllag*—which focuses all its many roles into a one-woman performance. For *Nocturne*, a composer's music, anchored by the script, conjures up for listeners its creator's recorded ambition.

The last of Gallagher's three musical-dramatic interludes, *Bohemians,* dramatizes the efforts of composers Michael W. Balfe (Dublin-born, 1808–1870) and William V. Wallace (Waterford-born; 1812–1865). In 1989 it was performed at Waterford's Garter Lane and Dundalk Arts Centre. As with *Nocturne*, Irish composers find success abroad. The two male leads play dashing, confident characters, paired against another strong female, Zigeunerin. The mid-nineteenth-century continental setting brings spectators into the drawing room, where she plays off the two men's skills before the audience, who will judge which of the two proves most deserving of acclaim. The two compete for her, while all three characters play incidental characters from Balfe and Wallace's careers. The contest ends in a tie; the two men race offstage together to write her an opera. Musical selections, as with the earlier interludes, enrich the play and transmit the appeal of the two men while introducing their work to yet another audience.

In *Shyllag*, a fifty-minute work performed by Gallagher in the one-woman role, the conceit of an actor taking on multiple roles, the integration of music to deepen mood, and the concentration of a determined female protagonist confronting a traditional culture all expand the playwright's scope. It opened in 1993 at Dublin's Andrews Lane; RTÉ aired a radio adaptation in 1999. Gallagher's Austrian studies in 1957 introduced her to refugees from 1956 Budapest. Her interest in Hungarian culture energizes this play; recordings by the folk ensemble Muzsikás enhance ambience even before the curtain rises. In Gallagher's most ambitious attempt to express synchronically and diachronically three generations of women over the past half century, she tackles exile, sexual liberation, Shakespearean role-playing, and Hungary before and after the Iron Curtain—to mention only the play's major concerns. Mother-daughter love, the inevitability of maturity, and the loss of innocence predominate in the monologues of Allwych, a Travelling Player—described in the notes as "[b]rave, mischievous, somewhat crazed" (373). Intertextual links among Shakespeare's roles, Allwych's travel anecdotes, post–World War II mores, Magyar allusion, and the continuing time shifts between Shyllag—Allwych's daughter—Allwych's mother, and various characters who flit in and out of Allwych's consciousness make this Gallagher's most challenging text. Ambiguously explained, with shades reminiscent of Beckett's verbose monologists enlivened through Allwych's many voices, she haunts "a railway station in Limbo" and waits for a train that never comes. Whether or not Allwych is lost in an inner space or an actual point of departure remains inconclusive. Despite this liminal indeterminacy, *Shyllag* humanizes the women and children abandoned through war to survive only as refugees so often throughout the twentieth century.

For *The Ring of Mont de Balison*, Gallagher offers a one-act commissioned as a community play for the Ranelagh Millennium Project. It was performed outdoors at Belgrave Square, Rathmines, in 1988. Gallagher begins with Cualann's Norman invasion and follows its evolution into present-day Ranelagh. Neighborhood amateurs filled dozens of roles, from the actual lord mayor of Dublin to the Norman garrison's lord. Gallagher includes dance, classical music, costumes, a mimed battle, and a fair. A cycle rally and acclaim for the capital city's nuclear-free zone climax the play, its generations linked by the story of a prized ring. Reminiscent of medieval drama in its localized references and incorporation of morality with mirth, the play continues Gallagher's workshop techniques that extend theatrical performance back into the crowd.

Dusty Bluebells returns to continental themes. Along with morality, this drama addresses performance itself. Women prisoners on Lush Island rehearse *The Mikado* while a German chemical firm proposes there a fertilizer factory. Ecological, farcical, and theatrical elements combine for an explosive finale, but the play diffuses its energy. As with *Labels*, social criticism uneasily meets bureaucratic satire. The loss of momentum within both lengthy plays weakens their cathartic conclusions. Her shorter works featured in *Fancy Footwork* transplant Gallagher's complex concerns into dramatic situations where, freed from overreliance upon contemporary urban critique, their creativity can flourish more exuberantly. *Dusty Bluebells* debuted at Damer Hall, Dublin, in 1987.

Other plays include *Midhir and the Firefly*—a dance and chorus piece inspired by the Irish legend of Midhir and Etain—and *Nasturtiums and Cherry Buns. The Nude Who Painted Back* appeared at the Fifth International Women Playwrights Conference at Athens and Delphi, in October 2000. A playlet, *Kalahari Blues*, debuted for Clonmel's Galloglass Theatre's 2001 autumn tour. Journalism and a story, "Pusakis at Paros," have also appeared.

CRITICAL RECEPTION

Launching Gallagher's novel, *Song for Salamander*, Irish poet Macdara Woods summed up its protagonist as "a Liberal caught up in the Corporate Fascist." He praised the book as "composed of marvelous visual moments and references, calling out to be translated into cinema" (typescript provided by Gallagher). A reviewer at the Web site Bibliofemme, while acknowledging the author's enthusiasm and way with words, rejected its fantastic inspiration: "Kafka taps deep into the human psyche in a way that leaves this novel standing on a hill waving half-heartedly at it." This 2004 novel, Gallagher's first work to be published abroad, should expand her audience beyond Ireland, where her workshops have introduced her to many students.

BIBLIOGRAPHY

Works by Miriam Gallagher

"Drama in Education: Is the Living Dramatist Dead or Alive?" *Irish Theatre Forum* 2, no. 2 (Spring 1998). http://www.ucd.ie/irthfrm/mgallagh.htm.

Fancy Footwork: Selected Plays. 2nd ed. Dublin: Society of Irish Playwrights, 1997.
Let's Help Our Children Talk. Dublin: O'Brien, 1977.
"Pusaki at Paros." *Artists Without Frontiers.* Members Page for Miriam Gallagher. http://artistswithoutfrontiers.com/mgallagher/index.html#.
"Shyllag: A Short Story." *Artists Without Frontiers: An On-Line Magazine* 1 (December 2003). http://magazine.artistswithoutfrontiers.com/archive/issue1/article_2_1.html.

SARAH GRAND
(1854–1943)

Tina O'Toole

BIOGRAPHY

Sarah Grand (Frances Bellenden-Clarke), "New Woman" writer and feminist activist, was born in Donaghadee, County Down, in 1854, the daughter of a naval coastguardsman. She grew up in County Mayo, but following her father's death in the 1860s, her family moved to Scarborough. Despite this remove, her Irish childhood had a profound effect on her writing career, and she ever after identified herself as Irish. Her semiautobiographical novel *The Beth Book* (1897) is set in Ireland.

Frances had a sporadic formal education, sent to school only at fifteen. There she formed a club in support of Josephine Butler's crusade to repeal the Contagious Diseases Acts, as a result of which she was expelled because of her religious scepticism and "forthright" manner. At sixteen she married David McFall, a thirty-nine-year-old widower and military surgeon to the Royal Irish Fusiliers. Her marriage created another link with Ireland, McFall being from Magherafelt. As a military wife, she traveled widely in the Far East, experiencing cultures far removed from home. Her acquaintance with her husband's medical knowledge enabled her to gain experience of another kind "not normally offered a Victorian girl" (Kersley, 37), an understanding of the body and of those diseases treated by a military surgeon.

In 1879 the McFalls moved to England, where he took up a post at the notorious Lock Hospital in Warrington. Frances's distress at her husband's complicity in the Lock system—part of the medical apparatus established by the Contagious Diseases Acts—added to her difficulties in this period. She was unhappily married, she was unfulfilled as a mother (her son, Archie, was born in 1871), and her feminist views made her unpopular locally. In *Ideala* (1888), her first novel, the eponymous heroine calls for meaningful work for women, decrying the domestic trap: "all this seems to me a grievous waste of Me!" (38). Frances continued with her writing and with efforts to have her work published. In so doing, she created a new role for herself, an independent personality whom she would later call "Sarah Grand."

Ideala, published anonymously at her own expense, was taken up by Richard Bentley, reprinted three times in 1889, and later reissued by Heinemann. Her second novel,

The Heavenly Twins (1893), was an overnight success, creating one of the sensations of literature. Reprinted by Heinemann six times in 1893, by 1894 it had sold twenty thousand copies in England (Cunningham, 177). Published by Cassell in the United States, it sold one hundred thousand copies (Mott, 182) and headed the best-seller list in 1894.

Frances left her family in the mid-1890s, changing her name to Sarah Grand. The Married Women's Property Act of 1882 meant that her earnings were her own, which was decisive in this move. In the 1890s, Grand's work was grist for the mill of the fledgling feminist movement. She later recalled this period warmly: "With these new friends I was in a new world. To hear them talk was like having doors opened and light shed on all that was obscure to me" (*The Heavenly Twins* [New York: Cassell, 1923], 28). A member of the Pioneer Club, she wrote for *Shafts*, her public lectures were in demand, and she wrote feminist essays and articles. She is credited with coining the term "the New Woman" to describe the new feminist heroine of the day.

However, by the early twentieth century, following the Wilde trials and the Boer War, public interest in the New Woman project had waned. Grand settled in Tunbridge Wells, where she kept up her political involvement, running several local suffrage societies. When the vote was won, a crowd of neighbors appeared with flowers and banners to escort her to the polls (Mangum, 192). She befriended the Dublin poet Katherine Tynan in the 1920s, who later described Grand as "a green oasis in the arid waste of Tunbridge Wells" (Kersley, 113). In 1920, she retired to live with Quaker friends in Bath. She served as mayoress of Bath from 1922 to 1929, and clearly relished her role as a pillar of society. Now firmly ensconced in the bosom of fashionable Bath, she had completed her journey from the subversive margins to the center of "respectable" British society. She died in Wiltshire in 1943, at the age of eighty-eight.

MAJOR WORKS AND THEMES

Sarah Grand's name is synonymous with New Woman fiction, and the writer's fortunes follow the ebb and flow of the genre itself. Grand was a key feminist writer and activist at the fin de siècle, and *The Heavenly Twins* developed a feminist aesthetic in fiction that involved a rethinking of traditional gender roles and posed a radical challenge to cultural and social mores. In a range of essays and short stories, mostly published in the feminist press, Grand tackles a variety of issues, such as marriage and the double standard, access to education for women, and the vote.

The 1890s are associated with questions about the relationship between art and life, and an investment in "Art for Art's sake." New Woman writers such as Grand opposed this trend, instead conflating social and artistic discourses, and refusing to see them as separate categories. Thus, the New Woman project is bounded by a sense of social duty not only to a community of women, but also to society at large, and by a commitment to writing with a purpose. Grand's heroines exist within a context of community—in direct opposition to the hero figure of novels by Henry Fielding, Oliver Goldsmith, and Tobias Smollet. Decisive action is difficult for her heroines, women living under the circumstances of late Victorian society, who cannot simply reject their socialization in the face of new ideologies. Grand explores the difficulties of balancing family responsibilities and the sense of duty to others instilled in women of this generation, engendering in such women a newly awakened feminist consciousness and sense of duty to themselves. The ambiguities of this situation are evident in the plot strategies of her novels and through the choices made by her protagonists, which are now sometimes read as inconsistencies or as rather weak compromises.

CRITICAL RECEPTION

The writings of the New Woman project have reemerged from the archives as a result of cultural projects of the second feminist movement in the 1970s, and the work of scholars such as Ann Ardis and Elaine Showalter. Before this, critics of New Woman material dismissed it as polemic, and reviews, such as one in the *Athenaeum* of November 2, 1897, dismissed Grand's work as "didactic," "preaching," and "moralizing" (743–44).

Unlike other writers of the period, mention of whose texts has been largely confined to footnotes, Sarah Grand's name occurs consistently in current scholarship relating to the period. Bonnell illustrates Grand's shift from a somewhat basic plea for equal rights within marriage to a broader platform that sees women as active agents within the world. Mangum illustrates the ways in which Sarah Grand used her very "middlingness," or the appearance of being nonthreatening, to disrupt (17–35). This device enabled her to carry a feminist message to a much wider audience than was reached by the works of more radical feminist writers such as Mona Caird. However, retrospectively, it has contributed to Grand's lack of prestige as a feminist and a writer in the current context. Throughout her work, Grand asserts that her New Woman protagonist is a sign of things to come. In one of her best-known passages, she writes, "Beth was one of the first swallows of the women's summer. She was strange to the race when she arrived, and uncharitably commented upon; but now the type is known, and has ceased to surprise" (*The Beth Book*, 527).

BIBLIOGRAPHY

Works by Sarah Grand

Adnam's [sic] *Orchard*. London: Heinemann, 1912.
Babs the Impossible. London: Hutchinson, 1901.
The Beth Book. 1897. Bristol: Thoemmes, 1994.
The Breath of Life. Manchester: Hygienic Health, n.d.
A Domestic Experiment. Edinburgh: Blackwood, 1891.
The Heavenly Twins. 3 vols. Privately printed, 1892. Ann Arbor: University of Michigan Press, 1992.
Ideala: A Study from Life. Privately printed, 1888. London: Heinemann, 1893.
"Mere Man." *Saturday Review*, January 8, 1901, 733–45.
The Modern Man and Maid. London: Marshall, 1898.
"The New Aspect of the Woman Question." *North American Review* 158 (1894): 270–76.
Our Manifold Nature. London: Heinemann, 1894.
Singularly Deluded. 1892. Edinburgh: Blackwood, 1893.
The Tenor and the Boy. London: Heinemann, 1899.
Variety. London: Heinemann, 1922.
The Winged Victory. London: Heinemann, 1916.

Studies of Sarah Grand

Ardis, Ann L. *New Women, New Novels: Feminism and Early Modernism*. New Brunswick, NJ: Rutgers University Press, 1990.
Bonnell, Marilyn. "Sarah Grand and the Critical Establishment: Art for [Wo]man's Sake." *Tulsa Studies in Women's Literature* 14, no. 1 (Spring 1995): 123–48.
Cunningham, A. R. "The New Woman Fiction of the 1890s." *Victorian Studies* 17 (1973): 177–86.
Davenport-Hynes, Richard. *Sex, Death and Punishment*. London: Fontana, 1991.

Kersley, Gillian. *Darling Madame: Sarah Grand and Devoted Friend.* London: Virago, 1983.

Mangum, Teresa Lynn. *Married, Middlebrow and Militant: Sarah Grand and the New Woman Novel.* Ann Arbor: University of Michigan Press, 1998.

Mott, F. L. *Golden Multitudes: The Story of Best-Sellers in the U.S.* New York: Macmillan, 1947.

LADY GREGORY (NÉE [ISABELLA] AUGUSTA PERSSE)
(1852–1932)

Martin F. Kearney

BIOGRAPHY

The twelfth of sixteen children, Isabella Augusta Persse was born on her Unionist father's Roxborough estate in County Galway. Educated privately, she married Sir William Gregory, former member of Parliament, in 1880; she was twenty-seven, he sixty-three. Their only child, William Robert, was born in 1881. The Gregorys visited Egypt that year, where Lady Gregory met Wilfrid Scawen Blunt, the first of her lovers. Widowed in 1892, Lady Gregory thereafter wore black. Her name and social position served Ireland and herself well. She met W. B. Yeats in 1894, and 1897 marked the first of his twenty summer visits to her Coole estate. Other writers, such as John M. Synge and Sean O'Casey, visited, too. Their discussions led directly to the Irish Literary Revival, which embraced Irish culture, art, and language. Her vital role in the establishment of an Irish national theater culminated in the 1904 founding of the Abbey Theatre; her play *Spreading the News* (1904) shared billing with a Yeats work on opening night. She served the Abbey over the years as patent holder, board member, playwright (more than forty plays), actor, and consultant. She took the Abbey Theatre Company to America in 1911–12, where she also lectured at universities, and where she had a brief affair with John Quinn. Among her literary works are translations of Irish sagas, collections of folktales, and translations of Irish poems. She spent much of her life trying to better the lives of Ireland's less fortunate via her nationalist/humanist art. The Coole Big House was not burned during the Troubles of the 1920s due to the Irish populace's high regard for her, although eventually it did suffer that fate. The "mother of Irish drama" died in 1932, from breast cancer.

MAJOR WORKS AND THEMES

A political writer, Lady Gregory touted national independence. Her first publication, *Arabi and His Household* (1882), supported the Egyptian nationalist Arabi Bey against Turkish rule. England's support of the Turks and the subsequent deportation of Bey mirrored Irish affairs, in her view, and the collection of essays she later edited, *Ideals in Ireland* (1901), placed her in the camp of Irish Nationalists. She next translated Irish mythology, *Cuchulain of Muirthemne* (1902) and *Gods and Fighting Men* (1904), presenting to the world Celtic myths integral to Irish Literary Revivalist literature. A major scholarly and creative achievement, Gregory's translations placed in the mouths of mythic figures the peasant speech, "Kiltartan," of the Coole region. These two books, along with her *Kiltartan History Book* (1909) and *Kiltartan Wonder Book* (1910), unify much disparate Irish myth, legend, history, and folklore. *A Book of Saints and Wonders* (1906) likewise focused on Irish personages of the distant past such as St. Brigit and St. Colum Cille. Each book was designed to transport Ireland's ancient past to contemporary Irish consciousness, concurrently exploring the "Irishness" of the Irish within an ethnic yet universal framework. More than just an Irish Nationalist, Lady Gregory also was a keen observer of human nature.

The greatness of Gregory's dramatic art rests precisely in its ability to deal simultaneously with the human experience and with the Irish experience. For example, the one-act play *The Rising of the Moon* (1903) illuminates the human condition of two native Irishmen while at the same time encouraging revolt against England. Similarly, the plays *Spreading the News, Kincora* (1905), and *The Gaol Gate* (1906) are anti-English, but their characters are always human first and Irish second. Gregory's experimental bent also gave birth to a number of Molière-turned-Kiltartan dramas such as *The Doctor in Spite of Himself* (1906) and *The Rogueries of Scapin* (1908). Ireland is again the fountainhead for *The Workhouse Ward* (1909) and *McDonough's Wife* (1913), illustrating Irish peasants' tragic lives and the phenomenon of "begrudgers," while adroitly evoking pathos from the protagonists' lonely plights. The recent historical past and the distant mythic past form the backdrops for *The Deliverer* (1911) and *Grania* (1912); the former deals with the fall of Charles Stewart Parnell, the latter with a young woman's disastrous endeavor to marry a young man, even though promised to an old hero (a common Gregorian theme perhaps influenced by personal experience).

The Kiltartan Poetry Book (1918) translates Irish folk poems. Culling the poems for this edition soon after the wartime death of her son, Gregory painfully was attuned to the reality that laments outnumber joyful poems through the ages. *Visions and Beliefs in the West of Ireland* (1920) followed, which was a culmination of decades of fieldwork. Her autobiography, *Seventy Years* (1974), albeit informative, can become entangled in details. Her *Journals* (1978, 1987), however, make for compelling reading, as therein Gregory's discerning eye fixes upon Coole Park and its tenants, the Anglo-Irish War, and the Troubles.

CRITICAL RECEPTION

Ideals in Ireland received a mixed welcome because it dealt with theoretical and political questions of the day. To some, it was obsessive and opinionated; to others, it justified Irish nationalism. W. B. Yeats thought *Cuchulain of Muirthemne* the best book to come out of Ireland in his lifetime, perhaps because it endeavored to unify diverse mythological materials and could inspire writers of the Irish Literary Revival (preface to *Cuchulain of Muirthemne*, 11). Some criticism averred that her translations of the Irish myths were free, that she misconstrued mythic features, and that her Kiltartan dialect was artificial. Herbert Fackler, however, argues that Lady Gregory never meant the translations to be accepted as literal, adding that her renderings of myths such as "The Fate of the Sons of Usnach" ingeniously reconciled difficulties concerning character motivation. Ulick O'Connor praises Gregory's development of a literary style based on speech patterns of the peasantry, first recorded in writing by Douglas Hyde. Saddlemyer (in "Image-Maker for Ireland") asserts that the significance of Gregory's study and collection of folklore cannot be overestimated. In her *Journals*, George Orwell perceived a rare breed: a member of the ruling class who identified with the oppressed peasantry. Mary Fitzgerald rates Gregory's autobiographical and historical works as highly as her folklore collections and translations.

Without doubt, Gregory's plays constitute her greatest literary contribution. From 1903 to her death almost thirty years later, her plays were popular with Abbey Theatre audiences. Although they were performed less frequently after 1932, Gregory's plays enjoyed a rebirth of favor with audiences after 1960. Widely respected (if infrequently performed) today by scholars and audiences, their renaissance is overdue. One-act plays were Gregory's forte, a little-used form before she experimented with it and shaped it into extremely powerful theater. Edward Kopper Jr., among many, believes her literary reputation rests with her briefer works. One of Gregory's earliest plays, *The Rising of the Moon*, was widely praised for its masterful dramatic technique, Thomas Hogan citing it as the best-written single act play ever (74). Though at times it is dismissed as a nationalistic production, most critics praise it highly and think it Gregory's most successful one-act play; for example, Kopper credits Gregory's consummate compression and composition of details (139). Early reviews of *Spreading the News* tended to focus on the play's humor and to type it as farce. Later critics such as Saddlemyer, Kopper, and Adams see this early comedy as a little gem with much intricacy, its curious upheaval probably to arise again in the cyclical fashion of nature. Gregory's dramatic realism and prose style greatly influenced other Abbey poetic dramas. *The Workhouse Ward*, yet another successful one-act comedy, is notable for its lively and comic war of words that some believe captures Irish character more truly than do the plays of Synge or O'Casey. Ernest Blythe informs us that this play was performed at the Abbey 241 times by 1962, second in number of all her plays' performances only to *The Rising of the Moon* (9). *The Gaol Gate*, another one-acter, is tragedy at its most touching in its consummate revelation of the disparity between English law and Irish identity. Comparing this play to the later *McDonough's Wife*, Kopper praises Lady Gregory's ability in each work to arouse hope within the depths of despair.

During Lady Gregory's lifetime, her dramas based on history and folklore, such as *The White Cockade, The Canavans* (1906), and *Dervogilla* (1908), were thought to be interesting additions to the Irish literary revivalist's cache of plays. *The Canavans*, generally, is regarded as Gregory's most successful full-length drama. Since her death, however, these plays have declined in popularity and literary esteem. Thus, they have been described variously as tedious, as closet drama, and as curiosities of early historical revisionism. Her plays based on Irish myth and legend, too, have been critically savaged. Her earliest endeavor in this area, *Kincora*, was attacked in its own time as banal, overworked, and verbose. *The Deliverer*'s literary weakness and uncharacteristic rancor mar its reputation, but its portrait of Parnell is praiseworthy. Far and away the most successful Gregory play based on myth is *Grania*. Its strengths reside in Gregory's abilities to make mythic characters human and to provide Grania with psychological complexity. Recent studies by Richard Cave, by Dawn Duncan, and by Cathy Leeney laud *Grania* and other Gregory tragedies as feminist vehicles wherein the tragic heroine's desires are given a dramatic vocabulary unequaled by any male playwright; the archetypal journey of the heroine is reinvented—the symbolic mission is inevitably successful; and open endings deliberately challenge the customary dramatic form of tragedy and thus lead to an aesthetic and thematic compromise.

Lady Gregory's literary reputation resides predominantly with her one-act plays of contemporary Irish life. Peasants are treated honestly, some might say to a fault, for human vices and virtues share Gregory's stage. Her strengths in these successful plays, Una Ellis-Fermor avers (139), are her natural talent unspoiled by training and her placing dramatic unity and structure above overt theory. The Irish Literary Revival's "mother" of Irish folklore and myth, Gregory did more to popularize these Irish subjects than did any of her contemporaries, a major coup, certainly. A controversial figure by 2005 (social class, politics, and gender issues with regard to herself and her work are rife), Lady Gregory is accurately placed by Anne Fogarty as a seminal writer in Irish modernism's canon; her impressive literary legacy is of considerable contemporary import (xiii).

BIBLIOGRAPHY

Works by Lady Gregory

Arabi and His Household. London: Kegan Paul, Trench, 1882.

A Book of Saints and Wonders, Put Down Here by Lady Gregory According to the Old Writings and the Memory of the People of Ireland. Foreword by Edward Malins. Gerrards Cross, UK: Smythe; New York: Oxford University Press, 1971.

Collected Plays 1: The Comedies. Edited by Ann Saddlemyer. Buckinghamshire, UK: Smythe; New York: Oxford University Press, 1971. (*Twenty Five, Spreading the News, Hyacinth Halvey, The Rising of the Moon, The Jackdaw, The Workhouse Ward, The Bogie Men, Coats, Damer's Gold, Hanrahan's Oath, The Wrens, On the Racecourse, Michelin, The Meadow Gate, The Dispensary, The Shoelace, The Lighted Window, A Losing Game.*)

Collected Plays 2: The Tragedies and Tragic-Comedies. Edited by Ann Saddlemyer. Gerrards Cross, UK: Smythe; New York: Oxford University Press, 1971. (*The Gaol Gate, Grania, Kincora, Dervorgilla, McDonough's Wife, The Image, The Canavans, The White Cockade, The Deliverer, The Old Woman Remembers.*)

Collected Plays 3: The Wonder and Supernatural Plays. Edited by Ann Saddlemyer. Gerrards Cross, UK: Smythe; New York: Oxford University Press, 1971. (*Colman and Guaire, The Travelling Man, The Full Moon, Shanwalla, The Golden Apple, The Jester, The Dragon, Aristotle's Bellows, The Story Brought by Brigit, Dave.*)

Collected Plays 4: The Translations and Adaptations. Edited by Ann Saddlemyer. Gerrards Cross, UK: Smythe; New York: Oxford University Press, 1971. (*Teja, The Doctor in Spite of Himself, The Rogueries of Scapin, The Miser, The Would-Be Gentleman, Mirandolina, Sancho's Master, The Poorhouse, The Unicorn from the Stars, Heads or Harps.*)

Cuchulain of Muirthemne: The Story of the Men of the Red Branch of Ulster. Arranged and Put into English by Lady Gregory. Preface by W. B. Yeats. Foreword by Daniel Murphy. Gerrards Cross, UK: Smythe; New York: Oxford University Press, 1970.

Gods and Fighting Men: The Story of the Tuatha de Danaan and of the Fianna of Ireland. Preface by W. B. Yeats. Foreword by Daniel Murphy. Gerrards Cross, UK: Smythe; New York: Oxford University Press, 1970.

Ideals in Ireland. London: At the Sign of the Unicorn; New York: Mansfield, 1902. (Editor.)

The Journals. Vol. 1, *10 October 1916–24 February 1925.* Edited by Daniel J. Murphy. Gerrards Cross, UK: Smythe, 1978.

The Journals. Vol. 2, *21 February 1925–9 May 1932.* Edited by Daniel J. Murphy. Essay "The Death of Lady Gregory" by W. B. Yeats. Afterword by Colin Smythe. Gerrards Cross, UK: Smythe, 1987.

The Kiltartan Book. Foreword by Padraic Colum. Gerrards Cross, UK: Smythe; New York: Oxford University Press, 1971. (*The Kiltartan Poetry Book, The Kiltartan History Book, The Kiltartan Wonder Book.*)

Lady Gregory's Diaries 1892–1902. Edited by James Pethica. Gerrards Cross, UK: Smythe; New York: Oxford University Press, 1996.

Mr. Gregory's Letter-Box 1813–1835. Foreword by Jon Stallworthy. Gerrards Cross, UK:
   Smythe, 1981; New York: Oxford University Press, 1982.
Our Irish Theatre: A Chapter of Autobiography. Foreword by Roger McHugh. Gerrards Cross,
   UK: Smythe; New York: Oxford University Press, 1972.
Over the River. London: Ridgway, 1888.
A Phantom's Pilgrimage, or Home Ruin. London: Ridgway, 1893.
Poets and Dreamers: Studies and Translations from the Irish. Foreword by T. R. Henn. Gerrards
   Cross, UK: Smythe; New York: Oxford University Press, 1974.
Seventy Years, 1852–1922: Being the Autobiography of Lady Gregory. Edited by Colin Smythe.
   Gerrards Cross, UK: Smythe, 1974; New York: Macmillan, 1976.
Sir Hugh Lane: His Life and Legacy. Foreword by James White. Gerrards Cross, UK: Smythe;
   New York: Oxford University Press, 1973. (Sir Hugh Lane's Life and Achievement, Case
   for the Return of Sir Hugh Lane's Pictures to Dublin, Sir Hugh Lane's French Pictures,
   and other material concerning the Lane Bequest.)
Sir William Gregory, An Autobiography. Foreword by Edward McCourt. Gerrards Cross, UK:
   Smythe, 1995.
Visions and Beliefs in the West of Ireland. With Two Essays and Notes by W. B. Yeats. Foreword
   by Elizabeth Coxhead. Gerrards Cross, UK: Smythe; New York: Oxford University Press,
   1970. (Collected and Arranged by Lady Gregory.)

Studies of Lady Gregory

Adams, Hazard. *Lady Gregory*. Lewisburg, PA: Bucknell University Press, 1973.
Blythe, Ernest. *The Abbey Theatre*. Dublin: National Theatre Society, 1962.
Butler, George F. "The Hero's Metamorphosis in Lady Gregory's *Cuchulain of Muirthemne*:
   Scholarship and Popularization." *Eire-Ireland* 22, no. 4 (Winter 1987): 36–46.
Cave, Richard Allen. "Revaluations: Representations of Women in the Tragedies of Gregory and
   Yeats." *Irish University Review* 34, no. 1 (Spring–Summer 2004): 122–33.
Coxhead, Elizabeth. *J.M. Synge and Lady Gregory*. London: Longmans, 1963.
———. *Lady Gregory: A Literary Portrait*. London: Macmillan, 1961.
Deane, Paul. "Mythical and Historical Irish Women of Strength as Portrayed by Lady Gregory."
   Notes on Modern Irish Literature 10 (1998): 51–56.
Duncan, Dawn. "Lady Gregory and the Feminine Journey: *The Gaol Gate, Grania, and The Story
   Brought By Brigit*." *Irish University Review* 34, no. 1 (Spring–Summer 2004): 133–44.
Ellis-Fermor, Una. *The Irish Dramatic Movement*. 1939. London: Methuen, 1954.
Fackler, Herbert. *That Tragic Queen: The Deirdre Legend in Anglo-Irish Literature*. Salzburg:
   University of Salzburg Press, 1978.
Fitzgerald, Mary. "Sean O'Casey and Lady Gregory: The Record of a Friendship." In *Sean
   O'Casey Centenary Essays*, edited by David Krause and Robert G. Lowery, 67–99. To-
   towa, NJ: Barnes and Noble, 1980.
Fogarty, Anne. "Introduction." *Irish University Review* 34, no. 1 (Spring–Summer 2004): viii–
   xiv.
Gillin, Edward. " 'Our Incorrigible Genius': Irish Comic Strategy in Lady Gregory's *Spreading
   the News*." *Colby Library Quarterly* 23, no. 4 (December 1987): 168–72.
Hawkins, Maureen. "Ascendancy Nationalism, Feminist Nationalism and Stagecraft in Lady Gre-
   gory's Revision of *Kincora*." In *Irish Writers and Politics*, edited by Okifumi Komesu
   and Masaru Sekine, 94–108. Gerrards Cross, UK: Smythe, 1989.
Hogan, Thomas. "Theatre." *Envoy* 2, no. 5 (April 24, 1950): 72–77.
Johansen, Kristin. "Creating an Historical Community: Lady Gregory's Work with the Irish Literary Revival." *Notes on Modern Irish Literature* 10 (1998): 46–50.
Knapp, James F. "Irish Primitivism and Imperial Discourse: Lady Gregory's Peasantry." In
   Macropolitics of Nineteenth-Century Literature: Nationalism, Exoticism, Imperialism,
   edited by Jonathan Arac, 286–301. Philadelphia: University of Pennsylvania Press, 1991.

Kohfeldt, Mary Lou. *Lady Gregory: The Woman Behind the Irish Renaissance.* London: Deutsch; New York: Atheneum, 1985.

Kopper, Edward A., Jr. *Lady Gregory: A Review of the Criticism.* Butler, PA: Kopper, 1991.

———. *Lady Isabella Persse Gregory.* Boston: Twayne, 1976.

Laurence, Dan H., and Nicholas Grene, eds. *Shaw, Lady Gregory and the Abbey: A Correspondence and a Record.* Gerrards Cross, UK: Smythe, 1993.

Leeney, Cathy. "The New Woman in a New Ireland? Grania after Naturalism." *Irish University Review* 34, no. 1 (Spring–Summer 2004): 157–71.

McCurry, Jacqueline. "From Domestic Warrior to 'Some Mild Modern Housewife': Lady Gregory's Transformation of the Deirdre Story." *Colby Quarterly* 28, no. 1 (March 1992): 34–38.

McDiarmid, Lucy. "The Demotic Lady Gregory." In *High and Low Moderns: Literature and Culture 1889–1939*, edited by Maria DiBattista and Lucy McDiarmid, 212–34. New York: Oxford University Press, 1996.

Mikhail, E. H. *Lady Gregory: An Annotated Bibliography of Criticism.* Troy, NY: Whitston, 1982.

Murphy, Daniel J. "Lady Gregory, Co-Author and Sometimes Author of the Plays of W.B. Yeats." In *Modern Irish Literature: Essays in Honor of William York Tindall*, edited by Raymond J. Porter and James D. Brophy, 43–52. New Rochelle, NY: Iona College Press, 1972.

Murphy, Maureen. "Lady Gregory: 'The Book of the People.' " *Colby Quarterly* 27, no. 1 (March 1991): 40–47.

O'Connor, Ulick. *All the Olympians: A Biographical Portrait of the Irish Literary Renaissance.* New York: Atheneum, 1984.

Orwell, George. "The Final Years of Lady Gregory." *New Yorker*, April 19, 1947, 108, 110.

Pethica, James. "Patronage and Creative Exchange: Yeats, Lady Gregory and the Economy of Indebtedness." In *Yeats and Women*, edited by Deirdre Toomey, 60–94. London: Macmillan, 1992.

Robinson, Lennox. *Ireland's Abbey Theatre: A History, 1899–1951.* London: Sidgwick and Jackson, 1951.

Saddlemyer, Ann. "Augusta Gregory, Irish Nationalist: 'After All, What Is Wanted But a Hag and a Voice?' " In *Myth and Reality in Irish Literature*, edited by J. Ronsley, 29–40. Ontario: Wilfrid Laurier University Press, 1977.

———. "Image-Maker for Ireland: Augusta, Lady Gregory." *The World of W.B. Yeats.* Eds. Robin Skelton and Ann Saddlemyer. Seattle: University of Washington Press, 1967. 161–68.

———. *In Defense of Lady Gregory, Playwright.* Dublin: Dolmen; London: Oxford University Press, 1966.

———. *Lady Gregory: Fifty Years After.* Gerrards Cross, UK: Smythe; Totowa, NJ: Barnes and Noble, 1987. (Editor, with Colin Smythe.)

Smythe, Colin. *A Guide to Coole Park, Home of Lady Gregory.* Foreword by Anne Gregory. Gerrards Cross, UK: Smythe, 1983.

Thuente, Mary Helen. "Lady Gregory and 'The Book of the People.' " *Eire-Ireland* 11, no. 5 (Spring 1980): 86–99.

———. "Lady Gregory's *Grania*: A Feminist Voice." *Irish University Review* 25, no. 1 (Spring–Summer 1995): 11–24.

———. "W.B. Yeats, Lady Gregory, and the Politics of Comedy." *Yeats: An Annual of Critical and Textual Studies* 15 (1997): 19–36.

Winston, Greg. "Redefining Coole: Lady Gregory, Class Politics, and the Land War." *Colby Quarterly* 37, no. 3 (June 2001): 205–22.

ANNE LE MARQUAND HARTIGAN
(1937–   )

Joseph Heininger

BIOGRAPHY

Anne Hartigan has led a many-faceted career as poet, playwright, painter, batik artist, and performer. The daughter of a father from Jersey, Channel Islands, and an Irish-Catholic mother from County Louth, Anne Hartigan (née Le Marquand) was born and raised in England. She studied fine art at the University of Reading, specializing in painting, and has lived in Ireland since 1962. At first she lived on her mother's family farm on the banks of the river Boyne with her husband, a farmer, and there began to raise a family of six children. She continued to paint, and in the 1970s, as her Web site account has it, "writing became an increasingly important part of her life. Writing was an outlet for creativity and passion and a link with an artistic world that she knew was out there somewhere." She was later divorced. Her first breakthrough was having a poem published in the *Irish Times* in 1975, and she won the Listowel Writer's Week Open Poetry Award in 1978. Her first two books of poetry, *Long Tongue* (1982) and *Return Single* (1986), were published by Beaver Row Press, Dublin. Two more books of poetry have followed, *Now Is a Moveable Feast* (1991) and *Immortal Sins* (1993), both published by Salmon. "Now Is a Moveable Feast" was also performed on Radio Telefís Éireann in 1980, produced by Dick Warner. The contemporary composer Eibhlis Farrell wrote a song cycle, "Songs of Death," for sections of this poem, and these were performed at the Hugh Lane Gallery in Dublin.

In addition to her poetry, she has written several plays: *Beds*, performed at the Dublin Theatre Festival in 1982, and *The Secret Game*, winner of the Mobil Prize for Irish playwrights in 1995. Her most well-known drama, *La Corbiere*, was first performed under the direction of Cathy Leeney at the Project Theatre, Dublin, in 1989, in an adaptation for a cast of six. It has since been presented as a one-woman show with two companion pieces, together referred to as her three "Jersey Lilies": *La Corbiere*, *Le Crapaud*, and *Les Yeux*, which premiered at the Beckett Centre, Trinity College Dublin, in September 1996. Her most recent one-act play, *In Other Worlds*, was performed on three continents in 2003; at Ohio Northern University, at the Edinburgh Fringe Festival, and at Otago University, New Zealand. Her paintings have been exhibited in one-woman shows at the Temple Bar Gallery in Dublin and other venues. She has given poetry readings and workshops in the United States, the United Kingdom, New Zealand, Hungary, Romania, and Ireland. She is a founder-member of the Women's Studies Forum at University College Dublin and is an active campaigner on behalf of women's rights issues. She currently lives in Dublin.

MAJOR WORKS AND THEMES

Although her major publications did not appear until the 1980s and 1990s, Anne Hartigan belongs to the generation of Irish women poets and playwrights who began to publish and to find their voices in Irish and international forums in the 1970s. She shares the feminist perspectives and the sense of necessary engagement against entrenched forms and habits of power manifested by the American poets and political activists Adrienne Rich and Muriel Rukeyser as well as her Irish near-contemporary, Eavan Boland, and later poets such as Medbh McGuckian and Paula Meehan. In her work for the theater, she is an experimentalist and a humanist. Her stagecraft, humor, and moving dramatic recitations are clearly related to the practice of writers such as Samuel Beckett and Harold Pinter.

For her own part, Anne Hartigan has developed a powerful style of address and vigorous individual treatments of themes such as female and male attachments to place and family traditions; the shaping force of place on personality; the pain of brokenness and ways of recovery from divorce and dispossession; and the need to face change and to create a self and satisfying work. She addresses these themes in her poems and plays, and is especially concerned with articulating them in relation to women's lives and the necessity for writers to discover and sound true, individual voices in their work. In *Clearing the Space: A Why of Writing*, her 1996 manifesto and meditation on artistic and personal creativity, she writes:

> If we write in our own voice, there can be no friction of competition between our writing and the writing of others. I am well aware that human beings want to struggle to the top, wherever that is, but in the making of art, this can be destructive to the work and the worker. This struggle is founded on an untruth. If we can have the straightforwardness to create with our own voice, the work forms its right self. . . . If we build our own writing, we add to the pattern. Our individual voice complements, harmonises, feeds and reconciles ourselves with all other voices, and is unique. Even if from where we are, we cannot see our place in the pattern. Our space is our own. We are founded on our own soil. No one else can write in your voice. (13–14)

In this work and elsewhere, Hartigan writes of the devaluation of women's contributions to society, of their conventional relegation to silence, sexual objectification, and powerlessness, and of the paradoxical powers of those who are considered defenseless or weak.

Her play *La Corbiere* is based on an episode in the history of World War II that has been overlooked by epic-writing historians. The play explores the fates of the French prostitutes who were imported during World War II to Jersey to entertain Nazi troops and drowned when they departed in a Dutch ship, which foundered. Experimentalist in staging and in dramatic presentation of character, the play primarily uses the women's voices to make a series of interwoven statements and laments, a deftly crafted chorus of sounds.

In this short play with nine voices, Hartigan brings to light what happened to these women in a haunting and evocative drama. The stage is tranformed into an echo chamber of overlapping voices and repeated phrases. The cumulative effect of the vocal fragments and repetitions is to make a litany of lamentation whose charged emotional tone and linguistic spareness are reminiscent of Samuel Beckett's plays and short prose pieces. *La Corbiere* was selected for inclusion in *Seen and Heard: Six New Plays by Irish Women*. In the introduction to this first anthology of plays by Irish women, the editor, Cathy Leeney, remarks that "Hartigan's 'La Corbiere'

> challenges the audience to enter a world of sounds and words that create a fractured series of beautiful and disturbing images. The play's poetry comes from the heart of the nightmare of war-torn Europe. Hartigan confronts us with the language of savage insult and obliteration, and uses the healing sea as a metaphor for the redemption of the lost women. Paradoxically, her abstract theatrical vision reaches deep into the tragedy and damage of war, and the will to negate it in the honour of remembrance. (viii–ix)

To demonstrate its remarkable qualities, one might select any of a number of passages from the ending of *La Corbiere*, which is both classical and contemporary in feeling and structure. It achieves a powerful blending of Greek tragic wisdom and echoes of the traditional Irish women's keening for the dead in its vocal commentary and dramatic presentation. As she laments for the drowned women, Marie-Claire, a survivor of the wreck, speaks:

> No one is coming with arms to dip. No strong arms to dip down you out from the sea's terror. No one. No white arms over the boat's side, to reach over the edge. No one searching. No eyes eager as searchlights, as La Corbiere light sweeps its arc over the storm. No one will lay you out in a quiet room. No one will light a candle at your head and feet. There will be no prayers. No one will push their boat out to take your bodies back to earth. You bob your last dance on the sea's foam. Flotsam. Rock and flow. Spreadeagled on the indifferent sea. No chrism to anoint your brow. No incense around a coffin of wood. No name in the newspaper, no name. Sorrow is a lost word. There are no tears. Can the salt sea weep? Only a harsh gull's cry. (*La Corbiere*, 192–93)

This passage achieves great dramatic power with its combination of references to the Irish rituals for the drowned in Synge's *Riders to the Sea* (1904) and allusions to the English rituals of Christian burial. These rituals of lighting candles and reciting prayers are invoked in the predominantly male war-literature tradition of the battlefields described in Wilfred Owen's elegiac World War I sonnet, "Anthem for Doomed Youth," and then wrenched from that context into the unfamiliar space of Marie-Claire's elegiac lament for the female noncombatant victims of La Corbiere and Jersey. With eloquence and linguistic spareness, *La Corbiere* explores the fates of these forgotten women, and, on a broader plane, urges due recognition of the combatants and noncombatants who were seen and continue to be seen as disposable persons in wartime. It is fitting that this French-named dramatic trilogy has been produced under the aegis of the Beckett Centre in Dublin.

In her verse, beginning with *Long Tongue*, she explores the conditions of women's lives and the landscapes that reflect human needs and desires. In the beginning, she often employed unrhymed quatrains, or, increasingly in her later work, lines of free verse and monologue. The early poems are often brief and witty, as in "Heirloom," which celebrates the speaker's love for her father, who used to tell her that, in bed, "it's always good weather" (12).

In her later work, in the longer poems "Omens" and "Penelope" in *Immortal Sins*, for example, she revisits the scenes of Greek myth. Hartigan dramatizes Penelope in old age asking whether her waiting and her sacrifices have been worthwhile. Penelope concludes that she is a queen and a fool, and asks, "Do only fools love?" (28).

Although she is most known for her poetry and plays, Hartigan writes some prose fiction. A notable example is "Pure Invention," a short story published in 1989, written as a parable of contention and contentment in marriage. Told from the wife's point of view, it is a story full of sly humor about the testy bonds of love and rivalry within a marriage. It has an oral folktale quality to it, and its humorous look at married life and the wit in the exchanges between the venturesome husband and the exasperated, strangely contented wife are reminiscent of Sean O'Casey's famous battles between Juno and her Paycock. In this short, amusing fable, Hartigan examines with a knowing and worldly wise tone the contest for the upper hand in a marriage.

In addition, she has used her paintings and drawings to illustrate her books of poems. For example, celebration, freedom of movement, physical grace, and strength are apparent in the detail from one of her paintings used as the cover art for the Salmon Press Poetry edition of *Immortal Sins*. Its primary colors are vibrant red and orange, and the dancing female figure recalls Matisse's late cutouts of dancers' silhouettes.

CRITICAL RECEPTION

When Anne Hartigan was asked by an interviewer in 1990, "Do you consider yourself an Irish poet?" she replied, "Yes, I do. Initially I was fearful of being criticized because of my English connections, but now I feel they're valid. So many Irish people have gone to England, why not celebrate someone who has come back? It's all linked up with identity. I feel Irish in my guts" (*Sleeping with Monsters*, 206). Her poems drew early attention from Irish poet and anthologist Brendan Kennelly, who praised *Long Tongue* for its "enthusiastic readiness to experiment with form, its lively, sensitive use of language, as well as a certain sharp lyricism that indicates an individual view and recording of experience" (3). In this, her first book, Hartigan became a mythmaker in her own right, citing the traditional Irish belief in the poet's possession of far-reaching powers. She wrote, "Long ago in Ireland the poet was thought to have fearful powers. It was a misfortune to have a poet in the family: doubly so if the poet were a woman, as her powers were twice as strong as a man's. A poet was recognized by the possession of an extra-long tongue" (*Sleeping with Monsters,* 206).

Patricia Haberstroh has devoted the most critical attention to Hartigan's work. She discusses Hartigan's poetry in conjunction with her examination of Eavan Boland, Nuala Ní Dhomhnaill, Paula Meehan, and their poetic projects, which are broadening the range of women's roles in contemporary Irish poetry to include "a much more expansive cast of characters" that "challenges many traditional female figures" (199). The fullest estimate so far is in Haberstroh, but her interesting discussion examines the poetry only and leaves the dramatic works untouched, as they are beyond the scope of her book. Dillon Johnston briefly mentions Hartigan among the poets who are changing the landscape of contemporary Irish poetry (xii). There is a need for much more extended critical discussion of Hartigan's poetry and plays, as well as her essays and other prose works.

BIBLIOGRAPHY

Works by Anne Le Marquand Hartigan

Plays

Beds. Dublin, 1982.
La Corbiere. Dublin, 1989.
Le Crapaud. Dublin, 1996.
Les Yeux. Dublin, 1996.
In Other Worlds. Ada, Ohio, 2003.
The Secret Game. New York, 2003.

Poetry

Immortal Sins. Dublin: Salmon, 1993.
Long Tongue. Dublin: Beaver Row, 1982.
Now Is a Moveable Feast. Dublin: Salmon, 1991.
Return Single. Dublin: Beaver Row, 1986.

Prose

Clearing the Space: A Why of Writing. Cliffs of Moher, Ire.: Salmon, 1996.
"Disillusion and Delight." In *The Irish Spirit*, edited by Patricia Monaghan, 130–36. Dublin: Wolfhound, 2003.
"Pure Invention." In *Territories of the Voice: Contemporary Stories by Irish Women Writers*, edited by Louise De Salvo, Kathleen Darcy, and Katherine Hogan, 79–85. Boston: Beacon, 1989. Reprinted as *A Green and Mortal Sound*. Boston: Beacon, 2003.

Studies of Anne Le Marquand Hartigan

Haberstroh, Patricia Boyle. *Women Creating Women: Contemporary Irish Women Poets*. Syracuse, NY: Syracuse University Press, 1996, 199–201.
Hartigan, Anne. Interview with Rebecca Wilson. In *Sleeping with Monsters: Conversations with Scottish and Irish Women Poets*, edited by Rebecca Wilson and Gillian Somerville-Arjat, 201–7. Dublin: Wolfhound, 1990.
———. http://www.annehartigan.com.
Johnston, Dillon. *Irish Poetry After Joyce*. 2nd ed. Syracuse, NY: Syracuse University Press, 1997, xii.
Kennelly, Brendan. Introduction to *Long Tongue*. Dublin: Beaver Row, 1982.
Leeney, Cathy. Introduction to *Seen and Heard: Six New Plays by Irish Women*. Dublin: Carysfort, 2001.

RITA ANN HIGGINS
(1955–   )

Rita Barnes

BIOGRAPHY

While hospitalized for tuberculosis as a young mother, Rita Ann Higgins began her writing career by reading books voraciously for the first time, starting with George Orwell's *Animal Farm* (1945) and Emily Bronte's *Wuthering Heights* (1847) (Wilson, 45). She recalls that reading these books was "a revelation," adding, "I had never read a book before. When I was growing up, all we had to read was *The Messenger* and the St. Jude Novena books" (Donovan, 16). She has said that she does not consider herself religious, but after a childhood steeped in such texts and the prayers she learned from her devoutly Catholic mother, she recognizes their poetic influence, especially due to their dissonance with her father's alcoholism (Wilson, 46).

Born in Galway City, Higgins is one of thirteen children. She stopped attending school at age fourteen, married at age eighteen, and has two children. Her early employment consisted of monotonous factory-line jobs, including work for multinational corporations that opposed unions. These experiences are later reflected in poems such as "When the Big Boys Pulled Out," in which women who spend their days separating nuts and washers are politicized; the plant soon closes. Many of Higgins's poems draw on firsthand knowledge of life on welfare and in menial jobs, and the attendant humiliations and inequities experienced in family and community life.

She began to write poetry at age twenty-seven, joining the Galway Writers Workshop. There she was encouraged to pursue her writing by Jessie Lendennie of Salmon Press, which later published Higgins's first four books. Her first, *Goddess on the Mervue Bus* (1986), resulted in the first of her many Arts Council writing bursaries. In 1987 she served at the Galway Library as Galway County's writer in residence. Her second book, *Witch in the Bushes* (1988), was followed by the Peadar O'Donnell Award in 1989. *Philomena's Revenge* was published in 1992. She earned a diploma in Women's Studies during her tenure as writer in residence at University College Galway. *Higher Purchase* (1996) was soon followed with a Poetry Book Society Recommendation in the United Kingdom for *Sunnyside Plucked: New and Selected Poems*. *An Awful Racket* appeared in 2001. Her four plays are *God-of-the-Hatch Man* (1990), *Face Licker Come Home* (1991), *Collie Lally Doesn't Live in a Bucket* (1995), and *Down All the Roundabouts* (1999).

After five rejected applications to the Aosdána (an organization of Irish artists nominated and selected by their peers for outstanding artistic achievement), she was elected in 1996. She refers to the application process by "the elitist Irish literati" as being "like welfare all over again. That sort of humiliation is what I want to write against" (Donovan, 16).

Higgins took a second degree at University College Galway in the Irish language in 1997, served as Offaly County writer in residence from 1997 to 1999 (editing the resulting volume *Out the Clara Road: The Offaly Anthology*), and was named the Cecil and Ida Green Honors Professor at Texas Christian University for 2000.

Her poems have been translated into French, German, Italian, Hebrew, Dutch, and Swedish. Her work has been widely anthologized, and she has toured and read her works internationally, earning a reputation as a leading poetic voice for working-class women and contemporary Irish urban experience. Higgins has given poetry workshops for prisoners in Ireland and England. Poems from her workshops at Sunderland Women's Centre and Washington Bridge Centre are published in the collection *Word and Image*, coedited by Higgins and Gráinne Sweeney.

MAJOR WORKS AND THEMES

Goddess on the Mervue Bus begins with an epigraph from Walt Whitman in praise of old women. To introduce her first book with the words of a non-Irish male poet reflects Higgins's insistence on defying expectations. She shares with Whitman a devotion to everyday subjects and, particularly, to the dignity and beauty of those outside mainstream society. The "goddess" of the title sets the tone for this collection's treatment of daily life in Galway, in which tongue-in-cheek mythical heroism is attributed to a scrap dealer's daughter.

The speaker in "Consumptive in the Library," the opening poem, is an aspiring poet who meets a tuberculosis patient in the Galway Library while reading Ulster poetry. Put off by her unwanted companion's cough, the speaker "moved to the medical section" (l. 29). Whether a real or imagined prelude to Higgins's own bout with the disease, the scene links her artistic beginnings to her period of medical confinement, meanwhile casting the contagion in terms of a suggested, if not overtly flirtatious, encounter. The poem characteristically intertwines the autobiographical and local scene with powerfully understated sexuality and humor. The collection as a whole explores Irish women's lives as mothers, wives, and daughters, aging women in the shops, women working together in factories, women thinking about sex, poetry, poverty, their dreams, their lives in housing projects. Men—chronically unemployed, estranged fathers, the "God-of-the-Hatch man" (the community welfare officer), and the rent man (to whom the book shares its dedication with Higgins's daughters and husband)—are more distant but are portrayed with emotional depth and sympathy for the social inequalities that befall them.

Witch in the Bushes continues to distinguish Higgins's poetry from self-consciously nationalistic Irish poetry. The elderly "Men with Tired Hair" in the opening poem watch from their windows in Galway's Prospect Hill, flatly waiting for "images pleasing and displeasing" (5). Higgins develops her distinct idiomatic voice in this volume, and in such poems as "It's All Because We're Working Class," "Women's Inhumanity to Women," and "Some People," there is an angry tone. "The KKK of Kastle Park," "The Blanket Man," and others dramatize and critique the socioeconomic divides within local communities.

In *Philomena's Revenge*, increasingly witty poems nevertheless sustain the poignancy and political edge of her early work. More confidently experimental approaches ("God Dodgers Anonymous," "People Who Wear Cardigans Are Subversive," "Dead Dogs and Nations") and poems about the suffering of contemporary Irish children ("Rain and Smart Alec Kids," "Safe Houses," and "Forgotten Prisoner") characterize this volume, which also reflects Higgins's experiences teaching in prisons ("They Believe in Clint Eastwood," "Four Steps Nowhere," "Name Calling," "H-Block Shuttle," and "His Shoulder Blades and Rome").

Higher Purchase is more ambitious in linguistic experimentation, in length, and in its forays outside the materials of direct experience, interspersed with poems employing Higgins's more characteristically familiar style and subjects. This method of organization, unlike a conventional division of a volume into thematic sections, suggests a seamlessness between the materials of local experience and classical reference, shifting easily between Galway slang and historical allusion. The pun on "hire purchase" (buying home furnishings via rental payments) in the title poem links material poverty, social stigma, and a mother's desire to better her children's standing in the eyes of their community. Poems drawing on literary reference, strikingly more abundant in this volume, include "Donna Laura," a dramatic monologue addressed to Petrarch, in which his lover speaks in the idiom of contemporary Ireland ("She Scalds the Arse Off Me," l. 13). The speaker in "The Flute Girls' Dialogue," likewise, snaps at Plato, " 'Discourse in Praise of Love' indeed" (l. 5). In "The Quarrel," Hera and Zeus squabble over his infidelities amid talk of dinner and teatime, with a nod to W. B. Yeats's "Leda and the Swan." As in previous collections, powerful narratives of individual women are prominent: "Mamorexia," "Breech," and "Mothercare" are among her most evocative works about the fragile mix of Irish cultural expectations and human limitations in motherhood, conveying a convincing balance of mature loving observation with clear social criticism.

An Awful Racket is dedicated to the poet's late nephew, whose death informs much of this volume but does not dominate it. "Black Dog Is My Docs Day" is the most directly elegiac work. The arrangement of the poems neither contains his death nor is overwhelmed by poems about it; rather, the poems are interwoven with scenes from Galway life in which painters disturb a household, a neighbor discusses his dogs, a woman grows more like her mother as she ages, and a family burns their estranged father's wardrobe for heating fuel. It is as if this arrangement of poetry couches personal tragedy in the context of a community's other aspirations and difficulties.

CRITICAL RECEPTION

Critics have praised Higgins for her wry wit, her ear for idiomatic expression, a straightforward style, and an unsentimentalized yet sensitive firsthand portrayal of the lower and lower-middle class in Galway City. She has been recognized for rendering the nature and particulars of Irish women's personal lives, especially their sexuality and their domestic and workplace experiences.

Patricia Boyle Haberstroh notes her freshness of style, pointing out that Higgins combines the mythic with the concrete poverty of daily life in modern Ireland (204–5). Haberstroh also observes that within scenes of conflict between men and women violence is often manifest in Higgins's works (206) and that Higgins is neither critical of nor condescending toward her subjects (207). Haberstroh sees Leland Bardwell as Higgins's predecessor among Irish women poets. She quotes Medbh McGuckian as saying that Higgins's best poems share "an epiphanic quality" with Nuala Ní Dhomnaill, Paul Durcan, and Paula Meehan. Characterizing Higgins's humor as sardonic, Haberstroh agrees with McGuckian that Higgins's style is mock-heroic (207).

In his analysis of the poem "Goddess on the Mervue Bus," John Hildebidle refers to this tendency as "myth-pillaging" and suggests Yeats's "Among School Children" as a precursor to the poem (35). Hildebidle characterizes Higgins as one who has taken "the Road of Bluntness . . . ready to announce her lack of university degrees. Distinctly an urban poet, she cannot readily avail herself of the model of [Patrick] Kavanagh. Oddly, her poetry reminds an American of William Carlos Williams, with a more overtly political edge." He argues that the seemingly prosaic quality of her language and narratives "do the work of a complex puzzle," and that her work "recolonizes familiar Irish poetic ground." The collection *Philomena's Revenge* "begins as a poetry of overheard voices . . . [but] soon becomes a poetry of sharp dialogue. . . . This Philomena is not from Greek legend but from the housing projects of Galway City, and her revenge is blunt and actual, if self-destructive." He rightly sees the volume as more technically mature and complex than her earlier works. According to Hildebidle, Higgins "resists easy labels. . . . Her acerbic eye cuts in all directions, not just against the 'patriarchal' ancestral voices of Irish poetry" (39).

Karen Steele sees Higgins's and Paula Meehan's insights into the commonplace as distinctly different from Eavan Boland's explorations of the "need to be ordinary" (317). For Higgins and Meehan, the quotidian can be alienating. Higgins's "celebratory discussions of sex . . . undermine traditional images of Irish femininity by playfully breaking the silence surrounding the taboo subject of Irish women's sensuality," using candid observation and humor (317). "I Want to Make Love to Kim Basinger" suggests "the closeting effect of compulsory heterosexuality in Irish culture," the "ubiquitous power of heterosexuality and patriarchy even in all-female spaces" such as the restroom and the bedroom (319). In "Mothercare," feminism and social class are brought to bear on the subject of adolescent pregnancy: "The subject of the poem—babies having babies—is a favorite among social and political conservatives who preach the message of sexual abstinence." Instead, Higgins "portrays the damaging effect of romanticizing motherhood" (320). The baby buggy becomes the ironic focus for the human drive for power, however small. The young mother's "unrealistic pledge to keep her pram 'immaculate' especially resonates for an Irish Catholic audience" (322) who grew up with the admonition for girls to model themselves on the Virgin Mary. Steele feels that Higgins is among a small group of contemporary Irish women poets who can "reshape the Irish imagination both inside and outside of the academy" (327), articulating ways "to challenge Irish social mores that silence discussions of or reflections on passion and desire" (318).

Kelli Elizabeth Moloy concurs. Their "new, powerful, independent, and often overtly sexual voices . . . move away from traditional and colonial representations of women toward representations of women as speaking subjects and tellers of previously unspeakable narratives."

Elizabeth Lowry contrasts Meehan's subtle and scholarly dexterity with Higgins's equally skillful directness and accessibility. She finds that Higgins's poems are minimalistic anecdotes using "flatness of expression" as a thematic tool, and that Higgins's poetic persona is self-mocking in autobiographical passages, undercutting her use of classical references with regional colloquialisms (92–93).

Sara Berkeley writes of *Sunny Side Plucked* that "some of the poems are too raw, and some don't live up to the single good idea of the title," such as "I Want to Make Love to Kim Basinger" ("Women In and Out of Love"). Berkeley sees more in *Higher Purchase*, "a sort of fairytale mixture of madness and glee, horror and pathos, with a Dylan Thomas twist to the language. . . . There's so much direct speech it's like an anthropologist's treasure chest [of] how Irish people spoke in the 1990s" ("Windy Bus Stop").

Higgins catalogs experiences by "listing grievances in a spiral of increasing frustration and surreal exaggeration," according to Katie Donovan (16). The influence of Catholic prayer influences their incantatory style.

Catherine Paul writes that Higgins eschews mystery (12) in recounting "events we could all do without yet find ourselves too often having to endure: views of sickeningly good-looking couples, excuses for unpayable rent, secrets one regrets telling one's friend, dealings with neutered cats, the unwanted mothering advice women give each other" (13). Paul finds that Higgins's poems "show a discrete distrust of poetry and the falsehoods it can protect" (13).

Molly McAnailly Burke sees later works indicative of Higgins's growing "access to the international language of literary power, from Greek and Roman classics to the analytical dialect of academic thought," in contrast to the observation of an Aosdána member that Higgins wrote "prose with short lines" rather than poetry (Web site).

Patrick Crotty points out "insistently good-humoured protests against social exclusion and the misuse of power in an increasingly brash and materialistic Ireland." He hears the voice "of a survivor quietly exhilarated by her own staying power but weighed down by the knowledge that others have lacked the resilience or the luck to come through." Her language exists "at a tiny, crucial remove from actual speech," with "haunting rhythms in monologues by edgy, earthy, unimpressed characters who understand suffering and are yet quick to see the funny side of things." He sees virtuosity in her later work: *An Awful Racket* is the best collection by "this laureate of the dispossessed" (64).

Carol Rumens is struck by Higgins's crafting of a personal poetic idiom from the very beginning of her career. Comparing Higgins to Paul Durcan, Rumens notes both the ability to "snatch a line from mass culture" and the indictment of religious hypocrisy, creating daring yet familiar persona, though recent works occasionally "stretch a point beyond its natural life-span, or widen the political or social comment into generalisation."

Such critiques are echoed in a review in *Stand UK* of *Sunnyside Plucked*, which stresses the prominence of anger in this collection. Her strength lies in "careful avoidance of any attempt at describing her subjects' emotions." Explorations of Irish Catholics are described as "witheringly witty." Decidedly in the oral tradition, the collection's poems are seen as succeeding on the page through innovative use of the vernacular (9).

BIBLIOGRAPHY

Works by Rita Ann Higgins

An Awful Racket. Tarset, UK: Bloodaxe, 2001.
Colie Lally Doesn't Live in a Bucket. 1995.
Down All the Roundabouts. 1999.
Face Licker Come Home. Galway: Salmon, 1991. Punchbag Theatre, Galway, 1991.
Fizz: Poetry of Resistance and Challenge. A Poetry Anthology Written by Young People. Galway: National University of Ireland, 2004. (Editor, with Sheila McDonnell and Pat Dolan.)
Goddess and Witch. Galway: Salmon, 1990.
Goddess on the Mervue Bus. Galway: Salmon, 1986.

God-of-the-Hatch Man. Punchbag Theatre, Galway, 1992.
Higher Purchase. Galway: Salmon, 1996.
Out the Clara Road: The Offaly Anthology. County Offaly: Offaly County Council, 1999.
Philomena's Revenge. Galway: Salmon, 1992.
Sunnyside Plucked: New and Selected Poems. Newcastle upon Tyne, UK: Bloodaxe, 1996.
Witch in the Bushes. Galway: Salmon, 1988.
Word and Image: A Collection of Poems. Sunderland: Arts Resource, 2000. (Editor, with Grainne Sweeney.)

Studies of Rita Ann Higgins

Berkeley, Sara. "From the Windy Bus Stop to the Reticent I." Review of *Higher Purchase. Irish Times,* June 8, 1996, 9.
———. "Women In and Out of Love." Review of *Sunny Side Plucked. Irish Times,* January 25, 1997, 8.
Boran, Pat. Review of *Goddess on the Mervue Bus.* http://www.ritaannhiggins.com/pat_boran.html.
Burke, Molly MacAnailly. "Educating Rita." *Sunday Independent,* March 16, 1997. http://www.ritaannhiggins.com/independent97.html.
———. "The Iron Fist." *Sunday Independent,* February 11, 1990. http://www.ritaannhiggins.com/independent90.html.
Crotty, Patrick. Review of *An Awful Racket. Irish Times,* June 23, 2001. http://www.ritaannhiggins.com/irish_times_02.html.
Donovan, Katie. "A Right Terror." *Irish Times,* November 7, 1996, 16.
Haberstroh, Patricia Boyle. *Women Creating Women: Contemporary Irish Women Poets.* Syracuse, NY: Syracuse University Press, 1996, 204–7.
Hildebidle, John. " 'I'll Have to Stop Thinking about Sex': Rita Ann Higgins and the Patriarchal Tradition." In *Contemporary Irish Women Poets: Some Male Perspectives,* edited by Alexander G. Gonzalez, 33–41. Westport, CT: Greenwood, 1999.
Horn, David. "The Genuine Article." Review of *An Awful Racket.* Bloodaxe Books. http://www.bloodaxebooks.com/00002.asp.
Lowry, Elizabeth. "The Home Front." Review of *Sunny Side Plucked. Poetry Review* (Winter 1996–1997): 92–93.
McGuckian, Medbh. "The Light of the Penurious Moon." Review of *Philomena Revenge. Honest Ulsterman* 85: 60–62. http://www.ritaannhiggins.com/mcguckian.html.
Moloy, Kelli Elizabeth. " 'Out of the Shambles of Our History': Irish Women and (Post)colonial Identity." PhD diss., West Virginia University, 1998. http://wwwlib.umi.com/dissertations/fullcit/9926667.
Odak, Shelia. Review of *An Awful Racket. Nua: Studies in Contemporary Irish Writing* 4, nos. 1–2 (Spring–Summer 2001): 219–21.
Paul, Catherine. "Rita Ann Higgins: A Moderator's View." *South Carolina Review* 32, no. 1 (Fall 1999): 12–14. http://www.clemson.edu/caah/cedp/Irelandarts.htm.
Review of *Sunny Side Plucked. Publishers Weekly,* February 24, 1997, 85.
Review of *Sunny Side Plucked. Stand UK,* March 1998. http://www.ritaannhiggins.com/stand.html.
Rumens, Carol. Review of *Goddess on the Mervue Bus, Witch in the Bushes,* and *Philomena's Revenge. Irish Times,* January 29, 1994, 9.
Steele, Karen. "Refusing the Poisoned Chalice: The Sexual Politics of Rita Ann Higgins and Paula Meehan." In *Homemaking: Women Writers and the Politics and Poetics of Home,* edited by Catherine Wiley and Fiona R. Barnes, 313–33. New York: Garland, 1996.
Wilson, Rebecca E. "Rita Ann Higgins." Interview. *Sleeping with Monsters: Conversations with Scottish and Irish Women Poets,* edited by Rebecca E. Wilson and Gillean Somerville-Arjat, 44–51. Edinburgh: Polygon, 1990.

NORAH HOULT
(1898–1984)

Karen O'Brien

BIOGRAPHY

Norah Hoult was born in Dublin of Anglo-Irish parentage. Her parents' untimely death resulted in her attending various boarding schools in England. After completing her education, Hoult pursued journalism. She joined the editorial staff of the *Sheffield Daily Telegraph* for two years and then worked for *Pearson's* magazine in London. As a journalist, Hoult wrote book reviews for the *Yorkshire Evening Post* and actively penned freelance assignments.

Scholartis Press takes credit for having discovered Hoult as an author. Her first book, *Poor Women!* (1928), a collection of short stories, was rejected nineteen times before being published by Scholartis and receiving critical acclaim. Hoult returned to Dublin from 1931 through 1937, where she continued writing novels, most notably *Holy Ireland* (1935) and *Coming for the Fair* (1937). While in Dublin, Hoult wrote a book review of Samuel Beckett's *More Pricks Than Kicks* (1934) for *Dublin* magazine, calling Beckett a "clever young man" who, basing his main character, Belacqua, in part on James Joyce's Leopold Bloom, "knows his *Ulysses* as a Scotch Presbyterian knows his Bible" (Harrington, 65). Hoult spent two years in America before returning to London in 1939. The last years of her life were spent at Jonquil Cottage in Greystones, County Wicklow, where she passed away in 1984.

MAJOR WORKS AND THEMES

Poor Women! brought Hoult critical acclaim as a new fiction writer. Including seven short stories, each titled for its main character, the volume studies the female cultural experience in the late nineteenth to early twentieth century and prewar Britain. "Violet Ryder," which was also printed separately as a novelette, follows the innocent consciousness of a seventeen-year-old girl from a lower-class upbringing who longs for wealth and love. The best story, "Bridget Kiernan," presents a twenty-five-year-old servant girl who fears that she may be pregnant out of wedlock.

Most of Hoult's work deals with issues of economy, sexuality, and religion. Marjorie Howes has observed that "one of her strengths as a writer lies in her ability to create characters whose thoughts and language inspire both the reader's sympathy and a sharp awareness of their limitations without direct authorial comment" (933). A strong sense of humanity is likewise recognizable in Hoult's first novel, but second book, *Time Gentlemen! Time!* (1930), dedicated to the memory of her mother, Margaret O'Shaugnessy. Edna, the wife of an alcoholic who is ushering the middle-class family into poverty, persists as one of Hoult's most memorable characters.

Holy Ireland (1935) examines the influence of religion on Irish family life in turn-of-the-century Dublin. Based on the history of Hoult's mother, it is the story of Margaret, a young woman who marries an English Protestant only to be persecuted for doing so by her Catholic father. After the parish priest makes sexual advances toward the young woman, she breaks from the Church, only to be castigated further by her father on his deathbed. *Coming from the Fair* (1937), its sequel, follows Margaret's brother, Charlie, the prodigal son, after his father's death in 1903 up to the Easter Rising. Hoult is lauded for presenting "a realistic account of the attitudes and manners of the Irish middle class of the period" (Welch, 250). *Father and Daughter* (1957) and *Husband and Wife* (1959), also set in Ireland, relate the experiences of the Mallory family of Shakespearean actors "travelling in the philistine Irish midlands" over an eleven-year period (Welch, 251).

Hoult wrote predominantly from a female perspective but was careful to describe herself as "anti-feminist": "I believe that feminism has done, on the whole, more harm than good to the true welfare of women" (quoted in Kunitz, 461). Cultural issues concerning women at the turn of the century and into the twentieth century were, in any case, her principal topics. In fact, Hoult's work was not spared by the Censorship Board, which banned at least one book by virtually every leading Irish writer between 1929 and the mid-1960s for containing controversial themes, such as the advocating of birth control (O'Gorman, 32).

Hoult's work, often thinly fictive, frequently captures the accuracy of thought and mood within historical moments and social contexts. For example, in *There Were No Windows* (1944) she recounts experiences with friends and fellow writers Ethel Colburn Mayne and Violet Hunt to describe the feelings about and impact of air raids during the London blitz (Johnson, 200). Furthermore, Hoult is grouped with novelists such as Kate O'Brien and Edna O'Brien, not only for being a great Irish writer, but also for being an author who deals with the oppressive facets of Catholic culture, such as "the Catholic hierarchy as authority, the Catholic school and the boarding-school filled with the presence of nuns, [and] the stifling religiosity of the home" (MacCurtain, 462).

CRITICAL RECEPTION

In the prefatory letter of *Poor Women!*, H. M. Tomlinson heralds, "I have never before heard of Norah Hoult, but there is no doubt, if she continues to write, that she is likely to be freely named whenever the best fiction is discussed" (vii). He contends that her short stories "are the unique manifestations which genius always gives us" and that her "gift for narrative is the right magic for story-telling" (vii). Hoult has achieved wide acclaim for her multidimensional character studies. Her skill for naturalistic description is a marked feature of her writing style. Often categorized with renowned Irish writers such as Samuel Beckett, Seán O'Faoláin, and Frank O'Connor, Hoult's work has yet to be fully recognized and placed among the classics.

BIBLIOGRAPHY

Works by Norah Hoult

Apartments to Let. London: W. Heinemann, 1931; New York: Harper and Brothers, 1932.
Augusta Steps Out. London: W. Heinemann, 1942.
Closing Hour. New York: Harper and Brothers, 1930.

Cocktail Bar. London: W. Heinemann, 1950.

Coming from the Fair. London: W. Heinemann, 1937; New York: Covici, Friede, 1937.

A Death Occurred. London: Hutchinson, 1954.

Ethel. London: W. Heinemann, 1933.

Farewell Happy Fields. London: W. Heinemann, 1948.

Father and Daughter. London: Hutchinson, 1957.

Father Hone and the Television Set. London: Hutchinson, 1956.

Four Women Grow Up. London: W. Heinemann, 1940.

Frozen Ground. London: W. Heinemann, 1952.

Holy Ireland. London: W. Heinemann, 1935; New York: Reynal and Hitchcock, 1936.

House Under Mars. London: W. Heinemann, 1946.

Husband and Wife. London: Hutchinson, 1959.

Journey into Print. London: Hutchinson, 1954.

The Last Days of Miss Jenkinson. London: Hutchinson, 1962.

Nine Years Is a Long Time. London: W. Heinemann, 1938.

Not for Our Sins Alone. London: Hutchinson, 1972.

A Poet's Pilgrimage. London: Hutchinson, 1966.

Poor Women! London: Scholartis, 1928.

Scene for Death. London: W. Heinemann, 1943.

Selected Stories. London: Fridberg, 1946.

Sister Mavis. London: W. Heinemann, 1953.

Smilin' on the Vine. London: W. Heinemann, 1941.

There Were No Windows. London: W. Heinemann, 1944.

Time Gentlemen! Time! London: W. Heinemann, 1930.

Violet Ryder. London: Elkin Mathews and Marrot, 1930.

Youth Can't Be Served. London: W. Heinemann, 1933; New York: Harper and Brothers, 1934.

Studies of Norah Hoult

Blain, Virginia, Patricia Clements, and Isobel Grundy, eds. *The Feminist Companion to Literature in English: Women Writers from the Middle Ages to the Present*. New Haven, CT: Yale University Press, 1990, 541.

Brady, Anne M., and Brian Cleeve, eds. *A Biographical Dictionary of Irish Writers*. New York: St. Martin's, 1985.

Commire, Anne, and Deborah Klezmer, eds. *Women in World History: A Biographical Encyclopedia*. Vol. 7. Waterford, CT: Yorkin, 2000, 505–6.

Harrington, John. *The Irish Beckett*. Syracuse, NY: Syracuse University Press, 1991, 65.

Hogan, Robert, ed. "Hoult, [Eleanor] Norah." *The Dictionary of Irish Literature*. 2nd ed. 2 vols. Westport, CT: Greenwood, 1996, 563–64.

Howes, Marjorie. "Public Discourse, Private Reflection, 1916–1970." In *The Field Day Anthology of Irish Writing*. Vol. 4, *Irish Women's Writing and Traditions*, edited by Angela Bourke, et al. New York: New York University Press, 2002, 923–1038.

Johnson, George M. "Ethel Colburn Mayne." *Dictionary of Literary Biography: Late-Victorian and Edwardian British Novelists*. Vol. 197. Detroit: Gale, 1999, 187–201.

Kunitz, Stanley J., ed. *Twentieth Century Authors: A Biographical Dictionary of Modern Literature*. New York: Wilson, 1955, 461.

MacCurtain, Margaret. "Recollections of Catholicism, 1906–1960." *The Field Day Anthology of Irish Writing*. Vol. 4, *Irish Women's Writing and Traditions*, edited by Angela Bourke, et al. New York: New York University Press, 2002, 570–601.

———. "Religion, Science, Theology and Ethics, 1500–2000." *The Field Day Anthology of Irish Writing*. Vol. 4, *Irish Women's Writing and Traditions*, edited by Angela Bourke, et al. New York: New York University Press, 2002, 459–753.

O'Gorman, Ronnie. "The Best Banned in the Land." *Galway Advertiser*, October 3, 2003, 32.

Rose, Jonathan, and Patricia J. Anderson, eds. *Dictionary of Literary Biography: British Literary Publishing Houses, 1881–1965*. Vol. 112. Detroit: Gale, 1991, 283–84.

Tomlinson, H. M. Prefatory Letter. *Poor Women!* by Norah Hoult. New York: Harper, 1929, vii–viii.
Welch, Robert, ed. *The Oxford Companion to Irish Literature*. Oxford: Clarendon; New York: Oxford University Press, 1996, 249–51.
Who Was Who: A Cumulated Index 1897–2000. London: A and C Black, 2002, 407.
Willison, I. R., ed. *The New Cambridge Bibliography of English Literature*. Vol. 4. Cambridge: Cambridge University Press, 1972, 605–6.

BIDDY JENKINSON
(1949–   )

Maureen E. Mulvihill

BIOGRAPHY

Irish-language poet, playwright, prose-fiction writer, and poetry editor, Biddy Jenkinson (a pseudonym) was born in Dublin, in 1949, according to scant and varying sources, and attended University College Dublin. Jenkinson, who enjoys speaking of herself in the third person, prefers not to discuss her personal life, explaining that a writer using a nom de guerre has no date or place of birth: "What is the point in creating a free spirit and then tying it down? Scholars will guess and detect; and anthologies will copy each other. It all has nothing to do with me. I prefer to wield a free pen." (All direct quotations from Jenkinson in this profile were graciously supplied by Jenkinson herself in e-mail correspondence with the author, April–August 2004; the author is grateful to Jenkinson for promptly supplying many timely amendments.)

Commenting on her concealed authorship, Jenkinson generously shared the following autobiographical facts: "My birth name is not a secret, but it is not relevant. The main reason I adopted a pen name was to leave my poems and writings as free as possible from the personality of a particular named and identified writer. The name I use is a family name, though I do use other identities, as well. 'Biddy' was a distant relative, long dead, a lady who had the reputation of having 'the sharpest tongue in the seven parishes [of Glendalough].' On account of this lady's sharpness, she remained unwed. As a child, I was thought to resemble her. Using an *'ainm cleite'* is a way of declaring that the work is neither confessional nor biographical. The composer of the poems accepts no limits except those imposed by the reach of her talent and the development of her skills. Poems start off on a clean page, in so far as that is possible." When asked which poets had influenced her work, Jenkinson named A. Glungheal, Aogan O Rathaille, Eochaidh, O hEodhasa, Eibhlín Dubh Ní Chonaill, John Donne, Piaras Feiriteir, and Jenny Strich. "I am especially interested," she added, "in the 'Leabhar Branach,' the sixteenth-century poembook of the O'Byrnes, compiled in Glenmalure during the late Bardic period in the *'dún'* of the O'Byrnes at Baile na Corra." Remarking on the dramatic rise of publishing women writers throughout Ireland in the last century, Jenkinson emphasized "opportunities."

Jenkinson's much-noted *ars poetica* and literary manifesto appear in her open letter to the editor of *Irish University Review* 21, no. 1 (Spring–Summer, 1991): 27–34. "The insistence that everything written in Irish be translated immediately into English [is most] peculiar (French would be more congenial!). Apart from an occasional English translation, permitted because of unusual circumstances, any shifts from Irish have been into French, German, Italian, Romanian, Turkish." And though she is sometimes referred to as a feminist poet, Jenkinson abjures all "isms": "Devotion to an 'ism' affects poetic vision."

Jenkinson's reverence for Ireland's early literary tradition is emphatically expressed in the Autumn 2004 edition of *Poetry Ireland*. In her review of the eighth volume of *Beathaisnéis* (Dublin: An Clochomhar Tta, 2003), a biographical adventure in Irish Ireland, undertaken by Diarmuid Breathnach and Máire Ní Mhurchú, she speaks thusly to modern readers: "Those for whom Irish literature is something written in English in the last few hundred years, might, as a token exercise in open-mindedness, run their fingernails along the spines of these eight volumes. Within the Irish tradition, those who preserve the record are revered. If we lose the past, how can we appreciate the present or imagine the future?" (Poetry Ireland Review 80 [Autumn 2004]: 39). For reliable information on Irish-language women writers, one of her special interests, Jenkinson recommends the booklist of her publisher Coiscéim, as well as the Cló Iar-Chonnachta Web site (http://www.cic.ie) and the three-volume anthology of poetry, prose, and drama (ca. 1900–2000), *Rogha an Chéid*, edited by Gearoid Denvir (Inverin, Ire.: Cló Iar-Chonnachta, 2000).

In addition to her own literary output, Jenkinson has been a capable editor of Irish poetry. The editor of the popular quarterly *Éigse Éireann/Poetry Ireland Review*, from Summer 2000 to Spring 2001, Jenkinson expressed sorrow in her first issue at having to turn away so much impressive poetry; of the 1,605 poems submitted, as many as 1,545 were declined.

Though she resided in Helsinki, Finland, in 2004, Jenkinson's home and principal residence is County Wicklow. One of her immediate projects is the creation of a garden that will translate themes from Irish literatures into horticultural language: "The line of yew trees across my field are for Suibhne, Mis, Mór and other possessed geniuses to leapfrog, and there are plenty of thornbushes for them to land in. The Fianna are represented by a straggling column of juniper trees climbing the hill. The persistent wind over Laidhre Mhór has decided that they will appear tired and wounded after a hunt. Visiting poets plant trees. Nuala Ní Dhomhnaill has a Turkish hazel. Seán Ó Tuama, a Ginko. The Rowans are all dedicated to the Muse." Also at her Wicklow home, Jenkinson tends to her pets and small animals, and preserves a bumblebee habitat. As the former cookery columnist for the Belfast newspaper *LÁ*, her interests also incline to the culinary arts.

MAJOR WORKS AND THEMES

As she has declared, "Love is the only possible theme for a writer. The writing itself is a matter of love. Recognition is no proper concern for a poet. . . . For my part, poetry takes the place of formal religious observance, as a way of loving whatever there may be." Three of her poems that have found particular favor are (using English-language titles) "The Sin of Giving Short Measure," "Spray," and "Silence." The closing, sad lines of "The Sin of Giving Short Measure" are memorably well wrought, even in translation:

I raise my pencil
to measure his head,

to leap over the memory of you
as I leaped over your death
by writing a death song.
The light on the line of his clavicle
expands till the room blurs with brightness.
All I have measured is my own lapse from humanity.
I stuff the gear into my bag
and stumble from the room
to pay the tears I owe you
to the streaming rain
with no restraint
with no artistry.

(http://www.atlantareview.com/Ireland/Jenkinso.htm.
Translated by Alex Osborne. Copyright Biddy Jenkinson, 1990)

At the *Poetry and Sexuality Conference*, hosted by the University of Stirling, Scotland (2004), Máire Ní Annracháin of the National University of Ireland presented a paper that emphasized an especially exciting strain in Jenkinson's work, "New Forms of Sovereignty: Echoes of the Goddess in the Gaelic Poetry of Biddy Jenkinson and Sorley McLean" (http://www.poetryconference.stir.ac.uk/se9.html).

An anthology of Jenkinson's poetry, *Rogha Dánta*, edited by Seán Ó Tuama and Siobhán Ní Fhoghlú, was issued by Cork University Press in 1999. Her plays, *Mise, Subhó agus Macco* and *Oh Rahjerum!*, were produced by the Belfast-based theater company Aisling Ghéar. Aisteoirí an Spidéil have also staged *Mise, Subhó agus Macco*. Coiscéim has recently published "Púca Púca," a story for naughty children, illustrated by Ríbó.

CRITICAL RECEPTION

Irish poet and translator Pearse Hutchinson, in his important and extended review of *Rogha Dánta*, an anthology of Jenkinson's poetry, judges Jenkinson "one of the best poets in Ireland" (http://www.munsterlit.ie/Swframe/SWNew1/rogha%20danta.htm). Hutchinson mentions her passion and humor, the rich color and variety of her writings, and most especially the *sound* of her verse, which displays a deep relish in language and the manifold poetic possibilities of Irish. "Biddy Jenkinson knows how to vary the tempo (the pressure)," writes Hutchinson, "as in two particular passages from *Mis ag Caoineadh Dubhrois*. Her ear for the different sound effects, the expressive possibilities of the language, is as near as makes no matter unerring. Musical doesn't only mean mellifluous, the guttural strength of Irish, perfectly fitting, comes into play. . . . The *joie de vivre* and also scorn in these poems are those of a poet *who can write*." Hutchinson also emphasizes Jenkinson's masterful skill in erotic content and lamentation.

Theo Dorgan, on his Web site, *Twentieth-Century Irish-Language Poetry*, notes that "we live in a changed landscape now. Biddy Jenkinson can forge, as she has done, a lapidary and rigorous language" (http://www.archipelago.org/vol7-3/dorgan.htm [2004]).

Jenkinson received a poetry prize from Oireachtas na Gaeilge and also from the Irish American Cultural Institute Butler Award.

*The author and the publisher gratefully acknowledge permission of Biddy Jenkinson
for the excerpt from "The Sin of Giving Short Measure."*

BIBLIOGRAPHY

Works by Biddy Jenkinson

Poetry

Amhras Neimhe. Dublin: Coiscéim, 1997.
Baisteadh Gintlí. Dublin: Coiscéim, 1987.
"Céaslóireacht: i.m., Gráinne a cailleadh 23.11.99." In "Write Now," *Irish Times*, December 9,
    2000. Weekend, 11. (With other verse, by Peter Sirr, George Siztes, Lorna Goodison, and
    Dag Andersson.)
Dán na hUidhre. Dublin: Coiscéim, 1991.
Mis. Dublin: Coiscéim, 2001.
Rogha Dánta. Edited by Seán Ó Tuama and Siobhán Ní Fhoghlú. Cork University Press, 1999.
    (An anthology of Jenkinson's poetry.)
Uiscí Beatha. Dublin: Coiscéim, 1988.

Prose Fiction (stories)

An Gra Riabhach—Gairscealta. Dublin: Coiscéim, 1999. (A collection of bawdy prose fiction.)

Plays, Published and/or Produced

Mise, Subhó agus Macco. In *Rogha an Chéid*. Indreabháin: Cló Iar-Chonnachta, 2000. Produced
    by the Aisling Ghéar theater company, Belfast, 2001, and by Aisteorí an Spidéil.
Oh Rahjerum! Dublin: Coiscéim, 1998. Produced by the Aisling Ghéar theater company, Belfast.
    Subsequent productions in Dublin and Galway.

Review & Commentary

"A Letter to an Editor." *Irish University Review* 21.1 (Spring/Summer 1991): 27–34.
 Review of *Beathaisnéis*. Vol. 8 (1983–2002), edited and compiled by Máire Ní Mhurchu argus
    Diarmuid Breathnach. Dublin: An Clóchomhar Tta, 2003.

Writings in Selected Anthologies

Bourke, Angela, Máirín Ní Dhonneadha, Siobhán Kilfeather, Maria Luddy, Margaret MacCur-
    tain, Gerardine Meaney, Mary O'Dowd, and Clair Wills, eds. *The Field Day Anthology
    of Irish Writing*. Vols. 4 and 5. Cork: Cork University Press, 2002.
Crotty, Patrick, and Andrew Crofts, eds. *Modern Irish Poetry*. Belfast: Blackstaff, 1995.
Donovan, Katie, A. Norman Jeffares, and Brendan Kennelly, eds. *Ireland's Women*. New York:
    W. W. Norton, 1994.
McBreen, Joan, ed. *The White Page/An Bhilleog Bhán; Twentieth-Century Irish Women Poets*.
    Cliffs of Moher, Ire.: Salmon, 1999.

Studies of Biddy Jenkinson

Hutchinson, Pearse. Review of *Rogha Dánta*. 2002. http://www.munsterlit.ie/Swframe/
    SWNew1/rogha%20danta.htm.
Siobhán, Ní Fhoghlú. Interview with Jenkinson. In *Ogma 8* edited by Micheál Ó Cearúill. Dublin:
    Counts, 2000, 62–69.

JENNIFER JOHNSTON
(1930–　　)

Shawn O'Hare

BIOGRAPHY

Jennifer Prudence Johnston was born in Dublin to Shelagh Richards (1903–1985) and Denis Johnston (1901–1984), the talented and respected playwright who authored a number of important plays, most famously *The Old Lady Says "No!"* (1929). Richards was a popular actress and later a television director. When Johnston was eight years old her parents separated and she and her brother, Michael, lived with their mother.

Johnston was educated at Park House School and as a teenager had aspirations to follow in the footsteps of her mother to be a stage actress. However, her mother was not keen on the idea, and eventually Johnston went on to attend Trinity College Dublin (TCD) instead. Johnston did not graduate from TCD but was later awarded an honorary degree.

In 1951, Johnston married Ian Smyth, a lawyer. The couple lived in Paris and London and had four children, two daughters and two sons. In 1976 she married David Gilliland, also a solicitor, and with his five children lived in Derry, close to the River Foyle. She continues to live in Derry.

At the age of thirty-five, Johnston started to write. With two young children at home, she realized that writing was the one thing she could do and still be available for her children's needs. The first book she wrote, *The Gates* (1973), was rejected by a number of publishers who believed the novel to be too short. However, when Johnston was forty, her second attempt at a novel, *The Captains and the Kings* (1972), was accepted for publication, and *The Gates* was published the following year. Since then Johnston has published eleven more novels, including the Booker Prize–shortlisted *Shadows on Our Skin* (1977) and the Whitbread Award–winning *The Old Jest* (1979). Her work has also appeared in a variety of collections, including *Finbar's Hotel* (1999).

Johnston has also written a number of plays, including *The Nightingale and Not the Lark* (1979) and *The Desert Lullaby* (1996). Four of Johnston's novels have been made into films: *How Many Miles to Babylon?* (1982), *The Christmas Tree* (1986), *The Dawning* (1988, based on *The Old Jest*), and *The Railway Station Man* (1992). She is a member of Aosdána, has served on the Abbey Theatre Board, and has won the Evening Standard First Novel Award.

MAJOR WORKS AND THEMES

At various times during her career, Johnston has been labeled a Big House novelist, a Troubles writer, and a master of psychology and character sketches. Her genius, of course, is that she can be all of those things. She is also recognized for her compact writing style. Many of her novels are fewer than 200 pages long, and her prose is smooth and spare.

Johnston's early reputation as a Big House novelist began with her first published novel, *The Captains and the Kings*, which is in many ways a typical Big House novel. It is the story of Charles Prendergast, a wealthy Protestant widower who lives in a large, run-down house—the Big House. It opens with two members of the police making their way to Prendergast's home on a September afternoon. The next scene flashes back to May, when we encounter Prendergast, who since the recent death of his wife, Clare, has resorted to living simply in the book-cluttered mess of his study. From the novel's opening pages, Prendergast is clearly a lonely old man, caught among childhood memories, thoughts of a cold marriage, a dysfunctional relationship with his daughter, Sarah, and old age, which for him has no friends and little direction. Prendergast's house has fallen into ruins as has his life. He befriends a young man from town, Diaramid Toorish, but that friendship eventually leads to a scandal when the teenager, who despises school and is about to be sent to Dublin by his parents, spends too much time at Prendergast's house. Diaramid's parents, as well as a number of people from the town, believe that Prendergast has imposed himself on Diaramid and that the two have had an inappropriate relationship. At the end of the story Diaramid's parents, along with the local priest and the police, confront Prendergast and the boy, warning the older man that he will be arrested and the boy Diaramid sent away. The novel concludes with Prendergast suffering a fatal heart attack as the police make their way to his house for the arrest.

Big House themes are continued in *The Gates*. In this story, Major MacMahon lives in a house described as being in the "English Italianate style." The major's niece, Minnie, comes from England to stay with him, and the physical state of Uncle Prionnsias (he suffers from chilblains and secretly drinks), as Minnie knows him, is representative of the crumbling of the house as well as of the declining Anglo-Irish society. Minnie falls in love with the son of an estate worker, Kevin, with whom she wants to change the direction of their lives, eventually coming up with a plan to reinstate the property's vegetable garden. When an obnoxious American couple offers to buy the estate's magnificent gates, which serve as the entrance to the driveway, Minnie and Kevin realize that they can use that money to fund their gardening project. However, Kevin just takes that money and runs off, leaving his past behind. Minnie is left to tell her uncle what has happened, although instead of being upset with her for selling the gates, Uncle Prionnsias and his niece realize that they have each other, which gives the novel a positive, if not upbeat, ending.

In her third novel, *How Many Miles to Babylon?* (1974), Johnston continues to explore the crumbling Irish Big House society. As in the earlier novels, Ireland's rigid class system (Anglo-Irish Protestant and Irish Roman Catholic) directly affects the lives of Johnston's characters. In this case, the story is about a friendship that begins in childhood between the aristocratic Alexander Moore and the local boy Jerry Crowe. Alexander is the narrator of the story, and it is evident early on that his overbearing mother, unchallenged by an ineffectual father, dictates the youngster's life. However, through their friendship and their mutual love of horses and night swimming in a nearby pond, the two young men form a bond of brotherhood. In fact, when Alexander is bullied by his mother to volunteer for World War I, so she can increase her status in the village, Jerry also joins the British military, and the two serve together, though, of course, Alexander is an officer. Unfortunately, Jerry sneaks away from his unit to go to the front to look for his missing father, and to save Jerry from being executed as a deserter, Alexander actually shoots and kills his best friend. Thus, the novel is narrated by Alexander as he awaits his execution for shooting a comrade.

Johnston's fourth novel, *Shadows on Our Skin*, departs from the Big House theme as the story focuses on a twelve-year-old boy, Joe Logan, who develops a crush on his teacher, Kathleen Doherty. Joe's home life is unhappy; his invalid father only tells stories about his glorious past of fighting for Irish freedom, and his mother is struggling to keep the family afloat financially and emotionally. Kathleen appreciates Joe's interest in poetry and befriends him, spending a lot of time with him and even taking some day trips with him. Joe's boyhood crush is challenged, however, when his older brother, Brendan (an Irish Republican Army member who recently returned to Derry from England), meets Kathleen. The two eventually fall in love, and when Joe learns that his brother will quit the IRA and go to England to wait for Kathleen, he tells his older brother that Kathleen is, in fact, engaged to a British soldier who is stationed in Germany. The novel ends, however, without the drama one would expect, though the ending also reflects the malaise of their lives and the situation in which they live.

While the setting is in a big house, on the coast south of Dublin, and the time frame is during the Irish War for Independence, *The Old Jest* signals a maturation in Johnston's writing, as psychology plays an increasingly important role. Orphaned, eighteen years old, soon to be attending Trinity College Dublin, and living with her aunt and aged grandfather in a decaying mansion, Nancy Gulliver is ready to enter the "adult" world. However, such a process is filled with complexities, whether it be defying the manners her aunt believes to be correct or being in love with a man, Harry, who loves another, more proper, young woman. Most revealing, though, is that Nancy is always looking for the father who abandoned her when she was young, always searching the face of every man she passes, hoping to recognize something. When she discovers that a transient has been hiding in her small, beachside bathhouse, she suspects that the middle-aged man, whom she calls "Cassius," who knows the area and the people quite well, is her father. As it turns out, Cassius is an IRA man, he even convinces Nancy to serve as a courier for him, and at the end of the novel the violence of the civil war becomes personal as Nancy's aunt Mary is present at a shooting at a racehorse track, and Cassius is shot to death. While the novel does encompass many of the traditional Big House themes, Nancy's relationships with those around her and her search for an identity anticipate Johnston's developing emphasis on her characters' interior lives.

Johnston's sixth novel, *The Christmas Tree* (1981), has a more contemporary setting. The story is narrated by forty-five-year-old Constance Keating, who is in the final stage of a losing battle with leukemia when she returns to Dublin from England to live in the home of her recently deceased father. With Constance is her nine-month-old daughter, and much of the novel centers on their relationship with the baby's father, a Polish Jew named Jacob Weinberg. As well as dealing with her own imminent death, Constance must also secure a future for her daughter, and much of the novel is about whether the father will return to take the baby or whether she will be left in the care of Constance's slightly overbearing sister, Bibi. The one person with whom Constance is able to connect is Bertie, a young woman from an orphanage who takes care of Constance as she grows weaker. In fact, Bertie actually completes the narrative after Constance dies.

For her seventh novel, *The Railway Station Man* (1984), Johnston uses a rural Donegal setting for the story about a midlife love affair between Helen Cuffe, a widow who moved to Donegal to pursue her painting ambitions, and Roger Hawthorne, an English eccentric who lost an eye and an arm in World War II. Helen has a strained relationship with her son Jack, and the tension is heightened when Jack and a friend called Manus come to visit, because the two are involved with the IRA (added to this is the fact that Helen's husband was an accidental victim of an IRA bombing in Derry). *The Railway Station Man* is really a novel about desires: Helen wants to be an artist, Roger wants to rebuild the railway stop in the small town, Helen and Roger want someone to love and someone to love them, and Jack wants to prove his worth to the Republican movement.

In *Fool's Sanctuary* (1987), Johnston returns to the Big House setting. This time the setting is Termon (the Irish word for "sanctuary"), a 300-year-old house that is the family estate for the Martins, an Anglo-Irish family with English roots. The various storylines of the novel are told with regret, and are recounted by Miranda Martin in her old age. She is remembering 1919, with the eighteen-year-old living at home with her father who, having gone against the long-standing Martin family tradition of English soldiering, dreams of making Ireland more ecologically sound by planting trees. As part of his commitment to Ireland and to the local area, the landowner funds the Dublin education of a local boy, Charlie, a Catholic, who goes to Dublin, takes up with the IRA, and Hibernicizes his name to Cathal. Miranda and Cathal fall in love, but that relationship is challenged when her brother, Andrew, and his friend Harry visit the home on leave from the British army. However, when Cathal receives the command that the two British officers must be killed, the abstract concept of death-murder-honor is put to a test. By the novel's end the characters realize that in revolutionary Ireland there is no such thing as a sanctuary, and, many years later, even in her advanced age, Miranda is still deeply affected by the events of her youth.

The struggle to come to terms with the events of the past is also the theme of Johnston's ninth novel, *The Invisible Worm* (1991). The novel's protagonist, Laura Quinlan, has a series of complex relationships with the people in her life. Middle-aged and without children, Laura lives the life of a spoiled, upper-class Protestant, surrounded by possessions but unhappy. Her husband, Maurice, is kind to her when she is ill, but as soon as she feels better he is quick to leave her alone at home while he takes advantage of his freedom in town. He introduces her to Dominic O'Hara, a defrocked priest and classics scholar, and he and Laura form a friendship that allows her to start to try to come to terms with her past. In fact, it becomes obvious that Laura's relationship with her parents has affected her the most. Her mother—wealthy Anglo-Irish and quirky—and her father—an Irish politician who eventually becomes a senator—have had a strained marriage. The most shocking aspect of the novel is that Laura was sexually abused by her father when she was growing up. In the end she seeks closure by burning the summer house where the abuse happened.

The Illusionist (1995) tells the story of Stella Macnamara and her oppressive marriage to Martyn Glover. Stella first met Martyn on a train, and soon thereafter they were married and living in the countryside outside of London. Martyn is a very secretive man who tells his wife little about his past or his family or even what he does daily. He even keeps a room in the home locked to prevent anyone from entering. All of this adds to his being an illusionist—a magician of sorts, who uses white doves in his act. Obsessed with controlling his wife, Martyn eventually forces Stella to quit work and stay at home. Later, however, Stella decides to pursue a career as a writer, even after Martyn tosses her typewriter out a window. When Stella decides that she has to leave her husband and return to Ireland, their daughter, Robin, decides to stay with her father. A terrorist bombing in London accidentally kills Martyn (as well as a car full of doves he has with him), and, appropriately for an illusionist, he is gone in a puff of smoke. Robin is unable to forgive her mother for leaving England, and they are both left with some of their illusions still intact.

Johnston's eleventh novel, *Two Moons* (1998), takes place in Killiney, the wealthy neighborhood south of Dublin, and is the story of three generations of women. Mimi and her daughter Grace share the house and are visited by Grace's daughter, Polly and her boyfriend. The boyfriend develops a crush on his girlfriend's mother, but Grace, an Abbey Theatre actress, is more obsessed with her craft, in particular Shakespeare. Meanwhile, Mimi is having regular conversation with an angel called Bonifacio di Longara, who is intent on convincing her to purchase expensive Gucci shoes. Ultimately, the novel is about how each of the characters comes to understand the issues she is facing: Mimi deals with death, Grace faces the combination of being middle-aged and an actress, and Polly learns that she must make her life decisions for herself and not be overly influenced by what her mother wants.

The search for the meaning of one's life is continued in Johnston's twelfth novel, *The Gingerbread Woman* (2000). Clara Barry is a Protestant from the Republic of Ireland and Laurence McGrane is a Roman Catholic from Northern Ireland. They meet one evening while he is walking his dog along Killiney Hill and she is taking a walk (though he thinks she is about to commit suicide). Both are going through difficult times in their lives: Clara is recovering from medical treatment for an undisclosed sexual ailment that she received from her previous boyfriend; Laurence, or Lar, as he is called, has lost his wife and daughter to an IRA bombing in the North. But they have different reactions to their predicaments. Clara is writing a novel in an attempt to move beyond her failed relationship with a man in New York City. Lar, trying not to feel lost and alone, frequently "talks" with his deceased wife, preserving her memory and continuing his commitment to her. Clara is also, seemingly, trapped by her upper-middle-class existence—her university education, being a lecturer in Irish literature, a childhood with a mother obsessed with making jam and gingerbread cookies (hence the title of the novel)—all the things that society accepts as the norm. The focus on the personal lives of the characters underscores the career-long shift in Johnston's writing from the larger Big House issues of societal differences and the crumbling of the Anglo-Irish ruling class to the personal problems and psychological situations of individual characters.

Despite its clever title, Johnston's thirteenth novel, *This Is Not a Novel* (2002), is, in fact, the story of three generations of a Dublin family. The narrator is Imogen Bailey, who is struggling to accept the drowning death of her brother Johnny, an Olympic-caliber swimmer. She was eighteen years old when it happened, and it caused her to have an emotional breakdown, as she stopped speaking to people and was eventually placed in a mental hospital. In trying to figure out how and why her family life fell apart, Imogen examines her past and comes to the conclusion that Johnny's schoolboy friend, Bruno Shlegel, played a role in the tragedy. Bruno had a disruptive impact on the entire family, including the maid, a Jew from Prague who resented Bruno for his German nationality. Although he cannot be directly blamed for Johnny's death, it is implied that the relationship between the two, countered with Bruno also showing interest in women, instigated Johnny's death. This idea is underscored by the fact that Imogen discovers through family papers that her uncle was forced to join the British military during World War I because his father feared that he was gay and thought joining the military would cure that. The young man was killed in combat. But at the novel's end, Imogen still does not have any answers, and she maintains her hope that somehow her brother did not drown and that he will someday return to the family.

CRITICAL RECEPTION

Jennifer Johnston's career as a novelist is long and distinguished. Early in her career many of her novels did have Big House settings, though they were always in some state of decline, which also often represented the emotional and psychological state of the characters. However, as her novels took on more contemporary settings, the Troubles of Northern Ireland began to play an important role in her work. More recently, Johnston's novels have detailed the inner struggles of her characters. David Burleigh argues that Johnston keeps readers "morally engaged" and that "her protagonists—the bereaved, the orphaned, the outcast—are all spirits struggling to enlarge themselves" (7). Much attention has also been given to Johnston's sparse writing style. Bridget O'Toole argues that "her economy of detail results in a certain nakedness in the drama between characters. Her medium is dialogue rather than evocation" (135). Andrew Parkin calls Johnston's style "precise and lucid" (316). The consensus is that Jennifer Johnston is one of the most significant Irish novelists of the twentieth century and that her themes and writing style validate such a reputation.

BIBLIOGRAPHY

Works by Jennifer Johnston

The Captains and the Kings. London: Hamilton, 1972.
The Christmas Tree. London: Hamilton, 1981.
The Desert Lullaby: A Play in Two Acts. Belfast: Lagan, 1996.
Finbar's Hotel. Edited by Dermot Bolger. San Francisco: Harcourt, Brace, 1999. (With Dermot Bolger, Roddy Doyle, Anne Enright, Hugo Hamilton, Joseph O'Connor, and Colm Toibin.)
Fool's Sanctuary. New York: Viking, 1988.
The Gates. London: Hamilton, 1973.
The Gingerbread Woman. London: Review, 2000.
How Many Miles to Babylon? London: Hamilton, 1974.
The Illusionist. London: Sinclair-Stevenson, 1995.
The Invisible Worm. London: Penguin, 1992.
The Nightingale and Not the Lark: A Play. Dublin: Raven Arts, 1988.
The Old Jest. London: Hamilton, 1979.
The Railway Station Man. London: Hamilton, 1984.
Shadows on Our Skin. London: Hamilton, 1977.
This Is Not a Novel. London: Review, 2002.
Two Moons. London: Review, 1998.

Selected Studies of Jennifer Johnston

Backus, Margot Gayle. "Homophobia and the Imperial Demon Lover: Gothic Narrativity in Irish Representations of the Great War." *Canadian Review of Comparative Literature* 21, no. 1 (March 1994): 45–63.
Benstock, Shari. "The Masculine World of Jennifer Johnston." In *Twentieth-Century Women Novelists*, edited by Thomas F. Staley, 191–217. Totawa, NJ: Barnes and Noble, 1982.
Berge, Marit. "The Big House in Jennifer Johnston's Novels." In *Excursions in Fiction: Essays in Honour of Professor Lars Hartveit on His 70th Birthday*, edited by Andrew Kennedy, 11–31. Oslo: Novus, 1994.
Burleigh, David. "Dead and Gone: The Fiction of Jennifer Johnston and Julia O'Faolain." In *Irish Writers and Society at Large*, edited by Masaru Sekine, 1–15. Totawa, NJ: Barnes and Noble, 1985.
Connelly, Joseph. "Legend and Lyric as Structure in the Selected Fiction of Jennifer Johnston." *Eire-Ireland* 21, no. 3 (Fall 1986): 119–24.
De Petris, Carla. "Landing from Laputa: The Big House in Jennifer Johnston's Recent Fiction." In *The Classical World and the Mediterranean*, edited by Giuseppe Serpillo, 334–43. Cagliari, Italy: Tema, 1996.

Fauset, Eileen. *Studies in the Fiction of Jennifer Johnston and Mary Lavin.* Ft. Lauderdale, FL: Nova Southeastern University, 1998.

Hargreaves, Tasmin. "Women's Consciousness and Identity in Four Irish Women Novelists." In *Cultural Contexts and Literary Idioms in Contemporary Irish Literature*, edited by Michael Kenneally, 290–305. Totowa, NJ: Barnes and Noble, 1988.

Imhof, Rüdiger. "A Little Bit of Ivory Two Inches Wide—The Small World of Jennifer Johnston." *Etudes Irlandaises* 10 (December 1985): 129–44.

Kirkpatrick, Kathryn, ed. *Border Crossings: Irish Women Writers and National Identities.* Dublin: Wolfhound, 2000.

Lanters, Jose. "Jennifer Johnston's Divided Ireland." *Dutch Quarterly Review of Anglo-American Letters* 18, no. 3 (1988): 228–41.

Lubbers, Klaus. "This White Elephant of a Place." In *Ancestral Voices: The Big House in Anglo-Irish Literature*, edited by Otto Rauchbauer, 221–37. Hildesheim: Olms, 1992.

Moloney, Caitriona. "An Interview with Jennifer Johnston." *Nua: Studies in Contemporary Irish Writing* 2, nos. 1–2 (Autumn 1998–Spring 1999): 139–49.

Mortimer, M. "The World of Jennifer Johnston—A Look at Three Novels." *Crane Bag* 4, no. 1 (Spring 1980): 601–7.

O'Toole, Bridget. "Three Writers of the Big House: Elizabeth Bowen, Molly Keane and Jennifer Johnston." In *Across a Roaring Hill: The Protestant Imagination in Modern Ireland*, edited by Gerald Dawe and Edna Longley, 124–38. Belfast: Blackstaff, 1985.

Parkin, Andrew. "Shadows of Destruction: The Big House in Contemporary Irish Fiction." In *Cultural Contexts and Literary Idioms in Contemporary Irish Literature*, edited by Michael Kenneally, 306–27. Totowa, NJ: Barnes and Noble, 1988.

Reisman, Mara. " 'She Heard the Shattering Glass': Explosion and Revelation in Jennifer Johnston's *The Railway Station Man.*" *Nua: Studies in Contemporary Irish Writing* 4, nos. 1–2 (2003): 89–111.

Watchel, Eleanor. "Jennifer Johnston Interview." *Queen's Quarterly* 104, no. 2 (Summer 1997): 319–29.

Winner, Anthony. "Disorders of Reading Short Novels and Perplexities." *Kenyon Review* 18, no. 1 (Winter 1996): 117–28.

MARIE JONES
(1955–)

Patrick Lonergan

BIOGRAPHY

Actor and playwright Marie Jones was born in east Belfast, Northern Ireland, and grew up in a predominantly Protestant working-class community. She became involved in acting from a very young age, performing as a teenager in James Young's popular review, *Little Boxes* (1968–1969). In 1976 she joined the Young Lyric Players at Belfast's Lyric Theatre, with which she has retained a strong association throughout her career.

In 1983, Jones joined with four other Belfast actors—Carol Scanlon, Eleanor

Methven, Brenda Winter, and Maureen McAuley—to found Charabanc Theatre (1983–1995). One of Ireland's first independent theater companies, Charabanc had an explicitly feminist orientation, having been established in response to its founders' perception that there was a lack of good roles for Irish actresses. This lack was partially due to the fact that Belfast theaters often passed over Northern Irish acting talent when casting plays, instead hiring actors from London or Dublin. But it was also because the Irish theater establishment tended to regard theater about or by women as being undeserving of funding, support, or critical attention. Throughout its twelve-year existence, Charabanc consistently challenged these biases.

Charabanc was originally conceived as a collective, but its members quickly organized themselves into individual roles, with Jones becoming the company's writer in residence. Her work was generally collaborative: the other company members would research issues of interest to the group and explore them in workshops, and Jones would develop their material into a coherent script. She also performed in most of the company's plays. Charabanc became successful in a very short period of time, touring internationally and attracting huge popular support—though it remained undervalued by Irish theater critics throughout its existence.

Jones resigned from Charabanc in 1990. With the director Pam Brighton she set up Dubbeljoint Theatre and also became involved in Replay Productions, a company dedicated to theater in education.

Jones's reputation grew steadily during the 1990s. Now writing entirely alone, she produced a series of plays that combined biting social critique—on issues such as Northern Irish sectarianism, globalization, and the persistence of sexism—with comedy, song, and exuberant theatricality. The most successful of these, *Stones in His Pockets* (1999), transferred to Broadway, winning a Tony Award.

Jones continues to live and work in Belfast, where she is married to Ian McIlhenny, the director of her most recent plays. She has received numerous awards for her work, including an honorary doctorate from Queen's University Belfast.

MAJOR WORKS AND THEMES

Marie Jones's work with Charabanc consistently focuses on issues of gender and social class. Using song and oral storytelling, the plays locate themselves within an Irish folk tradition of writing collaboratively from and for the community. Among Charabanc's best plays are *Lay Up Your Ends* (1983), about a group of women working in a Belfast linen factory, *The Girls in the Big Picture* (1986), which charts changing gender roles in Northern Ireland, and *Somewhere Over the Balcony* (1987), set in the nationalist Divis flats in Belfast.

Jones's first solo success was *A Night in November* (1994), in which Kenneth, a Northern Protestant, is so repulsed by the sectarianism and racism shown by Loyalist supporters during a football match between Northern Ireland and the Republic of Ireland that he decides to follow the Republic's team to the 1994 World Cup finals in the United States. The play is a monologue, with multiple parts performed by one actor; it focuses on a theme at the heart of Jones's work: the possibility of transformation. Kenneth rejects sectarianism while maintaining his Irish Protestant identity—and this transformation is mirrored in the style of performance, with the actor's movement from one role to another enacting the notion that identities need not be fixed.

In *Women on the Verge of HRT* (1996), two middle-aged Belfast women, Anna and Vera, travel to the Donegal hotel of Irish entertainer Daniel O'Donnell. In the naturalistic first half, the women discuss their unsatisfying relationships with men, and in the expressionistic second half, they sit on a cliff near the hotel and summon various people in their lives to account for themselves. The play concludes with a call for a reappraisal of Irish gender roles, challenging the notion that equality for Irishwomen has been achieved.

Stones in His Pockets charts the relationship of a Hollywood production team making a film about the Irish Land War with the residents of the Irish village in which the film is being shot. Jones draws a parallel between the nineteenth-century relationship of landlord, agent, and tenant being depicted in the film, and that of Hollywood producers using Irish mediators to exploit the villagers in the play. The play's two leading characters respond to that exploitation by deciding to make their own film about how poor treatment by the filmmakers provoked the suicide of a local resident. *Stones in His Pockets* is a triumph of theatricality, with all of the parts played by two actors, creating a contrast between exciting live performance and the homogenized superficiality of Hollywood film.

After the success of *Stones*, Jones reworked many of her earlier plays for production at the Lyric Theatre in Belfast. The most significant of these is *The Blind Fiddler* (2003), which focuses on a Belfast woman's attempts to come to terms with the recent death of her father. At the play's centre is the Catholic notion of sacrifice, with Jones paralleling the penance of Lough Derg pilgrims with compromises made for the sake of their children's prosperity by a Catholic couple in Belfast. The play proposes that sectarianism and social class are closely intertwined, which Jones embeds in a historical context by presenting the action *around* the Troubles, flashing back to the 1960s from post-ceasefire Ulster.

Jones's plays may not be noted for sophisticated narrative or characterization, but she deserves recognition for her ability to use theatrical performance to show how social roles may be overcome and for her commitment to bringing theater into contact with other forms of popular culture, notably music and folk tradition.

CRITICAL RECEPTION

Throughout her career, Marie Jones's work has had difficulty gaining the critical attention that it deserves. Many commentators use the commercial success of her plays as evidence of a lack of thematic sophistication, and she has frequently been accused of sentimentalizing and oversimplifying complex issues. These accusations are unfortunate: while Jones's drama may invite superficial interpretation, there is a clearly discernible commitment to social justice throughout her works. Furthermore, her plays are among the most theatrical currently being written in Ireland.

The first major treatment of Jones's work was a now seminal article by Victoria White, which argues that the Irish theatrical establishment was marginalizing Charabanc by treating it as catering only to a "minority audience" (34). White argues that critical responses to theater by Irish women are strongly predetermined by persistent prejudicial notions of gender roles, both in society and onstage.

Although the profile of Irish women dramatists has risen since 1990, when Jones left Charabanc, critical treatments of her work continued to place it in a marginal role, typically considering it only in the context of plays written by women or about Northern Ireland, rather than as a fully integrated part of the Irish repertoire. In part, this is because the popular success of *Women on the Verge of HRT* was unprecedented in Irish drama, and critics found themselves ill-equipped to consider a play that combines Brechtian alienation techniques with sentimentalized Irish ballads. More seriously, *A Night in November* was harshly criticized during its Dublin run for pandering to prejudices about Ulster Unionism.

The success of *Stones in His Pockets* appears to have reversed this trend somewhat, and Jones is now beginning to attract real critical attention. The thematic complexity of her work remains undervalued, however, as is her often unsettling interest in combining theatrical entertainment with genuine social engagement.

BIBLIOGRAPHY

Works by Marie Jones

Published Works

With Charabanc Theatre Company

The Hamster Wheel. In *The Crack in the Emerald: New Irish Plays*, edited by David Grant, 189–258. London: Hern, 1990.

Lay Up Your Ends (extract). In *The Female Line: Northern Irish Women Writers,* edited by Ruth Hooley, 54. Belfast: NI Women's Rights Movement, 1985.

Somewhere Over the Balcony. In *Postcolonial Plays—An Anthology*, edited by Helen Gilbert, 447–69. London: Routledge, 2001.

As Sole Author

A Night in November. London: Hern, 2001. (In same volume as *Stones in His Pockets*.)

Stones in His Pockets. London: Hern, 2001.

Women on the Verge of HRT. London: French, 1999.

Unpublished Plays

With Charabanc Theatre Company

The Girls in the Big Picture. 1986.

Gold in the Streets. 1986.

Now You're Talkin'. 1985.

Oul Delf and False Teeth. 1984.

As Sole Author

The Blind Fiddler. 2003.

Don't Look Down. 1992.

Eddie Bottom's Dream. 1996.

Hiring Days. 1992.

Ruby. 2000.

Weddins, Weeins and Wakes. 2001.

Studies of Marie Jones

DiCenzo, Maria. "Charabanc Theatre Company: Placing Women Center-Stage in Northern Ireland." *Theatre Journal* 45 (May 1993): 173–84.

Foley, Imelda. *The Girls in the Big Picture: Gender in Contemporary Ulster Theatre*. Belfast: Blackstaff, 2003.

Harris, Claudia W. "Reinventing Women: Charabanc Theatre Company." In *The State of Play: Irish Theatre in the 'Nineties*, edited by Eberhard Bort, 104–23. Trier, Ger.: WVT, 1996.

Lojek, Helen. "Playing Politics with Belfast's Charabanc Theatre Company." In *Politics and Performance in Contemporary Northern Ireland*, edited by John P. Harrington and Elizabeth J. Mitchell, 82–102. Amherst: University of Massachusetts Press, 1999.

Moylan, Pat. "Interview with Marie Jones." In *Theatre Talk*, edited by Lillian Chambers, Ger Fitzgibbon, and Eamonn Jordan, 213–20. Dublin: Carysfort, 2001.

von Goler, Hans. *Streets Apart from Abbey Street—The Search for an Alternative National Theatre in Ireland Since 1980*. Trier, Ger.: WVT, 2000.

White, Victoria. "Towards a Post-Feminism?" *Theatre Ireland* 18 (April–June 1989): 33–35.

MOLLY KEANE
(1904–1996)

Ann Owens Weekes

BIOGRAPHY

Molly Keane was born to the Skrine family in County Kildare, where she lived for five years before the family moved to County Wexford. She remembers her parents as very remote, her father spending time with the children only on Sundays; her mother, Moira O'Neill, a romantic poet from Antrim, mixed in neither local nor literary society. The five Skrine children were left to the care of nannies and governesses, but Molly remembers few hours of supervision. Her mother led morning prayers, then dogs were fed, two hours of class endured, and after lunch, the only meal the children took with their parents, they were free to fiddle with horses, dogs, and gardens. The housemaids and farmworkers were their friends. While her mother was religious and concerned about her children's modesty and good behavior, her father, an excellent horseman, taught the children that hunting mattered more than anything, a lesson revealed in all Keane novels.

The larger world of European tensions and Irish political struggles infringed but little on the Skrine household, until the family home, an ascendancy Big House, was burned down, in retaliation for Black and Tan atrocities. Molly's father refused to leave Ireland as his peers urged, believing the burning was political, not personal. Sent to boarding school in Bray during this time, Molly was disliked by her classmates, found academics uninteresting, but eventually came to enjoy English literature. Getting a job was never an option, she recalls: girls of her class stayed home until they married. Molly, however, was introduced to a wider world when she encountered the wealthy, sophisticated Perry family. This generous family welcomed her into their home for many months of hunting each year, and John Perry would later assist her to write plays.

The legend of Molly Keane's becoming a writer is well known, though indeed she told several versions. In one she averred that at seventeen she wrote her first novel, *The Knight of the Cheerful Countenance* (1926), to supplement her dress allowance, using the pseudonym M. J. Farrell to hide the embarrassing activity from her hunting friends. A productive writing career followed; she published ten novels between 1928 and 1952, plus a book of Irish sporting scenes, *Red Letter Days* (1933), and had three plays produced in London, all directed by John Gielgud. Although she would write one more play, Molly Keane retreated from the literature scene when her beloved husband, Robert Keane, died, and she struggled to care for her two young daughters. To many readers' delight, she began a second successful writing career in 1981 with the publication of *Good Behaviour*, a novel immediately acclaimed a classic. This has been followed by two more novels, a cookbook, and a book of Irish reminiscences. Molly Keane lived and died in Ardmore, County Waterford.

MAJOR WORKS AND THEMES

Forgotten in the British library since 1926, *The Knight of the Cheerful Countenance* was reissued in 1993. A beginner's novel, it introduces, nevertheless, the familiar Keane themes: the hunt, the upstairs-downstairs society of the Big House, the beautiful, plucky, unconventional girls, whom the author admires more than the good, sensible, dull ones. The romantic plot is predictable, serving only as rationale for the enthusiastic detailing of one rare, healthy, exciting hunt scene after another. The twilight of the Anglo-Irish ascendancy is the world Keane inhabits and records: affection for this society characterizes the early novels, with few insights into the cruelties of the system. *Young Entry* (1928) tells the story of Prudence Lingfield-Turrett's alienation from her adolescent girlfriend "Peter" as the latter becomes involved in romance. The novel moves quickly, carried by a witty dialogue and vivid descriptions of hunt and countryside. The suicide of the dismissed cook haunts Prudence but receives less attention throughout than the small dogs to whom Prudence and Peter devote themselves. In *Taking Chances* (1929), the last of this trio of novice novels, Keane moves from the successful romantic formula to near tragedy. Mary Fuller—a typical Keane woman—beautiful, sensuous, and dangerous, wrecks the marriage of her friend, as love becomes less like a game and more like the compulsive sport of hunting.

Sense of place, a constant in Keane's fiction, emerges fully in *Mad Puppetstown* (1931). The novel's first section depicts the golden childhood of Easter Chivington and her cousins Basil and Evelyn in an idyllic Ireland of devoted servants, mysterious mountains, and glorious hunts before the Great War and the Irish Troubles. British distrust of Irish servants is treated ironically, the distrust leading a British soldier into an ambush and sending the Chivingtons scurrying for safety to England. Discovering their mutual love of place, Easter and Basil return as adults to a neglected Puppetstown, jealously guarded by an elderly aunt and longtime retainer. Love of place, not romance, enables cousins, aunt, and retainer to share and restore Puppetstown.

Lady Honour, in *Conversation Piece* (1932), is the first of Keane's awful mothers, a series of vicious, elderly women who prey on the young or dominate them. The affection between Willow and her brother Dick seems excessive here and may signal

Keane's interest in forbidden love, a world that both interested and shocked her. The lesbian relationship of Jessica and Jane drives the plot of the following novel, *Devoted Ladies* (1934). Opening in fashionable London, a suitable setting for the brittle heroines, the novel quickly moves to the hunting scenes of Big House Ireland. Piggy, who effects the dramatic conclusion and "saves" the day for heterosexual love, is a marvelous portrait of Keane's unattractive innocents: greedy, selfish, lacking self-knowledge, madly desiring love, Piggy will be perfected in the Aroon of *Good Behaviour*.

In *Full House* (1935), *The Rising Tide* (1937), and *Loving Without Tears* (1951), Keane continues to develop superb portraits of cruel mothers: women whose gift is to charm and bind the very people they destroy. In *Full House*, Lady Olivia Bird, adored by her silly husband, dominates her children so completely that even when they see through her strategies, they are unable to leave her. A sad, humiliating situation with the governess is treated with insight and humor. Lady Charlotte is the evil genius of *The Rising Tide* who, like most of these Keane women, refuses to see the changes taking place in Ireland at the beginning of the century and also bullies her children into submission. Angel, in *Loving Without Tears*, is as manipulative as the other two mothers, but Keane concludes this novel in comic harmony.

Two Days in Aragon (1941) focuses on the threat to Anglo-Irish life, as Grania, the daughter of the Big House, has a secret affair with her nurse's son, Foley O'Neill, a member of an illegal Irish military unit. *Treasure Hunt* (1952), the last novel in Keane's first writing career, features a Big House after the Troubles, where the mad hilarity continues despite the family's being forced to take English, paying guests.

Three very good novels appeared in the 1980s: *Good Behaviour* (1981), *Time After Time* (1983), and *Loving and Giving* (1988). While her earlier works depicted both the charming and useless lives of the ascendancy, frantically involved with horses, dogs, and lovers to keep boredom at bay, the later novels reveal a savagery never fully concealed by the veneer of good behavior, a savagery bred from that very code, the only remaining proof of a dying, impoverished class's mistaken sense of superiority. Ignorance and utter lack of self-knowledge bolster this mistaken sense, turning the would-be models of good behavior into examples of stupidity and cruelty. In a brilliant stroke, Keane allows Aroon to narrate *Good Behaviour*, revealing, as she attempts to hide, her ignorance, greed, and ugly personality. Aroon's murder, in the first pages, of the Mummie she professes to love, sets the stage for the funniest, blackest of Keane's comedies. All three novels look back from a present in the 1970s or 1940s to the time of the characters' and Keane's own youth. All three jolt the reader with their mix of the mundane and the shocking, the comic and the tragic. Always characters in their own right, the beautiful houses of the earlier novels decay in these later years, revealing the hostile, dangerous face that money and confidence disguised in their youth. While horses and dogs remain an obsession, the beautiful, plucky girls of the past have been replaced by elderly, ugly, barren women. The last novels toll a death knell, not a lament, for Anglo-Ireland.

CRITICAL RECEPTION

Since the publication of *Young Entry*, reviewers have generally been appreciative of Molly Keane's novels; American critics found the fox-hunting life foreign but delighted in the antics of the ascendancy, while British and Irish reviewers saw Keane as a worthy successor to Somerville and Ross. The cruel acuity of her perception was noted, and her mixture of comic wit and poetic sensibility seen as delightful. Some early reviewers, however, recoiled at the "indecent" subject of *Devoted Ladies*; others found the "doggie" talk tedious. Reviewers of the three recent novels and of the reissue of the first eleven continue the praise but also take Keane's work more seriously. *Good Behaviour,* "with its mixture of the macabre and the mundane, the terrifying and the ridiculous," may well become a "classic among English novels," the *New York Times Book Review* proclaimed (Rachel Billington, August 9, 1981, 13). Caroline Blackwood applauds Keane's portraits of the "profoundly philistine" life of the Anglo-Irish, singling out "maternal cruelty" as a recurring theme ("Afterword," *Full House*, 320, 318). Polly Devlin sums up Anglo-Ireland in the early novels: "The 'real' Irish (the peasant Catholic Irish) seem only to enter this world—and thus Molly Keane/Farrell's faithful rendering—as a sub-species, good for opening gates and giving amusing, barely subservient lip service" ("Introduction," *The Rising Tide*, xi). Keane's work has not yet received the critical attention it deserves: the Big House motif and decline of the ascendancy, as well as Keane's black comedy and treatment of sexuality, are the foci of the more recent criticism.

BIBLIOGRAPHY

Works by Molly Keane

Conversation Piece. 1932. Reprint, London: Virago, 1991.
Devoted Ladies. 1934. Reprint, London: Virago, 1984.
Full House. 1935. Reprint, London: Virago, 1986.
Good Behaviour. London: Deutsch, 1981.
The Knight of the Cheerful Countenance. 1926. Reprint, London: Virago, 1993.
Loving and Giving. (Published in the United States as *Queen Lear*.) London: Deutsch, 1988.
Loving Without Tears. (Published in the United States as *Enchanting Witch*.) 1951. Reprint, London: Virago, 1988.
Mad Puppetstown. 1931. Reprint, London: Virago, 1986.
Molly Keane's Ireland. London: HarperCollins, 1994. (An anthology compiled by Keane and her daughter Sally Phipps.)
Molly Keane's Nursery Cooking. London: Macdonald, 1985.
Red Letter Days. 1933. Reprint, London: Deutsch, 1987.
The Rising Tide. 1937. Reprint, London: Virago, 1984.
Taking Chances. 1929. Reprint, London: Virago, 1987.
Time After Time. London: Deutsch, 1983.
Treasure Hunt. 1952. Reprint, London: Virago, 1990.
Two Days in Aragon. 1941. Reprint, London: Virago, 1985.
Young Entry. (Published in the United States as *Point-to-Point*.) 1928. Reprint, London: Virago, 1989.

Studies of Molly Keane

Adams, Alice. "Coming Apart at the Seams: *Good Behaviour* as an AntiComedy of Manners." *Journal of Irish Literature* 20, no. 3 (September 1991): 27–35.
Breen, Mary. "Piggies and Spoilers of Girls: The Representation of Sexuality in the Novels of Molly Keane." In *Sex, Nation and Dissent in Irish Writing*, edited by Eibhear Walshe, 202–20. Cork: Cork University Press, 1997.
Kreilcamp, Vera. "The Persistent Pattern: Molly Keane's Recent Big House Fiction." *Massachusetts Review* 28 (Autumn 1987): 453–60.

Lynch, Rachael Jane. "The Crumbling Fortress: Molly Keane's Comedies of Anglo-Irish Manners." In *The Comic Tradition in Irish Women Writers*, edited by Theresa O'Connor, 73–98. Gainesville: University of Florida Press, 1996.

O'Toole, Bridget. "Three Writers of the Big House: Elizabeth Bowen, Molly Keane, and Jennifer Johnston." In *Across a Roaring Hill: The Protestant Imagination in Modern Ireland*, edited by Gerald Dawe and Edna Longley, 124–38. Belfast: Blackstaff, 1985.

Weekes, Ann Owens. *Irish Women Writers: An Uncharted Tradition.* Lexington: University of Kentucky Press, 1990.

EVA KELLY

(1830–1910)

Katherine Parr

BIOGRAPHY

The poet Mary Ann Kelly, who came to be known as "Eva of the Nation," was born in Headford, County Galway. Her father, Edward, owned a farm in Killeen, Galway, and married Mary O'Flaherty of Headford. Kelly's maternal granduncle was a member of the United Irishmen, and her uncle, Martin O'Flaherty, was connected with Young Ireland. Yet the family tradition of revolutionaries dates back through centuries to the infamous pirate queen Graine Ui Maile, Grace O'Malley. Thus, it seems inevitable that Kelly would inscribe Irish history with her own brand of nationalism. She wrote poetry and prose for the Young Ireland newspaper the *Nation*, attaining her stature as a national poet.

Kelly first submitted poems to the *Nation* under the pseudonym "Fionouala," beginning in 1844. "The Leprechuan" describes the legendary Irish creature who hides his coveted gold. That poem was followed in 1845 by "The Irish Mother. A Story of '98," which commemorated the 1798 uprising. Acceptance of a third poem, "The Benshi," set Mary Ann Kelly on the road that would bring her fame, as well as profound sadness.

Kelly continued to write under the pseudonym "Fionouala" throughout the year 1845, exploring her identity as a national poet. Another published poem offers particular insight into her evolving self-image; "Grainne Maöl's Visit to Elizabeth" recalls a historic meeting between the legendary pirate queen and Elizabeth I. Kelly claimed descent from this Irish heroine, and, in her notebook, penned more than a half century after writing the poem, she ascribed her own rebellious spirit to that blood line. In 1846, for unknown reasons, Kelly adopted a new pseudonym, "Eva," an appellation that she would claim the rest of her life.

Kelly became increasingly involved with the Young Ireland movement and found inspiration in the historic events of the era. The rift between Daniel O'Connell and

Young Ireland, which occurred as a result of O'Connell's alliance with the Whig Party, impelled Kelly to write "Our Course" (1846), a poem that ascribed cowardice to Old Ireland. Another historical event surrounding Thomas Meagher's justification of violent resistance to colonial rule inspired Kelly's "To T.F. Meagher" (1846).

Another revolutionary leader, John Mitchel, also won Kelly's admiration with his own brand of fiery rhetoric. In 1848, Mitchel, an editor for the *Nation*, established a competing newspaper, the *United Irishman*. He enlisted notable writers from the *Nation*, including Kelly, although Kelly continued writing for the Young Ireland journal and contributed more poems, as well as letters and essays in which she advanced her own political and ideological views.

In 1848, the *Nation* ran Kelly's letter decrying Britain's suspension of habeas corpus. Confident of her standing as spokesperson, Kelly called government officials "plunderers and tricksters" and demanded action in the face of the blatant infringement on civil law. Her prose and poems also bore a feminist ideology, demanding equality for women and depicting that ideal in verse.

"Eva" also attended the trials of her friends, whom she regarded as heroes, and on a visit to Richmond prison, where Young Irelanders awaited trial, Kelly accepted a marriage proposal from Kevin O'Doherty, a medical student who cofounded the *Irish Tribune*. The engagement was kept a secret for her own protection. Convicted of treason, O'Doherty and other Young Irelanders remained in prison until June 1849, when police secretly transported them to a ship bound for the penal colony on Van Diemen's Land.

After O'Doherty's deportation, Kelly poured her energy into her writing. With a failed rebellion in the fall of 1848 and the disappearance of O'Doherty, Kelly suffered both the loss of an ideal and personal loss. Although her betrothed was granted a conditional pardon and they were married, Kelly endured bouts of depression. The couple's identification with Young Ireland forced their expatriation, so they traveled to Paris, where they lived with other exiles. While in France, Kelly felt keenly the separation from her family and homeland.

Eventually, a full pardon was granted to the convicted Young Irelanders, and the O'Dohertys were able to return to Dublin. In 1856, Kelly gave birth to her first son, William Joseph Kelly, at her mother-in-law's home in Monkstown. Dublin, however, was no longer friendly to the Young Irelanders, with Cardinal Cullen, head of Ireland's Roman Catholic community, denigrating them as conspirators.

Affiliation with Young Ireland had become a liability, and Kevin determined that the family would find a better life in Australia, where they emigrated in 1860. Kelly continued to compose and to translate poetry for a time. She contributed to the Poets' Corner of the Sydney *Freeman's Journal,* but eventually her career was eclipsed by that of her husband, who became a respected physician and politician. Her marital and maternal duties kept her from writing, and as Kelly disappeared from the literary scene, she also disappeared from the public sphere. One record especially reflects her evanescence: a journalist covering a function at Frascati, the O'Doherty home in Brisbane, wrote of the doctor's success and the future of his four sons, but included no mention of Kelly, neither as the poet nor as the woman who bore those sons (Patrick and Patrick, 241).

In 1877, Kelly traveled to San Francisco, leaving a manuscript of collected poems with publisher P.J. Thomas. She was bound for Philadelphia to enroll her eldest son in dentistry school and then on to Ireland where her second son, Edward, was enrolled in medical school. Upon her return through San Francisco, she found her first collection of poems published. Kelly returned again to Ireland in 1885, when O'Doherty was elected to Parliament, where he served briefly as member of Parliament for North Meath. Financial difficulties, however, forced the O'Dohertys to return to Brisbane, where his medical practice fell into bankruptcy.

Apart from exile and financial stress, Kelly faced other tragedies. She had given birth to eight children, but lost two babies in 1862 and 1864 and another in 1866. Within the decade 1890–1900, she lost her four sons and a granddaughter, and, in 1905, O'Doherty died, leaving his wife to depend on her only surviving child, Gertrude, who cared for her until her death, in 1910. In the final years of her life, Kelly was approached by a Father Hickey, who requested that she write a memoir of her affiliation with Young Ireland; although Kelly was unable to complete the memoir, she left a notebook with her plans for the volume. In July 1908, Father Hickey arranged a testimonial to raise money for her support, and, in Australia, another testimonial raised as much as 1,300 pounds (Patrick and Patrick, 264). Meanwhile, in Dublin, M. H. Gill published a second collection of her poetry (1909).

MAJOR WORKS AND THEMES

Early on, Kelly began to explore several themes that developed throughout her career. At the forefront were anticolonial sentiments, but she also maintained a predilection for Irish lore and Irish history. She wrote songs about expatriation during the time of famine emigration and Romantically inspired poems about the Irish landscape. Memory became a dominant poetic device. Her Young Ireland memories coalesce as a stream of consciousness in her later poems, and they appear again, more than fifty years after her career began, in her notebook, which is held today by the John Oxley Library in Brisbane. Although memory denotes personal recollections, Kelly utilized this device to forge a national memory or a collective unconscious for Ireland. She also wrote of Ireland's leaders, past and contemporary, including the legendary seventeenth-century piper Turlough Carolan. Her tributes to Thomas Davis, T. F. Meagher, and John Mitchel won her fame, although her criticism of O'Connell and the Loyal National Repeal Association brought her some infamy.

Her prose pieces called for the spirit of nationalism to rule over democratic governance and demanded an end to fighting among members of Young Ireland and O'Connell's Repeal Association. In a notable essay, "To the Women of Ireland" (1848), Kelly applied Mary Wollstonecraft's argument for responsible citizenship by women and chastised Dublin socialites for their disregard of famine victims. In this essay, Kelly demanded that women take an active role in the Irish cause, sacrificing life "if it be for Ireland's weal," and she shockingly stated that women should participate in the violence of revolution, directing her sisters to cast off the trappings of social propriety and to embrace the bloody work of independence.

CRITICAL RECEPTION

Kelly's earliest praise came from the *Nation*'s editor, Charles Gavan Duffy. Her first submission was esteemed as reflecting the "native character in language and structure." Her boldness, however, in asserting women's equality and in criticizing political leaders frequently received rebukes. Yet even after leaving Ireland for Australia, her international reputation as a poet survived. In 1877, *Poems by "Eva" of the Nation* was published in San Francisco, where the *San Francisco Monitor* had praised her poetic influence (December 12, 1876). The biographical preface to M. H. Gill's release of *Poems. By 'Eva' of 'The Nation,'* written by Justin McCarthy, recalls the affection with which the poet was held by her readers in Ireland and abroad. And in the same volume, Father Hickey, the priest who sought her out for the Dublin publication, added his praise for a "patriot poetess" (xxii).

BIBLIOGRAPHY

Works by Eva Kelly

Poems. By 'Eva' of 'The Nation.' Dublin: M. H. Gill, 1909.
Poems by "Eva" of the Nation. San Francisco: P. J. Thomas, 1877.

Studies of Eva Kelly

"Irish Literary Celebrities 5, Mary Izod O'Doherty." *Nation*, December 8, 1888, 3.
Luddy, Maria. "An Agenda for Women's History in Ireland, 1500–1900, Part II." *Irish Historical Studies* 28, no. 109 (May 1992): 19–37.
McCarthy, Justin. "Eva of the Nation." In *Poems. By 'Eva' of the 'Nation,'* edited by Seamus MacManus, xi–xxi. Dublin: Gill, 1909.
———. "Mrs. Kevin Izod O'Doherty (Eva Mary Kelly)." *Irish Literature*. Vol. 9. Chicago: DeBower-Eliott, 1904, 2675–77.
O'Connor, T. P., ed. "Eva Mary Kelly—Ellen Downing." *The Cabinet of Irish Literature: Selections from the Works of the Chief Poets, Orators, and Prose Writers of Ireland*. Vol. 4. London: Blackie, n.d., 145–48.
Patrick, Ross, and Heather Patrick. *Exiles Undaunted: The Irish Rebels Kevin and Eva O'Doherty*. St. Lucia: University of Queensland Press, 1989.
Thompson, Spurgeon. "Feminist Recovery Work and Women's Poetry in Ireland." *Irish Journal of Feminist Studies* 2, no. 2 (December 1997): 94–105.

RITA KELLY
(1953–   )

Joseph Heininger

BIOGRAPHY

Rita Kelly writes in both English and Irish, and her bilingual gifts as a writer reveal themselves in an English style that shows the enriching influence of the Irish language. She was born in Galway in 1953 and educated at St. Mary's Secondary School at the Convent of Mercy in Ballinasloe, County Galway. Her mother was born on the Castle Ellen estate near Athenry; prominent members of the Wilde family, including Edward and Oscar Wilde, spent holidays there. Rita Kelly began her education in Irish at an early age. She was taught by Thomas Fenton from the Kerry Gaeltacht, who was a cousin of the poets Padraig O Fiannachta and Nuala Ní Dhomhnaill (Rita Kelly, personal communication to Ann Owens Weekes; cited in Weekes, 169).

In 1972, she married the Irish-language poet Eoghan O Tuairisc. Her first book, *Dialann sa Diseart* (1981), consisting of poems in Irish, was written with her husband and records her life with him. Soon after, however, Eoghan O Tuairisc died in Caim, County Wexford, in 1982. Her husband's death proved to be a significant influence on her writing career, as demonstrated by the appearance of another book of poems in Irish, *An Bealach Eadoigh* (1984). Notably, *Fare Well: Beir Beannacht* (1990), a bilingual book of poems in English and Irish, contains several poems addressing O Tuairisc in an elegiac mode and other poems examining the changes in her life since his death.

Her first book of stories in English was *The Whispering Arch and Other Stories* (1986). More recently, she has published *From Here to the Horizon: Laois Anthology* (1999), a project undertaken during her time as writer in residence for County Laois. *Travelling West*, the largest collection of her poetry in English and Irish to date, appeared in 2000. She has also written a play, *Frau Luther* (1984), which was produced in London.

Rita Kelly won the *Irish Times* Merriman Poetry Award in 1975, the Sean O Riordain Memorial Prize for Poetry in 1980, and an Arlen House Maxwell House Prize for the short story. She was the recipient of an Arts Council bursary in 1985, and in the same year coedited *Poetry Ireland Review*. She has also participated in the National Writers' Workshops, has lived in New York City on the Upper West Side of Manhattan, and has taught creative writing in the United States. Her published writings encompass fiction, poetry, drama, and criticism. Her work has been translated into German, Dutch, and Italian and has occasionally been broadcast on radio and television in Ireland. Her poetry and fiction have been widely anthologized in Ireland and Britain. She lives on the River Barrow, between Athy and Carlow.

MAJOR THEMES

Rita Kelly's fiction explores the contours and avenues of traditional Irish life searchingly, with a keen eye for human complexity and the emotional nuances of her characters and their situations. Her stories in *The Whispering Arch* are typical of her themes: "Trousseau" deftly reveals the lives of a young postulant in a convent, Frances; her older friend and an enigmatic presence, Sister Oliver; and the authoritarian and condescending mother superior, Margaret. As Frances, the nun-to-be (the "Bride of Christ," as Sister Oliver drily calls her), is driven to town to choose her trousseau of brassieres and underclothes to wear under her new habit, Kelly uses dialogue and dramatic irony to create a sharply comic and bemused tone as the plot develops from early complications to final revelations. Mother Margaret, finding only an unsuitably casual male shop assistant to help with the delicate business at hand, inevitably makes a scene and makes a fool of herself. Sister Oliver, the coolly detached yet intensely watchful observer of these rites of passage, intervenes to buy for Frances, her mortified friend, who has left the shop to sit in the car by herself, "a soft nightgown, blue, and decidedly feminine" (30). Whether this gift is a clever gesture of sisterly solidarity against the rigidity of the convent's rules or whether it represents a more intimate, personal declaration is left to the reader to interpret. In the final scene, Kelly shows us Oliver's eyes flashing toward Frances in the car's mirror and writes, "Frances was disturbed by their intensity, their chill blue" ("Trousseau," 30).

This story is notable for its understated tone and omniscient point of view. It looks carefully beneath the comic surface of the nuns' shopping expedition to discover the currents of self-assertion and quiet resistance that characterize this group. Its sure touch for dramatic self-revelation and adroit mixture of comedy and moral serious-ness remind the reader of Jane Austen. Once again, Kelly observes the mores and competitions of a delimited social group in "En Famille," also from *The Whispering Arch*. Here the author puts one woman's suburban expectation of conformity to the test and shows the power of her conflicts with her sister and her husband to point the three adults toward the vast unhappiness that seems to await them. The showy and ex-pensive trappings of Barbara and James's house in town cannot hide their mutual lack of interest in their marriage, notwithstanding the imminence of a second child. The observant sister, Catherine, registers these nuances on her awkward visit to their household, one that tries very hard to display all the outward marks of middle-class domestic bliss.

In addition to her work in satiric and ironic modes and in modern versions of Jane Austen's social and moral arenas, Rita Kelly's fiction explores the theme of the unset-tling contacts between a challenging or cruel environment and a hypersensitive main character. A characteristic example is her anthologized story "Soundtracks." A short psychological narrative written in an impressionistic, Woolfian style, "Soundtracks" ex-plores a woman's mind on the verge of a breakdown as the noise of the train wheels, echoing through the station to which she has returned as an adult, presses on her ears. This story is an impressive rendering of a woman's disintegrating state of mind in a crisis. She is someone who has lived on the borders of groups all her life because at one point in her provincial girlhood, "Ruth had been accused of intelligence" ("Sound-tracks," 287).

In "The Intruders," the Irish students in a girls' school make fun of their first Irish-language teacher, an older local man, for his earnestness and social ineptitude. They swoon, however, for the handsome and dramatically gifted stranger from the Gaeltacht, Coilin. The story's denouement, a sensual encounter between Coilin and one of the students in a nearby wood, is well portrayed. The story's ending cleverly sends the reader back to the remote and even childish sense of time of the beginning, as the first sentence of the story now takes on an altered, perhaps ironic significance: "Irish was always somewhat virginal" (69).

Rita Kelly's poetry often touches on themes of brutality and tenderness in the rela-tions between family members as well as the range of emotions between lovers. Her narrative poem "The Patriarch" has been anthologized because of its handling of the theme of the father's brutality, its warping effects on human emotions, and the spread-ing infection it brings to family relations. The poem relates the ironic doubling back that takes place when violence takes possession of the heart and mind of the perpetra-tor of violence, and the ways in which violent acts always taint the doer. Kelly writes that if a person kills or butchers, he or she "must experience the trauma of killing and butchering" (19). A similar exploration of the lingering effects of early family patterns characterizes the later poem "The Glass Case," collected in her most recent volume, *Travelling West*. This poem attempts to humanize the fearsome paternal figure of the earlier poem and shows in its language and tone the effort the speaker makes to measure the lasting qualities passed down to the daughter by the father. It poignantly speaks of self-examination and of forgiveness of self and others in its last lines.

In addition to her poems on the legacies of cruelty and brutality, Kelly writes of the demands of loving and the loss of the beloved. In the title poem of *Fare Well: Beir Beannacht*, she addresses her departed husband, invoking classical parallels, naming the irises on the table as his mythical memorial flowers, and using to great effect the resources and resonances of the elegiac tradition. The poem concludes, however, by refusing to cling to any consolatory gesture, however small, and in so doing faces the utter inconsolability of such a loss. This poem registers the speaker's pain at knowing the finality of death. A later poem in this collection, "Your Voice Still Sounds," expresses a sense of reconciliation, of welcoming the fullness of the world. The speaker, who addresses the departed, offers a gift of self with her sense of growth and renewal. These poems indicate that Rita Kelly is an elegist of considerable powers. She is aware of death's shadow, yet her poetry records the sea's unexpected swelling full and wide with the renewed life force and the giving that marks her memory of the beloved.

CRITICAL RECEPTION

Critical estimates of Rita Kelly's writings have concentrated on her poetry, and most are reviews of her books rather than longer, formal scholarly essays. Brief mentions of her work, however, appear in two essays examining contemporary Irish poetry. Dennis O'Driscoll includes her in a list of "bilingual writers who have published in English and Irish," in the company of Micheal O'Siadhail, Michael Hartnett, Criostoir O Floinn, Eithne Strong, and Pearse Hutchinson (104). Alan Titley mentions her poetry as among the most interesting published in Irish today. He commends the "appropriate wordsmithiness" of her art in a reference to a host of contemporary poets working in Irish since the appearance of the Innti poets of the 1970s at University College Cork (Titley, 93). Medbh McGuckian provides an extensive treatment of the poems included in *Fare Well*.

Although her poetry and prose have attracted the attention of Irish and international reviewers, poets, and writers since 1981, there is a signal need for a longer study of her works in Irish and in English.

BIBLIOGRAPHY

Works by Rita Kelly

Poetry in Irish

An Bealach Eadoigh. Dublin: Coiscéim, 1984.
Dian Diseart. Dublin: Coiscéim, 1981. (With Eoghan O Tuairisc.)

Poetry in Irish and English

Fare Well: Beir Beannacht. Dublin: Attic, 1990.
From Here to the Horizon: Laois Anthology. County Laois: Laois, 1999.
"The Patriarch." In *Wildish Things: An Anthology of New Irish Women's Writing*, edited by Ailbhe Smyth, 19. Dublin: Attic, 1989.
Travelling West. Galway: Arlen House, 2000.

Fiction

"Soundtracks." In *Cutting the Night in Two: Short Stories by Irish Women Writers*, edited by
　　Evelyn Conlon and Hans-Christian Oeser. Dublin: New Island, 2001.
The Whispering Arch and Other Stories. Dublin: Arlen House, 1986.

Drama

Frau Luther. London, 1984.

Studies of Rita Kelly

McGuckian, Medbh. "Full of Consciousness." Review of *Fare Well: Beir Beannacht. Honest Ul-
　　sterman* 93 (1992): 76–78.
O'Driscoll, Dennis. "Comment: A Map of Contemporary Irish Poetry." *Poetry* 167, nos. 1–2 (Oc-
　　tober–November 1995): 94–106.
Titley, Alan. "Innti and Onward: The New Poetry in Irish." In *Irish Poetry Since Kavanagh*.
　　Dublin: Four Courts, 1996, 82–94.
Weekes, Ann Owens. "Rita Kelly." In *Unveiling Treasures: The Attic Guide to the Published
　　Works of Irish Women Literary Writers*. Dublin: Attic, 1993, 169–71.

MARY LAVIN
(1912–1996)

Maryanne Felter

BIOGRAPHY

　　Born in Walpole, Massachusetts, Mary Lavin spent at least the first nine years (dates
vary) of her life in the United States. But her mother, who was unhappy in the States,
returned with Mary to her home in Galway, after which the family moved to Dublin
in 1922. Mary was educated at Loreto Convent School; she did her MA (thesis on Jane
Austen) at University College Dublin (UCD) and began a doctoral program with plans
to do a dissertation on Virginia Woolf. However, writing her first story, "Miss Holland,"
while working on the dissertation gave Lavin the impetus to abandon the doctoral work
and focus on writing more stories and some poetry. She taught French at her old school
until she married lawyer William Walsh in 1942. They bought a farm with Lavin's inheritance, but when Walsh died in 1954, he left Mary with the farm and three small
children. Lavin worked the farm, raised her children, and wrote.

　　Lavin was the recipient of many awards. She won the James Tate Memorial Prize
in 1942; Guggenheim Fellowships in 1959, 1962, and 1972; the Katherine Mansfield-
Menton Prize in 1962; the Ella Lyman Fellowship in 1969; the Gold Medal from Eire

(Boston) in 1974; the Gregory Medal in 1974; the Irish American Foundation Award in 1979; and the Allied Irish Bank Award in 1981. In 1968, she received an honorary doctorate in literature from UCD, and in 1969, she married Michael MacDonald Scott. From 1964 to 1965 Lavin was president of Irish PEN (Poets, Playwrights, Essayists, Editors, and Novelists), and from 1971 until 1973 she served as president of the Irish Academy of Letters. She published her last story, "A Family Likeness," in *Irish University Review* in 1979. She died at the age of eighty in 1996.

MAJOR WORKS AND THEMES

Mary Lavin's opus consists of twenty books, including short stories and novellas, two children's books, and two novels, *The House on Clewe Street* (1945) and *Mary O'Grady* (1950). She herself said that she thought her novels were not her best work, but she is acknowledged by many twentieth-century critics to be a master of the short story. Stylistically, her stories are tightly constructed and deftly developed. Known for the power of their openings, the stories often have ambiguous or open-ended conclusions or ironic twists of plot. Critics have noted Lavin's disregard for historical issues so often found in Irish literature and her focus on the personal, the passionate, and the private. Most of her fiction centers around a number of themes: domestic situations, loneliness, widowhood, relationships, and families. Her characters tend to be middle-class; her settings are frequently ambiguous or only sketchily drawn. Her first book of stories, *Tales from Bective Bridge* (1943), which was lauded and promoted by Lord Dunsany, brought her to immediate attention. The stories turn on moments of perception by characters who are isolated and alienated, often even within relationships. The collection focused the themes and styles found in most of the later collections. From the start, Lavin was praised for her empathy for her characters, her ability to delve deeply into the human heart. The early collections showed fine crafting. Some critics say that her "middle work," including the collections *A Single Lady and Other Stories* (1951) and *The Patriot Son and Other Stories* (1956), is not representative of her best work. In these middle stories, intrusive narrators and surprise endings mar the grace and balance of her earlier style. In her later collections, however, *The Great Wave and Other Stories* (1961), *In the Middle of the Fields and Other Stories* (1967), and *Happiness and Other Stories* (1969), the general consensus is that Lavin returns to her earlier "impressionistic story," adding the autobiographical elements of the pain of her own widowhood. These later collections show Lavin at her best. When criticized for her lack of plot, Lavin responded with "Story with a Pattern." Here, the narrator/writer takes on a "poorly educated" self-styled critic who tells her, "Your endings are very bad. They're not endings at all. Your stories just break off in the middle. . . . My advice is to give your stories more shape, to give them more plot; to give them more pattern as it were" (Lavin, "Story with a Pattern" 205–7). In the process of giving the writer advice, the critic tells a plot-filled story, proving that Lavin herself could write such stories, had she so chosen. But Lavin's narrator justifies her own method: "I won't be able to find stories like this to tell. This was only one incident. Life in general isn't rounded off at the edges, out into neat shapes. Life is chaotic; its events are unrelated" (207). Lavin's fiction, in general, then, shows an emphasis on character often with an open-endedness or a lack of emphasis on plot, and a strong autobiographical element. She is sometimes called "old-fashioned," a realist who plays no literary games, sets off no stylistic fireworks, and is, generally, uninterested in formal experimentation. Most appreciated for her precision in handling the short form, her solid characterization, and the depth of her analysis of the human condition, Lavin has come to be considered one of the best short-story writers of the twentieth century.

CRITICAL RECEPTION

Most of the articles and books about Lavin begin by lamenting the fact that she has been so long overlooked in favor of writers who take on political and historical issues of the emerging and developing republic. But Gerardine Meaney, in *The Field Day Anthology*, calls Lavin "canonical" (5: 976) because of her inclusion in the original three-volume Field Day collection. Interest in Lavin seems to have peaked in the 1970s and 1980s, though some work continues to be done on her, especially on her neglected novels. From the start, reviewers compared her with Katherine Mansfield. Later they made sometimes unfavorable comparisons with "the three O's," Frank O'Connor, Liam O'Flaherty, and Sean O'Faolain, noting that Lavin's stories did not follow their focus on "Irishness." Lavin herself said that she found her models in continental fiction as well as in the work of Jane Austen and Virginia Woolf, both of whom she wrote about in graduate school; most of her stories transcend the nationalist agenda as well as the usual concern with either the peasant or the Anglo-Irish aristocracy of the Big House. As early as 1968, Robert Caswell argued for Lavin's place in the Irish canon in spite of her ignoring "the immediate reality of politics." The first full-length studies of Lavin's work were done by Zack Bowen (1975), A. A. Kelly (1978), and Richard Peterson (1978), with *Irish University Review* publishing a special Mary Lavin number in autumn 1979. Kelly's, Peterson's, and Bowen's books give good introductions to Lavin's work, including Bowen's long discussion of the two novels, general biographical information, some attention to the Irish backgrounds of the stories, and discussion of the themes. These early critics see both the stories and the novels as representative of traditional provincial Irish middle-class values, though Bowen does not discount the irony in Lavin's work. In an early work, Richard Peterson demonstrates the influence of Katherine Mansfield on Lavin's short stories. Augustine Martin, in "Prose Fiction, 1880–1945," says that Lavin "has fashioned perhaps the most complete fictional tapestry of middle Ireland about its daily business. Her mastery of organic form . . . enables her to record with unhurried vividness the tensions of family life on the big farm and in the small town, the drama of love and money, the attrition of time in human relationships, the heart as a lonely hunter" (1024). Though her novels have been seen as slow and plodding, the general critical consensus about her stories is that they are "as polished and neat, as perfectly detailed as a Dutch interior" (Brown, 32). Peterson in *Modern Fiction Studies* shows how Lavin learned from Katherine Mansfield's failures that "the distinction between experiencing the truth and being told the truth . . . greatly depends upon narrative control" (2). Richard Burnham studies the stories that were published in the *Dublin* magazine, starting with "Miss Holland" in 1939 and moving through to 1954, showing Seamus O'Sullivan's encouragement of the young writer and arguing that Lavin's association with O'Sullivan and the *Dublin* magazine gave her confidence and honed her skills. Janet Egleson Dunleavy has done textual work on "A Memory" and "Happiness," tracing the gestation and development of those stories through various versions and revisions. Her analyses of Lavin's working methods shed light on the stories as well as on Lavin's craftsmanship; Dunleavy uses her conversations with Lavin herself to discuss the author's methods and ideas. Mark Hawthorne's study of "Happiness" analyzes the narrative point of view and irony in the story and makes a good companion to Dunleavy's study. Catherine Murphy examines the way the "moments" in Lavin's fiction extend characters' and readers' understanding of the dimensions of reality, while Bonnie Kime Scott discusses a number of stories in relation to Lavin's "life of the female mind" (6). Marianne Koenig examines the relationship of the author to her form, showing the "distinction between early and later stories [in a] . . . body of work so consistent as Lavin's" (11). Jeanette Roberts Shumaker uses the Madonna myth to show how Lavin questions the ideology of patriarchy in "A Nun's Mother" (1944 version) and "Sarah." And Patricia Mezsaros argues that Lavin's novella *The Becker Wives* (1946) illustrates that her "vision of the woman as artist is both highly individual and one that finds its perfect embodiment in the short story form" (41). Mary Neary sees *The Becker Wives* as dramatizing the "Irish quest for identity," one that "dances on the edge of the abyss, tasting the terrifying, destructive, creative potential of the void" (7). And although Frank O'Connor commented early on that Lavin's "The Patriot Son" showed that she was wise in choosing not to write any other political stories (229), Regina Mahlke demonstrates that the focus of "The Patriot Son" and "The Face of Hate" "is not on the political events but on the inner conflicts of the protagonists" (4). Finally, in a recent article about *The House of Clewe Street*, Rachael Sealy Lynch reminds us that not only are Lavin's novels neglected but also that *Clewe Street* is a "relatively scathing commentary" (1) in which Lavin's use of irony and point of view works to criticize the conventional social milieu she has often for so long been assumed to support. Sarah Briggs in *Irish Studies Review* sums up Lavin's major contribution: the focus of the stories "is often on the experience of women—stories of small lives untold by other writers" (10).

BIBLIOGRAPHY

Works by Mary Lavin

At Sallygap and Other Stories. Boston: Little, Brown, 1947.
The Becker Wives and Other Stories. London: Joseph, 1946.
Collected Stories. Boston: Houghton Mifflin, 1971.
A Family Likeness and Other Stories. London: Constable, 1985.
The Great Wave and Other Stories. London: Joseph, 1961.
Happiness and Other Stories. London: Constable, 1969.
The House on Clewe Street. Boston: Little, Brown, 1945.
In a Cafe: Selected Stories. 1961. New York: Penguin, 1995.
In the Middle of the Fields and Other Stories. London: Constable, 1967.
The Lavin Collection, 1938–1972. SUNY-Binghamton Library Archives, Binghamton, New York.
Lavin Papers. Special Collections. University College Dublin.
A Likely Story. New York: Macmillan, 1957.
The Long Ago and Other Stories. London: Joseph, 1944.
Mary Lavin Papers 1953–1964. Southern Illinois University, Carbondale, Illinois.
Mary O'Grady. Boston: Little, Brown, 1950.
A Memory and Other Stories. London: Constable, 1972.
The Patriot Son and Other Stories. London: Joseph, 1956.
The Second Best Children in the World. Boston: Houghton Mifflin, 1972.
Selected Stories. New York: Macmillan, 1959.
The Shrine and Other Stories. London: Constable, 1977.
A Single Lady and Other Stories. London: Joseph, 1951.
The Stories of Mary Lavin. Vol. 1. London: Constable, 1964.

The Stories of Mary Lavin. Vol. 2. London: Constable, 1974.
Tales from Bective Bridge. Boston: Little, Brown, 1942.

Studies of Mary Lavin

Arkin, Steven. "Mary Lavin and Chekov: Something Autumnal in the Air." *Studies: An Irish Quarterly Review* 88, no. 351 (Autumn 1999): 278–83.

Arndt, Marie. "Narratives of Exile in Mary Lavin's Short Stories." *International Journal of English Studies* 2, no. 2 (2002): 109–22.

Asbee, Susan. "In Mary Lavin's 'The Becker Wives': Narrative Strategy and Reader Response." *Journal of the Short Story in English* 8 (Spring 1987): 93–101.

Bowen, Zack. *Mary Lavin*. Lewisburg, PA: Bucknell University Press, 1975.

Briggs, Sarah. "Mary Lavin: Questions of Identity." *Irish Studies Review* 15 (Summer 1996): 10–15.

Brown, Catherine Meredith. "Ireland in Many Moods." *Saturday Review of Books*, March 15, 1947, 32.

Burnham, Richard. "Mary Lavin's Short Stories in *The Dublin Magazine*." *Cahiers du Center d'Etudes Irlandaises* 2 (1977): 103–10.

Caswell, Robert W. "Irish Political Reality and Mary Lavin's *Tales from Bective Bridge*." *Eire-Ireland* 3, no. 1 (Spring 1968): 48–60.

———. "Mary Lavin: Breaking a Pathway." *Dublin* 6, no. 2 (1967): 32–44.

Church, Margaret. "Social Consciousness in the Works of Elizabeth Bowen, Iris Murdoch, and Mary Lavin." *College Literature* 7 (1980): 158–63.

Deane, Seamus. "Mary Lavin." In *The Irish Short Story*, edited by Patrick Rafroidi and Terence Brown, 237–48. Gerrards Cross, UK: Smythe, 1979.

Doyle, Paul A. "Mary Lavin: A Checklist." *Papers of the Bibliographic Society of America* 63 (1969): 317–21.

Dunleavy, Janet Egleson. "The Fiction of Mary Lavin: Universal Sensibility in a Particular Milieu." *Irish University Review: A Journal of Irish Studies* 7 (1977): 222–36.

———. "The Making of Mary Lavin's 'Happiness.' " *Irish University Review* 9, no. 2 (Autumn 1979): 225–31.

———. "The Making of Mary Lavin's 'A Memory.' " *Eire-Ireland* 12, no. 3 (Fall 1977): 90–99.

———. "Mary Lavin, Elizabeth Bowen, and the New Generation: The Irish Short Story at Midcentury." In *The Irish Short Story: A Critical History*, edited by James Kilroy, 145–68. Boston: Twayne, 1984.

———. "Men in Mary Lavin's Fiction." *Canadian Journal of Irish Studies* 2, no. 1 (1976): 10–14.

Harmon, Maurice. "From Conversations with Mary Lavin." *Irish University Review* 27, no. 2 (Autumn–Winter 1997): 287–94.

———, ed. Mary Lavin. Special issue, *Irish University Review* 9, no. 2 (Autumn 1979).

Hawthorne, Mark. "Words That Do Not Speak Themselves: Mary Lavin's 'Happiness.' " *Studies in Short Fiction* 31, no. 4 (Fall 1994): 683–88.

Kelly, A. A. *Mary Lavin: The Quiet Rebel*. Dublin: Wolfhound, 1978.

Koenig, Marianne. "Mary Lavin: The Novels and the Stories." *Irish University Review* 9, no. 2 (Autumn 1979): 244–61. Literature Resource Center. Galegroup. Cayuga Community College Library, Auburn, New York. Accessed June 18, 2004. http://www.galenet.galegroup.com.

Kosok, Heinz. "Mary: Lavin: A Bibliography." *Irish University Review* 9, no. 2 (Autumn 1979): 279–312.

Krawschak, Ruth. *Mary Lavin: A Check List*. Berlin: Author, 1979.

Lynch, Rachael Sealy. " 'The Fabulous Female Form': The Deadly Erotics of the Male Gaze in Mary Lavin's *The House of Clewe Street*." *Twentieth Century Literature* 43, no. 3 (Fall 1997): 326–38.

Mahlke, Regina. "Mary Lavin's 'The Patriot Son' and 'The Face of Hate.' " In *Studies in Anglo-Irish Literature*, edited by Heinz Kosok. Bonn: Bouvier, 1982. Literature Resource Center. Galegroup. Cayuga Community College Library, Auburn, New York. Accessed June 18, 2004. http://www.galenet.galegroup.com.

Martin, Augustine. "Afterword." *Mary O'Grady*. Hammondsworth: Penguin, 1986.

———, ed. "Prose Fiction, 1880–1945." In *The Field Day Anthology of Irish Writing*. Vol. 2, edited by Seamus Deane, Andrew Carpenter, and Jonathan Williams, 1021–27. Derry, Ire.: Field Day Publications, 1991.

Meaney, Gerardine. "Identity and Opposition: Women's Writing, 1890–1960." In *The Field Day Anthology of Irish Writing*. Vol. 5, *Women's Writing and Traditions*, edited by Angela Bourke, Mairin Ní Dhonneadha, Siobhán Kilfeather, Maria Luddy, Margaret MacCurtain, Gerardine Meaney, Mary O'Dowd, and Clair Wills, 976–80. Cork: Cork University Press, 2002.

Meszarnos, Patricia. "Woman as Artist: The Fiction of Mary Lavin." *Critique: Studies in Contemporary Fiction* 24, no. 1 (Fall 1982): 39–54.

Murphy, Catherine A. "The Ironic Vision of Mary Lavin." *Mosaic* 21, no. 3 (1979): 69–79.

———. "Mary Lavin: An Interview." *Irish University Review* 9, no. 2 (Autumn 1979): 207–24.

Murray, Thomas. "Mary Lavin's World: Lovers and Strangers." *Eire-Ireland* 7, no. 2 (Summer 1972): 122–31.

Neary, Mary. "Flora's Answer to the Irish Question: A Study of Mary Lavin's 'The Becker Wives.'" *Twentieth Century Literature* 42, no. 4 (Winter 1996): 516–25. Literature Resource Center. Galegroup. Cayuga Community College Library, Auburn, New York. Accessed June 18, 2004. http://www.galenet.galegroup.com.

O'Connor. Frank. *A Short History of Irish Literature: A Backward Look*. New York: Capricorn, 1968.

Peterson, Richard F. "The Circle of Truth: Stories of Katherine Mansfield and Mary Lavin." *Modern Fiction Studies* 24, no. 3 (1978): 383–94. Literature Resource Center. Galegroup. Cayuga Community College Library, Auburn, New York. Accessed June 18, 2004. http://www.galenet.galegroup.com.

———. *Mary Lavin*. Boston: Twayne, 1978.

Quinn, John, ed. "Mary Lavin." *A Portrait of the Artist as a Young Girl*. London: Methuen, 1987, 79–92.

Scott, Bonnie Kime. "Mary Lavin and the Life of the Mind." *Irish University Review* 9, no. 2 (Autumn 1979): 262–78. Literature Resource Center. Galegroup. Cayuga Community College Library, Auburn, New York. Accessed June 18, 2004. http://www.galenet.galegroup.com.

Shumaker, Jeanette Roberts. "Sacrificial Women in Short Stories by Mary Lavin and Edna O'Brien." *Studies in Short Fiction* 32, no. 2 (Spring 1995): 185–97.

Stevens, L. Robert. "An Interview with Mary Lavin." *Studies: An Irish Quarterly Review* 86, no. 341 (Spring 1997): 43–50.

EMILY LAWLESS
(1845–1913)

Matthew J. Goodman

BIOGRAPHY

Lawless has been read little since her death, and her work has nearly vanished from Irish literary collections. Even while alive, the Anglo-Irish writer never enjoyed the success that she deserved. Emily Lawless, eldest daughter of third Baron Cloncurry Edward Lawless and Elizabeth Kirwan of Castle Hackett, County Galway, was born in Lyons House, County Kildare, in 1845.

Whether at her ancestral home along the Liffey or on the feral coast of her family's summer home in County Clare, Emily Lawless's childhood days were spent outdoors, walking, painting, and swimming. The unsupervised days of youthful frolic provided Lawless with plenty of time for her entomological exploration, those scientific endeavors evolving into the naturalist elements that are embedded in her literary work. In a poem titled "An Entomological Adventure" (1897), Lawless recalls a childhood moment in which she snuck out of the house at night in order to observe a particular species of moth. Lawless's interest in science made her a keen observer of her surroundings, a trait that enriched the poetic landscapes within her work. A Lawless Irish landscape varies as cruelly as the weather, often symbolizing the imminence of one's fate. For her, it was impossible to separate the Irish landscape from its history and politics, specifically the resulting violence. At times the land is nurturing and allows for the prosperity of its inhabitants, but in other instances the landscape is wickedly unforgiving. Contrary to the Irish writers of her time who wrote to romanticize, Lawless's work was written from a naturalist standpoint.

Her writing career began in the early 1880s after she was persuaded by Miss Oliphant, Scottish novelist and friend of Emily's mother. After opting for an English setting in her earliest fiction, her ensuing novels, some of which are historical novels, were set in her native Ireland. Overtly present in her best works, feminist constructs are absent in her earliest novels, whose female characters are conservative. *A Chelsea Household* (1882) and *A Millionaire's Cousin* (1885) are predictable romances, in which the author applies satire to the traditional happy ending where marriage is imminent. Lawless's subsequent novel, *Hurrish* (1886), was criticized in Ireland yet celebrated in England. *Hurrish* marks the point at which Lawless's focus on the Anglo-Irish ascendancy is abandoned in favor of the Irish peasantry in County Clare. The emerging Irish Literary Revival looked upon the sympathy with which she treated English landowners and Irish peasants unfavorably, as it was deemed a travesty to grant any pardon to the English. Although the men and women of *Hurrish* are still quite conventional characters, Lawless's feminist eye opened widely in *Grania: The Story of an Island* (1892) and *Maria Edgeworth* (1904).

Lawless became a founding member of the United Irishwomen in 1910. She also supported the Irish Women's Franchise League (IWFL), Ireland's most prominent suffrage organization. The nationalist sympathies of the IWFL, however, did not suit Lawless's unionist politics. In 1905, five years prior to her role in the formation of the United Irishwomen, she was awarded a DLitt from Trinity College Dublin. Lawless's historical novels received considerable acclaim in England, where she published a number of journal articles regarding Irish history. Like the heroine of her novel *Grania*, Lawless, too, experienced the dour reality of an imposed isolation in her homeland. It was unfashionable to read Lawless's work, considering that Yeats and the Literary Revival popularized nationalist themes. The decline of her literary reputation is thus often attributed to her unionist politics. It did not help Lawless's case that she rejected the optimism of the Revival because she saw no hope for Ireland. For her, acknowledging Ireland's failed community, its rural poverty along with its violent political and religious differences, meant realizing the fateful self-destruction of the nation's people.

Lawless developed an addiction to the heroin she took for pain relief from 1905 until her death from a prolonged illness at her Surrey home in 1913. She spent the waning years of her life with friends in Surrey, occupying her time by tending to her garden. It was during this period that she wrote the majority of her poetry, as unremitting pain prevented her from writing novels.

MAJOR WORKS AND THEMES

For twenty years, following the publication of *A Millionaire's Cousin* (1895), Lawless's writing centered on her native Ireland. During this period she produced a history of Ireland, a collection of tales, and five novels. The absence of hope for Ireland's future is a recurring theme in Lawless's Irish works; as a result, Lawless chose to focus on the country's women and peasantry. Lawless wrote about Irish peasant life a decade before Literary Revival writers celebrated it. Her best fiction portrayed the Irish peasantry more realistically than Yeats had done in his work. *Hurrish*, her first Irish novel, is set during the Land League conflicts of the early 1880s. Lawless differed from the Literary Revival writers in that she was unbiased in her approach to the treatment of the contentious relationships between landowners and peasants. She hoped to promote an understanding of the Irish people for her English readers by revealing Irish feelings for landowners and the law. However, Lawless did not shy away from portraying the grim realities of peasant violence in Ireland.

Hurrish O'Brien, the strong, yet gentle, law-abiding farmer from the Burren in north Clare, does not possess any personal hatred. His mother is wholly different in that she is defined by both a hatred for England and a mistrust for landlords. Mat Brady, a nuisance in the Burren and Hurrish's sworn enemy, is the man that killed his sheep and terrorized his sister-in-law, Ally. Lawless reinforces Hurrish's passive nature as she explains that he would never intentionally harm Brady, although he acknowledges that the neighborhood would be better off if Mat Brady ceased to exist. Brady's hatred toward Hurrish culminates in his own demise after he shoots an errant bullet past Hurrish's head. Hurrish, in the grips of instinctive rage, kills Mat Brady with a single blow of his blackthorn. Lawless attempts to soften the violence by insisting that Hurrish would have given away everything he possessed in order to bring his rival back to life.

Major Pierce O'Brien, the landlord and magistrate representing the ascendancy, is scorned by his tenants throughout the novel because of what he stands for, despite

O'Brien's more than fair treatment of his tenants, which cannot alleviate their contempt. Major O'Brien, being fond of Hurrish and certain of his innocence, refuses to have Hurrish arrested. With this act of defiance, O'Brien immediately gains favor among the people. Although they are certain of his guilt, the people of the Burren wish to see their Irish brother escape justice, as doing so would be a small victory in their greater struggle.

While the women in *Hurrish* are relatively insignificant, Ally's refusal to marry Maurice Brady, Mat's brother and her aspiring suitor, causes Maurice to rant wildly on how her life would be insignificant if she chose not to marry. Through this scene Lawless introduces the theme of the woman's place as property in Irish society. Lawless's woman regains her voice through the heroine in *Grania: The Story of an Island*, yet even she is subjected to a speech regarding male dutifulness and female ingratitude. In *Grania* Lawless appears to be, for the first time, willing to address fully the isolation of the Irish woman and the country's peasantry. *Maria Edgeworth* is Lawless's other important feminist work.

Grania: The Story of an Island takes place on Inishmaan, a rocky oasis within the Aran Islands. Lawless's work was historically significant in that her visit to the Aran Islands preceded J. M. Synge's first visit by at least five years. Written in two volumes, the novel chiefly addresses the isolation of the Inishmaan people through the story of its heroine. Just as the title suggests, the island and the novel's female protagonist, Grania, exhibit comparable characteristics. The temperament of an aged Grania, in the novel's second volume, reflects the jagged rocks and dark crevices of Inishmaan. The novel begins with twelve-year-old Grania accompanying her alcoholic father, Con O'Malley, on a fishing expedition. Readers are able to view the Inishmaan landscape through Grania's youthful eyes. Lawless's heroine is ignorant about the landscape's history, choosing to observe what is most significant to her. She becomes aware of her father's drinking, acknowledges her disdain for the Shan Daly family, and recognizes her attraction to Murdough Blake, while coming to see Honor, her pious half sister, as a mother figure.

In the novel's second volume, an aging Grania's views on her tiny island are deliberate and less promising than those of her childhood. She readily acknowledges the isolation of her people and the meager position in which the island places them. With her father and mother now dead, Grania undertakes the household chores in their entirety, while caring for the ailing Honor. Lawless's heroine is allied with a physical strength that allows her to climb from the shoreline to the house with loads of kelp, exhausting work with which Murdough Blake, now her boyfriend, does not bother to offer to help. As part of the richest family on Inishmaan, Grania keeps close watch on the household turf supply because it is vulnerable to theft during the night. The island's susceptibility to nature's elements leaves the inhabitants of Inishmaan as vulnerable as the O'Malley turf supply.

That both Grania and her mother are considered foreigners in Inishmaan is never more evident than when Murdough and Grania travel to the market fairs in Galway. Murdough breaks a promise to Grania by leaving her alone among a people who are quick to mock her rustic appearance. As a result of his abrupt absence, Grania knowingly sells her goods for far less than their actual worth in order to flee from the bustling reality of an advanced Ireland, which frightens her. When retreating to the boats to wait for Murdough and the rest of their fellow travelers, Grania seeks refuge from a torrential downpour and encounters a local woman. The woman, as Grania notes, appears years older than her age would suggest. Grania does not allow the woman to haul the heavy pail of water from the shore to her house, and, taking it from her, Grania carries the load toward their dilapidated destination. The woman says nothing at all after Grania grabs the pail or after they are inside the house, where Grania sees a man lying drunk in the corner, muttering only insults and curses to his submissive, almost zombielike wife and to the small child he abruptly strikes. Lawless's heroine experiences an epiphany in which she acknowledges a significance in her being there, only to realize later that this was perhaps also a foreshadowing of things to come if she and Murdough were to marry.

Pained by her sympathy for the children and the woman in the house, she hastily heads to the shore in order to wait for Murdough and the others. Murdough arrives hours later and drunkenly stammers through an array of excuses. Murdough's incompetence and unreliability further propel Grania's self-sufficiency. She, like Honor, remains unmarried and unwilling to marry. Honor once explains to Grania that a woman's best option is to become a nun because married women are forced to endure the drinking and fighting that is so common among men, of which Murdough Blake and their father, Con, were precise examples. Grania's experience in the unpleasant household on the mainland has proved that things were no better for women outside of the island; however, Grania is unwavering in her opposition to Honor's piety, finding that escape to a convent is hardly an escape at all. By allowing her protagonist to discover similar instances of female oppression on the mainland, Lawless exposes the vulnerability and lack of freedom of women in late-nineteenth-century Ireland.

Marriage, as presented throughout *Grania*, is anything but advantageous for women. Honor tells Grania about the arranged marriage of Mary O'Reilly, how her father had discussed the price of his daughter's hand with the despicable suitor. Mary's willingness to commit suicide gravely reveals women's severely limited choices. The eldest women of the island discuss the unlikely marriage of Con O'Malley and Grania's mother, Delia Joyce, a woman who had no fortune and nothing of substance to offer Con O'Malley. Delia Joyce was physically attractive, noted to be wholly different from other women on Inishmaan, a foreigner. Unlike her mother, however, Grania's work ethic and wealth make her an attractive option for single men; for example, Murdough Blake often asks Grania for the money necessary to pay his debts. On one particular occasion late in the novel, Grania's refusal to give money and subsequent refusal to marry him send Blake into an angry tirade reminiscent of Maurice Brady's in *Hurrish*. Blake's intentions to marry Grania do not derive from an undying love; rather, he seeks financial stability. Lawless again makes the suggestion that women are property, a concept that allows for Grania's further isolation. Grania provides Murdough Blake with a final chance to prove that his intentions to marry are not fueled by monetary desires when she asks him to accompany her to Aranmore to fetch a priest in order for the dying Honor to be administered her last rites. After Murdough insists that an enveloping fog makes such a trip impossible, Grania leaves without him, drowning in the process. The strength and determination of Lawless's protagonist is copiously evident in her willingness to venture into the fog-laden sea in an attempt to take care of her sister's urgent spiritual needs.

CRITICAL RECEPTION

Relatively little has been written on Emily Lawless, although interest in her work has increased somewhat in recent decades. It is remarkable that a full-blown feminist study of her works has yet to appear. Her politics made her unfavorable among the majority in Ireland during her literary career. Lawless's *The Story of Ireland* was revised from a nationalist standpoint during the 1920s. Yeats, who included her historical novels *With Essex in Ireland* (1890) and *Maelcho* (1894) in his listing of the "Best Irish Books," criticized Lawless for being "in imperfect sympathy with the Celtic nature" (quoted in Brewer, 121). Her literary talent was never taken seriously among her Irish peers, as she was considered by the likes of Yeats and Synge to be a mere historian, and the public knew her best as a writer of historical fiction with Irish settings. British prime minister William Gladstone, in preparations for his arguments in favor of Irish Home Rule, favorably regarded Lawless's *Hurrish* as a "living reality" of the Irish people's estrangement from the law (quoted in Cahalan, 28).

In 1922, Ernest Boyd agreed with Yeats's views about the insignificance of Lawless's literary works, claiming that Lawless's prose was inferior and not worth the reader's time. The views of recent readers, however, are positive. James M. Cahalan has demonstrated that Lawless is "a pioneer among Irish women writers" and that "the work of . . . writers such as Kate O'Brien and Jennifer Johnston would be unimaginable if Lawless had not come before" (27). Cahalan's essay outlines "the cultural and critical difficulties that Lawless faced," surveys the role of gender in several of her works, and concludes by placing Lawless "in Irish literary tradition" (27). Essays by Betty Webb Brewer, Elizabeth Grubgeld, and Lisa Mills also praise Lawless's writing. Brewer's is a good survey of Lawless's career and shows that Lawless made a valuable contribution to Irish literary nationalism, while Grubgeld's and Mills's essays are more pointedly specific explorations of Lawless's works. Certainly, appreciation for Lawless's work, specifically its study from a feminist perspective, is long overdue. She should be looked on as a pioneering writer, historian, poet, and naturalist, one courageous enough to reveal a truthfully pessimistic portrait of Ireland, as opposed to the romanticized views of the popular writers of her time.

BIBLIOGRAPHY

Works by Emily Lawless

The Book of Gilly, Four Months out of a Life. London: Smith and Elder, 1906.
A Chelsea Householder. 3 vols. London: Low, 1882.
A Garden Diary—September 1899–September 1900. London: Methuen, 1901.
Grania: The Story of an Island. 1892. New York: Garland, 1979.
Hurrish: A Study. 2 vols. 1886. Edinburgh: Blackwood; Belfast: Appletree, 1992.
Maelcho: A Sixteenth-Century Narrative. 2 vols. London: Smith and Elder, 1894.
Major Lawrence, FLS. 3 vols. London: John Murray, 1887.
Maria Edgeworth. London: Macmillan, 1904.
A Millionaire's Cousin. London: Macmillan, 1885.
Plain Frances Mowbray, and Other Tales. London: John Murray, 1889.
The Story of Ireland. With some additions by Mrs. Arthur Bronson. London: Unwin, 1887.
Traits and Confidence. 1897. London: Methuen; New York: Garland, 1979.
With Essex in Ireland. Introduced by Stopford A. Brooke. London: Isbister, 1890.
With the Wild Geese. Introduced by Stopford A. Brooke. London: Isbister, 1902.

Studies of Emily Lawless

Boyd, Ernest. *Ireland's Literary Renaissance*. New York: Barnes and Noble, 1922.
Brewer, Betty Webb. " 'She Was a Part of It': Emily Lawless (1845–1913)." *Eire-Ireland* 18, no. 4 (Winter 1983): 119–31.

Cahalan, James M. "Forging a Tradition: Emily Lawless and the Irish Literary Canon." *Colby Quarterly* 27, no. 1 (March 1991): 27–39.

Grubgeld, Elizabeth. "Emily Lawless's *Grania: The Story of an Island.*" *Eire-Ireland* 22, no. 3 (Fall 1987): 115–29.

———. "The Poems of Emily Lawless and the Life of the West." *Turn-of-the-Century Women* 3, no. 2 (1986): 35–41.

Meaney, Gerardine. "Decadence, Degeneration and Revolting Aesthetics: The Fiction of Emily Lawless and Katherine Cecil Thurston." *Colby Quarterly* 36, no. 2 (June 2000): 157–76.

Mills, Lisa. "Forging History: Emily Lawless's *With Essex in Ireland.*" *Colby Quarterly* 36, no. 2 (June 2000): 132–45.

Sichel, Edith. "Emily Lawless." In *Nineteenth Century.* Vols. 19–20 (July 1914).

JOAN LINGARD
(1932–)

Joseph Heininger

BIOGRAPHY

Joan Lingard was born in Edinburgh, Scotland, and spent the formative years of her childhood living in Belfast, the setting for many of her novels for children and adults. Between the ages of two and eighteen she lived in East Belfast in a Protestant neighborhood, but then returned to Edinburgh, where she now resides. Although her family lived in a Protestant neighborhood, her upbringing was Christian Scientist, which left her feeling "an outsider" because she "became very much aware that all these denominations [Presbyterian, Church of Ireland, or Methodist] mattered greatly. . . . Each denomination seemed to me to feel a superiority over the other one" (Quinn, *Portrait,* 95). Her mother, with whom she was very close, developed cancer and died when Lingard was sixteen. After leaving school in Belfast with her senior certificate, she took a general certificate of education in 1954 at Moray House Training College in Edinburgh. In her early career, she worked as a schoolteacher in Belfast and in Scotland. Since 1963, she has published over forty books, among them many stories and novels for younger children and adolescents, and several novels for adult readers. She is also the author of a BBC television series, *Maggie,* adapted from her Maggie series of books set in Glasgow, and other scripts for BBC Scotland.

Lingard began to write at eleven years old, at her mother's urging, when she complained that she could not find enough to read: "From then on I wanted to be a writer, a novelist, and create stories of my own. It has always seemed to me that life is limited—we inhabit one body and see the world through our own eyes—but by writing, and reading, we can live in different worlds, get inside the skins and minds of other people, and, in this way, push out the boundaries of our lives" ("Joan Lingard," Penguin Web site). Her honors and awards include a Scottish Arts Council bursary and the German Buxtehuder Bulle Prize for Children's Literature in 1986. In 1998, she was awarded a Member British Empire (MBE) for services to children's literature. She is married and has three grown children and a grandson.

MAJOR WORKS AND THEMES

Joan Lingard writes about her characters' cultural and political inheritances, and the ways in which they "are shaped by the environment they have been born into or are growing up in, and also by the genes they inherit" ("Joan Lingard," Penguin Web site). Her preoccupation with boundaries, with her characters' attempts at crossing borders, and with the profound effects of prejudice, hatred, and displacement on human relations has continued throughout her career. It has found expression in novels dealing with universally recognizable adolescent experiences as well as the trials of war and the hatreds and misunderstandings spawned by sectarian attitudes. For example, she has shown the narrow presuppositions of an insular group of schoolgirls as they spy on their German teacher in 1944 Belfast in *The File on Fraulein Berg* (1980). In a radio interview with John Quinn, Lingard said, "We thought she was a German spy and we followed her all over Belfast noting her movements in a notebook. One morning she came into our class and said, 'Isn't it wonderful? Paris has been liberated!' We suddenly realised that she was on our side. Not long afterwards she left the school and we heard that she had gone to Palestine. We learned then that she was Jewish. We hadn't realised that and we had been horrible to her" (104).

In *The Twelfth Day of July* (1970), the first book in the Kevin and Sadie series of novels set in Belfast and London, her most popular and critically praised books for young people, Lingard explores the prejudice ingrained in children by traditional Catholic-Protestant cultural divisions in Northern Ireland and the escalation of tensions between these two groups as the day approaches for the Orange Lodges to commemorate "King Billy" at the Battle of the Boyne. The second book, *Across the Barricades* (1972), has become a modern classic and is frequently taught in secondary schools throughout the United Kingdom. It explores the pain and confusion resulting from violence between Protestant and Catholic factions in Belfast, even as Kevin and Sadie are drawn to one another. The last of the series, *Hostages to Fortune* (1976), finds them married, with a son, and living in England. The story deals with Kevin's job loss, their relocation, and the burden of helping Kevin's youngest sister, Cloddagh, who comes to them emotionally wounded by Northern Ireland's sectarian warfare and whose presence threatens to cause a rift between them.

In her fiction for adults, Joan Lingard explores the problems of identity, motive, and the effects of inheritance and uprooting on her characters. In *After Colette* (1993), a novel concerned with a woman's identification with the French writer Colette, and her family's quest to discover the reasons for her disappearance, Lingard uses an epigraph from Colette's *Jours gris*: "I belong to a country that I have left" (93). In *The Kiss* (2002), her most recent novel for adults, Lingard delves into the emotional lives of characters who find it difficult to control their artistic talents, familial duties, and sexual obsessions. The novel parallels the famous affair between Gwen John and Auguste Rodin with the attraction that a precocious Irish secondary student feels for her art teacher in contemporary Edinburgh. As a novelist, Lingard explores the continuing hold the past has on the present and the fault lines in human behavior, especially the erroneous assumptions people make about others based on their backgrounds, and the human costs of such misreadings.

CRITICAL RECEPTION

Most criticism of Lingard's fiction deals with her novels for young adults, for these books have established her reputation. From the Kevin and Sadie series, *Across the Barricades* (1972) has been singled out for commendation. Readers and critics praise her realism and lack of didacticism when addressing complex issues, whether arising in family life or between people brought up in different worlds. They also admire her subtle and evocative prose style, and her capacity for bringing the depths of a scene or the currents of a relationship to light with a telling selection of details.

In the interview with John Quinn, the author comments on the memories and impressions that inform her work, and the effects of childhood experiences on her imagination. Her fascination with border crossings and exile, and with her characters' attachments to divided homelands, has drawn attention from critics (Cleary, 112–19) who see the novels as excellent contributions to the literature of partition, especially in relation to Northern Ireland. She has also been claimed as a Scottish writer. *After Colette* has been excerpted in *The Picador Book of Contemporary Scottish Fiction*, and her works are read in Scotland's secondary schools.

Joan Lingard's novels reach a popular audience and are esteemed in Ireland and the United Kingdom. Most of her fiction, however, has not received due attention from North American readers.

BIBLIOGRAPHY

Works by Joan Lingard

After Colette. London: Sinclair-Stevenson, 1993.
Dreams of Love and Modest Glory. London: Sinclair-Stevenson, 1995.
Greenyards. New York: Putnam, 1981.
The Headmaster. London: Hodder, 1967.
The Kiss. London: Allison and Busby, 2002.
Liam's Daughter. London: Hodder and Stoughton, 1963.
The Lord on Our Side. London: Hodder, 1970.
The Prevailing Wind. London: Hodder, 1964.
Reasonable Doubts. London: Hamish Hamilton, 1986.
The Second Flowering of Emily Mountjoy. New York: St. Martin's, 1979.
Sisters by Rite. London: Hamish Hamilton, 1984.
A Sort of Freedom. London: Hodder, 1968.
The Tide Comes In. London: Hodder, 1966.
The Women's House. New York: St. Martin's, 1989.

Children's Novels

Kevin and Sadie Quintet

Across the Barricades. London: Hamish Hamilton, 1972.
Into Exile. London: Hamish Hamilton, 1973.
Hostages to Fortune. London: Hamish Hamilton, 1976.
A Proper Place. London: Hamish Hamilton, 1975.
The Twelfth Day of July. London: Hamish Hamilton, 1970.

Maggie Quartet

The Clearance. London: Hamish Hamilton, 1973.
The Pilgrimage. London: Hamish Hamilton, 1976.

The Resettling. London: Hamish Hamilton, 1975.
The Reunion. London: Hamish Hamilton, 1977.

   Eastern Europe Quartet

Between Two Worlds. London: Hamish Hamilton, 1991.
Natasha's Will. London: Hamish Hamilton, 2000.
Night Fires. London: Hamish Hamilton, 1993.
Tug of War. London: Hamish Hamilton, 1989.

   Other Children's Novels

Dark Shadows. London: Hamish Hamilton, 1998.
The File on Fraulein Berg. London: Julia McRae, 1980.
Lizzie's Leaving. London: Hamish Hamilton, 1995.
A Secret Place. London: Hamish Hamilton, 1998.

Interview with Joan Lingard

Quinn, John. Interview with Joan Lingard. *A Portrait of the Artist as a Young Girl*, edited by
    John Quinn, 93–109. Foreword by Seamus Heaney. London: Methuen, 1986, in associ-
    ation with Radio Telefís Éireann.

Studies of Joan Lingard

Anderson, Celia. "Born to the 'Troubles': The Northern Ireland Conflict in the Books of Joan
    Lingard and Catherine Sefton." *The Lion and the Unicorn* 21, no. 3 (Fall 1997): 387–
    401.
Cleary, Joe. *Literature, Partition, and the Nation-State: Culture and Conflict in Ireland, Israel
    and Palestine*. Cambridge: Cambridge University Press, 2002.
"Joan Lingard." Penguin, United Kingdom. http://www.penguin.co.uk/nf/Author/Author Page.
Taylor, Anne. *Joan Lingard: From Belfast to the Baltic*. Linden, UK: School Library Associa-
    tion, 1992.

DEIRDRE MADDEN
(1960–   )

Shawn O'Hare

BIOGRAPHY

Deirdre Madden was born in Belfast, Northern Ireland, on August 20, 1960, and
grew up in Toomebridge, County Antrim. In 1983 she graduated with honors from Trinity College Dublin with a BA and in 1985 completed an MA (with distinction) from
the University of East Anglia. She has published six novels and has won a number of
awards, including the Hennessy Award in 1980, the Rooney Prize for Irish Literature

in 1987, the Somerset Maugham Award in 1989, and the Listowel Kerry Ingredients Book Award in 1997, and was shortlisted for the Orange Prize for Fiction for women. In 1994 she was a writer in residence at University College Cork; she was a writing fellow at Trinity College Dublin in 1996–1997. Madden is a member of Aosdána, is married to the Irish poet Harry Clifton, and lives in Ireland and France.

MAJOR WORKS AND THEMES

Hidden Symptoms (1986), Madden's debut novel, is a story about the Troubles of Belfast and the devastating effect the violence has on Theresa Cassidy, a college student at Queen's University. Theresa is a Roman Catholic, and her twin brother, Francis, is killed by a group of Protestant extremists. His murder, understandably, shocks Theresa and forces her to reevaluate her life and her religion. Specifically, Theresa has a difficult time "turning the other cheek" and loving her enemies, who have killed him. In fact, those issues of trust and forgiveness affect not only Theresa's thoughts about her religion, but also the way she interacts with other people. Theresa's friend Kathy also faces a similar crisis of identity—she travels to London to meet the father who left her when she was a young child—though she eventually develops a better understanding of who she is and what she wants from life. Still, in Madden's claustrophobic Belfast, simple answers and realizations of identity are rare. Madden's reputation as a stylist—the smooth flow of her prose and her ability to evoke emotion through detailed images—is initiated in this work.

In *The Birds of the Innocent Wood* (1988), Madden continues to explore loss and isolation. Madden tells the stories of three women, a mother and her two daughters, and all three tales are rather dark and depressing. Jane, the mother, grew up an orphan and had a loveless marriage to James, which contributed to an unhappy life. Her daughters, Catherine and Sara, are forced to deal not only with the difficulties of their lives, but also with their mother's past as well, and the impact that had on their growing up. In many ways the novel is a study of the social pressure that women face in Ireland, and the hopelessness that the characters often face is a reminder of how male-dominated Ireland can be. Interestingly, Madden also avoids specifics in the novel, and never gives place names or dates. Such an approach does not deny the "Irishness" of the story, which clearly is set in Ireland, but instead suggests a universal quality that anticipates her future works.

Madden's third novel, *Remembering Light and Stone* (1992), takes place in Italy and is the story of Aisling, a young Irish immigrant. Aisling has lived in a small Italian village for five years, which is indicative of her personality: strong, individualistic, and stubborn. She is also very much in self-exile, a theme that is frequent in twentieth-century Irish writing. In fact, while she is able to note and express admiration for the beautiful Italian countryside, she cannot do the same for her native country. The implication is that Aisling is so lost and confused in her own world—a complex relationship with an American boyfriend, Ted, and the suicide of a cancer-stricken friend play a major role in this—that she finds it difficult to know who she is. This theme is also illustrated in Marina, Ted's ex-girlfriend, who spent her childhood constantly moving from place to place with her businessman father and thus lacks a clear identity. For Aisling, however, this way of thinking changes when she returns to Ireland and is able to understand herself better. Since the novel is told in the first person, Aisling's selfdiscoverings are all the more poignant and effective and make *Remembering Light and Stone* a powerful work.

In *Nothing Is Black* (1994), Madden brings the setting back to Ireland, and this time it is Donegal. The novel tells the story of three women: Nuala is in her thirties, is a new mother, owns a restaurant, and is a kleptomaniac; her cousin Claire, also in her thirties, is an artist; and Anna is a Dutch woman visiting Ireland during the summer who has a strained relationship with her grown-up daughter (when her ex-husband died, her daughter asked her not to come to his funeral). As in many of Madden's novels, the characters are searching for answers in their lives, and in *Nothing Is Black*, the women eventually do find some closure as Nuala reconnects with her family in Dublin, Claire dedicates herself more fully to her art, and Anna realizes that her daughter's problems are more about fear than malice. The novel's setting, rural and ruggedly beautiful County Donegal, plays an important role. Nuala felt that she should form a relationship with the native land of her mother, but, as with her mother, the mountains and fields of Donegal offered little to her. This fact was an important discovery for her. Claire is just as rootless, and although she grew up in Donegal, it means no more or less to her than other parts of Europe where she has lived. Anna, on the other hand, has made Donegal her safety zone; it is far from her troubles in the Netherlands, and it does not carry emotional baggage as it does for the other two women. In a sense, Anna is more at home in rural northwest Ireland, where she lives during the spring and summer, than the two Irishwomen. The novel's subtext, then, is that as Ireland becomes Europeanized, and as national borders become more and more invisible, many people may be left searching for, literally, their place in the world. *Nothing Is Black* is, on some levels, a novel that can be read and discussed in a postcolonial theoretical way, and it underscores Madden's development as an important voice of her generation.

In *One by One in the Darkness* (1996), Madden returns to a Northern Ireland setting, and, as in the earlier *Hidden Symptoms*, the Troubles of the North play an important role. In fact, the novel's three main characters—Helen, Cate, and Sally—lost their father to sectarian violence when he was murdered in the home of a fellow Sinn Fein member. Set in 1994, before the Irish Republican Army's ceasefire, the novel traces the paths taken by the three sisters. Cate has left County Antrim to take a job in London, where she works as a magazine editor. She leads a comfortable middle-class life—even changing the spelling of her name because "Kate" is too Irish—though she is pregnant and unmarried. Helen is a graduate of the law school at Queen's University Belfast and in the beginning of the novel is defending a man who shot a taxi driver because of religious reasons. Sally, the youngest, is a schoolteacher in a small town in County Antrim. While Helen and Sally are adjusting their lives to fit the changing North, Cate is able to return as an outsider—visiting for a week, which is the bulk of the novel—since living in London makes everything in Country Antrim seem new to her. In fact, her family cannot fully understand why she takes so much pleasure in driving through the countryside and spending time in decidedly Protestant villages. In many respects, *One by One in the Darkness* is Madden's most optimistic novel about the North, as its characters adapt to their changing country.

Madden's most recent novel, *Authenticity* (2000), moves away from the problems of the North and uses contemporary life in Dublin as a setting. In this story, William Armstrong, a successful and wealthy middle-aged lawyer who lives in Dalkey, meets Julia Fitzpatrick, a young aspiring artist, as he sits on a bench in St. Stephen's Green and she asks him to light her cigarette. She learns that William is contemplating suicide and follows him home to make sure he arrives unhurt. Eventually they become friends, though they have disparate experiences and economic situations. William, in fact, desires to be an artist and admires the life that Julia has. Julia's boyfriend, Roderic Kennedy, twenty years her senior and a well-established painter, warns her that a friendship with William, whom he sees as self-destructive, could negatively affect her. Roderic knows through experience how a complicated personal life can affect a person, and much of the novel traces his tense relationship with his bourgeois family, who do not understand his commitment to his art, the collapse of his marriage to an Italian woman, and his attempt to repair his relationship with their daughters. In the end, Roderic's advice turns out to be accurate as the friendship between Julia and William disintegrates.

CRITICAL RECEPTION

Madden's work has been well received by the critics, and, like Jennifer Johnston, she is noted for the clarity, subtlety, and precision of her writing style. Michael McLoughlin has argued that "Deirdre Madden must be one of the least hyped Irish writers, but she is one of those whose work deserves the most fanfare." Jerry White, author of "Europe, Ireland, and Deirdre Madden," notes that Madden's novels, "although wide-ranging in their subject matter, all engage with the ambiguities and difficulties faced by Ireland in the postcolonial era" (460). Unfortunately, most of Madden's novels have not been published in the United States, an injustice, as she is one of the most accomplished of contemporary Irish novelists. With the appearance of each novel, Madden's storytelling gets stronger. Though her early novels are fine works, they are narrow in scope and specific in place. A work such as *Authenticity*, however, represents an approach that moves beyond nationalities and national boundaries. It is to be hoped that U.S. publishers will soon realize that.

BIBLIOGRAPHY

Works by Deirdre Madden

Authenticity. London: Faber and Faber, 2002.
The Birds of the Innocent Wood. London: Faber and Faber, 1988.
Hidden Symptoms. London: Faber and Faber, 1986; New York: Atlantic Monthly Press, 1987.
Nothing Is Black. London: Faber and Faber, 1994.
One by One in the Darkness. London: Faber and Faber, 1996.
Remembering Light and Stone. London: Faber and Faber, 1992.

Studies of Deirdre Madden

De la Iglesia, Tamara Benito. "Born into the Troubles: Deirdre Madden's *Hidden Symptoms*." *International Journal of English Studies* 2, no. 2 (2000): 39–48.
McLoughlin, Michael. Review of *Authenticity*, by Deirdre Madden. *Sunday Business Post*, December 22, 2002. http://archives.tcm.ie/businesspost/2002/12/22/story333359.asp (accessed February 20, 2004).
Parker, Michael. "Shadows on a Glass: Self-Reflexivity in the Fiction of Deirdre Madden." *Irish University Review* 30, no. 1 (Spring–Summer 2000): 82–102.
White, Jerry. "Europe, Ireland, and Deirdre Madden." *World Literature Today* 73, no. 3 (Summer 1999): 451–60.

JOY MARTIN
(1937–   )

Susan Bazargan

BIOGRAPHY

Joy Martin (née Green) was born in Limerick and educated at Laurel Hill, a French convent, which appears in her first novel as well as in Kate O'Brien's fiction. Martin's mother was an Irish Catholic, her father an English Protestant, and the family lived "in a cottage on [her] grandfather's land" (Joy Martin, e-mail interview with the author, January 12–14, 2004). Martin's great-grandfather was John George O'Brien Kelly, Ireland's assistant land commissioner, who, from the end of the nineteenth century until the first decade of the twentieth, was responsible for transferring rented land from the powerful landlords to their long-abused tenants. O'Brien Kelly's three Georgian houses in County Limerick belonged to Martin's great-uncles and cousins. As a child, she had access to the great houses even though she was a rather poor relation (Martin, e-mail interview). Thus, from early on, she was tutored in the hierarchies of class in Ireland, a theme that would emerge in her fiction.

Despite her intellectual interests, Martin could not attend university because of financial constraints. Instead, she began working as a reporter for a local newspaper, then as a journalist in Dublin for the *Evening Press*. After her marriage, Martin spent fourteen years in Zambia and South Africa, where she was assistant editor of *Femina* and wrote for the *Times of Zambia*, Zambia Radio and TV, and the *Rand Daily Mail*, in Johannesburg. Returning to London, she worked as a scriptwriter for the BBC. Martin has been married twice and has two sons; she has been married to John Martin for twenty-five years. Her primary home is in Whitegate on Lough Derg in County Clare, but she also lives in London and Cape Town, South Africa (Martin, e-mail interview).

MAJOR WORKS AND THEMES

Martin's first publications were two works of nonfiction, which she published under her first married name, Joy Kuhn: *Twelve Shades of Black* (1976) and *Myth and Magic* (1978). The first book is a groundbreaking study in its attempt to make visible a segment of the black population usually effaced in South Africa. Twelve blacks (six men, six women) living in townships outside Johannesburg speak of their struggles and ambitions in a series of photo essays. Among them are a priest, a poet, an artist, and a detective sergeant. The interviews allow each person to voice his or her own story. Wally Serote, the poet, for example, speaks of his fear to "go into the white town" (33) and recalls being detained under the Terrorism Act of 1969. *Myth and Magic* tells the stories of several Shona stone sculptors living in Zimbabwe; photographs of their stunning carvings accompany the narratives. In Martin's final prose work, *The Elephant*

Man: The Book of the Film (1980), the interaction of word and image further illuminates the struggles of people living beyond the pale. Her study takes us behind the
scenes of the film's production and also contains details of John Merrick's life and his
disease.

As a novelist, Martin is primarily known for her historical fiction, which is based
not only on actual events in the history of Ireland but also beyond. Major historical up-
heavals and their impact on the lives of individuals constitute the main subject of her
fiction. Dominant themes include dispossession and the obsessive drive to right the
wrongs of the past. Romantic entanglements carry the plots of the stories, but Martin's
main interest is in the historical details and circumstances. She has conducted meticulous research, both archival and on location, to construct the backdrop of her stories'
developments. Ireland, in particular County Clare, is the exclusive setting of her first
novel, *A Wrong to Sweeten* (1986), which spans the years 1881–1893. Drawing on her
own family history, Martin tells the story of the O'Briens (descendents of Brian Boru,
last high king of Ireland) and their grand estate, Crag Liath, which is based on Clon-
macken, one of the houses owned by Martin's grandfather. In her Big House novel,
Martin takes us on a grand tour of East Clare, where she points out interesting land-
marks, such as Knockfierna, while introducing us to Irish lore and local myths. Family rivalries and jealousies but also deeper divisions in religious and political affiliations
are developed against a historical panorama that includes scenes of evictions and events
such as the Phoenix Park murders, the Land League activities, and Charles Stewart Parnell's fall from grace.

A Wrong to Sweeten serves as a prequel to Martin's fourth novel, *A Heritage of
Wrong* (1991). Although a "right" ending closes the family saga in 1917, the second-
generation members must first deal with more rivalries, passion, and deception as Crag
Liath once more becomes an object of desire. Whitegate and its environs are major settings, but metropolitan areas also feature in the novel as the characters' lives become
entangled in the era's major artistic movements, such as the Abbey Theatre, and political developments, such as the Easter Rising and the first World War.

In writing *The Moon Is Red in April* (1989), Martin turned to her grandmother's
family, the Cantillons, to tell the true story of Richard Hennessy (Martin, e-mail interview). In the novel, he appears as Richard O'Shaughnessy, who, evading the Penal
Laws in 1744, flees from Cork to France and fights in the Irish Brigade in the battle
of Fontenoy. He eventually settles in Cognac to become the founder of the Hennessy
Cognac business. In her third novel, Martin draws on the life of Ulick John de Burgh,
the fourteenth Earl of Clanricade, and his clandestine affair with one of his tenants (historically known as "Mrs. X"), which produced an illegitimate child. Ulick's castle Por-
tumna is only miles away from Martin's home in Ireland. "I used to wonder, walking
in that vicinity, how that outcast child must have felt," she remarks (Martin, e-mail interview). Martin brings to life these anonymous figures by giving identities to the
mother (Muraid Dillon) and child (Eva), who are evicted from their cottage. Like many
other characters in Martin's fiction, Eva passionately desires to claim her heritage and
her rightful family name and, in 1889, she travels to imperial Russia. To make Eva's
journey from East Galway to St. Petersburg plausible, Martin drew on the history of
de Burgh's ambassadorship to Russia and on the lives of many Irish and Scot women
who worked as governesses in that country (Martin, e-mail interview).

In creating Eva's story, Martin conducted research in Moscow and St. Petersburg.
Likewise, to trace the story of Laura, a photojournalist in *Image of Laura* (1992), Martin visited Berlin and even found the apartment where the real-life Laura had once

lived. Intergenerational conflicts and the fascination with the discovery of one's true heritage are the themes that once more emerge in this novel, which takes us from the 1930s to contemporary times in London, with tangential forays into Johannesburg, South Africa.

Martin has also published contemporary fiction under the pen name Mary Joyce. She is currently working on *Breaking the Butterfly*, a novel linking her experiences in southern Africa to modern Ireland (Martin, e-mail interview).

CRITICAL RECEPTION

Twelve Shades won a runner-up prize in the South African Literary Awards. Yet, "at the time of the book's publication," Martin writes, "many white people turned up their noses at it and children at school told my sons that 'Your mother writes books about kaffirs!' " (Martin, e-mail interview). After South Africa's independence, the book was greatly in demand as South African whites endeavored to learn more about the lives of black people.

Reviewers have found Martin's historical novels entertaining and intriguing. She has been commended for her meticulous research, which allows her to evoke the atmosphere of the period. Martin has also been praised as a gifted storyteller and journalist whose accurate observations of historical and geographical details render her fiction especially appealing to readers interested in Ireland and Irish history.

BIBLIOGRAPHY

Works by Joy Martin

Novels (Joy Martin)

A Heritage of Wrong. London: Grafton, 1991.
Image of Laura. London: HarperCollins, 1992.
The Moon Is Red in April. London: Weidenfeld and Nicholson, 1989.
Ulick's Daughter. London: Grafton, 1990.
A Wrong to Sweeten. London: Weidenfeld and Nicholson, 1986.

Novels (Mary Joyce)

Harlequin's Daughter. London: Headline, 1999.
The House by the Shore. London: Headline, 1997.

Prose (Joy Kuhn)

The Elephant Man: The Book of the Film. London: Virgin, 1980.
Myth and Magic. The Art of the Shona of Zimbabwe. Cape Town: Nelson, 1978.
Twelve Shades of Black. Photographs by Sylvie van Lerberghe. Cape Town: Nelson, 1976.

Studies of Joy Martin

The Munster Women Writers Project. http://www.evilpeanut.com/munsterwomen/project.htm (accessed December 29, 2003).
Weekes, Ann Owen. *Unveiling Treasures: The Attic Guide to the Published Works of Irish Women Literary Writers*. Dublin: Attic, 1993, 218–20.

MEDBH McGUCKIAN
(1950–   )

Sara E. Stenson

BIOGRAPHY

The third of six children, Medbh McGuckian was born to Hugh and Margaret Mc-Caughan in North Belfast. Her family resided in the Newington District, a small Roman Catholic area fraught with sectarian tension. Her father was a headmaster and part-time farmer in Ballycastle, County Antrim, her mother an influential art and music enthusiast. McGuckian attended Holy Family Primary School and Dominican Convent. She received her BA (1972) and MA (1974) from Queens University Belfast. At Queens, she studied under Seamus Heaney, with whom she built a strong working relationship. There she also met Michael Longley, and contemporaries such as Ciaran Carson, Paul Muldoon, and Frank Ormsby. Her first published poem, "Marriage," appeared in the *Honest Ulsterman* (June 1975). She taught school at the Dominican Convent and St. Patrick's School for Boys in East Belfast. She married John McGuckian, a teacher, in 1977. In 1979, her poem "The Flitting" was submitted under a male pseudonym and won England's prestigious National Poetry Competition. McGuckian has since earned a strong and sustained response from intrigued critics throughout her writing career, which began with the publication of two pamphlets of poetry, *Portrait of Joanna* (1980) and *Single Ladies* (1982).

McGuckian's accolades also include the Rooney Prize and the Alice Hunt Bartlett Award for her first major poetry collection, *The Flower Master* (1982). She was named the first female writer in residence at Queens University Belfast from 1985 to 1988. In 1984 her second collection of poetry, *Venus and the Rain*, was published (revised 1994). She edited an anthology of children's poetry, *The Big Striped Golfing Umbrella* (1985), for the Arts Council of Northern Ireland. *On Ballycastle Beach*, her third volume, was published in 1988. McGuckian was a visiting professor at Berkeley in 1991. In that same year, she won the Bass Ireland award, and her fourth volume, *Marconi's Cottage*, was short-listed for the prestigious *Irish Times*/Aer Lingus Award. *Captain Lavender*, her fifth major collection of poems, dedicated to her father, was released in 1995. She assisted with *The Field Day Anthology of Irish Women's Writing and Traditions* (2002) and worked as writer in residence at the University of Ulster, Coleraine.

She joined Aosdána, the selective Irish artists association, in the late 1990s. In 1997 her *Selected Poems* (edited by Dillon Johnston and Peter Fallon) became a Poetry Book Society recommendation. *Shelmalier*, based on the violent events of the 1798 rebellion, was released in 1998. The collection marks another turn since the 1994 release of *Captain Lavender* in which McGuckian continues to emphasize the political violence of past and present as well as the peace talks concerning the Troubles. The next three years were once again incredibly prolific for McGuckian, who continues to reflect on the situation in the North, starting with the publication of *Drawing Ballerinas*

(2001), which was followed by *The Face of the Earth* (2002). She was awarded the Tolman Cunard Prize for best single poem for "She Is in the Past, She Has This Grace." In 2002, Wake Forest University Press released *The Soldiers of Year II*, which contains selections from *Drawing Ballerinas* and *The Face of the Earth* in order to facilitate wider distribution of her work for her substantial and enthusiastic American readership. And most recently, her collection *Had I a Thousand Lives* (2003) appeared on the centenary of Emmet and Thomas Russell. McGuckian lives with her family in Belfast and Ballycastle, where she continues to write.

MAJOR WORKS AND THEMES

Daring, innovative, powerful, and even revolutionary, Medbh McGuckian is one of the most challenging and accomplished living Irish poets. Her work is unfalteringly original and ceaselessly challenging. McGuckian's poems form a montage of images that have been characteristically viewed as sensual, intricate, and dense, as well as illogical, flowery, and self-absorbed. Furthermore, it seems as if one cannot possibly react to her poetry in a neutral way. Readers are left stunned in awe of her marvels or frustrated from trying to derive meaning from her intricate, and at times apparently impenetrable, tapestries. While it is possible to grope for ways to describe McGuckian's style, the fact remains that her work requires readers to reconsider their own understanding of poetry, language, and the nature of the poetic voice.

McGuckian's 1979 win of England's National Poetry Competition for a poem based on a move from one house to another, "The Flitting," gave her national prominence. This achievement was followed by Anne Stevenson's formidable review of "The Portrait of Joanna," in which she was hailed as a "contemporary Irish Emily Dickinson" (952). Indeed McGuckian has found Dickinson's reinvention of language a revelation and has been influenced by Dickinson's ability to rebuke all that has come before. However, for McGuckian, the revolution does not appear as a stripping or paring down of language structure, but as a radical fragmentation and reformation of language that appears as a careful arrangement of provocative word couplings. The nature of her resistance lies in obliquity, which can dangerously become ambiguity, even obscurity. Quite unlike Dickinson, McGuckian's work has been repeatedly described as nonlinear, associative, and connoting "feminine," which she has not resisted. McGuckian is well aware of her tenuous position; in *Venus and the Rain* she claims that "this oblique trance is [her] natural way of speaking" ("Prie-Dieu," 29). In fact, readers often need a good deal of patience in approaching her challenging syntax and surprising shifts in registers of reference.

McGuckian explains that her impulse to write poetry is "tied up in self-defense, with the mind somehow conquering this awful emotional gut feeling of fear and anger" (Morris, 70). At their best, McGuckian's poems tempt and seduce readers into expecting to find something that swiftly escapes as it undergoes a startling metamorphosis. Through their unpredictable trajectories, McGuckian's poems make manifest the experiences of the emotional world, forcing readers to reconsider what they see. Furthermore, through her consistent invocation of female bodily experiences, familial relations, interiors, and images of reproduction, McGuckian confronts and displaces public and private realms.

The Flower Master, McGuckian's first major collection of poetry, explores and reinvents flower imagery. Using her own language of flowers, McGuckian represents the creation of poetry and human life. The collection's title poem depicts the art of creation as we learn "to stroke gently the necks of daffodils [to] make them throw their heads back to the sun" (41). Throughout the collection, McGuckian's harmonious and signature use of flora, gardens, and houses powerfully forms metaphors for bodily experiences such as childbirth and death. From the outset, images ebb and flow, constantly in flux, evocatively engaging readers in a powerful and ever-changing emotional world. Poet becomes artist in "The Seed Picture" and invokes the trope of a love letter or appears as a response to one. In "The Sun-Trap" the speaker has received a love letter from which she construes "at least the word for kisses" (30). In "The Sofa" the difficulty of writing poetry is masked by the speaker's initial decision not to open a love letter.

In *Venus and the Rain*, McGuckian reexamines feminine codes and symbols invoking female mythology and eroticism. She gives voice to the planet Venus, the moon, and other real and imaginary worlds. McGuckian explores the attraction between a series of binaries such as female/male, ocean/land, sun/moon, that dangerously threaten to fuse into one another. Similarly, in poems, such as "The Sitting," based on artistic ingenuity, a "dream-sister" signifies a split of self in relation to the creative process. Much of the collection centers on wintry, dark-blue, icy realms of night, though the scene appears to foster the beginnings of artistic creation rather than the ends of inspiration. Her poems explore womanhood in terms of birth, pregnancy, raising children, and relationships. "Venus and the Rain" depicts a trying process of creation.

In McGuckian's third major collection, *On Ballycastle Beach*, she continues to rework child and motherhood themes, though with a growing emphasis on mortality. She also engages in reflections about the nature of both linguistic and human creation. In a poem dedicated to Nuala Ní Dhomhnaill entitled "Harem Trousers," a poem gains the agency to desire a certain form: she has a poem dream about being written "without the pronoun 'I'" (40). In these poems she also continues to develop her keen sense of using language to create meaning. McGuckian dedicates the title poem to her father, poignantly anticipating loss.

McGuckian explores Irish poetry in the context of European poetic traditions in *Marconi's Cottage*, named after her summer cottage on the coast of Antrim, which was at one time inhabited by Guglielmo Marconi, inventor of the telegraph. Drawing on the work of Rainer Maria Rilke, Osip Mandelstam, and Marina Ivanovna Tsvetaeva, McGuckian reworks earlier themes of childbirth and artistic creativity within new compositional structures that include longer poems and a refreshed vocabulary. In "Clotho," McGuckian depicts her process for composing, dropping "three-quarters of [her] words" because she finds that she does not need them (50). Familiar images of the sea, sky, eyes, hands, colors, and home appear in even greater flux than before as chaos presents a stronger threat than before in poems such as "Gigot Sleeves," "The Most Emily of All," and "Breaking the Blue."

Captain Lavender contains a tonal shift toward addressing the Troubles and committing to the Irish cause. McGuckian composed the collection while running a creative-writing workshop with inmates who were suspected members of paramilitary groups in Maze prison. In "The Albert Chain," McGuckian evokes the image of her father from the perspective of a World War II veteran. In this poem and others she acutely reworks familiar images: flowers become berries dried at the stems, and an even greater storm threatens the home as the speaker claims, "I am going back into war, like a house I knew when I was young" (68).

Shelmalier marks yet another turn in McGuckian's thematic development. Though she previously refused to politicize her work, in this collection she addresses the bloody, historic 1798 rebellion. The collection's title draws its name from a barony in County Wexford and the name for an ancient group of waterfowl hunters. The word is the Anglicized version of "Siol Malure," meaning the seed, the people, the race, and the tribe. Again McGuckian maintains her characteristic difficulty by making overt historic references only in the title, author's note, and epigraph. McGuckian conjures new renderings of the relationship between past and present as she juxtaposes contemporary settings and seemingly autobiographical voices against a distant historical narrative. In an interview, McGuckian explains her need to write: "There are ghosts demanding to be heard, demanding that the truth be said, that I as poet should confront the past of my country" (Morris, 68). Her work appears as elegiac love poems that draw connections between personal and communal loss that afflict past battles and the ongoing Troubles.

In *Drawing Ballerinas* and *The Face of the Earth*, her most recent works, McGuckian again elicits historical events (such as the famine and the 1916 rising) and pairs them alongside recent struggles in the North in order to deconstruct contemporary events in terms of both historical precedence and future consequences. Throughout her poems in both collections, McGuckian carefully and cautiously examines the effects of violence and political unrest, unsure of the potential for lasting change through familiar guises of seduction, love letters, bodily sensations, and floral and weather imagery.

In *Drawing Ballerinas*, McGuckian deals with the emotional legacy of political terror. Instances of violence become hurricanes "whose presence or absence [is] the same" in the poem "At Mullaghmore" (11). Personal loss of a friend in the Abercorn Café explosion and Henri Matisse's reflections on war combine forces in "Drawing Ballerinas." In the title poem, McGuckian masterfully fuses images of ballerinas' bodies with victims of street violence; she explores the effects of political struggle for power upon individuals as "We are the focus of storms and scissor steps" (14). Themes or tropes of creation and the arts appear again, however, as tenuous in nature. In "Crumlin Road Courthouse," the speaker almost envisions lasting change, claiming that if the spires disintegrated from the tops of the churches and clouds could morph in form, he or she could divine "the river, the hospital, the citadel" (39).

The Face of the Earth (2002) likewise deals with the legacy of past political strife and current political climate in the North. In "Love Affair with Firearms," the past continually haunts the present in the form of memory and images. Photos turn brown and headlines blacken, speaking "of trenches, of who rose, who fell" (reprinted in *The Soldiers of the Year II*, 22). "Life as a Literary Convict" and "Filming the Famine" remain hesitant on hope, as they also reflect on current political realities while invoking the concern that creation has the power to oppress.

CRITICAL RECEPTION

From the beginning of her career, McGuckian has been recognized by some critics as doing something radically different. Since she is known particularly for her dense layering of images and seemingly obscure connections, the formal qualities of her poems resist easy interpretation and recognition and are, consequently, the source of ongoing critical debate. It should be noted that McGuckian's obliquity ultimately manifests itself in a resistance to familiar, objective frames of reference in both the physical world and that of language. Her fragmentation of established pictorial and linguistic systems of representation is not only rich and complex; it speaks toward a new form of autonomy and communication, and a new kind of poetry. In a recent interview with Helen Blakeman, McGuckian explains that poetry exists because the way we use language is "so inadequate" (63). Fittingly, critics have been primarily interested in the theoretical implications of McGuckian's lyrical style, her concerns with gender and sexuality, and her exploration of private and public realms.

One of the first to review McGuckian's work, Clair Wills maintains an interest in McGuckian's representation of private and public matters. In "The Perfect Mother" (1988), she examines McGuckian's representation of the mother figure and its relation to Catholic femininity in *The Flower Master* and *Venus and the Rain*. Wills identifies McGuckian's major polemic as that of an Irish Catholic female poet who is at once outside the major poetic tradition because of her gender, at odds with Catholicism's privileging of the mother as desexualized woman, and in conflict with nationalism's trope of the motherland. Through a consideration of McGuckian's poetry and interviews, as well as the work of Tom Inglis, Wills contends that McGuckian utilizes the roles of both mother and priest in order to challenge the authorial framework of Catholic Ireland. In *Improprieties: Politics and Sexuality in Northern Irish Poetry* (1993), she maintains that McGuckian reverts to the private and "domestic" since "the discourse of sexuality is the only public language to which, as a woman writer, she has legitimate access" (160). Wills identifies McGuckian's unidealized representations of motherhood, her depiction of woman's body as "the place of struggle," her emphasis on the daughter figure, and her acknowledgement of European poetic predecessors, all of which allow the poet to illuminate a future for Northern Ireland well beyond the dynamics of its relationship with patriarchal England (161). Thomas Docherty, like Wills, signals McGuckian's break with Irish national and cultural tradition. Calling upon Jean-Francois Lyotard's definition of postmodern artwork, he outlines the relationship between ritual and subjectivity in McGuckian's poetry and links her work with that of the surrealists.

Critics have been primarily interested in the relationship between McGuckian's lyrical style and gender in their consideration of her earlier work. Susan Porter seeks to place the poet in a postmodern tradition, which enables her to challenge her position as marginalized woman. Much like many scholars to follow, Susan Porter utilizes the work of Jacques Derrida—specifically his notion of disseminated meaning—to establish that McGuckian's poetry deconstructs binaries such as male/female, center/margin, and private/public. Porter considers imagery relating to women's bodies, childbirth, and the female arts; however, she privileges McGuckian's hymen imagery as particularly adept to destabilize established order.

Peggy O'Brien considers McGuckian's obliquity in relation to sexuality and sex. O'Brien also identifies several canonic precursors such as Dickinson, Marianne Moore, Hart Crane, and Walt Whitman. According to Eileen Cahill, McGuckian's "linguistic originality" is a by-product of her positioning apart from her contemporaries (265). Cahill applies postmodernist and contemporary feminist theory of Derrida's difference and Helene Cixous's ecriture feminine to suggest that McGuckian disturbs traditional binaries such as masculine/feminine. Mary O'Connor observes that McGuckian's challenging syntax stems from a "flight to the semiotic" (155). Haberstroh's *Women Creating Women* (1996) dedicates a chapter to McGuckian in which she examines her poetry in terms of gender and sexuality, identifying McGuckian's poetry as a feminine mode of speech. She uses the feminist contemporary theory of Cixous and Luce Irigaray to investigate the authority at play in McGuckian's conceptions of the "I" and the "you." Eunwon Han also indicates that McGuckian's writing is part of a feminine mode of speech as he examines her poetry in relation to Julia Kristeva's theory of the semiotic.

Alexander G. Gonzalez provides a rare close reading of individual poems, six from *The Flower Master* that focus upon the "married state—whether it be anticipated, enjoyed, or loathed" (44). Charles O'Neill explores the significance of McGuckian's image of the house in relation to Gaston Bachelard's *Poetics of Space* (1969).

Shane Murphy has sustained an interest in postmodern intertextuality, specifically with regard to McGuckian's poetic process as it gives rise to connections between past and present. In "Obliquity in the Poetry of Paul Muldoon and Medbh McGuckian" (1996), Murphy considers the ways in which McGuckian compiles lists of words she has read in literary autobiographies that she later uses for her poems as "palimpsestic double-writing" (97). Through an analysis of her textual appropriation or literary borrowing in "Gigot Sleeves," "Garo at the Gaumont," and "A Small Piece of Wood," he argues McGuckian inserts herself into a poetic tradition from which she has been previously excluded. Murphy's most recent work in the *Cambridge Companion to Contemporary Irish Poetry* (2003) claims that McGuckian's intertextual work "deterritorializes the English language" (200). Considering poems such as "The Truciler" from *Shelmalier*, Murphy exposes the poet's intertextual process as a way to describe her veiled commentary on identity politics.

Like Murphy's development of process, Guinn Batten has developed what she sees as the significance of absence in McGuckian's work. Batten's " 'The More with Which We are Connected': The Muse of Minus in the Poetry of Medbh McGuckian and Thomas Kinsella" (1997) claims that "absence" in the work of both poets allows them to bring poetry back to the roots of its "sexualized imagination" (2). Batten's most recent work compares McGuckian's poetry with Boland and Ni Chuilleanain in regard to the absence of the body (as it is conventionally rendered in poetry). Calling upon the work of postcolonial theorists David Lloyd and Gaytri Spivak, Batten claims that McGuckian's poetry stands as a "reincarnation" of the body politic in reference to Irish identity (179).

In "Ireland's Best" (1999), Katie Daniels compares McGuckian's *Shelmalier* with Eavan Boland's collection *The Lost Land* (1998) and Derek Mahon's *The Yellow Book* (1997) in relation to Irish patriarchal concerns. Helen Blakeman also considers "Shelmalier" among other poems in relation to metaphor and metonymy, which she defines through the work of Roman Jakobson and Jacques Lacan (2002). In " 'By Escaping and [Leaving] a Mark': Authority and the Poetry of Medbh McGuckian" (2002), Danielle Sered argues that McGuckian's authority is in fact a "radical . . . disruption of a traditional concept of authority" (273). As a radical alternative, the authority McGuckian establishes, according to Sered, cannot possess a center, or the the ability to name, nor can it control the multiple ways in which meaning is established by readers.

Robert Brazeau's work (2004) identifies McGuckian's poetry as avant-garde literature that works to "destabilize ideological discourses that delimit the role of women in contemporary Northern Ireland" (127). Brazeau uses the work of cultural critic Roland Barthes, contemporary feminist critics Julia Kristeva and Judith Butler, and the philosophy of Ludwig Wittgenstein to illustrate how language can redefine social mores.

Scholarship on McGuckian's work has responded in a variety of ways to her challenges at the level of language, gender, and political ideology. Throughout her newest volumes, McGuckian more openly refers to the North as she forces a collapse of past and present events; she also explores the dangers of artistic creation in the midst of troubled times or in their wake. Therefore, her recent poetry provides the material for an even greater outpouring of critical response, especially in relation to Ireland's identity and postcolonial theory.

BIBLIOGRAPHY

Works by Medbh McGuckian

Poetry

Captain Lavender. Oldcastle, Ire.: Gallery; Winston-Salem, NC: Wake Forest University Press, 1995.

Drawing Ballerinas. Oldcastle, Ire.: Gallery, 2001.

The Face of the Earth. Oldcastle, Ire.: Gallery, 2002.

The Flower Master. 1982. Oldcastle, Ire.: Gallery, 1993.

The Flower Master and Other Poems. Oldcastle, Ire.: Gallery, 1993.

Marconi's Cottage. Oldcastle, Ire.: Gallery; Winston-Salem, NC: Wake Forest University Press, 1991.

On Ballycastle Beach. 1988. Oldcastle, Ire.: Gallery, 1995.

Portrait of Joanna. Belfast: Ulsterman, 1980.

Selected Poems: 1978–1994. Oldcastle, Ire.: Gallery; Winston-Salem, NC: Wake Forest University Press, 1997.

Shelmalier. Oldcastle, Ire.: Gallery; Winston-Salem, NC: Wake Forest University Press, 1999.

Single Ladies. Budleigh Salterton, UK: Interim, 1982.

The Soldiers of Year II. Winston-Salem, NC: Wake Forest University Press, 2002.

Two Women, Two Shores: Poems by Medbh McGuckian and Nuala Archer. Baltimore, MD: New Poets, 1989. (Nuala Archer.)

Venus and the Rain. 1984. Oldcastle, Ire.: Gallery, 1994.

Other Works

"Crystal Night." In *My Self, My Muse: Irish Women Poets Reflect on Life and Art*, edited by Patricia Boyle Haberstroh, 135–37. Syracuse, NY: Syracuse University Press, 2001.

Horsepower, Pass By! A Study of the Car in the Poetry of Seamus Heaney. Coleraine, UK: Cranagh, 1999.

"Women Are Trousers." In *Border Crossings: Irish Women Writers and National Identities*, edited by Kathryn Kirkpatrick, 157–89. Tuscaloosa: University of Alabama Press, 2000.

"Rescuers in White Cloaks: Diary, 1968–1969." In Haberstroh, *My Self, My Muse*, 137–54.

Edited Work

The Big Striped Golfing Umbrella: An Anthology of Children's Poetry from Northern Ireland. Belfast: Arts Council of Northern Ireland, 1985.

Articles

"Don't Talk to Me about Dance." *Poetry Ireland Review* 35 (1992): 98–100.

"*Drawing Ballerinas*: Being Irish Has Influenced Me as a Writer." In *We Girls: Women Writing from an Irish Perspective*, edited by Liz Murphy. Sidney, Australia: Spanifex, 1996.

"Home." In *Hope and History: Eyewitness Accounts of Life in Twentieth-Century Ulster*, edited by Sophia H. King and Sean McMahon, 210–11. Belfast: Friar's Bush, 1996.

"Comhra, with a Foreword and Afterward by Laura O'Connor." *Southern Review* 31, no. 3 (1995): 581–614.

Interviews with Medbh McGuckian

Bohman, Kimberly S. " 'Surfacing: An Interview with Medbh McGuckian." *Irish Review* 1 (Autumn–Winter 1994): 95–108.

Blakeman, Helen. "'I Am Listening in Black and White to What Speaks to Me in Blue': Medbh McGuckian Interviewed by Helen Blakeman." *Irish Studies Review* 11, no. 1 (April 2003): 61–69.

Brandes, Rand. "A Dialogue with Medbh McGuckian in Winter 1996–7." *Studies in the Literary Imagination* 30, no. 2 (Fall 1997): 37–62.

Brown, John. *In the Chair: Interview with Poets from the North of Ireland.* Galway: Salmon, 2002.

McCracken, Kathleen. "An Attitude of Compassion." *Irish Literary Supplement* 9 (Fall 1990): 20–21.

McGrath, Niall. "The McGuckian Enigma: Interview with Medbh McGuckian." *Causeway* (Summer 1994): 67–70.

Somerville-Arjat, Gillean, and Rebecca E. Wilson, eds. *Sleeping with Monsters: Conversations with Scottish and Irish Women Poets.* Dublin: Wolfhound, 1990, 1–7.

Morris, Swanie. "'Under a North Window': An Interview with Medbh McGuckian." *Kenyon Review* 23, nos. 3–4 (Summer–Fall 2001): 64–74.

Sailer, Susan Shaw. "An Interview with Medbh McGuckian." *Michigan Quarterly Review* 32, no. 1 (1993): 110–27.

Studies of Medbh McGuckian

Allen, Michael. "The Poetry of Medbh McGuckian." In *Contemporary Irish Poetry: A Collection of Critical Essays*, edited by Elmer Andrews, 286–309. London: Macmillan, 1992.

Batten, Guinn. "Boland, McGuckian, Ni Chuilleanain and the Body of the Nation." In *The Cambridge Companion to Contemporary Irish Poetry*, edited by Mathew Campbell, 169–88. Cambridge: Cambridge University Press, 2003.

———. "'The More with Which We Are Connected': The Muse of Minus in the Poetry of Medbh McGuckian and Thomas Kinsella." In *Gender and Sexuality in Modern Ireland*, edited by Anthony Bradley and Maryann Gialanella Valiulis, 212–44. Amherst: University of Massachusetts Press, 1997.

Bendall, Molly. "Flower Logic: The Poems of Medbh McGuckian." *The Antoich Review* 48, no. 3 (Summer 1990): 367–71.

Blakeman, Helen. "Metaphor and Metonymy in Mebdh McGuckian's Poetry." *Critical Survey* 14, no. 2 (May 2002): 61–74.

Brazeau, Robert. "Troubling Language: *Avant-Garde* Strategies in the Poetry of Medbh McGuckian." *Mosaic* 37, no. 2 (June 2004): 127–44.

Burgoyne-Johnson, Jolanta. *Bleeding the Boundaries: The Poetry of Medbh McGuckian.* Coleraine, UK: Cranagh, 1999.

Cahill, Eileen. "'Because I Never Garden': Medbh McGuckian's Solitary Way." *Irish University Review* 24, no. 2 (Autumn 1994): 264–71.

Daniels, Katie. "Ireland's Best." *Southern Review* 35, no. 2 (1999): 387–402.

Docherty, Thomas. "Initiations, Tempers, Seductions: Postmodern McGuckian." In *The Chosen Ground, Essays on Contemporary Poetry of Northern Ireland*, edited by Neil Corcoran, 191–210. Bridgend, UK: Seren, 1992.

Gonzalez, Alexander G. "Celebrating the Richness of Medbh McGuckian's Poetry: A Close Analysis of Six Poems from *The Flower Master.*" In Gonzalez, *Contemporary Irish Women Poets*, 43–64.

———, ed. *Contemporary Irish Women Poets: Some Male Perspectives.* Westport: Greenwood, 1999.

———. "An Introduction to Reading Medbh McGuckian's Poetry: Close Analysis of 'The Chain Sleeper.'" *Notes on Modern Irish Literature* 9 (1997): 44–47.

———. "Older Women, Younger Men: Different Perspectives on the Use of Power in Nuala Ni Dhomhnaill's 'Flowers' and Medbh McGuckian's 'From the Dressing Room.'" *Notes on Modern Irish Literature* 12 (2000): 22–26.

Haberstroh, Patricia Boyle. "Medbh McGuckian." *Women Creating Women: Contemporary Irish Women Poets*, 122–59. Syracuse, NY: Syracuse University Press, 1996.

Han, Eunwon. "A Possibility of Women's Writings: A Study of Medbh McGuckian's Poems in the Context of J. Kristeva's Theory." *English Language and Literature* 42, no. 4 (1996): 791–811.

Jenkins, Alan. "Private & Public Languages." *Encounter* 59, no. 5 (November 1982): 56–63.

Johnston, Dillon. *Irish Poetry after Joyce*. Notre Dame, IN: University of Notre Dame Press, 1985, 1997.

McCurry, Jacqueline. "'Our Lady, Dispossessed': Female Ulster Poets and Sexual Politics." *Colby Quarterly* 27, no. 1 (March 1991): 4–8.

Murphy, Shane. "Obliquity in the Poetry of Paul Muldoon and Medbh McGuckian." *Eire-Ireland* 31, nos. 3–4 (Fall–Winter 1996): 76–101.

———. "Sonnets, Cantos and Long Lines: Muldoon, Paulin, McGuckian and Carson." In *Cambridge Companion to Contemporary Irish Poetry*, edited by Matthew Campbell, 189–208. Cambridge: Cambridge University Press, 2003.

———. "'You Took Away My Biography': The Poetry of Medbh McGuckian." *Irish University Review* 28, no. 1 (Spring–Summer 1998): 110–32.

O'Connor, Mary. "Medbh McGuckian's Destabilizing Poetics." *Eire-Ireland* 30, no. 4 (Winter 1996): 154–72.

O'Neill, Charles L. "Medbh McGuckian's Poetry: Inhabiting the Image." In Gonzalez, *Contemporary Irish Women Poets*, 65–78.

Porter, Susan. "The 'Imaginative Space' of Medbh McGuckian." *Canadian Journal of Irish Studies* 25, no. 2 (December 1989): 93–104.

Sered, Danielle. "'By Escaping and [Leaving] a Mark': Authority and the Writing Subject of the Poetry of Medbh McGuckian." *Irish University Review* 32, no. 2 (Autumn–Winter 2002): 273–86.

Sirr, Peter. "'How Things Begin to Happen': Notes on Eilean Ni Chuilleanain and Medbh McGuckian." *Southern Review* 32, no. 3 (Summer 1995): 450–67.

Stevenson, Anne. Review of McGuckian's early work. *Times Literary Supplement*, August 21, 1981, 952.

Wills, Clair. *Improprieties: Politics and Sexuality in Northern Irish Poetry*. Oxford: Oxford University Press, 1993.

———. "The Perfect Mother: Authority in the Poetry of Medbh McGuckian." *Text and Context* 3 (Autumn 1988): 91–111.

JANET McNEILL
(1907–   )

Tom Keegan

BIOGRAPHY

Janet McNeill was born in Dublin, but at the age of five she moved to Birkenhead, near Liverpool, and attended school there. In 1929 she graduated from St. Andrews University with an MA in classics. In 1933 she married Robert Alexander, after working for the *Belfast Telegraph* for two years, and moved to Lisburn, where she raised her four children. After many years of parenting, McNeill's career began to flourish with her winning of a 1951 BBC prize for playwriting, with *Signs and Wonders*, produced in Belfast that year. She served as chairman of the Belfast Centre of Irish PEN (Poets, Playwrights, Essayists, Editors, and Novelists) from 1956 to 1957 and was a member of the BBC Advisory Council from 1959 to 1964. She moved with her husband to England in 1964 and currently resides in Bristol.

MAJOR WORKS AND THEMES

A particularly prolific writer, Janet McNeill has published works for both adults and children ranging from articles and novels to plays and two opera libretti. Much of McNeill's work focuses on middle-class or upper-middle-class life, and her adult literature captures the subtle emotional shifts and predicaments of middle age, couched in the settings of the family and the nation. As she writes in her 1957 essay, "Seed, Root, and Stem," "the influence of country, of birth, of parentage, of heredity, of events, is undeniable, and in the ordering of our lives, inescapable. But there is in each man created a seed of original thought which, thrusting down into the nature of life before the womb, and up through all the over-lying accidental influences, can bear up the true stem of poetry and drama" (26). In this vein, *Tea at Four O'Clock* (1956) offers a scathing indictment of the bitterness and manipulation at work in middle-class Belfast life. The novel follows the domestic and psychological descent of Laura at the hands of her father and her older sister, Mildred. The theme of patriarchal domination ostensibly embodied in Mildred belies a more subtle theme of social domination, of ritual and domesticity—the novel ends with Laura, reduced to mental ruin, serving tea to Mildred's corpse.

McNeill's *The Maiden Dinosaur* (1964) again explores the themes of emotional sterility and social anguish, but has been regarded more recently as a lesbian novel, as the main character, schoolmistress Sarah Vincent, has been in love with her friend for several decades. *Talk to Me* (1965) revisits similar themes, utilizing the blindness of the main character, Alice, to address the confounding of communication and sympathy within this genteel society. Notably, McNeill turned almost exclusively to children's books after 1966—which she published substantially for the next decade. *Switch-On, Switch-Off and Other Plays* (1968) illustrates this movement into the realm of young adult fiction. The book contains an academic apparatus that includes a summary of each play's theme prior to the work. In the various plays the previously described themes of domesticity, alienation, and communication again appear. The play *Switch-On, Switch-Off and Other Plays* examines the networks of dependence within a family, nicely utilizing appliances as domestic barriers between individuals—for instance, the characters cannot hear one another over the din of the electric mixer. McNeill evokes a Beckett-like absurdism in *There's a Man in That Tree*, as characters attempt to come to terms with their own worldviews in light of one man's arboreal adventure. *Clothes-line* finds her critiquing the role of and reaction to advertising among housewives, while the themes of justice and judgment in society appear in both *Can I Help You?* and *Three from Four Leaves One*.

CRITICAL RECEPTION

For its elegant style and often-demure treatment of violent emotion, McNeill's work receives significant praise. However, her question, "Have we, perhaps, lingered too long in the Delectable Mountains with Yeats and Synge?" ("Seed, Root, and Stem," 28) has received mixed responses from artists and critics. Gerardine Meaney points out in *The Field Day Anthology* (vol. 5) that McNeill's "fiction is afforded no place in the Irish literary canon because of its definition in nationalist terms, but . . . can seem from the standards of literary England at the time to be quaintly regional and parochial" (1071). What we can see in the work of Janet McNeill is a literary precursor to the at-times droll, working-class-oriented poetry of the Irish 1980s. Discussing *The Maiden Dinosaur*, John Wilson Foster writes, "Without interiors, [McNeill's] people survive like animals from a previous age, dinosaurs in a zoo. They are the last of a species, of a generation and class born around the First World War and who lived through the Second World War" (242). This fatalism characterizes much of McNeill's work and illustrates her deft dismantling of the Victorian aesthetic in the face of an ever-graying, increasingly bleak social milieu.

BIBLIOGRAPHY

Works by Janet McNeill

Novels

As Strangers Here. London: Hodder and Stoughton, 1960.
A Child in the House. London: Hodder and Stoughton, 1955.
A Finished Room. London: Hodder and Stoughton, 1958.
The Maiden Dinosaur. London: Geoffrey Bles, 1964.
The Other Side of the Wall. London: Hodder and Stoughton, 1956.
The Small Window. London: Geoffrey Bles, 1967.
Talk to Me. London: Geoffrey Bles, 1965.
Tea at Four O'Clock. London: Hodder and Stoughton, 1956.

Collection of Short Works

A Light Dozen. London: Faber, 1957.

Children's Books

The Day Mum Came Home. London: Macmillan, 1977.
I Didn't Invite You to My Party. London: Hamilton, 1967.
The Magic Lollipop. London: Knight, 1974.
My Friend Specs McCann. London: Faber, 1955.
A Pinch of Salt. London: Faber, 1956.
Umbrella Thursday and a Helping Hand. Harmondsworth: Puffin, 1973.

Plays

Gospel Truth. Belfast: Carter, [1951?].
Signs and Wonders. 1951.
Switch-On, Switch-Off and Other Plays. London: Faber, 1968.

Essay

"Seed, Root, and Stem." *Threshold* 1, no. 4 (Winter 1957): 26–29.

Studies of Janet McNeill

Bourke, Angela, Mairin Ni Dhonneadha, Siobhan Kilfeather, Maria Luddy, Margaret MacCurtain, Gerardine Meaney, Mary O'Dowd, and Clair Wills, eds. *The Field Day Anthology* of *Irish Writing.* Vols. 4–5, *Women's Writing and Traditions.* Cork: Cork University Press, 2002.

Deane, Seamus, Andrew Carpenter, and Jonathan Williams, eds. *The Field Day Anthology of Irish Writing.* Vols. 1–3. Derry, Ire.: Field Day, 1991.

Foster, John Wilson. *Forces and Themes in Ulster Fiction.* Dublin: Gill and Macmillan, 1974.

Weekes, Ann Owens. "Janet McNeill." *Unveiling Treasures: The Attic Guide to Irish Women Writers.* Dublin: Attic, 1993.

PAULA MEEHAN
(1955–   )

Sara E. Stenson

BIOGRAPHY

Paula Meehan was born the eldest daughter of six in the northern part of Dublin's inner city. She received her early education from Whitehall House Senior Girls' School and eventually earned her bachelor's degree in English, history, and classical civilization from Trinity College Dublin. She also attended Eastern Washington State University, where in 1983 she received her MFA in poetry. Meehan won two Irish Arts Council bursaries and similar awards from the former Soviet Union and in Europe. Author of five volumes of poetry, Meehan has also written several plays, some especially for children. She received the Martin Tonder Award for Literature in 1996 and the Butler Award for Poetry from the Irish American Cultural Institute in 1998, and she has had two volumes of poetry short-listed for the *Irish Times* Literary Award. In the past, Meehan has been a fellow of the Robert Frost house in New Hampshire. She taught in Ireland at Trinity College and at University College Dublin, and is a member of Aosdána. Meehan works with numerous community-based writing workshops, including those with inmates from Mountjoy and Portalaoise prisons. She currently lives and writes in Dublin.

MAJOR WORKS AND THEMES

Meehan's work is steeped in a firm belief in the power of everyday revelations: that the quotidian has the ability to become visionary. Her own perspective has been shaped by a number of significant and differing influences. She is drawn particularly to the energy of American poets such as Robert Frost, Allen Ginsberg, Gary Snyder, and Lawrence Ferlinghetti. She also claims to gain stylistic influence from musicians such as Bob Dylan and Van Morrison. Russian poets have also left a strong impression on her, as have Irish poets such as Eavan Boland and Brendan Kennelly.

Meehan's efforts to highlight the lives of women and her commitment to transform the banal powerfully refute the metanarrative of nationalist history and offer a new version of Irish identity. Similarly to Eavan Boland, Paula Meehan chooses to work from her own sense of a personal history and she often tells women's stories in her poetry. She also claims to have been informed by the strong voices of the women in her family, such as her mother and grandmother. Throughout her work, Meehan consistently interrogates various episodes, spaces, and familial relations that form the memories of her own Dublin-based childhood. She frequently re-creates domestic spheres that are, of course, hardly without national significance for Irish women. Despite her numerous accounts of women and women's lives, Meehan resists being read as a feminist and prefers to conceive of her work as cross-gendered. Through its invigoration of the extraordinary in the commonplace, familial, and domestic, her work largely contributes to a national conversation concerning poetry.

Meehan's third major collection of poetry, *The Man Who Was Marked by Winter* (1991), showcases new forms of several poems that appeared previously in *Reading the Sky* (1984) and *Return and No Blame* (1986). The collection's most intriguing works stem from Meehan's childhood experiences, especially her relationship with her mother. "The Pattern"—one of her most famous poems—illuminates the tenuous and loving relationship between eldest daughter and mother through various vignettes in a Dublin flat. The mother scrubs the floor with Sunlight Soap, remakes an old dress for her daughter, and recalls the time she got caught by her own father wearing it out many years ago. The daughter subsequently recounts her own rebellion and by the poem's end, the mother formulates her own corrective. She promises to teach her daughter to follow "a pattern."

In "Buying Winkles," Meehan returns to her childhood theme, recounting trips to buy the boiled shellfish from women in Dublin. Meehan creates images of the odd sea creatures that, like the women who sell them, possess a fascinating glimmer-glow. She learns how to shell the fish and proudly carries a paper-wrapped bundle home. The poem marks an intimate time of learning and charting new territory for a young girl. Through "Buying Winkles," Meehan also manages carefully to evoke the mystery and charm of the act of writing poetry. For Meehan, both the creative process for the poet and the reading experience for the reader are entirely physical ones before they are intellectual. For her, poems live as re-creations of the poet's breath. In fact, she creates much of her work vocally, which helps to explain the wide variety in the stanza form, rhythm, and length of her work. As Meehan composes, lines formulate her major challenge. She tells John Hobbs in an interview, "Most of my solutions to the problems I set for myself are finding ways to spin them more energetically, to tighten them, to put as much pressure on them as I can" (60).

In *The Man Who Was Marked by Winter*, Meehan also initiates her lasting interest to render a number of destabilizing representations of romantic intimacy that are inevitably destroyed due to exterior social or natural forces. "The Leaving," for instance, presents an evocative twist on the nature of escape. Although she manages to provide means for the both of them, a woman's lover cannot leave, as he has "fallen so far down into himself" he cannot be reached (1). A woman makes the choice to leave in order to find safety for herself and her unborn child. The story is emblematic of the situation in the North; however, it powerfully resists any overt political connotations, as Meehan carefully crafts the poem in order to emphasize an individual's choice. "The Leaving" is one of Meehan's best-known works and is often among her anthologized poems.

The collection's title poem, "The Man Who Was Marked by Winter," was written at Robert Frost's house in New Hampshire. Meehan creates a powerful female ice goddess who takes a man's life, mysteriously marking him with a five-fingered gash. Meehan claims that Keats's "La Belle Sans Merci" (1819) was a major influence here, with a supernatural female power and the mortality of an innocent male. For Meehan, the role of the destructive goddess also provides an intriguing commentary on the nature of the poet and the muse. Splintered romantic relations between artist and muse appear again in her piece "Zugzwang," as an overbearing husband recounts the dissolution of his marriage. His wife is left broken, smothered, and objectified to the point that her own self-image is irreparably crushed.

The Man Who Was Marked by Winter also includes the poem that has brought Meehan the most amount of critical attention. "The Statue of the Virgin at Granard Speaks" recalls the tragic deaths of Anne Lovett and her secret child in 1984, which reignited a debate over abortion laws in Ireland. In Meehan's poem, the iconic statue of Mary comes alive, recounting the past year from a grotto near the actual home of Lovett in Granard, County Longford. The statue recalls the fifteen-year-old girl's struggle to give birth to a child whom no one knew she carried. As the girl desperately cries out, lying beside her dead baby in the bitter cold, Mary cannot, or will not, help her.

The Man Who Was Marked by Winter provides early evidence of Meehan's resourceful and daring use of a wide variety of material for inspiration, including Catholic hymns, the vernacular of her own Dublin-based working-class background, and folklore and myths from all over the world. Meehan, however, makes her own magic, creating her own fantasy world as she transforms the banal into something dreamlike and extraordinary. She states that her goal is ultimately to create a lasting, mysterious quality to her work so that it may have the power always to resist one reading, citing a Sufi traditional belief that poems can have seven unique readings (Hobbs, 53). The tone of her work often seeks to preserve a sense of multiplicity as she seems both to celebrate and to lament memories, relationships, and places often within the same location. Her poems themselves seem to change forms, much as the shapeshifter figures she creates.

Selections from her next major volume, *Pillow Talk* (1994), also appear alongside pieces from *The Man Who Was Marked by Winter* in the collection *Mysteries of the Home* (1996). In *Pillow Talk*, Meehan continues to develop similar intimacies of childhood and family in "A Child's Map of Dublin" and "My Father Perceived as a Vision of St. Francis." She also carefully designs pieces concerning broken lovers and betrayal, as in "Pillow Talk," "The Other Woman," and "Would You Jump into My Grave as Quick?" In "Not Your Muse," Meehan spins her earlier intrigue with Venus in "Fruit" to formulate a vivacious and boisterous response that rejects the possibility that the muse could be based on an actual woman.

Dharmakaya (2000) marks a substantial moment in Meehan's formal and thematic development. In the past she worked with Catholic rituals and various goddess figures, as well as shapeshifter influences from the Cuchulain cycle and Native American myths. In her most recent volume, however, Meehan invokes the Buddhist spiritual conception of consciousness to explore the turmoil of Dublin city, family, and intimate relationships. The volume's title is taken from the Buddhist *Book of the Dead* idea that when faced with death one sees a clear light of reality. Meehan examines how memories inform daily consciousness and become part of our bodies. "Breath" consistently reminds readers of the transitory nature of the immediate and highlights the significance of experiencing consciousness throughout the work.

Meehan's first play, *Mrs. Sweeney* (1999), originally produced in Dublin in 1997, centers on the loss of a daughter to AIDS. The play presents a revision of Sean

O'Casey's *Juno and the Paycock* (1924) and the King Sweeney legend. Her second play, *The Voyage* (1997), takes place on a famine ship, as a young girl shares her grand-father's gift for storytelling with fellow passengers, telling stories that recall and often change the myths of Tir na Nog, Oisin, and the Immramm. The play was part of the TEAM project, which sent it to Dublin inner-city schools whose children were deal-ing with the loss of their parents to AIDS. In September of 1999, Meehan's play *The Cell* was first produced at the City Arts Center in Dublin. Based on Meehan's en-counters with inmates during several writing workshops at Mountjoy and Portalaoise prisons, the play showcases the cramped quarters and tense relations among four fe-male inmates serving time for heroin possession.

Although Meehan has written plays relatively recently, she has worked with the the-ater for much longer. She cites Helene Cixous's conception of communal experience of theater as an important influence on her own work with the theater (O'Halloran and Maloy, 10). More specifically for Meehan, plays allow her to work easily through a guise of humor, unlike poetry. Lately, she has worked to create a children's play, *The Wolf of Winter*, which was produced in December 2003 at Dublin's Peacock Theater. Meehan presents a number of fairytale tropes; however, instead of utilizing one villain, she designs the townsfolk's greed as the evil force. As the play begins, a wolf enters the town and turns out to be a man who promises to bestow the village with many riches only if Jodie, a young girl, agrees to leave with him. Jodie's father hastily agrees to the trade, sending her off on a fantastical journey that reveals that she was actually raised by wolves. Her wild upbringing saves their lives as they run from hunters by the play's end.

CRITICAL RECEPTION

Surprisingly, no sustained study of Meehan's work has appeared despite her nu-merous volumes of poetry, various awards, and frequent appearances in anthologies. Early in her career her work received mixed reviews, including a series of essays in the *Irish Review*. Patrick Ramsey wrote a scathing appraisal of *The Man Who Was Marked by Winter*. Focusing especially upon "The Statue of the Virgin at Granard, Co. Longford," Ramsey cites theological "confusions" as evidence of Meehan's poor craft. Ramsey's unsubstantiated claims were later discredited by Peter Denman's reply, in which he validates Meehan's efforts to reinvoke a social crisis that remains unresolved. Subsequent reviews of Meehan's poetry admire her efforts to capture and display tu-multuous emotional worlds. Her newest collection of poetry, *Dharmakaya*, especially awaits serious critical attention.

Critical studies of Meehan's work usually draw their material from her poetry and consider her conceptions of femininity. Bernard McKenna focuses on a number of poems within her earlier collections, *The Man Who Was Marked by Winter* and *Pillow Talk*. McKenna identifies a recurring cycle throughout Meehan's work that moves first to recognition of a break or rupture, then to a moment of confrontation and subversion of the fracture, and finally to an image of a healing condition that provides the poten-tial for a nonfragmented character. McKenna studies the cycle formula in terms of community, continuity, and communion with the sublime. Examining "Coda" and "Fruit" in terms of women's communal relations and their sexuality, he then moves on to consider "The Pattern," "Night Prayer," and others in terms of women's legacy or intergenerational inheritance. Lastly he explores "Island" and "The Statue of the Vir-gin at Granard, Co. Longford" in light of women's communion with the sublime through traditional religious media and art.

Karen Steele is also drawn to Meehan's poem based on the statue of Mary in County Longford. Her essay provides a sociopolitical context that considers the role of Meehan and Rita Ann Higgins regarding Irish women's history and Irish women's identity. Steele claims that through their original representations of sexuality and motherhood, Higgins and Meehan subvert nationalist—or more specifically Yeatsian—conceptions of Mother Ireland in forceful ways that invigorate new conceptions of Irish identity. She examines Meehan's "The Statue of the Virgin at Granard Speaks" in light of two events from 1984–85, the death of Anne Lovett and the phenomenon of moving Marian statues.

Meehan has agreed to a number of interviews that have been published and have sparked a great deal of interest. In an interview with Eileen O'Halloran and Kelli Maloy, Meehan openly discusses her Dublin background, familial relations, influences, writing process for poetry and plays, as well as spirituality and use of the supernatural in her work. Meehan's interview with John Hobbs centers on her childhood and the poems she has created to reflect on her early experiences.

BIBLIOGRAPHY

Works by Paula Meehan

Plays

Cell: A Play in Two Parts for Four Actors and a Voice. Dublin: New Island, 2000. Presented by Calypso Productions, 1999.
Kirkle. TEAM Educational Theatre Company, 1995.
Mrs. Sweeney. In *Rough Magic: First Plays*, edited by Siobhan Bourke. Dublin: New Castle; London: Methuen, 1999.
The Voyage. TEAM Educational Theatre Company, 1997.
The Wolf of Winter. Peacock Theatre, Dublin, 2003.

Poetry

Dharmakaya. Manchester: Carcanet, 2000.
The Man Who Was Marked by Winter. Oldcastle, Ire.: Gallery, 1991; Cheney: Eastern Washington University Press, 1994.
Mysteries of the Home: Selected Poems. Newcastle Upon Tyne: Bloodaxe, 1996.
Pillow Talk. Oldcastle, Ire.: Gallery, 1991; Cheney: Washington University Press, 1994.
Reading the Sky. Dublin: Beaver Row, 1986.
Return and No Blame. Donnybrook: Beaver Row, 1984.

Interviews with Paula Meehan

Carney, Rob. "An Interview with Paula Meehan." *Atlanta Review* 2, no. 2 (1995): 49–58.
Dorgan, Theo. "An Interview with Paula Meehan." *Colby Quarterly* 28, no. 4 (December 1992): 265–69.
Gonzalez, Arias, and Mar Luz. " 'Playing with the Ghosts of Words': An Interview with Paula Meehan." *Atlantis* 22, no. 1 (June 2000): 187–204.
Hobbs, John. "An Interview with Paula Meehan." *Nua: Studies in Contemporary Irish Writing* 1, no. 1 (Autumn 1997): 53–68.
O'Halloran, Eileen, and Kelli Maloy. "An Interview with Paula Meehan." *Contemporary Literature* 43, no. 1 (Spring 2002): 1–27.

Studies of Paula Meehan

Brain, Tracy. "Dry Socks and Floating Signifiers: Paula Meehan's Poems." *Critical Survey* 8, no. 1 (1996): 110–17.

Colgan, Gerry. "The Wolf of Winter, Peacock Theatre, Dublin." *Irish Times*, December 16, 2003, 14.

Denman, Peter. "Right of Reply." *Irish Review* 16 (Autumn–Winter 1994): 123–26.

Kirkpatrick, Kathryn. Review of Paula Meehan's *Dharmakaya. Shenandoah* 51, nos. 2–3 (Fall 2001): 193–95.

McKenna, Bernard. "Battle Dressed to Survive: The Poetry of Paula Meehan." In *Contemporary Irish Women Poets: Some Male Perspectives*, edited by Alexander G. Gonzalez. Westport, CT: Greenwood, 1999.

Myers, Kimberley. "The Sexual Dialectic of Eavan Boland, Paula Meehan, and Nuala Ni Dhomhnaill." *South Carolina Review* 32, no. 1 (Fall 1999): 51–58.

O'Grady, Thomas. "Akhmatova on the Liffey: Paula Meehan's Lyrical Craft." *Colby Quarterly* 35, no. 3 (September 1999): 173–83.

Ramsey, Patrick. "Fragrant Necrophilia." *Irish Review* 15 (Spring 1994): 148–54.

Steele, Karen. "Refusing the Poisoned Chalice: The Sexual Politics of Rita Ann Higgins and Paula Meehan." In *Homemaking: Women Writers and the Politics of Home*, edited by Catherine Wiley and Fiona Barnes, 312–33. New York: Garland, 1996.

Trotter, Mary. "A Sort of Nationcoming: Invasion, Exile, and the Politics of Home in Modern Irish Drama." *Theatre Symposium: A Journal of the Southeastern Theatre Conference* 9 (2001): 95–106.

Weekes, Anne Owens. *Unveiling Treasures: The Attic Guide to the Published Works of Irish Women Literary Writers*. Dublin: Attic, 1993, 224–26.

MÁIRE MHAC AN TSAOI
(1922–   )

Cóilín D. Owens

BIOGRAPHY

Máire Mhac an tSaoi (pronounced Maurya WOK an Tee) was born in Dublin into a prominent Catholic, Gaelic, and nationalist family. Her father was Seán MacEntee of the Belfast old Irish Republican Army (IRA), a longtime Fianna Fáil Teachta Dála, a cabinet member, and Táiniste. Her mother, Margaret Browne, had three brothers, two of them distinguished clerics: Monsignor Pádraig de Brún, president of University College Galway, and Michael Cardinal Browne, master general of the Dominican Order. Both of her Browne grandparents were native speakers of Irish, and the family connection with the living language was maintained when "Father Paddy" (as Máire's spiritual father was affectionately known) built a summer home for the family at Dunquin, Dingle, County Kerry. Máire was educated at the local national school in Dunquin, where she acquired her passion for the language and culture of the Gaeltacht. Her education continued at Alexandra College, Beaufort High School, Rathfarnham, and University College Dublin, where she acquired a double degree in modern languages and Celtic studies in 1941. Until the end of the war she was a scholar at the Dublin Institute for Advanced Studies, which published her *Two Irish Arthurian Romances* (1946). She subsequently attended the Sorbonne on a scholarship (1945–1947) and won an Oireachtas Prize for her early Irish poetry. On her return, she qualified as a barrister and then joined the Department of External (now Foreign) Affairs, serving in Paris and Madrid as third secretary. She was soon promoted to first secretary and became part of the new United National section in New York from 1957 to 1960 and, during the following two years, to the European Community posting at Strasbourg. She resigned the service in 1962 and married Conor Cruise O'Brien. While pursuing her diplomatic career she was writing and translating: *Margadh na Saoire* appeared in 1956, and *A Heartful of Thought* in 1959. During the United Nations' intervention in Katanga, she visited the Congo and lived in Ghana (1962–1965) and New York (1965–1969). The O'Briens adopted two African children, Sean Patrick and Margaret, and have lived in Howth, County Dublin, and Duquin since 1969.

MAJOR WORKS AND THEMES

Margadh na Saoire (1956) was an impressive debut for an Irish-language poet. Comprising some forty poems, personal lyrics, experiments in traditional forms, and translations from English, Spanish, and French, it established Mhac an tSaoi as the leading lyricist writing in Irish. The poems conjoin the personal with the classical in the Irish formal tradition while expressing romantic themes in fresh and striking imagery. The poems are most eloquent when articulating the sense of loss, whether personal, of the people of the Gaeltacht, or of the Gaelic past. Thus, the most pleasing poems in this volume express the themes of lost or hopeless love ("Finit," "Labhrann Deirdre"), the passing of traditional life ("Ba Chuimhin Leis an Seanduine . . ."), or colonial exploitation ("Inquisitio 1484").

Her second book, *Miserere* (1971), is an English translation of Monsignor Pádraig de Brún's reflections on a series of pictures by Georges Rouault. An exercise of familial pietas, its citation of the Rouault legend, "Nous devons mourir, nous et tout ce ce qui est notre" (We are fated to die, we and all that is ours), seems also applicable to Mhac an tSaoi's own view of Irish language and culture.

In her second and third collections, *Codladh an Ghaiscigh* (1973) and *An Galar Dubhach* (1980), she abandons the formal experiments of her earlier poetry in favor of a more personal and maternal expression. Of the thirty lyrics, many are dedicated to her adopted children, recording their growth into adolescence.

An Cion go dtí Seo (1987) is a cumulative collection of these volumes, to which is added a further score of lyrics. It embraces a variety of subject and forms—religious meditations, eulogies for deceased friends and scholars, blessings for children, dedications to the younger Irish-language poets—and registers culture shock in the age of the worldwide media explosion.

Besides the poetry represented in these collections, Mhac an tSaoi has published many other poems, some short stories, and a range of scholarly essays and lectures on Celtic studies and modern and contemporary writing in Irish. She has contributed to various radio series and numerous symposia on Irish culture and history and is a leading critic and patron of younger Irish writers.

Her critical stance favors cautious experiment, respect for canonical standards of expression, and the integrity of the language, valuing its unique role as preserver of the national soul. She has subsequently modified this classical position, becoming less the critic than the patron of the younger generation of urban writers influenced by modernist and postmodernist trends. Thus, whereas she was inclined to chastise the untraditional use of language in the work of Seán O Ríordáin, she admits to a resigned acceptance or even an admiring enthusiasm for later writers such as Alan Titley, Nuala Ní Dhomhnaill, or the group associated with the Irish-language journal *Innti*. For their part, especially for the women writing since 1980, she is the singular voice writing in the bleak years of Ireland's previous political and cultural isolation.

In all of her work, the same themes and ideals persist: affectionate respect for family and intellectual mentors, the love of the people and landscapes of Corca Dhuibhne, and a deep loyalty to the traditions of classic Irish literature. Against these standards she views her own output as well as that of others. Thus, in her estimation, only three Irish writers of the present age reach the highest standards—Tomás O Criomthain, Máirtín O Cadhain, and Nuala Ní Dhomhnaill (*Southern Review*, 785).

CRITICAL RECEPTION

Margadh na Saoire (Market of Freedom) was universally praised for its sense of craft, its command of Munster Irish, and its erudition. Like the best examples of lyrical poetry from the Early Irish, Mhac an tSaoi's poetry is disciplined and understated. Her reviewers praise her controlled energy, her passion for the values in Gaeltacht culture rooted in pre-Christian Ireland, and her emulation of Old Irish metrics. Although the volume contains some juvenilia, its many fine lyrics show a disciplined shaping of inherited forms to modern subjects without dissolution into confessionalism. For all its emotional energy, the persona retains a tribal timbre. Subsequently, many of the poems from *Margadh*—such as "Caoindadh," "Do Shíle," "An Chéad Bhróg," "Oíche Nollag," and "Jack"—have become standard selections in Irish-language and school anthologies. Some of her critics wish for more extravagance, but all admire the manner in which she crafts the emotionally intense poems of love and family feeling.

At its periphery, her later work reflects images form the public sphere. Yet her personal universe takes its shape in highly refined phrases drawn from the pure idiom of authentic native speech. Her best poems, so full of personal intensity, are informed by the traditional love song and, behind that, the direct emotion of medieval Gaelic literature. The blend produces a classic elegance, unique in modern Irish poetry. Deeply committed to the language and cultural revival in Ireland, her work exhibits a fidelity to the ideals and discipline of that movement. To the next generation of Irish writers facing even more rapid and fundamental change than she encountered during her formative years, her criticism, counsel, and example are all reminders of the cultural stakes in the potential loss of the national language.

For their part, the next generation of Irish writers, especially the women, appreciate the complex, even paradoxical, example she sets: brought up among passionate cultural nationalists, trained by eminent Celticists to appreciate the impersonality of that tradition, she is the only one of her generation writing with a voice that is emotional, personal, and unambiguously feminine.

BIBLIOGRAPHY

Works by Máire Mhac an tSaoi

A Bhean Og On. Inverin, Ire.: Cló IarChonnachta, 2001.
An Cion Go Dtí Seo. Dublin: Sáirséal agus O Marcaigh, 1987.
An Galar Dubhach. Dublin: Sáirséal agus Dill, 1980.
"Ar Thóir Ghearóid Iarla." *Oghma* 2 (1990): 20–33.
Codladh an Ghaiscígh. Dublin: Sáirséal agus Dill, 1980.
A Concise History of Ireland. London: Thames and Hudson, 1972. (With Conor Cruise O'Brien.)

A Heart Full of Thought. Dublin: Dolmen, 1959. (Translations from the Irish.)

Margadh na Saoire. Dublin: Sáirséal agus Dill, 1956, 1971.

Miserere. Dublin: Gill and Macmillan, 1971. (Translations from the Irish of poems of Monsignor Pádraig de Brún.)

"The Origins of Poetry: Points of Comparison between Medieval Ireland and Early Greece." *Studia Hibernica* 24 (1984–1988): 7–28.

"Pádraig de Brún agus an Ghaeilge: Saol agus Saothar in Aisce." *Leachtai Cholm Cille* 23 (1993): 140–60.

Shoah agus Dánta Eile. Dublin: Sáirséal agus O Marcaigh, 1999.

"Writing in Modern Irish—A Benign Anachronism" and "In Celebration of the Irish Language." *Southern Review* 31, no. 3 (Summer 1995): 424–31, 772–85.

As *Máire Cruise O'Brien*

"An tOileánach: Tomás O Criomhthain (1865–1937)." In *The Pleasures of Gaelic Literature*, edited by John Jordan, 25–38. Cork: Mercier, 1977.

"The Female Principle in Gaelic Poetry." In *Women in Irish Legend, Life and Literature*, edited by S. F. Gallagher, 26–37. Totowa, NJ: Barnes and Noble, 1983.

"The Role of the Poet in Gaelic Society." In *The Celtic Consciousness*, edited by Robert O'Driscoll, 243–54. New York: Braziller, 1981.

The Same Age as the State. Dublin: O'Brien, 2003.

Interviews with Máire Mhac an tSaoi

Davitt, Michael. "Cómrá le Máire Mhac an tSaoi." *Innti* 8 (1984): 37–59.

Mac Reamoinn, Seán. "Athnuachan an Traidisiúin." *Comhar* 48, no. 1 (1989): 22–26.

Nic Dhiarmada, Bríona. "Bláthú an Traidisiúin." *Comhar* 46, no. 5 (1987): 23–29.

Studies of Máire Mhac an tSaoi

Buckley, Vincent. "Poetry and the Avoidance of Nationalism." In *Irish Culture and Nationalism*, edited by Oliver MacDonagh, W. F. Mandle, and Pauric Travers, 258–79. New York: St. Martin's, 1983.

Henry, P. L. *Dánta Ban: Poems of Irish Women Early and Modern.* Cork: Mercier, 1991.

O'Brien, Frank. *Filíocht Ghaeilge na Linne Seo.* Dublin: An Clóchomhar, 1968, 163–201.

ALICE MILLIGAN
(1866–1953)

Rita Barnes

BIOGRAPHY

Alice Milligan was born to a Methodist family in Omagh, County Tyrone. Her father was an antiquarian and member of the Royal Irish Academy as well as a successful businessman. She attended Methodist College, Belfast; Magee College, Derry; and King's College, London.

In Belfast, she founded the Irish Women's Association (1894), the Henry Joy Mc-Cracken Literary Society (1895), and the Irish Women's Centenary Union (1897) (Morris, "Becoming Irish?" 79). She wrote in 1893 that Irish literature cannot separate itself from politics (Hall, 62), and devoted her career to creating a Northern nationalist cultural identity.

With Ethna Carberry (Anna Johnston), Milligan created and edited a monthly newspaper, the *Northern Patriot* (1895), for the McCracken Society. When the society objected to Johnston's editorship because of her father's Irish Republican Brotherhood membership (Morris, "Becoming Irish?" n5), the pair established the *Shan Van Vocht* (1896–1899).

The Gaelic League awarded Milligan a prize in 1897 for her essay "How to Popularise the Irish Language" (O'Leary, 232). She supported the teaching of Irish with fund-raising tours of tableaux vivants and lantern shows on historical and legendary themes for Inghinidhe na hÉireann and the League (Trotter, 85; Boylan, 249).

She served as organizing secretary for the 1898 Centenary Committee in Belfast, earning appointment to the Centenary's national executive committee. Milligan advocated issuing of Irish cultural history diplomas by the League (O'Leary, 174). Her biography of Wolfe Tone appeared the same year.

In 1899 Milligan called for Gaelic League and Irish Literary Theatre (ILT) cooperation, suggesting that Yeats offer his dramatization of Ossianic myth (Trotter, 21). In February 1900, her play on the subject, *The Last Feast of the Fianna*, was performed at the Gaiety Theatre in Dublin for the Irish Literary Theatre's second season, with Edward Martyn's *Maeve* and *The Bending of the Bough*. Milligan's *The Deliverance of Red Hugh* (1901) fostered the collaboration she envisioned.

Milligan was appointed in 1906 to the league's steering committee, the Coiste Gno. Professional and personal friendships included John O'Leary, George Russell (AE), Roger Casement, and other cultural and political leaders (Kelly, 76).

An Anti-Partition League founder, Milligan continued to advocate for Irish unity despite increasing practical difficulties after partition. Milligan received an honorary DLitt from National University of Ireland in 1941. She died April 13, 1953, at Tyrcar, Omagh.

MAJOR WORKS AND THEMES

Milligan's earliest published work is a travelogue, *Glimpses of Erin* (1888), coauthored with her father. Its images of a rural Ireland untouched by politics contrast with those of her futuristic novel, *A Royal Democrat* (1890). Set in the 1930s, it concerns a British prince's shipwreck on the coast of Ireland and subsequent political awakening as a supporter of Irish independence.

During the 1890s, Milligan's writings for *Sinn Féin*, the *Irish Weekly Independent* (the column "Notes from the North"), *United Ireland*, and *United Irishman*, and her biography of Tone, all link myth and history to contemporary politics. *The Cromwellians*, an unpublished novel (begun in 1891) and her poetry, short fiction, and prose began using 1798 as a touchstone (Morris, "Becoming Irish?").

The *Northern Patriot* (1895) published poetry, fiction, and essays, including her own, emphasizing the North's role in national identity. After three months, the *Patriot* closed. The *Shan Van Vocht* (1896–99) became an influential journal recognized by contributors such as Yeats, AE, and James Connolly for its cultural and political commentary. The journal gave voice to Irish Nationalist feminism, criticizing male domination of Irish leadership (Innes, 136) and publishing primarily women authors, including Katherine Tynan and Nora Hoppner.

Milligan's touring tableaux vivants included "The Battle of Clontarf," "The Children of Lir," and "The Fairy Changeling"; scenes from Irish history, myth, and folklore popularized Nationalist imagery. Appropriating a Victorian genre, the tableaux became an organizing and educational tool.

The one-act *Last Feast of the Fianna* (1899) explores the legacy of divisive national conflict through the rift between Diarmuid and Finn. Oisin, Finn's son, became central to Milligan's political imagination. John O'Leary performed in the premier as a member of the Fianna. She unsuccessfully asked Douglas Hyde to translate *Last Feast* into Irish (O'Leary, 323). Risteárd Ó Foghludha's *Naoi nGearra* (*Nine Short Plays*, 1930) included Milligan's Ossianic trilogy.

The Deliverance of Red Hugh: A Play in One Act and Two Scenes (1901), notable for stylistic innovation, inspired George Russell (AE), Padraic Colum, and Yeats to work with the Fays (regarded as amateurs in their work with Inghinidhe na hÉirean). Inghinidhe planned its performance (with Milligan's *The Harp That Once*) to coincide with the Anglo-Irish-dominated Dublin Horse Show (Trotter, 92–93).

The Daughter of Donagh, published serially in *United Irishman* (1903), adapts Milligan's unpublished novel *The Cromwellians*. The melodrama concerns a dispossessed woman's manipulation of legal and social taboos in 1654. Rejected by the Abbey, the play was staged in 1905 in Cork. The theme of illegal marriage and dispossession appears also in her ballad "Lord Edward's Wife," set during Richard II's 1394 invasion. Ordered to banish his Irish family, Edward defiantly surrenders his property instead; Richard then hangs Edward's *seanachie* (storyteller).

Milligan's first inclusion in a volume of poetry occurs with AE's *New Songs* (1904). Her *Poems* appeared posthumously (1954) with an introduction by Henry Mangan and an appendix of her poetry publications. Representative is "Till Ferdia Came," comparing Ferdia's fatal battle with Cuchulainn to the conflict of the Irish Civil War, particularly the assassination of Michael Collins, and suggesting that foreign interests have goaded the Irish into destroying themselves.

CRITICAL RECEPTION

In her three pieces on Milligan, Catherine Morris analyzes Milligan's Protestant background and development of her political aesthetic, especially through her editorship and her writings concerning 1798; Morris examines unpublished and unfinished works, Milligan's reception as writer and political activist, and difficulties after partition.

Robbie Meredith explores how Milligan shaped Northern nationalism in the *Shan Van Vocht*. Prevailing images of the North saw industrial Belfast as representative, alien to Romantic Ireland. Coverage of northern perspectives, her own work using the Ulster cycle, and opinion pieces by diverse factions realized a more heterogeneous Revival.

C.L. Innes writes that poems in the *Shan Van Vocht* employ male perspectives; woman is "a lost or unattainable ideal, or an allegorical figure of Ireland . . . an unchanging essence" (136). AE includes Milligan in the 1904 anthology *New Songs* as one of eight leading younger Irish poets, commenting, "I enviously wish I could claim [these poems] as my own" (Weygandt, 116). Thomas MacDonagh names Milligan among poets worthy of Anglo-Irish literary historical study (990), entitling an essay about Milligan "The Best Living Irish Poet" because of her diverse Irish cultural credentials (Morris, "Belfast," 3).

Mary Trotter assesses Milligan's dramatic innovations as "a significant crossing of paths between Irish Literary Theatre high art and Gaelic League popular forms." Like Yeats, she achieves "aesthetic tension between grassroots Irish and avant-garde European modernist aesthetics" (24). Her tableaux mix politics with "tropes one would expect to find in a British pantomime" (89).

Christopher Morash places *Last Feast* among Revivalist plays that evoke "Shadwell's *Rotherick O'Connor* (1720) come back from the dead" (120–21), featuring upheaval of domestic life by apolitical supernatural forces (123).

Lennox Robinson calls *Last Feast* a "touching" play about "old age, the twilight of the Gods," with "very musical prose" and fine staging and costuming. He quotes the *United Irishman* that despite "wretchedly small" audiences, it "gave us the only glimpse we have seen of what the Ireland of pre-Christian days must have been" (15).

The English press praised *Last Feast* (Fallis, 91). The *Daily Express* deemed it "equivalent to the drama in ancient Gaelic literature. . . . If the aim of the Irish Literary Theatre is to create a national drama it is obvious that the development of Miss Milligan's method is the proper road to reach ultimate success" (quoted in Trotter, 23; O'Leary, 311).

Yeats reports that "with the exception of the *Irish Times* and our little Society papers," the play was widely praised in the Irish press ("*Last Feast*," 5). Yeats writes, Milligan's *Last Feast* "touched the heart as greater drama on some foreign theme could not," with populist and literary interests ("*Last Feast*," 4). Of *Red Hugh* (1901) Yeats comments, "I came away with my head on fire. I wanted to hear my own unfinished *Baile's Strand*, to hear Greek tragedy spoken with a Dublin accent" (quoted in Trotter, 93). He laments British drama's influences (*Samhain*, 6): "Without scenery it would resemble a possible form of old Irish drama" ("Plans and Methods," 4). By and with AE, he was then convinced to offer the Fays *Kathleen ni Houlihan* (Trotter, 93).

AE called Milligan "a girl of genius" for Irish theater, and "an elfish stage manager," creator of "little plays to help the infant Gaelic League" at "the infant beginnings of Irish dramatic art" (quoted in Mikhail, 137). Lady Gregory's review of ILT's second season mentions Milligan's "little play" (26). Padraic Colum refers to "that sterling young Ulster woman" (quoted in Mikhail, 61), recalling her "extraordinary disinterestedness and a sort of practicality, northern and womanly, that went with her vision and dream" (62).

BIBLIOGRAPHY

Works by Alice Milligan

The Daughter of Donagh: A Cromwellian Drama in Four Acts. United Irishman, December 5–26, 1903. Reprint, Dublin: Lester, 1920.

The Deliverance of Red Hugh. Weekly Freeman, March 13, 1902.

The Dynamite Drummer. Dublin: Lester, 1918. (With William Milligan.)

Glimpses of Erin. London: Ward, Lock, 1888. (With Seaton F. Milligan.)

Harper of the Only God: A Selection of Poetry by Alice Milligan. Edited by Sheila Turner Johnston. Omagh: Colourpoint, 1993.

Hero Lays. Dublin: Maunsel, 1908.

"How to Popularise the Irish Language." *Imtheacta an Oireachtais/Full Report of the Proceedings at the Oireachtas or Irish Literary Festival Held in the Round Room, Rotunda, Dublin, on May 17th, 1897*. Dublin: Gaelic League, 1897, 91. (As Geal na Gréine.)

The Last Feast of the Fianna. With Edward Martyn's *Maeve: A Psychological Drama in Two Acts.* Chicago: DePaul University Press, 1967.

"*The Last Feast of the Fianna.*" *Beltaine* 2 (1900): 18–21.

Life of Theobald Wolfe Tone. Belfast: Boyd, 1898.

Oisin and Padraic: A One-Act Play. Daily Express, November 11, 1899. Reprint, *Sinn Féin,* February 20, 1909.

Oisin in Tir-Nan-Og. Traslated by Tadgh Ua Donnchada. *Sinn Féin,* January 23, 1909.

Poems. Edited and with an introduction by Henry Mangan. Dublin: Gill, 1954.

"Prospects of the Irish National Literary Movement." *United Ireland,* December 19, 1896.

A Royal Democrat. London: Simkin, Marshall, 1890. (As Iris Olkyrn.)

Sons of the Sea Kings. Dublin: Gill, 1914. (With William Milligan.)

Two Poems. Dublin: Three Candles, 1943.

Two Poems of Triumph in Death. Dublin: Gaelic, 1917. (With Alice Furlong.)

In Anthologies

Armstrong, Isobel, and Joseph Bristow, eds. *Nineteenth-Century Women Poets: An Oxford Anthology.* New York: Oxford University Press, 1996.

Colum, Padraic. *Anthology of Irish Verse.* New York: Macmillan, 1922.

Cooke, John, ed. *The Dublin Book of Irish Verse.* Dublin: Hodges Figgis, 1909.

Hearon, Todd. *The Staged Irishman: Irish National Drama 1899–1904: A Critical Edition.* Carbondale: Southern Illinois University Press, 2003.

Kelly, A. A., ed. *Pillars of the House: An Anthology of Verse by Irish Women.* Dublin: Wolfhound, 1987.

MacManus, Anna Johnston. *We Sang for Ireland: Poems of Ethna Carbery, Seumas MacManus, Alice Milligan.* Dublin: Gill, 1950.

Meaney, Geraldine, ed. "Women and Writing, 1700–1960." In *The Field Day Anthology of Irish Writing.* Vol. 5, *Irish Women's Writing and Traditions,* edited by Angela Bourke, Mairin Ni Dhonneadha, Siobhan Kilfeather, Maria Luddy, Margaret MacCurtain, Gerardine Meaney, Mary O'Dowd, and Clair Wills. New York: New York University Press, 2002; Cork: Cork University Press, 2002.

Russell, George W., ed. *New Songs.* Dublin: O'Donoghue, 1904.

Studies of Alice Milligan

Boylan, Henry. "Alice Milligan." In *A Dictionary of Irish Biography.* 2nd ed. New York: St. Martin's, 1988, 249–250.

Concannon, Helena. *Women of Ninety-Eight.* Dublin: Gill, 1919.

Fallis, Richard. *The Irish Renaissance.* Syracuse, NY: Syracuse University Press, 1977.

Gregory, Lady Augusta. *Our Irish Theatre.* New York: Capricorn, 1965.

Hall, Wayne E. *Shadowy Heroes: Irish Literature of the 1890s.* Syracuse, NY: Syracuse University Press, 1980.

Harp, Richard. "No Other Place But Ireland: Alice Milligan's Diaries and Letters." *New Hibernia Review* 4, no. 1 (Spring 2000): 79–87.

———. "*The Shan Van Vocht* and Irish Nationalism." *Éire-Ireland* 24, no. 3 (Fall 1989): 42–52.

Innes, C. L. *Woman and Nation in Irish Literature and Society, 1880–1935.* Athens: University of Georgia Press, 1993.

Johnston, Sheila Turner. *Alice: A Life of Alice Milligan.* Omagh, N. Ire.: Colourpoint, 1994.

———. *Struggling for Light: A Biography of Alice Milligan.* Omagh, N. Ire.: Colourpoint, 1992.

Kelly, A. A., ed. Introduction to Milligan. In *Pillars of the House: An Anthology of Verse by Irish Women.* Dublin: Wolfhound, 1987, 76.

MacDonagh, Thomas. "The Best Living Irish Poet." *Irish Review* 4 (September–November 1914): 287–93.

Martin, Celeste. "Alice Milligan." In *Late Victorian and Early Edwardian Women Poets.* Vol. 240, *Dictionary of Literary Biography,* edited by William Thesing, 158–63. Detroit: Gale, 2001.

Meredith, Robbie. *"The Shan Van Vocht*: Notes from the North." In *Critical Ireland: New Essays in Literature and Culture*, edited by Aaron Kelly and Alan A. Gillis, 173–80. Dublin: Four Courts, 2001.

Mikhail, E.H., ed. *The Abbey Theatre: Interviews and Recollections*. Totowa, NJ: Barnes and Noble, 1988.

Morash, Christopher. *A History of the Irish Theatre, 1600–2000*. Cambridge: Cambridge University Press, 2002.

Morris, Catherine. "Alice Milligan and *Fin de Siècle* Belfast." In *The Cities of Belfast*, edited by Nicholas Allen and Aaron Kelly. Dublin: Four Courts, 2003.

———. "Becoming Irish? Alice Milligan and the Revival." *Irish University Review* 33, no. 1 (Spring–Summer 2003): 79–98.

———. "From the Margins: Alice Milligan and the Irish Cultural Revival, 1888–1905." PhD diss., University of Aberdeen, 1999. (Contains a complete chronological bibliographic listing for Milligan's published works.)

Obituary and bibliography. *Irish Book Lover* 32 (1953): 63–64.

O'Leary, Philip. *The Prose Literature of the Gaelic Revival, 1881–1921: Ideology and Innovation*. University Park: Pennsylvania State University Press, 1994.

Robinson, Lennox. *Ireland's Abbey Theatre: A History, 1899–1951*. London: Sidgwick and Jackson, 1951.

Russell, George W., ed. *New Songs*. Dublin: O'Donoghue, 1904.

Stewart, Bruce. "Alice Milligan." Princess Grace Irish Library (Monaco). Electronic Irish Records Dataset. http://www.pgil-eirdata.org/html/pgil_datasets/authors/m/Milligan,A. htm (2001).

Trotter, Mary. *Ireland's National Theaters: Political Performance and the Origins of the Irish Dramatic Movement*. Syracuse, NY: Syracuse University Press, 2001.

Weygandt, Cornelius. *Irish Plays and Playwrights*. Boston: Houghton Mifflin, 1913.

Yeats, William Butler. "The Irish Literary Theatre, 1900." *Beltaine* 2 (February 1900): 22–24.

———. *"The Last Feast of the Fianna, Maeve*, and *The Bending of the Bough* in Dublin." *Beltaine* 3 (April 1900): 4–6.

———. "Plans and Methods." *Beltaine* 2 (February 1900): 3–6.

———. "Windlestraws." *Samhain* 1. Dublin: Sealy, 1901. Reprint of nos. 1–7, London: Cass, 1970.

SUSAN L. MITCHELL

(1866–1926)

Paul Marchbanks

BIOGRAPHY

Susan L. Mitchell was born in 1866 in tiny Carrick-on-Shannon, County Leitrim, a town remembered fondly forty years later in her poem "Carrick." Her father's death when she was six led to her family's relocation to Sligo; she alone was removed to Dublin and there raised by two paternal aunts until a second move, to Birr, placed her under the care of a third aunt. In Mitchell's early thirties, an illness struck that eventually impaired her hearing; treatment of the ailment required yet another move, this time to London, where she stayed with the family of John B. Yeats, W. B. Yeats's father.

Soon after her illness, she joined artist and economist AE (George Russell) as assistant editor of the *Irish Homestead*, beginning a close friendship and professional relationship that would last until her death twenty-five years later. During this period, she created innumerable essays and poems—many published pseudonymously—for inclusion in the pages of the *Homestead* and then the *Irish Statesman*. While conjecture concerning the specific degree of intimacy between Mitchell and AE remains inconclusive, her death affected him profoundly. He felt her loss to such a degree that he found literary creation difficult for at least a year and, according to some, never did come to peace with her passing.

Professionally, their friendship was a mutually fruitful one. Mitchell's first poems appeared in publications edited by AE, and he provided support as she published two very different collections of her work in 1908. Though she never attained renown outside her Dublin circle, she proved a friend to many in the Irish Revival, her lampoons usually provoking only the intended chuckle from their subjects. George Moore proved a significant exception, his condescension toward Ireland earning him very tangible, poetic pokes from Mitchell, as well as a book-length portrait of the man and his works that was not a little acerbic.

She died at the age of sixty due to heart complications, removing from the Dublin literary scene one of the more independently honest checks on its growing tendency toward self-congratulation.

MAJOR WORKS AND THEMES

Mitchell's early artistic output was voluminous but largely invisible. In her editorial capacity at the *Freeman's Journal*, she helped AE quickly fill out with assorted essays what would have otherwise been a rather empty publication. This kind of work continued through to her death; that she wrote in the last two and a half years of her life close to two hundred pieces for AE's *Irish Statesman*—including assorted book and theater reviews—demonstrates the extent of her prolific output. Her familiar wit and comic sense teased all manner of subjects with a light but discerning touch, mocking in the same breath with which she praised. She considered a Brinsley MacNamara play to be depressing but illuminating, and concluded that G. B. Shaw's *St. Joan* was quite "alive" despite being rotund with every scrap of his "intellectual property down to the least egg-spoon" (Kain, 25–26, 27). In 1924, she vividly recalled the rioters at the Abbey's opening of *The Playboy of the Western World* (1907), comically remembering them as "ferocious defenders of our gentle characters" (Kain, 26).

Her poems first appeared in the holiday feature AE added to the *Irish Homestead* each year. *A Celtic Christmas* housed a number of her lyrics, such as the sombre "The Army of the Voice" (1902), "Ireland" (1905), and "Immortality" (1907), in addition to numerous unsigned satiric pieces. A few lyrics entered book form in *New Songs* (1904), a selection edited by AE that also included works by Padriac Colum and Alice Milligan. One of her more spontaneous and amusing verses, included in a pamphlet titled *THE ABBEY ROW, NOT Edited by W. B. Yeats* (a parody of a local theater journal overseen by Yeats), joined her friends' pieces in mocking those who had rioted at the opening of Synge's *Playboy* the night before. Mitchell's own jibe noted the inconsistency of those who, angered by the scandalous use of the word "shift," found no impropriety in attending "the Gaelic League, where men wear kilts" (Kain, 33).

The year 1908 became Mitchell's *annus mirabilis* when the successful *Aids to the Immortality of Certain Persons in Ireland* was quickly followed by *The Living Chalice*. The first collection laughed good-naturedly at everything from the suspect congratulations that Yeats and Lady Gregory gave one another in print to Yeats's notions concerning poetic drama and even to good friend AE's persistent mysticism. In "The Ballad of Shawe Taylor and Hugh Lane" she played with the 1905 furor over creating a municipal gallery for Dublin, and she poked hard that frequent exponent of British imperialism, Rudyard Kipling, in a parody of "Recessional" (1897) titled "Ode to the British Empire." Of prodigious length is a three-part ballad history of George Moore, Mitchell's target of choice. Here she satirized his self-aggrandizing professions of the distance between himself and the Catholic Irish people, not to mention his erratic and undependable support of the Gaelic language and the accompanying cultural revival. Nor does Moore's turn at mayor of County Mayo escape untouched. Still more comedy bookends the whole, including a sheet of upcoming titles such as *Supernatural Law in the Economic World* by AE and a sermon series by Edward Martyn entitled *Women of No Importance*, plus a faux group of rejected dedications and a list of characteristic foibles concerning such figures as Yeats and AE. A second edition of the collection appeared in 1913, complete with more satire of George Moore and his loud conversion to Protestantism, as well as two poems concerning the remembered *Playboy* crowd, one of which jabs at their facile conclusion that having a fictional Irishman commit fratricide somehow represents a slur on the nation's male population. The extended collection also included some serious poems such as the politically provocative "Ballad of Dermody and Hynes," which considers social injustice and Irish cowardice, and various others that bemoan English strictures on the Gaelic language or illuminate the growing discord between Ulster and the southern counties.

Mitchell's second collection, another that would be expanded and republished in 1913, assumed a more somber and this time spiritual tone as the Protestant poet explored her struggle to embrace a divine purpose. In the title poem the narrator mourns, with a cry akin to Lancelot's at the outset of the Grail quest, that the cup of life set at the biblical bridegroom's table has passed her by. The short poem ends, however, with an assertion that she has herself become the sought-after cup, one filled with the squeezed juice of her own life's pain, ready to be consumed by her God. In the next poem, "A Prayer," this "priestess of the Lord" requests heavenly inspiration. The words that follow throughout the collection accomplish a beautifully vivid reworking of Amergin's legendary oration, voice a distinct martial call to action, as in "To the Daughters of Erin" and "The Army of the Voice," and weave a bittersweet wreath of related Christmas lyrics.

Her engaging study of George Moore (1916) for the *Irishmen of Today* series placed analysis of the man and his art amid a colorful context of Mitchell's own reminiscences, coy commentary on other contributions to the series, and a sobering reflection on the devastating military response to the recent Easter 1916 rising. Mitchell's consideration of her central figure proves surprisingly balanced. Her longstanding dislike of Moore does indeed manifest itself; for instance, she criticizes *Hail and Farewell* (1911–14) for broadly mistreating Douglas Hyde and nearly all of his contemporaries, and she mocks Moore's grand public displays, which stirred nothing but his own hubris. To a chapter on his painting, she amusingly allots only two sentences. She does, however, praise much of his fiction. Though she maintains that women know far more than he about female character, she admits the warmth and strength of many of his heroines, including the well-known Esther Waters. *The Untilled Field* (1903) and *The Lake* (1905) also receive substantial praise as she lauds his temporary willingness to step outside his own pettiness. And given his obvious independence from most of Ireland's popular movements, she concludes that he could have injected a healthy dose of objectivity into the Irish consciousness, had his aspirations not been weighed down by arrogance.

Other memorable projects by Mitchell include *Leaguers and Peelers: or, The Apple Cart* (1911), a playlet that tackles the British proscription on using Irish Gaelic script in public places, and her organization in 1918 of an anthology of parodic, contemporary poetry that includes works by Oliver Gogarty, AE, and Lord Dunsany.

CRITICAL RECEPTION

AE's *New Songs* (1904), a book of poems by local writers, achieved a localized triumph. While Dubliners roundly praised it as a significant contribution to the Irish Revival, the new Londoner W. B. Yeats belittled AE's support of such amateurs and all but two of their poems; neither of the appreciated poems were by Mitchell. Yeats did elsewhere express, however, friendly regard for her work, including a parody of his "The Lake Isle of Innisfree" (1893), which begins "I will arise & run now and run to Grafton Street." Mitchell's *The Living Chalice* received commendation as a successful combination of "tenderness and beauty," in the words of the *Times Literary Supplement* (Kain, 76), and was supposed by the Dublin *Freeman's Journal* to have tapped into "the authentic sense of the deep mystery underlying the common things" (Kain, 76). The *Glasgow Herald* found in this, Mitchell's only wholly serious collection, that "Celtic" combination of the enigmatic and the sad, an emotional mix evoked by other female poets including Rose Kavanagh and Eva Gore-Booth (Kain, 15). Her study of George Moore found sympathetic readers in many who shared her disdain for Moore's congenital audacity, though one detractor, Douglas Goldring, thought her study too personal in nature (Kain, 85–86). AE's vocal defense of the book likely widened the gap between himself and its subject, as Moore was predictably offended by the book despite previous assertions that she could write "as she liked, take any liberties she would" (Joseph Hone, *The Life of George Moore* [New York: Macmillan, 1936], 330).

BIBLIOGRAPHY

Works by Susan L. Mitchell

Aids to the Immortality of Certain Persons in Ireland, Charitably Administered. Dublin: New Nation, 1908.
Christmas Poems. Privately printed, Christmas 1934. (With introductory poem, "In Memory of Susan Mitchell," by M. J. MacM[anus].)
Frankincense and Myrrh. Dublin: Cuala, 1912.
George Moore. Irishmen of To-Day series. Dublin: Maunsel, 1916.
"Leaguers and Peelers: or, The Apple Cart." *Irish Review* 1, no. 9 (October 1911): 390–406.
The Living Chalice and Other Poems, by Susan L. Mitchell, Being Number Six of the Tower Press Booklets, Second Series. Dublin: Maunsel, 1908.
Secret Springs of Dublin Song. Edited by Susan Mitchell. Dublin: Talbot, 1918. (An anthology of contemporary parodies.)

In Anthologies and Periodicals

AE, ed. *A Celtic Christmas*. (A holiday supplement to the *Irish Homestead*. Susan Mitchell contributed numerous poems in the years 1902–8.)
AE, ed. *New Songs . . . by Padriac Colum, Eva Gore-Booth, Thomas Keohler, Alice Milligan, Susan Mitchell, Seumas O'Sullivan, George Roberts, and Ella Young*. Dublin: O'Donoghue, 1904. (Susan Mitchell contributed five poems, including "Love's Mendicant.")
Cooke, John, ed. *The Dublin Book of Irish Verse*. Dublin: Hodges, Figgis, 1909. (Susan Mitchell contributed four poems, including "Amergin.")

Studies of Susan L. Mitchell

Bourke, Angela, Mairin Ni Dhonneadha, Siobhan Kilfeather, Maria Luddy, Margaret MacCurtain, Gerardine Meaney, Mary O'Dowd, and Clair Wills. "Susan Mitchell." In *The Field Day Anthology of Irish Writing*. Vols. 4 and 5, *Women's Writing and Traditions*, 568–69. New York: New York University Press, 2002.

Kain, Richard M. *Susan L. Mitchell*. Lewisburg: Bucknell University Press, 1972.

Pyle, Hilary. *Red-Headed Rebel, Susan L. Mitchell*. Dublin: Woodfield, 1998.

Russell, George W. "The Poetry of Susan Mitchell." *Irish Statesman*, March 27, 1926, 71–74.

Skelton, Robin. "Aide to Immortality: The Satirical Writings of Susan L. Mitchell." In *The World of W. B. Yeats: Essays in Perspective*, edited by Robin Skelton and Ann Saddlemeyer, 233–40. Dublin: Dolmen, 1965.

LADY MORGAN
(1776?–1859)

John J. Han

BIOGRAPHY

An enormously popular and controversial writer of the early nineteenth century, Lady Morgan (née Sydney Owenson) was born as the first child of Robert and Jane (née Hill) Owenson. Her father was an Irish actor–theatrical manager, and her mother was an English Methodist born of a tradesman. Exactly when and where Lady Morgan was born is unknown. One of the dates she provided is December 25, 1776, which is unverifiable. She was born either onboard ship or in Dublin. Morgan and her younger sister, Olivia, received a sporadic education at Protestant boarding schools near Dublin and finished school after their mother's death in 1789. As a student, Morgan read Shakespeare and Irish legends.

During 1798–1800, Morgan supported her family by working as a governess. Then, in 1801, she published her first work, *Poems, Dedicated by Permission to the Rt. Hon. Countess of Moira*, a volume of poetry. With the publication of her first novel, *St. Clair; or, the Heiress of Desmond* (1802), an imitation of Goethe's *Sorrows of Young Werther* (1774), she made writing her full-time occupation. The year 1805 saw the publication of *Twelve Original Hibernian Melodies, from the Works of the Ancient Irish Bards*, a collection of Irish songs, and of *The Novice of St. Dominick*, a historical novel set in sixteenth-century France.

Morgan's literary fame soared when she published the three-volume romance novel *The Wild Irish Girl* (1806), a nostalgic portrayal of Ireland's Gaelic past. Instantly Morgan became a literary and social celebrity in both Dublin and London, becoming popularly known as "Glorvina," the novel's Irish heroine. *The Wild Irish Girl* was followed by *The First Attempt; or, Whim of a Moment* (1807), a comic play; *Patriotic Sketches of Ireland* (1807), a collection of essays; *The Lay of an Irish Harp: or, Metrical Frag-*

ments (1807), a collection of ballads; and *Woman; or, Ida of Athens* (1809), a novel romanticizing a Greek heroine. *The Missionary: An Indian Tale* (1811), set in early colonial India, is a romantic novel condemning European imperialism and religious intolerance that inspired British romantic poets Lord Byron and Percy Bysshe Shelley. In 1812, she married English surgeon and philosopher Dr. Charles Morgan (later Sir Morgan). He shared Morgan's liberal nationalism, visited Europe with her three times, and coauthored some of her books. The couple had no children.

O'Donnel: A National Tale, a well-received novel focusing on Irish peasant life, came out in 1814. After the publication of *France* (1817), a travel narrative written after her visit to Paris, pro-English critics severely attacked Morgan for her nationalistic, liberal ideology. The *Quarterly Review* was at the forefront in those attacks. John Wilson Croker, a Munster barrister who had been at odds with Morgan since 1804, published a lengthy, malicious critique of *France* in the *Review*. Despite attacks by Tory publications, Morgan's popularity did not waver. She was paid 1,200 pounds by her publisher for the next novel, *Florence Macarthy: An Irish Tale* (1818). The success of *France* allowed her to write a similar book, *Italy*, which, when it came out in 1821, encountered another attack by Croker. In *The O'Briens and the O'Flahertys: A National Tale* (1827), a novel about the 1798 rebellion, Morgan continued to express her radical political ideas. Alarmed by her anti-English, anti-Protestant views, the British government put the Morgans under constant surveillance. *The Book of the Boudoir*, comprising Morgan's autobiographical sketches, came out in 1829. According to the author, *Passages from My Autobiography* (1859) is a trivial hodgepodge.

In 1837, Morgan's literary popularity earned her the honor of becoming the first woman writer to receive a literary pension (300 pounds) from the British government despite its recent suspicions; the citation commended her services to literature and to patriotism. In the same year, Morgan and her husband moved to London, where she devoted most of her time to social activities until her death in 1859. Her *Memoirs: Autobiographies, Diaries, and Correspondences* was published in two volumes in 1862.

MAJOR WORKS AND THEMES

Morgan's novels typically romanticize the Irish past, advance the Irish Nationalist cause, advocate Catholic emancipation, and promote democratic ideals. Among many of her works, the so-called Irish novels—*The Wild Irish Girl*, *O'Donnel*, *Florence Macarthy*, and *The O'Briens and the O'Flahertys*—are considered major. *The Wild Irish Girl* is an epistolary novel narrated by a young Anglo-Irish law student named Horatio. The son of an English lord, he comes to Ireland with a confirmed prejudice about the land and its people. His extended stay in Ireland confirms, however, that ideas received and formed in childhood can be erroneous. Learning to appreciate the natural landscape, cultural heritage, and language of Ireland, he discovers that the Irish are not semibarbarous and semicivilized people lacking graces that distinguish refined society. Horatio's romantic encounter with the Irish girl Glorvina—modeled after the author herself—is particularly enlightening to him: his own ancestors ruined the fortunes of Glorvina's royal family. The novel focuses not only on the ancient manners, modes, customs, and language of the Irish, but also on the root causes of Irish poverty and misery.

The historical romance *O'Donnel* is regarded as one of the first English novels to cast a governess as the protagonist. Miss Charlotte O'Halloran, the orphan of an Irish musician, marries a wealthy English duke, but he dies several weeks after the wedding.

Then she marries Roderick O'Donnel, and they regain his ancestral lands with the help of Lord Glenworth, an English Whig. In this novel, Morgan celebrates the rise of Ireland from silence, oblivion, and paralysis. She represents Irish aristocrats as Roman Catholics, defying the widely accepted notion that the ruling classes are Protestants. In this work, Morgan not only reclaims Ireland as a Catholic nation but also promotes her radical political ideology.

In *Florence Macarthy*, Morgan attempts to reconcile Catholics and Protestants. Lady Clancare, a Gael, is married to Fitzwater, a Norman; together they fight against Conway Crawley—a satiric rendering of John Wilson Croker, one of her most infamous critics—and his family. Crawley, who emerges as a venomous traitor collaborating with British imperialists, is a pretentious, arrogant, and pitiful person who is willing to trample on a frail woman or commit character assassination to seek his fortune.

The O'Briens and the O'Flahertys explores Irish political and religious factionalism at the end of the eighteenth century by focusing on the descendants of various ancient clans, including those of the O'Briens and the O'Flahertys. One of the characters, Murrough O'Brien, follows Lord Walter Fitzgerald, a passionate nationalist. Determining that a Catholic struggle against English colonial rule is futile, he turns to the strategy advocated by the Protestant Whig Henry Grattan, and then to the United Irishmen, the militant society formed by Wolfe Tone in 1791. The armed insurrection by the United Irishmen is quickly defeated, and O'Brien leaves Ireland for a military career in continental Europe. Unlike the O'Briens, characterized by fiery patriotism, the O'Flahertys embrace the ideals of nonviolence, order, and hierarchy.

CRITICAL RECEPTION

During her lifetime, Morgan's nationalistic fiction was popular in Ireland as well as in England and continental Europe. She had admirers in such contemporary writers as Sir Walter Scott, Percy Bysshe Shelley, Maria Edgeworth, and Lord Byron. At the same time, Morgan was under harsh attacks from Tory critics who regarded her radical ideology dangerous. Reviewing *Woman: or, Ida of Athens*, for instance, William Gifford dismisses the story as "merely foolish." According to Gifford, the novel's style and grammar are pitiable; its sentiments are "mischievous," "profligate," and "licentious and irreverent in the highest degree"; and the author's object of worship is Nature, not the creator of the universe (52). John Wilson Croker launches even more vicious attacks on Morgan and her works. In his 1817 review of *France*, published anonymously, he criticizes the book by pointing to bad grammar, blasphemy, indecency, and prerevolutionary ideology. He contends, "One merit, however, the title has—it is appropriate to the volume which it introduces, for to falsehood it adds the other qualities of the work,—vagueness, bombast, and affectation" (260). Then he compares her to John Hobhouse, author of the *Letters from Paris* (n.d.), both of whom promote "the reign of rebellion, plunder, and blood" (285).

Since the beginning of the twentieth century, critics have generally regarded Morgan as an important figure in early Irish fiction as well as in the political and cultural history of modern Ireland. However, Morgan's works have always received—and perhaps always will receive—mixed critical reception. George Paston discusses Morgan as one of the five minor celebrities of the nineteenth century. Despite her passion for high society, Paston notes, Morgan championed the cause of liberty and spoke for the oppressed (155). Pointing out that Morgan's life was more interesting than her art, Clara H. Whitmore contrasts her with Maria Edgeworth, who "has described the customs and manners of Ireland, and unfolded the character of its people in a manner that has never been equaled. But Lady Morgan, far inferior as an artist, has given fuller and more picturesque descriptions of the landscape of the country, and has made a valuable addition to the books bearing on the history of Ireland" (131–32). Thomas Flanagan, author of *The Irish Novelists, 1800–1850* (1959), considers Morgan one of the top five Irish novelists—alongside Maria Edgeworth, John Banim, Gerard Griffin, and William Carleton—in the first half of the nineteenth century. According to Flanagan, "Lady Morgan's novels afford us an understanding of the way in which cultural and political myth was created in nineteenth-century Ireland, and of the uses to which writers put the romantic conception of an immemorial Irish 'nation' " (47). Colin B. Atkinson and Jo Atkinson maintain that Lady Morgan takes an "honorable place" in literary history although she is not as significant as such women writers as Jane Austen or Charlotte Bronte (90). Seamus Deane observes that two women—Maria Edgeworth and Lady Morgan—"dominate Irish fiction in the first half of the nineteenth century" (90). Mary Campbell defends Morgan's significance in Irish literary history by pointing to her feminist and nationalist themes: "The role of woman in society and the rights of small nations to independence were her themes, and in spite of archaic language, pedantry and story telling tricks her concept of these two major issues is relevant, modern—and valid" (240). James M. Cahalan also comments that "the first major breakthroughs in the Irish novel were the fruits of the labors of two women, Maria Edgeworth and Sydney Owenson" (3). James Newcomer comments on the literary and historical significance of Morgan's works: "They exhibit a realistic understanding of troubled Ireland and a burning authentic impulse toward its betterment. It would be a loss to the Irish cause and to English letters if all that was left to us of Lady Morgan's generous writings were her name" (86). Kathryn Kirkpatrick notes that Morgan's novel not only "originates and predicts an Irish nationalism that perpetuates the violence from which it was born" but also "suggests a possible solution: a violent forgiveness" (xviii).

Despite a renewed interest in Morgan's life, works, and ideology, she has never recovered the kind of widespread popularity she enjoyed in her lifetime. Although new editions of *The Wild Irish Girl* (in 1999) and *The Missionary* (in 2002) have appeared, most of Morgan's works remain out of print. Fortunately, hypertexts of *The Wild Irish Girl*, *The Lay of an Irish Harp*, *O'Donnel*, and *Passages from My Autobiography* (excerpts) are available online.

BIBLIOGRAPHY

Works by Lady Morgan

Absenteeism. London: Colburn, 1825.
The Book of the Boudoir. 2 vols. London: Colburn, 1829. (With Sir Charles Morgan.)
The Book without a Name. 2 vols. London: Colburn, 1841. (With Sir Charles Morgan.)
Dramatic Scenes of Real Life. 2 vols. London: Saunders and Otley, 1833.
The First Attempts; or Whim of a Moment. London: Phillips, 1807.
Florence Macarthy: An Irish Tale. 4 vols. London: Colburn, 1818.
France. 2 vols. London: Colburn, 1817.
France in 1829–1830. 2 vols. London: Saunders and Otley, 1830.
Irish National Tales and Romances. London: Colburn, 1833.
Italy. 2 vols. London: Colburn, 1821. (With Sir Charles Morgan.)
Lady Morgan's Memoirs: Autobiographies, Diaries, and Correspondence. 2 vols. Edited by W. Hepworth Dixon. London: Allen, 1862.
The Lay of an Irish Harp: or, Metrical Fragments. London: Phillips, 1807.
Letter to Cardinal Wiseman. London: Westerton, 1851.

The Life and Times of Salvator Rosa. 2 vols. London: Colburn, 1824.
Luxima: A Tale of India. Revision of *The Missionary.* London: Westerton, 1859.
The Missionary: An Indian Tale. 3 vols. London: Stockdale, 1811.
The Novice of St. Dominick. 4 vols. London: Phillips, 1805.
The O'Briens and the O'Flahertys: A National Tale. 4 vols. London: Colburn, 1827.
An Odd Volume Extracted from an Autobiography. London: Bentley, 1859.
O'Donnel: A National Tale. 3 vols. London: Colburn, 1814.
Passages from My Autobiography. London: Bentley, 1859.
Patriotic Sketches of Ireland. 2 vols. London: Phillips, 1807.
Poems, Dedicated by Permission to the Rt. Hon. Countess of Moira. Dublin: Stewart, 1801.
The Princess; or, the Benguine. 3 vols. London: Bentley, 1835.
St. Clair; or, the Heiress of Desmond. London: Harding, 1802.
Twelve Original Hibernian Melodies. London: Preston, 1805.
The Wild Irish Girl: A National Tale. 3 vols. London: Phillips, 1806.
Woman and Her Master. 2 vols. London: Colburn, 1840.
Woman; or, Ida of Athens. 4 vols. London: Longman, 1809.

Studies of Lady Morgan

Atkinson, Colin B., and Jo Atkinson. "Sydney Owenson, Lady Morgan: Irish Patriot and First Professional Woman Writer." *Éire-Ireland* 15, no. 2 (Summer 1980): 60–90.
Cahalan, James M. *The Irish Novel: A Critical History.* Boston: Twayne, 1988.
Campbell, Mary. *Lady Morgan: The Life and Times of Sydney Owenson.* London: Pandora, 1988.
[Croker, John Wilson]. Review of *France*, by Lady Morgan. *Quarterly Review* 17 (1817): 260–86.
Deane, Seamus. *A Short History of Irish Literature.* Notre Dame, IN: University of Notre Dame Press, 1986.
Flanagan, Thomas. *The Irish Novelists, 1800–1850.* New York: Columbia University Press, 1959.
Gifford, William. Review of *Woman; or, Ida of Athens. Quarterly Review* 1 (1809): 50–52.
Kirkpatrick, Kathryn. *The Wild Irish Girl*, by Sydney Owenson, Lady Morgan. Edited with an introduction and notes by Kathryn Kirkpatrick. New York: Oxford University Press, 1999, vii–xviii.
Newcomer, James. *Lady Morgan the Novelist.* Lewisburg, PA: Bucknell University Press, 1990.
Paston, George. "Lady Morgan (Sydney Owenson)." In *Little Memoirs of the Nineteenth Century.* New York: Dutton, 1902, 95–155.
Whitmore, Clara H. *Woman's Work in English Fiction.* New York: Putnam's Sons, 1910.

VAL MULKERNS
(1925–   )

Virginia B. Mack

BIOGRAPHY

Val Mulkerns was born in Dublin to Esther (née O'Neill) and James Mulkerns. She attended the Dominican School on Eccles Street and upon completion of secondary school was employed as a temporary worker for the Irish civil service. During this time she began reading at the National Library at night and writing, mostly short stories in English, although she speaks Irish. In 1949, she left Ireland and went abroad, spending most of her time in England. After returning to Ireland in 1952, she was hired by Peadar O'Donnell as associate editor of the *Bell* (1952–54). Speaking of Mulkerns's role on the *Bell* and in the fight against censorship, James Plunkett, a close friend, characterized her as "involved with the rest of us [Sean O'Faolain, Frank O'Connor, Peadar O'Donnell] in trying to disperse the fog of obscurantism, 'hypocritical pietism in religion' [he uses O'Faolain's language here], censorship, lay priests, and traditionalism" (Plunkett, letter to the author, May 23, 1995). At the time of her employment on the *Bell* she had published a novel, *A Time Outworn* (1951), and five short stories and was writing a second novel, *A Peacock Cry* (1954). She now dismisses her early novels as "juvenilia" (Plunkett, letter). She married Maurice Kennedy in 1953, and soon after their marriage they moved to a home on Garville Road in Rathgar, where they lived for the rest of their married life. Their first child, Maeve, was born in 1954, at about the same time the *Bell* ceased publication and *A Peacock Cry* was published. A second child, Conor, was born in 1958, and a third, Myles, in 1959.

After her marriage and the birth of Maeve, Mulkerns's publication pattern shifted and literary production slowed. Instead she published book reviews in the *Irish Times*, and from 1969 to 1983 she wrote a weekly column for the *Evening Press*. In 1976 she began contributing to Irish Radio's *Sunday Miscellany*—a practice that she still continues. She also wrote fiction, dating the composition of some of the short stories of this period as early as 1965 (Mulkerns, interview with the author, July 23, 1997). However, none were published until the late 1960s, when David Marcus included the first of five in his "New Irish Writing" section of *The Irish Press*. She was awarded the A.I.B. Prize for Literature in 1984 for the publication of *Antiquities* (1978), *An Idle Woman* (1980), and *The Summerhouse* (1984). In 1992, her husband died after a long illness. She has edited a collection of his works with a critical introduction by Augustine Martin. In 1996, Mulkerns sold her house on Garville Avenue and moved to Dalkey, where she lives in a smaller house with a view of the sea.

MAJOR WORKS AND THEMES

Mulkerns was especially close to her father, James "Red" Mulkerns, who was in the garrison in the Four Courts during the Easter Rising and was subsequently interned at Frongoch in Wales. Because of her family's Nationalist political connections, her own involvement in the fight against censorship via her work on the *Bell,* and her own continuing interest in issues of importance to the Irish state as evidenced by the prevalence of direct Nationalist themes in her work, Mulkerns can clearly be regarded as a writer concerned with nationalism. She is equally concerned with questions of developing identity and of the woman artist's development in the New Irish State.

Mulkerns's first novel, *A Time Outworn*, was very well received. An excerpt from it appeared in *Harper's Bazaar* in August 1952, with an introduction by Frank O'Connor, who called it "the most interesting and significant [novel] to have come out of Ireland in twenty-five years" and referred to the young writer as "the first artistic voice of the post-Revolutionary generation" (110). The novel, set in Ireland in the late 1940s, is narrated by a young writer, Maeve Cusack. The plot traces Maeve's journey from Dublin to a small town in Tipperary and then to the West of Ireland. Next appeared *A Peacock Cry*, which is set in Connemarra and partially narrated by a fourteen-year-old girl, Clare Joyce. Clare is called "County Clare" by her siblings, suggesting a close relationship between character and place. The novel contains some of Mulkerns's best descriptions of place but it drew hardly any attention from critics.

The second major period of Mulkerns's writing is marked by the publication of *Antiquities*. In "An Irishman's Diary" Mulkerns said that *Antiquities* has three major themes: "the death of Romantic nationalism, the interaction of different generations in families on one another, and the vanishing of a physical Dublin that [she] knew as a child" (15). These three themes and the conflicting loyalties implicit in them form the core of her work in the second major phase. The collection is comprised of ten linked short stories set primarily in Dublin and spanning the period from 1916 to approximately 1978. In it, Mulkerns presents three generations of the Mullens family which, like her own, is closely linked to the New Irish State. The keystone story, "Special Category," is set after the 1916 rising at a prison in Cheshire where the grandfather has been interned; "The Torch," another story, tells of the murder of the granddaughter by the IRA. The first story in the collection, "A Bitch and a Dog Hanging," is included in *The Field Day Anthology* (vol. 3, 989–93).

Antiquities was followed by *An Idle Woman*, a collection of short stories set in Dublin in the late 1960s and 1970s. In three of these, Mulkerns explores the woman's relationship as writer to the literary establishment. The first woman, Theresa, in "The Open House," is a young woman who convinces her husband to buy a writer's house in fashionable South Dublin, thinking that she will also be able to move into his lifestyle. However, once inside she is again established in her wifely role, the "real" writers having abandoned the premises. The second, Mona Ambrose, in "You Must Be Joking," is a popular writer of "blockbuster" novels. She has fashioned for herself a pose that is based on a male role, characterized as a contemporary version of "Stage Irishry," and critiqued previously in Mulkerns's work in her representation of Dara Joyce in *A Peacock Cry*. Rosemary, the third, in "Still Life," is a wife who breaks free of the aesthetic standards of the critical male establishment. Thus these figures suggest three different stages of evolution in the development of the woman writer in relationship to the national tradition.

An Idle Woman was followed by *The Summerhouse*. The story takes place between the mid-1920s and the early 1970s and is told by five narrators from five different perspectives. It is set in the family home of the O'Donohues near Waterford, but memories of narrators take the reader back to the founding of the family, just as *Antiquities* takes the reader back to the founding moments of that family. Mulkerns uses the image of the house to explore ways in which people, and especially women, have been trapped in the male-determined space of the nation.

In *Very Like a Whale* (1986), Mulkerns turns to the twin themes of the movement of the woman away from the family and the environmental decay of Dublin. Set in Dublin in 1984, this novel of personal development juxtaposes options for the woman against options for Dublin itself as a major European city. The story is introduced from the perspective of twenty-seven-year-old Ben Ryan, whose return to Dublin after four years abroad is marked by great changes in both his family and the city. In his absence, his parents have separated, sold the family home, and moved to apartments. From Ben's perspective, Mulkerns shows us the problems of unemployment, drug abuse, poverty, and environmental damage that accompany economic growth. Through the novel we see Olivia, Ben's mother, growing away from Denis, her husband, and toward Stephen, her lover, until the novel concludes with her departure.

A Friend of Don Juan (1988), Mulkerns's latest collection, consists of thirteen stories in which she expands on her exploration of the efforts of the woman to gain access to the national tradition. In a significant step forward, the collection presents an argument for inclusion of minority voices into Irish identity. These groups include the older, unmarried woman in "The Zoological Gardens" and unwed mothers seeking abortions in "A Summer in London." They also extend beyond the realm of gender to religion, focusing on the Jewish minority in "A Friend of Don Juan," the Protestant minority in "End of the Line," and homosexuality in the priesthood in "Honda Ward."

CRITICAL RECEPTION

After Frank O'Connor's championing of *A Time Outworn*, little was said of Mulkerns's work until just before the publication of *Antiquities,* when a substantial interview by Caroline Walsh appeared in the *Irish Times.* James O'Brien compares her short stories in *Antiquities* to those of Maura Treacy and Kate Cruise O'Brien, focusing on the theme of social change and social values in the work of all three. Robert Hogan is also concerned with Mulkerns's short stories, comparing them favorably to those of Edna O'Brien. John Jordan, on the other hand, looks at Mulkerns's work within the context of other writers associated with the *Bell.* He especially praises "Memory and Desire" (from *An Idle Woman*), a story that deals with a homosexual attraction, saying Mulkerns's treatment of the theme illustrates the "creative force of understatement" (140).

Criticism of *Very like a Whale* looks at Mulkerns's work in relationship to that of novels by men. Katie Donovan, for example, compares it to Desmond Hogan's *The Ikon Maker* (1976). In a book-length study, Ulrike Paschel compares the environmental themes in *Very like a Whale* to the novels of Dermot Bolger and Roddy Doyle. Virginia Mack looks at diverse, normally incompatible, cultural elements, especially various aspects of gender and national identity in the novels and short stories.

BIBLIOGRAPHY

Works by Val Mulkerns

Antiquities: *A Sequence of Short Stories*. London: Deutsch, 1978.
A Friend of Don Juan. London: Murray, 1988.
An Idle Woman. Dublin: Poolbeg, 1980.
"An Irishman's Diary." Val Mulkerns comments upon *Antiquities*. *Irish Times*, May 20, 1978, 15.
A Peacock Cry. London: Hodder and Stoughton, 1954.
The Summerhouse. London: Murray, 1984.
A Time Outworn. London: Chatto and Windus, 1951.
Very Like a Whale. London: Murray, 1986.

Studies of Val Mulkerns

Donovan, Katie. *Irish Women Writers: Marginalized by Whom?* Letters from the New Ireland Series. Dublin: Raven Arts, 1988.
Hogan, Robert. "Old Boys, Young Bucks, and New Women: The Contemporary Irish Short Story." In *The Irish Short Story: A Critical History*, edited by James F. Kilroy, 169–215. Boston: Twayne, 1984.

Jordan, John. "The Short Story After the Second World War." In *The Genius of Irish Prose*, edited by Augustine Martin, 131–44. Dublin: Mercier, 1985.

Mack, Virginia B. "Challenging the Authority of the Lonely Voice: Val Mulkerns and the Technique of Radical Ambiguity." In *New Voices in Irish Criticism 3*, edited by Karen Vandevelde, 94–101. Dublin: Four Courts, 2002.

O'Brien, James. "Three Irish Women Story Writers of the 1970's." In *Literature and the Changing Ireland*, edited by Peter Connolly, 199–205. Gerrards Cross, UK: Smythe, 1982.

O'Connor, Frank. "A Tribute to Val Mulkerns." *Harpers Bazaar*, August 1952, 110.

Paschel, Ulrike. *No Mean City: The Image of Dublin in the Novels of Dermot Bolger, Roddy Doyle, and Val Mulkerns*. New York: Lang, 1998, 161–70.

Walsh, Caroline. "Saturday Interview: Caroline Walsh Talks to Novelist and Short-Story Writer Val Mulkerns." *Irish Times*, June 11, 1977, 11.

IRIS MURDOCH
(1919–1999)

Lisa Weihman

BIOGRAPHY

Iris Murdoch, philosopher and author of twenty-six novels, was born at 59 Blessington Street, Dublin, the only child of Anglo-Irish Protestant parents. Her father, Wills John Hughes Murdoch, was a cavalry officer during World War I, and later a civil servant in London; her mother, Irene Alice Richardson, known as Rene, was trained as an opera singer, but abandoned her career upon marriage. The family moved to London shortly after Iris's birth, first to Hammersmith and then to Chiswich. The family remained in close contact with relatives in Ireland throughout Iris's childhood, and as an only child, Iris was fascinated by the large, complex network of relatives in both Dublin and Belfast, whom she visited during school holidays. Peter Conradi's authorized biography of Murdoch begins with a chapter titled, "You Ask How Irish She Is?"—a fair question, given her short term of residence. Conradi's considered answer to this question is that it pleased Murdoch to be thought of as an Irish writer, and that she valued the association quite highly: "I'm *nothing* if not Irish," she remarked in later life. Ireland and Irishness are, Conradi claims, "a reference-point, a credential, somewhere to start out from and return to" (Conradi, 29). Blessington Street and her Irish relations inform her one historical novel set in Ireland, *The Red and the Green* (1965), which recounts one complicated family's relationships in the week leading up to the Easter Rising.

Murdoch was educated at the Froebel Demonstration School, Badminton, and then Oxford from 1938 to 1942, where she studied classics and briefly joined the Communist Party. In spite of later disillusionment and withdrawal from the party, her membership prevented her from studying in the United States in 1947. Murdoch worked for the Treasury in London from 1942 to 1944, and then with refugee relief through the

United Nations Relief and Rehabilitation Administration in Austria and Belgium, from 1944 to 1946. The experience of working with displaced persons in postwar Europe haunts her novels, and issues of personal, political, and intellectual exile or isolation are common themes in her work. In 1947, Murdoch attended Cambridge to study philosophy under Wittgenstein; a year later, she accepted a fellowship at St. Anne's College, Oxford, where she remained until 1963. From 1963 on, Murdoch devoted herself to writing, apart from a four-year lectureship at the Royal College of Art. Murdoch's experiences at Oxford, at Cambridge, and in postwar Europe connected her with many of the great minds of her day, including Raymond Queneau, Simone de Beauvoir, and Elias Canetti, with whom she had a love affair—one of many affairs with both men and women, including a serious attachment to the poet Franz Steiner. Murdoch married John Bayley in 1954, and the two remained together for the rest of her life. Bayley, a novelist and lecturer in English at Oxford, has written two memoirs of the marriage: *A Memoir of Iris Murdoch* (1998; published in the United States as *Elegy for Iris*, 2001) and *Iris and Her Friends* (2000). Both works focus on Murdoch's decline and eventual death in 1999 from Alzheimer's disease, and form the basis for the movie *Iris* (2001), directed by Richard Eyre and starring Kate Winslet and Dame Judi Dench.

MAJOR WORKS AND THEMES

Murdoch began writing in early childhood but did not conceive of herself as a novelist until after the war. *Under the Net* appeared in 1954, following Murdoch's first published work, a critical study of Sartre, whom she met in 1944. Murdoch's novels range across a wide literary terrain, from romances such as *The Sandcastle* (1957) to religious fables such as *The Bell* (1958) and *The Time of Angels* (1966). Psychoanalysis and sexual infidelity meet in *A Severed Head* (1961), which she adapted for the stage with J.B. Priestly and which was later made into a film. As with most novelists of her generation, the devastation of World War II and its aftermath are evident in her recurring themes, which include the abnegation of the self in the search for the Good, the journey toward spiritual enlightenment, the costs of emotional and political fanaticism, and the power structures that influence human behavior. Her most successful novels feature first-person male narrators, most notably in the Booker Prize–winning *The Sea, The Sea* (1978), which chronicles the moral choices and personal relationships of Charles Arrowby, a mercurial retired actor-director from the London theater scene who attempts to write his memoirs and rewrite his life. *The Sea, The Sea*, which is reminiscent of Shakespeare's *The Tempest*, is a mix of realism and gothic convention. Arrowby, a latter-day Prospero, seeks asylum by the sea but finds himself literally and figuratively haunted by his past and his own self-knowledge. As in many of Murdoch's novels, the characters are searching for large philosophical ideals by which to live their lives or make sense of their existence, and the subtext of much of Murdoch's work is the influence and power that people have on one another. Joyce Carol Oates comments that Murdoch's obsession is "*Self* as blinding, crippling, paralyzing, ludicrous: this seems to be Murdoch's position. She has said that the greatest art, like that of Shakespeare, is impersonal; it contemplates and delineates nature with a 'clear eye,' untainted by fantasy. Why subjectivity and even the private self's fantasies should be so abhorred by Murdoch, and denied a place, a weight, in the cosmos (for surely it is as "real" as the material world, or the collective fantasies we call culture), is never altogether clear in her philosophical writings or in her fiction" (186). Oates sees Plato's allegory of the cave as central to any understanding of Murdoch's work.

Another key influence on Murdoch's work is the power of myth in shaping one's personality and ethical responsibilities. One can trace the influence of Yeats in this respect, both artistically and personally; Murdoch finds Yeats's use of mythology attractive, and his diverse uses of Anglo-Irish ascendancy values echo in her own depictions of Ireland in her works. Ireland haunts many of Murdoch's novels, and in the 1950s she referred to the place as "something of a dream country where everything happens with a difference" (Conradi, 447). The Joycean short story "Something Special" represents the Dublin of her youth, the first draft of *A Severed Head* is set in the West of Ireland, and County Clare lies behind the fairytale gothic of *The Unicorn* (1963). Murdoch's only venture into the world of historical fiction is *The Red and the Green* (1965). The action chronicles the family of Andrew Chase-White, an Anglo-Irish cavalry officer awaiting active duty in World War I, whose mother, Hilda, follows an "atavistic" urge to abandon life in London for the suburbs of Dublin: " 'We Anglo-Irish families are so complex,' Hilda used often to exclaim with a kind of pride, as if complexity in families were a rare privilege. 'We're practically incestuous,' his Aunt Millicent had once added" (12). Literally incestuous, Dame Millicent Kinnard, Anglo-Irish mistress of Rathblane House and a posh Upper Mount Street address, is a ferocious interpretation of Cathleen ni Houlihan as femme fatale. The cigar-smoking, pistol-waving Millie hides a cache of weapons for Pat Dumay, a soldier in the Volunteer forces whose fanatical mix of self-loathing and preening self-regard leads to his martyrdom in the rising. There is a lot of Constance Markievicz in Murdoch's portrayal of Millie, who trades the remnants of ascendancy privilege to follow Pat Dumay into battle at Boland's Mills and ends the novel in poverty. Pat's ascetic, homoerotic impulses are channeled into a blind devotion to an Ireland that exists purely as a representation of his own will. Murdoch grapples with the psychology of totalitarian leadership, creating in Pat Dumay a character both repulsive and dangerously attractive.

CRITICAL RECEPTION

Iris Murdoch's long and prolific career attracted early and consistent attention from literary critics. The critic and novelist A. S. Byatt's *Degrees of Freedom: The Novels of Iris Murdoch* (1965) is the first major critical text, covering the first seven novels; Barbara Stevens Heusel argues in *Iris Murdoch's Paradoxical Novels: Thirty Years of Critical Reception* (2001) that Byatt's work is the "Ur-text" of Murdoch criticism (20). Like that of most early critics, Byatt's work addresses the degree to which Murdoch can be called a "philosophical" novelist and attempts to situate her work within a modernist rather than an emerging postmodernist canon. The first American book of criticism, Peter Wolfe's *The Disciplined Heart: Iris Murdoch and Her Novels* (1966), continued the conversation begun by Byatt regarding Murdoch's philosophical preoccupations. Wolfe finds that ethics and morality are "never presented as abstract doctrine" and thus partially refutes the notion that Murdoch is "philosophical" in the manner of Mann or Sartre (Wolfe, 34). Heusel outlines three distinct phases in Murdoch criticism: the "definitions" phase, from Byatt's text through Frank Baldanza's *Iris Murdoch* (1974), which is largely concerned with defining terms such as "philosophical novelist" and "realist"; a reappraisal of this approach by Richard Todd in *Iris Murdoch* (1984), among others, along with the ascendancy of Peter Conradi's concept of

Murdoch as a "moral psychologist," which characterizes Murdoch criticism in the 1980s; and a third phase of postmodern and gender analyses beginning with Elizabeth Dipple's and Deborah Johnson's studies in the late 1980s through the 1990s (Heusel, 8). An appreciation of paradox and ambiguity are central to any understanding of Murdoch's novels, which can be characterized as "philosophical" insofar as their primary preoccupations across the decades are an investigation into the nature of goodness and the limits of and responsibilities inherent in subjectivity. The formal experimentation of the late novels is of particular interest to postmodern critics, who look at her use of fragmentation, supernatural themes, and magical realism. As Heusel comments, "Murdoch's habit of writing novels to solve problems has left critics a rich heritage that cries out for continued critical analysis" (166).

Murdoch is widely regarded as the finest novelist of her generation, and she won many awards, including the James Tait Black Memorial Prize for *The Black Prince* in 1973, the Whitbread Literary Award for Fiction for *The Sacred and Profane Love Machine* in 1974, and the Booker Prize for *The Sea, The Sea* in 1978. She was named a Dame of the Order of the British Empire and the Royal Society of Literature's Companion of Literature in 1987, and Foreign Honorary Member of the American Academy of Arts and Sciences (1982), as well as receiving a National Arts Clubs Medal of Honor for literature (1990).

BIBLIOGRAPHY

Works by Iris Murdoch

Novels

An Accidental Man. London: Chatto and Windus, 1971.
The Bell. London: Chatto and Windus, 1958.
The Book and the Brotherhood. London: Chatto and Windus, 1987.
Bruno's Dream. London: Chatto and Windus, 1969.
A Fairly Honourable Defeat. London: Chatto and Windus, 1970.
The Flight from the Enchanter. London: Chatto and Windus, 1956.
The Good Apprentice. London: Chatto and Windus, 1985.
The Green Knight. London: Chatto and Windus, 1993.
Henry and Cato. London: Chatto and Windus, 1976.
The Italian Girl. London: Chatto and Windus, 1964.
Jackson's Dilemma. London: Chatto and Windus, 1995.
The Message to the Planet. London: Chatto and Windus, 1989.
The Nice and the Good. London: Chatto and Windus, 1968.
Nuns and Soldiers. London: Chatto and Windus, 1980.
The Philosopher's Pupil. London: Chatto and Windus, 1983.
The Red and the Green. London: Chatto and Windus, 1965.
The Sacred and Profane Love Machine. London: Chatto and Windus, 1974.
The Sandcastle. London: Chatto and Windus, 1957.
The Sea, The Sea. London: Chatto and Windus, 1978.
A Severed Head. London: Chatto and Windus, 1961.
Something Special (1957). London: Chatto and Windus, 1999.
The Time of the Angels. London: Chatto and Windus, 1966.
Under the Net. London: Chatto and Windus, 1954.
The Unicorn. London: Chatto and Windus, 1963.

An Unofficial Rose. London: Chatto and Windus, 1962.
A Word Child. London: Chatto and Windus, 1975.

Plays

The Italian Girl. London: French, 1968. (With James Saunders.)
Joanna Joanna: A Play in Two Acts. London: Colophon with Old Town, 1994.
The One Alone. London: Colophon with Old Town, 1995.
The Servants: Opera in Three Acts. London: Oxford University Press, 1981. (Libretto by Murdoch; music by William Mathias.)
A Severed Head: A Play in Three Acts. London: Chatto and Windus, 1964. (With J. B. Priestly).
Three Plays: The Black Prince, The Servants and the Snow, The Three Arrows. London: Chatto and Windus, 1973.

Poetry

Poems. Edited by Yozo Muroya and Paul Hullah. Okayama, Japan: University Education Press, 1997.
A Year of Birds. London: Chatto and Windus, 1978.

Philosophy

Acastos: Two Platonic Dialogues. London: Chatto and Windus, 1986; New York: Viking, 1987.
Existentialists and Mystics: Writings on Philosophy and Literature. Edited by Peter Conradi. London: Chatto and Windus, 1997; New York: Allen Lane, 1998.
The Existentialist Political Myth. Birmingham: Delos, 1989.
The Fire and the Sun: Why Plato Banished the Artists. 1977. New York: Viking, 1990.
Metaphysics as a Guide to Morals. London: Chatto and Windus, 1992; New York: Allen Lane/Penguin, 1993.
Sartre, Romantic Rationalist. 1953. London: Chatto and Windus; New York: Viking, 1987.
The Sovereignty of Good and Other Concepts. Cambridge: Cambridge University Press, 1967.

Studies of Iris Murdoch

Antonaccio, Maria. *Picturing the Human: The Moral Thought of Iris Murdoch*. Oxford: Oxford University Press, 2000.
Baldanza, Frank. *Iris Murdoch*. New York: Twayne, 1974.
Bayley, John. *Iris and Her Friends*. New York: Norton, 2000.
———. *Iris: A Memoir of Iris Murdoch*. London: Duckworth, 1998; London: Abacus, 2000. Published in the United States as *Elegy for Iris*. New York: St. Martin's, 2001.
Bove, Cheryl Browning. *Understanding Iris Murdoch*. Columbia: University of South Carolina Press, 1993.
Byatt, A. S. *Degrees of Freedom: The Novels of Iris Murdoch*. New York: Barnes and Noble, 1965.
Conradi, Peter. *Iris Murdoch, A Life*. London: HarperCollins, 2001.
———. *The Saint and the Artist*. London: HarperCollins, 2001.
Dipple, Elizabeth. "Fragments of Iris Murdoch's Vision: *Jackson's Dilemma* as Interlude." *The Iris Murdoch News Letter* 9 (August 1995): 4–8.
———. "The Green Night and Other Vagaries of the Spirit; or, Tricks, and Images for the Human Soul; or, The Uses of Imaginative Literature." *Iris Murdoch and the Search for Human Goodness*. Edited by Maria Antonaccio and William Schweiker, 138–68. Chicago: University of Chicago Press, 1996.
Gonzalez, Alexander G. "The Problem of Gender in Iris Murdoch's 'Something Special.'" *Journal of the Short Story in English* 21 (Autumn 1993): 19–27.

Heusel, Barbara Stevens. *Iris Murdoch's Paradoxical Novels: Thirty Years of Critical Reception.* New York: Camden House, 2001.

Johnson, Deborah. *Iris Murdoch.* London: Harvester, 1987.

Oates, Joyce Carol. "Sacred and Profane Iris Murdoch." *The Profane Art: Essays and Reviews.* New York: Dutton, 1983, 184–94.

Todd, Richard. *Iris Murdoch.* London: Methuen, 1984.

Wolfe, Peter. *The Disciplined Heart: Iris Murdoch and Her Novels.* Columbia: University of Missouri Press, 1966.

EILEAN NI CHUILLEANAIN
(1942–   )

Sara E. Stenson

BIOGRAPHY

Eilean Ni Chuilleanain was born in Cork City, the first of three children. Her parents, novelist Eilis Dillon and Cormac O'Chuilleanain, a professor of Irish at University College Cork, were major intellectual and artistic influences. Ni Chuilleanain attended Ursuline Convent and University College Cork, where she earned a BA in English and history in 1962 and an MA in English in 1964. She attended Oxford for the following two years, earning her BLitt in Elizabethan prose, with an emphasis on religious writing. Ni Chuilleanain wrote her thesis on the work of Thomas Nashe and finished her degree in 1969.

In 1966 she earned the *Irish Times* Poetry Award and began lecturing at Trinity College Dublin. Ni Chuilleanain currently teaches Renaissance literature at Trinity College, where she is also a fellow. She actively promotes the careers of promising Irish poets, starting with her organizing of poetry readings and the Irish Poetry Now exhibit in 1972. In that same year, her first poetry collection, *Acts and Monuments*, was published. In 1975, Ni Chuilleanain, along with Pearse Hutchinson, Macdara Woods, and Leland Bardwell, founded *Cyphers*, the distinguished Irish poetry journal that seeks to emphasize the links between Irish poetry and broader European traditions. Similar to the founding principles of *Cyphers*, a variety of languages, including Irish, Latin, French, and Italian, strongly influence Ni Chuilleanain's poetry. Her second collection of poetry, *Sites of Ambush* (1975), was followed by the release of *The Second Voyage* and *Cork* (both 1977). Ni Chuilleanain married poet and editor Macdara Woods in 1978. Their son, Niall, was born in 1983.

A revised version of *The Second Voyage* appeared in 1986. *The Magdalene Sermon* was published in 1989 and revised in 1991. Ni Chuilleanain has been the recipient of the Patrick Kavanagh Award and in 1992 won the O'Shaughnessy Prize for poetry. Her next major collections of poetry were *The Brazen Serpent* (1994) and *The Girl Who Married the Reindeer* (2001). Ni Chuilleanain lives in Dublin and Umbria.

MAJOR WORKS AND THEMES

Ni Chuilleanain has maintained a delicate relationship with the tradition of Irish poetry, especially regarding the legacy of poets from Munster. Although she often reflects on the place of her birth, her use of her native language can be deceiving. For Ni Chuilleanain, the polemic concerns the role of exile from Ireland as well as material that cannot be translated from Irish to English. Furthermore, as a female poet in a largely masculine tradition, she has had to negotiate her role between poet and subject, a tenuous position that she often represents in visual terms. Her poems most avidly explore the shifting nature of borders and intersections that manifest themselves as spiritual thresholds, translation of language, and distinctions between movement and stasis, and fear and wonder, and the line between water and earth. She often finds these intersections within the contexts of history, art, folktales, and the lives of women. In an interview with Kevin Ray she confirms that she is interested in the "sort of liminal thing about sacred space; things you do on the threshold" (65).

In *Acts and Monuments*, Ni Chuilleanain's poetic voice expresses pure fascination with the natural world and, subsequently, the very notion of being. Her particular vision in this collection explores the natural present through its intimate relation to the past. Ni Chuilleanain constructs seascapes and landscapes, at once haunting and inspiring, through which she invites readers to join with her in marveling at change as it slowly and consistently alters existence. Ni Chuilleanain also offsets the languid cadence of change with a sense of awe and reverence for the universe. Cold and unwelcoming, this world challenges survival. Therefore, these mediations often bring about an acute sense of isolation and loneliness.

The most pervasive and powerful symbol in the collection is water; it isolates, threatens, cleanses, and serves as a reminder of passing time. In "Lucina Schynning in Silence of the Night," water brings about consciousness as the speaker recalls "again the chirp of the stream running." In "Ferryboat," water is ominous and dangerous. The speaker recalls a "deaths-head" teaching the passengers how to fasten a lifejacket that "binds the buoyant soul to the sinking body." Threatening and isolating, perhaps the most powerful representation of an aqueous force comes about in "The Second Voyage," in which the Greek mythical hero Odysseus, desperate to find a hitching post, declares that his next journey will be on land, but that "the unfenced valleys of the ocean still [hold] him." He then reconsiders because he cannot follow through with the daily routine of life ashore. By the poem's end, he cannot distinguish between his tears and his sweat.

Ni Chuilleanain distinguishes between water and earth in one of her most well-known poems, "Family," in which she explains, "water has no memory" but "every stone recalls its quarry." The speaker's family and the natural world become distant in "Going Back to Oxford," in which the speaker describes a hostile university where the "toothmarks are showing where the sharp spires got me." Despite the dangers to survival and the languid sense of time change, the poet suggests that change must come at its natural pace as "going anywhere fast is a trap" ("Letter to Pearse Hutchinson").

In *Sites of Ambush*, Ni Chuilleanain develops a sense that patience and faithfulness not only allow for progress, but also enrich the spirit. She continues to work through themes of isolation and change, but with new subjects. In "The Lady's Tower," from her lofty position, the speaker appears as a keen observer of her surroundings; her overhead view is powerful, yet it also reminds her of the great distance between herself and the environment and also leads her to discover a sense of her own inevitable seclusion.

Ni Chuilleanain utilizes distance and isolation to develop intrigue and mystery in "The Absent Girl," in which, "conspicuous by her silences," woman becomes subject rather than speaker. Ni Chuilleanain reappropriates woman and resists objectifying her subject by deliberately creating a sense of mystery, which prompts readers to reconsider how others see this woman.

The poems in *Cork* accompany Brian Lalor's drawings of Cork City. She again takes on themes of isolation, change, aging, and death; however, this time they are internalized to a greater degree. Ten of these poems appear again in her later collection, *The Rose Geranium* (1981). Ni Chuilleanain also released a collection of her poetry, *The Second Voyage*, which contains poems from her three earlier volumes. Clair Wills's favorable review considers Ni Chuilleanain's adept abilities of constructing poems in a circular structure, which resists the possibility that motion can stop. The poet consistently subverts ways of seeing that attempt to fix or arrest motion in poems such as "A Gentleman's Bedroom." The "underside" inevitably surfaces through the guise of small "rustlings" and pervasive reminders of death, such as gravestones and graveyards.

The title of her next collection, *The Brazen Serpent*, originates from the Book of Numbers, in which Moses creates a brass snake to save the Israelites from the plague of fiery serpents. Themes of belief, perseverance, and transformation of the mystical into reality manifest themselves in a number of forms throughout the collection. Ni Chuilleanain asserts a growing emphasis on spirituality through meditations on Catholic saints, architecture, shrines, scholarship, and daily encounters, such as baking bread. The collection reflects on the death of Ni Chuilleanain's mother and sister, as she explores ways of speaking about the things families often cannot discuss. Personal tragedy fuels the vision of poems such as "The Fireman's Lift," a meditation on religious artwork in which the speaker beholds the Virgin Mary "spiraling" toward heaven as painters hoist a scene of Mary and the angels of heaven up high inside the dome of a church. Ni Chuilleanain transforms her immediate sense of awe at the image and the physical beauty of the angels lifting Mary up to heaven into metaphysical wonder: "This is what love sees, that angle." In "Vierge Ouvrante," which translates literally as the "opening virgin," the speaker beholds an image of a sacred statue while photographers snap cameras in the background, threatening to destroy the image. In her interview with Kevin Ray, Ni Chuilleanain reveals she intends the poem to be about "being a witness to human wickedness" (64).

Nuns often appear in these poems at the threshold between mortal life and divinity. In "The Real Thing," a nun searches for something solid, something true to verify the stories of the Bible and the tenets of her faith against the anonymity of her life and the "white sheet of history." In "Architectural Metaphor," a tour of church lands reveals a scene of a dying nun who remembers a scene in the graveyard from her youth.

Aging, change, and solitude return as Ni Chuilleanain's major themes in *The Magdalene Sermon*. Though several poems appear from the previous collection, the new ones suggest a significant development in terms of the articulation of the power of change. Female speakers appear more frequently in the volume, and, like the one in "The Bare Deal Board," stand up against powerful forces all around. The speaker recalls her own journeys as she studies the grooves in a piece of wood. Ni Chuilleanain explores women's spirituality and presents it in a particularly unadorned fashion in "Quarant Ore" and more convincingly in "J'ai Mal a nos Dents." The nun of the latter poem is sick and dying; despite her isolation, she tells her dentist, "I have a pain in our teeth." Ni Chuilleanain creates a startling end to the poem in which the nun is finally given back her body in death. In "The Informant," a woman describes her encounter with the mythical in such a matter-of-fact way that she subverts the authority of a disconcerting researcher. Even storytelling becomes the "lost art" of our grandmothers in the poem "History." Ni Chuilleanain also allows for women to find their voices and selves, as when Galatea comes alive and "a green leaf of language comes twisting out of her mouth." Ever subtle, Ni Chuilleanain is careful never to speak for her women subjects but rather to resort to implication through images and circumstance.

In her most recent collection, *The Girl Who Married the Reindeer*, she represents a female speaker once again in the title poem, which tells a tale based on a story from the Fenian cycle of Fionn mac Cumhaill and Sadb, Oisin's deer mother. Ni Chuilleanain's young girl gathers fruit on a hillside and returns home a year later for her sister's wedding, shortly after the birth of her child. A witch gives her powder, which causes her to forget her child and lover. He, in turn, curses the witch, and, as he dies, "Naked in death his body [is] a man's." Ni Chuilleanain allows for the reunion of mother and child, altering the original tale in which the father finds his son. Ni Chuilleanain not only renders the power of love between mother and son but also demolishes the divide between gender constructs.

Ni Chuilleanain's latest work stands as a stunning development in both style and content. Helen Emmit's review proclaims that it is her "finest achievement to date" and a "landmark in contemporary poetry" (477). Camille-Yvette Welsch admires her ability to create a world without the preconceptions of gender and imagination that "invokes mystery rather than confusion" (17). Ni Chuilleanain pursues the relationship between stasis and motion once again; however, at this point she also identifies several arenas where the two intersect and which become quite tangible for readers in poems such as "Borders," "Crossing the Loire," and "The Bend in the Road." "The Crossroads" illuminates the intersection between divinity and mortal life at the site of a blessed shrine. Ni Chuilleanain's superb skills of translating Irish as well as her sensitive ear for the vernacular are evident here, as in "Translation," "Gloss/Clos/Glas," "Kilcash" (based on an old Irish song), and "Hunger." Notions of the sacred and of everyday life blend as the points of view of statue and of visitors become one voice.

CRITICAL RECEPTION

Mysterious, careful, and courageous, Ni Chuilleanain safeguards the secret sources of her poetry and her writing process with the utmost concern. Reviewers and critics tend to see her work as elusive, but with a degree of reverence. For all her caution, she has earned a great degree of critical acclaim in Ireland. Ni Chuilleanain's poetry was included in anthologies early in her career; poets such as James Simmons admired her fascination with mystery and the horror of living. According to Robert Henigan, American reviewers were initially "at best, condescending," taking issue with work that appeared "not traditionally Irish," obtuse in its elliptical structure, and embedded with cliché (103). Henigan finds her early poems "easy to like but not easy to grasp" because of their complex mythical allusions and "womanly concerns," which are potentially "muted" by her writing techniques (103).

Ni Chuilleanain has in fact openly spoken of her need to keep both the sources of her material and her process for composing hidden. As she once told Kevin Ray, she admits to occasionally counting the syllables to her poems because "that's a conspicuous but inconspicuous and secretive thing one can do" (66). Critics also may well have been reacting to her fearless efforts to express the inexpressible. Ni Chuilleanian is drawn to render repeatedly that which makes us afraid, namely, horrific events and death. However, she also pursues that which we cannot explain: the supernatural, the divine, and that which is lost during translation. Seamus Deane explains that her emphasis on what cannot be translated questions "the very basis of Irish cultural nationalism, which after all, assumes the translatability of Irish spirit into English words"(6).

Peter Sirr translates or interprets Ni Chuilleanain's ways of seeing, claiming that both Ni Chuilleanain and Medbh McGuckian reject authority in their work, allowing imagination to take over. Ni Chuilleanain's poetry relies on the "clarity and attentiveness" of the gaze and the "details it illuminates" rather than on the "central government of an overt poetic personality" (450). Sirr's close analysis of poetic structure and tone reveals that Ni Chuilleanain deals with borders in both a thematic and formal sense of the term.

Patricia Boyle Haberstroh's foundational *Women Creating Women* (1996) investigates the borders between the sexes in the poet's work. Haberstroh's chapter on Ni Chuilleanain was one of the first to consider the poet's handling of gender and sexuality in relation to her representations of myth and language. For Haberstroh, the poet's illustration of Odysseus's fear of stasis is marked by his masculinity. Paul Scott Stanfield reads Ni Chuilleanain's poems in light of French feminist Luce Irigaray.

Kevin Ray's "Sites of Ambush: Eilean Ni Chuilleanain's Bordered Silences" investigates the relationship between secrecy and revelation in light of Freud's theory of the uncanny. Helen Emmit also utilizes Freud's theory of the uncanny to uncover how and why Ni Chuilleanain's animate world is linked to history and the feminine. She examines the poet's need to "recover" or "recuperate" Irish women and Irish history while simultaneously working to keep her efforts buried or hidden. Emmit concludes that Ni Chuilleanain's emphasis on the border between the familiar and the mysterious is also that same border between the interior and the exterior of the female body.

Dillon Johnston also studies representations of the body in Ni Chuilleanain's poetry. He compares her writing to Eavan Boland's in terms of their mutual concerns with sexuality and spirituality. He specifically deals with selections from *The Brazen Serpent,* such as "Fireman's Lift" and "An Architectural Metaphor," as they evoke her fascination with Baroque art and architecture. Johnston draws further connections between her poetry and Baroque art, the Counter-Reformation, and the language tradition, as well as the relationship between the spiritual and the corporeal, to emphasize Ni Chuilleanain's visionary rendering of the notion that we can only conceive of the spiritual through our bodies.

John Kerrigan considers the relationship between Ni Chuilleanain's place of birth and its impact on her work. Kerrigan holds that Munster Renaissance writer Daniel Corkery's three major themes (religious consciousness of the people, Irish nationalism, and the land) in his study of eighteenth-century Munster, *The Hidden Ireland* (1925), profoundly influence Ni Chuilleanain and her predecessors and contemporaries such as Michael Hartnett, Thomas McCarthy, and Sean Dunne. Kerrigan considers the breadth of her oeuvre in determining that her move from place-based content in *Acts and Monuments* and *Cork* to consider Ireland's links with Europe has to do with the "cultural geography" of the Hidden Ireland and a "global shrinkage" that has also affected her contemporaries (96). However, Kerrigan proclaims that the distinctively allusive quality of her work stems from her dealings with the Irish language and "Irish self-perceptions" (96).

Helen Kidd examines the ways in which Ni Chuilleanain's resistance of fixity signifies the poet's critique of the official institutions that previously proscribed a definition of Irishness and roles for women. Kidd examines the ways in which Ni

Chuilleanain inhabits the thresholds between fluidity and fixity, silence and annunciation, and Irish and English languages in order to highlight the marginalization, stereotyping, and silencing of women.

Guinn Batten examines the relationship among the poetry of Eavan Boland, Medbh McGuckian, and Eilean Ni Chuilleanain as they address the body of the nation. Batten argues that through her emphasis on traditional nomads (or the exile of the Irish in Europe) and the empowered *cailleach* figure, Ni Chuilleanain's representations subvert traditional patriarchal claims of Irish nationalism without reclaiming the authority also to represent a totalizing form of Irish identity.

Batten, Kidd, and Kerrigan's essays bring Ni Chuilleanain's challenge to traditional conceptions of Irishness to light and signal the types of studies that may perhaps be most prevalent in the future. Given the caliber of Ni Chuilleanain's most recent volume, it is to be hoped that critics will continue to discover the ramifications of her significant contribution to understandings of Irish poetry and identity.

BIBLIOGRAPHY

Works by Eilean Ni Chuilleanain

Poetry

Acts and Monuments. Dublin: Gallery, 1972.
The Brazen Serpent. Oldcastle, Ire.: Gallery, 1994; Winston-Salem, NC: Wake Forest University Press, 1995.
Cork. Dublin: Gallery, 1977.
The Girl Who Married the Reindeer. Oldcastle, Ire.: Gallery, 2001; Winston-Salem, NC: Wake Forest University Press, 2002.
The Magdalene Sermon. Oldcastle, Ire.: Gallery, 1989.
The Magdalene Sermon and Other Poems. Winston-Salem, NC: Wake Forest University Press, 1991.
The Rose-Geranium. Dublin: Gallery, 1981.
The Second Voyage. Dublin: Gallery; Winston-Salem, NC: Wake Forest University Press, 1977. Second edition. Dublin: Gallery, 1986; Winston-Salem, NC: Wake Forest University Press, 1989.
Sites of Ambush. Dublin: Gallery, 1975.

Translation

Ní Dhomhnaill, Nuala. *The Water Horse: Poems in Irish by Nuala Ni Dhomhnaill, with translations by Medbh McGuckian and Eilean Ni Chuilleanain*. Dublin: Gallery, 1999.

Other Works by Ni Chuilleanain

"Acts and Monuments of an Unelected Nation: The Cailleah Writes About the Renaissance." *The Southern Review* 31, no. 3 (Summer 1995): 570–80.
"Death and Engines." In *Choice*, edited by Desmond Egan and Michael Hartnett, 24–25. The Curragh: Goldsmith, 1979.
"Drawing Lines." *Cyphers* 10 (Spring 1979): 47–51.
"Forged and Fabulous Chronicles: Reading Spenser as an Irish Writer." *Irish University Review* 26, no. 2 (Autumn–Winter 1996): 237–51.
"Gaelic Ireland Rediscovered: Courtly and Country Poetry." In *Irish Poets in English*, edited by Sean Lucy, 44–60. Cork: Mercier, 1973.
Irish Women: Image and Achievement. Dublin: Arlen House, 1985. (Editor.)

"Love and Friendship." In *The Pleasures of Gaelic Poetry*, edited by Sean MacReamoinn, 49–62. London: Lane, 1982.

"Nuns: A Subject for a Woman Writer." In *My Self, My Muse: Irish Women Poets Reflect on Life and Art*, edited by Patricia Boyle Haberstroh, 17–31. Syracuse, NY: Syracuse University Press, 2001.

"Time, Place, and the Congregation in Donne's Sermons." In *Literature and Learning in Medieval and Renaissance England: Essays Presented to Fitzroy Pyle*, edited by John Scattergood, 197–216. Dublin: Irish Academic Press, 1984.

"The Voices of Maria Edgeworth's Comedy." In *The Comic Tradition in Irish Women Writers*, edited by Theresa O'Connor, 21–39. Gainsville: University Press of Florida, 1996.

"Wise and Well Spoken: Field Day Women and Translation." *Moving Worlds: A Journal of Transcultural Writings* 3, no. 1 (Spring 2003): 73–86.

"Woman as Writer: The Social Matrix." *Crane Bag* 4, no. 1 (1980): 101–5.

Interviews with Eilean Ni Chuilleanain

Consalvo, Deborah McWilliams. "An Interview with Eilean Ni Chuilleanain." *Irish Literary Supplement* 12, no. 1 (Spring 1992): 15–17.

Nordin, Irene Gilsenan. "The Weight of Words: An Interview with Eilean Ni Chuilleanain." *Canadian Journal of Irish Studies* 28, nos. 2–29, no. 1 (Fall 2002–Spring 2003): 75–83.

Ray, Kevin. "Interview with Eilean Ni Chuilleanain." *Eire-Ireland* 31, nos. 1–2 (Spring–Summer 1996): 62–73.

Williams, Leslie. " 'The Stone Recalls Its Quarry': An Interview with Eilean Ni Chuilleanain." *Representing Ireland: Gender, Class, Nationality*, edited by Susan Shaw Sailer, 29–44. Gainsville: University Press of Florida, 1997.

Studies of Eilean Ni Chuilleanain

Batten, Guinn. "The Body Politic: Boland, McGuckian, Ni Chuilleanain." In *The Cambridge Companion to Contemporary Irish Poetry*. Cambridge: Cambridge University Press, 2003, 169–88.

Conboy, Sheila. " 'What You Have Seen Is Beyond Speech': Journeys in the Poetry of Eavan Boland and Eilean Ni Chuilleanain." *Canadian Journal of Irish Studies* 16, no. 1 (July 1990): 65–72.

Deane, Seamus. "Poetry and Song, 1800–1890." In *The Field Day Anthology of Irish Writing*. Vol. 2, edited by Seamus Deane, Andrew Carpenter, and Jonathan Williams, 1–111. Derry, Ire.: Field Day, 1991.

Emmit, Helen V. " 'The One Free Foot Kicking Under the White Sheet of History': Eilean Ni Chuilleanain's Uncanny Landscapes." *Women's Studies* 29, no. 4 (August 2000): 477–94.

Foster, John Wilson. Review of *The Second Voyage. Eire-Ireland* 13, no. 4 (Winter 1978): 147–51.

Grennan, Eamon. "Real Things." *Poetry Ireland Review* 46 (Summer 1995): 44–52.

Haberstroh, Patricia Boyle. "Eilean Ni Chuilleanain." In *Women Creating Women*, 93–120. Syracuse, NY: Syracuse University Press, 1996.

Henigan, Robert. "Contemporary Women Poets in Ireland." *Concerning Poetry* 18, nos. 1–2 (1985): 103–15.

Johnston, Dillon. " 'Our Eyes and Writing Hands': Secrecy and Sensuality in Ni Chuilleanain's Baroque Art." In *Gender and Sexuality in Modern Ireland*, edited by Anthony Bradley and Maryann Gialanella, 187–211. Amherst: University of Massachusetts Press, 1997.

Kerrigan, John. "Hidden Ireland: Eilean Ni Chuilleanain and Munster Poetry." *Critical Quarterly* 40, no. 4 (Winter 1998): 76–100.

Kidd, Helen. "Cailleachs, Keen and Queens: Reconfiguring Gender and Nationality in the Poetry of Eilean Ni Chuilleanain, Nuala Ni Dhomhnaill, and Eavan Boland." *Critical Survey* 15, no. 1 (2003): 34–47.

Meaney, Geraldine. "History Gasps: Myth in Contemporary Irish Women's Poetry." In *Poetry in
Contemporary Irish Literature*, edited by Michael Kenneally, 99–113. Gerrards Cross,
UK: Smythe, 1995.

Nordin, Irene Gilsenan. " 'And/A Green Leaf of Language Comes Twisting Out of Her Mouth':
Eilean Ni Chuilleanain and the Quest Theme." *Irish University Review* 31, no. 2 (Autumn–Winter 2001): 420–30.

Ray, Kevin. "Sites of Ambush: Eilean Ni Chuilleanain's Bordered Silences." In *Contemporary
Irish Women Poets: Some Male Perspectives*, edited by Alexander G. Gonzalez, 123–34.
Westport, CT: Greenwood, 1999.

Sarbin, Deborah. " 'Out of Myth into History': The Poetry of Eavan Boland and Eilean Ni Chuilleanain." *Canadian Journal of Irish Studies* 19, no. 1 (July 1993): 86–96.

Sirr, Peter. " 'How Things Begin to Happen': Notes on Eilean Ni Chuilleanain and Medbh
McGuckian." *The Southern Review* 31, no. 3 (Summer 1995): 450–67.

Stanfield, Paul Scott. "How She Looks in That Company: Eilean Ni Chuilleanain as Feminist
Poet." In *Contemporary Irish Women Poets: Some Male Perspectives*, edited by Alexander G. Gonzalez, 103–21. Westport, CT: Greenwood, 1999.

NUALA NÍ DHOMHNAILL
(1952–   )

Oona Frawley

BIOGRAPHY

Born in Lancashire to physician parents, Nuala Ní Dhomhnaill moved to the Kerry
Gaeltacht at the age of five. This move led to an immersion in the Irish language that
not only provided her future work with its vocabulary and many of its settings, but also
exposed her to the rich inheritance of the Irish oral and literary traditions that is the
grounding force behind her poetry. After youthful attempts at writing poetry in English, Ní Dhomhnaill began writing in Irish, which, she discovered, felt far more natural and allowed her greater freedom of expression. Ní Dhomhnaill studied both Irish
and English at Cork University, where her work was published in *Innti*, the Irish poetry broadsheet. Following receipt of her BA and a higher diploma in education, Ní
Dhomhnaill left Ireland for Holland and Turkey, where she joined her soon-to-be husband, Dogon Leflef.

After several years of teaching English in Turkey, and after the birth of two of her
four children, Ní Dhomhnaill returned to live in Ireland, where she and her family have
continued to live, despite periods of time abroad. Besides regular returns to Turkey and
visiting professorships (at Boston College and New York University, for example), Ní

Dhomhnaill has traveled widely to lecture and to read her poetry in places as various as Japan, Nova Scotia, and, most recently, China. While her poetry is grounded in the almost mythical landscape of Kerry and the everyday landscape of the Dublin suburbs, its combination of the abstract and the concrete offers fertile ground for the absorption of the international material provided by such experiences. Ní Dhomhnaill was recently appointed the first Professor of Irish Poetry by the government of Ireland, and is increasingly recognized as one of Ireland's great poets in any language.

MAJOR WORKS AND THEMES

If every language is its own world, there is a sense of being an immediate tourist in writing in English about Ní Dhomhnaill's Irish poetry, because the Irish that is Ní Dhomhnaill's describes a world of dimensions quite different from those of the one we inhabit when we use English. Reading her poetry, then, even if in the translation that has made her work available to a larger, non-Irish-reading public, is an *immram*, a voyage like those that Irish scribes recorded centuries ago. The space delineated by Ní Dhomhnaill's poetic is one that, like Eavan Boland's, draws on received notions of women in Irish history and culture, but because of her commitment to the Irish language, Ní Dhomhnaill engages much more actively than English-language Irish poets with Irish poetic traditions, forms, and themes.

In his essay "The Poet," Ralph Waldo Emerson describes language as "fossil poetry," suggesting that could we trace words back through time, place, and millions of utterances, we would recover some primal utterance—each word a poem, profound and mystical. Emerson's idea provides a way of thinking about Ní Dhomhnaill's poetry in Irish—"the corpse that sits up and talks back," as she puts it in the title of one of her most famous essays. Untouched, she believes, by currents that influenced other European languages, and so reflective of a pristine archive as well as Ireland's colonial history, Irish is for Ní Dhomhnaill something those few steps closer to Emerson's "fossil poetry," but never fossilized, for this is poetic language that yanks what Ní Dhomhnaill claims is untouched Irish into the present, modernizes the myths, and creates a unique voice for women in Irish.

Newly returned to Ireland and not yet thirty when *An Dealg Droighin* (1981) appeared, Ní Dhomhnaill drew on centuries of oral tradition and mythology as well as more immediate, personal lore to devise a poetry that attempted to merge the mythic and folkloric with the modern. The resultant mix of medieval Irish, Christian, and international mythologies with a strong, contemporary woman's voice earned the author early acclaim.

By establishing an Irishwoman's voice so forcefully beyond the representation of woman as iconic emblem of land and nature, Ní Dhomhnaill disrupts Irish literary traditions. In other respects, as with *dinnseanchas*, or placelore, she continues Irish traditions. Ní Dhomhnaill's mapping of Irish-speaking Kerry and its historical female inhabitants (as in "In Memoriam: Elly Ní Dhomhnaill," *Pharaoh's Daughter*, 25), like her later mapping of Irish suburban life, establishes a continuum between past and present, between the mythological and the mundane, mining the Irish language for "fossil poetry." Ní Dhomhnaill offers an updated version of Irish *dinnseanchas* that, while it commemorates place and retrieves from the margins the Irish language, its speakers, and women in particular, does not allow stereotypical expectations to develop. Far from

depicting a West of Ireland primitive and wild as it was in J. M. Synge's initial idealized estimation, Ní Dhomhnaill depicts a landscape not only alive with mythology and
traditional Irish culture, but also—inevitably—steeped in modernity. While including
the modern in her vision of Ireland, Ní Dhomhnaill's poetry, in its commemoration of
landscape and place, continues the Irish tradition even while disrupting its stereotypes.

The sequence subsequently known as the "Mor poems" is an appropriate thematic
summary of the volume. Mor, a figure from the oral tradition of the Kerry Gaeltacht
resembling other Irish goddess-hag figures, allows Ní Dhomhnaill to grant permanence
to the oral tradition and to create a female voice then so frequently absent from Irish
literature. Mor is given added complexity by a modern psychological language, allowing the poet to express the dark, subconscious, and challenging side of feminine
power through an alter ego that is a contemporary, humanized goddess figure.

An innovation of the collection—and an indication of the directions Ní Dhomhnaill
would later take—is an insistence on female sexuality. Ní Dhomhnaill frequently in-
verts the traditional male poetic by writing love laments that express a physical as well
as an emotional longing for the man and his beauty. This eroticism Ní Dhomhnaill associates with pre-Christian Irish culture, and the collection several times reexamines
Christian tropes of woman's virginal purity.

Féar Suaithinseach (1984) revealed a deepening of similar themes. The influence
of early and medieval Irish literature remains a dominant force, in the shape of particular figures, such as Cuchulain, as well as in the more general reliance on and involvement with *dinnseanchas*. The concern with the mythological is tempered with a
strong realism and an insistence on bringing that realism to bear on the mythic. The
result is a sense of colliding worlds and times in many of the poems, as modernity and
the mythic are forced to converge. Rather than simply imposing a contemporary translation on Cuchulain's boyhood deeds, Ní Dhomhnaill more broadly translates Cuchulain himself into contemporary life, turning him, for example, into a young child bored
of awaiting his single mother outside of a pub. In making such details of modern Irish
life available to the mythic, Ní Dhomhnaill shows mythology's continued relevance.

With poems such as "Táimid damanta, a dheirféaracha" / "We Are Damned, My
Sisters" (*Selected Poems*, 15), this collection also advanced Ní Dhomhnaill's feminist
preoccupations. The poet gives voice to emblematic and iconic Irish female figures—
Sweeney's wife, Muirghil, and Medb, for example—as well as countless unnamed
women over the centuries, thus rewriting literary myth and history. However, rather
than reclaiming these figures to seize on their very iconicity as a source of inspiration,
Ní Dhomhnaill shatters stereotypes and insists on the realistic portrayal of women and
their physical sensuality, thus attempting to demonstrate what she perceives as the negative and pervasive impact of the Catholic Church on Irish mores.

Linked to this is a preoccupation with transformation and metamorphosis, themes
addressed through folklore on the abduction of children and women by fairies; through
cross-cultural myths; through the metaphor for the journey across space as a journey
of the self; and through a figure like the mermaid, which will gain increasing importance in Ní Dhomhnaill's poetic vision.

Rather than eliding the bawdy, violent, or transgressive elements from early Irish
mythology and writing, as Standish James O'Grady, Lady Gregory, and many others
did, Ní Dhomhnaill insists on the relevance of these elements to contemporary culture
and writes them back in to Irish literature. To visit the world of Ní Dhomhnaill's language is thus to enter a sensual landscape in which description of nature verges on the
primordial; here is a democracy where contemporary men and women, owners of Black

and Decker chain saws and sports cars, exist alongside mythological shape shifters, goddesses, hags, and the all-too-human heroes of Irish sagas.

The resulting poetry at once revives and challenges Irish traditions. The facility with which Ní Dhomhnaill moves between the modern world of suburban Ireland and Irish otherworlds demonstrates her commitment to exposing underrepresented aspects of Irish literary tradition. The breach between the mythological world and the world of our day-to-day lives is what the poet attempts to heal: we read that a child has been snatched back from the *sídh,* the fairy fort; we encounter the child wonder Cuchulain, hero of Ireland, left outside a pub; we might meet Queen Medbh and hear her complain of phone calls from the Badhbh, the vulture, telling her to come for breakfast armed with a bottle of wine. Ní Dhomhnaill's poetry opens the possibility of infinite worlds existing simultaneously, and insists on the relationship of myth to our lives— so that ultimately her poetry is not merely a resuscitation of but a creation of mythology.

Selected Poems: Rogha Dánta (1986/1988) was the first published volume of English-language translations of Ní Dhomhnaill's work. Michael Hartnett's translations from *Féar Suaithinseach* and *An Dealg Droighin* were first published in 1986, with a handful of Ní Dhomhnaill's self-translations; a 1988 volume followed, the translations accompanied with facing-page originals in Irish. Hartnett's versions, which worked to maintain the spirit of the originals, introduced Ní Dhomhnaill's poetry to a wider, English-language audience, and established the format in which much of her work would be published in the future.

Selected Poems included the Mor and Cuchulain series and so provided English-language readers with a sense of Ní Dhomnaill's irreverent and even carnivalesque dealings with myth and folklore. Ní Dhomhnaill's thematic focus on the otherworld and the lore of oral tradition comes through here, and while Hartnett's translations have occasionally been challenged as misrepresentative (as even Ní Dhomhnaill's own afterword to the 2000 edition tells us), there is an overall fidelity to the poet's themes.

Like *Selected Poems, Pharaoh's Daughter* (1990/1993*)* functioned as a breakthrough text for Ní Dhomhnaill. Comprised of translations from *An Dealg Droighin, Féar Suaithinseach,* and what would become *Feis* (1991) by thirteen well-known Irish poets—among them Seamus Heaney, Medbh McGuckian, and Paul Muldoon— *Pharaoh's Daughter* followed *Selected Poems* in presenting facing-page translations, and established Ní Dhomhnaill as the most esteemed Irish-language poet of her generation. With translations that reflect the styles and linguistic quirks of the individual poets, *Pharaoh's Daughter* brought Ní Dhomhnaill's poetic to the attention of an American and academic audience. Translations of the work that would become *Feis* indicated Ní Dhomhnaill's continued preoccupation with Irish myth and folklore, as well as displaying a matured take on the love poem, infused with the immediate physicality and eroticism apparent in earlier collections.

Feis's appearance marked a turning point in Ní Dhomhnaill's poetic. Where in earlier collections the meeting between the mythological and the modern offered an opportunity for metaphor that was often comic, here that meeting offers a more intense opportunity to examine psychological states. While earlier collections dealt with interiority, *Feis* goes further and shows a matured vision of the depth of the psychological disturbances inflicted by Irish history and the loss of the Irish language, as well as a more personal take on the effects of repression and depression. *Feis* also goes further in examining how myth and iconic creations merge with reality, if at all. Poems central to the collection and its aims are those that explode the mythological representation of Ireland as old woman/hag/colonized land or as goddess/virgin lover/emblem of a free nation. In pushing such icons to their realistic end, Ní Dhomhnaill shows not only how Irish history has used feminine imagery to fuel nationalism, but also how real Irish women, as a result, have suffered the consequences of being expected to function within the parameters of myth.

Ní Dhomhnaill's creation of a new mythology that draws on the old disrupts stereotypes of women, and of Irish women particularly, with a humor that is sudden, unapologetic, and aligned with another Irish tradition only infrequently engaged by Ireland's other major contemporary poets. Ní Dhomhnaill coyly challenges the patriotism inscribed in *aislings* of the eighteenth century : "Caitlín"/"Cathleen" (*Astrakhan Cloak*, 38–39), for example, that most perfect female representation of Ireland, is taken down from the pedestal, and not for a mere dusting, so that the trope of Ireland as eternally youthful and beautiful woman is shattered by a confrontation with the aging process. In "An tSeanbhean Bhocht"/"The Shan Van Vocht" (*Pharaoh's Daughter*, 128–31), Ní Dhomhnaill furthers her assault on these created images of Irish womanhood as Irish nation that have forced silence and invisibility upon Irishwomen. Her response here is to continue talking herself in order to overwrite, literally, the stereotype. In collapsing the old ideals by showing the hollowness of the forms and the silence this hollowness imposes, Ní Dhomhnaill clears the slate for a new Irishwoman, one who, rather than existing as a silent inspiration, is given a voice beyond allegorical representation of Ireland itself.

This voice restores to Irish literature a natural sensuality, and, in doing so, has given further life to those strong women of ancient Ireland who were elided by selective translations before and during the Revival. While part of this giving voice results in the speaking figures of "Caitlín" and "An tSeanbhean Bhocht," another part continues to focus on the *dinnseanchas* tradition of placelore, which Ní Dhomhnaill combines with what have been read as feminist tactics. In poems such as "Oileán"/"Island" (*Pharaoh's Daughter*, 40–43) and "Fear"/"Looking at a Man" (*Pharaoh's Daughter*, 140–43), for example, the poet reverses the tradition in which woman becomes landscape under the admiring and objectifying gaze of the male poet; the female poet here turns voyeur, unravelling the stereotype of woman as asexual virgin, becoming the amorous recorder of the beloved as physical object and displacing the idea of man as visual consumer of woman. Poem after poem insists on a natural female sexuality: in "An Bhean Mhídhílis"/"The Unfaithful Wife" (*Pharaoh's Daughter*, 104–9), we receive a matter-of-fact comic portrayal of the infidelities of an evening that refutes the notion of Irish womanhood as faithful and pristinely asexual.

Ní Dhomhnaill also reveals a continued preoccupation with what modernity has lost by distancing itself from myth and folklore. Like its medieval counterparts, the "*Immram*" (*Astrakhan Cloak*, 72–103) cycle of poems offers fantastical place, here in the shape of an otherworldly island that appears every seven years. The island becomes a containing symbol allowing Ní Dhomhnaill to explore our abandonment of belief in the otherworldly, which, she suggests, has led to the repression of aspects of ourselves that consequently emerge in inappropriate ways. Tourism and capitalism's exploitations of the mythological and folkloric, "*Immram*" suggests, keep not only such belief but also the past, particularly an Irish-speaking past, at a cynical remove; the poet here attempts to bridge this distance.

The Astrakhan Cloak (1992) continued what had proven to be a fruitful relationship between Paul Muldoon and Ní Dhomhnaill's poetry. That these translations from *Feis* appeared so soon after that volume's 1991 release confirmed Ní Dhomhnaill's status as one of the most significant Irish poets working in either Irish or English. Muldoon's playful, punning style matches Ní Dhomhnaill's own arch tone, and the result is an impressive collection that ranges from surreally realistic portraits of suburban domestic life to the otherworldly "*Immram*" cycle that accounts for a third of the book.

Cead Aighnis (1998), Ní Dhomhnaill's most recent Irish collection, which is dominated by the issue of the Irish language itself, offers a more politicized take on history. The mermaid on "dry land" becomes a physical emblem of the effect on the Irish psyche of losing the language and attempting to adjust to a new vocabulary and worldview. These poems can be comic in describing the inevitable clumsiness experienced by the mer-people on land, but there is a serious undercurrent to the sequence that extends to the collection in its entirety. In losing the Irish language, the Irish people have lost, she suggests, not only a vastly elastic means of expression, but also the ability to exist in and believe in another world that now seems foreign and impossible to us.

While Ní Dhomhnaill has always displayed a thorough awareness of Irish literary traditions, here an awareness of the bardic tradition of the poet's place within Irish culture is an added preoccupation. This is evidenced in poems whose themes are vision or the poet's ability to cross borders and transgress boundaries forbidden to others. These transgressions include her ability as a poet to retrieve details of the past— whether personal, ancestral, or broadly cultural—and so to transgress the limits of the present and gain access to the past.

Ní Dhomhnaill continues to demonstrate a keen ability to absorb modernity and postmodernity into what she has referred to as the "pre-modern" aspects of Irish culture so that, for example, psychoanalytical knowledge is applied to Ireland's mythological heroes and heroines. The theme that most frequently represents this merging of the past and present is, of course, the Irish language itself, which is used to express the postmodern condition. Ní Dhomhnaill thus not only forces recognition of traditional Irish poetic metrical and rhetorical forms, but has also worked to dispel the view of the Irish language itself as an outdated mode of expression. Her insistence on writing in Irish has long been recognized as a political act, and over the period of several decades, her writing can be seen to have played a part in the resurgence of interest in the Irish language.

With the appearance of *The Water Horse* (1999), translations drawn from *Feis* and *Cead Aighnis*, Ní Dhomhnaill's poetry received a further reconsideration and interpretation by leading Irish women poets. Eilean Ni Chuilleanain and Medbh McGuckian's translations are characteristic, and convey Ní Dhomhnaill's interest in a range of worldwide mythology and in the portrayal of woman as real, and not mere image. The volume also offers the first interpretation for an English-language readership of *Cead Aighnis*, Ní Dhomhnaill's latest and most ambitious volume to date.

CRITICAL RECEPTION

From early on, Ní Dhomhnaill has enjoyed popular and critical praise. That her poetry has elicited the attention of the major English-language poets in Ireland has increased her profile and granted her a wide audience in the United States, and particularly within Irish studies circles. In 1998, Seamus Heaney chose to pass Parnell's white-thorn stick, given him by Conor Cruise O'Brien, to Ní Dhomhnaill, the first Irish-language writer as well as the first woman accorded the honor. This is a certain indication of Ní Dhomhnaill's critical status.

Scholars have been particularly impressed with Ní Dhomhnaill's ability to transgress the artificial boundary set in place between the Irish language and modernity by the antiquating tendencies of the Irish Revival. While employing traditional Irish metrical schemes or drawing on her extensive knowledge of the *dinnseanchas* and folklore traditions, Ní Dhomhnaill has also long insisted on the contemporary. Irish is thus exposed as a living, breathing, and mutating language that also draws on a fount of tradition.

Irish studies scholars have found that Ní Dhomhnaill's work neatly dovetails with the obsessive reworking of the past so often cited as a theme, but they have had to draw up new parameters for Ní Dhomhnaill's inclusion of psychoanalytical and cultural theory in her poetry, as well as her unapologetic feminist tactics. Critics such as Angela Bourke draw attention to Ní Dhomhnaill's complex, feminist renderings of folklore that give voice to women historically silenced: fairy abductions, Catholic imagery and legend, and "contemporary" issues such as anorexia are all forced to merge in the poem "Féar Suaithinseach," Bourke demonstrates. Patricia Haberstroh examines Ní Dhomhnaill's work for explorations of "diverse images of the female" (187), and notes that "a fascination with miracles, whether in the fantastic stories of Irish folklore and biblical history or in the seemingly more ordinary birth of a daughter, blends the world of everyday experience with the transcendental world of religion, legend, and myth" (184).

Recent criticism, which has focused on issues of translation in relation to Ní Dhomhnaill's work, has brought psychoanalytic and postcolonial theory fruitfully to bear on her poetry, taking a cue from Ní Dhomhnaill's own essays and lectures. Mary O'Connor examines Ní Dhomhnaill's language and publications as transgressive of the boundary between Irish and English, thus acknowledging the issues and "effects of colonization and the consequent muddying of the linguistic waters" ("Lashings," 153). Frank Sewell argues that Ní Dhomhnaill "offers an optimistic, transformative vision for the good of the psyche, the individual, the nations, and even of the planet" (171); she uses the psychological energy of the hag (*cailleach*) and the goddess (*spéirbhean*) to represent the push/pull between psychological states experienced by the over-stretched contemporary woman—or man. Sewell points out, however, that while Ní Dhomhnaill's work "contains elements of Romanticism in . . . its rejection of rationalism and recourse to dreams, the unconscious and various aboriginal or tribal perspectives, it also displays a hard-earned, hard-nosed realism" (192). Seán Ó Tuama, despite praise for Ní Dhomhnaill's work, has remained unconvinced by Ní Dhomhnaill's reliance on psychology. Even Ó Tuama does not dispute, however, that Ní Dhomhnaill is the best Irish-language poet of the last century and that she has contributed much to the revival of Irish literary traditions.

BIBLIOGRAPHY

Works by Nuala Ní Dhomhnaill

An Dealg Droighin. Cork: Cló Mercier, 1981.
Cead Aighnis. Maynooth, Ire.: An Sagart, 1998.
Féar Suaithinseach. Maynooth, Ire.: An Sagart, 1984.

Feis. Maynooth: An Sagart, 1991.

Spíonáin is Róiseanna: Compáach don chaiséad cic L21 (Guth an ealaíontóra). Indreabhan: Cló
    Air-Chonnachta, 1993. (A compilation of earlier volumes.)

In Translation

The Astrakhan Cloak. Translated by Paul Muldoon. Mullingar: Gallery, 1992; Winston-Salem,
    NC: Wake Forest University Press, 1993.
Pharaoh's Daughter. Multiple Translators. Mullingar: Gallery, 1990. Rev. ed., Winston-Salem,
    NC: Wake Forest University Press, 1993.
Selected Poems. Translated by Michael Hartnett. Dublin: Raven Arts, 1986.
Selected Poems/*Rogha Dánta.* Translated by Michael Hartnett. 1988. Dublin: New Island, 2000.
The Water Horse. Translated by Medbh McGuckian and Eiléan Ní Chuilleanáin. 1999. Winston-
    Salem, NC: Wake Forest University Press, 2000.

Other Writings

Selected Essays of Nuala Ní Dhomhnaill. Edited by Oona Frawley. Dublin: New Island, 2005.
    "Why I Choose to Write in Irish: The Corpse That Sits Up and Talks Back." *New York
    Times Book Review,* January 8, 1995, 3, 27–28.

Studies of Nuala Ní Dhomhnaill

Bourke, Angela. "Fairies and Anorexia: Nuala Ní Dhomhnaill's 'Amazing Grass.'" *Proceedings
    of the Harvard Celtic Colloquium* 13 (1993): 25–38.
Cannon, M. Louise. "The Extraordinary within the Ordinary: The Poetry of Eavan Boland and
    Nuala Ní Dhomhnaill." *South Atlantic Review* 60, no. 2 (May 1995): 31–46.
Consalvo, Deborah McWilliams. "The Lingual Ideal in the Poetry of Nuala Ní Dhomhnaill."
    Eire-Ireland 30, no. 2 (Summer 1995): 148–61.
de Paor, Pádraic. *Tionscnamh Filíochta Nuala Ní Dhomhnaill.* Dublin: An Clóchomhar Tta, 1997.
Gonzalez, Alexander G. "Older Women, Younger Men: Different Perspectives on the Use of
    Power in Nuala Ni Dhomhnaill's 'Flowers' and Medbh McGuckian's 'From the Dress-
    ing Room.'" *Notes on Modern Irish Literature* 12 (2000): 22–26.
Haberstroh, Patricia Boyle. "Nuala Ní Dhomhnaill." In *Women Creating Women: Contemporary
    Irish Women Poets,* 160–224. Syracuse, NY: Syracuse University Press, 1996.
Léith, Caoimhín Mac Giolla. "Metaphor and Metamorphosis in the Poetry of Nuala Ní Dhomh-
    naill." *Éire-Ireland* 35, nos. 1–2 (Spring–Summer 2000): 150–72.
Manista, Frank C. "Representing Sublimity: Body as Paradox in the work of Nuala Ni Dhomh-
    naill." In *Contemporary Irish Women Poets: Some Male Perspectives,* edited by Alexan-
    der G. Gonzalez, 143–50. Westport, CT: Greenwood, 1999.
McWilliams, Jim. "Nuala Ni Dhomhnaill's Poetry: An Appreciation." In *Contemporary Irish
    Women Poets: Some Male Perspectives,* edited by Alexander G. Gonzalez, 135–42. West-
    port, CT: Greenwood, 1999.
Níc Dhiarmada, Bríona. "Immram sa tsícé: Filíoct Nuala ní Dhomhnaill agus próiseas an indib-
    hidithe." *Oghma* (1993): 78–94.
O'Connor, Mary. "Lashings of the Mother Tongue: Nuala Ní Dhomhnaill's Anarchic Laughter."
    In *The Comic Tradition in Irish Women Writers,* edited by Theresa O'Connor, 149–70.
    Gainesville: University of Florida Press, 1996.
———. "Sex, Lies and Sovereignty: Nuala Ní Dhomhnaill's Re-vision of *The Tain.*" *Working
    Papers in Irish Studies* 4 (1991–92): 1–10.
Ó Tuama, Séan. "Filíocht Nuala Ní Dhomhnaill: 'an Mháthair Ghrámhar is an Mathair Ghránna'
    ina cuid filíochta." *Léachtaí Cholm Cille* 17 (1986): 95–116.
Sewell, Frank. "Nuala Ní Dhomhnaill: Journeying to the Shrine." *Modern Irish Poetry: A New
    Alhambra.* Oxford: Oxford University Press, 2000, 149–98.

ÉILÍS NÍ DHUIBHNE
(1954–   )
Beth Wightman

BIOGRAPHY

Born in Dublin, Éilís ní Dhuibhne has described her younger self as a "quiet, timid and dull child with an obsessive interest in reading" who always planned to become a writer (Warwick). Her father was a native Irish speaker from Donegal, and ní Dhuibhne spoke Irish at school from the age of four; she attended Scoil Bhríde and Scoil Chaitríona in Dublin. However, her family did not speak Irish at home. Her childhood holidays were spent in Donegal among her father's family, including an aunt who became the model for "the Mad Aunt" Annie found in ní Dhuibhne's "Blood and Water" (1988) and *The Dancers Dancing* (1999). Ní Dhuibhne freely expresses her ties to the Irish language: "I feel a sense of personal connection with the Irish language apart from any ideological commitment—I am aware that I am only one generation away from a line of people who spoke Irish as their first language, and I do not want to be the one who breaks the linguistic link. I also love English and realize its value to me as a writer, and to all Irish writers. I like to feel that it is possible up to a point to write in the two languages of Ireland, and to cherish both of them" (ní Dhuibhne, e-mail message to the author, January 30, 2004).

After graduating with a degree in English from University College Dublin (UCD), ní Dhuibhne completed an MPhil and a PhD there in folklore and medieval literature, focusing on Irish ethnology and folklore. As part of her research, she collected stories from Irish-speaking *seanaithe* in Donegal and Kerry, including roughly a dozen from Donegal's John McCafferty, as well as urban legends in Dublin. This material comprises part of the archive at University College Dublin's Department of Folklore. Ní Dhuibhne has said that she resists using specific stories as the basis for her own, however: "I'm a bit of a purist—I'm not going to do up an existing story and make something else out of it. It's too good as it is" (Perry, 258).

Ní Dhuibhne's first short story, "The Green Fuse," was published as part of David Marcus's New Irish Writing series in the *Irish Press* (1974) when she was nineteen. Marcus continued to publish her stories, "and if he didn't publish them [she] threw them immediately into the wastepaper basket" (quoted in Perry, 249). She credits her involvement with the Women's Studies Forum at University College Dublin in the late 1980s with solidifying her sense of herself as an author. The forum, whose committee included poet Anne Hartigan and UCD academics Angela Bourke, Ailbhe Smyth, and Gerardine Meaney, among others, organized lectures and seminars on women's literature. As she herself has put it, working with the forum "convinced me of the importance of pursuing my writing career (perhaps I suspected that a lot of women with literary aspirations and talent gave up too soon?)" (ní Dhuibhne, e-mail message to the author, January 12, 2004). Smyth's Attic Press, a starting point for late-twentieth-century Irish women writers such as ní Dhuibhne who were later published by other presses, brought out her first collection of short stories, *Blood and Water* (1988), after she had finished her PhD and given birth to her first child: as she explains in an interview, "both events liberated me, somehow, and left me free to concentrate on my writing" (Warwick).

"I am a double agent," ní Dhuibhne told the *Irish Times* in 1999: "As well as writing, I work as a librarian . . . tidying up other people's writing," as an assistant keeper of (primarily literary) manuscripts at the National Library in Dublin. Her half-time position allows her to write full-time every other week, and to indulge her "addictions" to "literary gossip and news" and to gardening (ní Dhuibhne, "My Writing Day," *Irish Times Online,* July 10, 1999, http:www.ireland.com/newspaper/weekend/1999/0710/pfarchive.99071000028.html). Her literary tastes and influences, who have made increasingly prominent appearances in ní Dhuibhne's stories, run from short-story writers such as Richard Ford, Alice Munro, Anton Chekhov, and Ann Beattie to novelists such as Toni Morrison, A. S. Byatt, Charlotte Brontë, and David Lodge.

Ní Dhuibhne is married to retired folklorist Bo Almqvist, a Swede, and has two sons. Her family speaks primarily English at home, and occasionally some Irish and Swedish, although both of her sons attended all-Irish schools. They spend summers in Kerry, where ní Dhuibhne finds an ample supply of "the essential nutrients of literary creativity": "sleeping, dreaming and reading" (ní Dhuibhne, "My Writing Day"). She has published two novels in English and two in Irish, in addition to several volumes of short stories, two Irish-language plays, children's books (some under the name Elizabeth O'Hara), and scholarly articles on Irish folklore. She began writing children's fiction for her own children, initially fantasy stories about a boy named Ragnar (after her oldest son). A conversation with a friend who struggled to find books with female heroines for her daughters prompted ní Dhuibhne's "Scatterbrain Sally" series, set in Donegal in the late nineteenth century, which mixes Irish history and the complicated motions of female adolescence.

The list of literary prizes and bursaries bestowed on ní Dhuibhne thus far is long, and includes the Bisto Book of the Year Award in 1995 (for *The Hiring Fair*, a children's book), the Butler Award for Prose in 2000, and being shortlisted for the Orange Prize in 2000 (for *The Dancers Dancing*). She is currently at work on a new novel, tentatively titled *Splendour Falls.*

MAJOR WORKS AND THEMES

To some extent, ní Dhuibhne's writing reflects the duality of scholarship and domesticity that inflects her own biography. She chooses to write primarily short stories, which she has claimed are "structurally similar to the legend of oral tradition," the subject of her academic work ("Legends of the Supernatural," 150). While she eschews simply reworking Irish material into modern versions, her stories have often invoked folktale form and style. Ní Dhuibhne's work derives from her "love-hate relationship with Ireland" and from "the significance of what we call ordinary life. . . . She feel[s] like an historian of the emotional and psychological life of [her] time" (Warwick). Throughout, her work poses gendered alternatives to the forms and themes of Irish literary history.

The worlds of ní Dhuibhne's first collection, *Blood and Water* (1988), are defined by an economically depressed and socially questioning pre–Celtic Tiger Ireland, a place of poverty and labor strikes, of childhoods dominated by Catholic schools and mass and their bewildering moral codes. The title story introduces characters from and ideas about the urban/rural divide in Irish life that recur in *The Dancers Dancing*. The dog-killing woman in "Fulfillment" provides ní Dhuibhne's initial development of a cracked psyche and utterly unself-aware narrative voice that later appears in the form of Robin, the narrator of *The Bray House* (1990). "Midwife to the Fairies," ní Dhuibhne's frequently anthologized and probably most well-known story, integrates the alternative realities and forms of Irish folklore with "modern" Ireland, as a modern-day nurse assistant descended from a long maternal line of midwives encounters either a dangerously dysfunctional family or a fairy world—or both.

These short stories, written over the course of fifteen or so years, were quickly followed by ní Dhuibhne's first novel, *The Bray House*, a science-fictional story of a twenty-first-century female Crusoe on the desert island that Ireland has become after a nuclear disaster. The obvious ecological concerns in this dystopic novel exist alongside ní Dhuibhne's continuing interest in the gendered implications of narrative perspective and in what constitutes Irish culture after independence, after Samuel Beckett, and after Eamon de Valera's constitution. Robin, a myopic Swedish archaeologist who has mounted an expedition to post-holocaust Ireland, discovers a Victorian house buried under the ash that renders Bray a wasteland. Using the intact remnants of family life preserved in the house, she develops a wildly speculative "scientific" report about the house's inhabitants, deeply ironic in its assumptions and "conclusions" about Irish cultural values. The novel sets Ireland against a British nation that ignores the republic's very existence, and against British literary history (in the shapes of Daniel Defoe and Jane Austen). It also reads the Irish nation against a broader Europe, signified by Sweden, which alone among European nations has managed to survive and thrive after the uncontainable ecological devastation; Sweden served a similar rhetorical purpose in an early futuristic short story, "The Postmen's Strike" (in *Blood and Water*), and Scandinavia in general is a recurring setting in ní Dhuibhne's work. In the end, *The Bray House* reads twentieth-century gender expectations and conventions as persistently comical—if they weren't so clearly costly—Victorian ideals.

The short stories in *Eating Women Is Not Recommended* (1991) have resulted in ní Dhuibhne's categorization (alongside Evan Boland) as a "suburban" writer. Set in places like Rathmines and Rathgar, "The Bright Lights" and "See the Robbers Passing By" use descriptions of suburban space to foreground the efforts of socially marginalized young, female protagonists who mimic and adopt bourgeois mores. *Eating Women* also contains a number of stories with overtly feminist interests: "The Flowering" and "Needlework" articulate the limits and failure of female longing in terms of traditional women's "crafts." The self-consciously literary and time-bending "Wife of Bath" demonstrates the relevance of Alisoun's fifteenth-century pleasures and complaints to a twentieth-century Irish woman.

Following the model ní Dhuibhne developed in "Midwife to the Fairies," a modern folktale forms the structural thread of *The Inland Ice and Other Stories* (1997). In "The Search for the Lost Husband," sections of which open and close the collection and appear between discrete stories, a woman follows her enchanted lover-by-day-goat-by-night despite his exhortations to go home (to her father), only to get and reject him in the end. *The Inland Ice* brings an even more focused lens to ní Dhuibhne's by now characteristic explorations of female desire. Ní Dhuibhne has called them stories about "obsessive love" (Moloney 111). Predictably but not stereotypically vectored through men, with varying degrees of satisfaction, desire for this set of characters is muted, thwarted, compromised. They are, more often than not, Prufrockian middle-aged women, living Thoreau's lives of quiet desperation, who took "secure jobs" because they were few and far between, who got married and had children because that's what (Irish) women did. These stories depict Dublin's intellectual middle class—publishers, public-relations people, elected officials, literary agents, museum curators, teachers of English, librarians—more than the suburban landscape. They also portray women on the fringes of that class, seeking or trying to maintain some form of creative outlet. *The Inland Ice* still contains the occasional male protagonist or narrator (a serial rapist-killer, a gay man), and the male characters tend to claim similar causes for and suffer similar effects of their emotional malaise. But most distinctive in this collection's treatment of Irish masculinity are its dry discussions of the "new Irish man," the male Irish feminist who really isn't one at all (especially Michael in "The Woman with the Fish"). Their feminism usually operates as simply another version of male intellectual and social privilege, although the male characters don't understand this.

Ní Dhuibhne's Orange Prize–nominated novel, *The Dancers Dancing*, represents her most fully developed exploration of the intersections of language, landscape, gender, and place in Irish culture. Thirteen-year-old Orla Crilly, born and raised in Dublin, spends July 1972 in Tubber, County Donegal, the site of an almost iconographic summer Irish college and of her family's summer holidays: Orla's father comes from Tubber. A female bildungsroman, *The Dancers Dancing* sets its exploration of Irish womanhood within the context of Ireland's linguistic, political, spatial, and social divisions: English against Irish; North against South; urban against rural; middle and intellectual classes against working class; male against female; and what ní Dhuibhne has described as "premodern [against] postmodern" (Moloney, 104). Ní Dhuibhne co-opts W. B. Yeats's image of the dancer, which at the end of "Among Schoolchildren" (1927) connotes a kind of integration and synthesis, for her depiction of adolescent girls coming to understand their developing selves within the fractures of 1970s Irish culture. Here, ní Dhuibhne again parallels Eavan Boland in transforming an Irish literary tradition often predicated on a reductive gendering of land(scape), linking the physicality of the female Irish body with physical, political, and emotional landscapes in ways that demonstrate the wider scope of Irish womanhood.

The expansive quality of this novel remains in *Pale Gold of Alaska and Other Stories* (2000). These stories have more luxurious contours than the early material, but continue to develop ní Dhuibhne's considerable range of established concerns. This collection shares with *The Inland Ice* an interest in the complexities and vagaries of adult female desire, especially adulterous desire. Single women having affairs with married men, married women having affairs with single men, and married women having affairs with married men all figure in these stories, and all repeatedly signal the ultimate isolation of individuals. However, the stories are equally invested in the possibility of finding emotional fulfillment within barren emotional landscapes, described as at odds with often lush physical landscapes (like the American frontier in "The Pale Gold of Alaska" and the Wicklow Hills in "At Sally Gap"). In the Catholic prostitute who tells of the Irish Free State's institutionalized sexual hypocrisy ("Sex in the Context of Ireland") ní Dhuibhne continues to experiment with narrative voice. And while ní Dhuibhne frequently makes reference to her stories' literary antecedents and authorial influences in her work, "Oleander" comments self-consciously on the narrative craft to which she has committed herself, persistently aspiring to "the dense psychological detail of place and person and love" that the protagonist of "Oleander" attributes to Henry James and Richard Ford.

CRITICAL RECEPTION

Irish reviewers have long championed ní Dhuibhne's English-language work, beginning as early as 1992, when Gerardine Meaney's review of *Eating Women Is Not Recommended* and *The Bray House* appeared in the *Irish Literary Supplement*. Meaney praised both books' "unpredictability" and generic interventions with the short story and novel forms. Irish reviewers have been in agreement about *The Inland Ice and Other Stories*, admiring the collection's mix of folklore and realism. Des Traynor's review of *The Dancers Dancing* is effusive (in keeping with the novel's nomination for the Orange Prize), and ends with the question, "When is the world going to discover Éilís ní Dhuibhne?" (276). Michael Pratt, an American critic, did "discover" her in 2000 but finds her novel lacking; in fact, he ascribes to *The Dancers Dancing* only the clichéd faint praise of accurately depicting "a peculiarly Irish way of life," of "interest" that "lies in local culture." Anne Fogarty's almost contemporaneous assessment of *The Pale Gold of Alaska and Other Stories* is far more positive, and emphasizes the "capaciousness" of these stories, where "the psychology of love is shown always to be at odds with social convention and narrative expectations" ("Exploration").

Formal scholarly work on ní Dhuibhne has largely concurred with that done by reviewers on both the success of her innovations and her position within a newly emerging canon of Irish women writers. Carol Morris's 1996 study of *The Bray House* credits the novel with instituting an Irish "feminist genre" fictional tradition, "appropriat[ing] for feminist discourse . . . the anti-Utopian novel" and the masculine adventure tale (128). Derek Hand places the novel's postmodern narrative at the center of his discussion, arguing that its "main concern" is "the Irish obsession with 'texts' and interpretation" (110). Countering Gerry Smyth's suggestion in *The Novel and the Nation: Studies in the New Irish Fiction* (1997) that *The Bray House*'s value lies more in its ideological (and especially ecological) concerns than its aesthetic achievement, Hand stresses that the novel is deliberately "uneven . . . a conscious attempt to render the struggle for dominance of textual representations of Ireland" (111).

Smyth agrees with other critics of *The Bray House* that one of its overriding aims is "explod[ing] the myth of scientific rationalism" via the figure of Robin. He further asserts that the novel foregrounds the eroding "organic relationship with the local landscape" that once characterized Irish Gaelic culture (166, 167). Caitriona Moloney has similarly noted that "the deep fascination with landscape" on which Smyth focuses (166) is rewritten in *The Dancers Dancing* (Moloney 102). In Anne Fogarty's preface to her edition of *Midwife to the Fairies: New and Selected Stories* (2003), one of the more recent and most comprehensive discussions of ní Dhuibhne's work, she reads the increasing variety of locales in ní Dhuibhne's stories as "encourag[ing] a bifurcated, comparativist view of Irish society" (xv).

But for Fogarty, the fundamental principle of ní Dhuibhne's short fiction is that it sits "precariously positioned between tradition and modernity while never fully inhabiting either sphere" (x), reinforcing Hand's earlier observation that the interwoven folktale in *The Inland Ice* "makes clear ní Dhuibhne's understanding that at the heart of the Irish condition is an ongoing need to make creative and productive links between the past, the present, and the future" (103).

BIBLIOGRAPHY

Works by Éilís ní Dhuibhne

Literary Works in English

Blood and Water. Dublin: Attic, 1988.
The Bray House. Dublin: Attic, 1990.
The Dancers Dancing. Belfast: Blackstaff, 1999.
Eating Women Is Not Recommended. Dublin: Attic, 1991.
Hugo and the Sunshine Girl. Dublin: Poolbeg, 1991. (For children.)
The Inland Ice and Other Stories. Belfast: Blackstaff, 1997.
Ladies' Night at Finbar's Hotel. Edited by Dermot Bolger. London: Picador, 2000.
Midwife to the Fairies: New and Selected Stories. Cork: Attic, 2003.
The Pale Gold of Alaska and Other Stories. Belfast: Blackstaff, 2000.
The Uncommon Cormorant. Dublin: Poolbeg, 1990. (For children.)
Voices on the Wind: Women Poets of the Celtic Twilight. Dublin: New Island, 1995. (Editor.)

Literary Works in English for Children (as Elizabeth O'Hara)

Blaeberry Sunday. Dublin: Poolbeg, 1994.
The Hiring Fair. Dublin: Poolbeg, 1993.
Penny-Farthing Sally. Dublin: Poolbeg, 1996.
Sparkling Rain. Dublin, Poolbeg, 2003.

Works in Irish

Cailíní Beag Ghleann na mBláth. Dublin: Cois Life, 2003.
Dúnmharú sa Dainghean. Dublin: Cois Life, 2000.
Milseog an tSamhraidh agus Dún na Mban Trí Thine. Dublin: Cois Life, 1988.

Selected Critical Works

"Cruncher, Fatso, and Skyscraper Ted: Contemporary Irish Poetry for Children." *The Lion and the Unicorn* 21, no. 3 (September 1997): 415–25.
"Dublin Modern Legends: An Intermediate Type List and Examples." *Béaloideas* 51 (1983): 55–69.
"Legends of the Supernatural in Anglo-Irish Literature (Response to Brian Earls)." *Béaloideas* 60–61 (1992–3): 145–50.

Studies of Éilís ní Dhuibhne

Burke, Patrick. "A Dream of Fair Women: Marina's Carr's *The Mai* and Eilis ní Dhuibhne's *Dún na Mban Trí Thine*." *Hungarian Journal of English and American Studies* 2, no. 2 (1996): 123–27.
East, Louise. Review of *The Inland Ice and Other Stories*. http://www.ireland.com/newspaper/newsfeatures/1997/072.
Fogarty, Anne. "An Exploration of Eros." Review of *The Pale Gold of Alaska and Other Stories. Irish Times Online*, September 30, 2000. http://www.ireland.com/newspaper/weekend/2000/0930/pfarchive.00093000203.html.
———. "Preface." *Midwife to the Fairies: New and Selected Stories*. Cork: Attic, 2003, ix–xv.
Hand, Derek. "Being Ordinary—Ireland from Elsewhere: A Reading of Éilís ní Dhuibhne's *The Bray House*." *Irish University Review* 30, no. 1 (Spring–Summer 2000): 103–16.
Harrison, Bernice. Review of *The Pale Gold of Alaska and Other Stories. Irish Times Online*, April 7, 2001. http://www.ireland.com/newspaper/weekend/2001/0407/pfarchive.01040700245.html.

Maguire, Aisling. Review of *The Bray House*. *Irish Times*, May 5, 1990, Weekend, 8.

Meaney, Gerardine. "Beyond Eco-Criticism: A Review of Éilís ní Dhuibhne's *The Bray House* and *Eating Women Is Not Recommended*." *Irish Literary Supplement* 11, no. 2 (Fall 1992): 14.

Moloney, Caitriona. Interview with Éilís ní Dhuibhne. *Irish Women Writers Speak Out: Voices from the Field*, edited by Catriona Moloney and Helen Thompson, 101–15. Syracuse, NY: Syracuse University Press, 2003.

Morris, Carol. "*The Bray House*: An Irish Critical Utopia." *Études Irlandaises* 21, no. 1 (Summer 1996): 127–40.

Ní Mhainin, Aine. Review of *Dúnmharú sa Dainghean*. *The Sunday Business Post Online*, July 2, 2000. http://archives.tcm.ie/businesspost/2000/07/02/story290470.asp.

O Muiri, Pol. Review of *Dúnmharú sa Dainghean*. *Irish Times Online*, September 9, 2000. http://www.ireland.com/newspaper/weekend/2000/0909/pfarchive.00090900234.html.

Perry, Donna. Interview with Éilís ní Dhuibhne. *Backtalk: Women Writers Speak Out*, 245–60. New Brunswick, NJ: Rutgers University Press, 1993.

Pratt, William. Review of *The Dancers Dancing*. *World Literature Today* 74, no. 3 (Summer 2000): 596.

Smyth, Gerry. *The Novel and the Nation: Studies in the New Irish Fiction*. London: Pluto, 1997, 166–68.

Traynor, Des. Review of *The Dancers Dancing*. *Books Ireland* (October 1999): 276.

———. Review of *The Inland Ice and Other Stories*. *Books Ireland* (September 1997): 219–20.

Warwick, Nicola. "One Woman's Writing Retreat." Interview with Éilís ní Dhuibhne. 2001. http://www.prairieden.com/front_porch/visitng_authors/dhuibhne.html.

White, Victoria. Review of *Milseog an tSamhraidh* at the Samuel Beckett Center. *Irish Times Online*, October 16, 1997. http://www.ireland.com/newspaper/features/1997/1016/pfarchive. 97101600099.html.

ÁINE NÍ GHLINN
(1955–   )

Coleen Comerford

BIOGRAPHY

Áine Ní Ghlinn was born in County Tipperary. Written in the Irish language, Ní Ghlinn's poetry has also appeared in translation in various anthologies and textbooks, and her poems have also been aired on radio and broadcast on television. Ní Ghlinn has published three collections of poetry: *An Chéim Bhriste* (1984), *Gairdin Pharthais* (1988), and *Deora nár Caoineadh/Unshed Tears* (1996). Ní Ghlinn has also published two nonfiction works for teenagers and two children's books written in Irish. She has worked as a broadcaster with RTÉ and Raidió na Gaeltachta, and has also been a lecturer at Dublin City University. Ní Ghlinn won Oireachtas awards in 1985 and 1987, and was also given an award in 1987 by Duais Bhord na Gaeilge, Listowel Writers' Week.

MAJOR WORKS AND THEMES

Ní Ghlinn's poems deal with taboo subjects—such as child molestation and rape—with a direct, uncompromising voice. In "Yourself and Myself" (*Unshed Tears*, 9) the speaker is a young girl who is raped by her grandfather while playing house. The poem ironically juxtaposes images of childhood innocence ("We drank tea out of little toy cups") with the more ominous "game" of the grandfather, who suggests that the girl play Mammy, while he plays Daddy. In "Vomiting Sickness," the speaker suggests that the origin of a young girl's illness, which has puzzled her doctors, is "her father's seed," which causes her to vomit after every meal. Ní Ghlinn's verse deals with these issues in a confrontational style, matching the violence of the crimes with the violence of her imagery. In "Fear" (11), for example, the abused speaker's fear takes the shape of "a cat's corpse." In "Revenge" (19), the speaker carries a "sharp-edged" knife in her pocket, ready to murder the man who raped her.

In the collection *Deora nár Caoineadh/Unshed Tears*, a dual-language volume, almost every poem deals with incest and rape, aside from a series of poems that deal with emigration. The female subjects and speakers in this volume have complicated reactions to the violence they suffer. As the title of the collection suggests, many of the speakers and subjects are so overcome with shame and misery that they find it hard to release their painful emotions. In "Escape" (13), the subject attends the wake of the man who had raped her repeatedly and recalls his "slimy tongue" and "foul-smelling breath." After she leaves the room, she releases a horrific scream that had been caught in her throat for years. In "Tears" (39), the speaker asserts that she cannot weep, but acknowledges a "queue of tears" behind her throat, waiting to be released. "Picture" (41) deals with a mother and daughter who cannot talk about the father's molestation of the daughter. The daughter silently indicts the mother for allowing the abuse to continue, but neither can find the words to broach the horrifying subject.

Another common reaction to violent sexual abuse among the speakers and subjects of *Deora nár Caoineadh/Unshed Tears* is to disassociate themselves from the situation. In "I Went on Reading" (35), the speaker disturbingly continues to read her book while she is molested. In "Sanctuary" (43), the speaker mentally withdraws every time she is abused: "somewhere in the distance I hear your grunting." Ní Ghlinn's theme of disassociation in the face of violence culminates in two companion poems, "Schizophrenia I" and "Schizophrenia II," in which the speaker has so far removed herself from the reality of her dreadful situation that she has actually suffers from a personality disorder. The speaker's schizophrenia is a direct result of repeated sexual victimization, during which she would disassociate herself from the self that was being abused, hiding her "other" self "in the crack in the ceiling." "Schizophrenia I" deals with the initial crimes and the victim's disassociation from herself, while "Schizophrenia II" represents the victim's confused thoughts after being institutionalized.

The most disturbing reaction among the victims of *Deora nár Caoineadh/Unshed Tears* is identification with and dependence on the assaulter. In "Secret" (29), the speaker feels that she cannot tell anyone about the abuse and concludes by claiming that she cannot live without the "love" of her victimizer. In "Once a Week" (21), the speaker is molested by her stepfather, whose bed she returns to at least once a week for the "warmth of his sordid love," which she prefers to the loneliness she feels otherwise. The subject of "Blame" (24), who was first "seduced" by her father at age three, is raped by another man and impregnated at the age of thirteen. However, her attacker is acquitted because the judge believes that the girl, who would succumb to "any man's embrace," was to be held accountable. While the speaker is candid about the girl's promiscuity, she insists on the girl's honesty regarding the rape. Always frank, Ní Ghlinn speaks for the victim and acknowledges her promiscuous behavior without excusing it. The girl's behavior represents her stark, cruel reality: what choice, the poem demands, has this girl but to equate love with sex? *Deora nár Caoineadh/Unshed Tears* is a study of the victims of sexual abuse and the varying ways of coping with and surviving such a trauma. Whatever the victim's reaction, Ní Ghlinn's tone, while aggressive and accusatory, always retains a note of sympathy for the victim. Ní Ghlinn's most intense attacks, always directed at the attackers, defend the reaction of the victim and her right to aggression, rage, and retaliation.

CRITICAL RECEPTION

Ní Ghlinn's poems, both in the original Irish and in translation, have been published in many recent Irish poetry anthologies, such as *Wildish Things: An Anthology of New Irish Women's Writing* (1989), *Sruth na Maoile: Modern Gaelic Poetry from Scotland and Ireland* (1993), *An Crann Raoi Bhláth/The Flowering Tree* (1991), *Writing the Wind: A Celtic Resurgence: The New Celtic Poetry* (1997), and *Pillars of the House: An Anthology of Verse by Irish Women from 1690 to the Present*. Her poems have also appeared in various journals, including *Translation: The Journal of Literary Translation* (1989), *Poetry Ireland Review* (1994), and *The Bridge/An Droichead* (1989). While there is not much criticism on Ní Ghlinn's work, her inclusion in so many recent anthologies and journals suggests that she will soon attract more critical interest. Those who have written about Ní Ghlinn's work acknowledge her bold treatment of taboo subjects, her forthright style, and her dexterity with the Irish language.

BIBLIOGRAPHY

Works by Áine Ní Ghlinn

Poetry

An Chéim Bhriste. Dublin: Coiscéim, 1984.
Deora nár Caoineadh/Unshed Tears. Dublin: Dedalus, 1996.
Gairdin Pharthais. Dublin: Coiscéim, 1988.

Nonfiction for Teens

Daoine Agus Deith. Dublin: An Gum, 1995.
Mna as an nGath. Dublin: An Gum, 1990.

Children's books

Daifni Dineasar. Dublin: O'Brien, 2001.
Moncai Dana. Dublin: O'Brien, 2002.

Studies of Áine Ní Ghlinn

Crowe, Thomas Rain, Gwendal Denez, and Tom Hubbard, eds. *Writing the Wind: A Celtic Resurgence: The New Celtic Poetry*. Cullowhee, NC: New Native, 1997, 202–4.
Fitzmaurice, Gabriel, ed. *Irish Poetry Now: Other Voices*. Dublin: Wolfhound, 1993, 186–89.

Fitzmaurice, Gabriel, and Declan Kiberd, eds. *An Crann Faoi Bhláth/The Flowing Tree*. Dublin: Wolfhound, 1991, 294–99.

Kelly, A. A., ed. *Pillars of the House: An Anthology of Verse by Irish Women from 1690 to the Present*. 1987. Dublin: Wolfhound, 1997, 162–63.

McRedmond, Louis, ed. *Modern Irish Lives: Dictionary of Twentieth-Century Irish Biography*. Dublin: Gill and Macmillan, 1996, 228.

Weekes, Ann Owens, ed. *Unveiling Treasures: The Attic Guide to the Published Works of Irish Women Literary Writers*. Dublin, Ire.: Attic, 1993, 259–60.

White, Victoria. "Secrets and Lies." Review of *Deora nár Caoineadh/Unshed Tears*. *Irish Times*, October 5, 1997, 8.

MÁIRÉAD NÍ GHRÁDA
(1896–1971)

Coleen Comerford

BIOGRAPHY

Máiréad Ní Ghráda was born on a small farm in Kilmaley, County Clare. Irish was still spoken by many in Kilmaley while Ní Ghráda was growing up there, especially among the older generations, and Ní Ghráda's father, Séamus Ó Gráda, could recite passages from classic works in Irish. As a result, Ní Ghráda was raised to be bilingual and was educated in Kilmaley and at Mercy convent, in Ennis. She won a scholarship to study languages at University College Dublin (UCD) and pursued the canon of literature in Irish at the graduate level, also at UCD. Her master's thesis, "An Aoir sa Ghaeilge" ("Satire in Irish"), was directed by Douglas Hyde, Gaelic League founder and first president of Ireland after the establishment of the Irish Free State. Hyde became Ní Ghráda's mentor, and she became active in the Gaelic League while at UCD.

After university, starting about 1919, Ní Ghráda began publishing articles and reviews for literary magazines such as *An Branar*. Ní Ghráda also joined Cumann na mBan, the women's version of the Irish Volunteers, which supported male Republicans by providing sanctuary or trafficking in weapons. Her activities with this group once landed her in prison for obstructing traffic by collecting funds for the Gaelic League on Grafton Street, which increased her celebrity. The harrowing political and social climate of Ireland, especially from 1916, greatly influenced her literary work, which often seeks to expose the pretense and hypocrisy of Irish political and social practices, especially in terms of the role of women in traditional society.

During the turbulent years of the Irish Civil War, Ní Ghráda sided with the Free State, becoming the personal secretary to Ernest Blythe, a minister in the first Irish Free State government, from 1921 to 1923. Blythe later directed the Abbey Theatre, and Ní Ghráda wrote plays for the Abbey under his leadership. Ní Ghráda married Richard Kissane in 1923, and the couple later had two sons. Contrary to the social custom for married women, Ní Ghráda refused to give up her career after she was married.

In 1927, Ní Ghráda began working for 2RN, the predecessor to Radio Éireann, a public service under the jurisdiction of the Department of Posts and Telegraphs. Ní Ghráda was the first female mainstream radio announcer in Ireland or Britain. She earned the post of woman organiser despite the great prejudice against her as a married woman. Her application for employment was considered by the Civil Service Commission in 1926, and, despite the recommendation of the committee, Ní Ghráda was originally rejected because the minister of posts and telegraphs at the time, J. J. Walsh, refused to employ a married woman because he believed that married women could not provide "unbroken service" to a career outside of the home. Ní Ghráda's former boss, Ernest Blythe, countered Walsh's decision, arguing that since the published job description had never mentioned any objection to hiring a married woman and that since Ní Ghráda's qualifications were so outstanding, he must hire her. Another of Ní Ghráda's supporters, Major Brian Cooper, argued that the demands of the post, which included planning a children's hour and women's programming, would be better served by a married woman.

During her first two years at 2RN, Ní Ghráda served as a backup announcer for Seamus Hughes, in addition to producing women's and children's programming and managing the music library. However, in 1929 Ní Ghráda was promoted to regular announcer, which carried an enormous amount of responsibility, including performing many of her former duties. Ní Ghráda's work at 2RN is still considered pioneering, and she is credited with helping to pave the way for the more sophisticated broadcasting that came after the service was expanded in later years. Nevertheless, as a married woman, her position at 2RN was always uncertain, and she was forced to end her broadcast career in 1935, when Ní Ghráda's husband was offered reinstatement to service on the condition that his wife resign her post at 2RN.

Ní Ghráda turned to theater, in which she had been active as early as 1923. Drama became her genre of choice, and she wrote plays in Irish from the 1930s through the 1960s. Ní Ghráda was a well-known member of the literary scene in Ireland and worked with prominent artists such as Seán Ó Riada, Cyril Cusack, and Micheál Mac Liammóir.

MAJOR WORKS AND THEMES

Ní Ghráda's intent as a dramatist was to popularize theater in the Irish language. She succeeded in spite of the many challenges she faced. In 1923, An Comhar Drámaíochta, a theater co-operative, was formed to pursue the regular production of plays in Irish. Ní Ghráda was among its first members and actors. An Comhar Drámaíochta became a company in 1924 and performed plays at the Abbey, Peacock, and Gate theaters in Dublin.

In 1931, Ní Ghráda wrote for her Irish students at Kilmacud Domestic Science College a one-act comedy called *An Uacht* (*The Will*), which was produced by Micheál Mac Liammóir and performed at the Gate. The plot features a man who pretends to die in order to test his relatives while devising his will. Ní Ghráda's Irish version of an adaptation of a Tolstoy story, *Micheál,* was also produced by Mac Liammóir and performed at the Gate, and a year later the same play was performed at the Taibhdhearc Theatre in Galway. Ní Ghráda's *An Grá agus an Gárda* (*Love and the Policeman*), which was performed by An Comhar Drámaíochta at the Peacock and published in 1937, explores a theme that would become vital to her plays: marriage. As in *An Grá agus an Gárda,* marriage is seen from the feminine perspective in Ní Ghráda's plays.

With *An Grá agus an Gárda,* Ní Ghráda began to develop more complex dramatic plots. Unfortunately, her audience's weak understanding of the Irish language obliged Ní Ghráda to construct plays that could be understood through exaggerated gestures and mime. She began writing plays for the Abbey when it merged with An Comhar Drámaíochta in 1942, including *Giolla an tSolais* (1954), a three-act play set in a Kerry kitchen, which was also produced in Galway. The subject matter of this play involves malevolence brought on by what Eamon Ó Ciosáin has called a "Faustian deal" ("Máiréad Ní Ghráda"). Evil is vanquished by good, epitomized by the Virgin Mary.

Under the directorship of Ernest Blythe, Ní Ghráda wrote many short plays, which were arranged to follow plays in English; citing the audience's ignorance of Irish, Blythe would not risk longer plays in Irish as the main fare of the stage. Ní Ghráda introduced music to augment the audience's understanding of her plays, and Seán Ó Riada was called upon to create the musical accompaniment. Eventually, Ní Ghráda's plays became increasingly expressionistic. Using representational characters in *Giolla an tSolais*, she also experimented with using anonymous characters, more symbolic than realistic, as in *Mac Uí Rudai* (*Mr. Somebody*, 1963). Staged in 1961, it departs entirely from naturalistic theater, and exemplifies her later plays, which are typically very brief and expressionistic.

Ní Ghráda's most famous play, the two-act *An Triail* (*On Trial*, 1995) was produced in Irish in 1964, and in English in 1965, in the Eblana Theatre and deals with the fate of a young country girl impregnated by a married man. The young girl leaves home and gives birth at the ironically named Magdalen Laundry, after which she is betrayed by her father and tragically kills herself and her infant. *An Triail*, which is a fitting example of Ní Ghráda's interest in challenging oppressive social conventions and gender roles, especially with regard to women, addresses the controversial subjects of marital infidelity and unwed mothers and interrogates the methods that Catholic Ireland has devised to deal with such issues.

Among her many contributions to the canon of literature in Irish, aside from her work in the theater, Ní Ghráda wrote a volume of short stories and a science-fiction novel titled *Manannán* (1940). Throughout her career Ní Ghráda also wrote many textbooks for students of the Irish language, one of which, *Progress in Irish*, was widely used during her lifetime and is still used today. She translated many children's tales into Irish, including a translation of Peter Pan (*Tir na Deo*, 1938).

CRITICAL RECEPTION

Ní Ghráda has been recognized for her career as a broadcaster, her work in the theater, and her pioneering promotion of the Irish language. Ní Ghráda's plays, especially her shorter plays, have been staged frequently in drama festivals. *An Triail* was produced as part of the Dublin Theatre Festival in 1964, to favorable acclaim. *An Triail* has also been included recently as one of the plays studied by Leaving Certificate students in Ireland. The current surge of critical interest in Irish women's writing has found new interest in Ní Ghráda as a feminist model, which will undoubtedly increase the critical material devoted to her in English as well as in Irish.

BIBLIOGRAPHY

Works by Máiréad Ní Ghráda

An Bheirt Deartháir agus scéalta eile. Dublin: Oifig an tSoláthair, 1939.
An Grá agus an Gárda. Dublin: Oifig an tSoláthair, 1937.

An Triail. Dublin: Oifig an tSoláthair, 1995.
An Triail & Breithiúnas. Dublin: Oifig an tSoláthair, 1978.
An Uacht. Dublin: Oifig an tSoláthair, 1935.
Breithiúnas. Dublin: Oifig an tSoláthair, 1996.
D'Fhile nach Maireann: G.M.H. In *Nua-Fhili* 2, edited by S. Ó Céileachair. 1953–63. Dublin: Oifig an tSoláthair, 1968. Also in F. O'Brien, *Duanaire Nuafhilíochta.* Dublin: An Clochomhar, 1969.
Giolla an tSolais. Dublin: Oifig an tSoláthair, 1954.
Lá Buí Bealtaine. Dublin: Oifig an tSoláthair, 1954.
Mac Uí Rudai. Dublin: Oifig an tSoláthair, 1963.
Manannán. Dublin: Oifig an tSoláthair, 1940.
Micheál. Dublin: Oifig an tSoláthair, 1933.
On Trial. Dublin: Duffy, 1966.
Sügán Sneachta. Dublin: Oifig an tSoláthair, 1962.
Tir na Deo. Dublin: Oifig an tSoláthair, 1938.
Üll Glas Oíche Shamhna. Dublin: Oifig an tSoláthair, 1960.

Studies of Máiréad Ní Ghráda

Breathnach, D., and M. Ní Mhurchu. *Beatháisnéis a hAon.* Dublin: An Clóchomhar, 1986.
Comóradh Mháiréad Ní Ghráda (Leabhrán Cuimhneacháin). Coiste *Comórtha Mháiréad Ní Ghráda.* Kilmaley, Ire.: Leabrain Cuimhneachain, 1997.
Gorham, M. *Forty Years of Irish Broadcasting.* Dublin: Talbot, 1967.
Morgan, Eileen. "Unbroken Service: Máiréad Ní Ghráda's Career at 2RN, Ireland's First Broadcasting Station, 1927–35." *Eire-Ireland* 37, nos. 3–4 (Fall–Winter 2002): 53–78.
Ní Bhrádaigh, S. *Máiréad Ní Ghráda, Ceannródaí Drámaíochta.* Inverin, Ire.: Cló Iar-Chonnachta, 1996.
Ó Ciosáin, Eamon. "Máiréad Ní Ghráda: Biography." *Local Ireland.* http://www.local.ie/content/2488.shtml/ (accessed January 3, 1999).
———. "Máiréad Ní Ghráda agus a Saothar Liteartha." In *An Triail* agus *Breithiúnas*, by M. Ní Ghráda. Dublin: Oifig an tSoláthair, 1978.
Ó Ciosáin, Eamon. Preface to *An Triail.* Dublin: Oifig an tSoláthair, 1995.
Ó Siadhail, P. *Stair Dhrámaiocht na Gaeilge 1900–1970.* Indreabhán: Cló Iar-Chonnachta, 1993.
Welch, Robert. *The Oxford Companion to Irish Literature.* Oxford: Clarendon, 1996, 255.

EDNA O'BRIEN
(1930–   )

Sandra Manoogian Pearce

BIOGRAPHY

Edna O'Brien was born in the small rural town of Tuamgraney in County Clare. Like her famous country-girl characters, she left the rural countryside at age sixteen for the city of Dublin. There she attended the Pharmaceutical College of Ireland and qualified as a licentiate, but she soon discovered that writing was her passion and began working for the Irish Press in 1948. By 1951 she was married to Ernest Gebler and a year later her son Carlos was born; son Sasha came two years later. In 1959 she moved to London and began the novel that would change her quiet life, *The Country Girls*. It was rapidly published in 1960 and later won the Kingsley Amis Award. By 1964 O'Brien had published the next two novels of the trilogy and was divorced. In the years since, O'Brien has continued her prolific career, having published fifteen novels, nine short-story collections, one book of poetry, three plays, one biography, and assorted other works.

MAJOR WORKS AND THEMES

O'Brien's protagonists are often single women desperately searching for their identities in a sexually repressed Ireland. More recently, O'Brien's themes have become more overtly political. She has always been concerned with the land—historically and mythically—and the powerful emotions it evokes. The Country Girls Trilogy, comprised of *The Country Girls*, *The Lonely Girl*, and *Girls in Their Married Bliss*, catapulted Edna O'Brien to instant international success and to censorship at home. The Irish literary scene did not know what to make of her explicit sexual imagery and flamboyantly lyrical diction. Tame by American and European standards, Kate and Baba's antics in this first trilogy were viewed outside Ireland as innocent, even charming; Americans and Europeans loved the coming of age of these two daft, but wily, country girls and embraced O'Brien's darkly comic writing. At the same time some feminist readers chided O'Brien for the girls' unhealthy dependence on weak men. Her fourth novel, *August Is a Wicked Month* (1965), is the story of ironically named Ellen Sage, not wise in the ways of the heart, who has recently separated from her husband. O'Brien's images of spilt beads, missing glass, and a wounded bird are her early metaphors for Ellen's self-destructive nature. *Casualties of Peace* (1966), O'Brien's fifth novel, reveals Willa's story, interwoven with those of Tom and Patsy, boarders whose marital problems eventually engulf and destroy Willa. The tale's tragedy revolves around a mistaken identity and the gift of a fur coat from Willa's "coffee-coloured" and attentive lover, Auro.

Night (1972) enfolds a lyrical midnight soliloquy by Mary Hooligan, who spends a long, lonely night reviewing the depressing details of her life. O'Brien's stream of consciousness and earthy protagonist drew comparison to Joyce's Molly Bloom. Following a highly successful short-story anthology, *A Scandalous Woman and Other Stories* (1974), and an interesting autobiographical essay, *Mother Ireland* (1976), her next novel, *Johnny I Hardly Knew You* (1976), garnered rebuke. Nora is probably O'Brien's darkest heroine. We suspect that she is bordering on madness as she murders her lover, Hart. However, O'Brien's continued use of broken objects and wild animals—a choked mouse, a broken teacup, and a wild horse—all act as effective metaphors for Nora's crazed actions, adding some interest to this novel. *The High Road* (1988) departed somewhat from O'Brien's usual fare. It is a feminist retelling of Eden and the Passion story, chronicling the Spanish vacation adventures of Anna and her lesbian encounter with Catalina. Similar to the Christ-like imagery of Willa and Hart in previous novels, Catalina becomes the sacrificial victim. *Time and Tide* (1992) tells the tale of Nell, a divorced mother, trying to raise two boys, Paddy and Tristan, while hardly knowing herself. Early on, we learn of Paddy's death, a drowning aboard a sinking party boat. Nell begins to sink herself, drowning in a world of illicit relationships and drugs.

House of Splendid Isolation (1994), *Down by the River* (1997), and *Wild Decembers* (2000) comprise O'Brien's contemporary trilogy. *House of Splendid Isolation* is

O'Brien's political novel, the story of an older woman, Josie, who harbors an IRA terrorist, McGreevy. During their seven-day confinement a strange friendship develops. The novel is clearly antiwar and antiviolence, but many thought it much too sympathetic to McGreevy, perhaps modeled after a younger Gerry Adams. *Down by the River* marked another experiment: O'Brien fictionalizes the famous abortion X case of the fourteen-year-old Irish girl raped by her father's friend and ordered back from England, where she sought an abortion. Revealing her loathing of the Irish abortion laws and making them appear even more heinous, O'Brien has the girl's father commit the act. In *Wild Decembers*, Joseph Brennan and his once friend, now sworn enemy, Mick Bugler, fight over newly inherited land. Caught in the middle is Breege, Brennan's sister, but Bugler's lover. Containing some of O'Brien's famous dark comedy, it is ultimately a tragedy, partly ordained by a centuries-old legacy of doom whenever land is concerned. During this period Penguin published O'Brien's biography of James Joyce, the author she cites as her most influential mentor. O'Brien's latest novel, *In the Forest* (2002), is perhaps her darkest story yet. Set in the lush Irish countryside for which O'Brien is so famous, the novel contrasts that beauty with the harrowing tale of Michael O'Kane, an enormously troubled youth nicknamed "the Kindershreck," a man who terrifies young children and murders three innocent people. Again, O'Brien turns to a real event and uses it as the springboard for this ghastly psychological portrayal of a young killer.

CRITICAL RECEPTION

The Country Girls skyrocketed young, unknown Edna O'Brien to international fame. Banned in Ireland, the Country Girls Trilogy, *The Country Girls, The Lonely Girl*, and *Girls in Their Married Bliss*, caused a sensation. Ronan Bennett described Kate and Baba as "compelling creations of naivete and cunning, wisdom and daftness" and praised the new author for "the freshness of her talent and the honesty of her voice." The trilogy was repackaged with an epilogue in 1986 and again these new twenty pages caused a sensation for the tragic turn of events, drawing mixed reviews. Robert Hosmer Jr. liked it, seeing Kate and Baba "as two aspects of one developing personality," and perceived in the reissue a chance to reacquaint readers with the "fresh, captivating, occasionally lyrical prose; acute insight into the dynamics of human personality and behavior; vivid and articulate rendering of a fictional world of women ruined by their dependence on men" (1986 review, 12). Anatole Broyard, an admirer of the trilogy, found the epilogue wanting: "The style here is full of forced energy—slang, verbal jitters and epithets—in what seems a retrospective attempt to modernize the trilogy" ("Rotten Luck," 12). Writing back in 1966, the *Times Literary Supplement* (*TLS*) spoke of the author "endear[ing] herself to the literary world because she appeared to be writing with such naturalness and to have achieved an instinctive objectivity about the experiences of her country girls" (997). Some feel that O'Brien's best work remains with these three novels.

After the huge success of *The Country Girls*, *August Is a Wicked Month* disappointed. The *TLS* suggested that "an over-insistence on actual physical atonement for guilt" for Ellen resulted in "masochistic self-indulgence" and that while it is a "sadder and wiser exploration of happiness and guilt," it comes "dangerously near [to] exploiting emotion without professional discipline" (893). The *Atlantic Monthly* also criticized the "detached . . . dehumanized" story. Reviewer Brigid Elson delightfully predicted that *Casualties of Peace*, like its predecessors, would be banned in Ireland, but that "apparently it is a compliment in Ireland as all the best authors' works are unavailable there" (181). Elson went on to more specific praise, remarking that O'Brien's "rhetoric rarely flies too high. . . . Her characters' conversations and letters . . . are one deft step away from those of daily life." However, Elson criticized "her choice of symbols" (181), a notion shared by the reviewer for the *TLS*: "Miss O'Brien is now more sophisticated as a novelist and innocence and effervescence of style are no longer enough . . . despite her professionalism" (997).

Many critics lauded the seventh novel, *Night*, as an engaging tour de force. Vivian Raynor conceded that O'Brien was "outstanding in the current genre of liberated female writing" but warned that the writing in the novel "arouses pompous feelings of protectiveness" (4). Phoebe Adams was less guarded in her praise: "The effect is odd and not entirely satisfactory, but the prose . . . is remarkable. It glitters with surprises and ingenuities. It bubbles like a fountain of champagne and the entrancing game of words compensates for any vaporishness in the story" (103). Critics overwhelmingly panned *Johnny I Hardly Knew You*. Even Anatole Broyard, who lauded her last three, called this flatly a "bad novel," kindly contending that "even the most accomplished . . . occasionally make mistakes" ("One Critic's Fiction," 12).

American critics were highly complimentary of *A Fanatic Heart*, but these were the best stories of five collections and of twenty years, many of them published in the *New Yorker*. Michiko Kakutani of the *New York Times* praised its "earthy humor" and "firm sense of place," but thought it somewhat repetitious (C15). Mary Gordon's review in the *New York Times* was the most effusive: "She has—as only the finest writers can—created a world; she speaks in a voice identifiably and only hers. No voice could be less androgynous or more rooted in a land" (1).

O'Brien's tenth novel, *The High Road*, and one for which readers had to wait a decade, drew much critical response. Paul Gray virtually glorified it, comparing it to Thomas Mann's *Death in Venice* (1912) and suggesting that some "moments partake of the miraculous" (130). Robert Hosmer commended it: "Here she has rendered the landscape of a paradise before and after the fall" ("An Irish Medley," 250). Pearl K. Bell was less complimentary, censuring the novel for not offering "development or variety about this familiar character and her experience" (41). Terrence Rafferty presented the most comprehensive review, concluding, "this isn't by any means a completely satisfying novel, but its confusions are expressive, unsettling in weirdly memorable ways. Its mixture of self-regard and self-loathing is somehow elating" (94). During an interview, she admitted that it was her least favorite: "I don't think *The High Road* is realized. . . . It's imperfect. . . . I hadn't written for a long time. So I was groping to find my voice, but everyone is allowed a mistake" (Pearce, "An Interview," 7).

Lantern Slides earned rave reviews from American critics, winning the Los Angeles Times Book Review Prize for Fiction. David Leavitt agreed: "What distinguishes Ms. O'Brien's stories in *Lantern Slides* . . . is their lyrical voice and heartfelt pulsations"; Leavitt celebrated "her superb new collection [, which] continues the quest for origin and explanation that has preoccupied Ms. O'Brien these past decades. Though she covers no new ground here, she also digs deeper into the old ground than ever before, unearthing a rich archeology" (9). And London audiences acclaimed it: "On the subject of loneliness, O'Brien is excellent. The same precision with which she portrays landscapes applies to human emotions; there isn't a single character in these stories who is unconvincing. O'Brien continues to display acute powers of observation in a prose that is always neat and often immaculate" (Doughty, 616). This was O'Brien's favorite collection, and she extolled one story in particular: "There's a short story that I wrote in a single burst. It's called 'Brother.' It's a sister's incestuous love for her brother. I also like the title story" (Pearce, "An Interview," 8).

Critics either loved or hated *Time and Tide*. Marianne Wiggins, for example, hated it: "The author's sole point of view of the whole human mess is regrettably narcissistic" (60). Robert Hosmer Jr. on the other hand, loved it: "O'Brien's achievement in *Time and Tide* is so extraordinary that this eleventh novel may well eclipse the previous ten, even her first"; he calls the book "a haunting water poem, a heartfelt elegy engendered by the two most human emotions: love and loss" ("Down and Out," 25, 26). Ray Sawhill concurred, labeling it her "harshest yet most beautiful work. She has a touchy, rich theme: the sexuality of the bond between mothers and sons" (58).

While reviews were mixed, American critics primarily praised *House of Splendid Isolation*. Margo Jefferson celebrated O'Brien's "trying new things" (i.e., a political novel) and found that the famous O'Brien prose, "all lilt and sway and chant," helped move the plot and theme along despite "occasional allegorical excesses" (C18). Alice Hughes was even more effusive, calling "this intriguing and complex novel . . . no less than a history of contemporary Ireland. . . . a compressed and compassionate human history with no patently evil characters bearing easy political labels" (xlvi). Helen Thompson posited that the novel's strength and weakness lay in "the opening and closing internal monologues" of the child (179). The *New Republic* scathingly condemned the book as old, overworked, and overdone: "It makes no difference if we are reading the child's voice, or the main narrative, or Josie's uncle, an Irish Volunteer fighting against the British rule: it all sounds the same, solemn, portentous and clichéd" (Lee, 53).

Jose Lanters's astute review succinctly pinpointed both the strengths and weaknesses of *Down by the River*: "O'Brien is famous for the emotional intensity with which she can infuse her language, and the imagery in her latest novel is, as always, darkly and sultrily suggestive, at times perhaps (depending upon one's taste) excessively so" (135). Millicent Bell took O'Brien to task for making Mary "excessively mute and passive as a novelistic center" (613). However, Bell liked the father's characterization: "The rapist father is a triumph. . . . Whining, wily, self-excusing James MacNamara is a repulsive yet weirdly engaging personality" (614). Maria Alvarez scathingly denounced the book, which she believed "marred by problems of style and deficiencies of structure. . . . Had O'Brien given the narrative to her young heroine . . . the effort to capture a different viewpoint might have curbed her self-indulgent authorial intrusions and achieved the simplicity and the illusion of veracity that the tale demands" (22). Hosmer's review was the most comprehensive and balanced, citing O'Brien's "uncanny and sometimes profound ability to represent embodied female consciousness"; yet Hosmer conceded that the novel had "serious problems," that Mary "never really comes to life" (535).

Dermot Kelly highly praised *James Joyce,* this "labor of love": "O'Brien's fierce sense of solidarity with her subject can doubtless be traced to her own experience of censorship in her homeland. . . . But what she achieves with the poetic prose of this short biography is an extraordinary marriage of laser-like insights into the roots of the repressed culture and loving explorations of that feminine wisdom that is such an undeniable aspect of Joyce's genius" (703). Michael Patrick Gillespie commented, "Most Joyceans have already read the Ellmann biography. . . . Knowing that such people will be the most likely readers of any new biography must indeed be daunting for anyone undertaking such a project. O'Brien has responded to this challenge in a fashion that will either delight or enrage" ("Review," 697). And while Gillespie found the prose style "delightful," he was "uneasy" with some "inaccuracies" ("Review," 698).

Wild Decembers received praise as her best novel since *Time and Tide:* "Any reader can readily see that this novel will be vintage O'Brien—a dark, yet often comic, tale of betrayal, of characters and a land constrained by history, of flawed humans seeking compassion, requesting forgiveness and redemption" (Pearce, "Predictable" 20). Molly Winans loved the "entrancing rhythms and refrains . . . right from the first sentence," labeling this novel "stunning," at once "an intricate poem and a taut, suspenseful page-turner" (19). However, Jose Lanters chided O'Brien for being "stuck, in terms of themes and attitudes, in the 1950s," with female characters that fit too "easily into the traditional virgin/whore dichotomy, and are either passive, put-upon, and dependent, like Breege, or sexually voracious, like Rita and Reena" ("Review," 115).

Brooke Allen applauded the author of *In the Forest*, who has "juiced up her style to a new level of lushness and broadened her fictional scope to include not merely people within Ireland but Ireland itself: its history, politics, and character" (124). Caleb Crain's review was mixed: he liked the character of Kitty, "evidence that O'Brien can still write genuinely funny characters when she lets herself," but for the most part, Crain panned the book, convinced that O'Brien "doesn't have the same intuitive grasp of that crime" as she did of adolescent girls growing up in the country (11). Ronan Bennett lauded the novel as "spare, compelling and compassionate," forcing the country "to take a long, hard look at itself in April 1994 when the newspapers carried the accounts of tragic and horrific events" upon which this novel is based. Up to this point, Ireland liked "to think of itself as unlike anywhere in Europe . . . mobile phones without the muggings." Bennett praised the author for "breathing life into the murderous youth . . . making him terrifyingly and forlornly known to us."

BIBLIOGRAPHY

Works by Edna O'Brien

Arabian Days. Photography by Gerard Klijn. London: Quartet, 1977.
August Is a Wicked Month. London: Cape, 1965.
Casualties of Peace. London: Weidenfeld and Nicolson, 1966.
"A Cheap Bunch of Nine Flowers." In *Plays of the Year*. Edited by J. C. Trewin. New York: Ungar, 1963.
The Country Girls. London: Hutchinson, 1960.
The Country Girls Trilogy and Epilogue. New York: Farrar, Straus, and Giroux, 1986.
The Dazzle. London: Hodder and Stroughton, 1981.
Down by the River. New York: Farrar, Straus, and Giroux, 1997.
A Fanatic Heart: Selected Stories. New York: Farrar, Straus, and Giroux, 1984.
Girls in Their Married Bliss. London: Cape, 1964.
The High Road. New York: Farrar, Straus, and Giroux, 1988.
House of Splendid Isolation. New York: Farrar, Straus, and Giroux, 1994.
In the Forest. New York: Houghton Mifflin, 2002.
James Joyce. New York: Lipper/Viking, 1999.
Johnny I Hardly Knew You. New York: Doubleday, 1976.
Lantern Slides. London: Weidenfeld and Nicolson, 1990.
The Lonely Girl. New York: Random House, 1962.
The Love Object. London: Cape, 1968.
Mother Ireland. Photography by Fergus Bourke. London: Weidenfeld and Nicolson, 1976.
Mrs. Reinhardt and Other Stories. London: Weidenfeld and Nicolson, 1978.
Night. London: Weidenfeld and Nicolson, 1972.
On the Bone. Warwick: Greville, 1989.
A Pagan Place. London: Weidenfeld and Nicolson, 1970. Reprint, London: Faber, 1973.
Returning: A Collection of Tales. London: Weidenfeld and Nicolson, 1982.
A Scandalous Woman and Other Stories. London: Weidenfeld and Nicolson, 1974.
Seven Novels and Other Short Stories. London: Collins, 1978.

Some Irish Loving. New York: Harper and Row, 1979. (Editor.)

Tales for the Telling: Irish Folk and Fairy Stories. Illustrated by Michael Foreman. New York: Atheneum, 1986.

Time and Tide. New York: Farrar, Straus, and Giroux, 1992.

Virginia. London: Hogarth, 1981.

Wild Decembers. New York: Houghton Mifflin, 2000.

Zee and Co. London: Penguin, 1971.

Studies of Edna O'Brien

Adams, Phoebe. "Short Reviews: Books." Review of *Night*. *Atlantic Monthly*, February 1973, 103.

Allen, Brooke. "Thrilling Desperation." Review of *In the Forest*. *Atlantic Monthly*, March 2002, 124–26.

Alvarez, Maria. "Symbols of the Irish Soul." Review of *Down by the River*. *Times Literary Supplement*, September 27, 1996, 22.

Bell, Millicent. "Fiction Chronicle." Review of *Down by the River*. *Partisan Review* 64, no. 4 (Fall 1997): 612–14.

Bell, Pearl K. "Hopelessly in Love." Review of *The High Road*. *New Republic*, February 13, 1989, 40–41.

Bennett, Ronan. "The Country Girl's Home Truths." *Guardian*, May 4, 2002. http://books.guardian.co.uk/reviews/generalfiction/0,6121,709472,00.html (accessed November 10, 2003).

Broyard, Anatole. "One Critic's Fiction." Review of *Johnny I Hardly Knew You*. *New York Times Book Review*, January 1, 1978, 12.

———. "The Rotten Luck of Kate and Baba." Review of *The Country Girls: Trilogy and Epilogue*. *New York Times Book Review*, May 11, 1986, 12.

Cahalan, James. "Female and Male Perspectives on Growing Up Irish in Edna O'Brien, John McGahern, and Brian Moore." *Colby Quarterly* 31, no. 1 (March 1995): 55–73.

Carpenter, Lynette. "Tragedies of Remembrance, Comedies of Endurance: The Novels of Edna O'Brien." In *Essays on the Contemporary British Novel*, edited by Albert Wertheim and Hedwig Bock, 263–81. München: Hueber, 1986.

Carriker, Kitti. "Edna O'Brien's 'The Doll': A Narrative of Abjection." *Notes on Modern Irish Literature* 1 (1989): 6–13.

Crain, Caleb. "The Dead: Edna O'Brein's Novel Is about a Madman who Goes on a Killing Spree in Rural Ireland." Review of *In the Forest*. *New York Times Book Review*, April 7, 2002, 11.

Davies, Bonnie Lynn. "Re-constructucting the Brick Wall of Phallocentric Dis-Course: Nell Finds Her (M)Other Tongue in Edna O'Brien's *Time and Tide*." *Canadian Journal of Irish Studies* 22, no. 2 (December 1996): 73–81.

Doughty, Louise. "Restless Dreaming Souls." Review of *Lantern Slides*. *Times Literary Supplement*, June 8, 1990, 616.

Duncan, Dawn. "Edna O'Brien and Virginia." *Canadian Journal of Irish Studies* 22, no. 2 (December 1996): 99–105.

Dunn, Nell, ed. "Edna." In *Talking to Women*. London: MacGibbon and Kee, 1965, 69–107.

Eckley, Grace. *Edna O'Brien*. Lewisburg: Bucknell University Press, 1974.

Elson, Brigid. Review of *Casualties of Peace*. *Commonweal*, April 28, 1967, 181.

"Fiction." Review of *August Is a Wicked Month*. *Times Literary Supplement*, October 7, 1965, 893.

"Fiction." Review of *Casualties of Peace*. *Times Literary Supplement*, November 3, 1966, 997.

Gillespie, Michael Patrick. "Review." Review of *James Joyce*. *James Joyce Quarterly* 36, no. 3 (Spring 1999): 696–99.

———. " '[S]he Was Too Scrupulous Always': Edna O'Brien and the Comic Tradition." In *The Comic Tradition in Irish Women Writers*, ed. Theresa O'Connor, 108–23. Gainesville: University of Florida Press, 1996.

Gordon, Mary. "The Failure of True Love." Review of *A Fanatic Heart. New York Times Book Review*, November 18, 1984, 1.

Gray, Paul. "In Limbo with Love's Exiles." Review of *The High Road. Time*, November 21, 1988, 130.

Grogan, Maureen L. "Using Memory and Adding Emotion: The (Re)Creation of Experience in the Short Fiction of Edna O'Brien." *Canadian Journal of Irish Studies* 22, no. 2 (December 1996): 9–19.

Guppy, Shusha. "The Art of Fiction LXXXII: Edna O'Brien." *Paris Review* 92 (1984): 22–50.

Haberstroh, Patricia Boyle. "Edna O'Brien." In *Dictionary of Literary Biography: British Novelists Since 1960*, edited by Jay Halio. 14(2).2. Detroit: Gale, 1983, 572–80.

Haule, James. "Tough Luck: The Unfortunate Birth of Edna O'Brien." *Colby Library Quarterly* 23, no. 4 (December 1987): 216–24.

Hogan, Robert. "Old Boys, Young Bucks, and New Women: The Contemporary Irish Short Story." In *The Irish Short Story: A Critical History*, edited by James F. Kilroy, 169–215. Boston: Twayne, 1984.

Hosmer, Robert Ellis, Jr. "Book Reviews." Review of *The Country Girls Trilogy and Epilogue. America*, October 18, 1986, 169–215.

———. "Book Reviews." Review of *Down by the River. Cross Currents* 47, no. 4 (Winter 1997): 531–41.

———. "Down and Out in Life." Review of *Time and Tide. Commonweal* 127, no. 9 (October 23, 1992): 25–26.

———. "An Irish Medley." Review of *The High Road. America* March 18, 1989, 250–52.

Hughes, Alice. "History Behind the Headlines." Review of *House of Splendid Isolation. Sewanee Review* 106, no. 2 (Spring 1998): xlvi–xlvii.

Jefferson, Margo. "Edna O'Brien Takes Her Pen to a Wider Canvas." Review of *House of Splendid Isolation. New York Times*, July 13, 1994, C18.

Kakutani, Michiko. "Books of the Times." Review of *A Fanatic Heart. New York Times*, November 12, 1984, C15.

Kelly, Dermot. "Review." Review of *James Joyce. James Joyce Quartely* 36, no. 3 (Spring 1999): 701–3.

Kilroy, James F., ed. "Introduction." In *The Irish Short Story: A Critical History*. Boston: Twayne, 1984, 1–19.

Lanters, Jose. "Book Reviews." Review of *Down by the River. World Literature Today* 72, no. 1 (Winter 1998): 135.

———. "Review." Review of *Wild Decembers. World Literature Today* 75, no. 1 (Winter 2001): 115.

Leavitt, David. "Small Tragedies and Ordinary Passions." Review of *Lantern Slides. New York Times Book Review*, June 24, 1990, 9.

Lee, Hermione. "The Terror and the Pity." Review of *House of Splendid Isolation. New Republic*, June 13, 1994, 52–53.

Lynch, Rachel Jane. " 'A Land of Strange, Throttled, Sacrificial Women': Domestic Violence in the Short Fiction of Edna O'Brien." *Canadian Journal of Irish Studies* 22, no. 2 (December 1996): 37–48.

Lynch, Vivian Valvano. "Not Too Scrupulous This Time." A Review of Edna O'Brien's *James Joyce. Irish Literary Supplement* 19, no. 2 (Fall 2000): 10.

McMahon, Sean. "A Sex by Themselves: An Interim Report on the Novels of Edna O'Brien." *Eire-Ireland* 2, no. 1 (Spring 1977): 79–89.

Mitgang, Robert. "Many Faces of Love, Most of Them Unhappy." Review of *Lantern Slides. New York Times*, May 30, 1990, C17.

Morgan, Eileen. "Mapping Out a Landscape of Female Suffering: Edna O'Brien's Demythologizing Novels." *Women's Studies* 16, no. 2 (August 2000): 449–75.

O'Brien, Darcy. "Edna O'Brien: A Kind of Irish Childhood." In *Twentieth Century Women Novelists*, edited by Thomas F. Staley, 179–90. Savage, MD: Barnes and Noble Books, 1982.

O'Brien, Peggy. "The Silly and the Serious: An Assessment of Edna O'Brien." *Massachusetts Review* 28 (1987): 474–88.

O'Hara, Kiera. "Love Objects: Love and Obsession in the Stories of Edna O'Brien." *Studies in Short Fiction* 30, no. 3 (Summer 1993): 317–25.

Pearce, Sandra Manoogian. "An Interview with Edna O'Brien." *Canadian Journal of Irish Studies* 22, no. 2 (December 1996): 5–8.

———. "Redemption through Reconciliation: Edna O'Brien's Isolated Women." *Canadian Journal of Irish Studies* 22, no. 2 (December 1996): 63–71.

———. "Predictable, but Powerful: O'Brien's Domestic Tragedy." Review of *Wild Decembers*. *Irish Literary Supplement* 20, no. 1 (Spring 2001): 20–21.

Pelan, Rebecca. "Edna O'Brien's 'World of Nora Barnacle.'" *Canadian Journal of Irish Studies* 22, no. 2 (1996): 49–61.

Rafferty, Terrence. "Books: A Fresh Start." Review of *The High Road*. *New Yorker* January 30, 1989, 92–94.

Rafroidi, Patrick. "Bovarysm and the Irish Novel." *Irish University Review* 7, no. 2 (Autumn 1977): 237–43.

Raynor, Vivien. "A Sly County Girl Come to Town." Review of *Night*. *Book World, Washington Post*. January 7, 1973, 4.

Rooks-Hughes, Lorna. "The Family and The Female Body in the Novels of Edna O'Brien and Julia O'Faolain." *Canadian Journal of Irish Studies* 22, no. 2 (December 1996): 83–97.

Sawhill, Ray. "The Books of Summer." Review of *Time and Tide*. *Newsweek*, June 8, 1992, 58.

Schrank, Bernice, and Danine Farquharson. "Object of Love, Subject to Despair: Edna O'Brien's *The Love Object* and the Emotional Logic of Late Romanticism." *Canadian Journal of Irish Studies* 22, no. 2 (December 1996): 20–36.

Snow, Lotus. "'That Trenchant Childhood Route'?: Quest in Edna O'Brien's Novels." *Eire-Ireland* 14, no. 1 (Spring 1979): 74–83.

Thompson, Helen. "Book Reviews." Review of *House of Splendid Isolation*. *Review of Contemporary Fiction* 15, no. 1 (Spring 1995): 179–80.

Wiggins, Marianne. "Nell and Void." Review of *Time and Tide*. *Nation*, July 13, 1992, 60–62.

Wilhelmus, Tom. "Communities Perhaps." Review of *Wild Decembers*. *Hudson Review* 53 (2001): 697–98.

Winans, Molly. "A Dark Tale, Told in Singing Prose." Review of *Wild Decembers*. *Commonweal* 5 (May 2000): 19.

Wolcott, James. "Playgirl of the Western World." *Vanity Fair*, June 1992, 50.

KATE O'BRIEN
(1897–1974)

Elizabeth Gilmartin

BIOGRAPHY

Kate O'Brien was born in 1897 in Limerick to Thomas and Catherine O'Brien. The youngest daughter of nine children in a wealthy middle-class family, she was sent to Lauren Hill Convent in Limerick at age five, after her mother died. She received a BA in English and French from University College Dublin in 1919. After graduation, O'Brien moved to England, where she worked as a journalist for the *Manchester Guardian* and then taught for a term at St. Mary's Convent in Hampstead in 1921. Not caring for teaching, she then accompanied her sister and brother-in-law, Nance and Stephen O'Mara, to the United States for a fund-raising tour for Eamon de Valera in 1922. After she returned to England, O'Brien went to Spain for a year as a governess, or "Miss." Upon her return to England, she married Gustaaf Renier in 1923; the marriage was not an easy one and the couple divorced after only eleven months. O'Brien wrote the play *Distinguished Villa* (1926) in six weeks as part of a bet with a friend from college. The play was first performed at the Aldwych Theatre and received good reviews, as even Sean O'Casey sent a telegram saying "Dublin ventures to congratulate Limerick" (quoted in Walshe, 12). Her second play, *The Bridge* (1927), was produced at the Arts Theatre Club. Despite these early successes with theater, O'Brien's real success as a writer started when she began publishing novels.

In the late 1920s, O'Brien began working on a novel called *Without My Cloak* (1931), which won the Hawthornden and James Tait Black memorial prizes. Her next work, *The Ante-Room* (1934), is a sequel to *Without My Cloak*. Her next novel, *Mary Lavelle* (1936), based on her time in Spain, was banned by the Irish Censorship Board for its depiction of premarital sex between its young heroine and the married brother of her pupils. Then appeared *Farewell, Spain* (1937), which was banned in Spain for its criticism of Franco's regime; in addition to banning the work, Spain also banned O'Brien from entering the country until 1957.

During World War II, O'Brien worked for the Ministry of Information. *The Land of Spices* (1941) was also banned in Ireland for its fleeting reference to homosexuality. *The Last of Summer* (1942) was also converted into a play directed by Sir John Gielgud in 1944. At this time she also wrote reviews for the *Spectator* and edited a collection of essays, *The Romance of English Literature* (1943). Her historical novel, *That Lady* (1946), about Ana de Mendoza, stirred much interest as the novel was developed into the film *For One Sweet Grape*, in 1955, starring Olivia De Havilland and into a Broadway play starring Katherine Cornell. This enabled her to buy a house in Roundstone, County Galway, where she wrote *The Flower of May* (1953) and a work of nonfiction about St. Teresa of Avila (1951). Her last novel, *As Music and Splendour*, was published in 1958. Her last works were a travel book, *My Ireland* (1962), and a memoir, *Presentation Parlour* (1963). She died in Canterbury in 1974 and is buried in a Carmelite convent in Kent.

MAJOR WORKS AND THEMES

Like so many Irish writers, Kate O'Brien spent much of her adult life living away from Ireland, yet it remains the subject and setting of most of her novels. The main characters of all of her novels, even those set outside of Ireland, are Irish. These characters consistently face familial, political, religious, or social repression. Her characters often find themselves facing the choice between following their hearts or breaking a social or religious decree of some sort. That many of O'Brien's characters in this situation are female has led many scholars to consider O'Brien a feminist author, though this remains arguable. The idea of the forbidden love, which fascinated O'Brien, manifests itself in her work in adulterous or homosexual love. Her depiction of homosexuality, coupled with O'Brien's refusal to remarry, has led many scholars to believe she was a lesbian. Generally, the world reflected in O'Brien's work stifles its characters, and the tension of the novels lies in the characters' struggles to free themselves. Some of her characters are incapable of doing this, and her depiction of these realistic struggles and her refusal to provide the easy happy ending are her strongest appeals.

Without My Cloak and its sequel, *The Ante-Room*, tell the story of the Considine family, the most powerful family in Mellick, based on O'Brien's Limerick. Both focus on doomed love affairs. In the former, Denis loves the illegitimate daughter of a scullery maid, while his aunt Caroline does not love her husband, but someone else instead. Because of the social and religious restrictions of Victorian Ireland, neither love affair is destined for happiness. *The Ante-Room* continues to present doomed marriages and the torment of love that would be sinful if acted upon.

In *Mary Lavelle*, which was made into a movie called *Talk of Angels* (1996), O'Brien continues the exploration of the tension between illicit love affairs and Catholic teaching. Mary Lavelle falls in love with Juanito, the married brother of her charges in Spain, where she is a governess. O'Brien here shows Mary acting on her impulses and developing a physical relationship with Juanito, who has joined the revolutionary political movement. O'Brien uses the Spanish setting to critique Ireland, as her character can gain a type of freedom inaccessible in Ireland. In response to the banning of *Mary Lavelle*, O'Brien wrote her next novel, *Pray for the Wanderer* (1938), which portrays a male writer of "scandalous novels" who has left Ireland for England and returned to Ireland for a visit with family after a failed affair with a married woman. The novel focuses on the writer's inability to find acceptance in Irish society.

Though many of her novels contain autobiographical elements, *Pray for the Wanderer* and her next novel, *The Land of Spices*, have the most aspects of O'Brien's own life to them. Like *Pray for the Wanderer, The Land of Spices* was written in response to the banning of the previous book. It relates Anna Murphy's experience at a convent school similar to O'Brien's Laurel Hill. Also like *Pray for the Wanderer, The Last Summer* describes an artist's trip to Ireland, this time of an actress who discovers that her Irish relatives had disowned her father for marrying her actress mother. O'Brien, like Joyce, questioned the ability of artists to remain in Ireland's puritanical society.

O'Brien's novels often depict characters whose mothers have died or are in the process of dying. *The Last of Summer* and *The Ante-Room* each uses a dying mother as backdrop to the novel's action. In both novels this event forces the early maturity of the young Irish girls who are the main characters. These young women find themselves traveling through Europe, gaining educations and livelihoods, and navigating the difficulties of love relationships. In parallel fashion, the Irishness of the main characters is contrasted with the European traits of the other characters in a way that shows both the universality of their experiences and the uniqueness of their positions as Irishwomen in Europe. *As Music and Splendour* finally foregrounds the theme of homosexuality that has been present in the background in most of O'Brien's novels.

CRITICAL RECEPTION

O'Brien has been largely overlooked by scholars for many years, though a few important books about her appeared in the late 1980s and early 1990s. Individual essays that have been published in the past twenty years tend to focus on the feminism and lesbianism of her characters, her portrayals of bourgeois Ireland, her use of music and the other arts in her work, her use of Spain as a setting, and her similarity to other writers, such as Joyce. Three book-length studies, *Kate O'Brien: A Critical Study*, by Adele Dalsimer; *Kate O'Brien: A Literary Portrait*, by Lorna Reynolds; and a collection of essays entitled *Ordinary People Dancing*, edited by Eibhear Walshe, have been published since her death. Reynolds's book combines a critical assessment of each of O'Brien's novels with biographical information. As a personal friend of O'Brien's, Reynolds provides an interesting introduction to the author's life. The book is a bit marred by digressions, though, and tends to inform the reader as much about Reynolds's own life as it does about O'Brien's. Dalsimer's book, which provides a much more objective critical analysis of O'Brien's novels, argues for further scholarly consideration of O'Brien's work and suggests that scholars ignore her because of her "outsider" status: "Bourgeois in the Irish Peasant State, Irish in the English literary world, a Catholic who lived for many years in a Protestant country, and a writer whose final novel explicitly portrays a lesbian relationship, Kate O'Brien was relegated to literary oblivion" (xi). Walshe's collection, which sought to address the need for more discussion of O'Brien's work, includes an essay by Eavan Boland that highlights O'Brien's status as one of the few writers of the Irish middle class. Emma Donoghue's essay on O'Brien's lesbian fictions seeks to rise above the speculation on O'Brien's own sexuality and focus instead on her representation of lesbians. *Ordinary People Dancing* also shows the broad expanse of O'Brien's writing career through essays on her journalism and travel writing.

In *Five Irish Writers*, John Hildebidle explores the careers of lesser-known writers or writers, such as Elizabeth Bowen, whose Irish nationality had not formerly played an important part in the critical discussion about them. He sees detachment as the overriding theme of O'Brien's novels, particularly in the conflict her main characters have as they try to leave or escape the powerful love of their families and develop independent lives for themselves.

BIBLIOGRAPHY

Works by Kate O'Brien

The Ante-Room. London: Heinemann, 1934.
As Music and Splendour. London: Heinemann, 1958.
Distinguished Villa: A Play in Three Acts. London: Benn, 1926.
Farewell, Spain. London: Heinemann, 1938.
The Flower of May. London: Heinemann, 1953.
The Land of Spices. London: Heinemann, 1941.
The Last of Summer. London: Heinemann, 1943.
Mary Lavelle. London: Heinemann, 1936.
My Ireland. London: Batsford, 1962.
Pray for the Wanderer. London: Heinemann, 1938.
Presentation Parlour. London: Heinemann, 1963.
Teresa of Avila. Personal Portraits Series. London: Parrish, 1951.
That Lady. London: Heinemann, 1946.
Without my Cloak. London: Heinemann, 1931.

Studies of Kate O'Brien

Dalsimer, Adele. *Kate O'Brien: A Critical Study.* Dublin: Gill and Macmillan, 1990.
———. "A Not so Simple Saga: Kate O'Brien's *Without My Cloak*." *Eire-Ireland* 21, no. 3 (Fall 1986): 55–71.
Donoghue, Emma. " 'Out of Order': Kate O'Brien's Lesbian Fictions." In *Ordinary People Dancing*, edited by Eibhear Walshe, 36–58. Cork: Cork University Press, 1993.

Fogarty, Anne. "Other Spaces: Postcolonialism and the Politics of Truth in Kate O'Brien's *That Lady*." *European Journal of English Studies* 3, no. 3 (December 1999): 342–53.

Hildebidle, John. *Five Irish Writers: The Errand of Keeping Alive*. Cambridge, MA: Harvard University Press, 1989, 51–87.

Kiely, Benedict. "Love and Pain and Parting: The Novels of Kate O'Brien." *The Hollins Critic* 29, no. 2 (April 1992): 1–11.

Quiello, Rose. "Disturbed Desires: The Hysteric in Kate O'Brien's *Mary Lavelle*." *Eire-Ireland* 25, no. 3 (Fall 1990): 46–57.

Reynolds, Lorna. "The Image of Spain in the Novels of Kate O'Brien." In *Literary Interrelations: Ireland, England and the World*, edited by Wolfgang Zach and Heinz Kosok, 181–88. Tubingen, Ger: Narr, 1988.

———. *Kate O'Brien: A Literary Portrait*. Gerrards Cross, UK: Colin Smythe; Totowa, NJ: Barnes and Noble, 1987.

Ryan, Joan. "Class and Creed in Kate O'Brien." In *The Irish Writer and the City*, edited by Maurice Harmon, 125–35. Totowa, NJ: Barnes and Noble, 1984.

———. "Women in the Novels of Kate O'Brien: The Mellick Novels." In *Studies in Anglo-Irish Literature*, edited by Heinz Kosok, 322–32. Bonn: Bouvier, 1982.

Walshe, Eibhear. *Ordinary People Dancing: Essays on Kate O'Brien*. Cork: Cork University Press, 1993.

MARY O'DONNELL
(1954–)

Coleen Comerford

BIOGRAPHY

Mary O'Donnell was born in Monaghan. She studied philosophy and German at St. Patrick's College, Maynooth, and graduated in 1977. After her postgraduate studies in German, O'Donnell taught German and held various other positions, such as translator, library assistant, and drama critic for the *Sunday Tribune*. In 1994, she was the writer in residence at University College Dublin. She later fulfilled a residency in County Laois and edited the first *Laois Anthology of Writing*. In 2001, O'Donnell earned the James Joyce Suspended Sentence residency to Australia and participated in the Sydney International Writers' Festival. O'Donnell, also an experienced and well-known broadcaster, has created and presented several series of poetry programs for radio and has been the presenter for RTE Radio 1's weekly program *The Darkness Echoing*. She has also translated the work of Austrian poet Ingeborg Bachmann for publication.

O'Donnell is an accomplished novelist, short-story writer, and poet. Her poems have been published in various literary magazines and journals. She has received the Arts Council Literary Award, the William Aillingham Award, the Listowel Writers' Week Award, the VS Pritchett Short Story Award, and the Hennessey Literature Award. She has also been a prizewinner in the Cardiff International Poetry Competition and the

Austin Clarke Centenary Poetry Competition. She currently lives near Maynooth, County Kildare.

MAJOR WORKS AND THEMES

To date, O'Donnell has published three novels, four poetry collections, and a collection of short stories. Her first poetry collection, *Reading the Sunflowers in September*, was published in 1990, and her first collection of short stories, *Strong Pagans*, was published in 1991. Other poetry collections include *Spiderwoman's Third Avenue Rhapsody* (1993), *Unlegendary Heroes* (1998), and *September Elegies* (2003). Her poetry deals with love and its rituals, death, landscape and travel, and motherhood. Her poems are characterized by a meditative style and striking imagery.

O'Donnell is particularly interested in the unique circumstances that women face: marriage and its responsibilities and trials, childbirth and motherhood, and traditional roles inside and outside the home. The poem "Unlegendary Heroes" (22–24), from the eponymous volume, responds to a 1938 folklore survey conducted to record the local people of south Ulster. The poem reproduces a passage from this survey, which evidently recorded only the doings of male parish members. O'Donnell attempts to make up for the absence of female "heroes" in the survey. The women O'Donnell describes in this poem are "unlegendary" figures, such as Kathleen McKenna, who could "wash a week's sheets" and clothing, bake bread, and clean the house all in one day; Birdy McMahon, who reportedly walked to Monaghan for a sack of flour two days before she gave birth to her eighth child; and Phyllis McCrudden, twice a widow, who "raised five children and farmed her own land." Each figure is exceptional for her endurance, strength, and fortitude. O'Donnell celebrates the heroic nature of these women's daily survival, and insists that their existences and activities are as important as those of their male counterparts.

The subject of "Materfamilias" (32) is the speaker's grandmother, a woman who endured thirteen pregnancies, nine of which she carried to term. When questioned as to whether she would do it all again, the grandmother replies that once is enough for motherhood, which she describes as "the struggle between self and others." O'Donnell often characterizes motherhood as a devouring of the female self; while the woman is compelled to bear children, the energy expended in rearing them leaves her spent and wasted. Nevertheless, O'Donnell suggests that women's sense of feminine identity is largely associated with the ability to reproduce. This idea is central to O'Donnell's first novel, *The Light-Makers* (1992).

The Light-Makers is the story of Hanna Troy, a Dublin woman who is devastated by the infidelity of her husband, Sam. The story unfolds as Hanna wanders the streets of Dublin, killing time before an appointment with her new therapist at the Women's Centre. Hanna believes that her husband strayed from her as a result of their many failed attempts to have children. Sam's refusal to submit to a physical exam after Hanna's doctor concludes that nothing is wrong with her leads her to believe that he is rejecting her in a deeper sense as a woman and a potential mother. When Hanna discovers that Sam has impregnated his mistress, she is left to confront the fact the she is the one who cannot have children. Although she is a highly successful photographer, Hanna interprets her inability to be a mother as the ultimate failure of her womanhood. Interspersed with her reflections on her marriage are Hanna's memories of her own mother, a competent woman with a successful marriage, which intensify her sense of inadequacy. Sam and Hanna's unsuccessful marriage is ironically paralleled by their successful careers. Hanna and Sam are both adept creators: she of photographic images, he as architect of innovative buildings. Both are fixated on ideas of using light—both are "light-makers"—and light functions in the novel as a symbol for both truth and illusion, which perspective makes interchangeable. The novel ends as Hanna begins to discover self-worth and resolves to live only for herself.

In her 1999 novel, *The Elysium Testament*, O'Donnell's heroine is Nina, a talented architect who specializes in restoring grottos. As with Hanna, Nina's husband, Neil, has left her, and the novel is written as a series of letters to him that amount to an extended suicide note. The marriage begins to disintegrate after the birth of their second child, Roland. While Neil desperately wanted to have more children after Nina gave birth to their first child, Elinore, Nina was content with one child and is shocked and angry when she finds herself pregnant again, years later. Nina travels from Ireland to England to have an abortion, but changes her mind after phoning Neil. She has the baby for Neil's sake but never feels the natural attachment to Roland that she felt with Elinore. As Roland grows up, Nina is frightened by his seemingly mystical nature and is convinced that Roland can levitate, that he creates shrines in his bedroom to which he prays, and that he invents a mischievous "other" Roland. The reliability of Nina's first-person account is thrown into question by a series of letters her daughter writes to advice columns, which respond that her mother is intentionally abusing her younger brother verbally and physically. The fact that Roland is a terrified boy who has projected parts of himself onto his "evil" other self supports the possibility that Nina abuses him. Moreover, Nina never forgives Roland for his birth, and while she tries to love him she unconsciously punishes him for disrupting her life. When Roland is accidentally killed in the grotto Nina has been working long hours to restore, she feels responsible for his death. Ironically, Nina had begun to feel that she should love and protect Roland while the two explored the grotto together. While in *The Light-Makers* the narrator is obsessed with the idea that femininity and womanhood are intricately bound to motherhood and regrets the fact that she cannot have children, in *The Elysium Testament* the narrator obeys the same female impulse to reproduce but resents her motherhood to the extreme. Nina's grotto restoration is ironic; the grotto, a cavernous, sacred place, is a sort of symbolic womb, which she works to restore at the expense of her marriage and her family. It is there that she begins her adulterous affair with Ciaran, and there that her son is killed. Motherhood, this novel suggests, has both creative and destructive aspects. In the end, Nina decides not to kill herself, and instead pursue a relationship with John Holmes, a psychiatrist who has tried to help Nina through her grief. Nina also decides to give John her home, named Elysium, to use as a halfway house for his mentally ill patients.

CRITICAL RECEPTION

O'Donnell has won many prizes for her poetry and novels and has been hailed as one of Ireland's most exciting new writers. *The Light-Makers* was named the *Sunday Tribune* Best New Novel of 1992. *The Elysium Testament* was also received to great critical acclaim. O'Donnell has also been studied in the context of contemporary women's fiction in Ireland. Anne Fogarty looks at O'Donnell's novel *The Elysium Testament* and three other novels written by contemporary Irish women authors in terms of "the recent revolutionary and unprecedented alterations in Irish society" (61–62). Two of O'Donnell's novels—*The Virgin and the Boy* and *The Light-Makers*—are also discussed in the work of Christine St. Peter, who approaches *The Virgin and the Boy* as an example of the representation of sexual transgression in the context of the conflict between traditional Catholic Ireland and a radically changing nation. She discusses *The Light-Makers* as exemplary of the trend in contemporary Irish women's fiction toward "naturalization . . . of the presence of the women's movement(s) in Ireland" (161). While O'Donnell is lauded for her writing in itself, she has also been recognized as an important figure in popularizing women's fiction and women's issues in Ireland.

BIBLIOGRAPHY

Works by Mary O'Donnell

Fiction

The Elysium Testament. London, Trident, 1999.
The Light-Makers. Swords, Ire.: Poolbeg, 1992.
Strong Pagans. Swords, Ire.: Poolbeg, 1991.
The Virgin and the Boy. Swords, Ire.: Poolbeg, 1996.

Poetry

Reading the Sunflowers in September. Cliffs of Moher: Salmon, 1991.
September Elegies. Belfast: Lapwing, 2003.
Spiderwoman's Third Avenue Rhapsody. Cliffs of Moher: Salmon, 1993.
Unlegendary Heroes. Cliffs of Moher: Salmon, 1998.

Studies of Mary O'Donnell

Fogarty, Anne. "Uncanny Families: Neo-Gothic Motifs and the Theme of Social Change in Contemporary Irish Women's Fiction." *Irish University Review* 30, no. 1 (Spring–Summer 2000): 59–81.
St. Peter, Christine. *Changing Ireland: Strategies in Contemporary Women's Fiction*. New York: St. Martin's; London: Macmillan, 2000.
Wilson, Rebecca E., and Gillean Somerville-Arjat, eds. *Sleeping with Monsters: Conversations with Scottish and Irish Women Poets*. Dublin: Wolfhound, 1990, 18–25.

JULIA O'FAOLAIN
(1932–   )

Ann Owens Weekes

BIOGRAPHY

Julia O'Faolain was born into a family of writers and romantics; her mother, Eileen Gould O'Faolain, wrote children's stories; her father, Sean O'Faolain, was a distinguished writer and editor of the fine literary journal the *Bell*. Disillusioned by the protectionist, isolationist Ireland of the 1940s, Sean became a voice of dissent against the pruderies and pretensions of this Ireland, a voice that his daughter would echo. Eileen also shaped her daughter's perspectives by keeping her home until she was eight, audience for her own stories of fairies, pookas, and leprechauns. When she finally went to school, Julia incautiously revealed her knowledge and belief in the fairy world. The mockery of her skeptical peers determined her never to be caught out again, and from that time, she has turned a "cold eye" on all the myths of church and state, and indeed, of class. Her parents, she says, bequeathed her a fascination with magic and an inability to believe in it: the conjurer's art attracts, but she is alert to the sleight of hand rather than the pleasure of mystery.

MAJOR WORKS AND THEMES

Many of the stories in O'Faolain's first collection, *We Might See Sights!* (1968), were reprinted in *Melancholy Baby* (1978). The stories range through several levels and age-groups in Irish society and introduce a distinctive narratorial voice with an acute delight in penetrating pretension and an ability to paint a vivid picture with a few apt, original, and witty words. The title story is a haunting tale about the irrational nature of desire and the link between sexuality and violence. It is an accomplished, brief story whose theme O'Faolain explores in more detail in later work, particularly in novels. The pettiness of social distinctions, urged on children by their protective parents and teachers, another familiar O'Faolain theme, also appears here. A self-conscious young Catholic woman, struggling to realize an identity through sexuality, is the narrator in "A Pot of Soothing Herbs." Alluding to the hero of Irish myths, Cuchulain, and to the heroes of the Irish war against England, the author invites us to see the young woman's situation as both a continuation and a consequence of the Irish love of talk, of story, over action. "The Knight" delights in revealing the narcissistic qualities of the Knight of Columbus, bedecked in all his medieval grandeur. Fine social comedy and devastating powers of observation mark this first collection.

The next three books, *Godded and Codded* (1970), *Women in the Wall* (1975), and *Man in the Cellar* (1974), continue the social comedy and the focus on women's struggle for identity through passion, religious or secular. Sally, the protagonist of *Godded and Codded*, moves to Paris in search of sexual education and freedom from her dominating, repressive father. Godded and codded, the beautiful young woman finds lovers in plenty, but discovers that lovers leave when confronted with the tedium of pregnancy or age. *Women in the Wall*, a more substantial novel, mixes fact and fiction in the story of religious and secular passion in the war-torn world of sixth-century Gaul. The title story of *Man in the Cellar* is a remarkable fable of a woman's escape from an Italian bourgeois family that expects a wife, particularly an English Protestant one, to nourish her husband's machismo. O'Faolain's comedy succeeds, despite the drastic conclusions for many of the characters, because she distances her readers, refusing to allow identification with the objects of ridicule. In 1973, O'Faolain and her husband published *Not in God's Image: Women in History from the Greeks to the Victorians*, selections from documents relating to the legal status of women. This done, she says, she can now write of women without being bound by their political concerns (O'Faolain, interview with the author, Los Angeles, November 1985).

In *No Country for Young Men* (1980), the finest novel to date and short-listed for the Booker Prize, O'Faolain links the Troubles of the 1920s with those of the 1970s, as she weaves a pattern of gender and political intrigue rooted in Irish literature, history, and myth. The title and the plot undo Yeats and question both the historical and mythic record. Much of the complicated plot is embedded in the bog of Judith Clancy's mind. When her convent closes in the 1970s, Sister Judith, who was a young woman during the 1920s Troubles, is forced to live with her niece and nephew. The Diarmuid and Grainne story is replayed with the same tragic conclusion in the 1970s story of Grainne and Michael O'Malley and the American filmmaker James Duffy. The comedy here is largely restricted to the peripheral characters, and O'Faolain paints a sympathetic picture of both Grainne and Michael as Grainne struggles for passion and identity, and Michael for security. Repressed or distorted sexuality, the novel implies, in Irish myth, history, and fiction, erupts in physical violence.

Several short stories in *Daughters of Passion* (1982) also focus on sexual relations and marriage, the title story again linking violence and sexual denial. The past flashes through Maggie's mind as she endures a hunger strike for political status in Brixton prison. Involved in the Irish Republican Army almost by accident, Maggie, motivated by a mixture of jealousy and betrayal, kills a Special Branch investigator.

The Obedient Wife (1982) can be seen as an anatomy of a marriage, so detailed and penetrating is the analysis. Carla Verdi wishes to be a model mother and housewife as she attempts to bring up her son in a traditional Italian manner despite the chaos of her Los Angeles surroundings. Feeling rejected by her macho husband, Carla turns to Leo, a priest, who, sensitive to her every need, is the antithesis of her husband. Carla weighs the ties of marriage—the mutual responsibilities, the good and bad memories, the defining duties—against the excitement of a love affair and decides for marriage. Marco, Carla's husband, plays every card to persuade her to return to the life they have built in Italy, whereas Leo never makes demands. Carla sees Leo's restraint as evidence of an autonomy fatal to human relationships: needing only God, Leo cannot participate in a relationship built in large part from mutual need.

The Irish Signorina (1984) turns to the lover's side, as Anne Ryan visits the Italian family with whom her mother lived twenty-five years previously. Befriended by the family, Anne almost becomes her mother, her passion for her mother's ex-lover transcending her natural concerns of incestuous marriage. This exploration into forbidden love was followed by *The Judas Cloth* (1992). Covering the reign of Pius IX, 1846–78, this panoramic novel moves from Italy to France and introduces a wide cast of historic and fictional characters, including Nicola Santi, the pope's son. O'Faolain describes Machiavellian intrigue skillfully and wittily, re-creating historical scenes vividly, with detailed, authentic, and bloody descriptions of atrocities and betrayals. Characters in this too-large cast are not fully developed, however; hence, their behaviors are often unbelievable.

CRITICAL RECEPTION

Julia O'Faolain's original and apt description, insight into the complexities of human motivation and action, and acid sense of humor won attention, and usually acclaim, from the earliest stories. John Mellors finds *Man in the Cellar* "brilliantly disturbing," and notes the writer's manipulation of perspective, "so that you finally sympathize with the harpy, cancel your admiration of the sophisticated daughter of stuffy parents, and wonder whether the hero is not far sicker than the villain" (*Listener*, September 26, 1974, 416). Janet Egleson Dunleavy notes O'Faolain's "ability to draw a repulsive character with a few cruel strokes," but she laments that the writer uses satire for ridicule rather than forcing her readers to relate the characters to their own lives (*Irish University Review* 4, no. 2 [Autumn 1974]: 299–300); on the other hand, Theresa O'Connor sees O'Faolain's deployment of humor as an exploration of the human condition, similar to Joyce's in *Finnegans Wake*. Several critics consider the mystery of memory in *No Country for Young Men*. Some complain of "superfatted" descriptions or wallowing in violence, but others, Maurice Harmon for example, find O'Faolain's vision "harshly realistic," noting, "She sees the fury and the mire of human blood in an era when the supernatural was closer to human perception than it is now, when mystics apprehended the divine in terms of startling reality" (*Irish University Review* 5, no. 2 [Autumn 1975]: 324). "Skillfully spun and splendidly readable," William Trevor says of *No Country for Young Men*, "illuminated by a seriousness that is refreshing to encounter; though entertaining and rich in comedy, it eschews the trivial and is actually *about* something" (*Hibernia* 44, no. 23, June 5, 1980, 25).

BIBLIOGRAPHY

Works by Julia O'Faolain

Daughters of Passion. Middlesex: Penguin, 1982.
Godded and Codded. New York: Coward, McCann and Geoghegan, 1970. (Published in the United States as *Three Lovers*, 1971.)
The Irish Signorina. Middlesex: Penguin, 1984.
The Judas Cloth. 1992. Reprint, London: Minerva, 1993.
Man in the Cellar. London: Faber and Faber, 1974.
No Country for Young Men. Middlesex: Penguin, 1980.
Not in God's Image: Women in History from the Greeks to the Victorians. 1973. Reprint, London: Virago, 1979. (Edited with Lauro Martines.)
The Obedient Wife. 1982. Reprint, Middlesex: Penguin, 1983.
We Might See Sights. London: Faber and Faber, 1968.
Women in the Wall. 1975. Reprint, London: Virago, 1985.

Studies of Julia O'Faolain

Mastin, Antoinette. "Stephen Dedalus in Paris: Joycean Elements in Julia O'Faolain's *Three Lovers*." *Colby Quarterly* 30, no. 4 (December 1994): 244–51.
Moore, Thomas. "Triangles and Entrapment: Julia O'Faolain's *No Country for Young Men*." *Colby Quarterly* 27, no. 1 (March 1991): 9–16.
O'Connor, Theresa. "History, Gender, and the Postcolonial Condition: Julia O'Faolain's Comic Rewriting of *Finnegans Wake*." In *The Comic Tradition in Irish Women Writers*, edited by Theresa O'Connor, 124–48. Gainesville: University Press of Florida, 1996.
Weekes, Ann Owens. "Diarmuid and Grainne Again: Julia O'Faolain's *No Country for Young Men*." *Eire-Ireland* 21, no. 1 (Spring 1986): 89–102.

NUALA O'FAOLAIN
(1940–   )

Mary Fitzgerald-Hoyt

BIOGRAPHY

Born in Dublin on March 1, 1940, to Caitlin (also Katherine) and Tómas O'Faolain, Nuala O'Faolain was the second of nine surviving children of thirteen pregnancies. O'Faolain recalls a damaging, chaotic family life. Her father, known professionally as "Terry O'Sullivan," popular author of the social column "Dubliner's Diary" for the *Evening Press,* was frequently absent, leaving the family in poverty. Her mother, inhabiting an Ireland that was "a living tomb for women," became addicted to sleeping pills and alcohol.

A rebellious adolescent, O'Faolain was sent to boarding school at St. Louis's convent, County Monaghan. Though she won a scholarship to the National University in Dublin, her academic career was interrupted by personal problems, precipitating a painful episode doing menial work in England; she eventually completed her degree and earned scholarships that enabled her to study at the University of Hull and earn a BPhil at Oxford University.

Despite her successes as a university lecturer, a television producer for both BBC and RTÉ, and an opinion columnist for the *Irish Times*, O'Faolain was for decades plagued by self-doubt and dependence on alcohol and sleeping pills. Already a media celebrity in Ireland, she became internationally famous in 1996 with the memoir *Are You Somebody: The Life and Times of Nuala O'Faolain*, which was originally intended to be an autobiographical introduction to a collection of her *Irish Times* columns. O'Faolain's first novel, *My Dream of You*, appeared in 2001, and while at work on a second novel, she wrote a second memoir, *Almost There: The Onward Journey of a Dublin Woman*, in 2003.

After over a decade writing a weekly opinion column for the *Irish Times*, O'Faolain took a leave of absence, then returned to the paper briefly as a columnist for the weekend magazine supplement. She now divides her time between County Clare and New York.

MAJOR WORKS AND THEMES

In all of her books, O'Faolain writes of unmarried middle-aged women as socially disregarded, expected to be both sexually inactive and silent. The gulf between professional success and private unfulfillment is searingly rendered, but punctuated by linguistically arresting accounts of the places and people that both O'Faolain and Kathleen de Burca, her fictional travel writer, encounter. O'Faolain scrutinizes the intersection of personal, gender, and national identity.

Are You Somebody reveals the private trauma beneath O'Faolain's public persona as a journalist and television producer. The *Irish Times* columns included in the original Irish edition offer incisive commentary on topics ranging from an evening in a maternity hospital to Ireland's changing social landscape.

In attempting to reconcile herself with bitter family memories and the likelihood of personal solitude, O'Faolain concluded the original memoir with a breathtaking account of a Christmas spent alone on the Burren. In that landscape embedded with historical artifacts, O'Faolain finds a guardedly hopeful metaphor for her own life. She was blindsided, however, by the seismic changes that the book's unexpected popularity wrought in her life, bringing her sudden international fame and a staggering outpouring of support and affirmation from her readers, a phenomenon she describes in the "Afterwords" appended to the book when it was published outside of Ireland, minus the *Irish Times* columns, as *Are You Somebody: The Accidental Memoir of a Dublin Woman*.

In *My Dream of You*, expatriate Irish travel writer Kathleen de Burca, jolted by the sudden death of her closest friend and battered by the self-questioning of middle age, becomes intrigued by the real-life 1856 Talbot divorce proceedings, a case allegedly precipitated by an affair between Marianne Talbot, mistress of a Big House, and one of her Irish servants, William Mullan. Herself a wounded survivor of failed love affairs, Kathleen is attracted by what she believes was a love so passionate that it crossed ethnic and class boundaries and flourished amid the horrors of the Potato Famine. Wrenched out of her romantic illusions by the memorable Nan Leech, a local historian with Nationalist sympathies, and stunned by unexpected discoveries in her historical research, Kathleen must ultimately abandon her plan of writing a history or a historical novel about the Talbot case. *My Dream of You*, a novel with strong autobiographical influences, recalls *Are You Somebody* in its theme of self-discovery and self-acceptance. Kathleen must quell the ghosts of her past to find a direction for her future.

Although the novel was marketed as an old-fashioned "good read," such a designation is deceptive. O'Faolain employs metafictional techniques by including excerpts from *The Talbot Book*, Kathleen's unfinished historical novel. Further, not only is *My Dream of You* a midlife bildungsroman, but it also taps into cultural concerns of contemporary Ireland—the multiple interpretations of the past, the complex definitions of Irishness, the reconciliation of historical memory and future endeavor. Kathleen, an expatriate of long standing, feels compelled to go home not only to her family but to a country from which she has long been estranged. That Kathleen ends the book with speculation about Mullan's life and death as an American immigrant suggests her ability to move on with her own life, lonely and uncertain though it may be.

O'Faolain's next book, *Almost There: The Onward Journey of a Dublin Woman*, returns to memoir, tracing the six years following *Are You Somebody*. O'Faolain chronicles the impact of fame on her personal life, and as she did in the previous memoir, writes unflinchingly about the gulf between a successful career and a lonely private life. The misery following the end of her long relationship with Northern Irish journalist Nell McCafferty, the termination of an affair with a married man, and a new relationship with an American father of a young child are explored with painful candor. *Almost There* is an extraordinary glimpse into the life of "that specially unloved thing in a misogynistic society, a middle-aged woman with opinions." Just as O'Faolain described herself at the end of *Are You Somebody* as being between two places, the earth and the sky, she ends *Almost There* poised between two lives, two settings: a solitary life in her cottage in County Clare and her evolving relationship with her lover and his daughter in Manhattan.

CRITICAL RECEPTION

Are You Somebody was an immediate popular and critical success, hailed by Colm Tóibín as "likely to become a classic of Irish autobiography" (*Times Literary Supplement*, 15). The memoir elicited both a deep sense of personal identification from readers and the critical recognition that it was, as Eibhlín Evans noted, "an expression of a current, collective malaise." *Are You Somebody* voices the silences that lurked between public and private selves in 1950s and 1960s Ireland, and, in so doing, as Evans has commented, provides a corrective and a caveat to the contemporary Ireland of the so-called Celtic Tiger, one of whose cubs has been "a move to establish a type of pan-European parity of experience and identity," carrying with it the dangers of cultural alienation and loss of national identity.

My Dream of You, O'Faolain's first novel, was, like *Are You Somebody*, both a bestseller and a critical success. Catherine Lockerbie commented in the *New York Times* that the novel's traditional narrative style, accessible language, and provocative subject matter might have consigned it to being an "airport blockbuster," but its "intelligence" and O'Faolain's "awareness of the potential pitfalls" of writing such a novel make it distinctive (Web site 2001).

Almost There: The Onward Journey of a Dublin Woman was lauded as was its predecessor for its frank account of middle age. Mary O'Donoghue commented in the *Women's Review of Books* that O'Faolain's depiction of loneliness, "wrenching" in the first memoir, "reappears here, raw as a wound, in words as starkly beautiful as stripped bone." But ironically, O'Faolain's candor in self-revelation, which has often earned her praise for personal courage, aroused ad feminam attacks such as Caitlin Flanagan's (*Atlantic Monthly*) contemplating the possible "hypocrisy" of O'Faolain's feminism and Mick Heaney's (*Sunday Times*) questioning the wisdom of her confessions. Éilis Ní Dhuibhne (*Irish Times*), assessing O'Faolain's artistry rather than her personality, praised her ability to invest a personal story with "universal relevance," as well as her "intellectual depth [and] real literary education."

Nuala O'Faolain's writing scrutinizes such pressing contemporary issues as the nature of Irish identity, the place of Irishwomen in the Irish nation, and the myths that have shaped Ireland's self-image.

BIBLIOGRAPHY

Works by Nuala O'Faolain

Almost There: The Onward Journey of a Dublin Woman. New York: Riverhead, 2003.
Are You Somebody: The Accidental Memoir of a Dublin Woman. New York: Henry Holt, 1996.
Are You Somebody? The Life and Times of Nuala O'Faolain. Dublin: New Island, 1996.
My Dream of You. London: Michael Joseph; New York: Riverhead, 2001.

Studies of Nuala O'Faolain

Evans, Eibhlín. "Letters after the Fact: Responses to Nuala O'Faolain's *Are You Somebody?*" *Critical Survey* 14, no. 3 (2002): 51–63.
Lockerbie, Catherine. The *New York Times.* http://www.nytimes.com/gst/fullpage.html?res (accessed March 4, 2001).
Merkin, Daphne. "A Thorny Irish Rose." *New York Times Magazine*, February 18, 2001, 22–25.
Ní Dhuibhne, Eílis. "Voice at Full Power." *Irish Times*, March 22, 2003, 60.
O'Donoghue, Mary. "Alone in a Crowd." *Women's Review of Books* 20, no. 6 (March 2003): 9.
Toíbín, Colm. Review of *Are You Somebody. Times Literary Supplement*, November 29, 1996, 15.

MARY O'MALLEY
(1954–   )

Mary Fitzgerald-Hoyt

BIOGRAPHY

Mary O'Malley was born the eldest of ten children in Connemara, County Galway, a locale that permeates her poetry not only in its reverent attention to imagery of sea and terrain, but also in its awareness of the psychic pull of myth and history, the scars left by the alienation from native language. As she has noted in an autobiographical essay, " 'Between the Snow and the Huge Roses' " (in Haberstroh, *My Self, My Muse*), her father, a fisherman, and her uncle, a blacksmith, instilled in her an awareness of form and function, beauty and utility, that has served her well in the craft of poetry. Objects that surrounded her in childhood—Aran sweaters, fishhooks, nets, and so on—taught her "the need for craft and skill" and that "in the right combination of the two could lie the difference between life and death" (36). Her much-beloved grandmother, a gifted storyteller with a love for reading, nurtured her imagination and instilled in her the narratives of Irish history. O'Malley's recollection of her grandmother's house, where during the same visit she might hear stories of the potato famine as well as spirited participatory viewing of the television police drama *Kojak*, is mirrored in the younger woman's poetry, where contemporary popular culture coexists comfortably with folklore, myth, and history.

From an early age, O'Malley felt deeply her estrangement from her native language, noting that she was "raised between languages. . . . We spoke English, but almost the entire specialized vocabulary of the sea, the names of fish, rocks, birds, and plants, was in Irish" (37).

O'Malley attended University College Galway, where she later taught arts administration. For eight years she taught English at the New University of Lisbon, and Portugal is an evident influence in her first book of poetry, *A Consideration of Silk* (1990), which won the Hennessey Award. She was awarded an Arts Council bursary, which assisted her in the completion of *Where the Rocks Float* (1993).

The diversity of settings, characters, and voices in O'Malley's poetry is mirrored in her life experiences. She has been an active promoter and disseminator of literature and the arts, working as a radio and television writer and broadcaster, an organizer of the Cúirt Arts Festival, a director of the Galway Arts Centre, and a teacher, including in community writing workshops and prison; she has worked with the Clifden Community School Festival and the Letterfrack Environmental Centre. O'Malley has edited two collections of children's writing as well as *The Waterside Book* (1996), a collection of writings and artwork by people from Derry, where she completed a residency. She was elected to Aosdána, an honorary organization of creative artists. She has delivered lectures and readings in Europe and the United States, and most recently has toured with musician Sean Tyrell and actor Little John Nee in a well-received program of poetry and music.

O'Malley is married to Michael Gallagher, and they have two children, Oisín Joel and Tania Maeve. She lives in the Moycullen Gaeltacht, an Irish-speaking region in County Galway.

MAJOR WORKS AND THEMES

A Consideration of Silk evinces the breadth of vision, vividness of imagery, and far-reaching compassion that continues to inform O'Malley's poetry. The poems' impulse is often to forge connections between people and cultures, and Portugal, O'Malley's onetime home, is frequently featured, including the cultural and linguistic dislocations triggered by the return to Ireland. In the opening poem, "A Footspan of Sand," the Atlantic Ocean's shockingly cold water evokes nostalgia for the warm fecundity of Portugal, an awareness of belonging in neither place.

The geographical range of the poems—Russia, Chile, El Salvador, England, South Africa, and Angola, as well as Portugal and Ireland—is narrowed by their common exposure of injustice and suffering. O'Malley pricks the conscience and coaxes the sympathies by telling the stories of political refugees, torture victims, and workers exploited to sate the desires of the rich. O'Malley, the child of an island culture, continually warns against insularity, insisting on humanity's interdependence and connection. This impulse is particularly evident in her poems about women and gender. Biological imperatives, including sexual desire, are given hilarious treatment in "Gluttony" and "Hormones," but there are also harrowing reminders of how sex is used as a weapon, as in the chillingly unforgettable "Credo." The speaker raises the disturbing possibility that the price for the fulfilling sexual lives and happy maternity of some women is paid by those tormented and raped, as in El Salvador. Shocking, tender, and guilt-suffused, the poem asserts the ultimate redemption and triumph of the brutalized.

Whereas *A Consideration of Silk* reflects the uneasy transition between living in Portugal and returning to Ireland, *Where the Rocks Float* is immersed in the landscape, history, myth, and personal recollection of Connaught. Its four-section structure—"Ave," "The Cave," "The Boat Poems," and "The Grannuaile [*sic*] Poems"—begins with the poet's childhood in Connemara, where, despite her reverence for her family and the sea, she realizes her separation from both and finds a necessary but sometimes uneasy home in language. That the language is English and that her mentor is an English male poet complicate her self-discovery, for she must navigate the shoals of history, politics, and gender to find her own voice and vision, wherein Irish phrases and syntax bubble to the surface alongside the traditions of fiddle playing, quilt making, and petitioning for intercession at holy wells, reminiscent of Eavan Boland's description of language as "a kind of scar," a wound both healed and remembered. In "Tracing," dedicated to poet Richard Murphy and her own fisherman father, she declares her own territory. Just as Seamus Heaney's "Digging" blends admiration of his father's prowess as turf digger with the recognition that his own calling lies elsewhere, holding a pen instead of a spade, "Tracing" employs the imagery of boat building to describe the poet's discovery of her own calling.

"The Boat Poems" pay sometimes playful tribute to the varied craft that navigate the sea, frequently employing the boat as female speaker and witness to humanity's complex emotional relationships to each other and to boats, from a wife's jealousy of the hours her husband spends with his boat to the immigrant wrenched from the sea and digging tunnels beneath it in America. The sequence concludes with a tribute to Grace, or Granuaile, O'Malley, the sixteenth-century sea captain celebrated for her nautical prowess, daring, and defiance of English rule, yet long written out of Irish history. The final sequence of *Where the Rocks Float* is dominated by Granuaile's voice, and one senses a strong personal identification with a woman who, like Mary O'Malley herself, felt at home in neither gender's prescribed world.

The Knife in the Wave (1997), a bold, visionary collection, exudes a more confident voice and a willingness to experiment with form and subject, ranging from a series of poems written in couplets to three long sequences: "Miss Panacea Regrets," inspired by the poet's own pulmonary surgery, is a searing examination of postoperative pain and its inadequate palliatives; "The Joe Heaney Poems" were part of a documentary about a singer of the Irish traditional style known as *sean-nos*, whereby the singer remains impassive, masklike, a vessel for the song to enter; "The Seal Woman" is a reworking of the ancient *selchie* legend, whereby a seal was able to shape-shift into a woman. Whereas in earlier versions the woman is captured against her will and, despite her eventual affection for her captor and the children she bears him, never ceases to long for the sea, to which she eventually returns, in O'Malley's version the Seal Woman is a passionate, strong-willed soul whose return to land entails coaxing the sculpted mermaids from their perches on Galway City's buildings and bearing her lover away to her underwater world, which proves to be too heady and liberating for his landlocked mind. As Katie Donovan has pointed out, the poem also expresses O'Malley's dismay at the aesthetic damage done by Galway's urban development. The Seal Woman's lover is a builder, affiliated with the faceless architecture of contemporary cities and oblivious to the smoldering magic lurking beneath the old facades.

Women's voices and perspectives are likewise infused into old stories, so that we are given a different angle on the myth of Leda and the Swan and Yeats's rendering of it as well as an arresting view of the Virgin Mary. Passionate, brilliant, and outspoken, O'Malley's women try to extricate themselves from their consigned roles; their men, by turns domineering, unimaginative, and timid of change, are a poor match for them—though nevertheless seductive at times. Liberation—from physical pain, from confining social roles, from political oppression, from violence—echoes throughout this collection.

Asylum Road (2001) reveals O'Malley's increasing mastery of her craft, as she uses sharply honed and arresting imagery in the service of great uncertainties: the blessed curse of being a poet; the tormented delights of love; the sorrowful mysteries of innocents' suffering. Her previously demonstrated talent for blending breadth and narrowness of vision, so that a poem about a lost pet contains the same intensity and attention to detail as a meditation on the concurrent rifts and connections between cultures, is much in evidence. So, too, is a kaleidoscope of moods, so that O'Malley's frequent poems about the writing of poetry and the poet's vocation swoop from wry irony to arch playfulness to carnivalesque absurdity. As with many contemporary Irish writers, she wrestles with the issue of cultural identity, most pointedly in the deft "The Second Plantation of Connaught," which targets the invasion of Connemara by well-heeled, land-buying tourists trying to transform themselves into an illusory, essentialist Irishness. The haunting "In the Name of God and of the Dead Generations" probes Ireland's recent transformation from nation of emigrants to destination for immigrants, sympathetically linking the misery of coffin ship and lost language to recently arrived and often unwelcome refugees.

O'Malley's two most recent works, *The Boning Hall* (2002) and *Three Irish Poets: An Anthology* (with Eavan Boland and Paula Meehan, 2003), demonstrate her growing stature in contemporary Irish poetry. *The Boning Hall* blends an impressive collection of new poems with selections from the four earlier volumes. *Three Irish Poets*, edited by Eavan Boland, who herself has been instrumental in revolutionizing Irish poetry by being living proof that tradition notwithstanding, "woman" and "poet" are not mutually exclusive terms, showcases the works of three writers who, despite their differences in generation, locale, and style, have transformed the face of Irish poetry.

The new poems featured in *The Boning Hall* reveal O'Malley's versatility and range in style and subject. She pays tribute to women artists as diverse as Billie Holiday, Maria Callas, and Edna St. Vincent Millay, juxtaposing their creative brilliance and their private suffering. Old stories and images are refashioned, as in the stinging "The Ballad of Caitlin and Sean," which revisits the personification of Ireland as woman and England as conquering man. The myth of Demeter and Persephone, a frequent preoccupation in Eavan Boland's poetry, receives O'Malley's own imprint in "Persephone Astray" and the stunning "The Wineapple."

The emotional reach of these poems is likewise vast, from the hilarious "PMT—The Movie," in which Actaeon has the bad luck to encounter Diana and her nymphs in the throes of premenstrual tension, to the bitter lament for the dead of Bloody Sunday, " 'My role was that of an observer.' " A series of poignant poems, including "The Ice Age," "The Dinner Table," and "Songs from the Beehive," expresses the anguish of an unraveling love relationship.

In a return to one of her early loves, theater, O'Malley is currently engaged in playwrighting. She is also writing a self-described "memoir of place" about her childhood.

CRITICAL RECEPTION

The neglect of Mary O'Malley's poetry by literary critics would be astonishing were it not so often the lot of Irish women writers. To date, only one critical article has appeared: Bernard McKenna's " 'Such Delvings and Exhumations': The Quest for Self-Actualization in Mary O'Malley's Poetry." McKenna's study, based on O'Malley's first two collections of poetry, attempts to redress what he sees as an unjust attack on her work by Patrick Ramsey in the *Irish Review*. Praising her "intellectual subtleties, emotional depths, and a complex spirituality explored in a language sensitive to the details and intricacies of human behavior" (151–52), McKenna connects O'Malley to Richard Kearney's description of contemporary Irish culture as being in a period of "transition," pulled between " 'the claims of tradition and modernity' " (152).

McKenna identifies the search for identity as being at the heart of O'Malley's poetry. Linking her poetic impulse to early allegories of "spiritual pilgrimage," despite marked differences in style and sensibility, McKenna traces the ways in which O'Malley achieves "self-actualization" through her experiences of the Irish landscape, sensuality, motherhood, and the exploration of Irish ritual and myth, both pre- and post-Christianity. He notes her ability to transform the quotidian: "She finds the divine in the extraordinary experience of the ordinary and in the vital moments of the transfiguration of her world into something extraordinary" (171).

In the three volumes that have appeared since the publication of Bernard McKenna's essay, Mary O'Malley has proven herself to be one of Ireland's most outstanding contemporary poets. Though she is but ten years younger than Eavan Boland, who as a young writer was stunned to discover women's exclusion from written history and the

Irish literary canon, O'Malley stated in an interview that it never occurred to her to think her gender was an insurmountable obstacle to her chosen calling. Though noting that the term "woman writer" is still employed to disparage, when asked about feminism and writing she observed, "The great question for writers is that you be allowed to choose your own subject matter" (*The Writing Life*). Whereas Boland was impelled to assert the validity of domestic life as poetic subject, a stance that subjected her to critical assault, in an Ireland that has undergone seismic changes in the last few decades, O'Malley identifies writing about domestic concerns as a choice, but not an inevitable one, for those who are both women and writers.

BIBLIOGRAPHY

Works by Mary O'Malley

Asylum Road. Cliffs of Moher: Salmon, 2001.
The Boning Hall. Manchester, UK: Carcanet, 2002.
A Consideration of Silk. Galway: Salmon, 1990.
The Knife in the Wave. Cliffs of Moher: Salmon, 1997.
"Mary O'Malley." Interview. *The Writing Life.* Videocassette. Hosted by Jean Nordhaus. HoCoPoLitSo, 2004. Baltimore, MD: Howard Community College.
Three Irish Poets: An Anthology. Manchester, UK: Carcanet, 2003, 36–74.
"Weakness" and " 'Between the Snow and the Huge Roses.' " In *My Self, My Muse: Irish Women Poets Reflect on Life and Art*, edited by Patricia Boyle Haberstroh, 33–45. Syracuse, NY: Syracuse University Press, 2001.
Where the Rocks Float. Dublin: Salmon, 1993.

Studies of Mary O'Malley

Donovan, Katie. "Rhythms on each breath." *Irish Times*, May 22, 1997, 12.
McKenna, Bernard. " 'Such Delvings and Exhumations': The Quest for Self-Actualization in Mary O'Malley's Poetry." In *Contemporary Irish Women Poets: Some Male Perspectives*, edited by Alexander G. Gonzalez, 151–72. Westport, CT: Greenwood, 1999.

CHRISTINA REID
(1942–   )

Patrick Lonergan

BIOGRAPHY

Christina Reid was born into a Protestant family in working-class Belfast, Northern Ireland. Her childhood was spent predominantly in the company of women, with her time divided evenly between her parents' and maternal grandparents' homes. She has stated that the Unionist culture in which she was raised had a strong impact on her life and writing. Her memories of the annual July 12 Unionist commemoration of the Battle of the Boyne are an important influence on her work, as is the fact that many of her male relatives fought in the British army in the First and Second World Wars (Foley, 58–59). And although Reid grew up during a period in which sectarian tensions were relatively subdued in Northern Ireland, she has stated that she was aware of anti-Catholic discrimination and prejudice from a young age (Delgado, xvii–ix).

Reid left school when she was fifteen but returned to full-time education in 1980, when she took English, Russian studies, and sociology at Queen's University, Belfast. While at Queen's she also had her first successes as a writer, winning awards for *Tea in a China Cup* (1983) and *Did You Hear the One About the Irishman?* (written in 1980). These successes encouraged her to devote herself to writing full-time, and she withdrew from her studies.

In 1987, Reid moved to London with her three daughters, becoming writer in residence at the Young Vic from 1987 to 1989. Although she wrote prolifically during the 1980s, her output has slowed considerably since her move to London, and she produced only one full-length original work during the 1990s.

Although from a Unionist background and resident in England, Reid has consistently emphasized the Irish qualities of her work, particularly the linguistic uniqueness of her characters' Irish speech. She is also indebted to the Irish dramatic tradition, with Sean O'Casey a strong influence. It is, however, a sign of her work's richness that it is also often considered in the context of the highly politicized style of British drama popularized since the 1970s by Caryl Churchill and David Hare.

MAJOR WORKS AND THEMES

All of Christina Reid's original plays are set in working-class Belfast, with the lives of entire communities presented from the perspectives of the marginalized—women, people with disabilities, the unemployed, and others. Reid's plays reproduce many traditional Irish dramatic conventions: a strong focus on the theme of exile and homecoming, and action that is usually presented in a conservative narrative style that eschews innovation in favor of accessibility. Yet her writing is in many respects highly innovative. Reid was one of the first Irish writers to tackle the issue of racism, which she relates convincingly to Irish sectarianism and postcolonialism. Her inclusion of such forms of popular culture as stand-up comedy and music-hall makes her work a powerful challenge to the occasional elitism of the Irish theater. And, most important, she posits feminism as having the potential to transform Irish society in its entirety, offering liberation from sectarianism as well as sexism.

Reid's first produced play was *Tea in a China Cup*, which premiered in Belfast. It focuses on three generations of Belfast women, with action taking place against the backdrop of two military conflicts: the outbreak of the Second World War in 1939, and the early period of the Northern Irish Troubles in 1972. Reid presents these historical events from the perspective of her women characters, challenging received masculine views of militarism and heroism. Her presentation in the play of Sarah, a partially autobiographical figure forced into an unloving marriage, suggests that the limitations imposed on women by society are highly damaging, but often self-inflicted. Reid interestingly relates the restrictions suffered by women to the manner in which successive generations of her male characters die fighting for the British army—implying that working-class Belfast men are also manipulated into occupying damaging roles. The family heirloom of a china teacup in the play's title thus operates as a symbol for familial inheritance, as Reid considers whether an individual may liberate herself from a socially determined identity while remaining loyal to her traditions.

Did You Hear the One About the Irishman? was premiered in 1985 by the Royal Shakespeare Company. It concerns a doomed relationship between a middle-class Protestant woman and a working-class Catholic man. Despite the differences in the characters' backgrounds, Reid shows them to have much in common, including the fact that both are related to political prisoners on opposing sides of the conflict. The man and woman are told by their communities that their relationship is considered inappropriate and should end; they refuse to be intimidated by these threats and are murdered. This action is framed by occasional interruptions by a stand-up British comedian, who tells a series of offensive Irish jokes in a manner that at the time of the play's production remained commonplace on British television. The juxtaposition of the tragic story with this style of humor challenges the unwillingness of the British public to engage seriously with the Northern Irish Troubles, while also pointing to the absurdity of a conflict between factions who, Reid suggests, are in many ways indistinguishable.

Reid's most successful play, *Joyriders* (1986), is set in the Divis Flats, an impoverished nationalist community in Belfast. The play presents four teenagers—Arthur, Maureen, Tommy, and Sandra—on a youth training scheme housed in an abandoned linen mill, together with Kate, the scheme's administrator. All are deeply cynical about the effectiveness of the scheme, which is undermined as much by its participants' apathy as by governmental indifference. The play is framed by allusions to Sean O'Casey's *The Shadow of a Gunman* (1923): its opening scene is set in a theater where that play is being performed, and it ends with a death scene that consciously mirrors O'Casey's earlier work and contrasts with it simultaneously. Reid uses O'Casey to propose a continuity between pre-Independence Dublin and Belfast in the 1980s—which at that time was a provocative political statement. *Joyriders* also includes a number of songs that were written by teenagers living in the Divis Flats, showing that Reid's interest in politics was more than simply abstract: *Joyriders* is an excellent example of a playwright giving voice to the disenfranchised.

The Belle of the Belfast City (1989) opened in Belfast and presents three generations of women in a Protestant Belfast family who have come together on the eve of a major protest against the implementation of the 1985 Anglo-Irish agreement. The youngest of these women is Belle, a young black woman brought up mostly in London, who is visiting her Northern Irish relatives for the first time. Establishing a relationship between the racism experienced by Belle and anti-Catholic prejudice in Northern Ireland, Reid presents a challenging subplot in which a prominent Unionist politician manipulates a disabled youth for political gain. While the play resembles *Tea in a China Cup* in many ways, it is considerably more angry than Reid's previous works, representing the dominant form of Unionism in Northern Ireland as corrupt, racist, and self-serving. Yet it is also a surprisingly playful work, using song in a manner very reminiscent of Brendan Behan's *The Hostage* (1959). Reid's *My Name, Shall I Tell You My Name* (1989) was a success at the Dublin Theatre Festival. Originally produced for radio in 1987, it once again tackled the issue of racial tensions.

In 1992 Reid produced an adaptation of *Les Miserables* (1862); a play for children, *King of the Castle*, which is set on a bomb site in the 1950s, appeared in 1999. Her only major original work during that decade was *Clowns* (1996), a sequel to *Joyriders*. The linen mill that housed the youth training scheme in *Joyriders* has now been converted into a shopping center, where Arthur has opened a restaurant. Sandra has returned to Belfast for the center's opening, and it emerges during the play that she has been haunted by the ghost of Maureen for several years. The symbolic laying to rest of

Maureen's ghost makes *Clowns* one of the earliest dramatic attempts to come to terms with the increasing prosperity of Northern Ireland after the first IRA ceasefire of 1994. In *Clowns*, Reid considers the need for a balance between moving away from the past and remaining aware of the losses endured during the Troubles. This focus on the tension between the past and the future is one of Reid's recurrent themes, and in *Clowns* she deploys many other familiar aspects of her work, including stand-up comedy.

At the center of Reid's drama is an unwillingness to be restricted by socially determined roles, which means that despite its often depressing subject matter, her work is frequently uplifting and inspiring. Her inclusion of popular cultural forms such as music hall and comedy makes her plays highly enjoyable, both as narrative and as spectacle. Yet there is also an important thematic complexity in her work, which exposes the dynamics of imperialism as well as patriarchy.

CRITICAL RECEPTION

Although Reid is frequently included in academic considerations of political theater, her work has generally been omitted from studies and anthologies of Irish literature. In part this is due to the fact that, because Reid has produced relatively little work since 1989, she has been unable to maintain as high a profile as she enjoyed during the 1980s. Yet there are other explanations for the absence of an appropriate critical response to her work.

Reid herself has frequently suggested that her work's popularity could be explained by a "fashion" in the United Kingdom and the United States for plays about Northern Ireland (Eisner, D17). The level of interest in drama about the Northern Irish Troubles has truly declined somewhat since the middle of the 1990s, but it could be argued that Reid is ignored because her work highlights issues with which Northern Irish society remains uncomfortable. Imelda Foley draws attention to the way in which her plays use feminism to act as "a commentary on the lingering predicament of Northern Ireland and the failure not in addressing, but in implementing social change" (70). The difficulty in Northern Ireland of bringing about change—not to mention the struggle of women politicians to gain recognition in the Northern Ireland Assembly since 1998—shows that many of Reid's preoccupations remain unacknowledged and urgent.

Another explanation for her omission from most studies of Irish theater must be her focus on gender. It is increasingly clear that strong prejudices exist in Irish theater criticism against work by women, especially when that work enjoys commercial and popular success. Reid, together with Marie Jones and other Irish women writers, has been unjustly ignored for many years as a result of such prejudices.

International considerations of Reid continue to draw attention to the political aspects of her work, with many commentators offering interesting considerations of her use of Brechtian techniques. Her interest in community theater and theater-in-education further illustrates her commitment to genuine political activism through drama. Unfortunately, the relevance of Reid's politics to Irish life and theater remains largely unarticulated.

BIBLIOGRAPHY

Works by Christina Reid

The King of the Castle. In *New Connections 99: New Plays for Young People*, edited by Suzy Adriani, 453–514. London: Faber and Faber, 1999.

The Last of a Dyin' Race. In *Best Radio Plays of 1986*. London: Methuen, 1986, 39–72.
Plays 1. London: Methuen, 1997.

Studies of Christina Reid

Delgado, Maria M. "Introduction." In *Christina Reid Plays 1*. London: Methuen, 1997, vi–xxii.
Eisner, Jane. "Irish Unite on Theatre but Divide on Results." *Record*, September 11, 1986, D17.
Foley, Imelda. *The Girls in the Big Picture: Gender in Contemporary Ulster Theatre*. Belfast: Blackstaff, 2003.
Llewellyn-Jones, Margaret. *Contemporary Irish Drama and Cultural Identity*. London: Intellect, 2002.
Luft, Joanna. "Brechtian Gestus and the Politics of Tea in Christina Reid's *Tea in a China Cup*." *Modern Drama* 42, no. 2 (June 1999): 214–32.
McDonough, Carla J. " 'I've Never Been Just Me': Rethinking Women's Positions in the Plays of Christina Reid." In *A Century of Irish Drama—Widening the Stage*, edited by Stephen Watt, Eileen Morgan, and Shakir Mustafa, 179–92. Bloomington: Indiana University Press, 2000.
O'Dwyer, Riana. "The Imagination of Women's Reality: Christina Reid and Marina Carr." In *Theatre Stuff*, edited by Eamonn Jordan, 236–48. Dublin: Carysfort, 2000.
Roll-Hansen, Diderik. "Dramatic Strategy in Christina Reid's *Tea in a China Cup*." *Modern Drama* 30, no. 3 (Fall 1987): 389–95.

SOMERVILLE AND ROSS
(E.O.E. Somerville [1858–1949] and Violet Martin [1862–1915])

Ann Owens Weekes

BIOGRAPHY

Somerville and Ross was the name by which the cousins and literary collaborators Edith Oenone Somerville and Violet Martin published their fiction. The Somerville family came to Ireland in 1690 and established themselves in Castletownshend, County Cork, where they eventually built Drishane House. Edith was educated by governesses at home, and spent a term at Alexandra College, Dublin, and another at South Kensington School of Art, London. A keen artist, she overrode her family's protests to follow a cousin to Dusseldorf in 1891 and later studied art in Paris. The Martin family, which came to Ireland with Strongbow, built Ross House, County Galway, where Violet was educated by an aunt and a former hedge schoolmaster. The cousins met for the first time in January 1886 and thus began an extraordinary literary collaboration. The possibility and nature of such a collaboration were a source of critical curiosity from the beginning, but the cousins treated it as a natural outcome of the friendship of intellectual, artistic women. Edith recalled the conversational nature of their work: frequently they hit upon a proposition simultaneously, discussed, debated, and qualified it, and finally the purely fortuitous holder of the pen committed their ideas to paper. Violet loved to spend time in Castletownshend with the extended network of Somerville cousins; engaged in writing in Castletownshend, the women were frequently requested to forgo their "nonsense" and attend to their "real" duties of entertaining.

Both Anglo-Irish ascendancy families were devoted to hunting, dogs, gardens, and beautiful houses, and both women, in their lives and novels, were intensely—even defensively—loyal to their class and opposed to the forces that threatened it. But loyalty did not blind them to the class's gender injustices, which they—active in the suffragette movement—resented bitterly. Both were Unionists, Violet more so than Edith, who signed a clemency petition for the leaders of the 1916 rising. After the initial meeting, the women traveled extensively together, often commissioned to gather material for publication in London magazines; their most famous collection, *Some Experiences of an Irish R.M.* (1899), was originally requested by, and written for, the *Badminton* magazine. Unfortunately, the success of the short stories led to the writers' neglect of the serious novel: although *The Real Charlotte*, their masterpiece, won them acclaim in 1894, their pressing financial needs and lack of time made short stories more feasible than novels. Edith became mistress of Drishane when her mother died in 1895 and thereafter was engaged in multifarious activities, including horse dealing, cattle breeding, and art shows, and from 1903 to 1908 and again from 1912 to 1919, she was master of hounds to the West Carbery Fox-Hounds, a time-consuming, expensive responsibility but one very close to her heart. Violet died of a brain tumor in 1915, possibly caused by a fall from a horse in 1898, and Edith was bereft. Resorting to a medium in 1916, she believed that she made contact with Violet, who proclaimed their partnership to be merely interrupted, not ended; when she began to write again, Edith continued to publish under the names Somerville and Ross, insisting that Violet was a party to the creation. Edith was recognized as a woman of letters in 1932 with Trinity College's award of D. Lit and invited by W. B. Yeats to join the Irish Academy of Letters.

MAJOR WORKS AND THEMES

The decline of the ascendancy and the uneasy interaction between the Big House and tenants haunted Somerville and Ross's work from the start. *An Irish Cousin* (1889), their first novel, pictures the isolation and darkness of the west coast of Ireland, where the Sarsfield family's decay parallels that of their Big House, Durrus. The authors often employ the device of foreign innocent, to whom the complications of Irish politics and society must be introduced; Theo Sarsfield plays the part in this novel, arriving from Canada to the family home, where her Uncle Dominick has an irregular relationship with the servant, Moll. Attraction between the offspring of such a relationship and the legitimate offspring of the Big House is here and in other novels a source of conflict. Dominick rails against marriage between his son and Moll's daughter (perhaps also Dominick's) as an offense against class. Exposing his hypocrisy and his neglect of the very structures upon which class is built, the authors nevertheless usually conclude romances by pairing "appropriate" couples, those of the same class and creed. Supernatural or gothic elements appear in this work, as do vivid descriptions of house and country and excellent accounts of that Somerville and Ross delight, the Irish hunt.

Naboth's Vineyard (1891) features Irish village life, about which the authors knew little; hence, the characters are often stereotypes. Exploration of Irish hunger for land, a timely topic and one they knew well, begins here. A strong woman character is also introduced: Harriet, a mixture of good and evil, whose passionate desire for another man leads her to participate by omission in the murder of her husband. Harriet's actions—her vulgarity—are explained, as are the actions of other Somerville and Ross characters, as products of an inferior social class. Their first travel book, *Through Connemara in a Governess Cart* (1892), betrays the same tendency: the authors invent stock scenes as representations of the hilarious and ridiculous in Irish life, but they also present intimate, lively pictures of the countryside. An 1891 tour of Bordeaux produced *In the Vine Country* (1893); once again the authors observe from a height, but here the comic scenes are saved by self-mockery. Two more tours were made in 1893: *Beggars on Horseback* (1895), featuring Edith as the artist Miss O'Flannigan, the source of comedy, chronicles their visit to Wales; *Stray-Aways* (1920) recounts their tour of Denmark. A recurring feature in the travel books and novels is the authors' insistence on their difference from English women. The travel books appeared months, and sometimes years, after magazine publication.

The Real Charlotte (1894), begun in 1889, was not completed until 1893, fortunately, for, as Edith notes, once the novel was conceived, the characters were rarely out of their creators' minds. This long simmering contributed to the finely developed characters and the complex, ironic plot that made *The Real Charlotte* a masterpiece. Here, for the first time, the dialect is perfect, the accents and expressions throughout authentic and hilariously funny, the harvest of many hours of collecting phrases, words, and accents of family, servants, and local people. Charlotte Mullen, the title character, is a superb mixture of intelligence, greed, and passion, a plain and unlikable woman on the periphery of polite Anglo-Irish society. The novel spans a large spectrum of Anglo-Irish society: Sir Benjamin Dysart, owner of the Big House of Bruff, is senile and bullied by his attendant, the mad James Canavan; Christopher, the heir, is uninterested in the estate and in the complex land laws that ultimately transfer land from landlords to tenants; the English Lady Dysart, unaware of Irish dialectical nuances and behavioral patterns, fails to understand the many levels of society. Below the Dysarts is a chorus of country gentlemen, retired army officers, land agents, soldiers, and impoverished widows. Too many wives and daughters throng the parties, too few sons. All, with the exception of the Dysarts, struggle for land. All are well individualized by accent and expression. Beyond the pale, Charlotte's repressed and filthy Ferry Row tenants, ignored by all but their ruthless landlady, are an ominous sign of change to come. The entrance of pretty Francie Fitzpatrick initiates the usual attraction between inappropriate couples, but Charlotte's role moves this novel from romance to tragedy. Motivated by hunger for land and an arid passion for a worthless man, Charlotte is frighteningly mundane as she moves from callousness to cheating, stealing, and murder. Nothing is spared in the depiction of Charlotte's person and character, but finally the narrators express a generous understanding of the torture a plain, intelligent woman suffers in a society that values women's appearance and ignores their intelligence.

Unfortunately, the cousins never again wrote such a panoramic, penetrating novel, though they planned to do so. *The Silver Fox* (1898) first appeared in a newspaper, which, according to Edith, required weekly concluding sensations, and it thus lacks coherence. An unlikely romance dominated by superstition and legend, the novel runs true to the authors' habit of introducing English characters to the ways of Irish people but finally matches characters with "appropriate" partners of the same class and nationality.

In 1898, when the cousins were holidaying in France, *Badminton* magazine requested a series of short stories similar to the hunting/country stories published through the years. Thus were born the Irish resident magistrate and a comic series that would win the women huge popularity, particularly with the English, for whom they were written. The comedy results from the encounters of Major Yeates, the resident magistrate, an English gentleman, with Flurry Knox, his Irish landlord, with Flurry's extended family, which ranges from Lady Knox to Larry the Liar, a Knox auctioneer, and with the local people. The joke is often at the major's expense, but usually reader and major are at one, surprised and amused at the extraordinary antics of the Irish. Yeates develops from the innocent in *Some Experiences of an Irish R.M.* to become temporary master of hounds in *Further Experiences of an Irish R.M.* (1908), a real indicator of acceptance in this hunting society. The final series, completed the year of Martin's death, *In Mr. Knox's Country* (1915), reveals an aging Yeates and a dispossessed ascendancy in a post–land acts Ireland.

Pressed by their agent for the popular hunt stories, the cousins collected previously published stories into *All on the Irish Shore* (1903) and *Some Irish Yesterdays* (1906). A novel, *Dan Russel the Fox* (1911), is noteworthy only for its enthusiastic descriptions of the hunt. After Violet's death, Edith published *Irish Memories* (1917), a collection of family reminiscences begun and largely written by Violet. Edith published five more novels under both partners' names. *Mount Music* (1919) explores the relationship between Catholics and Protestants during the final years of the land transfer, 1894–1907. Although they have little sympathy with the land acts, the authors also delineate here, as in *The Real Charlotte*, the ineptness of the ascendancy. *An Enthusiast* (1921) features an idealistic Anglo-Irishman, Dan Palliser, who attempts to heal divisions during the time of the Black-and-Tan/Irish war. *The Big House of Inver* (1925) is the novel Violet Martin dreamed of writing, the novel of the decline of the ascendancy through debauchery, indifference, quarrels, and intermarriage with village girls. Shibby Pindy, whose name identifies her as a "side-shoot" of the Big House Prendeville family, is the last memorable Somerville and Ross character. Mistaken but, for all that, more worthy of respect than those around her, Shibby fights to restore house and family to their former grandeur—inevitably, a losing battle. *Inver* comes closest to *The Real Charlotte* in its penetration into character and its grasp of history. *French Leave* (1928) is a lighthearted romance that calls on Edith's student time in Paris, and *Sarah's Youth* (1938), written as Edith neared eighty, features a tomboy heroine who succumbs not to the romantic hero but to the lure of the hounds. Writing to the last, Edith also published an account of her trip to the United States, a biography of Charles Kendal Bushe—lord chief justice of Ireland and Somerville ancestor—and several collections of essays and memoirs.

CRITICAL RECEPTION

Initially Somerville and Ross's work received mixed reviews. The first novel was greeted as too gloomy, and *The Real Charlotte* was accorded an unsympathetic response. Favorable reviews soon followed, however, and by the time the R.M. stories were published, English reviewers were loud in their praise. The Irish audience—limited during the writers' lifetimes—declined almost totally during the 1940s and 1950s, and the work went out of print. The names and work of Somerville and Ross, however, continued to be essential in academic collections of Irish or Anglo-Irish writers. With the 1960s came a renewal of interest in ascendancy Ireland, and *The Real Charlotte* was recognized in both Ireland and England as a classic: V. S. Pritchett called it the best Irish novel of any period (*New Statesman*, May 24, 1968, 688). Interest was fostered on both sides of the Atlantic by the very popular British television R.M. series. Critical interest in Somerville and Ross increased in the 1990s and early 2000s: their humor still attracts attention, as does the hunt, but all aspects, including the hunt, are now analyzed to reveal the subtle class and cultural distinctions of both the passing Anglo-Irish and emerging Irish society. Some contemporary critics remark on the Big House versus "cabins" nature of Somerville and Ross's work, but most agree that their best work, *The Real Charlotte*, the *R.M.* series, and *The Big House of Inver*, deserve their high ranking in the canon of Irish literature.

BIBLIOGRAPHY

Works by Somerville and Ross

All on the Irish Shore. London: Longmans, Green, 1903.
Beggars on Horseback. Edinburgh: Blackwood, 1895.
The Big House of Inver. London: Heinemann, 1925.
Dan Russel the Fox. London: Methuen, 1911.
An Enthusiast. London: Longmans, Green, 1921.
French Leave. London: Heinemann, 1928.
Further Experiences of an Irish R.M. London: Longmans, Green, 1908.
Happy Days. London: Longmans, Green, 1946.
An Incorruptible Irishman. London: Nicholson and Watson, 1932.
In Mr. Knox's Country. London: Longmans, Green, 1915.
In the Vine Country. London: Allen, 1893.
An Irish Cousin. London: Bentley, 1889.
Irish Memories. London: Longmans, Green, 1917.
Maria and Some Other Dogs. London: Methuen, 1949.
Mount Music. London: Longmans, Green, 1919.
Naboth's Vineyard. London: Blackett, 1891.
Notions in Garrison. London: Methuen, 1941.
A Patrick's Day Hunt. London: Constable, 1902.
The Real Charlotte. London: Ward and Downey, 1894.
Sarah's Youth. London: Longmans, Green, 1938.
The Silver Fox. London: Lawrence and Bullen, 1898.
Slipper's ABC of Fox Hunting. London: Longmans, Green, 1903.
The Smile and the Tear. London: Methuen, 1933.
Some Experiences of an Irish R.M. London: Longmans, Green, 1899.
Some Irish Yesterdays. London: Longmans, Green, 1906.
The States through Irish Eyes. Boston: Houghton Mifflin, 1930.
Stray-Aways. London: Longmans, Green, 1920.
The Sweet Cry of Hounds. London: Methuen, 1936.
Through Connemara in a Governess Cart. London: Allen, 1892.
Wheel-Tracks. London: Longmans, Green, 1923.

Studies of Somerville and Ross

Cahalan, James M. "Humor with a Gender: Somerville and Ross and *The Irish R.M.*" In *The Comic Tradition in Irish Women Writers*, edited by Theresa O'Connor, 58–72. Gainesville: University of Florida Press, 1996.
Chen, Bi-Ling. "From Britishness to Irishness: Fox Hunting as a Metaphor for Irish Cultural Identity in the Writing of Somerville and Ross." *Canadian Journal of Irish Studies* 23, no. 2 (December 1997): 39–53.
Cowman, Roz. "Lost Time: The Smell and Taste of Castle." In *Sex, Nation, and Dissent in Irish Writing*, edited by Eibhear Walshe, 87–102. New York: St. Martin's, 1998.

Collis, Maurice. *Somerville and Ross: A Biography*. London: Faber and Faber, 1968.

Cronin, John. "'An Ideal of Art': The Assertion of Realities in the Fiction of Somerville and Ross." *Canadian Journal of Irish Studies* 11, no. 1 (June 1985): 3–19.

———. *Somerville and Ross*. Lewisburg, PA: Bucknell University Press, 1972.

Crossman, Virginia. "The Resident Magistrate as Colonial Officer: Addison, Somerville and Ross." *Irish Studies Review* 8, no. 1 (April 2000): 23–33.

Devlin, Joseph. "The End of the Hunt: Somerville and Ross's Irish R.M." *Canadian Journal of Irish Studies* 24, no. 1 (July 1998): 23–50.

Flanagan, Thomas. "The Big House of Ross-Drishane." *The Kenyon Review* 28 (January 1966): 54–78.

Greene, Nicole Pepinster. "Dialect and Social Identity in *The Real Charlotte*." *New Hibernia Review* 4, no. 1 (Spring 2000): 122–37.

McMahon, Sean. "John Bull's Other Ireland: A Consideration of *The Real Charlotte* by Somerville and Ross." *Eire-Ireland* 3, no. 4 (Winter 1968): 119–35.

Martin, David. "The 'Castle Rackrent' of Somerville and Ross: A Tragic 'Colonial' Tale?" *Etudes Irlandaises* 7, no. 2 (December 1982): 43–53.

Mooney, Shawn. "'Colliding Stars': Heterosexism in Biographical Representations of Somerville and Ross." *Canadian Journal of Irish Studies* 18, no. 1 (July 1992): 157–75.

Powell, Violet. *The Books and Background of Somerville and Ross*. London: Heinemann, 1970.

Power, Ann. "The Big House of Somerville and Ross." *The Dubliner* (Spring 1942): 43–53.

Pritchett, V. S. "The Irish R.M." In *The Living Novel and Later Appreciations*. New York: Vintage, 1947, 199–205.

Stevens, Julie Anne. "The Staging of Protestant Ireland in Somerville and Ross's *The Real Charlotte*." In *Critical Ireland: New Essays in Literature and Culture*, edited by Alan A. Gillis, 188–95. Dublin: Four Courts, 2001.

EITHNE STRONG
(1923–1999)

Joseph Heininger

BIOGRAPHY

Eithne Strong, née O'Connell, was born in Glensharrold, West Limerick, Munster, to Irish Catholic parents, both of whom were schoolteachers. She was first educated in an Irish-speaking school, Scoil Muiris, in Ennis, where she recalled hearing Irish poetry recited and became enchanted by its rhythms and meters. In 1942, at the age of nineteen, she moved to Dublin, worked for a year as a civil servant, and published her first poems in Irish in *An Glor*. There she met Rupert Strong, an English-born Protestant twelve years her senior, who was training at Trinity College Dublin as a Freudian psychoanalyst with John Hanaghan. At one point during their courtship, her parents came to Dublin and forced her onto a train to return to Limerick, an episode she described to Patricia Boyle Haberstroh as a "kidnapping" (*Women Creating Women*, 30, n4). She subsequently "escaped" her parents' house again, returning to Rupert Strong in Dublin. They married in 1943 against considerable continuing parental opposition. Shortly thereafter, they founded the Runa Press, an early publisher of poetry in Irish and English, with which she published her *Poetry Quartos* between 1943 and 1945. Later, Runa published her *Songs of Living* (1961) and became the first publisher of her remarkable long poem, *Flesh—The Greatest Sin* (1980).

Strong and her husband had nine children, the youngest of whom, Philip, was born with brain damage, in 1960. In 1986, Eithne Strong spoke to Rebecca Wilson about her efforts to raise a family and to write:

> The whole business of birth control wasn't really possible in those days. Then, when the children were very small, it was quite clear to me that their needs were more important. I really did feel the priority was to keep them and to be there. It seemed self-indulgent to go off to some little cubby-hole and exclude them. Also my youngest child, who was born in 1960, was mentally handicapped and that was always an extra tie. So I gave my energies to them rather than to anything else, although I was writing poetry and one or two pieces did get published. . . . As they grew older and became less dependent however I began to reassert myself. My poetry speaks of that struggle for space, and statements to my offspring that I'm not doing them any harm by searching out these new frontiers of my personality. And despite my youngest child's handicap my first book came out in 1961. (Wilson and Somerville-Arjat, 110)

When most of her children were grown, Strong attended Trinity College as a mature student and received a BA in Irish and English. She also earned a diploma in education from Trinity in 1975. Her first English collection, *Songs of Living* (1961), introduced her poems about the "Spae-woman." It was published with a laudatory but somewhat myopic introduction by Padraic Colum, in which he praised her "utterances of the priestess, the druidess, the sybil" (cited in Haberstroh, *Women Creating Women*, 31). She later published a novel, *Degrees of Kindred* (1979), and a collection of short stories, *Patterns* (1981). She continued to publish poetry collections, including *Sarah, in Passing* (1974) and *Flesh—The Greatest Sin* (1980), which won much praise. Strong's last collection of selected and new poems, *Spatial Nosing* (1993), was introduced by the contemporary Irish poet Mary O'Donnell.

Eithne Strong's other books of poems include *My Darling Neighbour* (1985) and, in Irish, *Cirt Oibre* [Working Rights] (1980) and *Fuil agus Fallaí* [Blood and Walls] (1983). Her last novel, *The Love Riddle* (1993), was based on her life and her marriage to Rupert Strong. After their marriage and settlement in Dublin, he practiced psychotherapy and she later taught in a Dublin school for twelve years. Rupert Strong died in Dublin in 1984. After she was widowed, Strong continued to write; some of her best later poems, such as "Tournesol" and "Spatial Nosing," address remembered experiences with her husband and her attempts to share bits of life with him. She broadcast her work frequently in Irish and English, worked in creative-writing workshops in Irish schools, and lectured in Ireland, England, Denmark, France, America, and Finland. Eithne Strong was a beloved mentor to many younger Irish writers and was a member of the executive committee of the Irish Writers' Union. She was also a member of Aosdána. Her death in 1999 in Dublin left the Irish literary world with a profound sense of loss.

MAJOR WORKS AND THEMES

Eithne's Strong's marriage to Rupert Strong was a shaping influence on her perspectives on loving, on human relationships, and on creativity. From him, she learned the attraction of ways of thought and approaches to experience that ran counter to the authoritarianism and restrictions of the Irish Catholicism she had learned as a girl. Strong's interests in psychology, identity, and creativity, especially in the seeds of conflict and sources of growth in human personality, are traceable to her need to go beyond the boundaries of provincial codes of thought and possibility. Her interests in the conditions of women's lives and in the opposition between the forces of eros and thanatos are expressed in many of her poems and short stories. She is a feminist but not a separatist. Rather, she holds that the interests of men and women are woven together:

> I happen to be a woman, so my experience is going to colour the way I write, but I haven't separatist views about that either. Sometimes I think men are a pain and sometimes I think women are a pain. I don't see how they can separate the human species that way. They happen to be there. . . . I think the human race has gone a bit berserk and it would do us no harm to dry up for a bit and review things. (Wilson and Somerville-Arjat, 114)

In her desire to surpass the boundaries of parochial experience, she searches out "the strangled impulse," as Patrick Kavanagh wrote in *The Great Hunger* (1942) when describing the root of Patrick Maguire's unhappiness, and makes inroads toward understanding self and others. Consequently, there is a restless energy and humor in much of her work.

The conflict between aging and the creative force of youth is a recurring theme in Eithne Strong's work. One finds it in poems such as "Making" as well as her excellent "Creaking of the Bones," a half-humorous, half-serious meditation on age and acceptance. The poem, a characteristic rhetorical encounter between the spirited, youthful self and the aged self that laments lost promise and diminished energy, sounds her best notes, as she reflects on age, which seems "a pleased assessment" rather than a "curtailment." As the poem ends, the speaker vows to accept her flawed self as it is and to acknowledge where it failed. She refuses to acclaim victories solely, but also greets and even sometimes applauds her "uncountable blanks." As Mary O'Donnell writes in her preface to *Spatial Nosing*, Strong's "The Creaking of the Bones" is thematically similar to W. B. Yeats's mature poems on aging, loss, and his "troubled heart," but her attitude of acceptance toward the "flawed self" departs from Yeats's habit of refashioning himself through language, gesture, and drama. Indeed, Strong's poem features a notable refusal to feed the heart on fantasy.

"Making," from *Let Live* (1990), shows the opposition between the erotic life drive, "the deathless lust to make," which is the province of the young, and the potent death drive to annihilation and extinction. The poem is always on the side of the inexplicable resurgence of life and sexual energy in the face of death and ends with phrases of wonder and welcome for the life force. Another theme in Strong's work is the effort to demystify and demythologize the body, often through the use of humor. The subject and the cheerful, wryly exasperated tone of her poem "Bottoms" reminds the reader of the domestic focus of poems by Paula Meehan and Rita Ann Higgins. In her prose fiction, Strong frequently explores the tortuous complexity of the actions people undertake to attain their heart's desires. In the short story "Thursday to Wednesday," published in *Patterns* (1981), two mature people who have met across the barrier of the woman's marriage acknowledge the fear of impropriety that accompanies their growing feelings. Their attempts at loving each other are thwarted by his fear of overstepping boundaries as well as the everyday demands of the woman's family.

A persistent and overarching idea in Strong's work is the necessity of, and the extreme difficulty of, escape from various constricting provincialisms of geography, culture, religion, and the proud human heart. It is the unifying theme of *Flesh—The Greatest Sin*, her long poem about the grinding debilitation of ordinary Irish people's lives and spirits by mistaken training in hatred of the flesh and antisexual attitudes. That "the greatest sin" is to be found in the temptations of the flesh and that constant mortification and repentance are the ordained human lot are the cruel lessons brought home to Nance, the unhappy and displaced daughter of the West of Ireland farmer Thomas Regan and his wife, Ellen. The poem exposes the crippling effects of such warping yet pervasive ideas on the lives of many, especially the women, who are taught to reject their physical beauty as the source of temptation and spiritual weakness. In a similar vein, Strong's writing explores the ways in which those who ought most to show the depth and truth of their Christian love can be portrayed as the most judgmental and envious of others' happiness. To cite one example, the curdling of charity into manipulative hatred and envy is revealed through the perspective of a bitterly jealous nun in the psychologically astute story "Bride of Christ," from *Patterns*.

CRITICAL RECEPTION

As noted earlier, in his 1961 introduction to *Songs of Living*, Padraic Colum commended Strong for writing "outside the context that much of women's poetry has to be read in" and praised her as a "druidess" and "sibyl" (31). More recently, the fullest treatment of Strong's poetry has appeared in Patricia Boyle Haberstroh's study *Women Creating Women: Contemporary Irish Women Poets*. In her discussion, Haberstroh situates Strong's work among that of her contemporaries and explores her poetry's significance for the next generation. While no book-length critical assessment of Strong's writings has yet appeared, contemporary Irish poets who have acquired the habit of looking back through their mothers, such as Eavan Boland and Paula Meehan, see a foremother in Eithne Strong and find inspiration in her life and work. For example, Mary O'Donnell praises Strong on a number of levels: "Strong was always wise, but the poems fan out in a multiplicity of directions. Love is a constant theme, right from the early days, but how it has been transmuted by cussed living, bargaining and the brinkmanship of human relationships!" O'Donnell continues, "Diversity of thought and impulse makes these poems radiate humanity, belief and a revelatory sense of justice. The inequities of human relationships is something this poet is particularly adept at exploring, and none too gently either, with flesh locked between the teeth as she tears back to the bone" (iii–xi).

Late in life, Strong wrote to an interviewer, Deborah M. Consalvo, discussing her fictional characters: "I am convinced writers continue to use permutations of their experiences in what they write" (Consalvo, "To Have the Right of Utterance," 18). Perhaps a passage from her last novel can serve as a summary statement of the centrality and power of loving in Eithne Strong's art: "Love was difficult. . . . It concerned itself with all people, not just lovers, with the nature of jealousy, with murderous rages, the urge to kill, how to confront and contain these titanic forces of the self, how to transform into constructive ways the energy that otherwise meant flooding blood and destruction" (*The Love Riddle*, 251).

Eithne Strong's poetry and prose reveal her lifelong refusal to shirk life's trials, her confrontation with reality and the truth of emotion, and her fortitude in the face of pain and disappointment. As poet and fiction writer, she accepts human frailty. Yet her writings still resound with the affirmation of human potential and demonstrate the power of art to illuminate experience.

BIBLIOGRAPHY

Works by Eithne Strong

Poetry in Irish

An Sagart Pinc. Dublin: Coiscéim, 1990.
Aoife faoi Ghlas. Dublin: Coiscéim, 1990.
Cirt Oibre. Dublin: Coiscéim, 1980.
Fuil agus Fallaí. Dublin: Coiscéim, 1983.

Poetry in English

Flesh—The Greatest Sin. 1980. Dublin: Attic, 1993.
Let Live. Galway: Salmon, 1990.
My Darling Neighbour. Dublin: Beaver Row, 1985.
Poetry Quartos. Dublin: Runa, 1943–45.
Sarah, in Passing. Dublin: Dolmen, 1974.
Songs of Living. Dublin: Runa, 1961.
Spatial Nosing: New and Selected Poems. Galway: Salmon, 1993.

Fiction

Degrees of Kindred. Dublin: Tansy, 1979.
The Love Riddle. Dublin: Attic, 1993.
Patterns, and Other Stories. Dublin: Poolbeg, 1981.

Other Writings

"Mullaghareirk: Aspects in Perspective." *Eire-Ireland* 28, no. 4 (Winter 1993): 7–15.
Padraic O Conaire, "Tetrach of Galilee." Translated by Eithne Strong. In *The Finest Stories of Pádraic O Conaire*. Dublin: Poolbeg, 1982, 35–42.

Studies of Eithne Strong

Colum, Padraic. Introduction to *Songs of Living*. Dublin: Runa, 1961, 7–8.
Consalvo, Deborah McWilliams. Review of *The Love Riddle*. *Irish Studies Review* 4, no. 3 (January 1996): 52–53.
———. " 'To Have the Right of Utterance': An Interview with Eithne Strong." *Celtic Pen* 2, no. 2 (Autumn 1995): 17–20.
Haberstroh, Patricia Boyle. "Eithne Strong." In *Women Creating Women: Contemporary Irish Women Poets*. Syracuse, NY: Syracuse University Press, 1996, 28–57.
———, ed. *My Self, My Muse: Irish Women Poets Reflect on Life and Art*. Syracuse, NY: Syracuse University Press, 2001.
Holmquist, Kathryn. "An Interview with Eithne Strong." *Irish Times*, November 3, 1993, 13.

O'Donnell, Mary. "Introduction." In *Spatial Nosing: New and Selected Poems*. Galway: Salmon, 1993, iii–xi.

Wilson, Rebecca E., and Gillean Somerville-Arjat, eds. "Interview with Eithne Strong." In *Sleeping with Monsters: Conversations with Scottish and Irish Women Poets*. Dublin: Wolfhound, 1990, 109–20. (Includes poems "Bottoms," "Tóineanna," "The Creaking of the Bones," "Gíoscán na Gnámh."

Wright, Nancy Means, and Dennis Hannan. "An Interview with Eithne Strong." *Irish Literary Supplement* 13, no. 1 (Spring 1994): 13–15.

MARY TIGHE (NÉE BLACHFORD)
(1772–1810)

Maureen E. Mulvihill

BIOGRAPHY

Anglo-Irish poet, novelist, and memoirist, Mary Tighe was born on October 9, 1772, in Dublin to an educated and privileged Protestant family. Both parents were decidedly bookish and literary. Tighe's father, William Blachford (variant, Blatchford), was a Protestant cleric and the keeper of books at the famous Marsh's Library in Dublin; formerly, he was chancellor of St. Patrick's Library, Dublin. Tighe's mother and first literary muse was Theodosia Blachford, née Tighe, a learned woman and a founding member of Irish Methodism; her English lineage included the earls of Darnley and also Edward Hyde, first Earl of Clarendon. Theodosia Blachford's important consultative, if not editorial and mentorial, role in Tighe's writings is valuably disclosed by Tighe herself in "Sonnet. Addressed to My Mother" . . . "to thee belong / The graces which adorn my first wild song," being Tighe's famous poetry book, *Psyche; or, The Legend of Love* (1805). The extent to which Theodosia Blachford materially assisted her precocious young daughter, both in her writings and in her career, is an attractive subject thus far unassessed by Tighe scholars.

In girlhood and adolescence, Mary Tighe was home educated by her mother, who introduced Tighe to classical literatures, mythology, and foreign languages and literatures; Tighe's many manuscripts, preserved principally at the National Library of Ireland, Dublin, and at Trinity College Dublin, display an aristocratic, calligraphic script and a familiarity with the contemporary formatting practices of literary manuscripts, suggesting that the Tighe family library included a good deal more than printed books.

In 1793, at the age of twenty, Tighe reluctantly entered into an arranged marriage with her first cousin, Henry Tighe (1771–1836) of Woodstock, Rosanna, County Wicklow, who represented the borough of Inistioge, County Kilkenny, in the Irish Parliament of 1790. This union soon proved strained and fruitless, and it was commonly thought that Mary Tighe enjoyed more felicitous hours with her husband's brother, the poet William Tighe, her eventual literary executor. For an interesting image of Mary

Tighe with (possibly) her husband, see a photograph of the painting *Mary Tighe, The Poet*, attributed to "G. Brooke," in *The Hamwood Papers of the Ladies of Llangollen and Caroline Hamilton, edited by Mrs G H Bell* (Eva Mary Hamilton Bell) (London: Macmillan, 1930). This is also the frontispiece of Linkin's edition of *Tighe* (2005).

Owing to the political interests of her husband and perhaps her own family connections in England, Mary Tighe resided in London during the first eight years of her married life. This documented fact of her biography is critical, as it suggests a great deal about the writer's literary development, her contacts and networks, and her exposure to London's many prominent English and Anglo-Irish writers. It is not unlikely that Tighe enjoyed some connection, however limited and distanced, to the rather large, public circle of the feminist polemicist and writer Mary Wollstonecraft. What is indisputably certain is that Tighe's many correspondents included the celebrated Anglo-Irish couple, Lady Eleanor Butler and Sarah Ponsonby, the storied Ladies of Llangollen. The couple's surviving papers at the National Library of Wales include a volume of manuscript poems by Tighe (microfilm reel 4, NLW MS 22985B, among others). In any case, Mary Tighe's principal work, *Psyche*, was published in London, and London was her first literary sponsor.

In about 1803, Tighe became ill with consumption (tuberculosis), a fairly common malady of the time. She wrote of her long illness in a poignant lyric of seven quatrains, "Verses Written in Sickness. *December*, 1804." After several years of suffering, Tighe succumbed in her thirty-seventh year on March 24, 1810, at the home of her beloved brother-in-law, William Tighe, in Woodstock, County Kilkenny; she was buried at Inistioge in Kilkenny. With profits from the commercial success of *Psyche*, the Tighe family generously built an addition to the orphanage in County Wicklow, suitably named in Mary Tighe's honor, the Psyche Ward. The family also contributed to the Methodist Home of Refuge in Dublin, which had been founded by Tighe's mother.

A sculpture of Mary Tighe in white marble by John Flaxman is displayed at the Tighe family mausoleum at Inistioge, County Kilknenny. A plaster model of the monument was bequested to the Kilkenny Archaeological Society in 1989, where it is on show in the Phelan Room at Rothe House, Kilkenny.

MAJOR WORKS AND THEMES

As Robert Hogan explains in his introductory essay in *A Dictionary of Irish Literature* (Westport, CT: Greenwood, 1979, 1996), most early Irish authors were naturally dual-language writers who wrote in Irish but published in English. Though Tighe's extant manuscripts are not written in Irish, but in English, scholars may locate some of her Irish-language manuscripts, in due course. It is entirely probable that she composed initially in Irish and also circulated her Irish-language manuscripts to a small Irish coterie. In any case, it may be said that Tighe's work is an indigenous Irish poetry to the extent that it was (reasonably) drafted, first, in Irish, that it drew upon Irish lore (though not exclusively, surely), and that it celebrated Ireland's beauty, especially the pastoral magnificence and transformative powers of Tighe's native Irish environs in Rosanna, County Wicklow. And while literary historians do not dispute Tighe's obvious poetic talents, Irish studies scholars are only beginning to probe the poet's Irishness. How "Irish" was Mary Tighe? To what extent, for example, did Tighe *live* as an Irish woman? It is rather surprising, even disappointing, that her work fails to engage, even covertly, with large political issues of her day, such as the rising of 1798 and the Act of Union on July 2, 1800.

Unlike a fair measure of Irish literature at this time, Tighe's is not an intellectual or polemical body of work, but chiefly a luxurious poetry of sensibility and imagination; hers is a world of myth, fable, legend, and faerie lore, much influenced by the revolutionary Romantic aesthetic of her day, as set out chiefly by Edmund Burke in his seminal *Philosophical Enquiry into the Origin of Our Ideas of the Sublime and Beautiful* (1756).

Tighe's small but diversified corpus of writings includes, foremost, her famous poetry book, *Psyche; or, The Legend of Love,* which she herself describes as "my first wild song" ("Sonnet / Addressed / To My Mother," line 3, 1811 ed., n.p., following Tighe's preface, [ix–xv]). Tighe's *Psyche* is a long allegorical verse epic in six cantos, extending to some 200 pages of printed text. It was inspired by the Cupid and Psyche legend of Apuleius and written in Spenserian stanza, a challenging poetic form for any writer. The entire manuscript was completed in 1795, according to Earle Vonard Weller (xix) and circulated among a selected coterie of family members and close acquaintances. An English-language, limited issue of the manuscript was then privately published in London in 1805. This small run of some fifty presentation copies was "Printed for James Carpenter, by C. Whittingham" (13 cm., 214 pp; 13 extant copies, Online Computer Library Center [OCLC] search, 2004). This was followed by *Psyche, with Other Poems* (quarto; imprint of Thomas Davison, Lombard St., Whitefriars, London), a posthumous issue that expanded the first printing with several additional short lyrics and sonnets. The third edition (1811) was graced by a lovely frontispiece portrait of Tighe, being Caroline Watson's engraving of John Comerford's portrait of Tighe after George Romney's "official" portrait of the poet (ca. 1794–95). Romney was the premier society portraitist at that time in high London circles. For what appears to be a generally reliable history of Tighe's *Psyche*, see Weller's *Keats and Mary Tighe* (1928), which provides a chronology of the volume's evolution from manuscript to print, and then on to multiple reprintings on both sides of the Atlantic (vii–xxiv).

Though principally valued today as a poet, Tighe was also a capable writer of fiction. *Selena* (ca. 1809), her unpublished autobiographical novel, extends to five volumes in manuscript, but, to date, it has received scant attention from Tighe scholars. In 1940, the manuscript was discovered, attributed, and added to the corpus of Tighe's writings. Of special interest to Tighe scholars today is her thirty-five-page memoir, *Mary: A Series of Reflections during Twenty Years*, posthumously printed in 1811 (possibly on the Tighe family home press) by Tighe's beloved family relative and confidant, William Tighe. Printed but not "published," Tighe's *Mary* is a case of a manuscript that was privately printed for a coterie of readers and family relations, but not published as a salable commodity on the literary market. Only two copies of Tighe's important *Memoir* are extant, one at the Houghton Library, Harvard University, the other at the National Library of Ireland, Dublin. What is especially remarkable about this text is its interleaving of miscellaneous, uncollected writings, principally poetry.

Tighe's corpus also includes a small body of uncollected verse, published in *The Amulet* (1827–28). Sections of her destroyed diary were reputedly copied by a relative, but Tighe scholars have yet to locate this valuable transcription.

English-language manuscript writings of Mary Tighe are preserved in the collections of the National Library of Ireland, Dublin; Trinity College Library, Dublin; the

National Library of Wales; Cambridge University Library, England; Edinburgh National Library, Scotland; and other recorded locations. Unrecorded, to date, are any of the poet's writings in her native language. Tighe's extensive correspondence (fifty-seven letters, 1802–ca. 1809) with Joseph Cooper Walker, an Irish antiquary, is preserved at Trinity College Dublin. The Chawton House Library for the Study of Women Writers (Hampshire, England) includes six bound manuscript journals of the Lucy and Henry Moore family of County Wicklow, whose 1809 and 1811 volumes consist of transcriptions of some of Mary Tighe's verse. This valuable acquisition was catalogued at the Chawton Library in 2004.

A handsome copy of the rare, limited-issue 1805 presentation copy of Tighe's *Psyche* is preserved in the library of the University of Illinois at Urbana (see OCLC for twelve additional locations, worldwide, as of 2005). The Lytton Strachey copy of Mary Tighe's *Psyche*, in the original binding, with original marbled endpapers, author frontis, and bookmark, and bearing Strachey's bookplate designed by Dora Carrington, is preserved in the Mulvihill Collection, New York City, an eventual gift to the Berg Collection, New York Public Library. Copies of Tighe's work on the antiquarian manuscript and book market, as of winter 2002, are announced by the *Kilkenny Archaeological Society Website* (http://216.147.42.229/saleroom.htm; November 2002 posting). The valuation (2002) of a third-edition copy of *Psyche*, at Ursus Rare Books, New York, was $2,250.

Tighe's Georgian-style mahogany writing desk (36 inches high × 21 inches wide), bearing a contemporary brass plaque ("Mary"), is in the present collection of the Dublin Writers Museum, 18 Parnell Square. The museum purchased the desk in 1994 for *IR.*£2100 at the auction of the Colonel C. K. Howard-Bury archive, Montrose Hotel, Dublin (Mealy's Auctioneers, Castlecomer, County Kilkenny). Affixed under the lift-up, slope top is a printed twenty-line elegy, possibly penned by Tighe's beloved family relative, poet William Tighe, *IN MEMORY OF* / **MARY** / *AUTHORESS OF* / **PSYCHE,** / *GIFTED AT HER BIRTH* / *With great Personal Beauty,.... **EPITAPH*** ("**REST**, Gentle Spirit, Dust consign'd to Dust").

CRITICAL RECEPTION

Mary Tighe was one of the most celebrated Irish women writers of her time. Though hers was a short, sad, and sickly life, Tighe's potential as a rising young poet of "witching tales," Irish ballads, the supernatural, and crafted allegorical verse was broadly noticed. With the success of *Psyche*, she soon became the darling of the Dublin and London literati, and she typically presented herself at various salons and events attired as a modern-day Psyche, in pastoral garb with a chaplet of roses. The Tighe vogue, which marked many literary circles shortly after Tighe's death, led to frequent reprintings of her work in Dublin, London, Edinburgh, and Philadelphia.

Yet Tighe was not beyond the reach of spiteful cavilers; her spirited response to absurd charges of obscenity, plagiarism, and bad writing provides a new and much-overlooked locus of Irish literary feminism, notwithstanding the contemporary identification of Tighe on the title page of *Psyche* as "Mrs Henry Tighe." In the preface to the 1811 posthumous edition of *Psyche*, penned shortly after the release of the book's first public issue in 1805, Tighe defends her poem as a decorous, if restrained, representation of erotic desire; indeed, her management of erotic moments in *Psyche*

("Oh, you for whom I write! . . . You know what charm, unutterably felt, / Attends the unexpected voice of Love:/ . . . You best can tell the rapture Psyche feels / When Love's ambrosial lip the vows of *Hymen* seals," canto I, verse 51, lines 1, 3–4, 8–9) illustrates a masterful, if coy, *ars interruptus*, a strategy that serves the dual purpose of erotic suggestion and female propriety, a strategy that thus releases Tighe from artistic fidelity to certain sexual content in her poem's parent text, Apuleius's classical legend of the Psyche myth. Also in her spirited reply to critics, Tighe justifies her method of "perplexed allegories" (Preface, 3rd ed. [1811], xii); her style may be ornate and florid, she all but admits, but at least it is readable by not retaining such "obsolete words which are to be found in Spenser and his imitators" (xii). Finally, responding to charges of plagiarism, Tighe explains that her reading habits have always been eclectic and that *Psyche* is "but the fruit of a much indulged taste" (xv).

Shortly after her death, Tighe's critical reputation swiftly began to build, with high assessments from such readers and critics as Sir James Mackintosh (*Memoirs*, edited by Robert J. Mackintosh, 2 vols. [London: Moxon, 1836], 2:195–96), William Howitt (*Homes and Haunts of the Most Eminent British Poets* [London: Routledge, 1847, 1894], 281–91), and George W. Bethune (*British Female Poets*, 1848, as discussed by Linkin, "More Than *Psyche*," 365–78). Tighe's *Psyche* was reprinted into the mid-1850s, and with the rise of Romanticism, Tighe and her work naturally enjoyed a robust popularity. But with the advent of Victorianism, Tighe fell out of favor as other literary vogues and writers came to the fore. Only in 1928, with Weller's important work on Tighe, was this Irish poet reclaimed from relative obscurity and her crowning chaplet of roses restored.

Current interest in Tighe, owing to a renaissance in Irish studies and in early women writers, focuses primarily on her status as an important, if newly recovered, pre-Romantic poet. And only recently have scholars valuably freed Tighe from the long shadow of John Keats, whose fairly broad use and adaptation of Tighe's imagery was initially documented in 1861 by Charles Cowden Clarke in the *Atlantic Monthly* and then in 1928 by Weller, whose close comparative study of the two poets identified "nearly four hundred parallel passages" (ix) between the 1811 issue of *Psyche* and the writings of Keats. Resulting from dedicated investigations into Tighe's life and work, launched by Weller in the last century, Tighe has been validated at last as an important poet in her own right. It is hoped that continuing scholarship on Tighe will soon assess the Irish character of her writings, as well as the broad career networks that made them so famous for a time.

For a continuing record of Tighe scholarship, see the online database *EirData: Electronic Irish Records Dataset* (Princess Grace Irish Library of Monaco, 2000; Present editor, Bruce Stewart).

BIBLIOGRAPHY

Works by Mary Tighe

Mary: A Series of Reflections during 20 Years. Posthumous publication; privately printed, 1811, but not published; not available as a vendible commodity on the Irish or English literary markets.

Psyche; or, The Legend of Love. A limited circulation coterie edition, 1795.

Psyche, with Other Poems. By the Late Mrs Henry Tighe. London, 1805 (limited issue, 50 copies). The 1811 edition (a handsome quarto), edited and readied for publication by William

Tighe, was the first public issue of Tighe's work on the London market; it was favored by subsequent reissues (e.g., 4th ed., octavo, 1812).

Selena. Unpublished autobiographical novel. 5 vols. ca. 1809.

Modern Editions and Facsimile Reprints of Tighe's Poetry, and Selections in Recent Anthologies

Bourke, Angela, Máirín Ní Dhonneadha, Siobhan Kilfeather, Maria Luddy, Margaret MacCurtain, Gerardine Meaney, Mary O'Dowd, and Clair Wills, eds. *The Field Day Anthology of Irish Writing.* Vol. 4, *Irish Women's Writing and Traditions.* 2002.

Carpenter, Andrew, ed. *Verse in English from Eighteenth-Century Ireland.* Cork, Ire.: Cork University Press, 1998.

Feldman, Paula, ed. *British Women Poets of the Romantic Period.* Baltimore, MD: Johns Hopkins University Press, 1997.

Feldman, Paula R., Brian C. Cooney, and James Harris. *The Life and Collected Poetry of Mary Tighe.* Baltimore: Johns Hopkins University Press, forthcoming.

Henchley, P., ed. *Works of Mary Tighe, Published and Unpublished.* Dublin: At the Sign of the Three Candles, 1957.

Kelly, A. A., ed. *Pillars of the House: An Anthology of Verse by Irish Women.* Dublin: Wolfhound, 1987, 1988.

Linkin, Harriet Kramer, ed. *The Collected Poems and Journals of Mary Tighe.* Lexington: University Press of Kentucky, 2005.

McGann, Jerome J., ed. *New Oxford Book of Romantic Period Verse.* Oxford: Oxford University Press, 1993.

Reiman, Donald H., ed. *Psyche; or, The Legend of Love.* Reprint, New York: Kessinger, 2004, 1978.

Wordsworth, Jonathan, ed. *Psyche, With Other Poems: 1811.* London: Woodstock, 1992.

Wu, Duncan, ed. *Blackwell Companion to Romanticism.* Oxford, UK: Blackwell, 1998.

———, ed. *Romantic Women Poets: An Anthology.* Oxford, UK: Blackwell, 1997.

Studies of Mary Tighe

Connolly, Claire. "Irish Romanticism, 1800–1830." In *The Cambridge History of Irish Literature.* 2 vols., edited by Margaret Kelleher and Philip O'Leary. Cambridge: Cambridge University Press, forthcoming.

Kilkenny Archaeological Society Web Site. http://216.147.42.229/saleroom.html. (Copies of Tighe's writings on the antiquarian rare book and manuscript market [2002]).

Lightbown, Mary. "Memorial to a Poetess." (John Flaxman's sculpture of Tighe.) *Old Kilkenny Review* 4, no. 5 (1992): 1195–1207.

Linkin, Harriet Kramer. "More Than *Psyche*: The Sonnets of Mary Tighe." *European Romantic Review* 13, no. 4 (December 2002): 365–78.

———. "Recuperating Romanticism in Mary Tighe's *Psyche.*" In *Romanticism and Women Poets: Opening the Doors of Perception,* edited by Harriet Kramer Linkin and Stephen C. Behrendt, 144–62. University Press of Kentucky, 1999.

———. "Romantic Aesthetics in Mary Tighe and Letitia Landon: How Women Poets Recuperate the Gaze." *European Romantic Review* 7, no. 2 (Winter 1997): 159–88.

———. "Romanticism and Mary Tighe's *Psyche*: Peering at the Hem of Her Blue Stockings." *Studies in Romanticism* 35 (Spring 1996): 55–72.

———. "Skirting around the Sex in Mary Tighe's *Psyche.*" *Studies in English Literature* 42, no. 4 (Autumn 2002): 731–52.

———. "Teaching the Poetry of Mary Tighe: *Psyche*, Beauty, and the Romantic Object." In *Approaches to Teaching Women Poets of the British Romantic Period,* edited by Harriet Kramer Linkin and Stephen C. Behrendt, 106–9. New York: Modern Language Association, 1997.

Mulvihill, Maureen E. "Laurels for Mary Tighe." *Irish Literary Supplement* 25, no. 1 (fall 2005): 19–20.

————. "Mary Tighe." *An Encyclopedia of British Women Writers*, edited by Paul Schlueter and June Schlueter, 620–21. New Brunswick, NJ: Rutgers University Press, 1998. (With primary and secondary bibliography [the first "modern" Tighe profile].)

O'Brien, Maeve. *Mary Tighe's "Psyche" and Apuleius's "Cupid and Psyche."* Forthcoming.

Weller, Earle Vonard. *Keats and Mary Tighe.* New York: Modern Language Association, 1928.

Wordsworth, Jonathan. "Mary Tighe." In *Visionary Gleam: Forty Books from the Romantic Period,* edited by Jonathan Wordsworth, 104–10. London: Woodstock, 1993.

KATHARINE TYNAN

(1861–1931)

Colette Epplé

BIOGRAPHY

Katharine Tynan grew up on the outskirts of Dublin in a middle-class Catholic family. Her father, Andrew Cullen Tynan, a prominent tenant farmer and entrepreneur, was a devout Parnellite, a quality he imparted to his daughter. She was particularly close to him and preferred his company over that of her invalid mother, Elizabeth Reily, whom she describes in one of her autobiographies, *Memories* (1924), as a "simple, innocent, narrow woman." Her father, who receives consistent praise in her memoirs, was very supportive of her education and exposed her to numerous writers and to the Nationalist cause when she returned from boarding school in 1874. When she was six years old, Tynan suffered from eye ulcers that, while leaving her severely myopic, did not interfere with her voracious reading and writing. After she moved back home, her father converted a room for her in the family house where she could focus on her literary pursuits; this room also served as a salon where she entertained popular intellectuals of the time.

At the age of twenty-four, and already a notable poet, she had a serendipitous meeting with the young William Butler Yeats, with whom she developed a successful working relationship and close friendship; in 1888 they published their first creative collaboration, *Poems and Ballads of Young Ireland.* They were mutually supportive of each other's poetry: Yeats encouraged her to write about what she knew, which added a new dimension to her work; Tynan provided useful contacts for Yeats in the literary and publishing worlds. As they grew older and their interests diverged, their friendship appears to have dwindled.

In 1893 Tynan married Henry Albert Hinkson, a barrister, in England, where they lived for the next eighteen years. During this time they had five children; however, their two eldest sons died in infancy. Overall, Tynan experienced great joy in domestic life—a sentiment echoed in her poetry. The family moved to Ireland in 1912 when Hinkson was appointed resident magistrate. Tynan remained a prolific writer throughout her marriage; as Hinkson's post offered little money, her writing significantly helped provide financial stability. After her husband unexpectedly died in 1919, her daughter, Pamela, became her companion, with whom she traveled widely in Europe, where Tynan worked as a journalist. She died in 1931 and is buried in England.

MAJOR WORKS AND THEMES

Tynan's numerous works of fiction provided economic success, but her role as a core member of the emerging Irish Literary Revival is what has garnered her the greatest fame. Producing more than 100 books of fiction, poetry, history, and autobiography, as well as editing some anthologies, she advanced the characteristic Revival concern with Irish cultural identity among a very large audience in Ireland and Britain; in addition, her works include her interests in Catholicism, feminism, and the situation of the poor.

Her fiction is comprised mostly of formulaic romances, which even she admitted as "potboiling"; she also produced idyllic sketches of the Irish peasant and peasant life for English audiences. While her novels were extremely popular, her poetry is what has earned artistic respect: in his 1930 introduction to *Collected Poems* AE wrote, "[she] was the earliest singer in that awakening of our imagination which has been spoken of as the Irish Renaissance" (vii).

Tynan's early poetry shows an eagerness to break with English literary traditions and to create a new Irish voice focused on Irish subjects and aimed at an Irish audience. Her later books of poetry, influenced by her strong belief in Catholicism, are works of religious devotion, often earning comparisons to Christina Rossetti; in his "List of 30 Best Irish Books," published in the *Daily Express* (February 27, 1895), Yeats praises her *Ballads and Lyrics* (1891), saying that she gives "a distinguished expression to much that is most characteristic in Irish Catholicism" (Alan Wade, ed. *The Letters of W.B. Yeats* [London: Hart-Davis, 1954], 246). Other prominent themes in her poetry are domestic bliss, the pain of losing a child, pastoral reflections, and meditations on war.

Her numerous works of autobiography offer insights into her life, friendships with central figures of the Revival, and the development of the Irish Literary Revival itself. Because she often quoted from private letters between herself and close friends—without their permission—her memoirs were considered controversial. Along with her own artistic endeavors, she was a respected editor of anthologies of Irish literature. As an editor of the second edition of *The Cabinet of Irish Literature: Selections from the Works of the Chief Poets, Orators, and Prose Writers of Ireland* (London: Gresham, 1902), she was responsible for the inclusion of contemporary authors, such as Yeats and Joyce, and the exclusion of previous choices that she believed had lost some of their original significance. In addition, she was a frequent contributor to numerous periodicals and magazines.

CRITICAL RECEPTION

While Tynan's poetry was praised by her contemporaries, the majority of her work has received little critical attention. Although since her death in 1931 she has figured durably in studies of the Irish Literary Revival, this is only as a presence in the background. The majority of contemporary criticism focuses on Tynan as an historic figure in the Revival, not as a contributing artistic force in her own right.

BIBLIOGRAPHY

Works by Katharine Tynan

The Admirable Simmons. London: Ward, Lock, 1930.
The Adventure of Carlo. London: Blackie and Son Limited, n.d.
The Adventures of Alicia. London: White, 1906.
Ballads and Lyrics. London: Paul, 1891.
Betty Carew. London: Smith, Elder, 1910.
Bitha's Wonderful Year. Glasgow: Robert Maclehose and Co. Ltd., 1922.
The Book of Flowers. London: Smith, Elder, 1909.
The Briar Bush Maid. London: Ward, Lock, 1926.
Castle Perilous. London: Ward, Lock, 1928.
A Cluster of Nuts: Being Sketches Among My Own People. London: Lawrence and Bullen, 1894.
Collected Poems. London: Macmillan, 1930.
Connor's Wood. London: Collins, 1933.
Countrymen All: A Collection of Tales. London: Maunsel, 1915.
Cousins and Others: Tales. London: Laurie, 1909.
Cuckoo Songs. London: Mathews, 1894.
The Curse of Castle Eagle. New York: Duffield, 1915.
A Daughter of Kings. New York: Benziger, 1905.
A Daughter of the Fields. London: Smith, Elder, 1900.
The Dear Irish Girl. London: Smith, Elder, 1899.
Delia's Orchard. London: Ward, Lock, 1931.
Denys the Dreamer. New York: Benziger, 1921.
Dick Pentreath. London: Smith, Elder, 1905.
Evensong. Oxford: Blackwell, 1922.
The Face in the Picture. London: Ward, Lock, 1927.
A Fine Gentleman. London: Ward, Lock, 1929.
The Flower of Peace. New York: Scribners, 1915.
Flower of Youth. London: Sidgwick and Jackson, 1915.
For the White Rose. New York: Benziger, 1905.
The Forbidden Way. London: Collins, 1931.
Freda. New York: Cassell, 1910.
The French Wife. London: White, 1904.
A Girl of Galway. London: Blackie, 1902.
The Golden Lily. New York: Benziger, 1902.
The Golden Rose. London: Nash and Grayson, 1924.
Grayson's Girl. London: Collins, 1930.
The Great Captain. New York: Benziger, 1902.
The Handsome Brandons. London: Blackie and Son Limited, n.d.
The Handsome Quaker and Other Stories. London: Bullen, 1902.
Haroun of London. London: Collins, 1927.
Heart o' Gold or The Little Princess. Toronto: The Musson Book Company Limited, n.d.
The Heiress of Wyke. London: Ward, Lock, 1926.
Herb O'Grace. London: Sidgwick and Jackson, 1918.
Her Father's Daughter. New York: Benziger, n.d.
Her Ladyship. London: Smith, Elder, 1907.
Her Mother's Daughter. London: Smith, Elder, 1909.
The Holy War. London: Sidgwick and Jackson, 1916.
Honey, My Honey. London: Smith, Elder, 1912.
The House. London: Collins, 1920.
The House of Crickets. London: Smith, Elder, 1908.
The House of Doom. London: Nash and Grayson, 1924.

The House of Dreams. London: Ward, Lock, 1934.
The House in the Forest. London: Ward, Lock, 1928.
The House of the Foxes. London: Smith, Elder, 1915.
The Infatuation of Peter. London: Collins, 1926.
Innocencies: A Book of Verse. London: Bullen, 1905.
An International Marriage. London: Ward, Lock, 1933.
Ireland. London: Black, 1909.
Irish Love-Songs. London: Unwin, 1892.
Irish Poems. New York: Benziger, 1914.
An Isle in the Water. London: Mathews, 1896.
John-A-Dreams. London: Smith, Elder, 1916.
John Bulteel's Daughters. London: Smith, Elder, 1914.
Julia. Chicago: McClurg, 1905.
A King's Woman. London: Hurst and Blackett, 1902.
Kit. London: Smith, Elder, 1917.
A Lad Was Born. London: Collins, 1934.
Late Songs. London: Sidgwick and Jackson, 1917.
The Land of Mist and Mountains: Short Stories. London: Unwin, 1895.
Life in the Occupied Area. London: Hutchinson, 1925.
A Little Book for John O'Mahony's Friends. Portland, ME: Mosher, 1909.
A Little Book of Common Courtesies. London: J.M. Dent & Co., 1906.
A Little Book of Manners. Dublin: The Talbot Press Ltd., n.d.
A Little Book of Twenty-four Carols. Portland, ME: Mosher, 1907.
A Little Radiant Girl. London: Blackie, 1914.
A Lonely Maid. London: Ward, Lock, 1931.
Lord Edward. London: Smith, Elder, 1916.
The Lost Angel. Philadelphia: Lippincott, 1908.
Louise de la Vallière and Other Poems. London: Paul, 1885.
Love of Brothers. London: Constable, 1919.
Love of Sisters. London: Smith, Elder, 1902.
The Lover of Women. London: Collins, 1928.
A Lover's Breast-Knot. London: Mathews, 1896.
The Luck of the Fairfaxes. London: Collins, Clear Type Press, 1905.
The Man from Australia. London: Collins, 1919.
Margery Dawe. London: Blackie, 1916.
Mary Beaudesert, V.S. London: Collins, 1923.
Mary Gray. London: Cassell, 1909.
Memories. London: Nash and Grayson, 1924.
The Merry Story Book: Stories for Little Folk. London: Wm. Collins Sons & Co. Ltd., n.d.
A Mésalliance. New York: Duffield, 1913.
The Middle Years. London: Constable, 1916.
A Midsummer Rose. London: Smith, Elder, 1913.
Miracle Plays. London: Bodley Head, 1895.
Miss Gascoigne. London: Murray, 1918.
Miss Mary. London: Murray, 1917.
Miss Phipps. London: Ward, Lock, 1925.
Miss Pratt of Paradise Farm. London: Smith, Elder, 1913.
The Moated Grange. London: Collins, 1925.
The Most Charming Family. London: Ward, Lock, 1929.
My Love's But a Lassie. London: Ward, Lock, 1918.
New Poems. London: Sidgwick and Jackson, 1911.
A Nun (Mother Xaviera Fallon). London: Paul, 1891.
Oh, What a Plague Is Love. London: Black, 1896.

The Other Man. London: Ward, Lock, 1932.

Paradise Farm. New York: Duffield, 1911.

Pat, the Adventurer. London: Ward, Lock, 1923.

Peeps at Many Lands: Ireland. London: A. & C. Black, 1927.

Peeps at Many Lands: Scotland & Ireland. NewYork: The Macmillan Company, 1921.

Peggy the Daughter. London: Cassell, 1909.

The Pitiful Lady. London: Ward, Lock, 1932.

The Playground. London: Ward, Lock, 1930.

Poems. London: Lawerence and Bullen, 1901.

Princess Katharine. New York: Duffield, 1911.

The Queen's Page. New York: Benziger, 1900.

The Rattlesnake. London: Ward, Lock, 1917.

A Red, Red Rose. London: Nash, 1903.

The Respectable Lady. London: Cassell, 1927.

Rhymed Life of St. Patrick. London: Burns & Oats, 1907.

The Rich Man. London: Collins, 1929.

The River. London: Collins, 1929.

Rose of the Garden. London: Constable, 1912; Indianapolis: Bobbs-Merrill, 1913.

Sally Victrix. London: Collins, 1921.

The Second Wife. London: Murray, 1921.

Shamrocks. London: Paul, 1887.

She Walks in Beauty. London: Smith, Elder, 1899.

Since I First Saw Your Face. London: Hutchinson, 1915.

The Story of Baron. Chicago: McClurg, 1907.

The Story of Cecilia. New York: Benziger, 1911.

The Story of Our Lord for Children. Dublin: Sealy, Bryers, 1907.

That Sweet Enemy. Philadelphia: Lippincott, 1901.

They Loved Greatly. London: Nash and Grayson, 1923.

Three Fair Maids. London: Blackie, 1909.

Twenty-five Years: Reminiscences. London: Smith, Elder, 1913.

Twenty-one Poems. Dundrum: Dun Emer, 1907.

Twilight Songs. New York: Appleton, 1927.

A Union of Hearts. London: Nisbet, 1901.

Victorian Singing Games. London: Folklore Society Library, University College London, 1991.

The Wandering Years. Boston: Houghton Mifflin, 1922.

The Way of a Maid. New York: Dodd, Mead, 1895.

The Web of Fraulein. London: Hodder and Stoughton, 1916.

White Ladies. London: Nash and Grayson, 1922.

The Wild Adventure. London: Ward, Lock, 1927.

The Wild Harp. London: Sidgwick and Jackson, 1913.

The Wind in the Trees. London: Richards, 1898.

Wives. London: Hurst-Blackett, 1924.

The Yellow Domino and Other Stories. London: White, 1906.

The Years of the Shadow. Boston: Houghton Mifflin, 1919.

Studies of Katharine Tynan

Boyd, Ernest A. *Ireland's Literary Renaissance.* New York: Lane, 1916.

Fallon, Ann Connerton. *Katharine Tynan.* Boston: Twayne, 1979.

Potts, Donna L. "Irish Poetry and the Modernist Canon: A Reappraisal of Katharine Tynan." In *Border Crossings: Irish Women Writers and National Identities*, edited by Kathryn Kirkpatrick, 79–99. Tuscaloosa: University of Alabama Press, 2000.

Rose, Marilyn Gaddis. *Katharine Tynan.* London: Associated University Presses, 1974.

LADY WILDE
(1821–1896)

Katherine Parr

BIOGRAPHY

Born into the Irish ascendancy, Jane Francesca Elgee was the granddaughter of Archdeacon Elgee, the rector of Wexford, and the daughter of Charles Elgee, a solicitor. Jane's place and date of birth, however, remain in doubt. She once recorded December 21, 1821, on an application for a grant, but she also claimed to have been born in 1826, dubious since her father's obituary places him in India, where he died, in 1825. Her biographers assume that she was born in Dublin when her parents lived at 6 Leeson Street. Nevertheless, Jane Elgee became one of nineteenth-century Ireland's most popular and respected writers. She was a poet, an essayist, and an accomplished translator.

Sara Elgee unable to afford tutors, bore the responsibility for her daughter's education. She set the foundation of her daughter's linguistic ability by hiring French and German governesses, and she relied on her brother-in-law Richard Waddy Elgee, a clergyman, for training Jane in the classics. Jane mastered ten languages and became a respected translator. In 1846, Jane witnessed the funeral of Young Ireland's Thomas Davis and was moved by the spirit of nationalism. She began writing for Davis's newspaper, the *Nation*, initially with letters signed "John Fanshaw Ellis" and subsequently with poems as "Speranza." Although her early poems were translations, the onset of the famine and news of deaths at Skibbereen inspired her first original poem, "Lament" (1846). The *Nation*'s editor, Charles Gavan Duffy, called it "thrilling" but irregular; her subsequent contributions became polished. By March 1847, she had attained status as a national poet.

In 1848, the summer of John Mitchel's conviction and deportation, Speranza wrote two articles for the *Nation:* "The Hour of Destiny" and "Jacta Alea Est" (The Die Is Cast). These became the focal point in Duffy's prosecution for treason. Called on to admit authorship of the infamous tracts, however, Jane refused to testify at his trial, although she claimed to have confessed authorship in a letter to the court. She is reputed to have stood at Duffy's trial and claimed her authorship in his defence, but it was Duffy's sister-in-law, Margaret Callan, who stood in the crowded courtroom and declared that she had authored the text. The association with the incident dampened Jane's Nationalist spirit, and "Speranza" ceased writing Nationalist poetry.

Despite her fiery poems against British rule in Ireland, Jane attended social functions sponsored by the British government at Dublin Castle. Her family disapproved of her association with Young Irelanders, and she began her translations and reviewed works by Irish writers. One very flattering account of Sir William Wilde's *The Beau-*

ties of the Boyne and Blackwater (1850) brought them together, and they married in 1851.

Lady Wilde gave birth to a son, William Robert Kingsbury, in 1852 and to a second son, Oscar Fingal O'Flahertie Wills, in 1854. The family moved into what would become famous as the site of Lady Wilde's salons, 1 Merrion Square, in 1855. A daughter, Isola Francesca Emily, was born in 1857. In January 1864, William Wilde was knighted, and after that event, Jane became Lady Wilde.

Although Jane produced no more poetry for the *Nation* after 1848, she continued to translate foreign texts and wrote several essays published in the *Dublin University* magazine. She also maintained her role as a social scion, where her salons won her fame. She considered herself and her husband geniuses and found her maternal duties limiting. Her sons, however, benefited from the social scene, where they were exposed to Dublin's intellectuals and artists. Young William became a solicitor and Oscar became internationally known for his own genius and wit.

Lady Wilde's brilliance as a poet and writer established her reputation as an intellectual, while her talent as a hostess brought her social acclaim, but with fame came notoriety. In 1864, her husband's infidelity resulted in suits brought by a patient, Mary Travers, one against Sir William for rape and a second for libel against Lady Wilde, who had written a letter to Travers's father, complaining of the daughter; both judgments went against the Wildes. In 1867, the Wildes were struck by the death of Isola at age ten, a tragedy that sent Jane into depression lasting three years. In 1874, Sir William Wilde died, leaving his financial affairs in disarray and Jane in debt. Although their house on Merrion Square was repossessed, her publications sustained her modestly. Lady Wilde then moved to London, to be near her sons, where she continued her salons, entertaining celebrities such as George Bernard Shaw and William Butler Yeats. If her own eccentricities invited detractors, her height at nearly six feet and her flamboyant dress brought ridicule. Furthermore, her sons' reputations added to her notoriety in London society. Her eldest, Willie, remained financially dependent on his mother although he had earned a law degree, and Oscar's embroilment in a homosexual scandal and subsequent imprisonment broke his mother's spirit. Her deathbed request to see her youngest son was denied, and she died, according to Oscar, brokenhearted in 1896.

MAJOR WORKS AND THEMES

Initially, Jane submitted only translations to the *Nation*, although these often reflected the revolutionary zeal of Young Ireland. As she began writing her own verse, however, two themes emerged—war with bloody retribution and divine revelation, especially with regard to her role as a poet. Like other Young Irelanders, Jane became caught up in news of worsening famine and shared the moral outrage that swept the country. In response, she began writing her own Nationalist ballads that denounced England and called for holy war, yet ironically, perhaps hypocritically, she also berated the Irish peasant who bore the brunt of famine and its accompanying disease. Among her early original poems, "The Young Patriot Leader" (1846) was followed by two poems that addressed reports of massive death and starvation from the famine. "Lament" and "A Supplication" captured the sentiments of the *Nation*'s readers, who watched helplessly as their country's population perished. The imagery in her verses included religious elements that reflected the Millenarian belief that redemption came only after suffering; thus, the famine became for Jane a divinely orchestrated event meant to purify the Irish, especially the peasantry who had indulged in the cardinal sins.

Jane's religious fervour carried over into her poems about the role of the poet and the nature of poetry. Her philosophy, taken from English Romanticism, places the poet central to the ultimate expression of truth. Because the poet stands proximate to the divine, as she believed, the poet is best able to perceive the truth in all matters. Jane believed that the poet's ultimate role was to teach truth and that her own genius as a poet, a self-reference she repeated in her philosophic discourses, set her apart from other women. She proclaimed more than once that as a poet she belonged to a divinely ordained class, as if anointed to speak for the masses.

Lady Wilde's prose, published after the infamous "Jacta Alea Est," was more moderate and reflected her keen and often humorous insights. She completed *The Memoir of Gabriel Beranger* (1880), which was begun by Sir William. *Driftwood from Scandinavia* (1884) arose from her travels with Sir William to Sweden, Denmark, and Germany. It contains a melange of Scandinavian history and legend with the author's personal observations on that society, and her sustained attacks on British society by contrast. Lady Wilde also collected William's notes on Irish myth, legend, and folk custom for publication as *Ancient Legends, Mystic Charms, and Superstitions* (1887) and subsequently *Ancient Cures, Charms, and Usages of Ireland* (1891). Other collections of Jane's essays appear in *Notes on Men, Women, and Books* (1891) followed by *Social Studies* (1893), where she recorded her observations on a variety of subjects, including history, religion, and literature, as well as women's roles as wives, mothers, and intellectuals. Curiously, she contradicted her own strongly feminist declarations with prescriptions for wives that reflected stifling Victorian social mores.

CRITICAL RECEPTION

Early in her career, Jane received high praise for her translations and her original poems, especially from her editor, Charles Gavan Duffy, who once praised her poetry as "virile" (see Duffy's *Four Years of Irish History 1845–1849: A Sequel to "Young Ireland"* [London: Cassell, Peter, Galpin, 1883], 94). Her later work, however, received severe criticism. In a review of *Driftwood from Scandinavia*, the *Academy* magazine panned the book, citing "inaccuracies and exaggerations" (quoted in Melville, 236). Her poetry was first collected and published in 1864 and praised in the *Dublin University Review* for its running commentary on the famine years. But the British were less favorable in assessing her work, which a member of the Royal Society of Literature called "strained and unnatural" (quoted in Melville, 20). Her book *Social Studies* received a lukewarm reception by the *Athenaeum* (Melville, 236); however, *Notes on Men, Women, and Books* received a favorable review that cited her essay on Calderon as among her best (*Athenaeum*, August 1891, 121). She also had included essays on Harriet Martineau, George Eliot, and Lady Blessington. Her final piece of writing signed as Speranza came in an 1878 pamphlet that she titled *The American Irish*, wherein she revived her antipathy for the British presence in Ireland and incited more denunciations. Of all her books, *Ancient Legends, Mystic Charms, and Superstitions* remains the best known and was acclaimed by William Butler Yeats for its insights into Celtic society (Introduction to *Irish Fairy and Folk Tales* [London: Scott, n.d.], xv).

BIBLIOGRAPHY

Works by Lady Wilde

Original Works

The American Irish. Dublin: McGee, [1879?].
Ancient Cures, Charms, and Usages of Ireland. 1891. Detroit: Singing Tree, 1970.
Ancient Legends, Mystic Charms, and Superstitions. 2 vols. 1887. London: Chatto and Windus, 1925.
Driftwood from Scandinavia. London: Bentley, 1884.
Memoir of Gabriel Beranger. London: Bentley, 1880.
Notes on Men, Women, and Books. London: Ward and Downey, 1891.
Poems. 1864. Dublin: Duffy, 1867; Glasgow: Cameron and Ferguson, 1870.
Poems by 'Speranza.' Dublin: Gill, 1907.
Social Studies. London: Ward and Downey, 1893.

Translations

The First Temptation or 'Eritis Sicut Deus.' Translated from Willhelmine Cantz. London: Newby, 1863.
The Glacier Land. Translated from Alexandre Dumas. London: Simms and McIntyre, 1852.
Pictures of the First French Revolution. Translated from Alphonse de Lamartine. London: Simms and McIntyre, 1850.
Sidonia the Sorceress. Translated from J. W. Meinhold, Parlour Library. Vols. 29–30; 2nd ed., London: Kelmscott, 1893; 3rd ed. London: Reeves and Turner, 1894.
The Wanderer and His Home. Translated from Alphonse de Lamartine. London: Simms and McIntyre, 1852.

Studies of Lady Wilde

Bremont, Anna, Comtesse de. *Oscar Wilde and His Mother.* London: Everett, 1911.
Byrne, Parick. *The Wildes of Merrion Square.* Edinburgh: Staples, 1953.
Howes, Marjorie. "Tears and Blood: Lady Wilde and the Emergence of Irish Cultural Nationalism." *Ideology and Ireland in the Nineteenth Century,* edited by Tadhg Foley and Sean Ryder, 151–72. Dublin: Four Courts, 1998.
Luddy, Maria. *Women in Ireland: A Documentary History 1800–1918.* Cork: Cork University Press, 1995, 252–54.
Melville, Joy. *Mother of Oscar: The Life of Jane Francesca Wilde.* London: Allison and Busby, 1990.
Tipper, Karen Sasha Anthony. *A Critical Biography of Lady Jane Wilde, 1821?–1896, Irish Revolutionist, Humanist, Scholar and Poet.* Woman Studies 34. Lewiston, NY: Mellen, 2002.
White, Terence de Vere. *The Parents of Oscar Wilde.* London: Hodder and Stoughton, 1987.
Wyndham, Horace. *Speranza.* London: Boardman, 1951.

SHEILA WINGFIELD
(1906–1992)

Coleen Comerford

BIOGRAPHY

Sheila Wingfield was born in Hampshire, England, daughter of Claude Beddington, a military officer, and Ethel Beddington, and attended school in Brighton, England. Wingfield once noted that her desire to become a poet emerged at the age of six, but during her youth and adolescence, her father, otherwise a cultivated man, strongly discouraged her interest in literature. Nevertheless, Wingfield pursued her interest in reading and writing, which she carried on without her parents' knowledge. She is noted for having secretly read a literary classic each night while growing up and for writing verses in the early morning, before her parents awoke. In this manner, Wingfield stealthily educated herself in literature and developed her talent in verse. Because of her father's disapproval, she could not associate with others in the field, and thus her poetic style was shaped exclusive of the advice or influence of other poets.

She married Marvyn Wingfield, ninth Viscount Powerscourt, in 1932 and bore two sons and one daughter. Wingfield's long personal association with Ireland began after her marriage, when she inherited a Queen Anne property in Ireland, which she renovated completely. When her in-laws died, Wingfield took charge of the remodeling and refurnishing of Powerscourt Castle in County Wicklow, a one-hundred-room Big House, while her husband farmed.

Wingfield's husband, like her father, was opposed to her study of literature and career as a poet. Also like her father, Wingfield's husband prevented her from keeping company with literary types. After marriage, she continued to write poems secretly, from three o'clock until seven o'clock in the morning. Wingfield was incredulous when her poems won acclaim from reviewers, and later when the Houghton Poetry Library of Harvard—which holds some of Wingfield's notebooks and tapes—expressed an interest in her work.

After her husband died, in 1973, she was finally free to practice her craft openly and socialize with reviewers and fellow poets. While Wingfield's seclusion from other writers was a source of grief during her youth and married life, critics have noted that Wingfield's isolation facilitated the growth of her unique voice and poetic approach.

MAJOR WORKS AND THEMES

Throughout her career, Wingfield published eight collections of poems and two memoirs, *Real People* (1952) and *Sun Too Fast* (1974, as Sheila Powerscourt). Her first book of poems, *Poems*, which appeared in 1938, established the settings, objects, and protagonists that would color and people her poems throughout her career. Her work is profoundly rooted in the Irish and English countryside. Other important influences, as Wingfield herself noted (Fraser, xvi), were world history, archaeology, folklore, and the classical Greeks. Wingfield's poems, populated by legendary heroes of mostly Western literature and religion, such as Greek heroes and biblical figures, reconstruct these heroes in terms of sense, feeling, and personality.

Reading Wingfield's poems, one may clearly detect the effects of her adolescent devouring of literary classics. While Wingfield told G. S. Fraser that "she has no philosophy" (xvii), her body of poems clearly exhibits a keen interest in the heroes and legends of classical and world literature and a fascination with time and the progression of history in general. Wingfield's poems, however they may contemplate the abstract, always return to the actual. In the poem "Odysseus Dying" (*Poems,* 15), from her first collection, the speaker reflects on what Odysseus must have thought as he lay on his deathbed. According to the speaker, Odysseus remembers "the wind" and "his old Father digging round a vine." This poem is typical of Wingfield's modern penchant for fusing the heroic and legendary with the ordinary, which is apparent in each volume of Wingfield's poetry.

Another theme that pervades Wingfield's work is the nature of time. Wingfield is interested especially in the idea of time as a continuum, which is thus readily traversable by the human imagination. Wingfield often suggests that all humanity is interconnected through time, and thus legendary figures loom as casually in the modern landscape as local farmers. She quite often presents time as an illusion, behind which all of humanity is related, and in this sense, the details of history seem arbitrary and overly personal. For example, in Wingfield's most recognized poem, *Beat Drum, Beat Heart* (1946), a long meditation on war that draws an analogy between soldiers and women in love, all soldiers from all wars are united by common emotions, desires, and desolation, while all women in love are similarly bound together. Wingfield's subjects are depersonalized to the point of universality, and the poems revolve around the fundamental themes that unite rather than divide humanity.

The theme of history as an endless continuum, readily decipherable in the land and the individual, is developed further in the poems of *A Cloud across the Sun* (1949). "Ireland" (75) suggests that Ireland "has no desolation, no empty feel" because pagan kings still roam the country. The poem "Any Troubled Age" (77) contemplates "how many times" across the ages terrible news has been brought home. In "Origins" the speaker claims, "Ancestors . . . make green my growth," and observes that ancient times seem mirrored in her temperament.

Wingfield's next collection, *A Kite's Dinner* (1954), further establishes her regard of history as circular rather than linear. "Everyman in the Wilderness" suggests the commonality of humankind and human experience, and "A Tuscan Farmer" celebrates the perpetual repetition of agrarian activities throughout the ages. "Janus" takes as its subject the well-known god, but for Wingfield he represents one who sees the past and the future at once.

The Leaves Darken (1964) further ponders the theme of time, as Wingfield explores the idea of history as preserved within the individual. The speaker of "On Being of One's Time" asserts that the rhythm of her body is composed of the beat of diverse histories and declares that she is not "committed" to her historical moment.

Wingfield followed *The Leaves Darken* with *Her Storms* (1974), *Admissions* (1977), and *Cockatrice and Basilisk* (1983). Her later poems are increasingly detached from her historical moment and contemporary consciousness, seeming even less personal than her previous work. "Glastonbury" and "Clonmacnois," from *Her Storms,* contemplate the eponymous places and their nameless inhabitants, both seemingly untouched by time. These books' poems are still peopled by heroes from the classical world, but Wingfield introduces Catholic saints and ancient Irish figures more often in her later volumes. Saint Brigid and Saint Francis are portrayed, as are Antigone and Teiresias, and Wingfield's speakers travel to Irish country towns and a museum in Dublin as well as Cologne and Nazareth. As if the drive behind her poetic work was to discover the essence of humanity, "No Instructions" (176), from her last volume, proclaims that we die as soon as we begin to learn "just what we are."

CRTITICAL RECEPTION

While Wingfield has received very little critical attention since the appearance of her early poems, which won acclaim from W. B. Yeats, James Stephens, and Walter de la Mare, those who have reviewed her work are consistently encouraging. G. S. Fraser remembers reviewing *A Kite's Dinner* with pleasure, and thinking that several of the poems in this volume deserved to be included in anthologies of twentieth-century poetry in English (xiii). Sir Herbert Read expressed great acclaim for *Beat Drum, Beat Heart,* which he praised as "the most sustained meditation on war that has been written in our time" (quoted in Fraser, xiii).

Richard Peterson regrets the lack of critical attention paid to Wingfield's work, while asserting that the positive response of Yeats, Stephens, de la Mare, Herbert Read, and Monk Gibbon has proved that her work is "worthy of the demanding reader" (155). Peterson's evaluation of *Admissions* is enthusiastic; he praises Wingfield's poems for their "precise craftsmanship and startling imagery," suggesting that *Admissions* is yet another reason the critics ought to pay more attention to Sheila Wingfield (154).

BIBLIOGRAPHY

Works by Sheila Wingfield

Poetry

Admissions: Poems 1974–1977. Atlantic Highlands, NJ: Humanities; Dublin: Dolmen, 1977.
Beat Drum, Beat Heart. London: Cresset, 1946.
A Cloud Across the Sun. London: Cresset, 1949.
Collected Poems: 1938–1983. New York: Hill and Wang, 1983.
A Kite's Dinner. London: Cresset, 1954.
The Leaves Darken. London: Weidenfeld and Nicolson, 1964.
Her Storms: Selected Poems 1938–1977. Atlantic Highlands, NJ: Humanities; Dublin: Dolmen, 1977.
Poems. London: Cresset, 1938.

Prose

Real People. London: Cresset, 1952.
Sun Too Fast. London: Bles, 1974. (As Sheila Powerscourt.)

Studies of Sheila Wingfield

Davis, Alex. " 'Wilds to Alter, Forms to Build': The Writings of Sheila Wingfield." *Irish University Review* 31, no. 2 (Autumn–Winter 2001): 334–52.
Fraser, S. G. Preface to *Collected Poems.* New York: Hill and Wang, 1983, xiii–xviii.
Peterson, Richard. Review of *Admissions. Eire-Ireland* 16, no. 1 (Spring 1981): 154–55.

SELECTED BIBLIOGRAPHY

Andrews, Elmer, ed. *Contemporary Irish Poetry: A Collection of Critical Essays*. London: Macmillan, 1992.

Ardis, Ann L. *New Women, New Novels: Feminism and Early Modernism*. New Brunswick, NJ: Rutgers University Press, 1990.

Armstrong, Isobel, and Joseph Bristow, eds. *Nineteenth-Century Women Poets: An Oxford Anthology*. New York: Oxford University Press, 1996.

Blain, Virginia, Patricia Clements, and Isobel Grundy, eds. *The Feminist Companion to Literature in English: Women Writers from the Middle Ages to the Present*. New Haven, CT: Yale University Press, 1990.

Boland, Eavan. "A Kind of Scar." In *A Dozen LIPPS*. Dublin: Attic, 1994, 72–92.

———. *Object Lessons*. New York: Norton, 1995.

Bort, Eberhard, ed. *Commemorating Ireland: History, Politics, Culture*. Dublin: Irish Academic Press, 2003.

———, ed. *The State of Play: Irish Theatre in the 'Nineties*. Trier: WVT, 1996.

Boss, Michael, and Eamon Maher, eds. *Engaging Modernity: Readings of Irish Politics, Culture, and Literature at the Turn of the Century*. Dublin: Veritas, 2003.

Bourke, Angela, Mairin Ni Dhonneadha, Siobhan Kilfeather, Maria Luddy, Margaret MacCurtain, Gerardine Meaney, Mary O'Dowd, and Clair Wills, eds. *The Field Day Anthology of Irish Writing*. Vols. 4–5. Cork: Cork University Press, 2002.

Boylan, Henry. *A Dictionary of Irish Biography*. 2nd ed. New York: St. Martin's, 1988.

Bradley, Anthony, and Maryann Gialanella Valiulis, eds. *Gender and Sexuality in Modern Ireland*. Amherst: University of Massachusetts Press, 1997.

Brady, Anne M., and Brian Cleeve, eds. *A Biographical Dictionary of Irish Writers*. New York: St. Martin's, 1985.

Brewster, Scott, Virginia Crossman, Fiona Becket, and David Alderson, eds. *Ireland in Proximity: History, Gender, Space*. London: Routledge, 1999.

Brown, John, ed. *In the Chair: Interview with Poets from the North of Ireland*. Galway: Salmon, 2002.

Brozyna, Andrea E. *Labour, Love, and Prayer: Female Piety in Ulster Religious Literature 1850–1914*. Montreal: McGill, 1999.

Buck, Claire, ed. *Bloomsbury Guide to Women's Literature*. London: Bloomsbury, 1994.

Cahalan, James M. *Double Visions: Women and Men in Modern and Contemporary Irish Fiction*. Syracuse, NY: Syracuse University Press, 1999.

———. *The Irish Novel: A Critical History*. Boston: Twayne, 1988.

———. *Modern Irish Literature and Culture: A Chronology*. New York: Macmillan, 1993.

Cairns, David, and Toni O'Brien Johnson, eds. *Gender in Irish Writing*. Philadelphia: Open University Press, 1990.

Campbell, Matthew, ed. *The Cambridge Companion to Contemporary Irish Poetry*. Cambridge: Cambridge University Press, 2003.

Cannon Harris, Susan. *Gender and Modern Irish Drama*. Bloomington: Indiana University Press, 2002.

Carlson, Julia, ed. *Banned in Ireland: Censorship and the Irish Writer*. Athens: University of Georgia Press, 1990.

Chambers, Lillian, Ger Fitzgibbon, and Eamonn Jordan, eds. *Theatre Talk*. Dublin: Carysfort, 2001.

Colman, Anne, and Medbh McGuckian, eds. *The Grateful Muse: Poems by Irish Women, 1716–1939*. Derry: Field Day, 1995.

Commire, Anne, and Deborah Klezmer, eds. *Women in World History: A Biographical Encyclopedia*. Waterford, CT: Yorkin, 2000.

Connolly, Claire, ed. *Theorizing Ireland*. Houndmills, UK: Palgrave Macmillan, 2003.

Connolly, Peter, ed. *Literature and the Changing Ireland*. Gerrards Cross, UK: Smythe, 1982.

Corcoran, Neil, ed. *The Chosen Ground: Essays on Contemporary Poetry of Northern Ireland*. Bridgend, UK: Seren, 1992.

Coughlin, Patricia, and Alex Davis, eds. *Modernism and Ireland: The Poetry of the 1930s*. Cork: Cork University Press, 1995.

Crowe, Thomas Rain, Gwendal Denez, and Tom Hubbard, eds. *Writing the Wind: A Celtic Resurgence: The New Celtic Poetry*. Cullowhee, NC: New Native, 1997.

Cullingford, Elizabeth Butler. *Ireland's Others: Gender and Ethnicity in Irish Literature and Popular Culture*. Cork: Cork University Press, 2001.

Dawe, Gerald. *Against Piety: Essays on Irish Poetry*. Belfast: Lagan, 1995.

Dawe, Gerald, and Edna Longley, eds. *Across a Roaring Hill: The Protestant Imagination in Modern Ireland*. Belfast: Blackstaff, 1985.

Deane, John F. *Irish Poetry of Faith and Doubt: The Cold Heaven*. Dublin: Wolfhound, 1990.

Deane, Seamus. *A Short History of Irish Literature*. Notre Dame, IN: University of Notre Dame Press, 1986.

Deane, Seamus, Andrew Carpenter, and Jonathan Williams, eds. *The Field Day Anthology of Irish Writing*. Vols. 1–3. Derry, Ire.: Field Day, 1991.

DeSalvo, Louise, Kathleen Walsh D'Arcy, and Katherine Hogan, eds. *Territories of the Voice: Contemporary Stories by Irish Women Writers*. Boston: Beacon, 1989.

Donoghue, Emma, ed. *The Mammoth Book of Lesbian Short Stories*. New York: Carroll and Graf, 1999.

Donovan, Katie. "Hag Mothers and New Horizons." *Southern Review* 31, no. 3 (Summer 1995): 503–14.

———. *Irish Women Writers: Marginalized by Whom?* Letters from the New Ireland Series. Dublin: Raven Arts, 1988.

Ellis-Fermor, Una. *The Irish Dramatic Movement*. 1939. London: Methuen, 1954.

Fackler, Herbert. *That Tragic Queen: The Deirdre Legend in Anglo-Irish Literature*. Salzburg: University of Salzburg Press, 1978.

Fallis, Richard. *The Irish Renaissance*. 1977. Syracuse, NY: Syracuse University Press, 1995.

Fitzmaurice, Gabriel, ed. *Irish Poetry Now: Other Voices*. Dublin: Wolfhound, 1993.

Fitzmaurice, Gabriel, and Declan Kiberd, eds. *An Crann Faoi Bhláth/The Flowing Tree*. Dublin: Wolfhound, 1991.

Fleming, Deborah, ed. *Learning the Trade: Essays on W. B. Yeats and Contemporary Poetry*. West Cornwall, CT: Locust Hill, 1993.

Foley, Imelda. *The Girls in the Big Picture: Gender in Contemporary Ulster Theatre*. Belfast: Blackstaff, 2003.

Foley, Tadgh, and Sean Ryder, eds. *Ideology and Ireland in the Nineteenth Century*. Dublin: Four Courts, 1998.

Foley, Timothy, Lionel Pilkington, Sean Ryder, and Elizabeth Tilley, eds. *Gender and Colonialism*. Galway: Galway University Press, 1996.

Frawley, Oona, ed. *Selected Essays of Nuala Ní Dhomhnaill*. Dublin: New Island, 2005.

Frehner, Ruth. *The Colonizers' Daughters: Gender in the Anglo-Irish Big House Novel.* Tubingen: Francke, 1999.

Fulford, Sarah. *Gendered Spaces in Contemporary Irish Poetry.* Bern: Lang, 2002.

Garratt, Robert F. *Modern Irish Poetry: Tradition and Continuity from Yeats to Heaney.* University of California Press, 1986.

Genet, Jacqueline, and Richard A. Cave, eds. *Perspectives of Irish Drama and Theatre.* Gerrards Cross, UK: Smythe, 1991.

Gillis, Alan A., ed. *Critical Ireland: New Essays in Literature and Culture.* Dublin: Four Courts, 2001.

Gonzalez, Alexander G., ed. *Contemporary Irish Women Poets: Some Male Perspectives.* Westport, CT: Greenwood, 1999.

———, ed. *Modern Irish Writers.* Westport, CT: Greenwood, 1997.

Goodby, John. *Irish Poetry Since 1950.* Manchester: Manchester University Press, 2000.

Graham, Colin. *Deconstructing Ireland: Identity, Theory, Culture.* Edinburgh: Edinburgh University Press, 2001.

Haberstroh, Patricia Boyle. "Literary Politics: Mainstream and Margin." *Canadian Journal of Irish Studies* 18, no. 1 (July 1992): 181–91.

———, ed. *My Self, My Muse: Irish Women Poets Reflect on Life and Art.* Syracuse, NY: Syracuse University Press, 2001.

———. *Women Creating Women: Contemporary Irish Women Poets.* Syracuse, NY: Syracuse University Press, 1996.

Hannan, Dennis, and Nancy Means Wright. "Irish Women Poets: Breaking the Silence." *Canadian Journal of Irish Studies* 16, no. 2 (December 1990): 57–65.

Harrington, John P., and Elizabeth J. Mitchell, eds. *Politics and Performance in Contemporary Northern Ireland.* Amherst: University of Massachusetts Press, 1999.

Harte, Liam, and Michael Parker, eds. *Contemporary Irish Fiction: Themes, Tropes, Theories.* Houndmills, UK: Macmillan, 2000.

Henigan, Robert. "Contemporary Women Poets in Ireland." *Concerning Poetry* 18, no. 1–2 (1985): 103–15.

Henry, P. L. *Dánta Ban: Poems of Irish Women Early and Modern.* Cork: Mercier, 1991.

Hildebidle, John. *Five Irish Writers: The Errand of Keeping Alive.* Cambridge, MA: Harvard University Press, 1989.

Hogan, Robert, ed. *Dictionary of Irish Literature.* 2nd ed. Westport, CT: Greenwood, 1996.

Hooper, Glenn, and Colin Graham, eds. *Ireland and Postcolonial Writing: History, Theory, Practice.* London: Palgrave Macmillan, 2002.

Hurtley, Jacqueline, Rosa Gonzalez, Ines Praga, and Esther Aliaga, eds. *Ireland in Writing: Interviews with Writers and Academics.* Amsterdam: Rodopi, 1998.

Hutton, Elaine, ed. *Beyond Sex and Romance: The Politics of Contemporary Lesbian Fiction.* London: Women's Press, 1998.

Hyland, Paul, and Neil Sammells, eds. *Irish Writing: Exile and Subversion.* New York: St. Martin's, 1991.

Hyrynen, Yvonne, ed. *Voicing Gender.* Tampere, Finland: University of Tampere Press, 1996.

Imhof, Rudiger, ed. *Contemporary Irish Novelists.* Tubingen: Verlag, 1990.

———, ed. *Ireland: Literature, Culture, Politics.* Heidelberg: Universitatsverlag C. Winter, 1994.

Innes, C. L. *Woman and Nation in Irish Literature and Society, 1880–1935.* Athens: University of Georgia Press, 1993.

Jeffers, Jennifer M. *Gender, Bodies, and Power: The Irish Novel at the End of the Twentieth Century.* London: Palgrave, 2002.

Johnson, Toni O'Brien, and David Cairns, eds. *Gender in Irish Writing.* Buckingham: Open University Press, 1992.

Johnston, Dillon. *Irish Poetry After Joyce.* 1985. Notre Dame, IN: University of Notre Dame Press, 1997.

Jordan, Eamonn, ed. *Theatre Stuff.* Dublin: Carysfort, 2000.

Jump, Harriet D., ed. *Diverse Voices: Essays on Twentieth-Century Women Writers in English.* London: Harvester Wheatsheaf, 1991.

Kelly, A. A., ed. *Pillars of the House: An Anthology of Verse by Irish Women from 1960 to the Present.* Dublin: Wolfhound, 1987.

Kelly, Aaron, and Alan A. Gillis, eds. *Critical Ireland: New Essays in Literature and Culture.* Dublin: Four Courts, 2001.

Kenneally, Michael, ed. *Cultural Contexts and Literary Idioms in Contemporary Irish Literature.* Totowa, NJ: Barnes and Noble, 1988.

———, ed. *Poetry in Contemporary Irish Literature.* Gerrards Cross, UK: Smythe, 1995.

———. *Irish Literature and Culture.* Savage, MD: Barnes and Noble, 1992.

Kester-Shelton, Pamela, ed. *Feminist Writers.* Detroit: St. James, 1996.

Kiberd, Declan. *Inventing Ireland: The Literature of a Modern Nation.* Cambridge, MA: Harvard University Press, 1995.

———. *Irish Classics.* London: Granta, 2000.

Kirkpatrick, Kathryn, ed. *Border Crossings: Irish Women Writers and National Identities.* Tuskaloosa: University of Alabama Press, 2000.

Lawrence, Karen, ed. *Decolonising Tradition: New Views of Twentieth-Century "British" Canons.* Carbondale: Illinois University Press, 1992.

Lazenbatt, Bill, ed. *Northern Narratives.* Newtownabbey, N. Ire.: University of Ulster Press, 1999.

Leeney, Cathy, ed. *Seen and Heard: Six New Plays by Irish Women.* Dublin: Carysfort, 2001.

Linkin, Harriet Kramer, and Stephen C. Behrendt, eds. *Romanticism and Women Poets: Opening the Doors of Perception.* Lexington: University Press of Kentucky, 1999.

Llewellyn-Jones, Margaret. *Contemporary Irish Drama and Cultural Identity.* London: Intellect, 2002.

Lloyd, David. *Anomalous States: Irish Writing and the Post-Colonial Movement.* Dublin: Lilliput, 1993.

Longley, Edna. *From Cathleen to Anorexia: The Breakdown of Irelands.* Dublin: Attic, 1990.

———. *The Living Stream: Literature and Revisionism in Ireland.* Newcastle: Bloodaxe, 1994.

Luddy, Maria. *Women in Ireland: A Documentary History 1800–1918.* Cork: Cork University Press, 1995.

MacDonagh, Oliver, W. F. Mandle, and Pauric Travers, eds. *Irish Culture and Nationalism.* New York: St. Martin's, 1983.

Madden-Simpson, Janet, ed. *Woman's Part: An Anthology of Short Fiction by and about Irishwomen 1890–1960.* Dublin: Arlen House, 1984.

Mahony, Christina Hunt. *Contemporary Irish Literature: Transforming Tradition.* New York: St. Martin's, 1998.

Marcus, David, ed. *Alternative Loves.* Dublin: Martello, 1994.

Mark, Alison, ed. *Contemporary Women's Poetry: Reading/Writing/Practice.* New York: Palgrave-Macmillan, 2001.

McBreen, Joan, ed. *The White Page/An Bhileog Bhán: Twentieth-Century Irish Women Poets.* Cliffs of Moher, Ire.: Salmon, 1999.

McCormack, W. J. *Ascendancy and Tradition in Anglo-Irish Literary History from 1789 to 1939.* Oxford: Clarendon, 1985.

———, ed. *The Blackwell Companion to Modern Irish Culture.* Oxford: Blackwell, 1998.

McCurry, Jacqueline. "'Our Lady Dispossessed': Female Ulster Poets and Sexual Politics." *Colby Quarterly* 27, no. 1 (March 1991): 4–8.

McDiarmid, Lucy, and Maria DiBattista, eds. *High and Low Moderns: Literature and Culture 1889–1939.* New York: Oxford University Press, 1996.

McRedmond, Louis, ed. *Modern Irish Lives: Dictionary of Twentieth-Century Irish Biography.* Dublin: Gill and Macmillan, 1996.

Meaney, Gerardine. "History Gasps: Myth in Contemporary Irish Women's Poetry." In *Poetry in Contemporary Irish Literature*, edited by Michael Kenneally, 99–113. Gerrards Cross, UK: Smythe, 1995.

Moloney, Caitriona, and Helen Thompson, eds. *Irish Women Writers Speak Out: Voices from the Field*. Foreword by Ann Owens Weekes. Syracuse, NY: Syracuse University Press, 2003.

Morash, Christopher. *A History of the Irish Theatre, 1600–2000*. Cambridge: Cambridge University Press, 2002.

Morgan, Kenneth, and Almut Schlepper, eds. *Human Rights Have No Borders: Voices of Irish Poets*. Dublin: Marino, 1998.

Morse, Donald E., Csilla Bertha, and Istrán Palffy, eds. *A Small Nation's Contribution to the World*. Gerrards Cross, UK: Smythe, 1993.

Moynahan, Julian. *Anglo-Irish: The Literary Imagination in a Hyphenated Culture*. Princeton, NJ: Princeton University Press, 1995.

Murphy, James H. *Catholic Fiction and Social Reality in Ireland, 1873–1922*. Westport, CT: Greenwood, 1997.

Murphy, Liz. *We Girls: Women Writing from an Irish Perspective*. Sidney, Australia: Spanifex, 1996.

Murphy, Maureen O'Rourke, and James MacKillop, eds. *Irish Literature: A Reader*. Syracuse, NY: Syracuse University Press, 1987.

Myers, James P., Jr., ed. *Writing Irish: Selected Interviews with Irish Writers from the* Irish Literary Supplement. Syracuse, NY: Syracuse University Press, 1999.

Napier, Taura S. *Seeking a Country: Literary Autobiographies of Twentieth-Century Irishwomen*. Lanham: University Press of America, 2001.

Ni Chuilleanain, Eilean, ed. *Irish Women: Image and Achievement*. Dublin: Arlen House, 1985.

———. "Wise and Well Spoken: Field Day Women and Translation." *Moving Worlds: A Journal of Transcultural Writings* 3, no. 1 (Spring 2003): 73–86.

Ní Dhomhnaill, Nuala. "What Foremothers?" *Poetry Ireland Review* 36 (Fall 1992): 18–31.

Ní Dhuibhne, Éilís, ed. *Voices on the Wind: Women Poets of the Celtic Twilight*. Dublin: New Island, 1995.

O'Brien, Peggy, ed. *The Wake Forest Book of Irish Women's Poetry: 1967–2000*. Winston-Salem, NC: Wake Forest University Press, 1999.

O'Connor, Theresa, ed. *The Comic Tradition in Irish Women Writers*. Gainesville: University Press of Florida, 1996.

Ó Tuama, Séan. *Repossessions: Selected Essays on Irish Literary Heritage*. Cork: Cork University Press, 1996.

Pelaschiar, Laura. *Writing the North: The Contemporary Novel in Northern Ireland*. Trieste: Parnaso, 1998.

Pendergast, Tom, and Sara Pendergast, eds. *Gay and Lesbian Literature*. Detroit: St. James, 1998.

Perry, Donna Marie, ed. *Backtalk: Women Writers Speak Out: Interviews*. New Brunswick, NJ: Rutgers University Press, 1993.

Pierce, David, ed. *Irish Writing in the Twentieth Century: A Reader*. Cork: Cork University Press, 2001.

Quinn, John, ed. *A Portrait of the Artist as a Young Girl*. London: Methuen, 1987.

Regan, Stephen, ed. *Irish Writing: An Anthology of Irish Literature in English 1789–1939*. Oxford: Oxford University Press, 2004.

Richards, Shaun, ed. *The Cambridge Companion to Twentieth-Century Irish Drama*. Cambridge: Cambridge University Press, 2004.

Rickard, John S., ed. *Irishness and (Post) Modernism*. Lewisburg, PA: Bucknell University Press, 1994.

Rosenthal, M.L. "Modern Irish Poetry: Some Notes by an Outsider." *Southern Review* 31, no. 3 (Summer 1995): 696–713.

Ryan, Ray. *Ireland and Scotland: Literature and Culture, State, and Nation 1966–2000*. Oxford: Oxford University Press, 2000.

———, ed. *Writing in the Irish Republic: Literature, Culture, Politics 1949–1999*. London: Macmillan, 2000.

Sage, Lorna, ed. *Cambridge Guide to Women's Writing in English*. Cambridge: Cambridge University Press, 1999.

Savage, Robert, ed. *Ireland in the New Century: Politics, Culture, and Identity.* Dublin: Four Courts, 2003.

Schirmer, Gregory A. *Out of What Began: A History of Irish Poetry in English.* Ithaca, NY: Cornell University Press, 1998.

Schlueter, Paul, and June Schlueter, eds. *An Encyclopedia of British Women Writers.* New Brunswick, NJ: Rutgers University Press, 1998.

Schrank, Bernice, and William Demastes, eds. *Irish Playwrights, 1880–1995: A Research and Production Sourcebook.* Westport, CT: Greenwood, 1997.

Sekine, Masaru, ed. *Irish Writers and Society at Large.* Totowa, NJ: Barnes and Noble, 1985.

Sewell, Frank. *Modern Irish Poetry.* Oxford: Oxford University Press, 2000.

Smyth, Ailbhe, ed. *Wildish Things: An Anthology of New Irish Women's Writing.* Dublin: Attic, 1989.

Smyth, Gerry. *Decolonisation and Literature: The Construction of Irish Literature.* London: Pluto, 1998.

———. *The Novel and the Nation: Studies in the New Irish Fiction.* London: Pluto, 1997.

St. Peter, Christine. *Changing Ireland: Strategies in Contemporary Women's Fiction.* New York: Palgrave, 2000.

Staley, Thomas F., ed. *Twentieth Century Women Novelists.* New York: Barnes and Noble, 1982.

Sullivan, Megan. *Women in Northern Ireland: Cultural Studies and Material Conditions.* Gainesville: University of Florida Press, 1999.

Thompson, Richard J. *Everlasting Voices: Aspects of the Modern Irish Short Story.* Troy, NY: Whitston, 1989.

Titley, Alan. *An tUrsceal Gaeilge.* Dublin: Clochomar, 1991.

———. "Innti and Onward: The New Poetry in Irish." *Irish Poetry Since Kavanagh.* Dublin: Four Courts, 1996.

Toomey, Deirdre, ed. *Yeats and Women.* London: Macmillan, 1992.

Trotter, Mary. *Ireland's National Theaters: Political Performance and the Origins of the Irish Dramatic Movement.* Syracuse, NY: Syracuse University Press, 2001.

Vance, Norman. *Irish Literature: A Social History.* Oxford: Blackwell, 1990.

von Goler, Hans. *Streets Apart from Abbey Street—The Search for an Alternative National Theatre in Ireland Since 1980.* Trier: WVT, 2000.

Walshe, Eibhear, ed. *Sex, Nation, and Dissent in Irish Writing.* Cork: Cork University Press, 1997.

Watt, Stephen, Eileen Morgan, and Shakir Mustafa, eds. *A Century of Irish Drama—Widening the Stage.* Bloomington: Indiana University Press, 2000.

Weekes, Ann Owens. *Irish Women Writers: An Uncharted Tradition.* Lexington: Kentucky University Press, 1990.

———. *Unveiling Treasures: The Attic Guide to the Published Works of Irish Women Literary Writers: Drama, Fiction, Poetry.* Dublin: Attic, 1993.

Welch, Robert. *Changing States: Transformations in Modern Irish Writing.* London: Routledge, 1993.

———, ed. *Irish Writers and Religion.* Savage, MD: Barnes and Noble, 1992.

———, ed. *The Oxford Companion to Irish Literature.* Oxford: Oxford University Press, 1996.

Westendorp, Tjebbe, and Jane Malinson, eds. *Politics and the Rhetoric of Poetry: Perspectives on Modern Anglo-Irish Poetry.* Amsterdam: Rodopi, 1995.

Wiley, Catherine, and Fiona R. Barnes, eds. *Homemaking: Women Writers and the Politics and Poetics of Home.* New York: Garland, 1996.

Wills, Clair. *Improprieties: Politics and Sexuality in Northern Irish Poetry.* Oxford: Clarendon, 1993.

Wilson, Rebecca E., and Gillean Somerville-Arjat, eds. *Sleeping with Monsters: Conversations with Scottish and Irish Women Poets.* Dublin: Wolfhound, 1990.

Zach, Wolfgang, and Heinz Kosok, eds. *Literary Interrelations: Ireland, England and the World.* Tubingen: Narr, 1988.

INDEX

Abbey Theatre: and Marina Carr, 62; and Mary Colum, 68; and Suzanne Day, 83; and Teresa Deevy, 84, 85, 86, 87; and Miriam Gallagher, 128; and Lady Gregory, 134, 136; and Susan L. Mitchell, 225; and Mairead Ni Ghrada, 265, 267

Abortion, 213, 235, 270, 282

Adams, Hazard, 136

Adams, Phoebe, 271

Adultery: and Nuala Ní Dhomhnaill, 252; and Eilis ní Dhuibhne, 259; and Máiréad Ní Ghráda, 267; and Kate O'Brien, 277, 278; and Mary O'Donnell, 281, 282; and Mary O'Malley, 288; and Lady Wilde, 320

AE (George Russell), 221, 222, 225, 226, 227, 315

Aisling tradition, 29, 107, 252

Allen, Brooke, 273

Alvarez, Maria, 272

Anderson, Linda, **9–11**

Androgyny, 271

Anorexia, 28, 254

Arjat, Gillean S., 4

Armstrong, C.D.C., 119

Atkinson, Colin B., 231

Atkinson, Jo, 231

Attic Press, 3, 256

Automatic writing, 76, 77

Balfe, Michael W., 129

Bannister, Ivy, **12–14**

Batten, Guinn, 205, 246

Baumann, Uwe, 118

Bayley, John, 237

Beckett, Mary, **14–17**

Bell, Millicent, 272

Bell, Pearl K., 271

Benét, William Rose, 71

Bennett, Ronan, 270, 273

Berkeley, Sara, **17–20**, 148

Bethune, George W., 312

Big houses: and Eavan Boland, 30; and Elizabeth Bowen, 39–43; and Geraldine Cummins, 77; and Maria Edgeworth, 111–14; and Mary E. Frances, 124; and Miriam Gallagher, 128; and Lady Gregory, 134, 135; and Jennifer Johnston, 158–62; and Molly Keane, 168–71; and Joy Martin, 198; and Nuala O'Faolain, 288; and Somerville and Ross, 298–302; and Sheila Wingfield, 323

Bildungsroman, 259, 288

Binchy, Maeve, **20–23**

Birmingham, Margaret, 128

Birth control, 152, 304

Bisexuality, 102, 103, 104

Blackwell, Bonnie, 113

Blackwood, Caroline, **23–26**, 171

Blakeman, Helen, 204, 205

Blythe, Ernest, 136, 265, 266, 267

Boland, Eavan, 1, 3, 6, **26–35**, 279, 291, 293–94

Bolger, Dermot, 18, 120

Bonnell, Marilyn, 133

Bourke, Angela, 4, **35–39**, 254

Bowen, Elizabeth, **39–44**, 279

Boyd, Ernest, 189

Boylan, Clare, **44–48**

Brazeau, Robert, 205

Brennan, Elizabeth, **48–51**

Brennan, Joseph, 107

Brennan, Maeve, 37

Brewer, Betty W., 189

Briggs, Sarah, 182
Brontë, Charlotte, 45
Brown, Catherine M., 181
Brown, Stephen, 74
Browne, Frances, **51–54**
Browning, Elizabeth Barrett, 2
Broyard, Anatole, 270, 271
Buck, Claire, 11
Burke, Molly M., 149
Burleigh, David, 163
Burnham, Richard, 181
Burns, Mike, 22
Butler, Marilyn, 109, 113
Byatt, A.S., 238

Cade, Elizabeth, 95
Cahalan, James M., 189, 231
Cahill, Eileen, 204
Callaghan, Mary Rose, **54–57**
Campbell, Mary, 231
Cannon, Moya, **57–61**
Carberry, Ethna, 220
Carleton, William, 112
Carr, Marina, **61–67**
Carr, Ruth, 11
Casey, Juanita, **67–69**
Catholic emancipation, 229
Cave, Richard, 136
Celibacy, 80
Cerquoni, Enrica, 65
Chessman, Harriet, 43
Child molestation, 263–64
Cixous, Helene, 214
Clee, Nicholas, 47
Clutterbuck, Catriona, 92
Coffey, Edel, 56
Colum, Mary, **69–72**
Colum, Padraic, 31, 69–70, 222, 304, 306
Communism, 236
Conradi, Peter, 236
Cooper, Brian, 266
Corbett, Mary Jean, 113
Corkery, Daniel, 113, 245
Crain, Caleb, 273
Croker, John Wilson, 229, 230
Cronin, Gearóid, 42
Cronin, John, 112
Crottie, Julia M., **72–75**
Crotty, Derbhle, 86
Crotty, Patrick, 149
Crowley, Jeananne, 86
Cummins, Geraldine, **75–78**, 83
Cunningham, A.R., 132

Dalsimer, Adele, 279
Daly, Ita, **79–82**
Daniels, Katie, 205
Davis, Thomas, 319
Day, Suzanne, 76, **82–84**
Deane, Seamus, 1, 37, 113, 231, 245
Deevy, Teresa, **84–88**
Denman, Peter, 214
Dent, Nick, 81
Devlin, Anne, 2, **88–94**
Devlin, Polly, 171
Dickinson, Emily, 201
Dillon, Eilis, **94–98**
Dipple, Elizabeth, 239
Divorce, 6, 140, 141, 269, 277, 287–88
Docherty, Thomas, 204
Donoghue, Emma, **98–102**, 104, 279
Donovan, Anne, 55
Donovan, Katie, 149, 235, 292
Dorcey, Mary, 81, **102–5**
Dorgan, Theo, 156
Doughty, Louise, 271
Dowden, Hester, 76
Downing, Ellen Mary Patrick, **106–9**
Duffy, Charles Gavan, 174, 319, 321
Duncan, Dawn, 136
Dunleavy, Janet, 181, 285
Dunne, Sean, 85, 87
Durcan, Paul, 19

Eagleton, Terry, 112, 113, 125
Edgeworth, Maria, **109–14**
Edwards, Ruth Dudley, **117–20**
Ellis-Fermor, Una, 137
Ellman, Maud, 43
Elson, Brigid, 270–71
Emerson, Ralph Waldo, 249
Emick, Katy, 47
Emmit, Helen, 244, 245
Enright, Anne, 2, **120–24**
Environmentalism, 234, 235, 258, 260, 290
Evans, Eibhlín, 288

Fackler, Herbert, 135
Farrell, Eibhlis, 140
Felter, Maryanne, 122
Feminism, 3, 4, 6; and Mary Beckett, 16; and
    Eavan Boland, 28, 30, 31, 33; and Angela
    Bourke, 35, 36, 37; and Elizabeth Bowen,
    43; and Marina Carr, 65; and Geraldine
    Cummins, 78; and Ita Daly, 82; and
    Suzanne Day, 83; and Mary Dorcey, 102–
    5; and Ellen Downing, 107; and Maria

Edgeworth, 113; and Mary E. Frances, 125; and Sarah Grand, 131–33; and Lady Gregory, 136; and Anne Hartigan, 141; and Rita Ann Higgins, 148; and Norah Hoult, 152; and Marie Jones, 164–67; and Eva Kelly, 173; and Emily Lawless, 185–89; and Medbh McGuckian, 204; and Paula Meehan, 212; and Alice Milligan, 220; and Lady Morgan, 231; and Eilean Ni Chuilleanain, 245; and Nuala Ní Dhomhnaill, 250–54; and Éilís Ní Dhuibhne, 258, 259, 260; and Máiréad Ní Ghráda, 267; and Edna O'Brien, 269; and Kate O'Brien, 277, 278; and Nuala O'Faolain, 289; and Mary O'Malley, 294; and Christina Reid, 295, 297; and Eithne Strong, 305; and Mary Tighe, 309, 311; and Katharine Tynan, 315; and Lady Wilde, 321
Field, John, 129
Field Day Anthology of Irish Writing (volumes 4–5), 5, 37, 200, 210
Fitzgerald, Mary, 136
Fitzgerald, Penelope, 122
Flanagan, Caitlin, 289
Flanagan, Thomas, 112, 114, 231
Fogarty, Anne, 137, 260, 282
Foley, Imelda, 297
Foster, John Wilson, 210
Fouéré, Olwen, 65
Fox, R.M., 87
Frances, Mary E., **124–26**
Fraser, G.S., 324, 325
Freud, Lucien, 23, 24
Frumkes, Lewis Burke, 21
Fryer, Charles, 77
Fulford, Sarah, 19

Gallagher, Miriam, **127–31**
Garfitt, Roger, 96
Gébler, Carlo, 81
Gibbes, E.B., 76
Gifford, William, 230
Gillespie, Michael Patrick, 272
Gilligan, Carol, 16
Gladstone, William, 189
Glastonbury, Marion, 55
Glendinning, Victoria, 39
Goldring, Douglas, 227
Gonne, Maud, 6
Gonzalez, Alexander G., 4, 6, 205
Gordon, Mary, 271
Grand, Sarah, **131–34**
Gray, Paul, 271

Gregory, Lady, **134–39**, 222
Grimshaw, Beatrice, 12

Haberstroh, Patricia B., 4, 60, 68, 143, 147, 204, 245, 254, 303, 306
Halio, Jay, 55, 56
Han, Eunwon, 204–5
Hand, Derek, 260
Harmon, Maurice, 285–86
Harris, Claudia, 65
Hartigan, Anne Le Marquand, **140–44**
Hartnett, Michael, 251
Haverty, Anne, 55
Hawthorne, Mark, 181–82
Hayden, Joanne, 122
Heaney, Mick, 289
Heaney, Seamus, 291
Henderson, Gordon, 67, 68
Henigan, Robert, 244
Heusel, Barbara S., 238, 238–39
Hickey, Father, 174, 175
Higgins, Rita Ann, **145–50**
Hildebidle, John, 148, 279
Hobbs, John, 215
Hogan, Robert, 235
Hogan, Thomas, 136
Hollingworth, Brian, 113
Hoogland, Renée, 43
Hopkins, Gerard Manley, 81
Hosmer, Robert, Jr., 270, 271, 272
Hoult, Norah, **151–54**
Howe, Stephen, 119
Howes, Marjorie, 153
Howitt, William, 312
Hughes, Alice, 272
Hutchinson, Pearse, 156

Incest, 19, 63–64, 238, 263–64, 270, 271, 272, 285
Infanticide, 267
Innes, C.L., 42, 221
Interfaith marriage, 125
Irigaray, Luce, 16, 245
Irish Civil War, 40
Irish folklore: and Angela Bourke, 35, 36, 37; and Marina Carr, 64; and Emma Donoghue, 99; and Lady Gregory, 135, 136, 137; and Marie Jones, 165–66; and Eva Kelly, 174; and Joy Martin, 198; and Alice Milligan, 221; and Eilean Ni Chuilleanain, 242; and Nuala Ní Dhomhnaill, 250, 251, 254; and Éilís Ní Dhuibhne, 256, 257, 258; and Mary O'Donnell, 281;

and Mary O'Malley, 290; and Mary Tighe, 309, 310; and Lady Wilde, 321
Irish language: and Angela Bourke, 35, 36; and Moya Cannon, 57–61; and Julia M. Crottie, 73, 74; and Eilis Dillon, 94; and Miriam Gallagher, 127, 128; and Lady Gregory, 134–36; and Rita Ann Higgins, 146; and Biddy Jenkinson, 154–56; and Rita Kelly, 175–78; and Máire Mhac an tSaoi, 216–18; and Susan L. Mitchell, 226, 227; and Lady Morgan, 229; and Val Mulkerns, 233; and Eilean Ni Chuil-leanain, 241–42, 244, 245, 246; and Nuala Ní Dhomhnaill, 248–54; and Éilís Ní Dhuibhne, 256, 257; and Áine Ní Ghlinn, 262–64; and Máiréad Ní Ghráda, 265–67; and Mary O'Malley, 290–93; and Christina Reid, 295; and Eithne Strong, 303–5; and Mary Tighe, 309

James, Henry, 16
Jefferson, Margo, 272
Jenkinson, Biddy, **154–57**
Johnson, Deborah, 239
Johnston, Denis, 158
Johnston, Dillon, 143, 245
Johnston, Jennifer, 1, **158–64**
Jones, Marie, **164–68**, 297
Jordan, John, 235
Joyce, James, 1, 68, 70, 71, 122, 270, 272
Joynt, Maud, 35

Kakutani, Michiko, 271
Kavanagh, Patrick, 1, 31, 305
Keane, Molly, **168–72**
Kearney, Eileen, 87
Kearney, Richard, 293
Keening, 36, 142
Kelly, A.A., 4
Kelly, Dermot, 272
Kelly, Eva, 108, **172–75**
Kelly, Rita, **175–79**
Kennelly, Brendan, 143
Kerrigan, John, 245, 246
Kersley, Gillian, 131, 132
Kiberd, Declan, 5, 37, 38, 96
Kidd, Helen, 245, 246
Kiely, Benedict, 113
Kipling, Rudyard, 226
Kirkpatrick, Kathryn, 231
Koenig, Marianne, 182
Kopper, Edward, Jr., 136
Kristeva, Julia, 16

Lanters, Jose, 272, 273
Lassner, Phyllis, 43
Lavin, Mary, 6, **179–84**
Lawless, Emily, **185–90**
Leavitt, David, 271
Lee, Hermione, 272
Leeney, Cathy, 136
Lendennie, Jessie, 104, 145
Leray, Josette, 42–43
Lesbianism, 43, 98–100, 102–5, 170, 209, 237, 269, 277, 278, 279, 288
Lewis, Gifford, 77
Lingard, Joan, **190–93**
Lockerbie, Catherine, 288–89
Logan, William, 33
Lojek, Helen, 92
London, Bette, 77
Longley, Edna, 33
Love, Barbara, 47
Lovett, Anne, 213, 215
Lowell, Robert, 24
Lowry, Elizabeth, 148
Lynch, Rachael, 182

Macaulay, Rose, 39
MacCurtain, Margaret, 4, 152
MacDonagh, Thomas, 221–22
Mac Intyre, Tom, 64
Mack, Virginia, 235
Mackintosh, Sir James, 312
Mac Liammóir, Michael, 266
MacNamara, Brinsley, 225
Madden, Deirdre, **193–96**
Madden-Simpson, Janet, 16, 77
Magical realism, 239
Mahlke, Regina, 182
Mahony, Christina Hunt, 104
Maja-Pearce, Adelware, 81
Maloy, Kelli, 215
Mangan, James Clarence, 52
Mangum, Teresa L., 132, 133
Marcus, David, 15, 16, 79, 233, 256
Markiewicz, Constance, 12
Martin, Augustine, 181
Martin, Joy, **197–99**
Masochism, 270
Mastectomy, 28
McAleese, Mary, 6
McBreen, Joan, 58
McCarthy, Justin, 74, 75, 108, 175
McCormack, W.J., 114
McDiarmid, Lucy, 4
McGuckian, Medbh, 3, 147, 178, **200–208**, 245

McKenna, Bernard, 214, 293
McLoughlin, Michael, 196
McNeill, Janet, **208–11**
Meaney, Gerardine, 181, 210, 260
Meehan, Paula, **211–16**, 293
Mellors, John, 285
Menstruation, 28
Meredith, Robbie, 221
Merriman, Victor, 65
Mezsaros, Patricia, 182
Mhac an tSaoi, Máire, **216–19**
Milligan, Alice, **219–24**
Miner, Valerie, 2
Miscarriage, 315
Mitchel, John, 173
Mitchell, Susan L., **224–28**
Moloney, Caitriona, 2, 4, 7, 12, 122, 260
Moloy, Kelli Elizabeth, 148
Monaghan, Patricia, 104
Moore, George, 225, 226, 227
Morash, Christopher, 222
Morgan, Lady, **228–32**
Morris, Carol, 260
Morris, Catherine, 221
Motherhood: and Ivy Bannister, 13; and Sara
    Berkeley, 18; and Caroline Blackwood, 25;
    and Eavan Boland, 28; and Mary Rose
    Callaghan, 54–55; and Anne Devlin, 91,
    92; and Anne Enright, 121–22; and Rita
    Ann Higgins, 147, 148; and Medbh
    McGuckian, 202, 204; and Paula Meehan,
    215; and Mary O'Donnell, 281, 282; and
    Mary O'Malley, 293
Mott, F. L., 132
Muldoon, Paul, 252–53
Mulkerns, Val, 15, **232–36**
Murdoch, Iris, **236–41**
Murphy, Catherine, 182
Murphy, Mike, 65
Murphy, Shane, 205
Murray, Christopher, 86, 87

Napier, Taura, 71
Nation, 70, 106–8, 172–75, 319, 320
Nationalism: and Maeve Binchy, 21; and
    Eavan Boland, 33; and Angela Bourke, 35;
    and Mary Colum, 69; and Anne Devlin,
    90; and Ellen Downing, 106–7; and Ruth
    Dudley Edwards, 118; and Mary E.
    Frances, 124, 125; and Lady Gregory,
    134–36; and Eva Kelly, 172–75; and
    Medbh McGuckian, 204; and Janet Mc-
    Neill, 210; and Paula Meehan, 211, 215;

and Máire Mhac an tSaoi, 216, 218; and
    Alice Milligan, 220–22; and Lady Morgan,
    229, 230, 231; and Val Mulkerns, 233–35;
    and Eilean Ni Chuilleanain, 245, 246; and
    Nuala Ní Dhomhnaill, 252; and Máiréad
    Ní Ghráda, 265; and Christina Reid, 296;
    and Katharine Tynan, 314; and Lady
    Wilde, 319, 320
Neary, Mary, 182
Newcomer, James, 112, 231
Ní Annracháin, Máire, 156
Ni Chuilleanain, Eilean, **241–48**
Ní Dhomhnaill, Nuala, 1, 6, 36, **248–55**
Ní Dhuibhne, Éilís, **256–62**, 289
Ní Ghlinn, Áine, 33, **262–65**
Ní Ghráda, Máiréad, **265–68**

Oates, Joyce Carol, 237–38
O'Brien, Edna, **268–76**
O'Brien, James, 235
O'Brien, Kate, 104, **276–80**
O'Brien, Peggy, 204
O'Carolan, Turlough, 128–29
O'Casey, Sean, 1, 277, 296
O'Connell, Daniel, 172–73
O'Connor, Frank, 85, 182, 233
O'Connor, Mary, 33, 204, 254
O'Connor, T.P., 108
O'Connor, Theresa, 285
O'Connor, Ulick, 135
Odone, Cristina, 22
O'Donnell, Mary, **280–83**, 304, 305, 306
O'Donnell, Peadar, 15, 16, 233
O'Donoghue, D.J., 125
O'Donoghue, Mary, 289
O'Driscoll, Dennis, 178
O'Faolain, Julia, 2, **283–86**
O'Faolain, Nuala, 1, **286–89**
Ogilby, Ann, 10
O'Halloran, Eileen, 215
O'Malley, Grace, 292
O'Malley, Mary, **290–94**
O'Neill, Charles, 205
O'Riordan, Kate, 7
Orwell, George, 136
O'Shea, Kitty, 55
O'Sullivan, Seamus, 181
O'Toole, Bridget, 163
O Tuama, Sean, 254

Padel, Ruth, 122
Parkin, Andrew, 163
Paschel, Ulrike, 235

Paston, George, 230
Patriarchy, 2; and Angela Bourke, 35; and
    Elizabeth Brennan, 49; and Anne Devlin,
    92; and Anne Enright, 121; and Rita Ann
    Higgins, 148; and Rita Kelly, 177; and
    Mary Lavin, 182; and Deirdre Madden,
    194; and Medbh McGuckian, 204, 205;
    and Janet McNeill, 209; and Eilean Ni
    Chuilleanain, 246; and Christina Reid, 297
Paul, Catherine, 149
Pearce, Sandra Manoogian, 272–73
Pearse, Patrick, 117, 118, 119
Peters, John, 81
Peterson, Richard, 181, 325
Plunkett, James, 15, 233
Pool, Gail, 47
Porter, Susan, 204
Postcoloniality, 6, 65, 113, 195, 205, 206,
    254, 295
Postnatal depression, 90
Pratt, Michael, 260
Pratt, Paula R., 104
Premenstrual tension, 293
Pritchett, V.S., 301
Promiscuity, 264
Prostitution, 141–42, 259
Pugh-Thomas, Claudia, 47

Quinn, John, 191, 192

Rafferty, Terrence, 271
Rahn, Suzanne, 95
Ramsey, Patrick, 214, 293
Ray, Kevin, 242, 243, 244, 245
Raynor, Vivian, 271
Rea, Anne, 92
Read, Sir Herbert, 325
Reid, Christina, 2, **294–98**
Reproductive rights, 6
Reynolds, Lorna, 278
Rhys, Jean, 6
Richardson, Maurice, 95
Rimo, Patricia, 71
Robinson, Lennox, 85, 222
Robinson, Mary, 6, 31
Rumens, Carol, 149
Ryan, W.P., 125

Saddlemyer, Ann, 4, 135–36
Salmon Press, 140, 143, 145
Sawhill, Ray, 272
Scaife, Sarahjane, 64, 65
Schoenberger, Nancy, 25

Scott, Bonnie Kime, 182
Scott, Sir Walter, 110, 111, 112
Sered, Danielle, 205
Sewell, Frank, 254
Shaw, George Bernard, 12, 225
Shumaker, Jeanette, 16, 182
Simmons, James, 244
Sirr, Peter, 245
Skidelsky, William, 122
Smyth, Ailbhe, 3, 16, 104
Smyth, Gerry, 16, 260
Somerville and Ross, 1, 77, **298–303**
St. Peter, Christine, 4, 81, 282–83
Stanfield, Paul S., 245
Steele, Karen, 148, 215
Sternlicht, Sanford, 71
Stevenson, Anne, 201
Stoppel, Ellen Kaye, 47
Strong, Eithne, **303–8**
Sullivan, Megan, 16

Thompson, Helen, 4, 7, 272
Tighe, Mary, **308–14**
Titley, Alan, 178
Toíbín, Colm, 288
Tomlinson, H.M., 152
Tracy, Robert, 113
Traynor, Des, 260
Trevor, William, 286
Trotter, Mary, 222
Tynan, Katharine, 132, **314–18**

Vigo, Jean, 89, 91

Wake Forest University Press, 4
Wallace, Clare, 65
Wallace, William V., 129
Walsh, Caroline, 235
Walsh, J.J., 266
Walshe, Eibhear, 279
Ward, Margaret, 4
Warner, Alan, 112
Waters, Maureen, 4
Watson, George, 112
Weekes, Ann Owens, 3, 4, 6, 104, 109, 113,
    122
Welch, Robert, 152
Weller, Earle V., 310, 312
Welsch, Camille-Yvette, 244
White, Jerry, 196
White, Victoria, 166
Whitlock, Pamela, 95
Whitman, Walt, 146

Whitmore, Clara H., 230–31
Widowhood, 180, 281, 304
Wiggins, Marianne, 272
Wilde, Lady, 108, **319–22**
Wilde, Oscar, 320
Williams, Richard D., 108
Wills, Clair, 204, 243
Wilson, Rebecca E., 4, 304
Winans, Molly, 273
Wingfield, Sheila, **323–25**
Wolfe, Peter, 238
Women's studies, 36, 113, 140, 145, 256
Wood, Chris, 92
Woods, Macdara, 130

Woolf, Virginia, 2
Workhouses, 73

Yeats, William Butler, 1; and Elizabeth Brennan, 49; and Lady Gregory, 134, 135; 225–27; and Emily Lawless, 189; and Alice Milligan, 222; and Susan L. Mitchell, 224–27; and Iris Murdoch, 238; and Éilís Ní Dhuibhne, 259; Mary O'Malley, 292; and Eithne Strong, 305; and Katharine Tynan, 314, 315; and Lady Wilde, 321

Zaleski, Jeff, 47

ABOUT THE EDITOR
AND CONTRIBUTORS

Rita Barnes is associate director of the Honors Program at Tennessee Technological University, where she teaches in the Department of English and serves as editor of three honors publications. She holds an MFA in creative writing and a PhD in English from the University of Massachusetts Amherst, where she completed her dissertation on Patrick Kavanagh.

Susan Bazargan is professor of English at Eastern Illinois University, where she teaches courses on postcolonial literatures in English and twentieth-century British and Irish literatures. She is the coeditor of *Image and Ideology in Modernist/Postmodernist Discourse* and has published articles on Virginia Woolf, W. B. Yeats, and James Joyce. She is currently working on a book-length manuscript, *Performative Joyce: A Study of Ulysses*.

Coleen Comerford teaches British and Irish literature at Mount Saint Mary Academy, an all-girls college preparatory school in Watchung, New Jersey. She recently earned her doctorate in English with a specialization in Irish Studies from State University of New York at Stony Brook. She has presented her work on Irish writers at numerous conferences. Her work focuses primarily on the interplay of literature, history, and myth in Ireland past and present, and on the analogous relationship between private and public histories.

Anthea Cordner received her BA and MA from the University of Newcastle upon Tyne, where she has been a graduate and tutorial assistant. She is currently visiting lecturer at the University of Sunderland. Her main areas of research are the prose writing of women from the North of Ireland, trauma theory, and regional and cultural theories, but her areas of interest extend into the contemporary novel and short story, Irish diaspora, and American literature. An article on Linda Anderson is forthcoming in the 2005 publication of *Crosscurrents*, a series following the links between Scotland and Ireland.

Claire Denelle Cowart teaches at Southeastern Louisiana University.

Christine Cusick recently completed a postdoctoral fellowship at Duquesne University and is currently an instructor of English at Slippery Rock University. Her interdisciplinary dissertation invoked an ecocritical framework to study memory of place in the poetry of Moya Cannon and Eavan Boland, in the landscape photography of Rachel Giese, and in Irish emigrant correspondence. Her article " 'Our language was tidal': Poetics of Place in the Poetry of Moya Cannon" is forthcoming from *New Hibernia Review.*

Colette Epplé teaches at Catholic University of America.

Maryanne Felter, professor of English at Cayuga Community College, teaches Irish drama and a survey of Irish literature. She has done work on a number of Irish women writers and has had her work published in the *Dictionary of Irish Literature, Modern Irish Writers, Nua,* and *Eire-Ireland.* Her most recent work on James Sullivan and the Film Company of Ireland has been published in *New Hibernia Review.*

Mary Fitzgerald-Hoyt is professor of English at Siena College. She is the author of *William Trevor: Re-Imagining Ireland* (2002). Her essays on such contemporary Irish authors as Eavan Boland, Ciaran Carson, William Trevor, Brian Friel, and Colm Toíbín have appeared in *Etudes Irlandaises, New Hibernia Review, Notes on Modern Irish Literature, Colby Quarterly,* the *Canadian Journal of Irish Studies,* and *Nua.* She is a regular reviewer for the *Irish Literary Supplement.*

Christie Fox is honors program coordinator and adjunct assistant professor of English at Utah State University. She received her PhD in folklore from Indiana University and has taught dramatic literature, folklore and mythology, and Western world literature. Her research interests and publications focus on Irish theater, particularly contemporary and avant-garde theater, and she is currently completing a manuscript on avant-garde Irish drama.

Oona Frawley is a research fellow at the Institute of Irish Studies, Queen's University, Belfast, where she is currently writing a book on Edmund Spenser's influence on Irish writers. She received her PhD from the Graduate School and University Center, the City University of New York. The author of *Irish Pastoral: Nature and Nostalgia in Irish Literature,* she is also the editor of *A New and Complex Sensation: Essays on Joyce's* Dubliners. She is the editor of the forthcoming *Selected Essays* of *Nuala Ní Dhomhnaill* and *New Dubliners: Stories to Commemorate Joyce's* Dubliners.

Elizabeth Gilmartin is a lecturer at Monmouth University in New Jersey. She received her doctorate from New York University in 2001 with a dissertation on J. M. Synge and Lady Gregory's use of the Anglo-Irish dialect. Her most recent article, "The Anglo-Irish Dialect: Mediating Linguistic Conflict," appeared in *Victorian Literature and Culture* in 2004. Other articles have appeared in *Foilsiu* and *College English Notes.* She is currently working on a book on the development of the Anglo-Irish dialect as a literary language.

Alexander G. Gonzalez, professor of English and SUNY Distinguished Teaching Professor, is the Irish literature specialist at Cortland College of the State University of New York. Educated at Queens College (City University of New York) and at the University of Oregon, where he received his doctorate, he has also taught at both these institutions, as well as at the University of California at Santa Barbara, at Ohio State

University, and at Pennsylvania State University as a Distinguished Scholar in Residence (summer 1991). He has authored two books, *Darrell Figgis: A Study of His Novels* (1992), and *Peadar O'Donnell: A Reader's Guide* (1996), and edited four more, *Short Stories from the Irish Renaissance: An Anthology* (1993), *Assessing the Achievement of J. M. Synge* (1996), *Modern Irish Writers: A Bio-Critical Sourcebook* (1997), and *Contemporary Irish Women Poets: Some Male Perspectives* (1999). In addition, he has published more than thirty articles in journals such as *Studies in Short Fiction*, *Irish University Review*, *Eire-Ireland*, *Colby Library Quarterly*, *The Journal of Irish Literature*, *Notes on Modern Irish Literature*, and many others. He is currently working on an essay that links Eavan Boland's poetry to R. G. Collingwood's aesthetic theory.

Matthew J. Goodman is currently studying literature at DePaul University. As an undergraduate at the University of Miami (Florida), he was involved with the *James Joyce Literary Supplement* and the "16th Irregular Miami J'yce Birthday Conference: Traditions and Innovations," a symposium that was held in the Bloomsday centenary year of 2004. His interests in Irish literature include the works of Samuel Beckett, Brian O'Nolan, Seamus Heaney, and James Joyce. Native American literature is also a significant literary interest, including the work of Sherman Alexie, Louis Owens, and Joy Harjo.

Patricia Hagen, professor of English at the College of St. Scholastica in Duluth, Minnesota, is the author of a book on the poetry of D. H. Lawrence and articles on Lawrence, John Fowles, and teaching business writing in Russia. With co-author Tom Zelman she has published two articles on Eavan Boland as well as *Eavan Boland and the History of the Ordinary* (2004).

John J. Han is professor of English at Missouri Baptist University, where he teaches American, minority, and world literature. He has written journal articles on Flannery O'Connor, Andrew Marvell, John Steinbeck, and Christian issues within higher education, and serves as founding editor of *Intégrité: A Faith and Learning Journal*. He also has written dozens of essays in such reference volumes as *An Encyclopedia to Catholic Literature*, *Writers of the American Renaissance*, *Asian American Autobiographers*, and *Asian American Novelists*.

Joseph Heininger is a lecturer in English at the University of Michigan, Ann Arbor. He has also taught at Hamilton College, St. Olaf College, Wayne State University, Eastern Michigan University, and the University of Rochester. He has published essays on Joyce, Heaney, Dante, and the Irish American poet R. T. Smith, as well as reviews of Irish, Irish American, and modern British literature. His essay "Teaching Joyce's *Ulysses* through British and Irish Popular Culture" appears in the Modern Language Association (MLA) volume *Approaches to Teaching Joyce's Ulysses* (1993). He is working on a book examining the development of a poetics of social and political witness in contemporary Irish writing. It discusses the ways in which poets try to articulate artistic and moral responses to acts of violence, and focuses on the work of Eavan Boland, Seamus Heaney, and Michael Longley in poetry, translation, and criticism.

Martin F. Kearney is a professor of modern Irish/British literature at Southeastern Louisiana University. His study *Major Short Stories of D. H. Lawrence: A Handbook* was published in 1998. He also has published essays in numerous scholarly journals, such as *Journal of English Studies* and the *College Language Association Journal*. His article "Robert Emmet and the Bold Mrs. Kearney: James Joyce's 'A Mother' as Historical Analogue" recently appeared in *Journal of the Short Story in English*. Additionally, he has published book reviews in *The D. H. Lawrence Review* and *Journal of English Studies*. Although his major focus is on the literature of James Joyce and D. H. Lawrence, his articles on such authors as Geoffrey Chaucer, Percy Shelley, and Nathaniel Hawthorne also have appeared in print.

Tom Keegan is a doctoral candidate in English at the University of Iowa. His research focuses on Irish postcoloniality and the rise and development of race in contemporary Irish cinema and literature.

Patrick Lonergan is a teaching assistant in the Department of English, National University of Ireland, Galway, where he completed a PhD on Irish theater and globalization in 2004. He reviews theater in the West of Ireland for the *Irish Times*, and is book reviews editor of *Irish Theatre* magazine. He was researcher for Druid Theatre's 2004 production of *The Playboy of the Western World* and is a founding member of the Council of Friends of the Dublin Theatre Festival. Recent academic articles include work on Martin McDonagh and Irish theater criticism (*Modern Drama*) and Sean O'Casey and the Irish Revival (*The Irish Revival Reappraised*, 2004). He has also published articles on Marie Jones, Billy Roche, and Anthony Trollope. At present, he is working on a collection of essays on the theater of Martin McDonagh.

Virginia B. Mack is assistant director of the William O. Douglas Honors College, Central Washington University, Ellensburg, Washington. She holds a PhD in Anglo-Irish drama and literature from University College Dublin, and her field of specialization is twentieth-century Irish writing with a special emphasis on women writers. Her doctoral thesis, "Woman and Nation: Val Mulkerns and the Aesthetics of Radical Ambiguity," is a study of the Irish writer Val Mulkerns. She has published work in the *Irish Literary Supplement* and *New Voices in Irish Criticism 3*.

Paul Marchbanks, a Jacob K. Javits fellow and PhD candidate at the University of North Carolina at Chapel Hill, will complete in 2005 a dissertation that attempts to pull issues involving intellectual/cognitive difference more fully into disability studies proper. Under the codirection of Weldon Thornton and Beverly Taylor, the larger project foregrounds fictional and sociohistorical representations of developmental disability (i.e., mental retardation) under the working title *Idiot Mine: Excavating Enlightened Intimations of Developmental Disability from 19th-Century Literature*. The future book includes close considerations of works by Mary Shelley, Charles Dickens, the Brontë sisters, Robert Browning, Joseph Conrad, and James Joyce. Forthcoming publications include essays in *New Hibernia Review* and *LISA*.

Claire McEwen is a doctoral student at the Research Institute of Irish and Scottish Studies, University of Aberdeen, Scotland. She studied literature at the University of Aberdeen and began her PhD in 2002 after graduating from the institute's MLitt program. She is researching contemporary Scottish, Irish, and Northern Irish women poets and their attempts to forge female identities within a fractured or dislocated nation(ality). She is particularly interested in the intersection of gender politics and discourses of national and female identity, the body and landscape, motherhood and sexuality, regional affiliation, and the diasporic experience.

Maureen E. Mulvihill, an elected member of the Princeton Research Forum, New Jersey, and formerly associate fellow, Institute for Research in History, New York City, is a dual specialist on early-modern Irish and English literatures. She earned a PhD at the University of Wisconsin (1983), with postdoctoral work at the Columbia University Rare Book School and at the Yale Center for British Art. She was an NEH Fellow in 1990 (Johns Hopkins University) and a Frances Hutner awardee (Princeton Research Forum) in 1995. Her book credits include *Poems by Ephelia* (New York, 1992, 1993), nominated for an MLA First Book Award by Rostenberg and Stern Rare Books, New York City; *'Ephelia'* (United Kingdom, 2003); *Thumbprints of 'Ephelia,'* a multimedia e-monograph (*ReSoundings*, Millersville, PA: Millersville University, 2001, 2004), http://www.millersville.edu/~resound/ephelia; and, in progress, *No More Lovely Lore: Irishwomen Writing Politically, Pre-1800* (working title). She also has published articles on Joseph Hindmarsh (*Dictionary of Literary Biography* 170); Eihblin Ní Chonaill, Mary Leadbeater, and Mary Tighe (*Encyclopedia of British Women Writers*, 1998); Trisha Ziff's Bloody Sunday exhibition (*New Hibernia Review,* Winter 2002); James Esdall, an Irish patriot publisher of eighteenth-century Dublin (*Oxford Dictionary of National Biography*, 2004); and, for recent issues of the *Irish Literary Supplement*, extended review essays on Mary Pollard's *Dublin Book Trade*, Brian Lalor's *Encyclopedia of Ireland* (digital version, *Irish Diaspora* Web site), the Oscar Wilde show (Morgan Library, New York City, digital version, *The Oscholars* Web site, June 2002), John Mahony's *Swift*, and Robert Hogan's *Thomas Sheridan*. Her illustrated essay on a multimedia research methodology for the study of early modern Irish women writers will appear in *Irish Literatures: Old & New Worlds*, edited by Maureen O. Murphy, 2 vols. (Greenwood, 2006). She also has written and designed multimedia Web pages of Lady Gregory (www.yeatssociety.org/coole.html) and on the Flight of Earls (www.theflightoftheearls.net/book_summary_andreviews.html). She is an advisory editor to the forthcoming *ABC-CLIO Encyclopedia of Irish-American Relations*, to which she is contributing profiles of Mary Robinson, Sir Michael Smurfitt, and Donald Keough. The Mulvihill Rare Book Collection will be a gift to the Berg Collection, NYPL, in 2006.

John L. Murphy, humanities professor at DeVry University, Long Beach, California, researches the literary history of two (usually separate!) ideas: purgatory and Irish republicanism. His essays and book reviews have appeared in *Comitatus*, the *European Joyce Studies Annual*, the *Hungarian Journal of English and American Studies, Iris Eireannach Nua*/the *New Hibernia Review*, the *Irish Literary Supplement,* and *Speculum*; he is contributing editor to the Belfast online journal the *Blanket*. Over a dozen of his entries on a variety of republican, cultural, Irish-language, and musical topics will be included in the *Encyclopedia of Irish-American Relations*. "The Jews in Ireland" and "The Influence of English upon Irish Literature" will appear in *Mediaeval Ireland: An Encyclopaedia*. He continues to investigate the rhetorical and actual tensions within fringe movements and their representation through republican ideology as expressed visually, orally, or in print and hopes to publish further on this subject.

Karen O'Brien is a PhD student in the Joint Doctoral Program in Drama and Theatre at the University of California, Irvine, and San Diego. She recently received a fellowship from Notre Dame University to participate in the Irish Seminar in Dublin and published a book review on the subject of gender in modern Irish drama in the *New England Theatre Journal*. Her research interests include Irish performance and nationalism.

Shelia Odak is a graduate student completing her PhD at Georgia State University. Her area of concentration is modern and contemporary British literature with an emphasis on Irish writers. She is currently completing her dissertation on the use of folklore, mythology, and fairy tales by contemporary Irish women authors.

Shawn O'Hare is an assistant professor of English at Carson-Newman College in Jefferson City, Tennessee, where he is also the founding editor of *Nua: Studies in Contemporary Irish Writing*, a biannual literary journal. He has published essays about Samuel Beckett, Roddy Doyle, Deirdre Madden, Frank O'Connor, Joseph O'Connor, James Plunkett, and Colm Tóibín. His book about the novels of Jennifer Johnston is forthcoming.

Tina O'Toole is teaching fellow in the Department of Languages and Cultural Studies, University of Limerick. She is general editor of the *Dictionary of Munster Women Writers 1800–2000* (Cork University Press, 2005), a bio-bibliographical dictionary of 600 English and Irish-language writers (http://www.ucc.ie/munsterwomen). She coauthored, with Linda Connolly, a study of second-wave Irish feminist activism, *Documenting Irish Feminisms* (2004). From 1999 to 2002 she was project researcher at the Women in Irish Society Project at University College Cork (http://www.ucc.ie/wisp), during which time she also held a travelling fellowship at the University of Ottawa. In 2002, she was awarded a government of Ireland postdoctoral fellowship to further her work on the New Woman literary and activist project of the 1890s. During 2003–4 she was a research fellow at the Institute of Irish Studies, Queen's University Belfast, and she has recently taken up a post in nineteenth-century British and Irish literature at the University of Limerick.

Cóilín D. Owens, professor of English at George Mason University, has edited *Family Chronicles: Maria Edgeworth's* Castle Rackrent, coedited *Irish Drama: 1900–1980*, and written numerous articles on Irish drama, language, and literature.

Katherine Parr is a lecturer at the University of Illinois, Chicago. She earned her doctorate from Northern Illinois University with the completion of her dissertation on the Irish poets Ellen Mary Downing ("Mary of the Nation") and Mary Ann Kelly ("Eva of the Nation"). Her article "Religious Affinity and Class Difference in Two Famine Poems from Young Ireland" appears in *Evangelicals and Catholics in Nineteenth-Century Ireland.*

Sandra Manoogian Pearce is professor of English at Minnesota State University, Moorhead. She has chaired the department for the last six years. In 1995 she brought Edna O'Brien to campus. Most recently Pearce has published articles on O'Brien and Joyce in the *James Joyce Quarterly, Colby Quarterly, Studies in Short Fiction*, and *Canadian Journal of Irish Studies*. Pearce is currently the secretary for the Midwest American Conference for Irish Studies.

Paige Reynolds is an assistant professor of English at the College of the Holy Cross in Worcester, Massachusetts, where she teaches modern and contemporary Irish literature. Her work has appeared in journals such as *Twentieth Century Literature*, *Modernism/Modernity*, *Irish University Review*, and *New Hibernia Review* (an essay for which she won the journal's 2003 Roger McHugh Award). She is currently completing a monograph tentatively titled *The Audiences for Irish Modernism*.

Rebecca Steinberger is assistant professor of English at College Misericordia, where she teaches courses in Shakespeare, Irish studies, medieval and Renaissance literature, and eighteenth-century and Restoration literature, among others. Currently, she is finishing a book, *Shakespeare and Twentieth-Century Irish Drama: Conceptualizing Identity and Staging Boundaries* (forthcoming), and has published on Brian Friel and Shakespeare's *Henriad*. She has given papers on an array of Irish writers, urban space, gender issues, and early-modern cultural studies in the United States, England, and Ireland. In addition, she is an associate editor of *Nua: Studies in Contemporary Irish Writing* and has guest-edited the special issue on Ireland and film. She has been named to *Who's Who Among America's Teachers* (2004) and is the recipient of four Faculty Development Summer Research Grants, a Strategic Initiative Competitive Grant, and a Willary Fellowship.

Sara E. Stenson is an adjunct professor in the Department of English at Boston College. Her interests include contemporary Irish writing and visual studies.

Ann Owens Weekes is associate professor of English at the University of Arizona, where she teaches Irish literature and has concentrated on the study of Irish women writers for many years. Her 1990 work, *Irish Women Writers: An Uncharted Tradition*, a discussion of writers from Maria Edgeworth to Julia O'Faolain, was the first work exclusively devoted to Irish women writers. This was followed in 1993 by *Unveiling Treasures: The Attic Guide to the Published Work of Irish Women Writers*, an introduction to the works and lives of more than 250 writers of fiction, poetry, and drama. She has written many articles on individual writers and is currently working on the fictional representations of women as mothers in twentieth-century Ireland.

Lisa Weihman is assistant professor of English at West Virginia University, specializing in twentieth-century British and Irish literature. She is currently working on a book project that explores women's coming-of-age fiction about the Irish nation. Previous publications include work on Oscar Wilde, women's narratives of the Easter Rising, and the novels of Elizabeth Bowen and Virginia Woolf.

Beth Wightman is assistant professor of English at California State University, Northridge, where she teaches postcolonial and twentieth-century British literature. Her current research focuses on the relations between space and visuality in writing by Irish and Caribbean women writers. Her work has appeared in *New Voices in Irish Criticism* (2000) and in the *Irish Literary Review*.

Gerald C. Wood is professor and chair of English at Carson-Newman College, where he also serves as film editor of *Nua: Studies in Contemporary Irish Writing*. He has written on various topics in literature and film, including Lord Byron, the horror film, and movie versions of American history. Wood edited a collection of one-act plays on Horton Foote (1989) and a casebook on Foote (1998), as well as the critical study *Horton Foote and the Theater of Intimacy* (1999). His most recent book was *Conor McPherson: Imagining Mischief*, published in 2003.

Thomas Zelman is professor of English at the College of St. Scholastica in Duluth, Minnesota. Since receiving his PhD from Indiana University in 1983, he has published on such disparate topics as advertising, the poetry of Robert Frost, and the Russian higher educational system. With Patricia Hagen, he has published two articles on Eavan Boland. Zelman and Hagen have also coauthored *Eavan Boland and the History of the Ordinary* (2004).